READING IMAGES AND TEXTS

UTRECHT STUDIES IN MEDIEVAL LITERACY

8

UTRECHT STUDIES IN MEDIEVAL LITERACY

READING IMAGES AND TEXTS

MEDIEVAL IMAGES AND TEXTS AS FORMS OF COMMUNICATION

PAPERS FROM THE THIRD UTRECHT SYMPOSIUM
ON MEDIEVAL LITERACY,
UTRECHT, 7-9 DECEMBER 2000

Edited by
Mariëlle Hageman *and* Marco Mostert

BREPOLS

D/2005/0095/106

ISBN 2-503-51437-5

Printed in the E.U. on acid-free paper

A British Library Cataloguing-in-Publication record is available for this book.

Contents

Preface

T his volume contains papers from an international symposium entitled "Reading Images and Texts: Medieval Images and Texts as Forms of Communication". The colloquium was held at the University of Utrecht (7-9 December, 2000). We want to thank all those present at the symposium for taking part in the lively discussions. Sadly, Michael Camille, who had spoken on "Reading the Textless Image: The Ceiling at St. Martin, Zillis", died shortly after the symposium and before he had been able to prepare his paper for publication. We are doubly sorry because his work had been one of the inspirations for the organization of the symposium.[1] His incisive remarks made in the course of the discussions have not made it into print.

The preparation of these proceedings has taken an inordinate amount of time. Fortunately, the papers published here are by no means outdated on the day the book is finally in print. A careful reader with a bibliographical bent may notice the odd absence of references to literature published in the last two or three years. The contributors have been given the option of updating their references, and some valiant efforts have been made. However, the editors have had to protect several contributors against the temptation of rewriting substantial parts of their texts. The published contributions therefore reflect the opinions contained in the papers as they were pronounced in December 2000, even when they had been revised in the light of the discussions. That the texts, published in the order in which they were delivered at the symposium, can stand the test of time is a tribute to the sound scholarship of their authors.

---

[1] We are thinking especially of his "Seeing and reading: Some visual implications of medieval literacy and illiteracy", *Art History* 8 (1985), pp. 26-49, but also of his "The language of images in medieval England, 1200-1400", in: *Age of Chivalry: Art in Plantagenet Wngland 1200-1400*, ed. J. ALEXANDER and P. BINSKY (London, 1987), pp. 33-40, of "Visual signs of the sacred page: Books in the Bible moralisée", *Word and Image* 5 (1989), pp. 111-130 and *Images on the Edge: The Margins of Medieval Art* (London, 1992).

A special word of thanks goes to the editors of *Word and Image*, who permitted Lawrence Duggan to reprint his "Was Art Really the 'Book of the Illiterate'?", published originally in 1989, without which his "Reflections" would be slightly harder to follow. We also thank Irene van Renswoude for her patient assistance before and during the colloquium.

Abbreviations

AASS   *Acta sanctorum quotquot toto orbe coluntur, vel a catholicis scriptoribus celebrantur, quae ex latinis et graecis aliarumque gentium antiquis monumentis collegit, digessit, notis illustravit* J. BOLLANDUS, ed. G. HENSCHENIUS, 1- (Antwerp, then Brussels, then Brussels and Paris, then Paris, 1643-).

BHG   *Bibliotheca Hagiographica Graeca*, 3rd edn., ed. F. HALKIN, 3 vols. (Brussels, 1957, repr. 1985: *Subsidia Hagiographica* 8a).

BHL   *Bibliotheca Hagiographica Latina Antiquae et Mediae Aetatis*, ed. SOCII BOLLANDIANI (Brussels, 1898-1899: *Subsidia Hagiographica* 6) and *Novum Supplementum*, ed. H. FROS (Brussels, 1986: *Subsidia Hagiographica* 70).

CCCM   *Corpus Christianorum: Continuatio Mediaevalis*, 1- (Turnhout, 1966-)

CCSL   *Corpus Christianorum: Series Latina*, 1- (1954-)

CSEL   *Corpus Scriptorum Ecclesiasticorum Latinorum*, 1-(Vienna,1866-)

MGH   *Monumenta Germaniae Historica*

    AA   *Auctores Antiquissimi*, 15 vols. (Berlin, 1877-1919)

    CAPP   *Capitularia Regum Francorum*, 2 vols. (Hannover, 1883-1897)

    CONC   *Concilia*, 1- (Hannover and Leipzig, then Leipzig, 1893-)

    EPP   *Epistolae (in Quarto)*, 1-8.1 (Berlin, 1887-1939)

    LL   *Leges (in Folio)*, 5 vols. (Hannover, 1835-1889)

    PP   *Poetae Latini medii aevi*, 6 vols. (Berlin, then Leipzig, München, Weimar, 1881-1979)

    SRG   *Scriptores rerum Germanicarum*

    SRM   *Scriptores rerum Merovingicarum*, 7 vols. (Hannover and Leipzig, 1884-1951)

PG   *Patrologiae cursus completus ... Series Graeca*, ed. J.P. MIGNE, 161 vols. (Paris, 1857-1936)

PL	*Patrologiae cursus completus ... Series Latina*, ed. J.P. MIGNE, 221 vols. (Paris, 1841-1864)
SC	*Sources Chrétiennes*, 1- (Paris, 1942-)

Reading Images and Texts:
Some Preliminary Observations
Instead of an Introduction

MARCO MOSTERT

I n recent years, the relations between images and texts have benefitted from
an increase in scholarly attention. In medieval studies, art historians, historians, codicologists, philologists and others have applied their methods and
questionnaires to the study of illuminated manuscripts and other works of art.[1]

---

[1] Cf. the publications listed in M. MOSTERT, "A bibliography of works on medieval communication", in: *New Approaches to Medieval Communication*, ed. M. MOSTERT (Turnhout,
1999: *Utrecht Studies in Medieval Literacy* 1), pp.193-318, at pp. 222-225 (Nos. 406-457). Apart
from the titles mentioned further down, to these publications may be added the following examples: A. STÜCKELBERGER, *Bild und Wort: Das illustrierte Fachbuch in der antiken Naturwissen-
schaft, Medizin und Technik* (Mainz, 1994); *L'Image: Fonctions et usages des images dans
l'Occident médiéval*, ed. J. BASCHET and J.-Cl. SCHMITT (Paris, 1996: *Cahiers du Léopard d'Or*
5); *Les images dans les sociétés médiévales: Pour une histoire comparée*, ed. J.-M. SANSTERRE
and J.-Cl. SCHMITT (Brussels and Rome, 1999: *Bulletin de l'Institut Historique Belge de Rome*
69); W.J. DIEBOLD, *Word and Image: An Introduction to Early Medieval Art* (Voulder, Colo-
rado, 2000); J.-Cl. SCHMITT, *Le corps des images: Essais sur la culture visuelle au Moyen Âge*
(Paris, 2002); *History and Images: Towards a New Iconology*, ed. A. BOLVIG and P. LINDLEY
(Turnhout, 2003: *Medieval Texts and Cultures of Northern Europe* 5); *Medieval Memory: Image
and Text*, ed. F. WILLAERT *et al.* (Turnhout, 2004), and *Seeing the Invisible in Late Antiquity and
the Early Middle Ages*, ed. G. DE NIE, K. MORRISON and M. MOSTERT (Turnhout, 2005: *Utrecht
Studies in Medieval Literacy* 14). More titles will be mentioned in the second edition of *New
Approaches to Medieval Communication*. Medievalists may also find inspiration in F. HASKELL,
History and its Images (New Haven, 1993), in *'Tweelinge eener dragt': Woord en beeld in de
Nederlanden (1500-1750)*, ed. K. BOSTOEN, E. KOLFIN and P.J. SMITH (Hilversum, 2001), or in
Imago narrat: Obraz jako komunikat w społeczeństwach europejskich, ed. S. ROSIK and P.
WISZEWSKI (Wrocław., 2002). The bibliography is huge.

These studies have shifted from a concern about the contents of the messages contained in the artifacts (e.g. an interest in iconography) to an interest in the ways in which they were communicated to their intended audiences. The perception of texts and images, their reception by contemporaries and by later generations have become topics in their own right. The analysis of individual manuscripts and works of art remains the basis for any consideration of their transmission and uses. Yet the time is approaching for an evaluation of the results of recent work in the light of the considerations elaborated by students of medieval communication. The interactions between non-verbal and verbal forms of communication, more in particular the relations between visual symbols other than writing and the recording of speech in writing, are important for the evaluation of both images and texts.

The title of the symposium of which you are about to read the proceedings was *Reading Images and Texts: Medieval Images and Texts as Forms of Communication*. According to some, medieval images may be 'read'. According to others, the perception of images is fundamentally different from that of texts. Do images have a morphology (colours, lines, planes), a syntax and semantics of their own? In other words: do both texts and images have a 'grammar'? Is it useful to speak of 'visual literacy'? The answers given to these questions vary according to the various disciplines involved. The subject of 'reading images' is usually addressed by art historians, because visual images tend to be privileged in investigations of this kind, and because these images are deemed to be the privileged territory of the art historian.[2] Clearly, the 'reading' of images is as complex and difficult a process as the reading of texts. The related subject of 'reading texts' is usually addressed by scholars of the written word: historians, literary historians, palaeographers and others. This symposium's organisers are convinced that images may be too important to be left to the art historians, just as written texts may be too important to be left to textual scholars. More often than not it seems as if art historians are deaf to what written texts have to say; similarly, historians and literary historians seem blind to the messages of images. To bring them together may not be altogether original; it may nevertheless result in considerations of the others' methods and approaches which might prove worthwhile. The reader will have to decide whether this is in fact the case.

A question which seems worth asking right at the start is: what is an image? Visual images may be understood as acts of communication meant to be per-

---

[2] See, e.g. *Reading Medieval Images: The Art Historian and the Object*, ed. E. SEARS and T.K. THOMAS (s.l., 2002).

ceived through the eye; for this to be possible, their information has to be fixed on a material support. There are, however, problems with this definition. The material support itself may transmit a message which may be different from that of the image one thinks to see. There is a clear distinction to be made between the face (*vultus*) and the head (*caput*) on which one sees the traits of the face. And there are images one is simply unable to see. The absence (or present absence) of an image may result in that image fulfilling unforeseen functions. Let us give an example. In the church of St. Eligius at Naples, one could see a fresco of the Virgin with blood painted on her face. A caption explained that, one day, a card player who had lost despite having invoked the name of the Virgin, had entered the church, and had given a blow to the holy image. And the image had started to bleed.[3] In another story, told by Thomas of Cantimpré (1201-1263/72), a man who had lost a game of dice had attacked Heaven with an arrow. Heaven, the image of our Saviour, had started to bleed.[4] In cases such as these, what is the image? All one can say is that, with some exceptions, images represent reality in a visual form. They may be symbols, and they may also serve the identification of the image with its model or prototype.[5]

Much can be said about images as symbols, e.g. about religious images, which may be elucidated by recourse to written texts. In the domain of these images a first answer may be sought to the question: what was the function of the image as intended by the patron? Religious images will have inspired veneration and devotion. They may also have confirmed a notion of the Church – or of power. However, we have grown accustomed to suppose political objectives almost anywhere, and we ought to ask if, in the practice of medieval political communication as it is described, e.g. in narrative sources, images are mentioned at all, and to what end? A recent reading of German historiographical sources written between the tenth and twelfth centuries by Gerd Althoff, someone who is sensitive to the manyfold forms of communication used in the resolution of political conflicts, did not result in a single instance of visual images being invoked as arguments, neither by secular lords, nor by there ecclesiastical

---

[3]   SUMMONTE, *Storia di Napoli* (Naples, 1601), 2, p. 267, quoted by L. ZDEKAUER, *Il gioco d'azzardo nel medioevo italiano: Con un saggio introduttivo di Gherardo Ortalli* (Rome, 1993), pp. 65-66.

[4]   Quoted by ZDEKAUER, *Il gioco d'azzardo*, p. 65, after Thomas of Cantimpré, *De apibus seu summum bonum*, 2 vols. (Douai, 1627), 2, p. 49 (*De lusore pro desperatione contra Deum sagittante*).

[5]   Cf. M. MOSTERT and J.-Cl. SCHMITT, "Analytical postscript", in: *Seeing the Invisible in Late Antiquity and the Early Middle Ages*, pp. 521-533.

colleagues.[6] More may be said about the reading of political images, but we ought to start from a reconstruction of the politics and the exercise of power of the time, rather than from the images to which we attribute political meanings. For can we be sure about those meanings? Were they present in the background, influencing those who took part in public rituals without these men and women being aware of that influence? Or were there indeed instances when the message contained in the images present was explicitly invoked? Similarly, the study of the uses of visual images by the missionaries of the early Middle Ages might tell us something about the perception of Christian images by pagan people who initially did not have any notion of the message those same images were meant to convey according to those who commissioned them. These considerations must surely have influenced the 'reading' of images.

Another problem is that of the support of the image. Clearly one has to distinguish between illuminated manuscripts, monumental architecture and funerary art. But what happens when an iconographical programme migrates from one support to another? Does it still have the same meaning for the beholder? That an image may migrate in this way suggests that the information contained in the image is more important than its material aspects. Even in the absence of a visible material support, an image may exist and have meaning, as in the example of the dice-player who pierced Heaven and made the blood of the Lord run. Nevertheless, the material support is important to the historian of images, because it allows the formulation of hypotheses about the audience reached by the image. In the early medieval insular world, laymen could see only very rarely the miniatures in illuminated manuscripts,[7] whereas sculpture, frescoes etc. were part of the liturgical setting of the church building, and could be viewed without too many restrictions.

The notion of the church building as a place where all the senses of the faithful were addressed, among other things by a relative abundance of visual images, raises the question: which are the constituent parts of an image? Different audiences, e.g. those composed of learned clerics and of lay people, may not have been able to perceive the various parts of a visual image in the same way. The case of manuscript illuminations is the least ambiguous: without

---

[6]   See G. ALTHOFF, *Spielregeln der Politik im Mittelalter: Kommunikation in Frieden und Fehde* (Darmstadt, 1997), with a rich bibliography in which figure studies of rituals and public ceremonies.
[7]   Cf. M.P. BROWN, *The Book of Cerne: Prayer, Patronage and Power in Ninth-Century England* (London, 1996), pp. 109-114, on the ritual of *aperitio aurium*, during which the miniatures were shown to the public.

knowledge of the written word, the image which accompanies a text may not be 'decoded' in its various parts. If the image is composed of letters, borrowed from the alphabet, the symbolic system developed to render speech visible, a reading of the image-text is necessary to arrive at the meaning intended by the patron, the artist or the scribe.[8] A similar problem arises when iconographies may be read on different levels. After a short period of instruction by a priest, a catechumen must have been able to interpret correctly the representation of, e.g. a baptism depicted in the apse of a church. But would the same catechumen have been able to interpret the palm branch held by a saint in that same representation? Or would he still need to ask someone who was literate? If such is the case, there are different levels of interpretation for different parts of a single image.

Learned clerics 'read' images in the light of iconographical and textual traditions to which the rest of the faithful did not have full access. What, then, is the role of tradition in the understanding of an image? Did the image 'talk' to the beholder of its own accord? Or was the science of letters necessary, if only because many images are provided with written captions to guide the understanding of those desirous to arrive at the mysteries of those images? Obviously an illiterate beholder, or a cleric who was not (or not yet) versed in the traditions manifest in the image, might feel emotions when regarding it. As the same iconographical programme may be executed in many different ways, the information contained in an image is not only of an 'intellectual' nature. Although the ways of drawing lines, of suggesting planes, or of painting colours were also indebted to traditions, it is clear that the observer may feel a sentiment of beauty, or find a meaning without reducing the image to an iconographical programme.[9] But how can we be sure if the emotions of those who were the contemporaries of the patrons are identical, or even similar, to our own? And how do we know for certain that the meaning we attribute to a visual image would be at least somewhat understandable to medieval men and women? We cannot know, except in those rare cases when literates wrote down their impressions of the images they saw.[10] Having read some of these texts,

---

[8]   Cf. L. KENDRICK, *Animating the Letter: The Figurative Embodiment of Writing from Late Antiquity to the Renaissance* (Columbus, Ohio, 1999).

[9]   J. BASCHET, J.-Cl. BONNE, M. PASTOUREAU and J.-Cl. SCHMITT, *Lire les images médiévales*, a volume to be published in the collection *L'atelier du médiéviste* (published by Brepols of Turnhout) will no doubt contain much of interest for this matter.

[10]   Cf. J. VON SCHLOSSER, *Quellenbuch: Repertorio di fonti per la Storia dell'Arte del Medioevo occidentale (secoli IV-XV) con un'aggiunta di nuovi testi e aggiornamenti critico-bibliografici a cura di János VÉGH* (Firenze, 1992). This work, published originally in 1896,

one may well wonder if medieval images are not radically different from modern images both as regards their intellectual content and their emotional or, if one wishes, sensual content.

What, then, is the relation between the image, the text and writing? Writing is a visual system representing speech, and because of its visuality, all writing is also image. This implies that every written text shares some of its aspects with images.[11] Hence the metaphor of reading may be useful to refer to the search for meaning in images as it does for that in texts. This suggests that the historians of the image might try having a look at the questions posed by the historians of reading,[12] so that these may be adapted to the study of images. If images can be regarded as symbols or representations to which different contemporary audiences ascribed different meanings, and if these meanings show a development over time, have a history, then the questions put by historians of reading seem, *mutatis mutandis*, if not identical then at least similar to those addressed during this symposium.

But why would we confine ourselves to the questionnaires of the historians of reading? Why not try to study images in the context of all forms of communication known to a particular society? We may study individual frescoes or other images present in church buildings, and learn much about the different ways in which these may have been 'read'. Imaging now the 'reading' of the whole of a church building, that of the entirety of images, smells, sounds, lights, words pronounced and chanted, rituals ... In a richly decorated church the faithful were attacked everywhere by visual, aural, tactile and olfactory sensations and even, when they partook of the sacrament, gustatory ones.[13] Unfortunately, the preliminary studies for a consideration of individual visual images in relation to all the other visual images present in a medieval church are still lacking – let alone the preliminary studies for considering the relations between the impressions made by images and other sensorial impressions.

---

remains a useful introduction.

[11]   See the observations of H. BELTING, "Das Bild als Text: Wandmalerei und Literatur im Zeitalter Dantes", in: *Malerei und Stadtkultur in der Dantezeit: Die Argumentation der Bilder*, ed. H. BELTING and D. BLUME (München, 1989), pp. 23-64.

[12]   Cf., e.g. *Storia della lettura*, ed. G. CAVALLO and R. CHARTIER (Bari, 1995), also available in French and English translation. On the development of the history of reading and the "fabrique du lisible", see H.-J. MARTIN, *Les métamorphoses du livre: Entretiens avec Jean-Marc Chatelain et Christian Jacob* (Paris, 2004), pp. 259-288.

[13]   Cf. H. WENZEL, *Hören und Sehen, Schrift und Bild: Kultur und Gedächtnis im Mittelalter* (München, 1995), pp. 95-127.

Is it possible, then, at least to attempt a series of case studies comparing the 'reading' of images and texts? For here, too, the moment for writing a synthesis has not yet arrived. It is possible, as the contributions to this volume show, to compare different techniques of 'reading', or to study iconographical and textual traditions.

The comparative study of the processes of finding meaning in images or texts is still a comparatively new field of research. What actually took place in the minds of (literate or illiterate) medieval people when they looked at images eludes us. Maybe this is because, compared to the study of the reception of texts, that of images is still lagging somewhat behind. How were images and texts perceived and understood by contemporaries? That is the question which lies at the centre of the contributions published here. Is it a question that can be answered only for individual images or texts? We will know that only after we have developed our research questions, and after we will have studied many more dossiers. If these proceedings will further future research on this topic, their publication will not have been in vain. The history of reading images and texts in the Middle Ages deserves all the attention currently bestowed on it, and more.

Corporeal Texts, Spiritual Paintings, and the Mind's Eye

HERBERT L. KESSLER

During the course of the twelfth and thirteenth centuries, churches in and around Rome came to be decorated with paintings derived ultimately from the great Early Christian memorial churches of St. Peter's and St. Paul's (fig. 1).[1] Of the dozen that still survive, the earliest is a modest church of ca. 1100 at Ceri just north of Rome, now dedicated to Santa Maria Immacolata,[2] and the best known and one of the latest is the basilica of San Francesco at Assisi.[3] Typically, members belonging to this group represent the Old Testa-

[1] Cf. J. GARBER, *Wirkungen der frühchristlichen Gemäldezyklen der alten Peters- und Pauls-Basiliken in Rom* (Berlin and Vienna, 1918); W. TRONZO, "The prestige of Saint Peter's: observations on the function of monumental narrative cycles in Italy", in: *Pictorial Narrative in Antiquity and the Middle Ages*, ed. H. KESSLER and M.S. SIMPSON (Washington, DC, 1986; *Studies in the History of Art* 16), pp. 93-112; H. KESSLER, "*Caput et speculum omnium ecclesiarum*: Old St. Peter's and church decoration in Medieval Latium", in: *Italian Church Decoration of the Middle Ages and Early Renaissance*, ed. W. TRONZO (Bologna, 1989), pp. 119-146 (reprinted in: H. KESSLER, *Studies in Pictorial Narrative* (London, 1994), pp. 393-432) and "L'antica basilica di San Pietro come fonte e ispirazione per la decorazione delle chiese medievali", in: *Fragmenta picta: Affreschi e mosaici staccati del Medioevo romano* (Rome, 1989), pp. 45-64 (reprinted in English in: KESSLER, *Studies in Pictorial Narrative*, pp. 452-477). It is possible that the Lateran basilica also played a role in establishing the Last Judgment as part of the scheme; in that case, the 'program' in the medieval churches should be understood as a synthesis of Rome's three Constantinian churches.
[2] N.M. ZCHOMELIDSE, *Santa Maria Immacolata in Ceri: Pittura sacra al tempo della Riforma Gregoriana* (Rome, 1996), and E. PARLATO and S. ROMANO, *Roma e il Lazio*, 2nd edn. (Milan, 2001).
[3] H. BELTING, *Die Oberkirche von San Francesco in Assisi: Ihre Dekoration als Aufgabe und die Genese einer neuen Wandmalerei* (Berlin, 1977).

ment on one wall, beginning with a single scene of the Creation of the Cosmos and continuing through Genesis, and end with the Exodus from Egypt; and they depict the New Testament across the nave, starting with the Annunciation to Mary and ending with Christ's post-Resurrection appearances. Often, they picture the Adoration of the Twenty-Four Elders on the apsidal arch and the Last Judgment on the reverse façade. In most of the derivatives, as in the Early Christian basilicas, *tituli* accompany the paintings.[4]

The memorial churches have long since been destroyed: St. Peter's in 1506 and 1606 for the construction of the great church still on the spot and St. Paul's by fire in 1823. Scholars have often turned to the derivatives, therefore, to help reconstruct the fourth/fifth-century decorations, which otherwise are known principally through seventeenth-century watercolour copies (figs. 2-3, 6, 12-13, 20).[5] They have recognized that the copying of the paintings and mosaics in Rome's two apostolic basilicas was provoked, initially at least, by the revival of the *ecclesiae primitivae forma* during the period of the Gregorian Reform and that the result was the establishment of a more or less consistent framework for church decoration in the region.[6] Several scholars have also highlighted the originality of the 'copies', pointing out that the revival of Early Christian sources was only one element operating in these paintings.[7]

An important aspect distinguishing the later churches from their models is the intensification of the typological references within the narratives. Thus, in the late twelfth-century paintings in San Giovanni a Porta Latina,[8] the unity of

---

[4]   Cf. H. KESSLER, "Diction in the 'Bibles of the illiterate' ", in: *World Art: Themes of Unity and Diversity*, ed. I. LAVIN (Philadelphia, 1989), vol. 2, pp. 297-308 (reprinted in: KESSLER, *Studies in Pictorial Narrative*, pp. 33-48).

[5]   The frescoes of Old St. Peter's are known only from two watercolors by Domenico Tasselli (MS Vatican, Biblioteca Apostolica Vaticana [henceforth BAV], Vat. A 64 ter), copied and described in Giacomo Grimaldi's *Descrizione della Basilica antica di S. Pietro in Vaticano* (MS BAV, Barb. lat. 2733), ed. R. NIGGL (Vatican City, 1972). Those in St. Paul's are preserved in a set of seventeenth-century watercolors (MS BAV, Barb. lat. 4406) and an early nineteenth-century drawing by J.B. d'Agincourt (MS BAV, lat. 9843, f. 4r). See S. WAETZOLDT, *Die Kopien des 17. Jahrhunderts nach Mosaiken und Wandmalerein in Rom* (Vienna and Munich, 1964).

[6]   Cf. H. TOUBERT, *Un art dirigé: Réforme grégorienne et iconographie* (Paris, 1990); KESSLER, "*Caput et speculum*", and ZCHOMELIDSE, *Santa Maria Immacolata*.

[7]   See especially TRONZO, "Prestige of Old St. Peter's"; KESSLER, "*Caput et speculum*"; and ZCHOMELIDSE, *S. Maria Immacolata*.

[8]   P. STYGER, "La decorazione a fresco del sec. XII della chiesa di S. Giovanni ante Portam Latinam", *Studi Romani* 2 (1914), pp. 261-328; J. WILPERT, *Römischen Mosaiken und Malereien der kirchlichen Bauten vom IV bis XIII Jahrhundert* (Freiburg i.B., 1916); G. MATTHIAE a.o., *S. Giovanni a Porta Latina e l'oratorio di S. Giovanni in Oleo* (Rome, s.a.); M. MANION, "The frescoes of S. Giovanni a Porta Latina in Rome", unpublished Ph.D. dissertation, Bryn Mawr

all Scripture is introduced at the very start of the decoration, appropriately by John himself (fig. 4). In a church memorializing his martyrdom in Rome, the Evangelist is portrayed in the place of honour to the right of the altar holding a book on which the opening words of his Gospel are displayed: "*IN PRINCIPIO ERAT VERBUM*" ("In the beginning was the Word"; Io 1, 1); and the source text and paradoxically also the realization is illustrated at the head of the Old Testament series (fig. 5), with the appropriate *titulus*: "*IN PRINCIPIO CREAVIT D[EUS] TERRAM*" ("In the beginning, God created the earth"; Gn 1, 1).[9] A watercolour copy of the first field of the right wall in St. Paul's[10] (fig. 6) leaves no doubt that the specific iconography of the Creation scene in San Giovanni a Porta Latina was taken from the Early Christian imagery.[11] Flanked by sun and moon, John's Creator/Logos appears in a starry orb and stretches out his hands toward personifications of light and dark enclosed in mandorlas. The dove of the Holy Spirit descends over the waters and dry land beneath him.[12] Moreover, in San Giovanni a Porta Latina alone, and not in St. Peter's, St. Paul's, or in any other later version, the second genesis, Christ's incarnation, is pictured directly below the Creation of the world. In the Annunciation to Mary (fig. 7), succeeding words from John's Gospel preface are realized: "*Et Verbum caro factum est, et habitavit in nobis*" ("So the Word became flesh; he came to live dwell among us"; Io 1, 14).[13] In this way, at the very start of the decorative series, inscriptions and superimposed pictures assert the harmony of the Old and New Testa-

College (Bryn Mawr, 1972); and M. MANION, "The frescoes of S. Giovanni a Porta Latina: The shape of a tradition", *Australian Journal of Art* 1 (1978), pp. 93-108.

[9]   John the Baptist is portrayed at the left, the Evangelist's counterpart; undoubtedly he originally displayed the "*Ecce agnus Dei*" on the scroll he holds, an allusion to the Lamb of God pictured directly above. A close counterpart to the apsidal composition survives in San Martino ai Monti; cf. J. OSBORNE, "A Carolingian *agnus Dei* relief from Mola di Monte Gelato, near Rome", *Gesta* 33 (1994), pp. 73-78. San Giovanni a Porta Latina had become a possession of the Lateran in 1144-1145; though dedicated to the Saviour, the Lateran basilica was also the church of the two Johns. Cf. S. DE BLAAUW, *Cultus et decor: Liturgia e architettura nella Roma tardoantica e medievale*, 2 vols. (Rome, 1994), 1, pp. 161-169, 210.

[10]   MS BAV, Cod. Barb. 4406, p. 25.

[11]   The beginning of the Old Testament sequence in St. Peter's is not recorded; presumably, though, like the later half, it was nearly identical to that in St. Paul's.

[12]   The Lamb of God in the Barberini copy was not a feature of the medieval painting.

[13]   The same set of connections is made in the Chapel of St. Thomas at Anagni, which is related to San Giovanni a Porta Latina also in other ways; however, there, the Annunciation is in the second register below the Creation and John the Evangelist, presenting the opening words of his Gospel, is portrayed in the embrasure of the portal across the room. Cf. H. KESSLER, "L'oratorio di San Tommaso Becket", in: *La Cripta della Cattedrale di Anagni* (Rome, 2001), pp. 89-95.

ments, which John 'the Divine' had himself perceived with special acumen,[14] offering a form of elevated understanding that, during the Middle Ages, was considered a form of 'spiritual seeing'.[15]

In at least one other instance in San Giovanni a Porta Latina, words and a pictorial juxtaposition make the relationship between Old and New Testament specific (fig. 8). Taken literally, the verse inscribed beneath the Expulsion of Adam and Eve from Paradise refers only to the source of humankind's sin: "*INMORTALEM DECUS PER LIGNUM PERDIDIT HOMO CAELIS*"; "Man lost the immortal splendour of heaven by the wood" can be construed simply as an allusion to the punishment meted out when Adam and Eve ate from the tree of the knowledge of good and evil.[16] But a long tradition going back to Irenaeus of Lyon († after 178) held that wood from the tree in Paradise was used to make the cross on which Christ died.[17] In San Giovanni a Porta Latina, that tradition is confirmed visually by the Crucifixion depicted directly below. Moreover, a pictorial motif underscores the association between the Expulsion from Paradise and the Crucifixion. The gold, gem-encrusted walls of Eden (fig. 9) identify the lost "*decus caelis*" as the Heavenly Jerusalem to which humankind will be returned at the end of time.[18] The Book of Revelation describes the celestial city as built of "pure gold, bright as clear glass ... adorned with jewels [and with] twelve gates made of pearls" (Apc 21, 18-21); and the eleventh-century Last Judgment panel in the Vatican Museum (fig. 10) as well as the closely related depiction in Ceri both represent the blessed enclosed within an ornamented precinct quite like the Eden in San Giovanni a Porta Latina.[19] In this

---

[14] See J. HAMBURGER, *St. John the Divine: The Deified Evangelist in Medieval Art and Theology* (Berkeley and Los Angeles, 2002). I wish to thank Professor Hamburger for allowing me to consult his study before publication.

[15] For an overview, see H. KESSLER, " 'Facies bibliothecae revelata': Carolingian art as spiritual seeing", in: *Testo e immagine nell'alto medioevo*, 2 vols. (Spoleto, 1998: *Settimane di studio del Centro italiano di studi sull'alto medioevo* 41), 2, pp. 533-584 (reprinted in: H. KESSLER, *Spiritual Seeing* (Philadelphia, 2000), pp. 149-189).

[16] MANION, "Shape of Tradition", p. 104 and TRONZO, "Prestige of Saint Peter's", pp. 109-110.

[17] Cf. H.M. VON ERFFA, *Ikonologie der Genesis: Die christlichen Bildthemen aus dem Alten Testament und ihre Quellen*, 2 vols. (Munich, 1989), 1, pp. 114-119.

[18] *La dimora di Dio con gli uomini (Ap 21, 3): Immagini della Gerusalemme celeste dal III al XIV secolo*, ed. M. GATTI PERER (Milan, 1983).

[19] W. PAESELER, "Die römische Weltgerichtstafel im Vatikan: Ihre Stellung in der Geschichte des Weltgerichtsbildes in der römischen Malerei des 13. Jahrhunderts", *Kunstgeschichtliches Jahrbuch der Bibliotheca Hertziana* 2 (1938), pp. 313-393; V. PERI, "La Tavola Vaticana del Giudizio Universale: Nota sulla data e sul tema apocalittico", *Atti della Pontificia Accademia di Archeologia, Rendiconti* 39 (1966-1967), pp. 169-183; ZCHOMELIDSE, *Santa Maria Immacolata*, pp. 149-159. R. SUCKALE, *Das mittelalterliche Bild als Zeitzeuge*

way, the pictures assert, Christ's sacrifice on the Cross and its re-enactment in the Mass celebrated in the church would restore the "the immortal splendour of heaven".

Though not unique, the typological references in the caption accompanying the scene of the Expulsion in San Giovanni are exceptional. Generally, the *tituli* in the medieval churches underscore the actuality of the events pictured and, as in the case of the Creation and Annunciation or Expulsion and Crucifixion in San Giovanni a Porta Latina, the theological relationships of Old and New Testament events are established pictorially, either by such interpolated elements as the Christ-Creator in resplendent Eden or through such meaningful juxtapositions as that of the tree and cross. In other words, the texts offer a literal account and the pictures an interpretive reading.

A good example is the depiction of Joseph Pulled from the Well and Sold to the Ishmaelites in Santa Maria Immacolata at Ceri (fig. 11).[20] The (fragmentary) caption reads simply: "... *ANIS IOSEP DAT[UR] ISMAELITIS*" ("Joseph is given to the Ishmaelites"). The picture, however, conflates into one composition two moments that, in St. Paul's, were pictured in a more discursive fashion in separate compositions (figs. 12 and 13).[21] Joseph is pulled from the circular well. The brother at the left grabs his hip, the one on the right his arm, while the others watch what is transpiring and discuss it. At the same time, the bearded, oldest brother (cloak fastened at the shoulder) accepts payment from a bald, half-naked Ishmaelite who clutches a moneybag in his left hand. Another of the Ishmaelites (who have arrived on two camels) takes Joseph away.

Although the merger of two episodes required the painters at Ceri to effect certain economies, for instance, to eliminate the second figure of Joseph, a secondary subject is introduced that was not in the source pictures (or any of the other copies). In the lower left corner, one of the brothers is shown displaying Joseph's coat of many colours to another. The interpolated vignette cues a Christian reading of the Old Testament story. The two men, and indeed the others discussing the wicked deed behind them, recall nothing so much as the soldiers dividing Christ's garment in depictions of the Crucifixion, a good example being the somewhat earlier painting in Sant'Angelo in Formis (fig. 14).[22] What is more, a late twelfth-century compendium of *tituli*, the *Pictor in Carmine*, includes just this event as a type for the Crucifixion:[23] "*Fratres*

(Berlin, 2002), pp. 12-122.
  [20] ZCHOMELIDSE, *Santa Maria Immacolata*, pp. 63-64.
  [21] MS BAV, Cod. Barb. 4406, pp. 47 and 48.
  [22] Cf. O. MORISANI, *Gli affreschi di S. Angelo in Formis* (Naples, 1962), fig. 44.
  [23] M.R. JAMES, "*Pictor in carmine*", *Archaeologia*, 94 (1951), pp. 141-166 and A. ARNULF,

Ioseph nudant eum tunica talari et polimita" ("Joseph's brothers strip him of his long and colourful tunic").

Likewise, the prominent representation of one brother receiving the money-bag calls to mind Judas accepting the thirty pieces of silver, another connection the *Pictor in Carmine* makes: *"Spondet Iudas Iudeis pro XXX argenteis de proditione Christi. Fratres Ioseph uendunt eum Ismaelitis negotiatoribus pro XX argenteis"* ("Judas promises the Jews to betray Christ for thirty pieces of silver. Joseph's brothers sell him to the Ishmaelite merchants for twenty pieces of silver").[24]

These references to Christ's passion allow for the reading of Joseph's odd posture, his arms outstretched and body twisted, as an allusion to the crucified Christ. And they account for the strigillation of the well from which Joseph is lifted; a common feature in Early Christian sarcophagi, strigillation character-izes Christ's tomb at Sant'Angelo in Formis (fig. 15). Again, the *Pictor in Carmine* supports the interpretation, offering as a parallel for the Entombment of Christ the scene of: *"Ioseph a fratribus mittitur in cisternam ueterem"* ("Jo-seph is put into an old well by his brothers").[25] Among the patriarchs, Joseph was long regarded as the type of Christ par excellence. He assumed a particu-larly important position in biblical exegesis at the turn of the twelfth century. The contemporary exegete and Abbot of Montecassino Bruno of Segni (1045/49-1123), for instance, elaborated the entire story of Joseph in terms of Christian history. For him, the coat of many colours signified Christ's divine nature, covering his humanity; and the blood of the goat used to stain it was a symbol of the dead Jesus.[26]

Indeed, by figuring the literal account of the Old Testament event provided in the *titulus* with a typological reading of it, the painting recapitulates Christ's incarnation. It interprets and completes the words from Jewish history just as Christ did in his very person. The same pattern is evident also in the distichs of the *Pictor in Carmine*; although organized according to the chronology of Christ's life, the verses themselves are straightforward and descriptive.

Versus ad picturas: Studien zur Titulusdichtung als Quellengattung der Kunstgeschichte von der Antike bis zum Hochmittelalter (Munich and Berlin, 1997), pp. 273-286.

[24] JAMES, *"Pictor"*, p. 160.

[25] JAMES, *"Pictor"*, p. 162.

[26] *Expositio in Genesim*, ed. in: MIGNE, *PL* 164, col. 219: *"Per haedum, quem occiderunt, Christi mortem, per tunicam vero, quam in ejus sanguine tinxerunt, carnem sanguine proprio cruentatam designamus ... Fecit autem pater huic filio suo dilecto tunicam polymitam, per quam, carnem, qua divinitas induta est, intelligimus"*. Zchomelidse noted Bruno of Segni's interest in the acts of mercy, imagery that is featured in the Last Judgment on the reverse facade (ZCHOMELIDSE, *Santa Maria Immacolata*, p. 158).

When captions in the Italian churches convey explicit typological meanings, they consistently do so, not for obscure subjects as might be supposed, but
rather for pictures that could prove problematic because they involve the expec-
tation of seeing God with human eyes. Thus, the words "Man lost the immortal
splendour of heaven by the wood" beneath the Expulsion from Eden in San
Giovanni a Porta Latina refer to the belief that one punishment for the sin of
Adam and Eve was humankind's eternal banishment from the sight of the Lord.
And, read with the Crucifixion below, the same caption reminds the viewers
God did become visible again when he assumed flesh and lived on earth.

Likewise, the well-established Trinitarian significance of the scene of
Abraham Greeting the Angels hardly seems to have required verbal reinforce-
ment. In San Pietro a Valle at Ferentillo,[27] completed about twenty years after
San Giovanni a Porta Latina, the typology would, in any case, have been clear
enough without any text; the foremost messenger dressed in green is distinguished from his two winged companions clad in red (fig. 16). The very fact
that the Trinity disclosed to Abraham is represented in a picture, however, is
precisely the problem; the mystery revealed to Abraham at this moment was not
manifested physically, but rather spiritually. Bruno of Segni stressed this point.
Abraham, he wrote, did not see the Trinity itself but, through *worshipping* the
unity of God when he greeted the three messengers, he acknowledged the Tri-
une Deity.[28] At Ferentillo, therefore, words were added to make that point.
Although badly damaged, the caption was clearly a version of the Ambrosian
reading of the event "*tres videt et unum adoravit*", repeated by Peter Damian
(ca. 1007-1072), Rupert of Deutz (ca. 1070-1129/30), and other contemporaries: "*TRE ... N ... CU[M] ME ... VIDET CO ... LAUDET ET UNAM*".[29]

Picture and *titulus* convey the same idea even more forcefully in San
Giovanni a Porta Latina (fig. 17). As in Ferentillo, one of the angels is distin-

---

[27] A. SCHMARSOW, "Romanische Wandgemälde der Abteikirche S. Pietro bei Ferentillo",
Repertorium für Kunstwissenschaft 28 (1905), pp. 391-405; E. WÜSCHER-BECCHI, "Sopra un
ciclo di affreschi del Vecchio e Nuovo Testamento nella Badia di S. Pietro presso Ferentillo",
Atti della Pontificia Accademia Romana di Archeologia (Rome, 1906), pp. 199-221; A. ORAZI,
L'abbazia di Ferentillo (Rome, 1979); *L'Umbria*, ed. A. PRANDI a.o. (Milan, 1979); and H.
KESSLER, "The icon in the narrative", in: IDEM, *Spiritual Seeing*, pp. 19-28.

[28] *Expositio in Genesim*, 18, ed. in: MIGNE, *PL* 164, cols. 193-194: "*Ecce enim, quod ante
id temporis omnibus incognitum fuerat, in Trinitate Deum cernit, et in unitate adorat; non quod
Trinitatem ipsam viderit; sed quia per hoc, quod viderat, in Trinitate, et unitate Deum cognoscere meruit; unde cum tres viderit, attamen nonnisi unum adorat, nonnisi unum Dominum
vocat*".

[29] Peter Damian, *Antilogus contra Judaeos*, 25, ed. in: MIGNE, *PL* 145, col. 43; Rupert of
Deutz, *De glorificatione Trinitatis et Processione Sancti Spiritus*, 31, ed. in: MIGNE, *PL* 169,
cols. 94-95.

guished from the others, but Abraham averts his eyes from the messengers. He worships the one and three, but does not see the mystery with his physical senses. The caption makes the point explicit: *"DEUM MENTE VIDENS COLUIT"* ("Seeing God in his mind, [Abraham] worships him").

The *titulus* beneath the depiction of Moses at the Burning Bush in Ceri serves the same cautionary purpose (fig. 18). Another classic Christian typology,[30] alluded to in the Gospel of Luke to prove the possibility of resurrection (Lc. 20:7), God's appearance to Moses on Mount Horeb was a watershed moment in sacred history. Bruno of Segni, for instance, wrote of it that "Now the mysteries commence, now the sacred meanings are revealed",[31] arguing that one of those mysteries is the relationship to the other *terra sancta*, Eden, from which Adam and Eve were ejected, the scene pictured directly above in Santa Maria Immacolata (fig. 19).[32] He also maintained that the commandment to Moses to remove his sandals refers to the garments the first couple wore outside Paradise, the skin of dead animals. And, following an ancient line of exegesis, he saw in the bush-not-consumed-by-fire the Virgin "who conceives through the Holy Spirit, without desire of the flesh and without sexual passion".[33] Thus, the tree and serpent featured in the same field at Ceri allude to the sin depicted above, which also featured a tree and a serpent, and to the punishment for that sin, which included exile from God's presence.

Seeing God is at the very core of the first part of the story:

> There the Lord *appeared* to him in the flame of a burning bush. Moses *noticed* that, although the bush was on fire, it was not being burnt up; so he said to himself, "I must go across to *see* the wonderful *sight*. Why does not the bush burn away?" When the Lord saw that Moses had turned aside to *look*, he called to him out of the

---

[30] Cf. Th. ALIPRANTIS, *Moses auf dem Berge Sinai: Die Ikonographie der Berufung des Moses und des Empfangs der Gesetzestafeln* (Munich, 1986); F. BOESPFLUG, "Un étrange spectacle: Le Buisson ardent comme théophanie dans l'art occidental", *Revue de l'art* 97 (1992), pp. 12-31; and N. ZSCHOMELIDSE, "Das Bild im Busch: Zu Theorie und Ikonographie der alttestamentlichen Gottesvision im Mittelalter", in: *Die Sichtbarkeit des Unsichtbaren: Zur Korrelation von Text und Bild im Wirkungskreis der Bibel: Tübinger Symposium 1999*, ed. B. JANOWSKI and N. ZCHOMELIDSE (Stuttgart, 2002).

[31] *Expositio in Exodum*, III, ed. in: MIGNE, *PL* 164, col. 237: *"Jam incipiunt mysteria, jam revelantur sacramenta"*.

[32] *Expositio in Exodum*, III, ed. in: MIGNE, *PL* 164, col. 237: *"Locus enim in quo stas, terra sancta est; in terra sancta non licet habere calceamenta, non licet indui pellibus mortuorum; ideo enim Adam in paradiso nudus exiens zona pellicea indutus est"*.

[33] *Expositio in Exodum*, III, ed. in: MIGNE, *PL* 164, col. 237: *"Haec autem visa est ardens, sed non arsit, quia sine qarnis concupiscentia, sine libidinis aestu, sancto Spiritu obumbrata concepit"*.

bush, "Moses, Moses". And Moses answered, "Yes, I am here". God said, "Come no nearer; take off your sandals; the place where you are standing is holy ground". Then he said, "I am the God of your forefathers, the God of Abraham, the God of Isaac, the God of Jacob". Moses covered his face, for he was afraid to *gaze* on God. (author's emphasis)

In St. Paul's the two moments were pictured in separate fields. In the first, Moses confronts only the Hand of God, symbolizing the divine voice (fig. 20). At Ceri, the hand is attached to a whole figure, transforming the event into a vision of the God-made-man. Christ appears at the centre of an enormous green oval filled with vine-like branches and red flames.[34] Nonetheless, the patriarch seems to hear God, not see him with physical sight. Moses looks upward and beyond the Saviour who is pictured more or less facing toward the viewer.

It is no surprise that the Lord's appearance to Moses at Horeb necessarily prompted speculation about the nature of God's visibility. The episode was cited in a much-circulated prologue to the Book of Revelation.[35] Rupert of Deutz speculated that God appeared in the bramble because fire offered a worthy metaphor for God, who was uncircumscribable and invisible, adding that the fire that did not consume the bush in which it appeared also served as an allegory of Christ's dual nature: *"subauditur Christus Deus et homo"*.[36]

This is precisely the claim made by the *titulus* beneath the painting in Santa Maria Immacolata: *"[DEU]S E[ST] ET HOMO QUEM SACRA FIGURAT IMAGO"*. The only caption in the church that refers explicitly to the painting itself, the *titulus* is, in fact, the second line of a couplet recorded in the *Inscriptionum Christianarum libellus* by Hildebert of Lavardin (1056-1134)[37] and also in a

[34] The sexual implications of Christ appearing in the bush alongside Moses transforming the serpent into a stiff rod are obvious.

[35] D. DE BRUYNE, *Préfaces de la Bible Latine* (Namur, 1920), p. 263.

[36] *In Exodum Commentariorum*, I.12.3, ed. in: MIGNE, *PL* 167, cols. 578-79: *"Deus invisibilis, qui nec loco circumscribitur, nec ullis sensibus corporis percipitur, quoties visibiliter hominibus apparet, rebus ipsis congruam assumit speciem, propter quas apparere dignatur .... Totus enim hic ignis, subauditur Christus Deus et homo, novem in utero ejus mensibus habitavit, et levem carnis vel animae ejus stipulam sive fenum, non solum non combussit, verum etiam majore cum virginitatis honor gratiaque formati exinde hominis, quem assumpsit, perenniter illustravit"*.

[37] Ed. in: MIGNE, *PL* 171, col. 1283; Cf. R. BUGGE, *"Effigiem Christi, qui transis, semper honora*: Verses condemning the cult of sacred images in art and literature", *Acta ad Archaeologiam et Artium Historiam Pertinentia* 6 (1975), pp. 127-139; H. KESSLER, "Real absence: Early medieval art and the metamorphosis of vision", in: *Morfologie sociali e culturali in Europa fra tarda antichità e alto medioevo*, 2 vols. (Spoleto, 1998: *Settimane di studio del Centro italiano di studi sull'alto medioevo* 45), 2, pp. 1157-1211 (reprinted in: KESSLER, *Spiritual Seeing*, pp. 104-148); ARNULF, *Versus ad picturas*, pp. 273-286; KENDALL, *Allegory*

florilegium of *tituli* by Baudri of Bourgueil (1046-1130) (both contemporaries of Ceri who knew one another)[38] and that William Durandus (1230/31-1296) later took over in his *Rationale*: "*NEC DEUS EST NEC HOMO, PRAESENS QUAM CERNIS IMAGO, SED DEUS ET HOMO QUEM SACRA FIGURAT IMAGO*".[39] ("The image that you see is neither God nor man in the flesh, but it is God and man in the flesh which the sacred image depicts".) In a sense, the Christ pictured in the bush replaces the first line of the verse. The *titulus* derived from the second line, warns the viewer that the figure of the Divine Being, which Moses himself saw only in his imagination, is only an *imago*.

In the written compendia and in all extant works, the cautionary caption is always applied to devotional images, Christ in Majesty or the Crucifixion. Why was it added to the Old Testament narrative at Ceri? As in the case of the scene of Abraham Greeting the Three Angels, the reason has to do with the dangers inherent in the theme itself, which involves the envisioning of God. Not only does the "*sacra imago*" reveal the Christian truth underlying the Jewish theophany, but it also represents what Moses himself saw in his mind's eye when he looked at the burning bush. Because humankind's direct vision of God was sacrificed through Adam's and Eve's sin, a clear distinction had to be drawn between physical seeing and mental imagining.[40] Together, word and image reinforce the belief that all material depictions seen through the physical sense of sight can only be *figures* of God.

Because God became visible in Christ, events from the Gospels generally did not present the same difficulty to image-makers. Nonetheless, in San Giovanni a Porta Latina and at Ferentillo, depictions of eschatological themes or New Testament subjects that, themselves, involved veneration induced the painters to introduce devices that alert viewers to the fact that what they are allowed to see is only an image of God, not God himself. In the Last Judgment on the reverse façade of the former, for instance, Christ's face was painted on a separate panel set into the plaster (figs. 21 and 22) to make clear that, just as Abraham and Moses saw only a physical metaphors of the Deity, so too those in the church are not really viewing God. Only the blessed would see at the

---

of the Church, p. 81; and ZCHOMELIDSE, "Bild im Busch".

[38] ARNULF, *Titulusdichtung*, p. 298.

[39] *Rationale divinorum officiorum*, ed. A. DAVRIL and T. THIBODEAU (Turnhout, 1995: CCCM, 140), p. 35. Durandus was probably the source for the inscription around Christ on the altar in the Chapel of St. Firmin at St. Denis; cf. J. FORMIGÉ, *L'abbaye royale de Saint-Denis: Recherches nouvelles* (Paris, 1960), pp. 124 ff. Only the base of the altar is an authentic medieval work, however; the inscription, like the figures, is a nineteenth-century creation.

[40] See C. HAHN, "*VISIO DEI*: Changes in medieval visuality", in: *Visuality Before and Beyond the Renaissance: Seeing as Others Saw*, ed. R. NELSON (Cambridge, 2000), pp. 169-194.

Lord's face, and they, only at the end of time. As Augustine (354-430) pointed out, on Judgment Day, the saved would apprehend

> through a direct vision and not through a dark image, as far as the human mind elevated by the grace of God can receive it. In such a vision, God speaks face to face to him whom He has made worthy of this communion. And here we are speaking not of the face of the body but of that of the mind.[41]

The same explicit artificiality in the faces of Christ and Mary in the Crucifixion scene in San Giovanni a Porta Latina is to be understood in terms of the long history of the Crucifix as a devotional image and John the Evangelist's special role in the development.[42] An outsized composition close to the door on the right wall, the Crucifixion would have provided a special focus;[43] the enlarged depiction in the late eleventh-century decorations of Sant'Urbano alla Caffarella in Rome, also derived from St. Peter's, offers a parallel (fig. 23).

Following a long tradition, Sant'Urbano pictures two patrons venerating the Crucifixion scene.[44] It is quite possible that the Crucifixion in San Giovanni also included a donor portrait in the destroyed lower portion. Even if it did not, however, the image's devotional aspect was so well established that the need would have been felt to distinguish the picture from the celestial reality it stands for. The cross itself was sufficient to conjure up Christ in the minds of the faithful, as Einhard (ca. 770-840) reported in the ninth century, citing Jerome's (ca. 350-420) report that, when Paula prostrated herself before the cross in Jerusalem:

---

[41] *De Genesi ad litteram*, 12, 26, ed. I. ZYCHA (Vienna, 1894: CSEL 28), 1, p. 420: *"Ibi uidetur claritas Domini, non per uisionem significantem, siue corporalem, sicut uisa est in monte Sina, siue spiritualem, sicut uidit Isaias, uel Johannes in Apocalypsi: sed per speciem, non per aenigmata, quantum cam capere mens humana potest, secundum adsumentis dei gratiam, ut os ad os loquatur deus ei quem dignum tali colloquio fecerit; non os corporis, sed mentis"*; tr. J. TAYLOR, *St. Augustine, The Literal Meaning of Genesis*, 2 vols. (New York, NY, 1982: *Ancient Christian Writers* 41-42), 2, p. 217.

[42] Styger actually found a fragment of the wooden panel, presumably painted with the portrait of Mary, beneath an iron hook.

[43] K. NOREEN, *Sant'Urbano all Caffarella: Eleventh-Century Roman Wall Painting and the Sanctity of Martyrdom*, unpublished Ph.D. diss., Johns Hopkins University (Baltimore, 1998).

[44] E.g., the ninth-century painting at San Vincenzo al Volturno which pictures the Abbot Epyphanius at the foot of the cross; cf. J. MITCHELL, "The crypt reappraised", in: *San Vincenzo al Volturno*, 1, ed. R. HODGES (London, 1993), pp. 75-114.

"... she adored Christ as if she saw the Lord still suspended there". And we believe that we too ought to do this, namely to prostrate ourselves before the cross and, with our inner eye open, to adore him, who is suspended on the cross.[45]

The presence of John the Evangelist only underscored the scene's evocative power. The Apostle is partially preserved at the right of the composition, where remains of his right arm are sufficient to establish that he was pictured with his hand raised to his face in a gesture of meditation, much as in the depiction in Sant'Angelo in Formis (fig. 14). Recalled in this way, John's ability to contemplate Christ's divinity in his "mind's eye" even at the nadir of the Lord's earthly existence must have contributed to the need to insert the icon into the Crucifixion scene.[46]

An attached panel was also introduced on the triumphal arch at San Pietro a Valle to distinguish God's face, pictured among the seven lamps of gold and angels as described in the Book of Revelation (fig. 24). Here, too, the 'one like the son of man' was pictured on a separate panel attached to the painted plaster by metal hooks, leaving no doubt that the image was merely an evocation of God's face (fig. 25). In the narratives of Christ's life on the nave wall, moreover, a similar device was deployed in episodes involving worship to warn viewers not to confuse facsimiles of God with the Divinity itself. Thus, the scene of Christ's Entry into Jerusalem at the centre of the third register (fig. 26), the citizens emerge from the arched gateway to hail the Lord and one of them lays a cloak down before him. The context of veneration created by these figures is reinforced by Zacchaeus, who, according to Luke, "being a little man, could not see what [Jesus] looked like. So he ran on ahead and climbed a sycamore-tree in order to see him" (Lc 19:1-10). The figure of Christ breaks from the narrative direction and is shown front-faced and bearing a gemmed cross nimbus. Enthroned side-saddle on an ornamented blanket, he holds a scroll in one hand and blesses with the other. These features were adopted from Rome's most famous icon of Christ, the *Acheropita* in the Lateran, now badly abraded but known through many copies, including the fine panel in the cathedral at Sutri, which is contemporary with Ferentillo (fig. 27).[47] The reference to

---

[45] *On the Adoration of the Cross*, in: *Charlemagne's Courtier: The Complete Einhard*, ed. and tr. P.E. DUTTON (Toronto, 1998), p. 174.

[46] Cf. J. O'REILLY, "St. John as a figure of the contemplative life: Text and image in the art of the Anglo-Saxon Benedictine reform", in: *St. Dunstan: His Life, Times, and Cult*, ed. N. RAMSAY a.o. (Woodbridge, 1992), pp. 165-185.

[47] See H. BELTING, *Likeness and Presence: A History of the Image before the Era of Art*, tr. E. JEPHCOTT (Chicago, 1994), pp. 64-68 and *passim*, and most recently the essays by S. ROMANO, M. ANDALORO, W. ANGELELLI, and E. PARLATO in: *Il volto di Cristo* (catalogue of an

the Lateran icon would not have been missed by the faithful in San Pietro a Valle; a bust-length version of the *Acheropita* is the focus of a prayer niche on the adjacent wall near the altar in San Pietro a Valle (fig. 28). When Christ is shown in an episode involving adoration, then, the painter quoted an icon to remind those who contemplated the scene that what they see is merely an image.

The danger that viewers might also be induced by the worshipping kings in the Adoration of the Magi to confuse the picture with the reality behind it led to the incorporation of another famous icon in the scene directly above the Entry (figs. 29 and 30). Here, however, it is Mary who is presented as an image, in this case, as the Maria Avvocata (e.g. the version from the Roman church of Sta. Maria in Ara Coeli, fig. 31);[48] those looking at the painting of the Adoration see, not the Mother of God, but only a picture of her.[49]

The uppermost scene on the central axis of the New Testament wall in San Pietro a Valle also involved worship. It pictured Christ enthroned in heaven being adored by angels. Unfortunately, too little of it is left to determine how the face of God, shown enthroned in majesty, was rendered.[50] Clearly, though, it capped an anagogical ascent on the central axis of the north wall, beginning with the nadir of Christ's earthly life when he arrived in Jerusalem at the start of his Passion, moved upward to the moment he was recognized by the pagan kings, and culminated in the celestial realm (in line with the triumphal arch but illuminated by windows) where the heavenly minions eternally sing his praise. Like the scenes of Abraham and the Angels and Moses at the Burning Bush at Ceri, which also involve veneration or the Crucifixion in San Giovanni a Porta Latina, the Entry into Jerusalem and Adoration of the Magi in San Pietro a Valle near Ferentillo include cautions against confusing physical seeing with mental meditation.

Appropriately, Old Testament subjects in the medieval churches generally rely on words of warning and New Testament episodes on pictures of icons. In all of these cases, however, the problem of what one is seeing in the paintings was not eliminated; it was only shifted. Descriptive texts, typological pictures,

exhibition), ed. G. MORELLO and G. WOLF (Rome, 2000), pp. 36-52. Cf. KESSLER, *Spiritual Seeing*, pp. 26-28.

[48] BELTING, *Likeness and Presence*, pp. 314-329 and *passim*, and G. WOLF, *Salus Populi Romani: Die Geschichte römischer Kultbilder im Mittelalter* (Weinheim, 1990).

[49] The *Maria Avvocata* may have been pictured in a niche on the left side of the apsidal arch, the counterpart of Christ *acheropita* at the right. The two images were often paired, as in the most famous replica, the triptych in Tivoli (Duomo); cf. MATTHIAE, *Pittura romana*, 2, pp. 58-60.

[50] KESSLER, *Spiritual Seeing*, pp. 19-21.

and icons remind viewers that corporeal words and spiritual images can stimulate their minds to a higher, inner vision. But, while the mental pictures might
lead to the threshold of the highest spiritual plane, they can not penetrate it. To
see God required a 'third type of vision', what Augustine called intellectual
seeing, which was not dependent on either words or images.[51]

A reminder of this tenet was introduced at San Giovanni a Porta Latina
between the declarations of *"IN PRINCIPIO"* that, in text and picture, so emphati-
cally declare the unity of sacred history and hence the very possibility of elevated seeing.[52] It was provided by a second portrait of John the Evangelist between the standing apostle holding his gospel and the pictorial realizations of his
words in the Creation and Annunciation (fig. 32). Now largely lost, this portrait
showed the Evangelist writing his Gospel, his eagle bearing a book inscribed:
"ALTA PENETRA[S] CELUM TU MENTE IOANNE[S]" ("John, you rise above heaven
with your elevated mind"). Displayed by the bird believed to be capable of flying higher than any other creature, the text asserted the widely-held claim that,
of all men, John alone had been privileged to rise above this world and, in truth,
see God. In a church dedicated to the one evangelist capable of seeing the creation of the world, the incarnation of the Word, and the end of time–Scriptural
moments all pictured in San Giovanni a Porta Latina – John's privileged ability
to see with the highest form of vision is explicitly asserted.[53]

The very prologue that cites Moses at the burning bush as an example of
spiritual seeing attributes the more elevated mode of vision to John:

Another way is intellectual, for example, as when, revealed by the Holy Spirit, we
understand by the intellect of the mind the truth of the mysteries as it is, in which
way John saw those things that are related in this book. For, he did not merely see
figures of the spirit but he understood their meaning in his mind.[54]

---

[51] *De genesi ad litteram*, 12, c. 26, ed. J. ZYCHA (Vienna, Prague and Leipzig, 1894: CSEL
28, 1), p. 420.

[52] See H. KESSLER, *"Facies bibliothecae revelata"*, pp. 533-594 (reprinted in: IDEM,
Spiritual Seeing, pp. 149-189).

[53] E.g. Jerome, *Epistle* 53, 4, ed. in: MIGNE, *PL* 22, col. 543: *"Iohannes rusticus, piscator,
indoctus? et unde illa, obsecro: 'in principio erat Verbum, et Verbum erat apud Deum, et Deus
erat Verbum'"*.

[54] *"Alia intellectualis, quando uidelicet spiritu sancto 'reuelante' intellectui mentis
ueritatem misteriorum sicut est capimus, quomodo uidit iohannes, quae in hoc libro referuntur.
Non enim figuras tantum spiritu uidit, sed et earum significata mente intellexit"* (ed. DE BRUYNE,
Préfaces, p. 263).

Moreover, John's superior contemplative powers were elaborated with particular interest by Carolingian theologians. Alcuin (ca. 730-804) wrote in his commentary on John's Gospel:

> And so he is elevated far before the three other Evangelists; these you see, as it were, on the earth conversing with the human Christ, while him you see mounting above the cloud which covers the entire earth and reaching the liquid light of heaven where he beheld, with a most acute and powerful mind, the Word in the beginning, God issuing from God, light from light.[55]

Margaret Manion has pointed out that the very text inscribed on the book in San Giovanni a Porta Latina is Carolingian in origin; a nearly identical verse occurs in the Majestas Domini in the Codex Aureus of St. Emmeram in Munich,[56] dated 870:[57] "*Scribendo penitras caelum tu mente, Iohannes*". The same idea is repeated in the *titulus* to the portrait of John (f. 97r):

> *Cum sancto penitras arcana labore, Iohannes,*
> *Quae nullus potuit hominum nec mentis acumen*
> *Alta sophya nitens unquam penitrare legendo*
> ...

Recently, Paul Dutton and Edouard Jeauneau have demonstrated that these *tituli* were most likely composed by John Scotus Eriugena (ca. 810-ca. 877), whose ideas about John are also set out in his *Commentary* on John's Gospel.[58] More than a mere mortal, John ascended to the third heaven and there perceived the totality of sacred history and the mystery of the Trinity.[59]

---

[55] *Commentarium in Joannem*, 1, ed. in: MIGNE, *PL* 100, cols. 741 ff.; tr. M. SCHAPIRO, "Two Romanesque drawings in Auxerre", in: *Studies in Art and Literature for Belle Da Costa Greene*, ed. D. MINER (Princeton, 1954), pp. 331-349 (reprinted in: M. SCHAPIRO, *Romanesque Art* (New York, 1977), pp. 306-327). The claim that John alone had penetrated time and space to view the entirety of sacred history had a strong influence on depictions of him. An early ninth-century ivory in the Metropolitan Museum of Art in New York, for instance, depicts John holding an open book with the first words of his Gospel inscribed on it, an eagle above his head, and a verse from the *Paschale Carmen* of Sedulius: "*MORE VOLANS QUILE VERBUM PETIT ASTRA [IOHAN]NI[S]*" ("Flying like an eagle, the word of John aspires to the heavens"). See C. LITTLE, "A new ivory of the court of Charlemagne", in: *Studien zur mittelalterlichen Kunst 800-1250: Festschrift für Florentine Mütherich zum 70. Gesburtstag* (Munich, 1985), pp. 11-28.

[56] MS Munich, Bayerische Staatsbibliothek, Clm, 14000, f. 6v.

[57] Cf. W. KOEHLER and F. MÜTHERICH, *Die Karolingischen Miniaturen*, 5: *Die Hofschule Karls des Kahlen* (Berlin, 1982), pp. 175-198.

[58] Ed. in: MIGNE, *PL* 122, cols. 283 ff.

[59] See also, Haimo of Auxerre, *Homily IX*, ed. in: MIGNE, *PL* 118, cols. 54-75; Bruno of

John's special role in seeing all of sacred history as a unity accounts for the fact that, of all the derivatives of St. Peter's and St. Paul's, only San Giovanni a Porta Latina breaks with the system of opposing Old Testament and New on facing walls and organizes the narratives in parallel, continuous registers.[60] The church on earth dedicated to the Evangelist reflects the celestial Church that he alone saw when he penetrated the heavens.[61]

The point that true intellectual vision is needed to enter the super-celestial realm is made in at least one other of the churches derived from the apostolic basilicas, not in the overall structure as in San Giovanni, but rather in specific details. The opening image in San Pietro a Valle at Ferentillo (fig. 33) is clearly derived from the traditional composition based on the Early Christian programs and reiterated at Ceri and San Giovanni a Porta Latina (figs. 5 and 6); however, it introduces a new feature, a scroll borne by two angels and inscribed: "*PRINCI-PIO CELU ET TERRA[E] FECISSE FIGURAM*".[62] Inspired by a Virgilian passage,[63] the hexameter verse varies the opening words of the Book of Genesis to suggest that what is shown in the depiction is not heaven and earth itself but only the outward appearance (*figura*) of the heaven and earth.[64] Augustine may have been the immediate source for the concept, specifically his account in the *City of God* of the new creation that is to follow the Last Judgment:

> When the judgment shall be finished, then this heaven and this earth shall cease to be, and a new heaven and a new earth shall begin. But this world will not be utterly consumed; it will only undergo a change; and therefore the Apostle says: The form [*figura*] of this world passeth away, and I would have you to be without care. The form [*figura*] goes away, not the nature.[65]

Segni, *Commentaria in Joannem*, I, ed. in: MIGNE, *PL* 165, cols. 451-461. Bruno of Segni, it should be noted, may have played an important role in the theology of twelfth-century painting.

[60] John was featured, not only in the several portraits and the Crucifixion, but also in the final scene on the left wall showing Christ at the Sea of Tiberias.

[61] This contradicts Marilyn Lavin's suggestion that a liturgical procession can be tracked in the narrative structure: M. LAVIN, *The Place of Narrative: Mural Decoration in Italian Churches, 431-1600* (Chicago, 1990), p. 28.

[62] Angels bearing a scroll appear, as well, in the slightly later church of San Nicola a Castro dei Volsci; unfortunately, only the letters: "*AUCTOR*" are legible in the inscribed text. See: A. MARABOTTINI, "Affreschi del XIII secolo a Castro dei Volsci", *Commentari* 6 (1955), pp. 3-17; and KESSLER, "St. Peter's", pp. 461-462.

[63] "*Principio caelum ac terram camposque liquentes*" (*Aen.*, 6, 724). I thank Edouard Jeanneau and Brian Stock for considering this *titulus* for me.

[64] Cf. the classic essay by E. AUERBACH, "Figura", in: *Neue Dantestudien* (Istanbul, 1944), pp. 11-71.

[65] Augustine, *De civitate Dei*, 20, 14: "*Peracto quippe judicio tunc esse desinet hoc coelum et haec terra, quando incipiet esse coelum novum et terra nova. Mutatione namque rerum, non*

This reading of the beginning of history as also the end is supported by the changes made in the traditional composition at San Pietro a Valle. In contrast to the symmetrical, almost passive disposition of the Creator in the opening scenes in all the other churches, the Creator is pictured turning toward the left, not to create Light (now lost) but to banish it with an emphatic gesture. Moreover, reference to the disappearance of this world at the end of time is made by the angels unrolling the scroll, surely an allusion to Revelation 6, 14: "the sky vanished, as a scroll is rolled up". Although less commonly included in Western representations than in Byzantine depictions, angels unfurling the rotulus of the firmament are pictured in the ninth-century Last Judgment at Müstair (fig. 34),[66] a painting sometimes associated with St. Peter's, and in the chapel of St. Sylvester in SS. Quattro Coronati dedicated in 1246, that is, less than half a century after San Pietro a Valle.[67] At Ferentillo, then, the roll is both the firmament created on the second day to separate heaven from earth and Scripture itself, embodying God's word – the *"Logos"* of John's Gospel. In his *Commentary* on Genesis, the ninth-century theologian, Remigius of Auxerre (ca. 841-ca. 908) had already made the link:

> The firmament signifies the holy scripture, as the Apocalypse gives its meaning. Those above it, the angels, always have God before their eyes and have no need for scripture; those below, humans, are taught by divine scripture, without which they would know nothing of the celestial realm.[68]

Indeed, at Ferentillo, the angels are above the firmament/scroll and fix their eyes on the Creator himself.

---

omni modo interitu transibit hic mundus. Unde et Apostolus ait, Praeterit enim figura hujus mundi, volo vos sine sollicitudine esse. Figura ergo praeterit, non natura"; tr. J. HEALEY, *St. Augustine, The City of God*, 2 vols. (London, 1950), 2, p. 289.

[66] B. BRENK, *Tradition und Neuerung in der christlichen Kunst des ersten Jahrtausends. Studien zur Geschichte des Weltgerichtsbildes* (Vienna, 1966).

[67] MATTHIAE, *Pitturae*, 2, pp. 146-153.

[68] *Commentarius in Genesim*, ed. in: MIGNE, PL 131, col. 57: *"Mystice firmamentum sanctam significat Scripturam, sicut in ejus significatione in Apocalypsi dicitur: et coelum recessit sicut liber involutus: aquae multae populi sunt. Tunc ergo firmamentum in medio aquarum factum est, quando Scriptura divina populis innotuit. Aquae quidem super firmamentum significant angelicas catervas quae bene super firmamentum esse dicuntur, quia, Deum semper prae oculis habentes, non indigent legali institutione neque evangelicis praeceptis. Quae vero sub firmamento sunt aquae, homines significant qui divinis edocentur praeceptis, sine quibus ad coeleste regnum pervenire nequeunt"*.

When Moses, John, and Paul rose to the third heaven, they actually had penetrated this firmament. Other humans, if they were so blessed, would have to wait until Judgment Day when this firmament would yield to a new heaven. As Augustine described in his *Confessions:*

> Or who except thou, O our God, made that firmament of the authority of thy divine Scripture to be over us? As it is said: For the heaven shall be folded up like a book; and is even now stretched over us like a skin. For thy holy Scripture is of more eminent authority, since those mortals departed this life, by whom thou dispensed it unto us. And thou knows, O Lord, thou knows, how thou with skins did once apparel men, so soon as they by sin were become mortal. Wherefore has thou like a Skin stretched out the Firmament of thy book, that is to say those words of thine so well agreeing together; which by the ministry of mortal men thou spread over us.... Other Waters also there be above this Firmament, immortal they be, as I believe, and separated from all earthly corruption. Let those super-celestial peoples, thine angels, praise thee, yea, let them praise thy name: they, who have no need to gaze up at this firmament, and by reading to attain the knowledge of thy word. For they always behold thy face there and do read without any syllables measurable by time, what the meaning is of thy eternal will.[69]

Displaying the words *"CAELUM"* and *"TERRA"*, the roll displayed by the angels in San Pietro a Valle is to be understood, first of all, as the firmament that separates the visible world from heaven above. Beginning with the *"PRINCIPIO"*, the text inscribed on it initiates the dual reading of Scripture – Augustine's "words so well agreeing together" – that is manifested in the subsequent paintings and that elevates the viewer spiritually to the upper limit of visuality. But, like the tunics of dead flesh symbolizing Adam and Eve's mortality and Moses's sandals, the roll made of skin is a barrier to the full apprehension of the Deity. The "firmament of the authority of divine Scripture", it asserts as clearly as any

---

[69] *S. Aureli Augustini Confessiones*, 13, 16-17, ed. M. SKUTELLA (Stuttgart, 1981), pp. 340-341: *"Aut quis nisi tu, deus noster, fecisti nobis firmamentum auctoritatis super nos in scriptura tua diuina? caelum enim plicabitur ut liber, et nunc sicut pellis extenditur super nos, sublimioris enim auctoritatis est tua diuina scriptura, cum iam obierunt istam mortem illi mortales, per quos eam dispensasti nobis. et tu scis, domine, tu scis, quemadmodum pellibus indueris homines, cum peccato mortales fierent. Unde sicut pellem extendisti firmamentum libri tui, concordes utique sermones tuos, quos per mortalium ministerium superposuisti nobis.... Sunt aliae quae super hoc firmamentum, credo, inmortales et a terrena corruptione secretae. Laudent nomen tuum, laudent te supercaelestes populi angelorum tuorum, qui non opus haben suspicere firmamentum hoc et legendo cognoscere verbum tuum; vident enim faciem tuam semper et ibi legunt sine syllabis temporum, quid velit aeterna voluntas tua"*; tr. *St. Augustine's Confessions ... With an English Translation by William Watts, 1631*, ed. W.H.D. ROUSE, 2 vols. (Cambridge, Mass. and London, 1951: *The Loeb Classical Library*), 2, p. 403.

other element in the twelfth- and thirteenth-century paintings that corporeal texts and spiritual images are useful; but to join the angels in direct contemplation of God's face, human sight is inadequate. Only the mind's eye can make the leap.

Fig. 1   Rome, St. Paul's Outside the Walls (painting by G.B. Panini). National
Museums and Galleries of Wales, Cardiff.

Fig. 2   Rome, St. Peter's, right wall of nave (watercolour by Domenico Tasselli). Vatican, Biblioteca Apostolica, Cod. A 64 ter, f. 13r.

Fig. 3   Rome, St. Peter's, left wall of nave (watercolour by Domenico Tasselli).
Vatican, Biblioteca Apostolica, Cod. Barb. Lat. 2733, ff. 113-114.

Fig. 4   Rome, San Giovanni a Porta Latina, apse (after Wilpert).

Fig. 5   Rome, San Giovanni a Porta Latina, Creation of the Cosmos (after Wil-
         pert).

Fig. 6   Rome, St. Paul's Outside the Walls, Creation of the Cosmos (watercolour). Ms Vatican, Biblioteca Apostolica, Cod. Barb. 4406, p. 25.

Fig. 7   Rome, San Giovanni a Porta Latina, Annunciation (after Wilpert).

Fig. 8   Rome, San Giovanni a Porta Latina, Expulsion and Crucifixion (after Wilpert).

Fig. 9   Rome, San Giovanni a Porta Latina, Crucifixion.

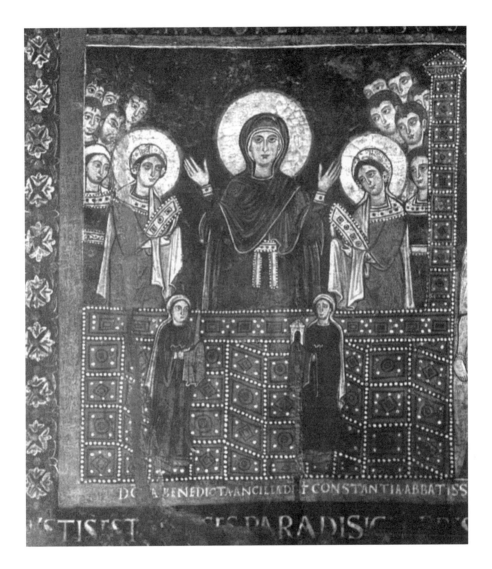

Fig. 10 Vatican, Pinacoteca, Last Judgment (detail).

Fig. 11 Ceri, Santa Maria Immacolata, Joseph Sold to the Ishmaelites (photo-
          graph by the author).

Fig. 12 Rome, St. Paul's Outside the Walls, Joseph Put into Well (watercolour).
MS Vatican, Biblioteca Apostolica, Cod. Barb. 4406.

Fig. 13 Rome, St. Paul's Outside the Walls, Joseph Sold to the Ishmaelites (watercolour). MS Vatican, Biblioteca Apostolica, Cod. Barb. 4406.

Fig. 14 Sant'Angelo in Formis, Crucifixion.

Fig. 15 Sant'Angelo in Formis, Entombment (after Morisani).

Fig. 16 Ferentillo, San Pietro a Valle, Abraham and the Three Angels (ICCD).

Fig. 17 Rome, San Giovanni a Porta Latina, Abraham ad the Three Angels (af-
        ter Wilpert).

Fig. 18 Ceri, Santa Maria Immacolata, Moses and the Burning Bush (after Zchomelidse).

Fig. 19 Ceri, Santa Maria Immacolata, Expulsion and Moses and the Burning
        Bush (photograph by the author).

Fig. 20 Rome, St. Paul's Outside the Walls, Moses and the Burning Bush (watercolour). MS Vatican, Biblioteca Apostolica, Cod. Barb. 4406.

Fig. 21 Rome, San Giovanni a Porta Latina, Last Judgment (after Wilpert).

Fig. 22 Rome, San Giovanni a Porta Latina, Last Judgment (detail) (photograph
　　　by the author).

Fig. 23 Rome, Sant'Urbano alla Caffarella, Crucifixion (photograph by the author).

Fig. 24 Ferentillo, San Pietro a Valle, apsidal arch (photograph by the author).

Fig. 25 Ferentillo, San Pietro a Valle, apsidal arch (detail) (ICCD).

Fig. 26 Ferentillo, San Pietro a Valle, right wall, Entry into Jerusalem (ICCD).

Fig. 27 Sutri, Duomo, Christ (after *Il Volto di Cristo*).

Fig. 28 Ferentillo, San Pietro a Valle, apsidal wall, niche, Christ (ICCD).

Fig. 29 Ferentillo, San Pietro a Valle, right wall, Adoration of the Magi (ICCD).

Fig. 30 Ferentillo, San Pietro a Valle, right wall, Adoration of the Magi (detail) (ICCD).

Fig. 31 Rome, Santa Maria in Ara Coeli, *Maria Avvocata*.

Fig. 32 Rome, San Giovanni a Porta Latina, John the Evangelist (photograph by
        the author).

Fig. 33 Ferentillo, San Pietro a Valle, Creation of the Cosmos (ICCD).

Fig. 34 Müstair, Cloister of St. John, Last Judgment (detail) (after Gnädiger and
        Moosburger).

Was Art Really the "Book of the Illiterate"?[1]

LAWRENCE G. DUGGAN

Pictures are used in churches so that those who are ignorant of letters may at least read by seeing on the walls what they cannot read in books (*codicibus*).

What writing (*scriptura*) does for the literate, a picture does for the illiterate looking at it, because the ignorant see in it what they ought to do; those who do not know letters read in it. Thus, especially for the nations (*gentibus*), a picture takes the place of reading. ... Therefore you ought not to have broken that which was placed in the church in order not to be adored but solely in order to instruct the minds of the ignorant.[2]

Pope Gregory the Great (590-604) wrote these words sometime around the year 600 in two separate responses to the iconoclastic activities of Bishop Serenus of Marseilles. The apparent simplicity of Gregory's analogy is deceptive. Did he, for example, consider it only a metaphor, or did he literally

[1]   This essay is a slightly corrected reprint from *Word & Image*, 5.3 (1989), pp. 227-251. I am grateful to the editors of this journal for the permission to republish.
[2]   *S. Gregorii Magni registrum epistularum libri VIII-XIV*, ed. D. NORBERG (Turnhout, 1982: *CCSL* 140A), IX, 209 and XI, 10, pp. 768, 873-876: "*Idcirco enim pictura in ecclesiis adhibetur, ut hi qui litteras nesciunt saltem in parietibus uidendo legant, quae legere in codicibus non ualent*" and "*Nam quod legentibus scriptura, hoc idiotis praestat pictura cernentibus, quia in ipsa ignorantes uident quod debeant, in ipsa legunt qui litteras nesciunt; unde praecipue gentibus pro lectione pictura est ... . Frangi ergo non debuit quod non ad adorandum in ecclesiis sed ad instruendas solummodo mentes fuit nescientium collacatum*". A complete if stilted translation of the letters may be found in: *Selected Epistles of Gregory the Great*, tr. J. BARMBY (repr. Grand Rapids, 1976: *Select Library of Nicene and Post-Nicene Fathers*, 2nd series, 13), pp. 23, 53-54. There have been many speculations as to whom Gregory had in mind when he spoke of *gentes*. See, for example, J.W. THOMPSON, *The Literacy of the Laity in the Middle Ages* (Berkeley, 1939: *University of California Publications in Education* 9; repr. New York, 1966), p. 23, n. 86: "Gregory's use of *idiotae* and *gentes*, here, makes it appear that he had in mind the lower classes and especially the foreign (i.e., the German) element in the population".

believe that illiterates can 'read' pictures? If so, what did he mean by the verb 'to read'–private silent reading, reading aloud, or some kind of group activity perhaps engaging both illiterates and literates? Did he think of the 'reading' of books and the 'reading' of pictures as fully or only partly comparable? In other words, can 'reading' pictures only remind one of what one already knows or can it also, like the reading of books, convey essentially new information? Although another letter of Gregory's uses this comparison only in the first, restricted sense, that does not necessarily exclude the second possibility here.[3] Is the word *scriptura* in the second letter to be rendered broadly as 'writing' or narrowly as applying only to Sacred 'Scripture'? Did Gregory think that only religious pictures were thus 'readable'? While some might contend that he meant nothing more, the use of *codices* in the first letter would tend to support the broader translation 'writing'; but that argument will not dispel all questions on this point, much less on all the others.

Whatever Gregory wished to say, and whether or not he would be amazed by these endless ruminations, these words may well be the most weighty ever penned by a churchman in the history of Western art. If Ernst Kitzinger was right to declare that "in the entire history of European art it is difficult to name any one fact more momentous than the admission of the graven image by the Christian Church",[4] then Gregory's authoritative defence of images provided for religious art "a sanction which should be regarded as one of the crucial events in the history of art".[5] Most scholars would agree that it became *the* classic statement of the Western attitude on the question.[6] If this is true, it is odd that scholars have devoted little study to the historical fate of this dictum.[7]

---

[3]   In a letter to Secundinus which was interpolated into Gregory's register in the eighth century, there appears towards the end a sentence which suggests that Gregory may have had in mind only the recollective function of pictures (*"Et dum non ipsa pictura quasi scriptura ad memoriam filium Dei reducimus ..."*); but it should be noted that Gregory was here considering only pictures of Christ. The text of the letter is in *S. Gregorii Magni registrum epistularum*, Appendix X, pp. 1104-1111; the quotation appears on p. 1111.

[4]   E. KITZINGER, "The cult of images before iconoclasm", *Dumbarton Oaks Papers* 8 (1954), p. 85.

[5]   K. CLARK, *Moments of Vision and Other Essays* (New York, 1981), p. 40.

[6]   Besides the several references given by H. KESSLER, "Pictorial narrative and Church mission in sixth-century Gaul", *Studies in the History of Art* 16 (1985), p. 89, n. 3, see also W. LOWRIE, *Art in the Early Church* (New York, 1947); A. Grabar, *Christian Iconography: A Study of Its Origins* (Princeton, 1968), p. 93; E.H. GOMBRICH, *The Story of Art*, 11th edn. (New York, 1966), pp. 92, 95; and many others.

[7]   This is noted by M. CAMILLE, "Seeing and reading: Some visual implications of medieval literacy and illiteracy", *Art History* 8 (1985), p. 26. For some references, see V. GRUMEL, "Images (cult de)", in: *Dictionnaire de théologie catholique* (Paris, 1899-1950), 7.1,

It is the first intention of this paper to provide a more comprehensive coverage than has hitherto been available of the various repetitions of, variations on, and departures from Gregory's specific belief that the illiterate can read pictures just as the literate can read books. I say 'more comprehensive' rather than 'comprehensive' because the more I look, the more I find, a search that could know no limit and never issue in publication. But I believe I have collected more references than has yet been done. If it seems that often little attention is given to the development or context of the many adumbrations of this idea, this is partly because of limitations of space, but mainly because of the failure of the original author to say much more of relevance than is quoted here.

But my purpose is not merely to chronicle the success of Gregory's adage, but also to ask whether it is true. Can the illiterate in fact read pictures in the same way that the literate can read books? In the last few years this problem has captured considerable scholarly interest which will be discussed later. It will be argued here that in certain fundamental ways illiterates cannot read pictures just as literates can read books. Finally, the significance not only of the error of the dictum, but also of its durability over the next millennium and a half will also be explored.

I

A most practical and convincing demonstration of papal authority is the extent to which Gregory's idea has been quoted, repeated, slightly modified, reduced to formulae, and so little questioned over the course of the ages, even though papal authority has never been claimed for the realm of perception and

pp. 766-844, especially pp. 768-774, 797-799, 812; L. GOUGAUD O.S.B., *"Muta praedicatio"*, *Revue bénédictine* 42 (1930), pp. 168-170; G. LADNER, "Der Bilderstreit und die Kunst-Lehren der byzantinischen und abendländischen Theologie", *Zeitschrift für Theologie* 50 (1931), pp. 1-23; O. THULIN, "Bilderfrage", in: *Reallexikon zur deutschen Kunstgeschichte*, ed. O. SCHMITT (Stuttgart-Waldsee, 1937-), 2, pp. 562-572; J. KOLLWITZ, "Bild und Bildtheologie im Mittelalter", in: W. SCHÖNE, J. KOLLWITZ and H. FREIHERR VON CAMPENHAUSEN, *Das Gottesbild im Abendland* (Wittin and Berlin, 1959), pp. 109-138; J. PELIKAN, *The Christian Tradition: A History of the Development of Doctrine: II. The Spirit of Eastern Christendom (600-1700)* (Chicago, 1974), pp. 91-145; W.R. JONES, "Art and Christian piety: Iconoclasm in medieval Europe", in: *The Image and the Word: Confrontations in Judaism, Christianity and Islam*, ed. J. GUTMANN (Missoula, 1977), pp. 75-105. The important article by H. GRUNDMANN, "*Litteratus-illiteratus*: Der Wandel einer Bildungsnorm vom Altertum zum Mittelalter", *Archiv für Kulturgeschichte* 40 (1958), pp. 1-65 (repr. in his *Ausgewählte Aufsätze* (Stuttgart, 1976-1978: *MGH Schriften* 25), vol. 3, pp. 1-66), notes simply that Gregory's dictum was often repeated in the Middle Ages (p. 7).

aesthetics, even though Gregory antedates by many centuries the earliest arguments for any kind of papal infallibility, and even though he might have been
shocked by the independent vitality taken on by an idea he never developed and
perhaps never meant as anything more than a metaphor. But then the whole
notion has rarely been critically examined, and even then sometimes on rather
different grounds. In whatever form, it has usually been simply repeated in the
context of a debate centred on a much wider range of issues and to which it was
always subordinate.

The source of Gregory's idea is an intriguing and complex problem in its
own right. Three of the fourth-century Eastern Fathers–Nilus, Basil, and Gregory of Nyssa–made remarks that might have inspired Gregory; but aside from
the difficulty that Gregory on his own admission knew no Greek and was consequently acquainted with these Fathers at best in Latin translation if not oral
distillations, the more compelling fact is that, although they likened pictures to
books, none of these men asserted straight out that the illiterate can read pictures, but suggested rather that pictures function only to remind viewers of what
they already know. Both Basil and his brother Gregory of Nyssa, however,
employed in a Christian context the ancient topos of likening the *spoken* word
and pictures as instruments of communication. For Basil, "what the sermon
shows of the story through hearing, the silent picture puts before the eyes by
imitation"; for Gregory of Nyssa, the silent picture on the wall "speaks".[8] Such

---

[8]   For the sake of the printer and the reader I offer the Latin texts rather than the Greek
(with emphasis added at the appropriate places): Nilus, *Epist. lib.* IV, 61 (Olympiodoro Eparcho),
ed. in: PG 79, cols. 577-580 ("*ut litterarum rudes, et divinarum Scripturarum lectionis nescii
figurae conspectu rerum optime gestarum eorum, qui vero Deo legitime dervierunt, teneant, et
ad eorum res gloriosas atque praeclaras, per quas terram pro coelo, et visibilibus invisibilia
praeferentes certatim properent*"); Basil, *Homilia*, XIX (*In sanctos quadraginta martyres*, 2, ed.
in: PG 31, cols. 507-510 ("*Nam et res in bello fortiter gestas saepe tum oratores, tum pictores
exprimunt, illi quidem eas sermone ornantes, hi vero ipsas depingentes in tabellis, et utrique non
paucos ad fortitudinem exitarunt*. Quae enim historiae sermo per auditum exhibet, ea ob oculos
ponit silens pictura per imitationem. *Hunc ad modum et nos astantibus in memoriam revocemus
virorum virtutem, eorumque gestis velut in conspectum adductis, qui generosiores sunt,
animoque ipsis conjunctiores, eos ad aemulationem exstimulemus*"; Gregory of Nyssa, *De S.
Theodoro martyre*, ed. in: PG 46, cols. 739-740 ("*... solet enim etiam pictura tacens in pariete
loqui, maximeque prodesse ...*"). In defiance of the scholarly consensus, Gregory's knowledge
of some Greek has been vigorously asserted by J.M. PETERSON, *The Dialogues of Gregory the
Great in Their Late Antique Cultural Background* (Toronto, 1984: *Pontifical Institute of
Medieval Studies, Studies and Texts* 69), pp. 189-191; but see the review by P. MEYVAERT in
Journal of Ecclesiastical History 37 (1986), pp. 112-114. The study of the language and thought
of Gregory has now been eased by the publication of the *Thesaurus sancti Gregorii Magni*,
Series A Formae, and Concordantiae, ed. CETEDOC (Turnhout, 1986: *Corpus Christianorum
Thesaurus patrum latinorum*). On the Cappadocian Fathers, see the excellent discussion in G.

similitudes, especially if they had been conventionalized, could well have in-spired Pope Gregory, who then went one step further by analogizing the *written* word with pictures. The very ambiguity of 'word', capable of oral or written expression, would encourage such elaboration, particularly since the written word was so often–but not always–read aloud.

As for Western, Latin authors with whom Gregory would have been more familiar, here too there are problems. Augustine castigated those who tried to read pictures instead of the Scriptures, for, he seems to imply, it is far more likely that they will misread pictures than 'read' them correctly, to say nothing of their neglect of Holy Writ.[9] Clearly for Augustine pictures do not enjoy parity with books. His contemporary Paulinus of Nola (353/354-431) is more frequently invoked as a predecessor of Gregory, but he too does not say what Gregory does.

> This was why we thought it useful to enliven all the houses of Felix with paintings on sacred themes, in the hope that they would excite the interest of the rustics by their attractive appearance, for the sketches are painted in various colours. Over them are explanatory inscriptions, the written word revealing them outlined by the painter's hand. So when all the country folk point out and read over to each other the subjects painted, they turn more slowly to thoughts of food, since the feast of fasting is so pleasant to the eye. In this way, as the paintings beguile their hunger, their astonishment may allow better behaviour to develop in them. Those reading the holy accounts of chastity in action are infiltrated by virtue and inspired by saintly example.[10]

Paulinus accepts the necessity of written inscriptions to disclose the meanings of the paintings, which presumably cannot otherwise be 'read' accurately if at all. Furthermore, 'reading' here is a complex activity which Paulinus antici-pates will engage a group of people talking with each other. Perhaps Gregory

---

LANGE, *Bild und Wort: Die katechetischen Funktionen des Bildes in der griechischen Theologie des sechsten bis neunten Jahrhunderts* (Würzburg, 1969), pp. 13-38, esp. pp. 13-15, 28-30. One problem with tracing the influence of the Cappadocians with respect to this theme is that even in Byzantine sources documented references to them occur only from the eighth century onward (see *ibid.*, p. 15 and n. 10).

[9] Augustine, *De consensu evangelistarum*, I, cc. 9-16, PL 34, cols. 1049-1053. See the discussion of this passage in R. BERLINER, "The freedom of medieval art", *Gazette des beaux-arts*, 6th series, 28 (1946), pp. 273-274.

[10] Poem 27 of *The Poems of St. Paulinus of Nola*, tr. P.G. WALSH (New York, 1975: *Ancient Christian Writers* 40), pp. 580-590, p. 291. On Paulinus see W.H.C. FREND, "The two worlds of Paulinus of Nola", in: IDEM, *Religion Popular and Unpopular in the Early Christian Centuries* (London, 1976: *Collected Studies* 45).

had these other features in mind–contiguous written explanations, group discussion, and the literacy of at least some members of the group–but he does not say so in either of the two letters to Serenus.

Bede makes interesting use of Gregory's idea in at least three separate places. In a homily for the feast of Benedict Biscop he defends depictions of sacred stories for instructive as well as ornamental purposes, so that "those who are not capable of reading words may learn the works of our Lord and Saviour by looking at these images".[11] But in describing the pictures with which Benedict had adorned the monastery of Wearmouth-Jarrow Bede talks about their function slightly differently:

> in order that all men who entered the church, even if they might not read, should either look (whatsoever way they turned) upon the gracious countenance of Christ and His saints, *though it were* but in a picture; or might call to mind a more lively sense of the blessing of the Lord's incarnation, or having, *as it were*, before their eyes the peril of the last judgment, might *remember* more closely to examine themselves[12]

(emphasis added). Finally, in his treatise *On the Temple* of Solomon Bede drew upon the Greek as well as Gregory to characterize pictures as "living Scripture" for the illiterate. But note the whole passage:

> Now if it was permissible to lift up a brazen serpent on a piece of wood so that the Israelites who beheld it might live, why should it not be allowable to recall to the memory of the faithful by a painting that exaltation of our Lord Saviour on the cross through which he conquered death, and also his other miracles and healings through which he wonderfully triumphed over the same author of death, and especially since their sight is wont also to produce a feeling of great compunction in the

---

[11] Bede, *Homelia* I, 13, ed. D. HURST, in: *Bedae Venerabilis opera homiletica - Opera rhythmica*, ed. D. HURST and J. FRAIPONT (Turnhout, 1955: *CCSL* 122), p. 93: "*... adportauit nunc pincturas sanctarum historiarum quae non ad ornamentum solummodo ecclesiae uerum et ad instructionem intuentium proponerentur aduexit uidelicet ut qui litterarum lectionem non possent opera domini et saluatoris nostri per ipsarum contuitum discerent imaginum*". (The older edition of this sermon is listed as *Homelia* 17 in *PL* 94, col. 228, with the variant reading of "*lectione*" for "*lectionem*".) On the complex question of Bede's indebtedness to Gregory, see P. MEYVAERT, *Bede and Gregory the Great* (Jarrow on Tyne, 1964: *Jarrow Lecture* 1964), pp. 13-19, reprinted in his *Benedict, Gregory, Bede and Others* (London, 1977: *Collected Studies* 61).

[12] *Vita sanctorum abbatum monasterii in uyramutha et gyruum*, 6, in Bede, *Opera historica*, ed. and tr. J.E. KING, 2 vols. (London and New York, 1930: *Loeb Classical Library*), 2, pp. 405-407.

beholder, and since they open up, as it were, a living reading of the Lord's story for those who cannot read? For the Greek for *pictura* is indeed "living writing".[13]

Bede thus restricted his meaning in two different ways. First, he appends *quasi* to the 'living Scripture' image, suggesting that it was for him a metaphor, not literal truth. But 'quasi' is ambiguous, interpretable either negatively as hesitation or positively as affirmation that looking at pictures is 'like' reading. Second, Bede also says that these pictures work to "recall to the memory of the faithful" the Crucifixion and other sacred stories. They remind the viewer of what he already knows. This central problem of memory, reading, and learning is one to which we shall return again and again.

In the extensive debates about iconoclasm under both Charlemagne and Louis the Pious, Gregory's particular point about the value of images for the illiterate was usually swamped by the many other complex issues involved.[14] One or the other letter of Gregory to Serenus was often quoted–by Pope Hadrian I to the Council of Nicaea in 787 and Charlemagne, the *Libri Carolini*, the synod of Paris of 825, Agobard of Lyons, and the Irish monk Dungal in his reply to Claudius of Turin–all without further elaboration.[15] But there are three exceptions. In his *De exordiis* Walafrid Strabo (*c*. 808-849) discoursed at some length on the utility of pictures for the simple, dubbing them "a certain kind of writing for the unlettered" ("*pictura est quaedam litteratura inlitterato*"); but

---

[13] Bede, *De templo*, ed. in: *Beda Venerabilis, Opera exegetica, 2A*, ed. D. HURST, (Turnhout, 1969: CCSL 119A), pp. 212-213. I have used the translation of this passage given in P. MEYVAERT, "Bede and the church paintings at Wearmouth-Jarrow", *Anglo-Saxon England* 8 (1979), p. 69.

[14] For a detailed survey, see E.J. MARTIN, *A History of the Iconoclastic Controversy* (London, 1930; repr. New York, 1978), pp. 222-273; T.F.X. NOBLE, "John Damascene and the history of the iconoclastic controversy", in: *Religion, Culture, and Society in the Early Middle Ages: Studies in Honor of Richard E. Sullivan*, ed. T.F.X. NOBLE and J.J. CONTRENI (Kalamazoo, 1987: *Studies in Medieval Culture* 23), pp. 95-116; and D.F. SEFTON, "The popes and the holy images in the eighth century", *ibid.*, pp. 117-130. For a careful discussion of Charlemagne's own views, see G. HAENDLER, *Epochen karolingischer Theologie: Eine Untersuchung über die karolingischen Gutachten zum byzantinischen Bilderstreit* (Berlin, 1958: *Theologische Arbeiten* 10).

[15] *Sacrorum conciliorum nova et amplissima collectio*, ed. J.D. MANSI, new edn. by J.B. MARTIN and L. PETIT, 53 vols. (Arnheim and Leipzig, 1901-1927), 12, p. 1060 and 13, pp. 786-787; *Libri Carolini*, II, 23, ed. H. BASTGEN (Hannover, 1924: *MGH Concilia* 2, *Supplementum*), pp. 81-82, and in: *Concilia aevi Karolini*, 2.2, ed. A. WERMINGHOFF (Hannover and Leipzig, 1908; *MGH Concilia* 2.2, repr. Hannover, 1979), pp. 487-488, 527-529; Agobard of Lyon, *Opera omnia*, ed. L. VAN ACKER (Turnhout, 1981: CCCM 52), pp. 171-172 (c. 22 of his *De picturis et imaginibus*); Dungal, *Responsa contra perversas Claudii Taurinensis episcopi sententias*, ed. in: PL 105, cols. 468-469.

his choice of the qualifying *quaedam* implies possibly a certain reserve about the literal possibility of reading pictures, a suspicion underscored by the rest of the passage.[16] The stance in the *Libri Carolini* was, on second inspection, even more curious. After quoting Gregory's letters at length in Book II, chapter 23, without comment but with evident approbation, exactly one book later the authors scoffed at the notion of the comparability of pictures with Holy Writ.[17] So too did Hrabanus Maurus (†856), abbot of Fulda and archbishop of Mainz, in a poem addressed to Hatto of Mainz.[18] Pictures, they all agreed, can only remind and so at best are a poor substitute for the written word. This scorn was of course directed at the Greeks and particularly the second Council of Nicaea of 787,[19] but it could have been taken as indirect criticism of Gregory. Whether anyone was aware of this cannot be said. But neither then nor, with very few

---

[16] Walafrid Strabo, *De exordiis et incrementis quarundam in observationibus ecclesiasticis rerum*, ed. A. BORETIUS and V. KRAUSE, in: *Capitularia regum Francorum* 2.3 (Hannover, 1960: MGH, *Capitularia regum Francorum* 2.3), p. 484: "*primum quidem, quia pictura est quaedam litteratura inlitterato, adeo ut quidam priorum legatur ex picturis didicisse antiquorum historias. ... Et videmus aliquando simplices et idiotas, qui verbis vix ad fidem possunt perduci, ex pictura passionis dominicae vel aliorum mirabilium ita compungi, ut lacrimis testentur exteriores figuras cordi suo quasi lituris impressas. Igitur sicut omnia munda mundis, coinquinatis autem et infidelibus nihil mundum, quia coinquinata sunt eorum et mens et conscientia, ita males omnes viae offensionis plenae sunt; et sicut boni etiam malis bene, sic mali etiam bonis male utuntur*".

[17] III, 23, ed. in: MGH, *Concilia* II, pp. 150-153, especially p. 153: "*Pictores igitur rerum gestarum historias ad memoriam reducere quadammodo valent, res autem, quae sensibus tantummodo percipiuntur et verbis proferuntur, non a pictoribus, sed ab scriptoribus conprehendi et aliorum relatibus demonstrari valent. Ac per hoc absurdum est dicere: 'Non contraeunt pictores Scripturis, sed quicquid Scriptura loquitur hoc demonstrant'*". See also the stimulating essay by C. CHAZELLE, "Matter, spirit, and image in the *Libri Carolini*", *Recherches Augustiniennes* 21 (1986), pp. 163-184, especially pp. 178-179.

[18] Ed. in: E. DÜMMLER, *Poetae Latini aevi Carolini*, 2 (Berlin, 1884: MGH *Poetae Latini medii aevi* 2), No. 38, p. 196: "*Nam pictura tibi cum omni sit gratior arte, / Scribendi ingrate non spernas posco laborem. / Psallendi nisum, studium curamque legendi, / Plus quia gramma valet quam vana in imagine forma, / Plusque animae decoris praestat quam falsa colorum / Pictura ostentans rerum non rite figuras. / Nam scriptura pia norma est perfecta salutis / Et magis in rebus valet, et magis utilis omnis est, / Promptior est gustu, sensu perfectior atque / Sensibus humanis, facilis magis arte tenenda. / Auribus haec servit, labris, obtutibus atque, / Illa oculis tantum pauca solamina praestat*".

[19] More precisely, it was based on Western mistranslations and misunderstandings of the Greek position (see MARTIN, *Iconoclastic Controversy*, pp. 228-229), for in fact the Second Council of Nicaea had affirmed only the reminder value of images: "For the more these are kept in view through their iconographic representation, the more those who look at them are lifted up to remember and have an earnest desire for the prototypes", tr. in: *Icon and Logos: Sources in Eighth-Century Iconoclasm*, tr. D.J. SAHAS (Toronto, 1986: *Toronto Medieval Texts and Translations* 4), p. 179.

exceptions, later would anyone launch a direct assault on Gregory's words until the Reformation.

These complexities in the tradition and evolution of Gregory's idea in the early Middle Ages were parallelled by those in the High Middle Ages. Gregory continued of course to be quoted without additional comments, as for example in the *Decretum* and *Panormia* of the canonist Ivo of Chartres (†1116), the *Decretum* of Gratian, and the *Sic et non* of Peter Abelard.[20] Someone who had a decidedly vested interest in Gregory's position was the twelfth-century artist of the St Albans Psalter, who began his depictions of the life of Christ with this paraphrase of Gregory, the only words in the text:

> For it is one thing to venerate a picture and another to learn the story it depicts, which is to be venerated. The picture is for simple men what writing is for those who can read, for those who cannot read see and learn from the picture the model they should follow. Thus pictures are, above all, for the instruction of the people.[21]

New variations also appeared, often based on new comparisons. In his *Disputatio Between a Christian and a Jew*, Abbot Gilbert Crispin of Westminster (1085-1117) has the Christian assert that "just as letters are shapes and symbols of spoken words, pictures exist as representations and symbols of writing".[22] When Abbot Peter the Venerable of Cluny (1122-1156) described writing as "a silent preacher" ("*taciturnus praedicator*"), he could just as easily have been discussing pictures.[23] Honorius Augustodunensis, writing in the first half of the twelfth century, enthusiastically personified all parts of the church, comparing the windows, for instance, with teachers (*doctores*). He gave three reasons for pictures in churches, of which the first was that they were the "*laicorum litteratura*".[24] His substitution of *laici* for Gregory's *illiterati* is significant, for, as Michael Clanchy and others have shown, it was precisely at this time that this old equation was in social reality beginning to break down with the gradual rise of lay literacy.[25] That did not stop Albertus Magnus a century later from

---

[20] Ivo of Chartres, *Decretum*, III, 41, and *Panormia*, II, 36, *PL* 161, cols. 206 and 1093; Gratian, *Decreti pars tertia, De consecratione*, III, 27, ed. E. FRIEDBERG, *Corpus iuris canonici* (Leipzig, 1879; repr. Graz, 1959), 1, p. 1360; Peter Abelard, *Sic et non: A Critical Edition*, ed. B. BOYER and R. McKEON (Chicago, 1976), q. 45, p. 209.

[21] Quoted in CAMILLE, "Seeing and reading", p. 26.

[22] Quoted *ibid.*, p. 32.

[23] *The Letters of Peter the Venerable*, ed. G. CONSTABLE, 2 vols. (Cambridge, Mass., 1967), 1, p. 39.

[24] Ed. in: *PL* 172, col. 586.

[25] See R.V. TURNER, "The *miles literatus* in twelfth- and thirteenth-century England: How rare a phenomenon?", *American Historical Review* 83 (1978), pp. 928-945, especially pp. 930-

calling pictures the *"libri laicorum"* in an Advent sermon.[26] About the same time Sicard of Cremona (1160-1215) applied the phrase *"litterae laicorum"* to sculpture and carvings as well as pictures.[27] *"Laicorum scriptura"* was the description given by Johannes Beleth (†1202) in his *Summa de ecclesiasticis officiis* with the following extraordinary justification: "for as Gregory says, what writing is for a cleric, a picture is for the layman".[28] Now Gregory had written nothing of the kind; but it was in such pat phrases, accurate or not, that he was being remembered in the twelfth and thirteenth centuries. This distortion speaks volumes about the creative powers of memory and about the curious fate of an idea which survived because it was useful.

The problem of reading, learning, and memory which Bede had touched on also came directly to the fore in the High Middle Ages. It is unclear whether the synod of Arras was being deliberately cautious in 1025 in declaring that "the simple and the illiterate in church who cannot gaze upon this [i.e., the Crucifixion] through the Scriptures may contemplate it through certain features of a picture",[29] nor was the sermon delivered by Bishop Gerard of Arras-Cambrai (1013-1048) any more helpful when he remarked that "the less educated and illiterate in the church, who cannot understand written biblical texts, form a mental impression of them through the painting's delineation".[30] Sicard of Cremona was in his way being as imprecise as Bede on a crucial issue in his phrasing: "for whatever has been written or sculpted was written for our instruction (Rom. 15), words, I say, commemorative of things past, indicative of

---

931; M. CLANCHY, *From Memory to Written Record: England, 1066-1307* (Cambridge, Mass., 1979), pp. 175-201, especially pp. 177-181.

[26] Albertus Magnus, *Opera omnia*, ed. A. BORGUET (Paris, 1890-1899), 13, p. 18. This, so far as I know, is the only pronouncement Albert made on this subject.

[27] Ed. in: *PL* 213, col. 40.

[28] Johannes Beleth, *Summa de ecclesiasticis officiis*, c. 85, ed. H. DOUTEIL (Turnhout, 1976: CCCM 41A), pp. 154-155: *"Sed quoniam ea, que hucusque diximus, ad clericos maxime pertinere uidentur, nunc pauca dicenda sunt de laicorum in duobus consistit: In picturis et in ornamentis. 'Nam', ut ait Gregorius, 'quod est clerico littera, hoc est laico pictura'. Picturarum autem alie sunt supra ecclesiam ut gallus uel aquila, alie extra ecclesiam ut in fronte forium bos et leo, alie intra ecclesiam ut yconie, statue et figure et diuersa picturarum genera, que uel in uestibus uel in parietibus depinguntur"*. See also c. 164, pp. 321-322: *"Hec ideo dicimus, ut sciatur, qualis in ecclesia debet depingi, quod et de unoquoque apostolarum et multorum aliorum sanctorum est sciendum similiter. Aliter enim mentiremur nos in littera laicorum, scilicet in picturis"*. This is the same work printed in *PL* 202 as the *Rationale divinorum officiorum*.

[29] C. 14, ed. in: *Sacrorum conciliorum nova et amplissima collectio*, ed. MANSI, 19, p. 454.

[30] I have used the translation in B. STOCK, *The Implications of Literacy: Written Language and Models of Interpretation in the Eleventh and Twelfth Centuries* (Princeton, 1983), pp. 136-137.

things present and future".[31] The question whether for Bede and Sicard pictures served anything beyond a mnemonic function, i.e. reminding one of what one already knew, is not resolvable on the basis of these texts. Nor can one be quite sure about the final meaning of the relevant text most commonly cited in connection with this whole issue, the *Rationale divinorum officiorum* of William Durandus, bishop of Mende (†1296). The meaning seems quite straightforward until the very last sentence:

> Pictures and ornaments in churches are the lessons and scriptures of the laity. Whence Gregory: It is one thing to adore a picture, and another by means of a picture historically to learn what should be adored. For what writing supplieth to him who can read, that doth a picture supply to him who is unlearned, and can only look. Because they who are uninstructed thus see what they ought to follow; and things are read, though letters be unknown ... we worship not images, nor account them to be gods, nor put any hope of salvation in them; for that were idolatry. Yet we adore them for the memory and remembrance of things done long ago.[32]

It was evidently St. Bonaventure (1221-1274) who introduced an indubitable distinction in this discussion between reading (or learning) and memory in his equally famous tripartite defence of religious art:

(1) They [images] were made for the simplicity of the ignorant, so that the uneducated who are unable to read Scripture can, through statues and paintings of this kind, read about the sacraments of our faith in, as it were, more open scriptures.
(2) They were introduced because of the sluggishness of the affections, so that men who are not aroused to devotion when they hear with the ear about those things which Christ has done for us will at least be inspired when they see the same things in figures present, as it were, to their bodily eyes. For our emotion is aroused more by what is seen than by what is heard.
(3) They were introduced on account of the transitory nature of memory, because those things which are only heard fall into oblivion more easily than those things which are seen.[33]

---

[31] *Mitrale sive de officiis ecclesiasticis summa*, ed. in: PL 213, col. 40: *"Fiunt autem hujusmodi, ut non solum sint ornatus ecclesiarum, sed et iam litterae laicorum. Quaecunque enim scripta, vel sculpta sunt, ad nostram doctrinam scripta sunt [Rom. 15], litterae, inquam, rememorative praeteritorum, indicativae praesentium et futurorum"*.

[32] William Durandus, *Rationale divinorum officiorum*, Book I, tr. J.M. NEALE and B. WEBB, *The Symbolism of Churches and Church Ornaments* (Leeds, 1843; repr. New York, 1973), p. 53, and excerpted in: *A Documentary History of Art*, ed. E.G. HOLT, 3 vols. (Garden City, 1957-1966), 1, pp. 121 ff.

[33] In his commentary on the *Sentences* of Peter Lombard, lib. III, dist. IX, art. 1, q. 2, concl.,

It will be noted, however, that Bonaventure, like others before him, used the qualifier *quasi*, although not in relation to the act of 'reading' itself, but rather to his own phrase "more open scriptures".

As springboard for his reflections, Aquinas employed, like Bonaventure, the same passage in the standard handbook of theology, Peter Lombard's *Book of Sentences* (3.9), and a tripartite rationale for images:

> There were three reasons for the institution of images in churches. First, for the instruction of simple people, because they are instructed by them as if by books. Second, so that the mystery of the Incarnation and the examples of the saints may be the more active in our memory through being represented daily to our eyes. Third, to excite feelings of devotion, these being aroused more effectively by things seen than by things heard.[34]

Although Aquinas too sets apart the recollective function of images (if not quite as insistently as Bonaventure), what is most conspicuous is his conservative, almost wary, view of art and the *simplices*. Far from asserting that they can read pictures, he stresses their passive role in *being instructed* by pictures *as if* by books–yet another qualification. The simple are, presumably, to receive proper guidance from the clergy. Unfortunately, we cannot determine whether Aquinas was moved by a genuine perception that ordinary people cannot really read pictures, a pastoral concern that they might all too easily misread pictures, or a clerical fear that danger lies in according the laity such liberty. Whatever his reasons (which are not mutually exclusive), Aquinas, as was so often the case with him, did not follow the crowd.

There were of course critics of high medieval ecclesiastical art, particularly its ostentatiousness. The most celebrated of them was Bernard of Clairvaux (1090-1153), who in his *Apologia* excoriated the waste of precious materials in monasteries that could be used to feed the poor, the detraction from the true worship of God to which images can tempt the pious, the distraction from the study of Scripture, and so on–but never, significantly, does Bernard deny Greg-

---

in his *Opera omnia* (Quarrachi, 1882-1902), 3, p. 203. I have used the translation in C. GARSIDE Jr., *Zwingli and the Arts* (New Haven, 1966), p. 91.

[34] *Commentum in IV Sent., lib. III, dist. IX, art. 2, sol. 2 ad. 3um*, in his *Opera omnia*, 25 vols. (Parma, 1852-1872), 7, p. 109.

ory's premise that the illiterate can 'read' religious art.[35] Neither did the many other critics of religious art in the high and late Middle Ages.[36]

The most direct criticism of Gregory's idea before the Reformation came from Bernard's *bête noire*, the Abbot Suger (*c.* 1081-1151), ruler of the royal monastery of St.-Denis and by times of France itself as regent. In his tract on his administration of St.-Denis, there occurs a curious passage. Suger is describing the richly decorated panels of the main altar:

> And because the diversity of the materials such as gold, gems and pearls is not easily understood by the mute perception of sight without a description, we have seen to it that this work, which is intelligible only to the literate, which shines with the radiance of delightful allegories, be set down in writing. Also we have affixed verses expounding the matter so that the allegories might be more clearly understood.[37]

What does Suger mean by saying "this work, which is intelligible only to the literate"? That only those who understand the meaning of the panel can be called literate, that only literate people are intelligent enough to understand, or that only those who can read have access to the key to comprehension? If Suger meant the last, as seems probable, he was implicitly criticizing Gregory, but he otherwise makes nothing of it. Nor did anyone else in the later Middle Ages. Suger was not, however, the only patron to have fastened explanatory words to the images he commissioned.[38]

Complexity reigned in the late Middle Ages as well, if of different sorts. The passage in Lombard's *Sentences* that had inspired both Bonaventure and

[35] In his *Apologia ad Guillelmum abbatem*, ed. in his *Opera omnia*, ed. J. LECLERCQ and H.M. ROCHAIS, 8 vols. (Rome, 1957-1977), 3, pp. 61-108. A complete translation of Bernard's "Apologia to Abbot William" by M. CASEY appears in: *The Works of Bernard of Clairvaux*, 1, *Treatises* 1 (Washington, 1970: *Cistercian Fathers Series* 1), pp. 33-69, and partial translations may be found in: *Life in the Middle Ages*, ed. G.G. COULTON (Cambridge, 1967), 4, pp. 169-174, and in: *Documentary History of Art*, ed. HOLT, 1, pp. 18-22. One modern historian nevertheless draws the untenable inference that "It must be remembered that Bernard recognized the Church's role in education – thereby accepting the use of illustrations for the illiterate" (J. PHILLIPS, *The Reformation of Images: Destruction of Art in England, 1535-1660* (Berkeley and Los Angeles, 1973), p. 20, n. 29).

[36] See M.R. JAMES, *"Pictor in carmine"*, *Archaeologia* 94 (1951), pp. 141-166, especially pp. 141-142, 144-145; G.G. COULTON, *Art and the Reformation*, 2nd edn. (Cambridge, 1953), pp. 330-336, 371-387; O. VON SIMSON, *The Gothic Cathedral*, 2nd edn. (New York, 1962: *Bollingen Series* 48), p. 44, n. 60; JONES, "Art and Christian piety", pp. 83-95.

[37] *Abbot Suger and the Abbey Church of St.-Denis and Its Treasures*, ed., tr., and annotated by E. PANOFSKY (Princeton, 1946), p. 63.

[38] See COULTON, *Art and the Reformation*, p. 392.

Aquinas evidently did nothing for Alexander of Hales (†1245), Richard of
Middleton († *c.* 1305), Duns Scotus (†1308), William of Ockham († *c.* 1349),
Thomas of Strasbourg († *c.* 1350), Bernardinus of Siena (†1444), Dionysius the
Carthusian (†1471), or Gabriel Biel (†1495), none of whom quotes Gregory in
this context or alludes to art and the illiterate.[39] (Neither had Peter Lombard, it
should be mentioned.) Jan Hus in his impressively learned gloss on the same
text only quotes Gregory without additional comment.[40] And just as Bonaventure on this matter was not followed by his fellow Franciscans Duns Scotus,
Ockham, and Bernardino of Siena, neither was Aquinas invariably followed by
later Dominicans. At least two did quote him without acknowledge-
ment–Giovanni Balbo (John of Genoa) († *c.* 1298) in his influential *Catholicon*
and Rainerius of Pisa († *c.* 1350) in his *Pantheologia*.[41] But Antoninus of Florence (†1459) in his *Summa* neither cites this passage from Aquinas nor devel-
ops this idea in any way, even though he does cite the relevant passages from
Gregory's letters and various texts from Aquinas' *Summa theologica* on images.[42] The other most distinguished Dominican of the late Middle Ages, Cardinal Cajetan (Thomas de Vio, 1469-1534), in his commentary on Aquinas'

[39] Petrus Lombardus, *Sententiae in IV libris distinctae*, 3rd edn., III, 9, c. un., *"De
adoratione humanitatis Christi"*, (Rome, 1971-1981: *Spicilegium Bonaventurianum* 4-5), 2,
pp. 68-71; Magistri Alexander de Hales, *Glossa in quatuor libros Sententiarum Petri Lombardi*,
4 vols. (Quaracchi, 1951-1957), 3, pp. 104-116; Richardus de Mediavilla, *Super quatuor libros
Sententiarum Petri Lombardi quaestiones subtilissimae*, 4 vols. (Brixen, 1591; repr. Frankfurt,
1963), 3, ad III, dist. 9; Joannes Duns Scotus, *Opera omnia*, ed. nova, 26 vols. (Paris, 1891-1895:
repr. Farnborough, 1969), 14, pp. 384-400; William of Ockham, *Opera plurima* (Lyons, 1494-
1496; repr. Farnborough, 1962), *ad loc. cit.*; Thomas of Strasbourg, *Commentaria in IIII libros
sententiarum* (Venice, 1564; repr. Ridgewood, 1965), *ad loc. cit.*; Bernardino of Siena, *Opera
omnia*, 9 vols. (Quaracchi and Florence, 1950-1965), 7, *ad loc. cit.*; Dionysius the Carthusian,
Opera omnia, 42 vols. (Monstrolii, 1896-1913), vol. 23, *ad loc. cit.*; Gabriel Biel, *Collectorium
circa quattuor libros Sententiarum*, ed. W. WERBECK and U. HOFMANN, 5 vols. (Tübingen,
1973-1984), 3, pp. 186-195.
[40] *Mag. Joannis Hus Super IV. Sententiarum*, ed. W. FLAJSHANS and M. KOMÍNKOVÁ
(Prague, 1905), pp. 414-423.
[41] Joannes Balbus, *Catholicon* (Mainz, 1460; repr. Farnborough, 1971), s.v. *"Imago"*;
Rainerius of Pisa, *Pantheologia seu Summa theologiae* (Venice, 1486), fol. IIV, s.v. *"Adoratio"*.
Balbus is quoted by M. BAXANDALL, *Painting and Experience in Fifteenth-Century Italy: A
Primer in the Social History of Pictorial Style* (Oxford, 1972), p. 41, and M.R. MILES, *Image as
Insight: Visual Understanding in Western Christianity and Secular Culture* (Boston, 1985),
p. 66, without indication of his debt to Aquinas. For a recent discussion of Balbus, see G.
POWITZ, "Zum 'Catholicon' des Johannes de Janua: Das Autorexemplar und die Tradition der
Exemplare des Franciscus de Agaciis", *Archivum Fratrum Praedicatorum* 53 (1983), pp. 203-
218.
[42] *Sancti Antonini Summa theologica*, 4 vols. (Verona, 1740; repr. Graz, 1959), *Pars* III, tit.
12, c. 9, cols. 542-545, *"De multiplici adoratione, scilicet latriae, et duliae, et hyperduliae"*.

Summa spoke of pictures as *"codices populorum"* and left it at that.[43] In the fifteenth century another Dominican, Michele da Carcano, hewed very closely to Bonaventure rather than Aquinas in his gloss.[44] Other Dominicans followed neither. Giovanni Dominici commended paintings and sculptures to the families of his native Florence because "these representations are the books of the man on the street",[45] and a century later Savonarola in one sermon called images in churches books of the illiterate, but his loose understanding of the word 'reading' will be taken up later.[46] Another Dominican much influenced by Savonarola in general, Ambrosius Catharinus or Lancelotto Politi (†1553), was more careful than his master, In a *Disputation on the Cult and Adoration of Images* he viewed their strength as *"libri idiotarum"* in stimulating memory, edification, and devotion.[47] Among the Dominicans, in short, there obtained no 'party line' on the issue; but then, like everyone else, they gave it no great thought.

It may therefore not be wise to press too far the imputation of an active role to illiterates by Bonaventure and of a passive one by Aquinas. The great churchman Jean Gerson (†1429), for example, in his *Summa* offers a précis of Bonaventure's triple schema. Images developed first "because of the simplicity of the ignorant, so that those who do not know how to read the Scriptures may read them in pictures".[48] Yet in a Christmas sermon he cleaves much more to Aquinas' position, clearly out of fear of misconstruction by the untutored. Images, he said there, are made "for no other reason than for showing the plain people who are ignorant of the Scriptures what they must believe. Therefore one must prevent acceptance as true of any untrue representation which expounds the Scriptures incorrectly".[49]

---

[43]   Cajetan's *Commentaria* is most readily available in the "Leonine edition" of Aquinas's *Opera omnia* published in Rome from 1882 onwards under the initial patronage of Pope Leo XIII. The relevant passage appears in Cajetan's remarks on *Summa theologica*, III, 25, 3, vol. 11, p. 281.

[44]   Quoted in BAXANDALL, *Painting and Experience*, p. 41.

[45]   Quoted in J. LARNER, *Culture and Society in Italy 1290-1420* (New York, 1971), p. 284.

[46]   Girolamo Savonarola, *Prediche sopra Ezechiele*, ed. R. RIDOLFI (Rome, 1955), 1: 375, No. 27: "*Le figure delle chiese sono i libri di questi tali [fanciulli], e però si vorria provvedere anche meglio che li pagani*", see below, p. 100.

[47]   Ambrosius Catharinus, "*Disputatio de cvltv et adoratione imaginvm*", in: *Enarrationes, assertiones, disputationes* (Rome, 1551-1552; repr. Ridgewood, 1964), cols. 121-144, especially 128-130, 134.

[48]   Jean Gerson, *Summa theologica* (Venice, 1587), *lib.* I, art. 12, fol. 30r: "*Ex hoc quaeritur, quare imagines introducte sunt in ecclesia? Solutio: propter simplicium ruditatem: vt qui scripturas legere nesciunt legant in picturis*".

[49]   Quoted in BERLINER, "Freedom of medieval art", pp. 282-283. The Latin text of this sermon is printed in Gerson's *Opera omnia*, ed. L.E. DU PIN, 5 vols. (Antwerp, 1706), 2, p. 947,

A similarly sophisticated awareness of the dangers of misreading can be seen in two other sources, both from England around 1400. The first is the well-known dialogue *Dives and Pauper* of unknown authorship. It is most telling that the very first question which Dives, a rich layman desirous of understanding and fulfilling the Ten Commandments, puts to Pauper, a well-read mendicant, is how to read images, which "been ordeynyd to been a tokene and a book to the lewyd peple, that they moun redyn in ymagerye and peynture that clerkys redyn in boke, as the lawe seyzt, De. con. di. iii, Perlatum ...".[50] (Note that Gratian's *Decretum*, not Gregory, is cited as the source here.) Pauper proceeds to instruct him, including a cautionary chapter on the many ways in which the Crucifixion is typically 'read' and the dire consequences which result:

> And so oon woord is referryd to dyuerse thynggys and this blyndzt mechil folk in here redyngge, for they wenyn that alle the preyerys that holy cherche makyzt to the cros that he made them to the tree that Crist deyid on or ellys to the cros in the cherche, as in that antiphene, O crux splendidior. And so for lewydnesse they been deseyuyd and wurshepyn creaturys as God hymself.[51]

A sermon from another English priest about the same time is even more reserved:

> we see that painting, if it be true, without a mixture of lies, and not too eager at abundant feeding of men's wits, and not an occasion of idolatry for the people, serves but to read the truth, as naked letters to a scholar.[52]

This precision and caution grew out of contemporary Lollard concern with images. Interestingly, on our subject Wycliffe was uncharacteristically moderate. He spoke of images as *"libri laicis"* ("books for the laity"), quoted Gregory with approval, and held that "it is evident that the images may be made both well and ill".[53] His legacy to the Lollards was thus ambiguous. Although they,

---

and the original French version is in his *Oeuvres complètes*, ed. P. GLORIEUX, 10 vols. in 11 (Paris, 1960-1973), 7, p. 963.
   [50] *Dives and Pauper*, Commandment I.i, ed. P. HEATH BARNUM (Oxford, 1976: *Early English Text Society* 275), pp. 82-83.
   [51] *Ibid.*, Commandment I.iv, pp. 87-89. The quotation appears on p. 89.
   [52] *Reliquiae antiquae*, ed. T. WRIGHT and J.O. HALLIWELL, 2 vols. (London, 1843; repr. New York, 1966), 2, p. 50. This modernized rendering appears in BERLINER, "Freedom of medieval art", p. 279. See pp. 95-101 below for further discussion of the various conceptions of 'reading' in this text.
   [53] The principal germane texts are Sermon 17 in *Iohannis Wyclif Sermones*, ed. I. LOSERTH,

too, often quoted Gregory to Serenus, they usually focused on his condemnation of the worship of images. Like the Carolingians, they devoted little attention in their iconoclastic concerns to our specific topic. Even their occasional condemnations of images as "a book of error to the lay people" or "false ymagys and bokis of heresye worthi to be destroyed" accepted the premise that images could be 'read', which was precisely why they were so fraught with danger.[54]

These attacks elicited various orthodox responses, of which two are of some interest in this context. Thomas Netter (*c.* 1377-1430), provincial of the English Carmelites and spiritual adviser of King Henry V, in a lengthy treatise quoted both Gregory and Bede and equated Scripture and pictures in a novel way: "he who would forbid images to the laity will next forbid Scripture to the clergy. For what is writing but a certain picture and an image of a word of the mind or voice?"[55] The controversial Reginal Pecock (*c.* 1393-1461), bishop of Chichester, composed one of the most detailed defences in Western literature of the value of religious images and indeed of their manifold superiority to the word. He was also one of the most consistently precise writers on images as books of the illiterate, which he always described as "rememoratijf signes", "seable rememoratijf signes", or "rememoratijf visible signes", i.e. reminding the viewer of what he already knew. Nowhere does he even imply that they could serve anything more than a mnemonic function.[56] But at least at one point

4 vols. (London, 1887-1890), 2, pp. 125-126, and in the tract *"De mandatis divinis"* in *Wyclif's Latin Works*, 22 (London 1922; repr. New York, 1966), pp. 154-166. For thorough recent discussions of Wycliffe's position, see W.R. JONES, "Lollards and images: The defense of religious art in later medieval England", *Journal of the History of Ideas* 34 (1973), pp. 29-30, and M. ASTON, "Lollards and images", in her *Lollards and Reformers: Images and Literacy in Late Medieval England* (London, 1984), pp. 135-192, especially pp. 137-143, 177.

[54] The two phrases appear, respectively, in JONES, "Lollards and images", p. 33, and *Fasciculi Zizaniorum Magistri Johannis Wyclif cum tritico, ascribed to Thomas Netter of Walden, Provincial of the Carmelite Order in England, and Confessor to King Henry the Fifth*, ed. W.W. SHIRLEY (London, 1858: *Rolls Series* 5), p. 364. In addition to this work and the two articles just cited, see also *Fifteenth-Century Prose and Verse*, ed. A.W. POLLARD (New York, 1964), pp. 97-174, especially pp. 133-134 (the examination of William Thorpe, priest, by Archbishop Thomas Arundel of Canterbury).

[55] Thomas Waldensis, *Doctrinale antiquitatum fidei catholicae ecclesiae*, 3 vols. (Venice, 1759; repr. Farnborough, 1967), 3, pp. 916-917, 925-927.

[56] Reginald Pecock, *The Repressor of Over Much Blaming of the Clergy*, ed. C. BABINGTON, 2 vols. (London, 1860: *Rolls Series* 19), 2, 136-137, 145, 148, 161-167, 170, 182, 214-215. See also *The Donet*, ed. E.V. HITCHCOCK (London, 1921: *Early English Text Society, Old Series* 136), p. 121: "*And so it is not agens the first comaundement of god in moyses tablis ymagis to be had as bokis or kalenders to remembre and to bring into mynde the biholder vpon hem that he folewe cristis lijf and holi seintis lijfis ...*" (spelling partially modernized).

he too introduces confusion by describing Holy Writ and other devout works as "heerable rememoratijf signes".[57] Did he really intend to suggest that Scripture can only remind us of what we already know, or was he perhaps tempted by the urge to draw a neat parallel with the "seable rememoratijf signes" of pictures? Although the latter is probable, it is not clear.

The problem associated with images and their abuses stirred up fewer controversies in Bohemia, mainly because so many more and graver issues were at stake there, but the words of one early Czech reformer bear on our theme. Matthew of Janov (*c.* 1355-1393) denounced at great length excesses in popular devotion to images, but in the end he approximated Wycliffe's moderate position: "yet by this I intend not to deny that images may reasonably be made and placed in the church, since all Holy Church holdeth thus, and men commonly say that such images are the lay folk's Bible". He was nevertheless to recant this errors in 1389 and was suspended from preaching for six months.[58]

A very different form of criticism was already arising in Italy among the early humanists. Petrarch expressed the attitude succinctly in his will of 1370 in which he bequeathed a painting by Giotto, "whose beauty amazes the masters of the art, though the ignorant cannot understand it".[59] The spirit behind that attitude was captured by Boccaccio in the *Decameron* (VI, 5) where he wrote that Giotto "brought back to life that art which for many centuries had been buried under the errors of those who in painting had sought to give pleasure to the eyes of the ignorant rather than to delight the minds of the wise".[60] Petrarch's denial that ordinary people can read art did not, of course, spring from any effort on his part to view things from their point of view. On the contrary, it originated in an *a priori* contempt for the masses and the general 'intellectualization' of art in the early Renaissance.[61]

---

[57] *Repressor*, 2, 209: *"Mankinde in this lijf is so freel, that forto make into him sufficient remembraunce of thingis to be profitabli of him remembrid he nedith not oonli heerable rememoratijf signes, (as ben Holi Scripture and othere deuoute writingis,) but he nedith also therwith and ther to seable rememoratijf signes".*

[58] COULTON, *Art and the Reformation*, pp. 376-378; M. SPINKA, *John Hus at the Council of Constance* (New York, 1965), pp. 24-26. On iconoclasm and the Hussite movement, see H. KAMINSKY, *A History of the Hussite Revolution* (Berkeley and Los Angeles, 1967), pp. 18, 170, 175, 183, 192-193, 209, 230-231, 243, 250, 252, 254, 262, 299, 306, 338, 377, 439; JONES, "Art and Christian piety", pp. 91-95.

[59] Quoted in LARNER, *Culture and Society in Italy*, p. 276.

[60] Quoted in *ibid.*, p. 276, and M. BAXANDALL, *Giotto and the Orators: Humanist Observers of Painting in Italy and the Discovery of Pictorial Composition 1350-1450* (Oxford, 1971), p. 60.

[61] See J. LARNER, "The artists and the intellectuals in fourteenth-century Italy", *History* 54 (1969), pp. 13-30. For a thoroughly refreshing view, see BAXANDALL, *Giotto and the Orators*,

It should be remarked, however, that this marked disdain for the ignorant receded among later Renaissance writers. Alberti's treatise *On Painting* from the 1430s, for instance, is entirely different, as this typical passage reveals: painting "alone is equally pleasing to both learned and unlearned; and it rarely happens in any other art that what pleases the knowledgeable also attracts the ignorant".[62] Later Renaissance discussions often followed Leonardo's assertion of the superiority of painting to poetry, from which he drew the following conclusions:

> Now look what a difference there is between listening for a long time to a tale about something which gives pleasure to the eye and actually seeing it all at once as works of nature are seen. Moreover, the works of poets are read at long intervals; they are often not understood and require many explanations, and commentators very rarely know what was in the poet's mind; often only a small part of the poet's work is read for want of time. But the work of the painter is immediately understood by its beholders.[63]

Giovanni Battista Armenini (1533?-1609) went even further and applied these concepts to religious art as well in his *On the True Precepts of the Art of Painting*, published in 1586:

> Writings speak to us and move us, and paintings do the same, but yet they are different in that poetry requires study, time and knowledge to be understood, whereas painting stands always revealed to persons of every quality and type. Writings do not help him who lacks memory or judgment; but painting is always apprehensible and is understood by all but the completely blind.
>
> By simulating, one represents the image, the passions, the martyrdom, and death of the holy men who were devoted to God. And so one can say that through this means the illiterate come to know the true and direct path to their salvation.[64]

---

pp. 59-63, 97 (e.g. "St. Augustine had notoriously preferred to be condemned by the grammarians rather than not to be understood by the vulgar. The humanists consciously reversed this attitude; they were committed to a neo-classical literary elite whose activity must necessarily pass over most people's heads" (p. 59) or "Petrarch's references to contemporary art are few and usually as superficial as his reference here to Simone Martini" (p. 63)).

[62] Leon Battista Alberti, *On Painting and On Sculpture: The Latin Texts of De pictura and De statua*, ed. and tr. C. GRAYSON (London, 1972), p. 65. See also pp. 61 and 79.

[63] *Paragone*, 26, in *The Literary Works of Leonardo da Vinci*, 3rd edn., rev. by J.P. RICHTER and I.A. RICHTER (London, 1970), 1, 60.

[64] Giovanni Battista Armenini, *On the True Precepts of the Art of Painting*, ed. and tr. E.J. OLSZEWSKI (New York, 1969), pp. 102, 106, respectively.

Such ideas about the objective and immediate capacity of any onlooker to apprehend paintings were Renaissance elaborations of ancient comparisons of poetry and painting which may have owed something to Scholastic discussions of the relativity of words (as in Hugh of St. Victor), but little or nothing to Gregory and his commentators.[65]

It would be erroneous to think that everyone agreed with these ideas, as indeed two contemporaries of Armenini did not. Romano Alberti, secretary of the Roman Academy of Painters, Sculptors, and Architects, in his *Tract on the Nobility of Painting* (1585) asserted only the reminder value of art with explicit reference to Gregory the Great and the Second Council of Nicaea of 787.[66] Similarly, in his *Treatise on the Art of Painting* (1584), sometimes called "the Bible of Mannerism", Gian Paolo Lomazzo compared painting and writing only insofar as they acted to preserve memories.[67]

By this time religious art had come under widespread, direct, and successful attack from the Protestant Reformers. On this point Luther was, as he so often was, conservative, and in fact, far from viewing images as troublesome or blasphemous, he dreamed of a complete picture Bible which "would be, and would be called, a lay Bible".[68] Furthermore,

---

[65] See R.W. LEE, "*Ut pictura poesis*: The humanistic theory of painting", *Art Bulletin* 22 (1940), pp. 197-269 (separate repr., New York, 1967); J.R. SPENCER, "*Ut rhetorica pictura*", *Journal of the Warburg and Courtald Institutes* 20 (1957), pp. 26-44; BAXANDALL, *Giotto and the Orators*, pp. 16, 24-27, 39-44, 59-64, 122-125. For later developments, see W.G. HOWARD, "*Ut pictura poesis*", *Publications of the Modern Language Association* 24 (1909); C. DAVIS, "*Ut pictura poesis*", *Modern Language Review* 30 (1935), pp. 159-169; R. PARK, "'*Ut pictura poesis*': The nineteenth-century aftermath", *Journal of Aesthetics and Art Criticism* 28 (1969), pp. 155-164; and J. GRAHAM, "*Ut pictura poesis*: A bibliography", *Bulletin of Bibliography and Magazine Notes* 29 (1972), pp. 13-15, 18. On Hugh of St. Victor, see the remarks of BERLINER, "Freedom of medieval art", pp. 276-277, and below, pp. 99-100.

[66] Romano Alberti, *Trattato della nobilità della pittura*, ed. P. BAROCCHI, *Trattati d'arte del Cinquecento fra Manierismo e Controriforma*, 3 vols. (Bari, 1960-1962), 3, p. 229. On Alberti, see J. SCHLOSSER. *Die Kunstliteratur: Ein Handbuch zur Quellenkunde der neueren Kunstgeschichte* (Vienna, 1924), p. 348.

[67] Gian Paolo Lomazzo, *Scritti sulle arti*, ed. R.P. CIARDI, 2 vols. (Florence, 1973), 2, p. 13. On Lomazzo, see SCHLOSSER, *Kunstliteratur*, pp. 352-353.

[68] *Passional*, in: *D. Martin Luthers Werke: Kritische Gesamtausgabe*, 10.2 (Weimar, 1907), p. 458: "*Ich habe fur gut angesehen das alte Passional buechlin zu dem bettbuechlin zu thun, allermeist umb der kinder und einfeltigen willen, welche durch bildnis und gleichnis besser bewegt werden, die Goettlichen geschicht zu behalten, denn durch blosse wort odder lere, wie Sant Marcus bezeuget, das auch Christus umb der einfeltigen willen eitel gleichnis fur yhn prediget habe ... . Und was solts schaden, ob ymand alle furnemliche geschichte der gantzen*

Pictures contained in these books we would paint on walls for the sake of remembrance and better understanding, since they do no more harm on walls than in books. ... Yes, would to God that I could persuade the rich and the mighty that they would permit the whole Bible to be painted on houses, on the inside and outside, so that all can see it. That would be a Christian work.[69]

Most of the other Reformers aggressively rejected religious images, but usually because God had forbidden graven images and because the Reformers insisted on the primacy of His Word, not because they grasped that Gregory had erred on the educative value of art for the illiterate. Their critique, in short, derived from the vantage-point of heaven rather than of the people. Thus in 1523 the Swiss priest Ludwig Hätzer published *The Judgment of God Our Spouse as to How One Should Hold Oneself toward All Idols and Images, According to the Holy Scriptures*, in which he refuted four arguments traditionally advanced on behalf of images. In reply to the third, "They are books for laymen", Hätzer only verges on a non-religious rejection of the idea: "That is human folly. Gregory says such things, but God does not. Indeed, God says completely otherwise. God repudiates images, and you want to teach from the book which God has repudiated".[70] In similarly rejecting images for theological reasons as idols and abominations, Martin Bucer of Strasbourg alluded to the common people only insofar as they were misled and bilked by the cult of images.[71] Rather like Augustine before him, Calvin appears to have scorned images because they teach falsehoods, not because they cannot teach at all.[72] Calvin's identification of Gregory's dictum with the Catholic position was indirectly echoed sometime later by John Whitgift, archbishop of Canterbury (1583-1604), in his defence of the reading of Scripture: "Do you think that there cometh no more knowledge or profit by reading the scriptures than doth by 'beholding of God's creatures'? Then let us have images again, that they may be laymen's books, as the papists call them. ...".[73] Two Reformers, however, explic

---

Biblia also lies nach einander malen yn ein buechlin, das ein solch buechlin ein leyen Bibel were und hiesse?".

[69] "Against the Heavenly Prophets in the Matter of Images and Sacraments" (1525), ed. C. Bergendoff in: *Luther's Works*, ed. H.T. Lehmann *et al.*, 55 vols. (Saint Louis, then Philadelphia, 1958), 40, p. 99.

[70] Garside, *Zwingli and the Arts*, pp. 109-115; the quotation is on p. 114.

[71] "*Grund und Ursach auss gotlicher schrifft der neüwerungen an dem nachtmal des herrn, so man die Mess nennet, Tauff, Feyrtagen, bildern und gesang in der gemein Christi*", pp. 185-278 in: *Martin Bucers Deutsche Schriften*, ed. R. Stupperich, 9 vols. in 11 (Gütersloh, 1960-1995), 1, especially pp. 269-274 ("*Ursach darumb die bilder sollen abgestelt werden*").

[72] *Institutes*, Bk. I, ch. 11, especially 5-7.

[73] *The Works of John Whitgift*, ed. J. Ayre, 3 vols.(Cambridge, 1851-1853: *Parker Society*

itly ridiculed Gregory's maxim. In 1525 Zwingli asserted the worthlessness of pictures without words: "If now you show an unbelieving or unlettered child images, then you must teach him the Word in addition, or he will have looked at the picture in vain ... the story must be learned only from the Word, and from the painting one learns nothing except the form of the body, the movements or the constitution of the body or face".[74] Several years earlier, in 1521, Karlstadt launched a frontal assault on Gregory and what he called the "*Gregeristen*" and even more radically denied that images can remind, much less teach, and in support of his view he retranslated Habakkuk 2:19. Whereas the modern Revised Standard version renders the crucial words as "can this give revelation?", Karlstadt made sure that Scripture said what he thought: "Is it possible that it [an image] can teach?"[75] But precisely because Karlstadt took such radical stances on nearly everything, his criticisms did not pass into the mainstream.

Catholic apologists sometimes answered these charges of the Reformers, sometimes not. One of the most ample and curious on the subject of our concern was Thomas More's *Dialogue Concerning Heresies* (1529), in which he cleverly says that the heretics themselves call images "laymen's books" and that they are very right to do so. More's exposition is worth quoting at length:

> For where they say that images be but laymen's books, they cannot yet say nay but that they be good books, both for laymen and the learned too. For as I somewhat said unto you before, all the words that be either written or spoken be but images representing the things that the writer or speaker conceiveth in his mind: likewise as the figure of the thing framed with imagination, and so conceived in the mind, is but an image representing the very thing itself that a man thinketh of. ... Now if I be too far from you to tell it you, then is the writing not the name itself but an image representing the name. And yet all these names spoken, and all these words written be no natural signs or images but only made by consent and agreement of men, to betoken and signify such thing, whereas images painted, graven, or carved, may be so well wrought, and so near the quick and to the truth, that they shall naturally, and much more effectively represent the thing than shall the name either spoken or written. For he that never heard the name of your master, shall if ever he saw him be brought in a rightful remembrance of him by his image well wrought and touched to the quick. And surely saving that men cannot do it, else, if it might commodiously be done, there were not in this world so effectual writing as were to express all things in imagery. ... But now, as I began to say, since all names written or spoken be but images, if ye set aught by the name of Jesus written or spoken,

46-48), 3, p. 32.

[74] GARSIDE, *Zwingli and the Arts*, pp. 172-173.

[75] C.C. CHRISTENSEN, *Art and the Reformation in Germany* (Athens, Ohio, 1979), pp. 32-33.

why should ye set nought by his image painted or craven that representeth his holy person to your remembrance, as much and more too, as doth his name written? Nor these two words *Christus crucifixus*, do not so lively represent [to] us the *remembrance* of his bitter passion, as doth the blessed image of the crucifix, neither to [a] layman nor unto a learned [man].[76]

The emphasis I have added, however, implies that More conceived of the comparability of words and images exclusively, or at least principally, in terms of their great recollective function only.

The great reform Council of Trent (1545-1563) proceeded far more cautiously on this issue. To what extent Protestant criticisms affected the Fathers of the Council is not clear, for Gerson, Janov, and other late medieval churchmen had expressed their apprehension and alarm over abuses connected with images for a good century before the Reformation. In its last session in December 1563 the Council of Trent promulgated a long decree on images which proclaimed their manifold worth when properly venerated, particularly their didactic value in imparting to the people the truths of the faith. It explicitly and repeatedly stressed the necessarily passive role of the people and the role of religious art as an adjunct in teaching them. In its repeated insistence on these points Trent went well beyond Aquinas' conservatism. The Fathers were palpably animated by pastoral, clerical, or hierarchical considerations as well as by the urge to respond to a recent outburst of iconoclasm in France; but whether they actually thought about whether non-literates could read pictures cannot be said.[77] The text is as follows:

Moreover, let the bishops diligently teach that by means of the stories of the mysteries of our redemption portrayed in paintings and other representations the people are confirmed in the articles of faith, which ought to be borne in mind and constantly reflected upon; also that great profit is derived from all holy images, not only because the people are thereby reminded of the gifts and benefits bestowed on them by Christ, but also because through the saints the miracles of God and salutary examples are set before the eyes of the faithful, so that they may give God thanks for those things, may fashion their own life and conduct in imitation of the

---

[76] *The English Works of Sir Thomas More*, ed. and tr. W.E. CAMPBELL, with Introduction and Notes by A.W. REED, 2 vols. (a facsimile reproduction of the Tastell edition of 1557 together with translation) (London and New York, 1931), 2, pp. 20-21. See also p. 264: "... images be the books of lay people, wherein they read the life of Christ".

[77] This particular point is unfortunately not mentioned in the otherwise thorough and convincing article by the late H. JEDIN, "Entstehung und Tragweite des Trienter Dekrets über die Bilderverehrung", *Tübinger Theologische Quartalschrift* 116 (1935), pp. 143-188, 404-429, reprinted in his *Ausgewählte Aufsätze und Vorträge*, 2 vols. (Freiburg etc., 1966), 2, pp. 460-498.

saints and be moved to adore and love God and cultivate piety. ... And if at times it happens, when this is beneficial to the illiterate, that the stories and narratives of the Holy Scriptures are portrayed and exhibited, the people should be instructed that not for that reason is the divinity represented in picture as if it can be seen with bodily eyes or expressed in colours or figures.[78]

The effect of the Tridentine decree on public religious art was immediately discernible in many quarters. The great Spanish Jesuit Francesco de Suarez (1548-1617) was even more guarded than Aquinas in his *Commentary* on the *Summa Theologica*.[79] The celebrated reforming archbishop of Milan, St. Charles Borromeo (1538-1584), issued *Instructions on Ecclesiastical Fabric and Ornamentation* which in their cautious severity surpassed those of Trent.[80] Several decades later his cousin, Cardinal Federigo Borromeo (1564-1631), who also held the see of Milan and founded the Ambrosian Library, wrote a draft in Italian and a final version in Latin of a work entitled *De pictura sacra*. Towards the conclusion he discusses the various usages of images by Christians. In this connection he twice invokes the name of Gregory the Great: first, with respect to the capacity of images to excite and deepen our contrition; second, with reference to their employment as aids for the instruction of the ignorant masses in the sacred mysteries, "as the same Pope Gregory wrote".[81]

---

[78] *Canons and Decrees of the Council of Trent*, tr. H.J. SCHROEDER (Rockford, 1978). Sess. 25, decree "On the invocation, veneration, and relics of saints, and on sacred images", p. 216. The Latin text is in: *Conciliorum oecumenicorum decreta*, ed. G. ALBERIGO *et al.*, 3rd edn. (Bologna, 1973), p. 775: "*Illud vero diligenter doceant episcopi, per historias mysteriorum nostrae redemptionis, picturis vel aliis similitudinibus expressas, erudiri et confirmari populum in articulis fidei commemorandis et assidue recolendis; tum vero ex omnibus sacris imaginibus magnum fructum percipi, non solum quia admonetur populus beneficiorum et munerum, quae a Christo sibi collata sunt, sed etiam quia Dei per sanctos miracula et salutaria exempla oculis fidelium subiiciuntur, ut pro iis Deo gratias agant, ad sanctorumque imitationem vitam moresque suos componant, excitenturque ad adorandum ac diligendum Deum, et ad pietatem colendam. ... Quodsi aliquando historias et narrationes sacrae scripturae, cum id indoctae plebi expediet, exprimi et figurari contigerit; doceatur populus, non propterea divinitatem figurari, quasi corporeis oculis conspici, vel coloribus aut figuris exprimi possit*".

[79] *Commentaria ac disputationes in tertiam partem D. Thomae*, Disput. LIV, "*De usu et adoratione imaginum*", in: *Opera omnia* (Paris edn.), 18, pp. 595 ff., especially pp. 596, 598.

[80] S. Carlo Borromeo, *Instructiones fabricae et supellectilis ecclesiasticae*, c. 17, in: *Trattati d'arte del Cinquecento*, ed. BAROCCHI, 3, pp. 42-45. For a careful discussion of the practical consequences of Tridentine legislation on art, see E. WATERHOUSE, "Some painters and the Counter-Reformation before 1600", *Transactions of the Royal Historical Society*, 5th series, 22 (1972), pp. 103-118.

[81] Card. Federico [*sic*] Borromeo, *De pictura sacra*, ed. C. CASTIGLIONI (Sora, 1932), Bk. II, c. 12 ("*Diverso uso delle immagini presso i Cristiani*"): "*L'antichità usò le immagini per i vari scopi, e anzitutto a ridestare qual sentimento di dolore che ognuno deve sentire nell'animo per*

Knowingly or not, Cardinal Federigo Borromeo had just added a new twist to the whole tradition by linking Gregory and Trent. With one small clause he had harmonized two texts, 'modernized' Gregory, and buttressed the Tridentine decree with his authority.

The Gregorian dictum on art and the people basically disappeared from conciliar and synodal legislation for at least the rest of the sixteenth century,[82] and when it reappeared at the council of Narbonne in 1609 it assumed the form of images as "books of the rude and unlearned" (*"rudium & imperitorum libri"*), quickly followed by all the Tridentine restrictions.[83] The spirit of Trent lived on into the eighteenth century. The superb, usually comprehensive ecclesiastical encyclopedia compiled by the Franciscan Lucio Ferraris (†1763) is uncharacteristically terse on the subject of images. Most of the space is given over to quotation of the Tridentine decree and to considerations of what may or may not be depicted. On the uses of images Ferraris says tersely that they are "of very great necessity and utility in the Church". He then adduces several authorities, including Pope Gregory II and the Council of Trent, but not Gregory the Great.[84]

But the dictum was not so easily driven underground (if that was in fact Trent's intention) and survived elsewhere. In his *Dialogue on the Errors of the Painters* (1564) Giovanni Andrea Gilio cited Gregory approvingly and excoriated the painters for their massive irresponsibility.[85] Charles Borromeo's reforming counterpart in Bologna, Gabriele Paleotti (1566-1597), quoted not only Gregory several times in his *Discourse on Sacred and Profane Images* (1582),

---

le proprie colpe, e ciò lo attesta San Gregorio. Inoltre pensavano di poter con questo mezzo ammaestrare la moltitudine ignorante nei sacri misteri, come scrisse lo stesso papa Gregorio. Intedevano ancora di tributare alle immagini quel culto che le scuole e i dottori acconsentono; al qual proposito San Basilio dice che non solo in privato ma anche pubblicamente egli venerava le immagini e che ciò era istituzione e tradizione apostolica". This modern edition was prepared by collating the Italian and Latin texts.

[82] See *Sacrorum conciliorum nova et amplissima collectio*, ed. MANSI, 34, pp. 118, 164-165, 184-190, 589-590, 687, 824, 888-889, 989-990, 1135-1138, 1292, 1345, 1413-1416, 1458-1459.

[83] *Ibid.*, p. 1485.

[84] Lucio Ferraris, *Bibliotheca canonica, juridica, moralis, theologica ...*, 10 vols. (Venice, 1770), 5, pp. 25-29. The quotation occurs at 5, 27, 30: *"Imaginum usus est maximae necessitatis, & utilitatis in Ecclesia. Gregorius II. Epist. 12. Concil. Senonens. cap. 14. Conc. Mogunt. IV. cap. 42. Conc. Trid. cit. sess. 25. decreto"*. On Pope Gregory II (715-731), see E. CASPAR, "Papst Gregor II. und der Bilderstreit", *Zeitschrift für Kirchengeschichte* 52 (1933), pp. 28-89, who includes a new edition of Gregory's letters.

[85] Giovanni Andrea Gilio, *Dialogo nel quale si ragiona degli errori e degli abusi de'pittori circa l'istorie*, ed. BAROCCHI, *Trattati*, 2, pp. 25, 108.

but also St. John Damascene and Basil the Great, drawing on the latter to call images "mute books or popular scripture". He also noted the similarity of the Greek words for painter and writer.[86] These terms reappeared seventy years later, together with the Greek "living Scripture", in the *Tract on Pictures and Sculpture, Their Use and Abuse* (1652), by Giovanni Domenico Ottonelli and Pietro da Cortona.[87] One fascinating variation on the whole Gregorian theme appeared not long after the conclusion of Trent in a Latin work entitled *On Pictures and Sacred Images* (1570), written by Johannes Molanus (Jan Vermeulen), a professor of theology at Louvain. In defence of images he quoted Gregory, Bede, Thomas Netter, and other sources, and he inclined to emphasize how little error images had actually caused. He would seem to have been reacting as much against the strictures of Trent as those of the Protestants.[88] Images "are not only the books of the laity and the unlettered", he wrote, "but also of the most learned and most holy men". True, he continued, "certain books are written for the more simple (*rudioribus*), others for the more learned", and simple folk cannot derive as much as educated people can from a particular work. Nevertheless, "there are images, but very few in number, whose principal signification and representation is grasped by the learned alone. Among them are the revelations described by St. John in the Book of the Apocalypse".[89]

A final curious and ironic twist in the effect of Trent on the Gregorian dictum appeared more than two hundred years later. In 1786 the Habsburg Archduke of Tuscany, Leopold, as vigorously reform-minded as his mother

---

[86] Gabriele Paleotti, *Discorso intorno alle imagini sacre e profane*, ed. BAROCCHI, *Trattati*, 2, pp. 142-143, 208, 226. On Paleotti, who became the first archbishop of Bologna when it was elevated to metropolitan status in 1582, see P. PRODI, *Il Cardinale Gabriele Paleotti (1522-1597)*, 2 vols. (Rome, 1959-1967), and for a comparison of Carlo Borromeo and Paleotti, see E. COCHRANE, "New light on Post-Tridentine Italy: A note on recent Counter-Reformation scholarship", *Catholic Historical Review* 56 (1970), pp. 310-311.

[87] Giovanni Domenico Ottonelli and Pietro Berrettini (= Pietro da Cortona), *Trattato della pittura e scultura, uso et abuso loro (1652)*, ed. V. CASALE (Treviso, 1973), p. 53.

[88] Joannes Molanus, *De historia SS. imaginum et picturarum, pro vero earum uso contra abusus, libri quattuor*, 3rd edn., rev. by J.N. PAQUOT (Louvain, 1771), pp. 31-33, 60-61, 66-73, 87-91.

[89] *Ibid.*, p. 68: "*Libri quidam scribuntur pro rudioribus, quidam pro doctioribus. In uno quoque & eodem libro, quaedam tantum doctioribus & capacioribus subserviunt, quaedam vero & plebi. Sic & Imagines pleraeque statuuntur, ut quod in eis principaliter significatur, facile rudis populus aut assequatur, aut assequi possit, ita tamen ut multa magis propter doctos & capaciores addantur, quam propter rudiores. Sunt etiam Imagines, sed perpaucae, quarum principalis significatio & repraesentatio a solis doctis intelligitur. Inter quas sunt Revelationes a beato Joanne in Apocalypsi descriptae. Ex iis enim lectis parum intelligit simplex plebecula, ac proinde multo minus ex iis depictis*".

Maria Theresa and his brother Joseph, ordered the convening of a great ecclesiastical assembly at Pistoia for the sweeping reformation of the Church in his realms. During the debates on whether statues ought to be draped, the minutes record that a statement by the bishop of Colle prompted this reply: "the illustrious Signor Advocate Cavaliere Paribene observed that according to the Council of Trent images are the book of the ignorant, in which they read the stories of the deeds of the saints ...".[90] Trent was now being credited with a formula which it had not only not originated, but may have taken some trouble to avoid! Just as Federigo Borromeo had harmonized Gregory with Trent, so now Trent was harmonized with Gregory.

Despite these survivals of the medieval dictum in the early modern period, it does not appear to have been as commonplace as it was in the Middle Ages and the Renaissance. Protestant criticism and official Catholic caution had evidently taken their toll. Curiously, these tacit and explicit criticisms of Gregory's position do not seem to have moved modern scholars. With very few exceptions (to be mentioned below) none of the modern authorities consulted in the preparation of this essay raises a single doubt about the veracity of Gregory's dictum.[91] Any of them could answer with some justice that it is not the business of the art historian to pose such a question, just as a historian of theology cannot, *qua* historian, ask whether Anselm's argument for the existence of God or Aquinas' views on *succubi* are actually true. This analogy is not perfect, however, for whereas the truths of theology are not demonstrable, the questions raised here about art and its relationship to the beholder can be rationally investigated, and the answers can tell us much about the intentions and perceptions of artists and viewers alike. But few scholars have looked at it this way. Like Ludwig Hätzer, Meyer Schapiro once drew nigh the difficulty in a passing

[90] *Sacrorum conciliorum nova et amplissima collectio*, ed. MANSI, 38, p. 1167: "*L'illustriss. sig. avvocato cav. Paribeni osservò, che secondo il concilio di Trento le immagini sono i libri per gl'ignoranti in cui leggono la storia delle azioni dei santi ...*".

[91] See, for example, C.R. MOREY, *Early Christian Art* (Princeton, 1942); LOWRIE, *Art in the Early Church*, pp. 32-36; R. ARNHEIM, *Art and Visual Perception* (Berkeley, 1954); ID., *Toward a Psychology of Art* (Berkeley, 1966), ID., *Visual Thinking* (Berkeley, 1969); M. BRION, "Introduction" to: *The Bible in Art* (New York, 1956), p. 10 ("pictures and sculptures have an extraordinary power to educate the mind and stir the emotions".); A. GRABAR, *Martyrium: Recherches sur le culte des reliques et l'art chrétien antique*, 3 vols. (Paris, 1943-1946; repr. London, 1972), 2, p. 321; ID., *Christian Iconography: A Study of Its Origins* (Princeton, 1968), p. 93; S. RINGBOM, *Icon to Narrative: The Rise of the Dramatic Close-up in Fifteenth-Century Devotional Painting* (Abo, 1965: *Acta Academiae Aboensis* A 31.2), pp. 11-22; J. BRONOWSKI, *The Visionary Eye: Essays in the Arts, Literature, and Science*, sel. and ed. P.E. HRIOLTI and R. BRONOWSKI (Cambridge, Mass., 1978), especially the chapters entitled "Art as a Mode of Knowledge" and "The Speaking Eye, the Visionary Ear".

observation in his *Words and Pictures*, but he made nothing of it.[92] Rudolf Berliner did not proceed from his appreciation of "how difficult it is to understand the intentions of an unrationalistic art through a rational approach" to put himself in the place of the viewer.[93] In summarizing Gregory's "classical expression" of Western attitudes, Walter Lowrie quotes from one of the letters to Serenus and follows it with this cryptic remark: "Strangely enough, there is no evidence that a contrary opinion was ever expressed in Rome. Certainly it did not prevail".[94] In fact, the view regnant among the great majority of twentieth-century scholars was embodied in this classic paragraph by Emile Mâle:

> To the Middle Ages art was didactic. All that was necessary that men should know–the history of the world from the creation, the dogmas of religion, the examples of the saints, the hierarchy of the virtues, the range of the sciences, arts and crafts–all these were taught them by the windows of the church or by the statues in the porch. The pathetic name of *Biblia pauperum* given by the printers of the fifteenth century to one of their earliest books, might well have been given to the Church. There the simple, the ignorant, all who were named "*sancta plebs Dei*", learned through their eyes almost all they knew of their faith ... . Through the medium of art the highest conceptions of theologian and scholar penetrated to some extent the minds of even the humblest of the people.[95]

Lest this forthright statement seem too extreme to be typical, it may be noted that the phrase *biblia pauperum*, whose origin Mâle correctly indicated, has been attributed to Gregory by at least three scholars (one of them Gerhart Ladner);[96] that the phrase 'book of the illiterate' has been conflated with *biblia*

---

[92] M. SCHAPIRO, *Words and Pictures: On the Literal and the Symbolic in the Illustration of a Text* (The Hague and Paris, 1973), p. 11: "In the archaic periods of classical and medieval art painters often felt impelled to inscribe their paintings with the names of the figures and even with phrases identifying the action, although according to a common view supported by the authority of church fathers, pictures were a mute preaching to the illiterate".

[93] BERLINER, "Freedom of medieval art", p. 264.

[94] LOWRIE, *Art in the Early Church*, p. 36.

[95] E. MÂLE, *The Gothic Image: Religious Art in France of the Thirteenth Century*, tr. D. NUSSEY (New York, 1958), p. VII.

[96] J. GUTMANN, "Preface" to *The Image and the Word*, p. 2; JONES, "Art and Christian Piety", p. 84; LADNER, "Bilderstreit", p. 19. On the *biblia pauperum*, see *Biblia pauperum: Facsimile Edition of the Forty-Leaf Blockbook in the Library of Esztergom Cathedral*, introduction, notes and subtitles by E. STOLTÉSZ, tr. L. HALÁPY (Budapest, 1967), pp. VI-VIII, XXV-XXVII; M. BERVE, *Die Armenbibel: Herkunft, Gestalt, Typologie* (Beuron, 1969), pp. 7-9; and A. HENRY, *Biblia Pauperum: A Facsimile and Edition* (Aldershot, 1987), pp. 3-38, especially pp. 3-4 and 17-18.

pauperum by two other scholars (one of them Coulton);[97] and that for the phrase *muta praedicatio* ('mute sermon') with which Dom Louis Gougaud intituled his handy florilegium on this whole subject he provided no instance before 1911.[98]

Within the last fifteen years or so a major change has occurred as all the complexities of 'reading' and 'seeing' have come under the knife as leading subjects of dissection in several disciplines. The polyhedral Gregorian dictum, now a venerable proverb in the lexicon of Western scholars for a millennium and a half, has nevertheless held on tenaciously. It is revealing that two recent scholars of distinction, Hans Belting and Michael Baxandall, who have directed their attention precisely to the viewers of art in the Middle Ages and the Renaissance, nowhere take up this issue in their otherwise stimulating treatises.[99] Other scholars have raised the question in some form but pushed it only so far. Franz Bäuml's article, "Varieties and consequences of medieval literacy and illiteracy", appeared in 1980. Although he raises the subject of our concern, what he says is brief and elusive:

> Of course, it is obvious that pictures could not always have served the purpose suggested by Pope Gregory. But his dictum also immediately suggests the familiar attribute of medieval art that a picture must be "read"–an appropriate description of the function of medieval pictorial art produced prior to the second half of the twelfth century.[100]

Margaret Aston also confronts the issue in her paper, "Devotional literacy", published in 1984. She attempts to comprehend the dictum in its cultural context and seems to conclude that it is right and that it is we with our twentieth-century blinders who really cannot understand it aright.[101] Michael Camille's

---

[97] R. STEINBERG, *Fra Girolamo Savonarola, Florentine Art, and Renaissance Historiography* (Athens, Ohio, 1977), p. 51 ("... sacred pictures, as Savonarola was not the first to suggest, are after all the Bible of the poor and the illiterate ..."); COULTON, *Art and the Reformation*, p. 293.

[98] GOURGAUD, *"Muta praedicatio"*, p. 168.

[99] H. BELTING, *Das Bild und sein Publikum im Mittelalter: Form und Funktion früher Bildtafeln der Passion* (Berlin, 1981), pp. 91-92; BAXANDALL, *Painting and Experience*, pp. 40-56. Baxandall, in fact, in his more recent *Patterns of Intention: On the Historical Explanation of Pictures* (New Haven, 1985), pp. 2-5, 43-44, argues that because vision is "the most precise and vivid faculty given us by God", its particular precision enabled it "to expound holy matter clearly" (pp. 43-44).

[100] *Speculum* 55 (1980), pp. 237-265. The quotation appears on p. 259.

[101] M. ASTON, "Devotional Literacy", in: *Lollards and Reformers*, pp. 101-133, esp. pp. 114-119.

"Seeing and reading: Some visual implications of medieval literacy and illiteracy" is excessively slippery in the many meanings he attaches to the word 'literacy', but on the issue which occupies us he bares deep feelings in his testy gloss on Suger's inscriptions for his panels: "Such are the inscriptions devised by that typical esoteric *litteratus* of the twelfth century, Abbot Suger of St. Denis, who in lavishing images and words on his new church specifically excludes those unable to read ...".[102] In her book *Image as Insight* Margaret Miles very sensibly notes, first, that the message intended by the commissioner or executor of a work of art is rarely if ever the message received by the viewer (of whatever stripe) and, secondly, that words, however problematical, are by nature more precise than images as instruments of communication.[103] Miles does not go far enough, however, to question whether the people can literally read art (despite her populist as well as feminist ideological concerns) and whether the dictum is right (even though she quotes Durandus and Giovanni Balbo without comment).[104] The nine scholars who gathered in Baltimore in 1984 to focus on *Pictorial Narrative in Antiquity and the Middle Ages* confessed its complexity and their perplexity, but none suggested that the dictum was wrong.[105] Neither here nor in his earlier *Das Bild und sein Publikum im Mittelalter* did Hans Belting venture any doubts,[106] and in his paper Herbert Kessler goes to considerable lengths to 'save' Gregory, as it were, by deemphasizing the gap between literates and non-literates, interposing literate intermediaries, and effectively 'reading' Paulinus of Nola into Gregory's text.[107] Even more recently an entire number of *The Journal of Interdisciplinary History* was devoted to twelve papers on the theme of "The Evidence of Art: Images and Meaning in History". Although in their "Introduction" Theodore K. Rabb and Jonathan Brown take it as axiomatic that works of art are of themselves "elusive" and "indeterminate" and thus require more precise analysis through words, they do not address our concern directly, nor do any of the contributors.[108]

---

[102] CAMILLE, "Seeing and reading", especially pp. 32-37. The quotation appears on p. 34.
[103] MILES, *Image as Insight*, pp. 6, 28-35.
[104] *Ibid.*, p. 66. For her concern with perception of religious art by the uneducated, see pp. XI, 5, 7-9.
[105] *Pictorial Narrative in Antiquity and the Middle Ages*, ed. H.L. KESSLER and M. SIMPSON (= *Studies in the History of Art* 16 (1985)), pp. 7-8.
[106] H. BELTING, "The new role of narrative public painting of the Trecento: *Historia* and allegory", in: *ibid.*, pp. 151-168, especially p. 151.
[107] KESSLER, "Pictorial narrative", pp. 75-91, particularly pp. 76, 80, 85-88.
[108] *The Journal of Interdisciplinary History* 17.1 (1986). The introductory remarks appear on pp. 1-6; see especially pp. 1-2.

A few scholars have bucked the conventional wisdom. G.G. Coulton, both an artist and an historian by training, expressed sensible doubts some time ago.[109] The most frontal assault has come recently from the pen of Avril Henry:

> Even recently the suggestion has been repeated that the *Biblia Pauperum* was to instruct the illiterate "even as the facades of cathedrals instructed Villon's mother" (a suggestion which implies comprehension of the pictures without their texts!). The surprisingly persistent notion that the medieval visual arts were designed to *instruct* the unlettered is based on a misconception. Little medieval art is merely instructive. Our modern response to medieval typology is sufficient evidence that pictures in this mode only 'instruct' if you already know what they mean. They then act as reminders of the known truth. It is not a bit of good staring at a picture of a man carrying two large doors on the outskirts of a city and expecting it to suggest the risen Christ. You are likely to take him for a builder's merchant or a removal man unless you already know that this is always Samson with the gates of Gaza and that, like Christ, he has, as it were, broken gaol. If you stare at a depiction of two self-consciously naked people picking fruit you are likely to mistake them for apple-gathering nature-worshippers if you do not already know (as most people do even today) that this is Adam and Eve, whose temptation and fall prefigures Christ's resistance to temptation.[110]

Rather less confrontative is E.H. Gombrich, who just a few years ago put forth a more nuanced view:

> The decisive papal pronouncement on this vital issue was that of Pope Gregory the Great, who wrote that "pictures are for the illiterate what letters are for those who can read". Not that religious images could function without the aid of context, caption and code, but given such aid the value of the medium was easily apparent. Take the main porch of the cathedral of Genoa. ... The relief underneath ... represents the martyrdom of St. Lawrence. ... Without the aid of the spoken word the illiterate, of course, could not know that the sufferer is not a malefactor but a saint who is marked by the symbol of the halo, or that the gestures made by the onlookers indicate compassion. But if the image alone could not tell the worshipper a story he had never heard of, it was admirably suited to remind him of the stories he had been told in sermons or lessons.[111]

---

[109] COULTON, *Art and the Reformation*, chaps. 14-15 (entitled, respectively, "The people's mind" and "The poor man's bible").

[110] HENRY, *Biblia Pauperum*, pp. 17-18.

[111] E.H. GOMBRICH, *The Image and the Eye: Further Studies in the Psychology of Pictorial Representation* (Ithaca, 1982), pp. 155-157.

Gombrich had been edging toward this position for some time. In 1969 he wrote that

> it is in the nature of things that images need much more of a context to be unambiguous than do statements. Language can form propositions, pictures cannot. It seems strange to me how little this obvious fact has been stressed in the methodology of art history. ... The means of visual art cannot match the statement function of language. Art can present and juxtapose images, even relatively unambiguous images, but it cannot specify their relationship.[112]

Once a certain critical mass of scholars does begin to attack a problem, controversies and schools inevitably arise. Let me mention but one significant contribution from the substantial literature that is now appearing. In his *Deeper into Pictures* (1986) Flint Schier has probed many of these interrelated issues with lucidity of thought and expression. He criticizes two major "heresies" (the "semiological" and the "illusionist") for muddying these waters in our times and classifies Gombrich (albeit an earlier Gombrich) as holding an untenable position between these two schools. Schier's own position, which he lays out in 200 pages, cannot be adequately summarized here. Nevertheless, one may for the purposes of this paper fairly characterize part of his argument as being that since pictures, unlike natural languages, "have no grammatical rules, natural or conventional", one can at the very most 'recognize' rather than 'read' what he defines as 'icons' in a very precise way.[113] However much he may disagree with Gombrich on other matters, Schier fundamentally agrees with him on this one: pictures cannot be 'read' as books can.

II

The reader will have sensed by now that my sympathies lie with the views of Coulton, Henry, Gombrich and Schier, whatever the differences among them in manner and vigour of formulation. While Leonardo, Baxandall, and others

---

[112] E.H. GOMBRICH, "The evidence of images", in: *Interpretation: Theory and Practice*, ed. C.S. SINGLETON (Baltimore, 1969), p. 97. Cf. also his earlier *Art and Illusion: A Study in the Psychology of Pictorial Representation*, 2nd edn. (Princeton, 1961), pp. 62, 227, 240, 393-394. Gombrich's iconoclastic position among art historians was recognized by S. and P. ALPERS, "*Ut pictura noesis*? Criticism in literary studies and art history", *New Literary History* 3 (1972), pp. 448-454, who also express their doubts about 'reading' images (p. 446).

[113] F. SCHIER, *Deeper into Pictures: An Essay on Pictorial Representation* (Cambridge, 1986), *passim*, but chaps. 4, 5, and 8 in particular.

rightly insist that pictures can present in a *coup d'oeil* what words can do only at length, if at all, the other side of the coin is that pictures as instruments of precise communication fall far short of words, that a mark of that disparity is that pictures inevitably must be made intelligible in words to the intellect (but not necessarily to other parts of the psyche), and that pictures cannot be 'read' in the same way as, or as fully as, books. Let us consider the different examples adduced by Henry and Gombrich of Adam and Eve and of St. Lawrence. If these relatively simple depictions cannot be read correctly without prior knowledge of the story and recognition of the context, imagine what difficulties were presented to an illiterate medieval viewer of a complex scene based on the many stories in the Old Testament and the New? One either knew already what was depicted, or else one could not learn from the image alone anything of elementary value. Imagine a Tuscan peasant coming upon Masaccio's *Tribute Money* in the Brancacci Chapel, or a Roman considering *The Entry into Jerusalem* in Duccio's Maestà, or an English pilgrim in awe before Michelangelo's *Last Judgment*, or a German nobleman astonished by Donatello's *Mary Magdalene*. None of these people could learn from the painting or sculpture what it was about. They could be reminded of what they already knew, they might be moved to tears or wonder, they might be struck by a novel feature of the rendition, they might experience the presence of the divine–but these were all experiences open to the literate as well as the illiterate.

But the position of literates and illiterates is entirely different. Let me give another illustration. In connection with this study I read about the depiction at Tours of St. Martin Healing the Leper.[114] I learned much about it, its background, and its significance. Were I at Tours, I could learn a great deal, if not quite as much, about the pictures by reading the accompanying verses by Venantius Fortunatus. If I looked only at the pictures, I might possibly guess what they were about; but then, if I knew what they were about, it would be because I already knew what they were about. In this case I would be able to read the signs correctly, but I would not learn anything new as a result. They would only remind me of something I already knew. This is very different from my being able to read the words on the walls or in the article, for these word-signs tell me much I did not know and can, in addition, suggest to me new interpretations of the pictures which I alone would not have conceived. By comparison, the illiterate cannot read the picture-signs so as to gain new knowledge, and by definition he cannot read words. He may happen to identify correctly in the picture what he already knows, he may easily misconstrue it, he can 'read into' it all sorts of interpretations shaped by his previous experi-

---

[114] KESSLER, "Pictorial narrative", pp. 76-84.

ence–but without help from someone (or something) else he can learn nothing new and possibly cannot even guess correctly the primary meaning of the painting. I, on the contrary, can add to my knowledge by reading texts. I may misread a text and mistake an author's precise meaning; but however imperfect they are, words are inherently more precise than images and can convey new knowledge.

But before writing off the idea of reading pictures as mistaken we should heed the words of a perceptive modern historian of medieval literacy: "past ideas must be analyzed in their own terms before they are assessed in modern ones".[115] Specifically, we must remember that Gregory lived in an age of extremely limited literacy, an age of oral culture in which reading aloud was still the norm, and in which, therefore, the boundary between hearing and reading was not as great as it has come to be since the seventeenth and eighteenth centuries. As a man of the early Middle Ages, Gregory may have understood the mentality of his unlettered contemporaries in ways which we have not yet reconstituted and probably never can. But some tentative speculations on what Gregory might have meant and how he perceived reality may be ventured here, assuming for the moment that he did think art could do more than simply remind and that it could be read as books can be read.

First, Gregory was speaking of religious art depicting figures and scenes from the Old Testament, the New Testament, and more recent Christian history, stories which he could well have assumed constituted the common stock of knowledge for both the literate and the illiterate alike. Had he reflected on how people ordinarily acquired this knowledge at a young age through sermons and stories, he would have realized that most literates learned most of this from others before they could read and that they thus shared with the unlettered not only this knowledge, but also the way they both came by it. Furthermore, in the early Middle Ages, as in many a situation of restricted literacy, the lettered reader would continue to depend heavily on a teacher as mediator and, hence, like illiterates, to learn through the ear. Finally, reading aloud was the custom, and so reading was ordinarily (but not exclusively) aural as well as visual. It was a truism often repeated through the ages that hearing served to correct the fallibility of sight.[116] In this light the gap between literates and illiterates might

---

[115] M. CLANCHY, "Literate and illiterate; hearing and seeing: England 1066-1307", in: *Literacy and Social Development in the West: A Reader*, ed. H.J. GRAFF (Cambridge, 1981), p. 21.

[116] J. GOODY, "Introduction", in: *Literacy in Traditional Societies*, ed. J. GOODY (Cambridge, 1968), p. 13; W.J. ONG, *The Presence of the Word* (New Haven, 1967), pp. 176-191; IDEM, *Orality and Literacy: The Technologizing of the Word* (London and New York, 1982), pp. 2, 24, 34, 36, 41, 50, 75, 119, 140-141.

not seem all that great, similarities might appear to overshadow differences, and comparison and analogy could more easily come to mind than would contrast and antithesis. The conventional ancient topos of assimilating word and picture would in fact by its very weight of tradition have deflected Gregory from reflecting on the truth of his pithy dictum.

The second speculation revolves specifically around what Gregory may have understood by "books" and "learning" and their relationship to each other. Today reading is normally a silent activity with many purposes, a principal one of which is to gather information in a world of constantly growing facts and data. Reading is largely divorced from speech, hearing, memory, and the age-old pursuit of wisdom. (Who speaks of wisdom in the modern university?) By comparison, as a churchman Gregory was well acquainted with the passages in Scripture which enjoin the reader or listener to "take the book and eat it".[117] However a modern Biblical fundamentalist (or, more exactly, literalist) might construe such words, the ordinary Jew or Christian knew that to 'eat' meant on a metaphorical level to 'take to heart' or to 'make a part of oneself' and that the first essential step to such ingestion was memorization. 'Reading' a book, particularly a holy or wise book, therefore implied memorizing it, reading was closely associated with memory, and so by extension reading could remind one in a sense of what one already knew. Furthermore, as Father Walter Ong has pointed out, in all the ages before the invention of printing, manuscripts were not easy to read, each manuscript was unique because of the copying process, and the preparation of indexes was not ordinarily worth the effort. Refinding material was very difficult, which encouraged memorization, which in turn encouraged reading aloud as an aid to memorization.[118]

However much Gregory may have conflated memory with other mental processes, the Scholastics of the high Middle Ages did not in theory, and for that reason when they averred that laypeople could somehow read pictures they presumably meant that people were thereby doing something more than simply recalling what they already knew. But from a practical point of view, memory was still inextricable from learning, which may help to explain why the Scholastics kept on repeating and modifying Gregory's idea. Let us reflect on Johannes Beleth and his remarkable attribution to Gregory of the contemporary figural analogy *clericus: litteratus: :laicus: illiteratus*. It was an understandable distortion. Beleth doubtless remembered that he had read something of the sort somewhere in Gregory–but where, and how to check it? Because of intervening improvements in script Beleth was not in quite as intimidating a position as

---

[117] Ez 3, 1-3; Ier 15, 16; Apc 10, 9-10.
[118] GOODY, *Literacy*, p. 14; ONG, *Orality*, pp. 119, 124.

Bede four centuries before, who in his collection of Gregory's works was faced with around 2,100 folios weighing between 90 and 100 pounds (with covers); but Beleth still had nothing like Migne's handy, printed, two-volume, seven-pound edition complete with indexes.[119] Unable to check very quickly, Beleth thus 'remembered' Gregory in a distinctive way which helps to explain his and other variations on Gregory's words.

A different text from the high Middle Ages might be adduced at this juncture not only to help us understand Gregory and his *traditores* (meant as both 'followers' and 'traitors'), but even to exculpate them. The author is everyone's favourite twelfth-century *locus classicus* on tyrannicide, courtiers, humanism, and the papal monarchy, John of Salisbury (*c.* 1115-1180), and the text is the *Metalogicon*:

> The word 'reading' is equivocal. It may refer either to the activity of teaching and learning (*discentis*), or to the occupation of studying written things by oneself. Consequently, the former, the intercommunication between teacher and learner, may be termed (to use Quintillian's word) the 'lecture' (*praelectio*); the latter, or the scrutiny by the student, the 'reading' (*lectio*), simply so called.[120]

Now several scholars have intimated that 'reading' in the Gregorian dictum should be understood in the first sense as the activity of teaching and learning, an activity which requires an intermediary.[121] If this is so, it is odd that neither Gregory nor any of his successors ever chose the more precise and appropriate *praelectio*; and although *lectio* can have this meaning, it is indefensible to aver that it must bear only or primarily this interpretation or even that texts were habitually read aloud in the Middle Ages. As Paul Saenger has brilliantly shown, the growth of silent reading, already encouraged by the monastic culture of the early Middle Ages, was greatly accelerated by the Scholastic culture of the high Middle Ages.[122]

---

[119] MEYVAERT, "Bede and the church paintings", p. 75.

[120] Save for one correction, I have followed the translation given in *The Metalogicon of John of Salisbury*, Bk. I, c. 24, tr. D.D. McGarry (Berkeley and Los Angeles, 1962), pp. 65-66. The Latin text is as follows: "*Sed quia legendi uerbum equiuocum est, tam ad docentis et discentis exercitium quam ad occupationem per se scrutantis scripturas; alterum, id est quod inter doctorem et discipulum communicatur, (ut uerbo utamur Quintiliani) dicatur praelectio, alterum quod ad scrutinium meditantis accedit, lectio simpliciter appelletur*" (*Ioannis Saresberiensis episcopi Carnotensis metalogicon*, ed. C.C.J. WEBB (Oxford, 1929), pp. 53-54). The germane passages in Quintilian's *Institutes* are 1, 2, 15; 1, 5, 11; and 2, 5, 4.

[121] KESSLER, "Pictorial narrative", pp. 76, 80, 85-88; CAMILLE, "Seeing and reading", pp. 32-37; STOCK, *Implications of Literacy*, p. 522.

[122] P. SAENGER, "Silent reading: Its impact on late medieval script and society", *Viator* 13

To rescue us from being overwhelmed by the bewildering overcomplication of these issues of reading, learning, and memory, there exists another twelfth-century text, the one which most directly treats all these matters, the *Didascalicon* of Hugh of St. Victor (1096/1097-1141), the German count who left his mark on the intellectual life of Paris. Reading, in fact, is his central theme, as he announces in the Preface:

> The things by which every man advances in knowledge are principally two–namely, reading and meditation. Of these, reading holds the first place in instruction, and it is of reading that this book treats, setting forth rules for it.[123]

Besides distinguishing clearly between reading and meditation, Hugh also emphasizes that both are ways to advance in knowledge. From Scripture, however familiar the text, one can learn at several levels. Part Two of the *Didascalicon*, he says, will show

> how Sacred Scripture ought to be read by the man who seeks in it the correction of his morals and a form of living. Finally, it instructs the man who reads in it for love of knowledge, and thus the second part too comes to a close.[124]

Far from denying the mnemonic function of reading Scripture, Hugh underlines its importance because of the fallibility of our memories and the necessity of our truly 'knowing' Scripture, ingesting it, making it part of our very being, and acting on it. This is the deepest kind of knowledge, but not the only kind. We can learn by reading all sorts of new things, including "new elementary facts" ("*nova rudimenta*"),[125] and the object of a thorough drilling in the seven liberal

---

(1982), pp. 367-414. Similarly, *lesen* in Medieval German can mean both 'private reading' and 'reading aloud': M.G. SCHOLZ, *Hören und Lesen: Studien zur primären Rezeption der Literatur im 12. und 13. Jahrhundert* (Wiesbaden, 1980), pp. 36 ff., 70 ff., and ID., "On presentation and reception: Guidelines in the German strophic epic of the Late Middle Ages", *New Literary History* 16.1 (Autumn 1984), pp. 137-151, especially pp. 137 and 141. This whole issue was devoted to the theme of "Oral and written traditions in the Middle Ages".

[123] Hugh of St. Victor, *Didascalicon de studio legendi*, ed. C. H. BUTTIMER (Washington, D.C., 1939: *Catholic University Studies in Medieval and Renaissance Latin* 10), preface, p. 2. I have used the translation of J. TAYLOR, *The Didascalicon of Hugh of St. Victor: A Medieval Guide to the Arts* (New York, 1961), p. 44.

[124] *Ibid.*, preface, p. 2 of the Latin text and pp. 44-45 of the English translation.

[125] *Ibid.*, Bk. V, ch. 1: "Therefore, let the student prepare himself once and for all by fixing these matters in the forefront of his mind, in certain little formulae, so to say, so that thereafter he will be able to run the course before him with free step and will not have to search out new elementary facts as he comes to individual books" (p. 120 of the translation, p. 94 in the Latin text).

arts is to enable us to learn by ourselves. According to Hugh, then, we can learn to read by ourselves and, more to the point, by reading acquire new knowledge, precise knowledge of new information, as well as deepen what we already know. Unfortunately, Hugh does not apply his sophisticated understanding of reading, remembering, and learning to the idea of 'reading' pictures, and it would be imprudent to speculate on his views. It is nonetheless essential to note that a thinker of the high Middle Ages formulated all these relevant distinctions, which therefore cannot be dismissed as anachronistic impositions on the past of purely modern categories. Hugh's was a particularly complex understanding of these processes, but it can hardly have been unique.

Admittedly, however, most propagators of the dictum were far less precise in their use of the word 'read'. In addition to the many instances already adduced one may add the following. Having in one sermon alluded to images in churches as books of the unlearned, Savonarola demonstrated in another his latitudinarian understanding of the act of reading:

> Read the things of God which excite you to His love. But you say, "I don't know how to read". Do you want me to show you a good book for you which you do know how to read? Take the crucifix into your room; let that be your book ... Take, then, the crucifix for your book, and read it, and you will see that will be the best remedy for preserving the light in you.[126]

The anonymous English priest of the late fourteenth century cited earlier used 'read' in more ways than was suggested by that quotation, which itself suggests daringly that "painting serves but to read the truth, as naked letters to a scholar".[127] He seems to impute to objects like paintings and books the capacity actively to read out the truth to passive observers. In addition, in his denunciation of miracle plays the priest also rehearsed the argument of their partisans that men 'read' the will of God better in a play than in a painting, "for this is a deed [dead] bok, the tother a quick". Not so, he answers, for miracle plays are "made to deliten men bodily than to ben bokis to lewdis men". Therefore, he concludes, "I preye thee rede enterly in the book of lyf that is Crist Jhesus" how

---

[126] Savonarola, *Prediche sopra Ruth e Michea*, No. 25, ed. V. ROMANO, 2 vols. (Rome, 1961), 2, p. 277: "*Leggi cose di Dio e chi ti eccitino allo amore suo. Ma tu che di': – Io non so leggere –. Vuo' tu che io t'insegni uno buono libro per te, che tu lo saprai leggere? Tieni el Crucifisso in camera tua: Questa sia el tuo libro. Non fare comme colui che tiene figure disoneste in camera sua, che incitano a libidine. Credi a me, che noi siamo mossi da'sensi. Tieni adunque el Crucifisso per tuo libro, e leggi quello, e vedrai che questo sarà ottimo remedio a conservarti questo lume*".

[127] See above, p. 79.

to achieve salvation.[128] He might have added, but did not, that one can also 'read' the Book of Nature, a common trope from Augustine to Thomas Browne.[129]

A great deal turns in the end on the answers to two questions. First, was the dictum in any of its forms intended to be understood literally rather than only metaphorically? That is very difficult and usually impossible to discover in most cases. Second, was the analogy between reading pictures and reading books, illiterates and literates, meant to hold *only* insofar as both books and pictures were, in Pecock's words, "rememoratijf signes", or were pictures viewed as comparable to books in further ways, especially as vehicles of new information? Unfortunately, few in the Western tradition were as careful as the great Byzantine expositor, St. John Damascene (*c.* 675-749), whose whole position is accurately encapsulated in this sentence: "an image is, after all, a reminder: it is to the illiterate what a book is to the literate, and what the word is to hearing, the image is to sight".[130] Bishop Pecock came closest to this clarity, but even he muddied the waters at one place by choosing tidiness over clarity. As for the others, the caution of Bede, Aquinas, Durandus, and many others implies perhaps that they considered images to have memorial worth comparable to that of books, but nothing more. Gregory's own position will probably never be clarified. Bonaventure apparently introduced a decided distinction between the function of images to stimulate the memory of beholders, simple and learned, and to serve as the books of the illiterate–but literally, and in what way? At almost every turn where there is not confusion there is failure to cut through the thicket of issues, and so the muddied waters have spread in time.

In the end, therefore, I would still contend that after making all possible allowance for the mind and the situation of Gregory and the many *traditores* of his dictum, they were still wrong insofar as they intended to say that images can do more than remind and deepen what one already knows.

---

[128] *Reliquiae antiquae*, 2, pp. 46, 50.

[129] J.M. GELLRICH, *The Idea of the Book in the Middle Ages: Language Theory, Mythology, and Fiction* (Ithaca, 1985), pp. 29-30.

[130] John of Damascus, *De imaginibus oratio* I, ed. in: PG 94, tr. in: *Iconoclasm: Papers Given at the Ninth Spring Symposium of Byzantine Studies, University of Birmingham, March 1975*, ed. A. BRYER and J. HERRIN (Birmingham, 1977), p. 183 (which incorrectly lists the column number in PG 94 as 1258). See also John of Damascus, *Exposition of the Orthodox Faith*, c. 16, tr. S.D.F. SALMOND (repr. Grand Rapids, Mich., 1976: *Select Library of Nicene and Post-Nicene Fathers*, 2nd series 9), p. 88, and *St. John Damascene on Holy Images*, tr. M.H. ALLIES (London, 1898), pp. 12-13, 19, 39-40, 47, 67, 87, 93, 96, 97, 117.

III

If I am right, what is the significance of this misconception and its historical success down to the present?

First, it sheds considerable light on Gregory's authority, which in these
matters (not to mention others) was so great by the later eighth century that
Pope Hadrian I in his letter to Charlemagne quoted several letters of Gregory.[131]
No one in the Middle Ages who in effect criticized Gregory's idea ever named
him in the same context, and it is reasonable to suppose that his authority over-
awed others who might otherwise have developed doubts. It has recently been
convincingly argued that Pope Hadrian I's teaching on images led to the quiet
suppression of the *Libri Carolini* at the court of Charlemagne for the rest of the
Middle Ages.[132] If Hadrian I exerted this much influence, how much more was
that of Gregory? Analogously, to some degree we all fall into the trap of accepting something because so-and-so said it. The anti-papal glee with which
certain Protestant Reformers openly attacked Gregory is equally comprehensi-
ble. What is not so understandable is the acceptance of, and continuing variations on, Gregory's theme by modern scholars, most of whom would shudder
at the merest mention of papal authority in matters of faith and morals, but have
in effect conceded it to Gregory, if not to other popes, in matters aesthetic.

Second, the dictum prompts some reflections on the nature of 'high' or
'learned' culture and its relationship to 'popular' culture. This has come to be
an area of considerable concern to historians in recent decades, especially to
those of the medieval and early modern periods. The problem regrettably lends
itself to simplistic thinking, especially of a bipartite division or 'two-tiered
model' in which 'learned' and 'popular' are usually regarded in antithetical
terms, and this in turn encourages categorization according to one's preju-
dices.[133] Under the influence of Protestantism and the Enlightenment, for instance, many scholars have dismissed the cult of the saints as having had a

---

[131] See above, p. 70.

[132] A. FREEMAN, "Carolingian orthodoxy and the fate of the *Libri Carolini*", *Viator* 16
(1985), pp. 65-108.

[133] For some recent critiques of this kind of thinking, see C. GINZBURG, *The Cheese and the
Worms: The Cosmos of a Sixteenth-Century Miller*, tr. J. and A. TEDESCHI (Harmondsworth,
1982), pp. XIV-XXIV; T. TENTLER, "Seventeen authors in search of two cultures", *Catholic
Historical Review* 71 (1985), pp. 248-257, a review of the seventeen contributions to *Faire
croire: Modalités de la diffusion et de la réception des messages religieux du XIIe au XIVe siècle*
(Rome, 1981); and M. LAUWERS, "'Religion populaire', culture folklorique, mentalités: Notes
pour une anthropologie culturelle du moyen âge", *Revue d'histoire écclésiastique* 82 (1987),
pp. 221-258.

popular origin which lamentably, in their eyes, percolated upwards into the learned Church and so corrupted pristine Christian belief. Peter Brown has convincingly demonstrated as untrue not only this belief, but also the idea that "the worship of icons rose like a damp stain from the masses".[134] Sister Charles Murray has also brilliantly exposed biased 'high-low' thinking on the issue of art and early Christianity.[135] Several years ago Jacques Le Goff presented a thesis about *The Birth of Purgatory* which has been justly taken to task for its prejudiced outlook and approach.[136] 'High-low' thinking evidently pervades our conceptualization about much of the past in ways we are only beginning to appreciate.

In this context, in dividing viewers into the lettered and the unlettered Gregory the Great thought essentially in bipartite terms, but only to some extent in antithetical terms. For it is revealing that Gregory as an educated man justified religious art by asserting its educative value for the common man. It is not necessarily all that important that he adduced this reason first, for he might have been thinking of an ascending series of arguments in accordance with good rhetorical principles, or from another point of view he might have wanted to begin with what was peculiar to illiterate viewers and then pass on to the effects which could be experienced by all beholders. Still, he evidently felt a strong urge to defend 'high culture' by showing its connection to 'popular culture', and furthermore he was probably confident that the argument would somehow appeal to Bishop Serenus. Gregory's attitude contrasts markedly with that of Boccaccio and Petrarch–the first's depreciation of the traditional concern of artists "to give pleasure to the eyes of the ignorant rather than to delight the minds of the wise", the second's frank denial of the ability of the masses to understand art. Both regard learned and popular culture as antitheses, and neither is concerned about the usefulness of the higher culture for the lower. Greg-

---

[134] P. BROWN, *The Cult of the Saints: Its Rise and Function in Latin Christianity* (Chicago, 1982), pp. 12-22, and ID., "A Dark-Age crisis: Aspects of the iconoclastic controversy", *English Historical Review* 87 (1973), pp. 16-17: "If anything, it was the elite of the Byzantine world whose needs were more effectively satisfied by the cult of icons than were those of the supposed masses of the population" (p. 17).

[135] C. MURRAY, "Art and the early Church", *Journal of Theological Studies*, N.S. 28 (1977), pp. 303-345. This article was reproduced as chap. 1 in her *Rebirth and Afterlife: A Study of the Transmutation of Some Pagan Imagery in Early Christian Funerary Art* (Oxford, 1981: *British Archaeological Reports, International Series* 100).

[136] J. LEGOFF, *La naissance du Purgatoire* (Paris, 1981; Eng. tr. *The Birth of Purgatory*, tr. A. GOLDHAMMER (Chicago, 1984)); A.J. GUREVICH, "Popular and scholarly medieval and cultural traditions: Notes in the margins of Jacques LeGoff's book", *Journal of Medieval History* 9 (1983), pp. 71-90; and G.R. EDWARDS, "Purgatory: 'Birth' or evolution?", *Journal of Ecclesiastical History* 36 (1985), pp. 634-646.

ory's concern was of course pastoral, whereas Boccaccio and Petrarch had no such interest, even if they were both clerics.

At the same time, however much Gregory believed that religious art served the people, his misapprehension reveals his failure, or his inability, to place himself in the position of an illiterate looking at a religious image. Given the evolution of Christian art up to this time and his feelings about its legitimacy, Gregory had no incentive to take a critical stance which could have undermined his own thinking. He had a vested interest in maintaining, and no interest in discarding, an opinion which he possibly learned rather than formulated on his own. He stood in a developing tradition in the West which he greatly reinforced by the authority of his words, however misleading they may have been.

What about the Scholastics and their contributions to the tradition? There is much significance in their substitution of *laici* for Gregory's *illiterati* precisely at the time that such an identification was beginning to break down, and in their careful distinction between memory and learning which they did not apply to the Gregorian dictum. These salient facts underscore the truism that intellectuals deal with ideas, that these ideas have a force and a logic of their own which do not necessarily have much to do with extramental reality, and that intellectuals habitually think they understand 'the people' much better than in fact they do (when they bother to think about the people in the first place). Many readers will verify this from their own observations in the present, but for some reason we are loath to apply these lessons of our experience to people in the past. One can understand both the early humanists' defensive contemptuousness for the ignorant and the later humanists' preoccupation with neoclassical ideas about poetry and painting, words and things, and the clarity of the Book of Nature as mirrored in naturalistic art. What is hard to fathom is the attitude of so many mendicants, whom Peter Burke has described as "amphibious or bi-cultural, men of the university as well as men of the marketplace".[137] Yet even they who were supposedly in close touch with the people left little evidence that they noticed that simple folk cannot 'read' art.[138]

Finally, what of the even more peculiar developments of the nineteenth and twentieth centuries, not only the persistence of the dictum and the comparative lack of criticism (despite all the interest in 'the people'), but scholars' further

---

[137] P. BURKE, *Popular Culture in Early Modern Europe* (London and New York, 1978), pp. 70-71; see also p. 101.

[138] As for the commonplace that late medieval preachers habitually integrated pictures into their sermons as ways of teaching the people, the paucity of such references in the sources (at least English sources) is remarked by COULTON, *Art and the Reformation*, pp. 317, 566; and G.R. OWST, *Literature and Pulpit in Medieval England*, 2nd rev. edn. (New York, 1961), pp. 47-55, 136-148. See also HENRY, *Biblia Pauperum*, p. 18.

variations on the Gregorian theme as well? This is of course a vast and intricate problem of modern cultural history which warrants separate treatment on its own, and so four modest suggestions will have to suffice here. First, one of the astute adages which I find confirmed again and again is that "whether or not history repeats itself, historians repeat each other".[139] In light of this review of the peregrinations of Gregory's idea, this bit of wisdom should itself perhaps be modified to read "whether or not history repeats itself, thinkers repeat each other, more or less". Second, in the nineteenth century the Romantic movement wrought unparalleled havoc with this idea, just as it did with other fanciful concepts about the Middle Ages with which teachers of medieval history still have to contend–The Age of Faith, The Glory of Knighthood, The Wonder of Chivalry, Aquinas as the Acme of the Middle Ages, and all those other Beautiful (and therefore, of course, True) ideas. In connection with our particular theme one need mention only three famous book titles–Ruskin's *Bible of Amiens*, Morris' *Art of the People*, and above all Hugo's *Notre-Dame de Paris*, in whose view, "up until Gutenberg, architecture was the chief, the universal form of writing. It was the Middle Ages which wrote the final pages in the book of granite, which had been begun in the Orient and carried on by Ancient Greece and Rome".[140] Such Romantic notions live on, perhaps not always repeated in such bald form, but surviving nonetheless in more attenuated and hence more insidious form; and unless they are dispassionately dissected, they will go on being repeated generation after generation.[141] Although medievalists

---

[139] Variously ascribed to Max Beerbohm and Herbert Asquith (D.H. FISCHER, *Historians' Fallacies: Toward a Logic of Historical Thought* (New York, 1970), p. 25). In a different way, William Ivins, Jr., wrote that "Most of what we think of as culture is more than the unquestioning acceptance of standardized values" (W. IVINS, *Prints and Visual Communication* (Cambridge, Mass., 1953), p. 4).

[140] John Ruskin, *The Bible of Amiens*, in: *The Works of John Ruskin*, 39 vols. (London, 1903-1912), 33, pp. 113-114, 124; Victor Hugo, *Notre-Dame of Paris*, tr. J. STURROCK (Baltimore, 1978), especially Bk. III, chs. 1 and 2; Bk. IV, ch. 5; Bk. V, chs. 1 and 2; Bk. VI, ch. 2 (pp. 123, 128, 149, 174, 186-202, and 213 of this edition; the quotation appears on p. 200); William Morris, *The Art of the People: An Address delivered before the Birmingham Society of Arts, February 19th, 1879* (Chicago, 1902). Hugo's ideas live on, as in V. BROMBERT, *Victor Hugo and the Visionary Novel* (Cambridge, Mass., 1984), ch. 3, "The living stones of Notre-Dame".

[141] One has only to think of the titles of the many books published by P. MACKENDRICK since 1960: *The Mute Stones Speak ...*, *The Dacian Stones Speak*, *The Greek Stones Speak*, etc. Doubtless MacKendrick means 'speak' metaphorically, but this flaccid usage nevertheless perpetuates the confusion. For recent examples, see E.L. EISENSTEIN, *The Printing Revolution in Early Modern Europe* (Cambridge, 1983), pp. 34-35 ("Not only did printing eliminate many functions previously performed by stone figures over portals and stained glass in windows ... . The favorite text of the defenders of images was the dictum of Gregory the Great that statues

know, for example, that 'The Age of Faith' is a highly misleading characterization, it seems nearly impossible, despite all our best efforts, to extirpate it from the textbooks, much less from the popular consciousness.

A third factor is the twentieth-century academic preoccupation with words, both their limitations and their hidden meanings, as witness linguistic analysis in philosophy, semiotics and deconstructionism in literary studies, and a general fascination with numbers as more precise instruments for the apprehension and statement of the truth. In many quarters, words are regarded, consciously or unconsciously, as having to be 'interpreted' rather than 'read', and so the former gap between them and pictures has for many scholars narrowed appreciably or even disappeared. We have gone too far in this direction of depreciating words. While some literary texts do indeed require a search for 'subtexts' and other opaque or covert meanings, it is dangerous to extend this attitude to all words and texts, if only because we run the risk of developing into a neo-Gnostic priesthood which alone can discern the *real* meaning of a text–and every modern academic is culturally programmed to know how wicked all priests are. Words are not perfect and never can be, but they will always remain our most precise, if ever defective, mode of communication. By comparison, pictures can be interpreted as artifacts and be very useful also as 'sources' and as stimulants of new insights, but their correct interpretation can be corroborated only by reference to other sources, by allusion to what one already knows, and by the use of words to conduct an intelligible and fruitful discussion of the meaning of individual pictures. Pictures cannot 'speak' clearly, only words can. That is the long and the short of it.

A final speculation is this. In the modern age perhaps the historical disciplines, and the relatively new field of art history in particular, have had an unspoken, perhaps unconscious, vested interest in perpetuating this dictum

served as 'the books of the illiterate'".); P. LASLETT, *The World We Have Lost*, 3rd edn. (New York, 1984), p. 235 ("The most important messages for the society were, of course, religious, and in medieval Christianity the pictures in the windows and on the walls of the churches told with wearisome repetitiveness the story which everyone had to know for the sake of his or her salvation".); V.A. KOLVE, *Chaucer and the Imagery of Narrative: The First Five Canterbury Tales* (Stanford, 1984), p. 45; J. VAN ENGEN, "The Christian Middle Ages as an historiographical problem", *American Historical Review* 91 (1986), p. 549 ("The methods employed to teach religious ideas and practices included, especially, materials now studied by art and literary historians: mystery plays developing out of the mass, wall paintings as 'books for the illiterate', vernacular sermons, saints' lives in epic form, and so on. A difficult area, this, and one in which historians often must work from hints rather than solid sources".). As the final sentence indicates, Van Engen understands that there are problems in general with these methods, and it must also be admitted that Eisenstein and Kolve seem to speak only or primarily of the mnemonic function of pictures as 'books'; but none of these authors addresses the fundamental question raised here.

because it posits the utility of art for the people. Art has often been useful for, and popular with, the people, although frequently in more complicated ways than we first imagine.[142] But do we really have anything to fear if we at last admit that Gregory and his many disciples erred in regarding art as the book of the illiterate?

---

[142] For an intelligent discussion, see COULTON, *Art and the Reformation*, pp. 338-342, 365-370.

Reflections on "Was Art Really the 'Book of the Illiterate'?"[1]

LAWRENCE G. DUGGAN

In 1981 the old saw about art as "the book of the illiterate" suddenly piqued my interest. Ultimately, my extensive researches resulted in an article published in *Word & Image* in 1989. In it, I sought not only to trace the origins and history of this dictum, but also to ask whether it was in fact true that illiterates could read in images what literates could read in books. I found that the *fons et origo* of this idea was Pope Gregory the Great (590-604) and that it had undergone a long, sometimes curious, even tortuous evolution down to the present. I also argued that no matter how one attempted to interpret, contextualize, or rationalize this notion, in the end we had to "admit that Gregory and his many disciples erred in regarding art as the book of the illiterate".[2] This peroration was evidently too much to stomach for the readers consulted by the half-dozen or so distinguished journals to which I had submitted the essay for consideration. These reviewers concurred that the argument was too controversial, brash, or just plain absurd. One scholar with whom I had publicly debated the issue in 1986 was Herbert Kessler. Although then, as presumably now, he disagreed with

---

[1] In this revised version of the paper I have endeavoured to address the questions and incorporate the suggestions offered at the conference in Utrecht, particularly those of Michael Camille, Michael Curschmann, Herbert Kessler, John Lowden, Henry Mayr-Harting, Rosamond McKitterick, Karl Morrison, Marco Mostert, and Sophie Oosterwijk. To all of them I offer heartfelt thanks.

[2] L.G. DUGGAN, "Was art really the 'Book of the Illiterate'?", *Word & Image* 5 (1989), pp. 227-251, at p. 251, and reprinted in this volume at p. 63. Further references to this article will be made to the reprint only.

me, it was ironically through his good offices that the article finally appeared in
Word & Image.

Nevertheless, since its appearance eleven years ago, although I have encountered many references to it in notes,[3] I have seen almost no discussion of the
issues it raises, I have received almost no communications about it, and I was
once greeted with studied coolness by a colleague in art history and his wife
when I asked them for their response. Two art historians whom I recently infor-
mally consulted offered entirely different impressions of its reception. The one
thought that the essay was so "fundamental" and its thesis so obvious that it had
passed into the conventional wisdom without further discussion, whereas Dale
Kinney thought that although the article is frequently cited, no one has really
addressed the issues it raises or the implications it suggests, especially their
incompatibility with the views of others such as Kessler and Celia Chazelle. One
of the few positive comments in print I have discovered is from Robin Cormack,
who describes my contribution to the discussions of Gregory's dictum as "particularly helpful".[4] Although Brendan Cassidy does not cite my work explicitly
in his "Introduction" to *Iconography at the Crossroads*, he seems implicitly to
agree when he quotes approvingly Dr. Johnson's riposte to Boswell, "Painting,
Sir, can illustrate, but cannot inform".[5] On the other hand, in his *Violence and
Daily Life: Reading, Art, and Polemics in the Cîteaux Moralia in Job*, Conrad
Rudolph remarks in a footnote to the conclusion that he is "in fundamental dis-
agreement with the recent studies by Chazelle ... and Duggan", but he does not
elaborate.[6] A revealing early visceral reaction came about six months after the

---

[3]   E.g. C. CHAZELLE, "Pictures, books, and the illiterate: Pope Gregory I's Letters to
Serenus of Marseilles", *Word & Image* 6 (1990), pp. 151-153, nn. 3-5, 32, 34, 37-38, 40, 54;
H.L. KESSLER, " 'Facies bibliothecae revelata': Carolingian art as spiritual seeing", in: *Testo e
Immagine nell'Alto Medioevo*, 2 vols. (Spoleto, 1994: *Settimane di Studio del Centro Italiano di
Studi dell'Alto Medioevo* 41), 2, p. 533, n. 2; L. NEES, "Art and architecture", in: *The New
Cambridge Medieval History*, 2: *c. 700-c. 900*, ed. R. MCKITTERICK (Cambridge, 1995), p. 818,
n. 64; J. LOWDEN, "The beginnings of biblical illustration", in: *Imaging the Early Medieval
Bible*, ed. J. WILLIAMS (University Park, PA, 1999), p. 56, n. 120; D. HOOGLAND VERKERK,
"Biblical manuscripts in Rome 400-700 and the Ashburnham Pentateuch", in: *Imaging the Early
Medieval Bible*, p. 98, n. 2; EADEM, "Moral structure in the Ashburnham Pentateuch", in: *Image
and Belief: Studies in Celebration of the Eightieth Anniversary of the Index of Christian Art*, ed.
C. HOURIHANE (Princeton, 1999), p. 74, n. 17.
[4]   R. CORMACK, *Painting the Soul: Icons, Death Masks and Shrouds* (London, 1997),
p. 227, n. 39.
[5]   *Iconography at the Crossroads: Papers from the Colloquium Sponsored by the Index of
Christian Art, Princeton University, 23-24 March 1990*, ed. B. CASSIDY (Princeton, 1993), p. 8.
Boswell's Life of Johnson, new edn. (London, 1953), p. 1313 (June 1784, aet. 75).
[6]   C. RUDOLPH, *Violence and Daily Life: Reading, Art, and Polemics in the Cîteaux
Moralia in Job* (Princeton, 1997), p. 125, n. 42 (on p. 126).

publication of the article. At a conference at Princeton in March 1990, Michael Camille called it "a recent diatribe which usefully collects together texts but fails to address the visual aspects of the equation".[7] Camille was more measured in his criticism by the time he spoke at Spoleto in 1993, where he said that "A useful corrective to Duggan's totally textual and therefore limited vision of the issue is given in Kessler, "Diction in the 'Bibles of the Illiterate' ".[8] The latter essay, published originally in 1989 and reprinted in 1994, represented Kessler's oral refutation of my paper in 1986.[9] Apart from these few references, for years I have therefore assumed that I had said unpalatable things and was being studiously ignored in reprisal. I am still not sure what to make of it all. Neither is Celia Chazelle, who has been lumped with me by one scholar and contrasted with me by another.

But let us move from the *Rezeptionsgeschichte* of the article to the reception of texts in the Middle Ages.

First, let me reaffirm my belief that Gregory the Great and his followers were wrong. To be sure, others before Gregory had said somewhat similar things about art as the book of the illiterate. Yet Gregory generally gets the credit because of the crispness of his formulation and his distinctive authority as pope. To recollect his authoritative status, we need only mention labels like 'Gregorian chant', 'Gregorian Sacramentary', and 'Gregorian water', all of which assign to Gregory things for which he was sometimes at best only partly responsible.

Was he wrong on the matter at issue, pictures as the books of the illiterate? Many scholars like Conrad Rudolph in effect insist that he was not. As in 1989, I continue to find it amusing that so many of them "would shudder at the merest mention of papal authority in matters of faith and morals, but have in effect conceded it to Gregory, if not to other popes, in matters aesthetic".[10] Gregory was simply a human being who could be wrong and make mistakes, and I would suggest that he did so from time to time.

Allow me to probe this point in two different ways. First, it was a staple of late antique and medieval Christian thinking that a passionate husband is an adulterer to his wife. James Brundage has recently shown that what seems to us

---

[7] M. CAMILLE, "Mouths and meanings: Toward an anti-iconography of medieval art", in: *Iconography at the Crossroads*, p. 44, n. 4.

[8] M. CAMILLE, "Word, text, image and the early Church Fathers in the Egino Codex", in: *Testo e Immagine*, 1, p. 84, n. 29.

[9] H. KESSLER, "Diction in the 'Bibles of the Illiterate' ", in: *World Art: Themes of Unity and Diversity: Acts of the XXVIth International Congress of the History of Art (Washington, 10-15 August 1986)*, ed. I. LAVIN, 3 vols. (University Park, PA, 1989), 2, pp. 297-308, repr. in: H. KESSLER, *Studies in Pictorial Narrative* (London, 1994), pp. 33-48.

[10] DUGGAN, "Art", p. 102.

a curious notion is not rooted in the New Testament so much as in Stoic philosophy. When theologians and canon lawyers in the High Middle Ages were casting about for an appropriate Christian authority to adduce in its support, they found it in the so-called *Responsa Gregorii* – probably spurious texts, we now think, but sufficient then in their authority because they were attributed to Gregory the Great.[11] Whatever Gregory might have thought of this idea, we would not agree with it.

Now there is a very different matter in which we do know Gregory's position, and on this most of us would again not concur with him. Several years ago I published an essay on Charlemagne and the forcible conversion of the Saxons to Christianity.[12] Much of it was devoted to exploring the long period of religious and cultural preparation culminating in Charlemagne's drastic decision that the Saxons must convert to Christianity or die. Among those people most crucial in shaping this climate of thinking was a long line of bishops. They took seriously their obedience to the Great Mandate imposed by Christ to spread the gospel to all nations, and put great pressure on rulers like Clovis not only to convert, but to exert pressure on their subjects to convert. Gregory took this one step further by exhorting the recently converted King Ethelbert of Kent (560-616) to

> increase your righteous zeal for their conversion; suppress the worship of idols; overthrow their buildings and shrines; strengthen the morals of your subjects by outstanding purity of life, by exhorting them, terrifying, enticing, and correcting them ...[13]

Gregory was urging the king to calculated violence against specific pagan objects. In dispensing advice to Augustine, the first archbishop of Canterbury (597-604/609), Gregory pulled back somewhat from this position:

> tell him what I have decided after long deliberation about the English people, namely that the idol temples of that race should by no means be destroyed, but only the

---

[11] J.A. BRUNDAGE, "The married man's dilemma: Sexual morals, canon law, and marital restraint", *Studia Gratiana* 28 (1998), pp. 149-69, especially p. 167; on the authenticity of the *Responsa Gregorii*, see IDEM, *Law, Sex, and Christian Society in Medieval Europe* (Chicago and London, 1987), pp. 140-141 and the references given there.

[12] L.G. DUGGAN, " 'For force is not of God'? Compulsion and conversion from Yahweh to Charlemagne", in: *Varieties of Religious Conversion in the Middle Ages*, ed. J. MULDOON (Gainsville, Fla., 1997), pp. 49-62.

[13] Beda, *Historia Ecclesiastica Gentis Anglorum*, I, c. 32, ed. as: *Bede's Ecclesiastical History of the English People*, ed. and tr. B. COLGRAVE and R.A.B. MYNORS (Oxford, 1969), p. 113.

idols in them. Take holy water and sprinkle it in these shrines, build altars and place relics in them. For if the shrines are well built, it is essential that they should be changed from the worship of devils to the service of the true God.[14]

But even to a fellow bishop Gregory was urging a policy of selective destruction of things – of idols, but not of their repositories. It is of great interest, then, that a century and a half later Boniface († 754), the 'Apostle to the Germans', followed Gregory's advice to Ethelbert, not Augustine, in cutting down sacred trees and shrines among the Frisians and the Hessians, including the mighty Oak of Jupiter (i.e. Thor) at Geismar.[15] Several decades later, Charlemagne, ever a man of bold action, went one step further from the destruction of things to the destruction of people in his promotion of Christianity. What Gregory the Great would have thought of his own contribution to the incremental espousal of violence in the onward march of Christianity one can only wonder.

It will doubtless be objected that in this instance Gregory was addressing a question of policy and not epistemology, as in the two famous letters to Bishop Serenus of Marseilles. Let us then suppose that if Gregory did not actually make a mistake, perhaps he did not express himself as well as he might have. After all, this has happened time and again in the history of human thought and expression. Consider Epicurus (341-270 BC), for example, and the peculiar disparity between his actual teachings and the popular understanding of the term 'epicurean'. Epicurus can hardly be blamed for the survival of some of his writings and not of others. In those that are extant, however, he does not state the core of his philosophy as well as he might – to avoid pain rather than to pursue pleasure – and thus contributed inadvertently to widespread misconstrual of his position. Perhaps Gregory the Great similarly did not articulate as precisely as he might his position on images as the books of the illiterate.

The objection will also be voiced that Gregory did not mean his words to be interpreted in these ways, and that what he wrote should not be construed literally or wrenched from its context. Perhaps not, but the indisputable facts are that both did occur with respect to his written words on images as well as on conversion policies. Although Gregory cannot be blamed for what Charlemagne chose to do, Gregory did contribute significantly to the creation of that climate of opinion on which Charlemagne acted. As for our insistence on the distinction

---

[14] *Ibid.*, I, c. 30, ed. pp. 106-107.

[15] Willibald, *Vita Bonifatii*, cc. 5-6, 8, ed. in: *Briefe des Bonifatius – Willibalds Leben des Bonifatius nebst einigen zeitgenössischen Dokumenten*, ed. and tr. R. RAU (Darmstadt, 1968: *Ausgewählte Quellen zur deutschen Geschichte des Mittelalters* 4b), pp. 488, 494-495, 508-512; English tr. in: *The Anglo-Saxon Missionaries in Germany*, tr. C.H. TALBOT (New York, 1954), pp. 41, 45-46, 55.

between the literal and the metaphorical interpretations of Gregory's words, this typically modern binary opposition was probably inapplicable in the Middle Ages because of the well-developed method of fourfold interpretation of Scripture. In that approach to interpretive thinking not only were the literal and the metaphorical compatible; it easily encouraged movement from one to the other. And in reply to the possible further objection that here we are not dealing with the interpretation of Scripture as such, we must remind ourselves that Gregory the bishop was living and working in a highly sacralized culture suffused with allusions to and evocations of the Bible at almost every turn. This was certainly the case with the images with which we are dealing.

There is yet another possibility we need to consider as well, i.e. the unspoken assumptions behind Gregory's ideas about reading as not being a solitary and silent activity, but rather a communal and aural one. In my article I suggested this possibility when I asked what did Gregory "mean by the verb 'to read' – private silent reading, reading aloud, or some kind of group activity perhaps engaging both illiterates and literates?"[16] I did not explore then what I had posed as a rhetorical question, so allow me to do so now by looking at four different texts illustrating the reception of both images and words by 'interpretive communities' in worlds quite different from our own. We shall work our way backwards in time.

In his *Autobiography*, Benvenuto Cellini (1500-1571) tells us that upon near-completion of his *Perseus and Medusa* in 1554, his patron, Cosimo I, Grand Duke of Tuscany, responded in this way:

> For all that the work strikes us as being very beautiful it still has to please the people. So, my dear Benvenuto, before you give it the finishing touches I wonder if you would do me the favour of opening the screen, a little, for half a day, so that it can be seen from my piazza. Then we shall be able to hear what the people think of it.

Cellini complied, and his record of the popular reaction comes as no surprise:

> And then, as God would have it, as soon as it was shown, the people praised it with such unrestrained enthusiasm that I was given some consolation. They never left off attaching verses to the posts of the doors ... On that day, when it was on show for a few hours, more than twenty sonnets, all praising my statue to the skies, were attached to the posts. After I had covered it up again, every day a host of sonnets were attached there, and with them Latin and Greek verses as well, since it was vacation

---

[16]   DUGGAN, "Art", p. 64.

for the University of Pisa and all the celebrated professors and scholars rivalled each other in what they wrote.[17]

According to Cellini, this kind of reaction was hardly unusual. Earlier he tells us that the dedication of Michelangelo's New Sacristy at San Lorenzo in Florence occasioned the composition of more than a hundred sonnets, but that Bandinello's botched *Hercules and Cacus* elicited more than a thousand sonnets, "all abusing that clumsy abortion".[18] Vilification evidently comes forth far more readily than praise.

In 1311, Duccio di Buoninsegna (ca. 1255-1319) completed his enormous altarpiece, the *Maestà*, for the cathedral in Siena. Its placement there was recorded by one of the city's chroniclers:

> And on the day that it was carried to the Duomo the shops were shut, and the bishop conducted a great and devout company of priests and friars in solemn procession, accompanied by the nine signiors, and all the officers of the commune, and all the people, and one after another the worthiest with lighted candles in their hands took places near the picture, and behind came the women and children with great devotion. And they accompanied the said picture up to the Duomo, making the procession around the Campo, as is the custom, all the bells ringing joyously, out of reverence for so noble a picture as this. And this picture Duccio di Niccolò the painter made in the house of the Muciatti outside the gate *a Stalloreggi*. And all that day they stood in prayer with great alsmgiving for poor persons, praying God and His Mother, who is our advocate, to defend us by their infinite mercy from every adversity and all evil, and keep us from the hands of traitors and of the enemies of Siena.[19]

This was an event bringing together the entire community, lay and clerical, male and female, rich and poor, accompanied by much music and presumably many words, for both a holiday and a holy day to pray that this sacred image might protect Siena against its many enemies.

Just two years earlier, in 1309 Jean de Joinville (1225-1317) completed what Queen Jeanne of Navarre had asked him to write, a life of King St. Louis IX. He begins his account in this revealing way:

---

[17] Benvenuto Cellini, *Autobiography*, tr. G. BULL (Harmondsworth, 1956), pp. 364-65.

[18] *Ibid.*, pp. 336, 379.

[19] G. MILANESI, *Documenti per la storia dell'arte senese*, 3 vols. (Siena, 1854), 1, p. 169; tr. in: C.E. NORTON, *Historical Studies of Church-Building in the Middle Ages* (New York, 1880), pp. 144-145.

> In the name of God Almighty, I, Jean, Lord of Joinville, Seneschal of Champagne, dictate the life of our good King, Saint Louis, ... so that it may be set down in due order for the edification of those to whom this book is read.[20]

This one sentence tells us that this book, the first biography by a layman in French, in both its composition and its reception involved more than one person and both the mouth and the ear as well as the eye and the hand.

This passage quite possibly also reminds one of the famous section in Book VI of Augustine's *Confessions* (VI, c. 3) in which he describes coming upon Ambrose reading silently.[21] Instead of dwelling on this much analysed text, let us turn instead to the book that Ambrose may have been reading and which in any event was the central text for Ambrose, Gregory the Great, and all those other early Christians, some of whom were inspired to create that new product of late antique Christian civilization, the illuminated Bible.

And so we turn to the Bible itself. A reading from the Gospel according to Saint Matthew, chapter the 5th, beginning at the 43rd verse: "Jesus said, 'You have heard that it was said, "Thou shalt love thy neighbour, and shalt hate thy enemy" ' ". We literates accustomed to thinking of the Bible as a book to be read might be struck by Jesus' words "heard" and "said". "Said" may be ambiguous, as in "the book says", but "heard" is not. Perhaps Jesus meant to call attention to the disparity between what the text actually says and what people think it says. For Leviticus 19, 18 clearly enjoins us only to "Love thy neighbour as thyself" and speaks neither of hate nor of enemies (and, incidentally, it also reminds us that the law of love first appears in the Old Testament, not the New, no matter what many Christians prefer to believe). It is the sixth time in the opening chapter of the Sermon on the Mount that Jesus speaks in this way – "You have heard that it was said" – but this is the first and only instance in which he was perhaps pointing to a misunderstanding or even perversion of the original text. On killing, adultery, divorce, oaths, and revenge, Jesus quotes the original Old Testament passage accurately. Underscoring received distortions of the law was therefore not the reason for his choice of this repeated mode of allocution. Instead, Jesus is reminding us of how his presumably Hebrew audience came to learn and understand the scriptures either principally or secondarily – through hearing and probably usually as a communal experience. This was doubtless true for women and children, who were presumably present at the

---

[20] Jean de Joinville, *Life of Saint Louis*, I, c. 1, tr. in: *Joinville and Villehardouin, Chronicles of the Crusades*, tr. M.R.B. SHAW (Harmondsworth, 1963), p. 167.

[21] Cf. B. STOCK, *Augustine the Reader: Meditation, Self-Knowledge, and the Ethics of Interpretation* (Cambridge, Mass., and London, 1996), p. 7 and *passim*.

Sermon on the Mount as they certainly were at the miracle of the loaves and fishes. But this common aural experience was true also for Jewish males school- ed in the scriptures. Men heard these words recited and chanted by others repeat- edly, and they heard the words of God as they reverentially recited them by themselves. Hearing the sacred text was an integral part of the experience. What was true for Jews was no less true for Christians.[22]

The Bible. In thinking about this paper and mining medieval and Renais- sance sources illuminating the subject of interpretive communities, I had not thought about looking to the Bible itself until I heard a sermon given by the rector of my church, in which he referred to this passage from Matthew. Sud- denly it clicked. It was so obvious, particularly since it was the Scriptures and the whole realm of religion that formed the backdrop of Gregory the Great's famous formulation and of so much modern scholarship on 'art' in late antiquity and the early Middle Ages.

If we reorient ourselves to the Bible, to the world of Gregory and of the Middle Ages, we can again find in medieval texts confirmation of these intima- tions about how God's Word was received. Consider *The Book of Margery Kempe*, the first autobiography in English. In one place Margery (ca. 1373-ca. 1440) speaks of "conversing about scripture, which she learned in sermons and by talking with clerks".[23] Later she begs Almighty God to slake her hunger for His Word by sending her a priest to read Scripture to her. God, having been properly approached, was evidently happy to oblige. A priest came to her in Lynn and "for the most part of seven or eight years" read to her not only the Bible, but also "many a good book of high contemplation", including "doctors' commentaries on it, St. Bride's book, Hilton's book, Bonaventura's *Stimulus amoris*, *Incendium amoris*, and others similar".[24] Although no one would argue that Margery Kempe was in any respect typical, her testimony reminds us yet again that in her world sight and sound, reading and hearing, were intermingled in ways we need always to bear in mind, especially when we are trying to figure out whether art was really the "book of the illiterate".

This brings us back to Gregory the Great, this time in his approach to the Bible itself. Michael Camille has pointed out a particularly pertinent passage in Gregory's own writings.[25] In the epistolary preface to his *Homilies on the Gos-*

---

[22] Cf. W.A. GRAHAM, *Beyond the Written Word: Oral Aspects of Scripture in the History of Religion* (Cambridge, 1987).

[23] *The Book of Margery Kempe*, c. 14, tr. B.A. WINDEATT (Harmondsworth, 1985), p. 65.

[24] *Ibid.*, c. 58, pp. 181-182. For another parallel passage, see *ibid.*, c. 17, p. 75.

[25] CAMILLE, "Word, text, image", p. 85.

pels, addressed to Bishop Secundinus of Taormina, Gregory wrote the following:

> As part of the sacred ceremonies of the Mass, from those which are customarily read on certain days in this church, I made an exposition of forty readings from the Gospels. And the already dictated exegesis of certain of them was read aloud to the attendant congregation by the scribe, but the explanation of certain others I delivered before the people myself, which was collected in writing (*excepta*) as I spoke. But certain brothers, burning with passion for the sacred Word, recopied them before I could follow my plans for correcting what I had said.[26]

Camille characterizes the import of this brief passage for our purposes as illustrating "complex and problematic relations between the oral production of [Gregory's] writings, their aural reception and their eventual visual transcription as writing". Initially I was not so sure. I assumed that these *lectiones* on the Gospels, collected as *homilia*, were sermons of an exegetical type well known, for example, in the writings of the Cappadocian Fathers and John Chrysostom (second half of the fourth century). Things were not that complicated – so I thought. But questions arose upon further reflection. Why would Gregory have his scribe read these prepared *lectiones* to the congregation instead of doing so himself, particularly if the scribe was not a priest? If Gregory did so because of his notoriously poor health, why would he then deliver his as yet unwritten homilies himself? Why should he evidently have so little control over the production of the definitive text of words which he had delivered *ex tempore*? Is this really plausible, or is Gregory employing a classical literary trope – perhaps to apologize proleptically for imperfections in his style? Or is it possible, as I suggested earlier, that Gregory has simply expressed himself poorly here? There may be logical answers to all these questions, but they do not readily come to mind. Therefore we should beware of our assumptions about how Gregory dealt with Scripture.

And so, too, with Gregory and images. It has recently been pointed out that Kurt Weitzmann, that *doyen* of late antique and early Christian art, and his disci-

---

[26] Gregorius Magnus, *Homilia in Evangelia*, ed. R. ÉTAIT (Turnhout, 1999: *Corpus Christianorum, Series Latina* 141), p. 1: "*Inter sacra missarum sollemnia, ex his quae diebus certis in hac ecclesia legi ex more solent, sancti euangelii quadraginta lectiones exposui. Et quarumdam quidem dictata expositio assistenti plebi est per notarium recitata, quarumdam uero explanationem coram populo ipse locutus sum atque ita ut loquebar excepta est. Sed quidam fratres, sacri uerbi feruentes, antequam ad propositum modum ea quae dixeram subtili emendatione perducerem transtulerunt*". I have amended Camille's slightly confusing translation in his "Word, text, image", p. 85.

ples made fundamental assumptions about early Christian painting. One of them was that "narrative art began in texts"[27] and that words were "in or near almost all medieval pictures". The latter quotation is from one of Weitzmann's students, Herbert Kessler, who significantly goes on to ruminate on "precisely what Gregory and his followers thought could be learned from *these pictured texts*".[28] But were "pictured texts" that common at the time of Gregory himself? A watchword of historians is that "chronology and geography are the eyes of history". John Williams and John Lowden have recently argued that Weitzmann got the order wrong: large-scale pictures inspired illustrated Bibles, not vice versa. Words were not *ab initio* in a close physical nexus with, and increasingly in juxtaposition to, images, but became so only gradually.[29] The implication is that the kind of association between word and images to which Kessler alludes, which was indeed characteristic of later medieval art, was still infrequent in Gregory's own age and took root firmly only from the Carolingian period onwards, having passed in some sense through the unusually complex filter of Insular art.[30] In short, it is anachronistic to think of a late antique Gregory in this medieval way, and therefore misleading to contextualize and rationalize his words about pictures as the "books of the illiterate" in this manner. Kessler's governing premise in his refutation of my original argument seems wrong.

Yet if I am right, it is exactly this point which helps to explain why Gregory's dictum caught on so readily in the Middle Ages and has enjoyed such tenacious vitality down to the present. Later established medieval patterns with the nearly ubiquitous juxtaposition of images and texts came to inform, but also distort, the understanding and interpretation of Gregory's dictum, and to perpetuate that distortion.

If Gregory's commentators and advocates were thus in yet another respect wrong – even if understandably so – do I still maintain that Gregory himself was wrong? Rather than repeat the final sentence of my original essay which so thoroughly vexed the reviewers and later readers, allow me to cite again an incomparably higher authority than myself, Dr Samuel Johnson: "Painting, Sir, can illustrate, but not inform".

---

[27] This apt phrasing is from J. WILLIAMS, "Introduction", in: *Imaging the Early Medieval Bible*, p. 4.

[28] KESSLER, "Diction in the 'Bibles of the Illiterate' ", p. 33. Emphasis added.

[29] WILLIAMS, "Introduction", pp. 1-8, and LOWDEN, "The beginnings", especially pp. 52-58.

[30] I am particularly grateful to John Lowden for his help in phrasing this distillation of his ideas as precisely as possible.

Paradise and Pentecost[1]

CLAUDINE A. CHAVANNES-MAZEL

Ever since early Christianity, Christians have sought to turn the written word into images. Whatever reasons there were – and whatever measures were taken in the past to suppress the seemingly irresistible wish to pic-torially represent Scripture – Christian imagery has a productive history indeed. Many stories told in the Gospels were visually standardized and frozen into a single image as early as the third century. The iconography of Pentecost, how-ever, was established somewhat later. Although the Descent of the Holy Ghost was a crucial event in the legitimation of Christendom, it was an event without much human activity, taking place while the participants sat still and prayed. Despite the mighty wind and fiery tongues, the filling of the apostles with the Holy Ghost – the key moment – is difficult to picture because of its static char-acter. For this reason, as we shall see, in rendering the event the dogmatic im-port was soon to overshadow the historical narrative.

The Descent of the Holy Ghost on the fiftieth day after Jewish Pesach – or, for most Christian denominations, fifty days after Christ's Resurrection – is told in the Acts of the Apostles.[2] The twelve apostles, sitting together in prayer in an upstairs room, play the leading parts. Also present are Mary and a few

[1] This paper was written in 2001. I thank Henry Mayr-Harting and Mayke de Jong for their valuable suggestions.
  [2] Act 2, 1-5 (King James version): "And when the day of Pentecost was fully come, they were all with one accord in one place. And suddenly there came a sound from heaven as of a rushing mighty wind, and it filled all the house where they were sitting. And there appeared unto them cloven tongues like as of fire, and it sat upon each of them. And they were all filled with the Holy Ghost, and began to speak with other tongues, as the Spirit gave them utterance. And there were dwelling at Jerusalem Jews devout men, out of every nation under heaven".

other women. Suddenly there is the sound of a rushing, mighty wind and "cloven tongues like as of fire ... sat upon each of them" (Acts 2, 3). The whole world, "Jews, devout men, out of every nation under heaven" (Acts 2, 5), is in attendance when, inspired, the apostles start to speak in all and every language.

Today, Pentecost or Whitsun is not a major festival in the Christian Church. In patristic times, however, it marked an important point of departure in the Christian story: the beginning of the New Law and the founding of the Church itself. For this reason, St. Jerome (ca. 350-420) labels the first part of Acts *"Ecclesiae initia in Ierusalem"*. It was from that very moment that the apostles were to go and preach all over the world (cf., e.g. Mt 28, 19) enabling not only Jews but people from every nation, class and religion to convert by their own free will and to believe in the Jewish Messiah.

I will focus here on the visualization of the birth of the Church, the Christian community, which promises Paradise to all humankind. I will argue that Paradise and Pentecost became strongly related visually towards the end of the Middle Ages.[3]

Pentecost is not found among the events painted in the early Christian Roman catacombs. Nor is it represented on smaller objects of art until the late sixth century. The earliest extant representations come from the Eastern empire: the Rabbula Codex transcribed in the monastery at Beth Sagba, Mesopotamia,[4] and one of many Syrian *ampullae* brought to the West in the sixth and seventh

---

[3]   An abundant literature exists on the iconography of Pentecost. Fundamental studies are: A. GRABAR, "Le schéma iconographique de la Pentecôte", in: IDEM, *L'art de la fin de l'antiquité et du Moyen Age*, 3 vols. (Paris, 1968), 1, pp. 615-627 (originally published in Russian in: *Seminarium Kondakovium* 2 (Prague, 1928), pp. 223-239); S. SEELINGER, *Pfingsten: Die Ausgießung des Heiligen Geistes am fünfzigsten Tage nach Ostern* (Düsseldorf, 1958); A. ESMEIJER, "Cosmos en *theatrum mundi* in de Pinkstervoorstelling", *Nederlands Kunsthistorisch Jaarboek* 15 (1964), pp. 19-44; S. SEELIGER, "Pfingsten" in: *Lexikon der christlichen Ikonographie*, ed. E. KIRSCHBAUM, 8 vols. (Rom etc., 1968), 3, cols. 415-423, with bibliography; G. SCHILLER, *Ikonographie der christlichen Kunst*, 4.1: *Die Kirche* (Gütersloh, 1976), pp. 11-33 and pls. 1-85, gives, apart from an extensive overview, an ample amount of illustrations. Recent contributions are: E. LEESTI, "The Pentecost illustration in the Drogo Sacramentary", *Gesta* 28.2 (1989), pp. 205-216, and P. LOW, "The city refigured: a Pentecostal Jerusalem in the San Paolo Bible", in: *The Real and Ideal Jerusalem in Jewish, Christian and Islamic Art*, ed. B. KÜHNEL (Jerusalem, 1998), pp. 265-274.

[4]   MS Florence, Biblioteca Laurenziana, Cod. Plut. I, 56, f. 14v. According to its colophon, the manuscript was copied by the monk Rabbula in the monastery of St. John at Beth Sagba in 586. Facsimile by C. CECCHELLI, G. FURLANI and M. SALMI, *The Rabbula Gospels* (Olten and Lausanne, 1959). K. WEITZMANN, *"Loca sancta* and the representational arts of Palestine", *Dumbarton Oaks Papers* 28 (1974), pp. 31-55. Weitzmann argues that the miniature reflects a monumental composition, apparently of a niche casting a shadow. The chapel of the Holy Spirit in the Sion Church in Jerusalem may have been the prototype.

centuries.[5] Both witnesses seem confusing at first sight, as they show a parallel between Pentecost and Christ's Ascension, two events which until the fifth century were celebrated on the same day.[6] Amid the standing apostles is the Virgin Mary, her arms stretched out in prayer. The presence of the Mother of God underlines the two natures of Christ, an issue much debated at the time. Although it is not her main role here, Mary also personifies the Church.[7]

The Church was often depicted in the person of a woman. In her fundamental study on the representation of *Ecclesia* in early Christian iconography, Marie-Louise Thérel stresses that, although it is a woman who represents the Christian community, she is not necessarily identical with the Virgin Mary. Often she is an emblematic antique personification, a veiled middle-aged woman. As such she appears in the two mosaics near the entrance of the church of Santa Sabina and in the Adoration mosaic of the triumphal arch in the Santa Maria Maggiore, both in Rome.[8] The apostles Peter and Paul may also stand for the Church: Peter for the *Ecclesia ex Circumcisione* and Paul for the *Ecclesia ex Gentibus*. The idea was familiar in monumental art in the early fifth century, when the mosaic in the apse of the church of Santa Pudenziana in Rome was created.

After the iconoclastic period of the eighth and ninth centuries, when the imaging of the Christian narration had been in jeopardy, Pentecost was initially rendered as a strictly male event in both East and West: Mary was no longer depicted as part of the congregation. She was, however, to return in an impressive manner in Western representations of Pentecost.

---

[5] Monza, Cathedral Treasury, ampulla no. 10, reverse. A. GRABAR, *Les ampoules de Terre sainte* (Paris, 1958), p. 42.

[6] R. CABIÉ, *La Pentecôte, l'évolution de la cinquantenaire pascale au cours des cinq premiers siècles* (Tournai, 1965); J. DANIÉLOU, "Grégoire de Nysse et l'origine de la fête de l'Ascension", in: *Kyriakon: Festschrift Johannes Quasten* , ed. P. GRANFIELD and J.A. JUNGMANN, 2 vols. (München, 1970), 2, pp. 663-666.

[7] St. Augustine, *Enchiridion de fide, spe et caritate*, 34, 10, ed. J. BARBEL (Düsseldorf, 1960: *Testimonia* 1): "*Ecclesia quae imitans eius matrem quotidie parit membra eius et virgo est*". See H. RAHNER, *Symbole der Kirche: Die Ekklesiologie der Väter* (Salzburg, 1964), pp. 63-64; M.-L. THÉREL, *Les symboles de l' "Ecclesia" dans la création iconographique de l'art chrétien du IIIᵉ au VIᵉ siècle* (Rome, 1973); K. DELAHAYE, *Erneuerung der Seelsorgsformen aus der Sicht der frühen Patristik* (Freiburg i. Br, 1958), translated into French under a better title, as: *Ecclesia Mater chez les Pères des trois premiers siècles: Pour un renouvellement de la Pastorale d'aujourd'hui* (Paris, 1964); SCHILLER, *Ikonographie* 4.1, pp. 84-89.

[8] THÉREL, *Les symboles*, pp. 106-109 and 124.

The Iconography of Pentecost in the East

In the East, the iconographical scheme for Pentecost was drawn up according to those of several distinct and recognisable assemblies. Usually (following the story told in Acts), the twelve apostles sit together talking or praying. They are arranged in single files left and right, with Peter and Paul towards the centre, and are looking towards each other. An early example is an icon from Mount Sinai,[9] previously assigned to the seventh to ninth centuries, but dated by Kurt Weitzmann in the ninth or tenth century.[10] In the apostles' midst a little golden dove hovers. Heaven, in the form of a medallion, encloses a bust of Christ from which tongues of fire issue in broad streams. It is important to note that the groups of apostles are aligned on a slightly curved ground. According to Weitzmann, the semicircle derives from the mosaic in the cupola of the church of the Twelve Apostles in Constantinople.[11] It is, however, also the classical way of rendering a gathering.[12]

The ninth century was a creative period: an architectural setting was added to the iconography of Pentecost. Although the gathering of the apostles remained the subject of the story, the upper room in which they had come together – the *coenaculum* or cenacle – gained importance both visually and symbolically.[13] Antique personifications were not the only sources to which a Byzantine artist could turn to enhance a historic moment with dogmatic symbolism. He could adapt other well-known formulas to meet the requirements of his subject. By suggesting iconographical parallels between the seating arrangements of the apostles and that of other groups of seated dignitaries, artists did not only increase the intrinsic meaning of the latter. They also turned the communal room in which the apostles gathered into an instrument for making the biblical event topical. They compared it with contemporary meetings such as Church councils and other clerical conclaves. One can understand the definitive

---

[9] No. B. 45.

[10] K. WEITZMANN, *The Monastery of Saint Catherine at Mount Sinai: The Icons*, 1: *From the Sixth to the Tenth Century* (Princeton, 1976), pp. 73-76 and pls. XXX, XCIX-CI; SCHILLER, *Ikonographie der christlichen Kunst*, 4.1, pl. 4.

[11] K. WEITZMANN, "Narrative and liturgical gospel illustrations", in: IDEM, *Studies in Classical and Byzantine Manuscript Illumination* (Chicago and London, 1971), p. 261.

[12] It is reminiscent of the *stibadeion* or semicircular bench, common in classical and early Christian pictures as e.g., in the scene of the Last Supper in the Rossano Gospels, in the Vienna Genesis, and in the mosaic of the S. Apollinare Nuovo in Ravenna.

[13] Ch. WALTER, *L'iconographie des conciles dans la tradition byzantine* (Paris, 1970: *Archives de l'orient chrétien* 13), pp. 209-212.

exclusion of female attendance in Eastern depictions of Pentecost: these types of clerical meetings simply did not allow for the presence of women.

The Pentecost gathering may assemble around an empty throne, the *Hetoimasia*, on which the Holy Ghost has alighted.[14] A miniature in a copy of St. Gregory of Nazianzus's Homilies (from Constantinople, now in Paris), is among the earliest surviving examples of a *Synthronon* (fig. 1).[15] The image refers directly to the early council tradition, in which an empty throne was placed in the room as proof of Christ's omnipresence (fig. 2). Symbol replaces theophany.[16] The assembled dignitaries compared their conclave formally to Pentecost, hoping for the same divine inspiration as that bestowed upon the apostles. Charles Walter, when discussing this conformity, also pointed out the resemblance with the liturgical disposition of the *cathedra* and stand in the apse of early Christian churches.[17]

Ultimately, but still before the end of the ninth century, the semicircle of apostles in the Eastern iconographical tradition assumed the form of a horse-shoe. The foreground of the images was usually occupied by various tribes, the "devout men out of every nation". These could also be represented by one old man standing in the middle of the open space in the foreground, holding a cloth with twelve scrolls or leaves in his hands, with the word "*kosmos*" written above his head. This tradition can be found in a treatise written on Mount Athos by the monk Dionysius of Fourna (1670-1744), who prescribes an old man in a grotto as a symbol of the cosmos. In images of Pentecost the old man was sometimes replaced by Joel, who prophesied the Descent of the Holy Ghost:

---

[14] WALTER, *L'iconographie des conciles*, ch. 5: "les analogies de l'iconographie des conciles dans l'art chrétien", pp. 187-214; N. OZOLINE, "La Pentecôte du Paris grec. 510: Un témoignage sur l'église de Constantinople au IXe siècle", *Rivista di archeologia cristiana* 63 (1987), pp. 245-255.

[15] MS Paris, Bibliothèque Nationale, grec 510, f. 355r, made in Constantinople for the Emperor Basil II around 880. See S. DER NERSESSIAN, "The illustrations of the Homilies of Gregory of Nazianzus, Paris grec. 510: A study of the connections between text and images", *Dumbarton Oaks Papers* 16 (1962), p. 206; *Byzance: L'art byzantin dans les collections publiques françaises*, catalogue of an exhibition (Paris, 1992), No. 258. An even earlier example of a Hetoimasia is the Chludov Psalter, MS Moscow, State Historical Museum, 129, made in Constantinople in the middle of the ninth century, with later additions. Facsimile by M.V. SCEPKINA, *Miniatjury Khludovskoi Psaltiri* (Moskova, 1977). See *The Utrecht Psalter in Medieval Art*, ed. K. VAN DER HORST a.o., catalogue of an exhibition (Utrecht, 1996), No. 2.

[16] In reference to this tradition, the first Vatican Council of 1869 had a gilded empty throne made by Virginio Vespignani to hold a manuscript of the Gospels (MS Vatican, Biblioteca Apostolica, Urb. lat. 10) during the assembly. The Gospel according to St. John was laid open at the opening words "*In principium erat verbum*".

[17] WALTER, *L'iconographie des conciles*, pp. 209-212, 236.

"And it shall come to pass afterward, that I will pour out my spirit upon all flesh" (Joel 2, 28 and Acts 2, 17).[18] Apparently, the scheme with its separate groups of people and the empty grotto in the foreground was understandable to the Byzantine beholder, although it is very different from the biblical narrative on which it was ultimately based. Evidently, through its iconography Pentecost was seen as a cosmic event with a strongly dogmatic character rather than a mere historical moment (cf. fig. 3).

Fixed in the ninth century, the Eastern iconography of Pentecost hardly changed afterwards. This elicited the remark from Grabar:

> Il n'y a probablement pas de scène évangelique qui ait moins nourri l'imagination créatrice des artistes byzantins: depuis le IXe siècle, ils répètent invariablement le même schéma dépourvu de toute vraisemblance réaliste.[19]

The Iconography of Pentecost in the West

Looking at an early fifteenth-century triptych in the Utrecht Museum Het Catharijneconvent (fig. 4), one might be led into believing that the Western iconography of Pentecost obediently followed Byzantine models.[20] The wooden panels show the stylistic elements typical of the Middle Rhine region.[21] The central part of the altarpiece is now lost; the two remaining wings are covered on both sides with lively and colourful scenes taken from the life of Christ. The Descent of the Holy Ghost, on the inside of the wing painted on a golden background, takes place in an open, round room. A turreted entrance with an enormous door in the centre of the picture accentuates that the building is closed. Inside, the twelve apostles sit in prayer around a central figure, the Virgin

---

[18] Translation: "The descent of the Holy Spirit. A house: the twelve apostles are sitting in a circle. Below them is a small chamber in which an old man holds before him in his hands, which are covered by the veil, twelve rolled scrolls; he wears a crown on his head, and over him these words are written: The World. Above the house is the Holy Spirit in the form of a dove; a great light surrounds it, and twelve tongues of flame come down from it and rest on each of the apostles" (quoted from *The Painter's Manual of Dionysius of Fourna*, tr. P. HETHERINGTON (London, 1978), pp. 40, 103).

[19] A. GRABAR, "Le schéma iconographique", p. 615.

[20] Utrecht, Museum Catharijneconvent, inv.-nos. 25-28. S. BEEH-LUSTENBERGER, in: *Die Parler un der schöne Stil 1350-1400: Europäische Kunst unter den Luxemburgern*, ed. A. LEGNER catalogue of an exhibition, 7 vols. (Köln, 1978), 1, pp. 262-263 (with bibliography).

[21] G. Bott sees a direct relationship with workshops in Cologne: G. BOTT, "Beobachtungen am Siefersheimer Altar in Darmstadt", in: *Vor Stephan Lochner: Die Kölner Malerei van 1300 bis 1430*, catalogue of an exhibition (Köln, 1974), pp. 46-47.

Mary. The formal resemblance to the Byzantine composition of a Russian icon of the sixteenth or seventeenth centuries (fig. 3 and Colour Plate 1) is striking. The door in the foreground of the Utrecht retable matches exactly the open space in the Orthodox icon, and the apostles are grouped in a similar way. However, the meaning of the retable must be different. Mary's presence requires an explanation. Moreover, the firmly shut door suggests the opposite of an open space. Why is there formal similarity between the two images when there is a more than probable difference in meaning? Or could the open space and closed door possibly mean the same thing? To answer these questions, we must go back and investigate the iconographical development of the rendering of Pentecost in the Latin West.

Since iconoclasm, the West has imitated its Byzantine neighbour willingly whenever it suited its purpose. A good example is the Benedictional commissioned by bishop Aethelwold of Winchester (963-984) (fig. 5).[22] Although the Anglo-Saxon miniaturist had a different sense of style and space, the miniature echoes the Byzantine scheme in every way. The twelve apostles sit in a semicircle facing each other, and fiery tongues come from the Dove hovering above them in a mandorla. Little towers left and right are shadowy reminders of the holy cenacle. Western artists, however, because of the lack of an iconic tradition, were free to create their own images of Pentecost. They did so, and varied according to symbolic interpretations the East could not have imagined.

1. Peter is Represented as the Central Figure

A first Western predilection when depicting Pentecost is the principal place given to St. Peter at the centre of the group of apostles. Peter was the apostle who addressed the crowd immediately after the Descent of the Holy Spirit. Most important, however, is that he was the first apostle, the rock upon which Christ said he would build the Christian Church (Mt 16, 18-19) (fig. 6). The predominance of Peter seems to express the wish to underline the primacy of the Roman patriarch within the Christian world. In Rome, however, Paul was revered almost as much as Peter. Until the late twelfth century, the composition with Peter and Paul as the two protagonists of the Church remained alive side by side with that in which Peter is the more notable of the two.

---

[22] MS London, British Library, Add. 49598, f. 67v. R. DESHAM, *The Benedictional of Aethelwold* (Princeton, 1995: *Studies in Manuscript Illumination* 9), pp. 89-92 and colour plate 26.

2. The Central Composition

Instead of a semicircle or a curved row of apostles, the West seems at times to prefer a rounded composition for Pentecost, with groups of apostles sitting in a circle or facing the crowd.[23] According to Schiller, this reflects both the cosmic character of the event and the togetherness or oneness of the group.

A circular composition may require the accentuation of its centre. An example is the Pentecost miniature in the Codex Egberti, made on the Reichenau around 980, now in the library of Trier (fig. 7).[24] The apostles sit in the upper row and overlook a crowd of people standing with their backs to the spectator. In the middle of the image is a small octagonal basin looking like a well, with little golden round bread rolls in it; above it is written *"communis vita"*, communal life, a reference to Acts 2, 44: "And all that believed were together and had all things common ...". Henry Mayr-Harting detects a direct influence of the Gorze reform of monastic life, which started in the diocese of Metz in the 930s.[25] Indeed, establishing a form of *vita communis*, or a community of living and worship, was an essential feature of this reform, which had considerable influence on monastic life in the Ottonian empire.

[23] Schiller finds the earliest example in the San Paolo Bible (SCHILLER, *Christliche Ikonographie* 4.1, pp. 18-19 and pl. 17). For a thorough discussion of the miniature, see: P. LOW, "The city refigured", pp. 265-274, and H. SCHADE, "Studien zu der karolingischen Bilderbibel aus St. Paul vor den Mauern in Rom, 2. Teil", *Wallraf-Richartz Jahrbuch* 22 (1960), pp 24-43. Schiller discusses the round composition on pp. 20-22. Additional examples can be found in manuscripts from the Echternach school: MS Bremen, Staatsbibliothek b 21, f. 72v, and MS Gotha, Landesbibliothek I. 19, f. 112v. See A. BOECKLER, *Das goldene Evangelienbuch Heinrichs III.* (Berlin, 1933), Abb. 173, 185.

[24] H. SCHIELE, *Codex Egberti der Stadtbibliothek Trier: Voll-Faksimile-Ausgabe und Textband* (Basel, 1960); G. FRANZ and F.J. RONIG, *Codex Egberti der Stadtbibliothek Trier: Entstehung und Geschichte der Handschrift* (Wiesbaden, 1984), p. 49 and pl. 3. The text above the miniature reads: "*SPIRITUS HOC EDOCENS. LINGUIS HIC ARDET ET IGNE*"; below: "*QUA CAUSA TREMULI CONUENIUNT POPULI*"; the text in the middle reads: "*COMMUNIS UITA*".

[25] H. MAYR-HARTING, *Ottonian Book Illumination*, 2 vols. (London, 1991), 1, pp. 83-86 and 2, pp. 79-80. On the Gorze reform, see K. HALLINGER, *Gorze-Kluny: Studien zu den monastischen Lebensformen und Gegensätzen im Hochmittelalter*, 2 vols. (Roma, 1950-1951: *Studia Anselmiana* 22, 25), 2 esp. chapter 4: "Die Stellungname zur Frage des Zentralismus", pp. 736-764; *L'abbaye de Gorze au Xe siècle*, ed. M. PARISSE and O.G. OEXLE (Nancy, 1993), and J. NIGHTINGALE, *Monasteries and Patrons in the Gorze Reform: Lotharingia c. 850-1000* (Oxford, 2000). An ivory book cover now in the J. Rylands Library Manchester, also from the Trier region, shows the same iconography. See F. STEENBOCK, *Der kirchliche Prachteinband im frühen Mittelalter von den Anfängen bis zum Beginn der Gothik* (Berlin, 1965), No. 110, Abb. 150.

The central position of the basin full of bread might also be an early example of an iconography that was to become very common later in the Middle Ages. The *communis vita* can also be a metaphor for the Christian Church, established on the day of Pentecost through baptism by the Holy Ghost, thanks to Christ's Redemption. Christ's sacrifice, announced during the Last Supper, may be symbolized by the golden bread rolls in the Reichenau miniature.

The idea of the Church or Christian community and its relationship with the events of Pentecost is symbolized in a different way in an early twelfth-century manuscript with Pericopes from Echternach (fig. 8).[26] The Pentecost miniature shows a composition similar to that from the Reichenau, but the basin and the crowd have been replaced by the Tree of Life from the garden of Eden, bearing twelve golden flowers. The parallel between these ideas (Paradise, Redemption, Church and Pentecost) must have been relatively easy to understand, since it dates back to early Christianity. St. Ambrose (ca. 340-397), in his *De Spiritu Sancto*, identifies the "pure river of water of life" from Paradise (Apc 22, 1) with the Holy Ghost: *"Flumen est spiritus sanctus"*.[27] The house of God on earth – the Church – refers to the house of God in heaven – Paradise. The founding of the Christian Church at Pentecost was made possible because of Christ's sacrificing his body through the Crucifixion. Paradise, the Fountain of Life, the Tree of Life and the Cross, standing in an enclosed garden, gradually develop a single meaning with various interchangeable interpretations.

---

[26] MAYR-HARTING, *Ottonian Book Illumination*, 2, p. 187; BOECKLER, *Das goldene Evangelienbuch*, pp. 69-72 and Abb. 180, 182-184; *Het geïllustreerde boek in het Westen*, catalogue of an exhibition (Brussels, 1977), No. 9 and pl. 1.

[27] *De Spiritu sancto* I, c. XVI, 156, ed. in: *Patrologiae cursus completus ... Series latina*, ed. J.P. MIGNE, 221 vols. (Paris, 1841-1864) (henceforth *PL*) 16, col. 740: *"Spiritum sanctum flumen esse magnum, cujus munere mystica Jerusalem irrigatur"*); I, c. XVI, 157, *ibidem*: *"Ergo flumen est spiritus sanctus, et flumen maximum, quod secundum Hebraeos de Jesu fluxit in terris, ut ore Esaiae accepimus prophetatum. Magnum hoc flumen, quod fluit semper"*; III, c. XX, 153-154, col. 812: *"Ergo flumen est Spiritus"*. Apc 22, 1: "And he shewed me a pure river of water of life, clear as crystal, proceeding out of the throne of God and of the Lamb". The relation Pentecost-Apocalypse is visualized *in extenso* in the Sherborne Missal, MS Alnwick Castle, Northumberland, Library of the Duke of Northumberland 450, dated AD 1396-1407 (U. REHM, *"Accende lumen sensibus*: illustrations of the Sherborne Missal interpreting Pentecost", *Word and Image* 10 (1994), pp. 230-261.

The parallel with Paradise was to have a long and fecund life.[28] In Hraba-nus Maurus's (780-856) famous encyclopedia *De universo* (or, as the author called it, *De rerum naturis*), the correlations between water, or, more specifi-cally, the *"fons vitae"* (the source of all virtue: *"initium omnium bonorum, et origo virtutum"*), the four gospels, the enclosed garden and the Church are manifold. The word *paradisus*, Hrabanus explains in the chapter *"De paradi-so"*, is synonymous with *hortus*. Paradise is virtually identical with the Church. In its centre is a well, from which four streams originate; they are the four gos-pels. The streams from paradise carry the image of Christ, who irrigated the Christian Church with his word and his baptism.[29] The significance of water compared with Christ's house, the grace of the Holy Ghost, and with eternal life is clarified in the chapter *"De fontibus"*.[30]

Both East and West adopted the idea of the Cross standing in the paradisia-cal garden as the symbol of salvation and as the fountain of life. It occurs in both manuscript painting and monumental art. A few examples may suffice. The beautiful little Harbaville Triptych, now in the Louvre but made in tenth-century Constantinople, shows the Cross standing on flowers with a backdrop of flourishing plants, while heavenly stars surround its top (fig. 9). The mosaic in the apse of the church of San Clemente in Rome (ca. 1130) displays the Crucifixion framed by scrolls of acanthus leaves as symbols of Paradise; four streams spring from the base of the Cross, and deer have come to slake their

---

[28] The Persians, the Jews, and the Christians thought paradise a beautiful *hortus conclusus* with clear water, shadow, sunshine, birds and the smell of sweet honey. The Christians understood the four rivers from Gn 2, 10 to water their paradise from a mountain; Church Fathers like St. Augustine (*De civitate dei* 13, 21, ed. B. DOMBART and A. KALB (Turnhout, 1955: CCSL 48, p. 404): *"paradisum scilicet ipsam ecclesiam"*) and St. Ambrose (*Liber de Paradiso* 3, 13, ed. in: *PL* 14, col. 296) took over the pre-Christian images of deer, peacocks, doves etc. drinking from a spring and compared them with the soul who slakes his thirst from the fountain of paradise (A. THOMAS, "Brunnen" in: *Lexikon der christlichen Ikonographie*, 1, cols. 331-336).

[29] *De Universo* XII, 3, ed. in: *PL* 111, col. 334: *"Paradisus Ecclesia est: sic de illa legitur in Canticis canticorum: Hortus conclusus soror mea sponsa. A principio autem plantatur para-disus: quia Ecclesia Catholica a Christo, qui est principium omnium, condita esse cognoscitur. Fluvius de paradiso exiens imaginem portat Christi de paterno fonte fluminis, qui irrigat Ecclesiam suam verbo praedicationis, et dono baptismi (...) Item allegorice quatuor paradisi flumina quatuor sunt Evangelia ad praedicationem in cunctis gentibus missa"*.

[30] *De Universo*, ix, 9, ed. in: *PL* 111, col. 317: *"Fons quoque aut Dominum Christum mys-tice signifiact, aut gratiam Spiritus sancti, aut Baptismi lavacrum, aut originem virtutum. Nam Christus signifiact in eo, quod in Genesi legitur, fontem esse in medio Paradisi, unde quatuor flumina procedebant, hoc est, quatuor Evangelia de fonte salutaris procedentia ad irrigationem generis humani. Item fons Spiritus sancti gratiam designat in eo, quod Dominus dicit in Evan-gelio: Qui biberit aquam, quam ego do, fiet in eo fons aquae salientis in vitam aeternam"* and col. 318: *"Fons ergo originem virtutem significat"*.

thirst. Right under the foot of the Cross, the Serpent is slain (fig. 10). Christ crucified once stood on top of the so-called Moses Well in the Carthusian monastery of Champmol near Dijon, carved by Claus Sluter around 1400 (fig. 11). The life-sized prophets remain *in situ* in what has been a hospital since it was built. They are as witnesses to a better world, imperturbed by the sometimes harrowing sounds of the patients around them. The most complex example of the association of ideas discussed here can be found in a manuscript containing the *Horloge de Sapience*, a French translation of Henricus Suso's (ca. 1295-1366) *Horologium sapientiae*. The manuscript dates from the 1460s and is illustrated by the François Master and his circle (fig. 12). At the centre of a cycle of scenes from Christ's passion, an enclosed garden with a central fountain promises the Paradise Christ died for, shown on the left in the miniature. The Crucifixion does not take place on Mount Calvary, but rather in a church building decorated with golden *fleurs-de-lis*.

The all-encompassing idea of the Tree of Life as a centre piece in the gathering of the apostles at Pentecost was to be amplified. The Church, as a metaphor for the Christian community, was considered to be a continuation of the Jewish temple, and a replacement at the same time. The upper room in which, according to the Acts of the Apostles, the Descent of the Holy Spirit had taken place, had been a palpable construction. How could one imagine the Church as Heaven and Paradise, if human actions could take place inside it? The Descent of the Holy Ghost upon the apostles took place inside a building. Through this event the building became a paradisiacal place. How was this double meaning visualized and emphasized?

3. The Tree of Life as the Axis of the World

The Tree of Life as a symbol of earthly Paradise could also be considered as the axis, the spindle of the world. On the authority of the prophet Ezechiel, the world's central point (the "*umbilicus mundi*") was Jerusalem: "The city of Jerusalem I have set among the nations, with the other countries round her" (Ez 5, 5). There once had been a real column in Jerusalem to mark the world's centre. In the seventh century, Abbot Adamnan of Iona (ca. 624-704) gave one of the oldest descriptions of Jerusalem in his redraft of the travel-record of the monk Arculf. In *De locis sanctis*, Adamnan speaks of:

> a very tall column which stands in the middle of the city. ... During the summer solstice at noon the light of the sun in mid heaven passes directly above this column and shines down on all sides, which demonstrates that Jerusalem is placed at the centre of the earth. This

explains why the psalmist used these words to sing his prophecy of the holy places of the Passion and Resurrection which are in Aelia. "Yet, God, our King, of old worked salvation in the midst of the earth". This means "in Jerusalem", which is called the "Mediterranean" and the "Navel of the Earth".[31]

Christians saw the presence of the column in conjunction with the passage from Ezechiel as justification for centring maps on Jerusalem (cf. fig. 13).[32] And so we find images of Pentecost with the apostles assembled around the pivot of the universe. The cosmos is present amongst the apostles just as it was in Eastern representations of the same events, in which a the personification of the cosmos was standing in their midst. A sacramentary from the Cathedral Treasury in Mainz, made there around 1000, arranges the twelve apostles around a central tall column (fig. 14). This column doubles as the middle one of seven beams of light, representing seven fiery tongues descending from heaven; the Dove of the Holy Ghost hovers on the column's top.[33] The Benedictional of Archbishop Robert, in Rouen since the eleventh century, includes a lively representation of Pentecost on f. 29v (fig. 15).[34] Compared to the Benedictional of Aethelwold (fig. 5), a column and coloured atmospheric striations have been added to the miniature. Desham hesitates about this column and suggests a relation with the apostolic "columns" of the Church,[35] but we now know that the column emphasizes the cosmic nature of the event.

[31] Adamnan, *De locis sanctis*, I, 11.1-4, ed. D. MEEHAN *Adamnan, De locis sanctis*, (Dublin, 1958: *Scriptores latini Hiberniae* 3), p. 56. The translation is after by J. WILKINSON, *Jerusalem Pilgrims before the Crusades* (Warminster, 1977), pp. 93-116, at p. 99.

[32] J.F. NIEHOFF, "*Umbilicus mundi*: Der Nabel der Welt: Jerusalem und das Heilige Grab im Spiegel von Pilgerberichten und -karten, Kreuzzügen und Reliquiaren", in: *Ornamenta Ecclesiae*, catalogue of an exhibition, 3 vols. (Köln, 1985), 3, pp. 53-72 (with bibliography); M. WERNER, "The Cross-carpet page in the Book of Durrow: The cult of the True Cross, Adamnan, and Iona", *Art Bulletin* 72 (1990), pp. 202, 205; *The History of Cartography*, 1: *Cartography in Prehistoric, Ancient and Medieval Europe and the Mediterranean*, ed. B. HARLEY and D. WOODWARD (Chicago and London, 1987), p. 340, and the bibliography on pp. 369-370. J.M.F. VAN REETH, "The Paradise and the city: Preliminary remarks on Muslim sacral geography", in: *Across the Mediterranean Frontiers: Trade, Politics and Religion, 650-1450*, ed. D.A. AGIUS and I.R. NETTON (Turnhout, 1997: *International Medieval Research* 1), pp. 235-254.

[33] MS Mainz, Diözesanmuseum, Cod. Kautsch Nr. 4, f. 108v. See: *Vor dem Jahr Tausend: Abendländische Buchkunst zur Zeit Kaiserin Theophanou*, catalogue of an exhibition (Köln, 1991), No. 22 (with bibliography).

[34] MS Rouen, Bibliothèque Municipale, Y. 7. D.N. DUMVILLE, *Liturgy and the Ecclesiastical History of Late Saxon England* (Woodbridge, 1992: *Studies in Anglo-Saxon History* 5), pp. 87 ff.. Dumville dates the manuscript to the second quarter of the eleventh century. Anton von Euw keeps to the end of the tenth century: A. VON EUW, "Rouen, Bibliothèque municipale, Ms. Y 7", in: *Vor dem Jahr Tausend*, No. 46, p. 158.

[35] DESHAM, *The Benedictional of Aethelwold*, p. 268.

The Pentecost iconography also developed associations with Paradise. In the Bertold Missal, commissioned by Bertold, abbot of Weingarten around 1200-1235, the significance of the Pentecost scene is further enhanced (fig. 16).[36] The four streams of Paradise have been added in the corners, and we are almost in Paradise. At the end of the thirteenth century, the diptych from the golden altar now in Bern was made for the Hungarian King Andreas III. It shows influences from both East and West (fig. 17).[37] Although we see the old-fashioned Eastern Pentecost, the Tree of Life rather than the personification of the world is situated in its centre.

4. From a Single Column to the Seven Pillars of Wisdom

The single column, when not understood as the axis of the world, is an odd and at times uneasy phenomenon, as in the miniature of the eleventh-century Bernulphus codex, made on the Reichenau and now in Utrecht (fig. 18).[38] Its central place makes the column an almost hostile object between the two groups of apostles. Indeed, the Reichenau masters often omitted it, as in an early eleventh-century sacramentary.[39] This uneasiness is expressed in the monumental forms of the Pentecost image in the Stavelot Retable in Paris (fig. 19).[40] Now in the Cluny Museum, but manufactured for the abbey of Stavelot around 1160, the gilded altarpiece is a *magnum opus* of the goldsmiths of the Meuse Valley. The building in which the scene takes place is supported by seven columns. Renewed in the nineteenth century, these columns are faithful copies of the original columns. The middle column, however, supports

[36] MS New York, Pierpont Morgan Library, M. 710. R.G. CALKINS, *Illuminated Books of the Middle Ages* (London, 1983), pp 180-197, and colour plate 14. See also M. VAN VLIERDEN, *Utrecht, een hemel op aarde* (Utrecht, 1988; *Clavis Kunsthistorische Monografieën* 6), chapter "De Wereldorde", pp. 16-25.

[37] P. HUBER, *Bild und Botschaft: Byzantinische und venezianische Miniaturen zum Alten und Neuen Testament* (Zürich, 1973), pp. 147-148 and 191, pls. 1-27.

[38] MS Utrecht, Museum het Catharijneconvent, ADM h 3. Evangelistary, Reichenau, mid-eleventh century. See H.W.C.M. WÜSTEFELD, *Middeleeuwse boeken van het Catharijneconvent*, catalogue of an exhibition (Utrecht, 1993), No. 6, pp. 30-31; A. KORTEWEG, "Der Bernulphuscodex in Utrecht und eine Gruppe verwandter spätreichenauer Handschriften", *Aachener Kunstblätter* 53 (1985), pp. 35-76.

[39] MS Paris, Bibliothèque Nationale, lat. 18005, f. 94v. MAYR-HARTING, *Ottonian Book Illumination*, 2, pp. 80-81.

[40] P. BLOCH, "Zur Deutung des sog. Koblenzer Retabels im Cluny-Museum", *Das Münster* 14 (1961), pp. 256-261. The retable was in Koblenz in the nineteenth century, hence the German name 'Koblenzer Retabel'.

nothing but air and seems a displaced component of the design.[41] Peter Bloch, an eminent specialist in typology, seems right in supposing a symbolic meaning of this middle column. Together the columns symbolize the seven pillars of wisdom (Prv 9, 1: "Wisdom hath builded her house, she hath hewn out her seven pillars"). The Old Testament Temple of Wisdom is the Christian Church of the New Law. Honorius of Autun (ca. 1180-ca. 1137), closely associated with the theological schools of the Liège region, was one of the first to stress the parallel between the seven pillars and the seven gifts of the Holy Ghost. In his *Speculum ecclesiae* he writes:

> *Hae sunt VII columnae quibus domus sapientiae fulcitur quia donis VII spiritus sancti Ecclesiae, quae est domus, insignitur.*[42]

These are the seven pillars upon which the house of wisdom is built, and because of the seven gifts of the Holy Spirit the Church, which is the house, shines forth in all her glory.

The seven gifts of the Holy Spirit from Isaiah 11, 2 will rest upon the rod out of the stem of Jesse:

And the spirit of the Lord shall rest upon him, the spirit of wisdom and understanding, the spirit of counsel and might, the spirit of knowledge and of the fear of the Lord.

The chain of associations could be lengthened and turned from abstract ideas to concrete persons. Ever since St. Jerome connected the *"virgo"* of Isaiah 7, 14 with the *"virga"* of Isaiah 11, 1, the Virgin Mary has had a place within the lineage of Jesse and David.[43] Combining the two prophecies, one might surmise that Mary would be depicted receiving the seven gifts of the Holy Ghost. However, it was not until the twelfth century that, due to Bernard of Clairvaux (ca. 1090-1153) amongst others, the veneration for the Virgin Mary became

---

[41] In 'remaking' the retable in the 1930s, the goldsmith B. Witte 'improved' the original design by omitting the middle column. See BLOCH, "Zur Deutung", p, 257.

[42] Ed. in: *PL* 172, col. 962.

[43] Is 7, 14: "Behold, a virgin shall conceive and bear a son, and shall call his name Immanuel"; Is 11, 1: "And there shall come forth a rod out of the stem of Jesse, and a branch shall grow out of his roots". Jerome, *Commentarium in Isaiam prophetam, IV*, 11, ed. in: *PL* 24, col. 144: *"Nos autem virgam de radice Jesse, sanctam Mariam Virginem intelligamus, quea nullum habuit sibi fruticem cohaerentem; de qua et supra legimus: Ecce Virgo concipiet et pariet filium"*.

more articulated.[44] Sometime in the twelfth century Mary returned among the apostles in the iconography of Pentecost, taking the place of the column or of St. Peter.

The most illuminating picture, visualizing the long chain of exegetical commentaries in a single image, can be found in the Gospels of Henry the Lion, transcribed and illustrated in Helmarshausen around 1185 (fig. 20).[45] The Virgin Mary sits in the middle of the group of apostles, while seven doves hover above their heads. They represent the seven gifts of the Holy Ghost; each is named individually in golden capitals on a purple background. In the same cosmic moment they symbolize the seven pillars of the temple, with the fiery tongues acting as the temple's roof. Mary represents the Christian temple, the Church, upon which the seven gifts have come to rest. Since early Christian times, as we have seen, *Ecclesia* had been a female personification without being identified necessarily with Mary.[46] Thus, both *Ecclesia* and Mary could stand at Christ's right-hand side under the Cross in many Carolingian and Ottonian miniatures and ivories. It is only in the twelfth century that the visual arts combine the two women into a single venerable image of Mary.[47]

After the middle of the twelfth century, the central position of Mary was a matter of course in the Western iconography of Pentecost. She became the personification of the Church and the focus of veneration by the apostles. Her central position received extra weight because a crown was posed upon her head. This was not because she happened to be there when the Holy Ghost descended from heaven, nor because she was Christ's mother, and not even because she had become *Ecclesia*. It was rather because she, as *Ecclesia*, was the bride of Christ. As *Ecclesia*, Mary represents the spouse from Paul's letter tot the Ephesians: "Husbands, love your wives, even as Christ also loved the Church, and gave himself for it" (Eph 5, 25).[48] And as *Ecclesia*, she also sits in the middle of the Christian community in pictorial representations of Pentecost.

---

[44] For the worship of the Virgin Mary in medieval society and its impact on the arts, see the excellent: *Marie: Le culte de la Vierge dans la société médiévale*, ed. D. IOGNA-PRAT, E. PALAZZO and D. RUSSO (Paris, 1996).

[45] MS Wolfenbüttel, Herzog August Bibliothek, Cod. Guelf. 105 Noviss. 2°, f. 112v and MS München, Bayerische Staatsbibliothek, Clm 30055. Cf. *Heinrich der Löwe und seine Zeit: Herrschaft und Repräsentation der Welfen 1125-1235*, catalogue of an exhibition, ed. J. LUCKHARDT and F. NIEHOFF (München, 1995), No. D 30, pp. 206-210 (with bibliography).

[46] RAHNER, *Symbole der Kirche*, and THÉREL, *Les symboles de l'Ecclesia*.

[47] There are a few earlier exceptions, notably in England, the best known being the Gospel book from Bury St. Edmunds of ca. 1120-1140 (SCHILLER, *Ikonographie*, 4.1, fig. 33).

[48] Eph 5, 23-26: "For the husband is the head of the wife, even as Christ is the head of the church .... Husbands, love your wives, even as Christ also loved the church, and gave himself for it; that he might sanctify and cleanse it with the washing of water by the word".

As both bride and mother of Christ, she is a virgin: the enclosed garden, the *hortus conclusus*, is her attribute.

Bearing this in mind, let us turn again to the Eastern iconography of Pentecost, with its open space in the middle (as in the thirteenth-century retable in Bern (fig. 17)) and compare this to the altarpiece from the Middle Rhine now in the Utrecht Museum Catharijneconvent (fig. 4). The formal and seemingly accidental similarity turns out to possess a strong iconological meaning, even if the empty dark space has been replaced by a firmly closed door. The *hortus conclusus* is an attribute of Mary, not in her role of *Ecclesia* but as bride and virgin. The garden also refers to Paradise. In the Bern altarpiece, the dark space that represented all humankind in the world, also represents Paradise because of the Tree of Life in its centre.

A miniature from the Pericopes of Kuno of Falkenstein dating from 1380, in the Cathedral treasury of Trier, has transformed the idea into a symbolic image (fig. 21).[49] In the lower half a fountain stands in an open space with the inscription "*communis vita*", and four streams run underneath its basin. In the fountain, small round loaves of bread are being eaten by the community, and even a dog gets his share (cf. Mt 15, 27: "yet the dogs eat of the crumbs which fall from their masters' table"). In the upper half, Mary is the central person of a Pentecost scene. The parallel between the Virgin and the fountain of communal life is emphasized. In a woodcut in an illustrated printed book of hours, Mary and the apostles have come to join the Christian community around the fountain, drinking from its heavenly liquid (fig. 22). The dove of the Holy Ghost has spread its wings above them, and fiery tongues melt with the contents (wine, blood, fire) of the fountain.

By Way of Conclusion

A church as a paradisiacal garden to the community was revisualised near Amsterdam, as witnessed by the Gothic Growth Project in the polder at Almere (fig. 23). Martinus Boezem (born Leerdam, 1934), artist and professor of Fundamental Form Studies at the Department of Architecture at the Technical University of Delft (1979-1986), in 1980 filled the heaven with doves. They had first eaten pigeon seed laid out as the outline of a cathedral. In this way, the

---

[49] MS Trier, Domschatz, 6, completed 5 May 1380. See *Die Parler und die schöne Stil*, 1, p. 265; F.J. RONIG, "Die Buchmalerei-Schule des Trierer Erzbischofs Kuno von Falkenstein", in: *Florilegium artis: Beiträge zur Kunstwissenschaft und Denkmalpflege: Feschrift für Wolfgang Götz*, ed. M. BERENS a.o. (Saarbrücken, 1984), pp. 111-115.

doves carried the cathedral up to heaven. In 1987, Boezem planted 174 Italian poplars according to the original ground plan of the cathedral of Reims, 150 meters long and 75 meters wide. A cathedral grows towards the light, just as trees do, he explained. Every town grows and has its own history. The newly-built city of Almere, however, situated in one of the large, recent polders in the IJsselmeer at the centre of the Netherlands, was laid out in one go. Boezem was asked to give the town a work of art. As he told a journalist, this city was built on newly acquired land, taken from the sea. "A city without history needs a cathedral. But a medieval church takes a hundred years to be completed. Poplars need thirty years, so that is why I planted the poplars".[50] In the same interview he recalled his difficulties with bureaucracy, but also with the deer that came to rub their antlers against the young trees, and with the sheep he had rented to graze the land, but that subsequently disappeared. Although Boezem may not have been familiar with the symbolic meaning of sheep and deer, medievalists are: they have their place in paradise on earth. They help to remind us that the image of the Green Cathedral, with all its ideology and modern concepts, has its textual roots firmly in the writings of the Church fathers. Only by reading them do we grasp the Cathedral's seminal meaning.

---

[50] "De geest wil vliegen" ("The spirit wants to fly"): Interview by B. STIGTER in *NRC-Handelsblad*, 9 September 1996, "Cultureel supplement", p. 1. See also: *Boezem*, ed. E. VAN DUYN and F. WITTEVEEN (Bussum, 1999), pp. 73-80 and Nos. 145, 275.

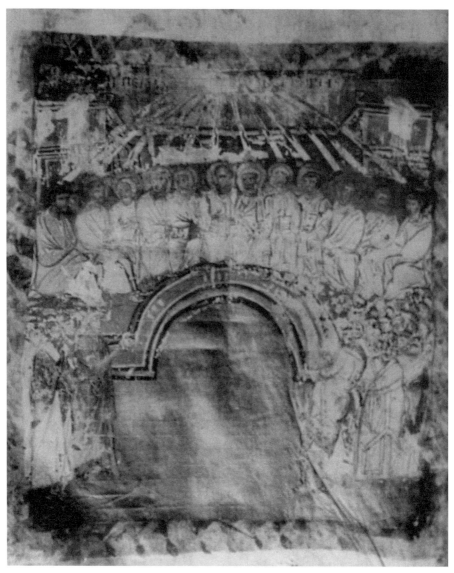

Fig. 1   Pentecost, from a copy of Gregory of Nazianzus, *Homilies*, datable to
ca. 880, MS Paris, Bibliothèque Nationale, grec 510, f. 301r. Cliché
Bibliothèque nationale de France, Paris.

Fig. 2   First council of Constantinople, from Gregory of Nazianzus, *Homilies*, MS Paris, Bibliothèque Nationale, grec 510, f. 335r (ca. 880). Cliché Bibliothèque nationale de France, Paris.

Fig. 3   Russian icon, seventeenth century, present whereabouts unknown. See
also Colour Plate 1.

Fig. 4   Pentecost, retabel from the Middle Rhine region, early fifteenth century. Utrecht, Museum Het Catharijneconvent.

Fig. 5   Pentecost. Benedictional of Æthelwold, MS London, British Library,
         Add. 49598, f. 67v.

Fig. 6   Pentecost. Sacramentary of St. Gereon, ca. 1000. Ms Paris, Bibliothèque Nationale, lat. 817, f. 77r. Cliché Bibliothèque nationale de
France, Paris.

Fig. 7   Pentecost with *communis vita* in the centre. Codex Egberti, ca. 980. MS
Trier, Stadtbibliothek 24, f. 103r.

Fig. 8   Pentecost with Tree of Life in the centre. Pericopes from Echternach,
early twelfth century. MS Brussels, Bibliothèque Royale, 9428, f. 104v.

Fig. 9   Harbaville Tryptich, ivory, late tenth century. Back, wings closed. Paris, Musée du Louvre.

Fig. 10 Apse, Church of San Clemente, Rome, ca. 1120-1130.

Fig. 11 Claus Sluter, Well of Moses, Chartreuse de Champmol, Dijon, 1395-
1406.

Fig. 12 Henricus Suso, *L'Horloge de sapience*, ca. 1450-1460. MS Brussels,
Bibliothèque Royale, IV 111.

Fig. 13 Map of the world, centred on Jerusalem; from an English psalter of the first half of the thirteenth century. MS London, British Library, Add. 28681, f. 9r.

Fig. 14 Pentecost from a sacramentary from Mainz, around 1100. MS Mainz,
Domschatz (Diözesanmuseum), Cod. Kautzsch 4, f. 108v.

Fig. 15 Pentecost with column in the centre. Benedictional of Robert de Ju-
    mièges, second quarter of the eleventh century. MS Rouen, Bibli-
    othèque Municipale, Y 7, f. 29v.

Fig. 16 Pentecost. Bertold Missal, ca. 1200-1235. MS New York, The Pierpont
Morgan Library, M 710, f. 64v.

Fig. 17 Diptych of King Andreas III of Hungary, 1290-1296. Chrystal miniatures on lime wood, cameos, pearls, etc. Detail left wing: Pentecost.
Bern, Historisches Museum, Inv. Nr. 301.

Fig. 18 Pentecost with one column. Evangelistary (Bernulphus codex), Reichenau, ca. 1040-1050. MS Utrecht, Museum Het Catharijneconvent, ABM
h 3.

Fig. 19 Pentecostal altarpiece (Stavelot Retable), gilded copper on wood, ca.
1060-1070, 7 columns. Paris, Musée de Cluny, Cl. 13247.

Fig. 20 Pentecost, Gospels of Henry the Lion, 1185-1188, MS Wolfenbüttel, Herzog August Bibliothek, Cod. Guelf. 155 Noviss. 2° / München, Bayerische Staatsbibliotheek, Clm 30055, f. 112v.

Fig. 21 Gospels of Kuno of Falkenstein, *c.* 1380. Pentecost and fountain. MS Trier, Domschatz 66.

Fig. 22 Pentecost, with fountain of wine or fire, woodcut from the *Grandes Heures Royales*, printed by Vérard (Paris, after 20 August 1490). New York, The Pierpont Morgan Library, PML 127725 (ChL 1523B), f. a5r.

Fig. 23 Marinus Boezem, Gothic Growth Project ('Green Cathedral'), in Almere-East, Flevoland, Parcel KZ 45. 1978/1987-present. 174 Italian poplars (*Populus nigra italica*), stone, concrete, shells. After E. VAN DUYN and F. WITTEVEEN, *Boezem* (Bussum, 1999), pp. 76-77.

Changing Perceptions of the Visual in the Middle Ages: Hucbald of St. Amand's Carolingian Rewriting of Prudentius

WILLIAM J. DIEBOLD

In 1977, François Dolbeau published a previously unknown account of the life and death of the early Christian martyr Cassian written by the late Carolingian schoolmaster Hucbald of Saint Amand (*ca.* 840-930).[1] Dolbeau noted that Hucbald's prose account of Cassian's martyrdom was closely dependent on Prudentius's (348-*ca.* 405) poem of *ca.* 400 describing the same events.[2] While Hucbald's *Passio Cassiani* has not been ignored by subsequent scholars,[3] neither has it attracted great interest, in large part because it seems so expected – yet more evidence of two well-known phenomena: the special Carolingian interest in Prudentius and, more generally, in late antique Christian authors. Nor has the extensive similarity between Prudentius's late antique model and its Carolingian copy encouraged scholars to study Hucbald's text in detail. In this paper I argue that a comparison between model and copy is nonetheless rewarding for the study of late antique and early medieval visual culture. In both Prudentius's poem and Hucbald's prose text, vision and the visual arts play a central role. By paying close attention to what Hucbald retained

---

[1]   *BHL* 1626d. F. DOLBEAU, "Passion de S. Cassien d'Imola composée d'après Prudence par Hucbald de Saint-Amand", *Revue Bénédictine* 87 (1977), pp. 238-256.

[2]   *BHL* 1625. *Peristephanon* IX, in: *Aurelii Prudentii Clementis Carmina*, ed. M. CUNNINGHAM (Turnhout, 1966: *CCSL* 126), pp. 326-329. For an English translation, see: *The Poems of Prudentius*, tr. M. EAGAN (Washington, DC, 1962: *The Fathers of the Church* 43).

[3]   The text is discussed in J. SMITH, "The hagiography of Hucbald of Saint-Amand", *Studi Medievali*, 3rd series 35 (1994), pp. 517-542, and EAD., "A hagiographer at work: Hucbald and the library at Saint-Amand", *Revue Bénédictine* 106 (1996), pp. 151-171.

from Prudentius and what he altered, we can gain a particularly sharp insight into the similarities and differences between late antique and Carolingian ideas about images. In particular, Hucbald's text provides evidence of what I believe is a distinctively Carolingian worry about the power of images.

The Spanish-born Prudentius composed many didactic and devotional poems; these include the collection known as the *Peristephanon*, written just around the year 400 and comprising 14 poems devoted to various Italian and Spanish martyrs.[4] The *Peristephanon*'s ninth poem, at 106 lines one of the shorter ones, is devoted to the martyrdom of the obscure Saint Cassian, who had apparently died a century or more earlier in one of the pre-Constantinian persecutions of Christians.[5] On a pilgrimage to Rome, the poet came to the northern Italian town of Imola and made his devotions at the saint's shrine there:

> I was stretched out on the ground, prostrate before the tomb, which holy   5
> Cassian, the martyr, honours with his consecrated body.
> While in tears I reflected on my wounds and all the labours
> Of my life and the pricks of grief,
> I lifted my face to heaven, and there stood opposite me
> An image of the martyr painted in coloured hues.[6]   10

Prudentius goes on to describe the picture, which showed the saint surrounded by countless boys, pricking him with the styluses they normally used to take down their school lessons on wax tablets. At this point, the pilgrim questions the sacristan (*aedituus*) of the shrine. Prudentius does not specify what he asked, but presumably it was the subject of the grotesque image. Almost all the rest of the poem is the sacristan's answer, which tells the story of Cassian's martyrdom at considerable length and in much gory detail. (Readers should be

---

[4]   Recent book-length studies of the *Peristephanon* are M. ROBERTS, *Poetry and the Cult of the Martyrs: The* Liber Peristephanon *of Prudentius* (Ann Arbor, 1993) and A.-M. PALMER, *Prudentius on the Martyrs* (Oxford, 1989).

[5]   For the history of Cassian and his cult, see: M. BLESS-GRABHER, *Cassian von Imola* (Bern, 1978: *Geist und Werk der Zeiten* 56). This useful book traces the Cassian legend from its origins into the twentieth century and examines Prudentius's poem in special detail. Hucbald's text was apparently unknown to Bless-Grabher. The recent and thorough study of Cassian's cult in the exhibition catalogue *Divo Cassiano – Il culto del santo martire patrono di Imola, Bressanone e Comacchio*, ed. A. FERRI (Imola, 2004) appeared too late to be considered in this article.

[6]   *Peristephanon* IX, 5-10; tr. in: S. GOLDHILL, "Body/politics: Is there a history of reading?", in: *Contextualizing Classics: Ideology, Performance, Dialogue: Essays in Honor of John J. Peradotto*, ed. T. FALKNER, N. FELSON, and D. KONSTAN (Lanham, 1999), p. 114.

warned that this tale of a teacher martyred by his students can be tough going for delicate professorial ears.)

Cassian was a schoolmaster, specializing in the teaching of shorthand. He was not a popular instructor:

> Harsh at times were his rules, and the wearisome lessons
> Aroused the dread and anger of the youthful mob.[7]   25

During a persecution, he was identified as a Christian. When the Roman magistrate learned Cassian's profession, he decreed that the future saint's punishment was to be given back to his pupils:

> "Take him away", cried the judge; "Remove him hence as a culprit
> And give him to the children he was wont to flog.
> Let them make sport of him as they will; let them torture him freely,
> And in their master's blood make red their truant hands.   40
> It is a joy to think that the harsh schoolmaster will furnish
> Amusement for the pupils he so often curbed.[8]

Cassian's pupils took to the task and bound his hands. Some threw their writing tablets at him, breaking the wooden frames on his face; others poked him with their sharp iron styluses. The description is graphic and its pathetic power is strengthened as the students taunt Cassian, saying:

> You should not be displeased at our marks; it was you who commanded
> That never in our hands we hold an idle stylus.
> We do not ask for the holiday now you so often refused us,   75
> O grudging teacher, when you kept us in your school.[9]

They ask Cassian to look over the marks they are making on his body to "See if we have made any mistakes in our letter formation for you to correct".[10] Christ in heaven finally brings a merciful end to the saint's torture by granting him death. At this point, the sacristan breaks off his narration of Cassian's story and speaks to the pilgrim about the painting of the saint: "These are the things, stranger, that you admire, expressed in clear colours; that is Cassian's glory".[11]

---

[7] *Peristephanon*, IX, 24-25; tr. EAGAN, p. 184.
[8] *Peristephanon*, IX, 37-42; tr. EAGAN, p. 185.
[9] *Peristephanon*, IX, 73-76; tr. EAGAN, p. 187 (slightly modified).
[10] *Peristephanon*, IX, 79-80; tr. GOLDHILL, "Body/politics", p. 117 (slightly modified).
[11] *Peristephanon*, IX, 93-94; my translation.

The sacristan also urges the pilgrim to pray to the saint. Prudentius writes that he obeyed, embracing the tomb and weeping, before continuing his pilgrimage to Rome.

This extraordinary text invites a variety of analyses. For example, in its representation of death through writing instruments and letter-like wounds, Prudentius's late antique poem literally proves the Apostle Paul's claim that the letter kills (II Cor 3, 6); it also provides an uncanny foreshadowing of Franz Kafka's twentieth-century exploration of the same subject in his story *In der Strafkolonie (In the Penal Colony)*.[12] I will confine my analysis to only one aspect of the text, one consequence of its genre. For whatever else it is, Prudentius's poem is an *ekphrasis*, a verbal description of a work of visual art. Much recent literature, written at both the theoretical and historical levels, has recognized the special importance of *ekphraseis* to art-historical inquiry.[13] Thus Simon Goldhill, introducing his deep and subtle reading of *Peristephanon* 9, has written that Prudentius speaks to "problems which are integral to the highly contested journey towards iconoclasm".[14] For Goldhill, these problems include the status of Christian cult images such as that of Cassian in the light of the Second Commandment's prohibition on visual representation and the Christian understanding of older, pagan images.

Goldhill places the poem in a late fourth-century historical context, one in which the question of images was "a topic of some debate". He is certainly right that the status of images was very much at issue around 400; indeed, it is an issue that is explicitly addressed in other poems by Prudentius. Goldhill cites two passages from Prudentius's poem against the Roman orator Symmachus. In the first, the emperor Theodosius (ruled 379-395) strongly defends images, and especially pagan images, claiming that they retain lasting value even in a Christian era. But elsewhere in the text, Theodosius's sons, Honorius

---

[12]   For three recent and sophisticated literary-critical readings of *Peristephanon*, IX, see: ROBERTS, *Poetry*, pp. 132-148; GOLDHILL, "Body/politics", pp. 89-120, esp. pp. 109-118; and R. COPELAND, "Introduction: Dissenting critical practices", in: *Criticism and Dissent in the Middle Ages*, ed. R. COPELAND (Cambridge, 1996), pp. 1-23, esp. pp. 6-12 (I am grateful to Michael Camille for calling this last article to my attention). While all of these studies are excellent and I have learned much from them, they in no way exhaust the poem; in particular, none pursues the interpretive directions hinted at in my text.

[13]   From a wealth of recent literature, I cite two studies I have found clear and helpful: L. JAMES and R. WEBB, " 'To understand ultimate things and enter secret places': Ekphrasis and art in Byzantium", *Art History* 19 (1991), pp. 1-17 (on the general problem of medieval *ekphraseis*) and L. NEES, "Theodulf's mythical silver Hercules vase, *Poetica Vanitas*, and the Augustinian critique of the Roman Heritage", *Dumbarton Oaks Papers* 41 (1987), pp. 443-451 (on a Carolingian *ekphrasis*).

[14]   GOLDHILL, "Body/politics", p. 111.

(r. 395-423) and Arcadius (r. 383-408), give a much more negative assessment of images, calling them fictions. In *Contra Symmachum* the image question is explicitly problematized; the images in *Peristephanon* 9, by contrast, are unproblematic because they are portrayed in a uniformly positive way. Thus, Prudentius represents the picture of Cassian's martyrdom in straightforward terms and praises it for its ability to make him feel strong emotions:

> I lifted my face to heaven, and there stood opposite me
> An image of the martyr painted in coloured hues,   10
> Bearing a thousand blows, torn over all his limbs,
> Showing his skin ripped with minute points.
> Countless boys round him – pitiful sight![15]

Here, pictorial representation seems to have fallen away. It is the boys pricking Cassian that are the miserable sight, not the painting of the boys' actions.

The image of Cassian in Prudentius's poem is transparent; it is also author-itative, since the sacristan gives it his imprimatur:

> I consulted the sacristan who said "What you see, stranger, is no empty old-wives' tale. The picture recounts a history which is recorded in books and demonstrates the true faith of olden times".

> *Aedituus consultus ait: "Quod prospicis, hospes,*
> *non est inanis aut anilis fabula.*
> *Historiam pictura refert, quae tradita libris*
> *ueram uetusti temporis monstrat fidem.*[16]   20

The sacristan tells the pilgrim that he has before his eyes not an "empty old-wives' tale" (*"inanis fabula"*, i.e. something expressed orally), but rather a *historia* also known from books. The sacristan thus places the picture on the same plane with the written content of books and distinguishes it from the lower (because oral and feminine) plane of women's fables. Similarly in lines 93-94, cited earlier, the sacristan tells the pilgrim that what he has seen, ex-pressed in clear colours, is Cassian's glory. There is no hint here of any limits on painting's ability to represent Christian truths. Prudentius, writing shortly after Theodosius's establishment of Christianity as the state religion of the

---

[15]   *Peristephanon*, IX, 9-13: *"erexi ad caelum faciem, stetit obuia contra/fucis colorum picta imago martyris/plagas mille gerens, totos lacerata per artus, ruptam minutis praeferens punctis cutem./Innumeri circum pueri (miserabile uisu)"*; tr. GOLDHILL, "Body/politics", p. 114.
[16]   *Peristephanon*, IX, 17-20; tr. GOLDHILL, "Body/politics", p. 113 (slightly adapted).

Roman empire (381), is triumphalist. While his presentation of writing in *Peristephanon* 9 invites a deconstructive reading, with words – the very material of which the text is constituted serving as the instrument of Cassian's death – the poem's attitude towards the visual is confident, sure, unproblematic.

This late antique, Prudentian view of images stands in contrast to that found in Hucbald of Saint Amand's version of the Cassian story. Hucbald, born around 840, spent much of his life as a monk in the northern French monastery of Saint Amand, first as a pupil of the famous teacher Milo and then as his successor as head of the school there. He died in 930, at the age of ninety.[17] Hucbald's account of Cassian's passion, while explicitly indebted to Prudentius's poem, is in prose. Hucbald claimed he did this to make Prudentius's poetry more accessible to his students. Julia Smith, however, has rightly pointed out that Hucbald's text is no easy read, as he deploys a full range of sophisticated rhetorical devices.[18] Since there is no evidence of a cult of Cassian in Carolingian Francia (such cults being the reason Hucbald wrote his other saint's lives), it seems likely, as Smith has proposed, that Hucbald composed the text for school use, a sign of both mordant wit and pedagogical acumen.

Hucbald greatly expanded upon Prudentius's poem, not by adding more information about the events surrounding Cassian's death, but by giving the death narrative an extensive frame. The Carolingian text began with a now-lost preface that discussed the virtues of prose over poetry. This was followed by an account of salvation history from Adam to the present, including a discussion of the persecutions that caused Cassian's death, and a long etymological disquisition on the origins of Cassian's name in the aromatic shrub *cassia* (cinnamon) mentioned in the Psalms and the Song of Songs. Then came Hucbald's retelling of the tale from Prudentius, which takes up somewhat less than half the text's length. Hucbald ended by discussing the hagiographer's three audiences: his students, his readers, and God.[19]

I will pay attention only to the section of Hucbald's text in which he revises Prudentius. In particular, I am interested in the way Hucbald's representation of images rewrites the late antique poem. In brief, my argument will be that, in contrast to Prudentius's poem, Hucbald's early tenth-century text shows a characteristically Carolingian worry about the power of images.

A good place to begin our analysis is to look at Hucbald's version of the scene in which the pilgrim begins to look at the martyr image of Cassian:

---

[17]   On Hucbald, see F.-J. KONSTANCIAK, "Hucbald v. St.-Amand", in: *Lexikon des Mittelalters* 5 (Munich and Zurich, 1991), cols. 150-151.

[18]   SMITH, "Hagiography", p. 531.

[19]   This outline is based on that in DOLBEAU, "Passion", pp. 243-244.

I lifted my eyes to God, when suddenly I see his painted image, marvellous (but really more miserable) in appearance.

... oculos ad *Deum* erexi, *cum subito* pictam *ipsius* imaginem *conspicio* visu *mirabilem sed plus* miserabilem ...[20]

A comparison with lines 9-13 of *Peristephanon* 9 makes clear how closely Hucbald often followed his model (underlined words show direct borrowings from Prudentius). Not only are the two texts close verbally, they are also close conceptually. It is very difficult to distinguish them by the way they present images. Indeed, Hucbald's text may be even more favourable to the power of pictures than Prudentius's, since Hucbald allows the painting's appearance to be both "*mirabilis*" and "*miserabilis*".

But in comparing a second passage from the Carolingian text with its model, we can see some doubt on Hucbald's part about the veracity of images:

> When the sacristan was asked what these things meant, he answered: "What you see, stranger, is no empty old-wives' tale; rather, the picture, accurate in its various colours, shows a true story of an earlier age, known not from fleeting words but from truthful books. The master whose image you look at here was famous, out- standing in educating the young".

> *Percunctatus igitur ianitorem hec quidnam portenderent [praetenderent?] respon- dit: "O* hospes, *illud quod cernis* non est inanis fabula *vel* anilis, sed veram mon- strat historiam *evi antiquioris* pictura variis colorum limata fucis, non fugacibus verbis sed veracibus cognitam libris. Hic etenim cuius effigiem contueris magister fuerat insignis ac* puerilibus praefuerat studiis.[21]

As noted above, the parallel passage in Prudentius is quite straightforward. The sacristan tells the pilgrim that what he sees is not an old woman's tale ("*inanis fabula*"), but that the picture tells a story – a story that has the sanction of being recorded in books and shows the true faith of old. Prudentius's simple direct- ness contrasts with Hucbald's need to insist upon everything. Hucbald copies Prudentius's nice juxtaposition of *inanis* and *anilis* and his contrast between the oral *fabula* and written *historia*. But he then repeats the point, portraying the fleeting words of the old wive's tales (and the sacristan's story?) as inferior to authoritative, truthful books. This repetitive duplication signals the Carolingian

---

[20] DOLBEAU, "Passion", p. 251; my translation.
[21] DOLBEAU, "Passion", p. 251; my translation.

need to reassert at every opportunity the very things that Prudentius took as given.

A further instance of Hucbald's need to emphasize the ability of pictures to tell the truth is found in another subtle but significant rewriting of his model. In Prudentius's poem, the picture tells a story and that story shows the true faith of old. Hucbald uses almost the same vocabulary, but to a different end. For him, the picture shows a true story, and it is that truth conveyed by the (here accurate, but potentially doubtful) picture on which he concentrates his attention. "... rather, the picture, accurate in its various colours, shows a true story of an earlier age, known not from fleeting words but from truthful books". Prudentius's "true faith of olden times" is no longer of interest, the claim about truth having been shifted to the picture and the story it tells. For Hucbald, living in the aftermath of the Carolingian debates about the status of images sparked by Byzantine iconoclasm, it is no longer possible simply to take for granted, as does Prudentius, the truth of images. Instead, that truth needs to be insisted upon precisely because it is debatable. For the Carolingian author, this particular image happens to be truthful. For Prudentius, images were truthful by nature.

A similar concern about representation is apparent in the periphrasis, not found in Prudentius, with which the sacristan in Hucbald's text starts to tell the tale of Cassian's martyrdom. Prudentius's sacristan begins his story with a simple declarative sentence: "He was outstanding in educating the young".[22] In Hucbald's version, by contrast, there is an intervening qualification, as the sacristan reminds the pilgrim that he is seeing not Cassian himself, but his "*effigies*": "The master whose image you look at here was famous". This literal-minded insistence that works of art are representations is very much part of the Carolingian language of art. It is, for example, the main position of the *Libri Carolini*, the late eighth-century treatise on images written for Charlemagne by Theodulf of Orléans (750/60-821) to respond to Byzantine iconodulism. A chief argument of the *Libri Carolini* is that images are not identical with what they represent, but are rather manufactured, artist's fictions. It is often claimed that the *Libri Carolini* were an anomaly, without significant influence on Carolingian image practice or understanding. There is almost no direct evidence that the text was read during the ninth century. I would nevertheless argue that its theory that images can only serve as decoration or to recall past events was the standard Carolingian one.[23]

[22] *Peristephanon*, IX, 21; my translation.
[23] The bibliography on the *Libri Carolini* is immense. For a recent review, including a study of the reception of the text in the Carolingian period, see the introduction to: *Opus Caroli*

    This is not a case I can make fully in this paper, but I would like to point to
a small, yet significant relationship between Hucbald's text and the *Libri
Carolini*. In describing the painting of Cassian, Hucbald says the picture was
"*variis colorum limata fucis*", a phrase translated above as "accurate in its
various colours". In classical Latin, *fucus* usually had a tinge of deceit about it;
the word was used for cosmetics and, more generally, for coloured things that
masked surfaces.[24] This made it an appropriate word for an artist's paints, and
this is how Prudentius himself used it in line 10 of *Peristephanon* 9. Given
Prudentius's favourable attitude towards the visual in his poem about Cassian's
death, it is hard to see his use of *fucus* as connoting deception. But what is the
meaning of *fucus* when it reappears in Hucbald? There the word has a more
negative connotation, as it typically did in the Carolingian period. As part of
the larger research project of which this paper forms a part, I have compiled a
concordance to all Carolingian texts that discuss what we would call art. Leaving the *Libri Carolini* aside for the moment, there are only two other instances
in Carolingian literature where *fucus* is used to talk about images. One occurs
in a description of heaven in the prose life of St. Amandus by Hucbald's
teacher, Milo († 871/872);[25] in the other, the word is used in its technical sense
of reddish dye.[26] *Fucus*, then, is unusual in Carolingian writing about art –
except in the *Libri Carolini* and related texts produced as part of the Carolingian response to the Byzantine image debate: there, *fucus* appears 16 times, in
almost every instance in an explicitly negative context. For example, here is
Theodulf contrasting the Carolingian position on images with that of the
Byzantines:

> Since they place almost all their hope in images, they differ greatly from the holy
> and universal Church, which places its hopes not in the colours of a picture (*pictu-*
> *rae fucus*) or in the work of a craftsman's hands.[27]

---

regis contra synodum (Libri Carolini), ed. A. FREEMAN (Hannover, 1998: *MGH Concilia* 2,
Supplementum 1), pp. 1-93.
   [24]   *Oxford Latin Dictionary*, ed. P. GLARE (Oxford, 1982), s.v. "*fucus*", esp. 4 and 5;
A Latin Dictionary, ed. C. LEWIS and C. SHORT (Oxford, 1879), s.v. "*fucus*", esp. II B and III
   [25]   *BHL* 341b: Milo of S.-Amand, *Sermo legendus in Transitu seu Depositione [S. Amandi]*,
ed. B. KRUSCH in: *Passiones vitaeque sanctorum aevi Merovingici*, ed. B. KRUSCH and W.
LEVISON (Hannover, 1910: *MGH Scriptores Rerum Merovingicarum* 5), p. 463.
   [26]   Ed. in: MIGNE, *PL* 138, col. 266.
   [27]   *Opus Caroli regis*, p. 417. Other appearances of *fucus* in the *Libri Carolini* are *Opus
Caroli regis*, pp. 149, 205, 206, 214, 229, 260, 287, 296, 298, 493, 535, and 540. The word also
appears once in the *Libellus* assembled for the use of the council of Paris in 825 (ed. in: *MGH
Concilia* 2, p. 541) and once in Jonas of Orléans's (before 780-843) *De cultu imaginum* (ed. in:
MIGNE, *PL* 106, col. 340).

In the Carolingian context, then, Hucbald's use of *fucus* signals his mistrust of images.

A further comparison between Prudentius and Hucbald shows a similar difference on the question of images. Again, for Prudentius pictures are straightforward:

> These are the things, stranger, that you admire, expressed in clear colours; that is Cassian's glory.

> *Haec sunt quae liquidis expressa coloribus, hospes,*
> *miraris, ista est Cassiani gloria.*[28]

For the late antique poet, representation is transparent; Cassian's glory is fully equivalent to its depiction in painting. Not so for Hucbald:

> "This was the triumph of the precious martyr Cassian, this the playful malice of the youthful gang, this the delectable spectacle for the impious persecutor". When he saw these things represented in the church in various colours, the venerable poet Prudentius knew them to be true, not only from the testimony of his host, but also from the aid of that martyr to him in everything that he sought from God through the merits of his [Cassian's] suffering.

> *"Hic fuit triumphus Cassiani pretiosi martiris, hec ludibunda cohortis malitia*
> *puerilis, hoc delectabile impii spectaculum persecutoris". Hec Prudentius poeta*
> *venerabilis, dum in basilica ipsius conspiceret* coloribus *depicta variis, vera esse*
> *non solum attestatione cognovit sui hospitis, sed etiam auxilio eiusdem martiris*
> *sibimet de omnibus que a Deo per eius expetiit merita suffragantis.*[29]

Like Prudentius, Hucbald begins by stating the facts of Cassian's life and noting that they were depicted in the painting. Again, however, Hucbald has his doubts: neither the visual image of the saint's life nor the verbal account of that life by the sacristan is sufficient. Instead, the verifying force comes from the martyr's aid to the poet. Reality lies in deeds rather than in images or words. This idea has no parallel in Prudentius's text; it is a purely Carolingian interpolation. It is especially noteworthy because, as Smith has noted in her synthetic account of the full range of Hucbald's hagiography, Hucbald was conspicuously uninterested in miracles and the other earthly proofs of sanctity that were

---

[28]   *Peristephanon*, IX, 93-94; my translation.
[29]   DOLBEAU, "Passion", p. 254; my translation.

the stock in trade of most Carolingian hagiographers. "Turning his back on those forms of saintly assistance which alleviated the misery of the current human condition, Hucbald viewed saints' patronage as an exclusively spiritual matter".[30] The general truth of Smith's claim is not in doubt. It highlights how, in his *Passion of Cassian*, the problems posed by visual representation caused Hucbald to break from his normal pattern of thought.

In contrast to his model, Hucbald's account of Cassian's martyrdom shows considerable worry about the transparency and efficacy of images. Those worries are part of a general concern by the Carolingian clergy about the power of images. The best known witness to that concern is the *Libri Carolini*, but what is more significant is the widespread Carolingian acceptance of the *Libri Carolini*'s strict limits on images. Carolingian images, uniquely in the history of Western art, are never represented as misbehaving, as speaking, moving, or acting like real people.[31] Early in the Carolingian period, Theodulf insisted that images were purely human creations, without special powers. To an astounding degree, that position became the standard Carolingian one, countering a strong Western tendency to animate works of art. As a result, there are more miracle-working images in short texts by Gregory of Tours (*ca.* 540-594) (to say nothing of Byzantine saints' lives) than there are in the entire corpus of Carolingian literature.[32]

To this point my argument has rested on some very close (arguably too close) readings of a single Carolingian text; the differences that I have pointed to between the ways in which Prudentius and Hucbald represented images are admittedly subtle. Yet there is one important exception. Prudentius describes the 'crime' that led to Cassian's condemnation by the Roman magistrate laconically: "he disdained to pray at the altars".[33] In the parallel passage in Hucbald's text, however, Cassian delivers an attack on idols:

---

[30] SMITH, "Hagiography", p. 523.
[31] Cf. J.-M. SANSTERRE, "Attitudes occidentales à l'égard des miracles d'images dans le haut moyen âge", *Annales ESC* 53 (1998), pp. 1219-1241. Although I do not think that all of Sansterre's conclusions can be derived from the meagre evidence, his article is filled with remarkable analyses as well as valuable references to the primary and secondary bibliography. For the evidence that the tendency to animate images is more or less universal, see: D. FREEDBERG, *The Power of Images* (Chicago, 1989).
[32] For the early medieval Western evidence, see: SANSTERRE, "Attitudes"; for a more general survey of Eastern and Western medieval attitudes towards images, see the sources collected in H. BELTING, *Likeness and Presence: A History of the Image before the Era of Art*, tr. E. JEPHCOTT (Chicago, 1994), pp. 491-556.
[33] *Peristephanon*, IX, 32: "... *aris supplicare spreuerat* ..."; my translation.

[Cassian] claims that the vain idols are mute, deaf, and without sense; and he vowed he will never give the honour due to the one, true God to sculptures or, better put, demons.[34]

Prudentius's altars become Hucbald's idols. Why?

At a basic level, of course, it is unsurprising for a Christian author to reject idolatry. Nor is Hucbald's language unusual. The condemnation of idols as vain, mute, deaf, and without sense is common in Carolingian writing.[35] Also typically Carolingian is Hucbald's insertion of idols into a text that does not require them. Carolingian saint's lives as a genre are obsessively concerned with idols. Yet this elevated concern about idols is strange, because literal idolatry was not a major problem in Carolingian life. Although on the borders of their empire the Carolingians were encountering pagans who might be considered idolaters, there is no geographical pattern to the Carolingian textual preoccupation with idolatry. Texts from border regions are no more likely to condemn idolatry than are those from the Carolingian heartland, where idolatry had not been an issue for centuries. Also striking is the literalness of the Carolingian conception of the idol. While even the earliest Christian writers (for example, Tertullian (*ca.* 150-*ca.* 230)) had already construed the Biblical prohibitions on idolatry as a metaphor for all sorts of prohibited behaviour, the Carolingians typically had a completely material understanding of idolatry (see, e.g. Hucbald's literal-minded claim that idols are vain and without speech, sense, or hearing).

Why were Carolingians obsessed with idols and especially with asserting that they were without power? I believe the Carolingian representation of the prohibited idol can tell us much about the Carolingian conception of the sanctioned image. This Carolingian concern comes not (or not only) from their contact with pagans, but from their worries about the legitimacy of Christian

---

[34]   DOLBEAU, "Passion", p. 252: "*Qui [Cassianus] discussus christianum se esse respondit, idola vana muta et surda ac sine sensu asserit, nec honorem soli Deo vero debitum se sculptilibus immo magis demonibus numquam allegavit persolvere*"; my translation.
[35]   E.g. Anskar, *Vita sancti Willehadi*, ed. G.H. PERTZ, in: *Scriptores rerum Sangallensium; Annales, chronica et historiae aevi Carolini*, ed. G.H. PERTZ *et al.* (Hannover, 1829: *MGH Scriptores* 2), p. 380 (*BHL* 8898); *Alia vita [Thuribii]*, ed. in: *Acta sanctorum* April 2 (Antwerp, 1675), p. 419 (*BHL* 8346); *Acta vitae et martyrii [S. Carauni martyris]*, ed. in: *Acta sanctorum* May 6 (Antwerp, 1688), p. 751 (*BHL* 1565); Adso of Montier-en-Der, *Vita prolixior [S. Mansueti episc. Et conf.]*, ed. in: *Acta sanctorum* September 1 (Antwerp, 1746), p. 639 (*BHL* 5209); Hrabanus Maurus, *De universo*, ed. in: MIGNE, *PL* 111, col. 226. There is no study of Carolingian conceptions of idolatry. Such a study will be part of a book I am writing on Carolingian visual culture. In that book I will make the arguments of this and the following paragraph in more detail and with much fuller documentation.

images. These worries arose in the eighth and ninth centuries because of Carolingian engagement with Byzantine and Roman debates over the proper status of the image. This explains an unusual aspect of Carolingian writing about forbidden pagan idols: its almost perfect correspondence with Carolingian writing about accepted Christian images. Texts such as the *Libri Carolini* are like the texts on idols in their insistence that images are manufactured and have no special powers. The special Carolingian concern with idols, then, is an aspect of their concern about their own image practice.[36]

This claim cannot be argued decisively in a short paper. However, we find additional evidence for it if we turn from Carolingian texts about images to the images themselves. It is odd, given the lack of any evidence for a cult of St. Cassian outside Italy, that we have two Carolingian representations of his passion. One of these is verbal, Hucbald of St. Amand's text; the other is visual, found in a manuscript of Prudentius's writings made in the region of Lake Constance around 900.[37] In this book, *Peristephanon* 9 is illustrated by three miniatures, with each miniature subdivided to show two separate moments in the story. The first miniature represents the poem's frame narrative: in one part, Prudentius and the sacristan at Imola meet and talk; in another, the pilgrim kneels before Cassian's church and prays. The second shows, at the top, Cassian teaching a group of schoolboys and, at the bottom, the saint being led before the Roman magistrate who turns him over to his pupils for punishment. The third miniature (fig. 1) illustrates the climax of the saint's life, as many schoolboys stab him to death while an angel at upper right carries the saint's soul to heaven, where it is received by the hand of God. At the upper left, a nude male figure on a pedestal, an idol, watches over the proceedings. The presence of this idol is remarkable. Just as we must be surprised that, unmotivated by Prudentius's text, an idol was added by the Carolingian hagiographer Hucbald to his story, so we must be surprised that the same figure, equally unmotivated by the text, was added by the Carolingian miniaturist to his illus-

---

[36]   Cf. M. McCormick, "Textes, images et iconoclasme dans le cadre des relations entre Byzance et l'Occident carolingien", in: *Testo e Immagine nell'alto medioevo, ?* vols (Spoleto, 1994: *Settimane di studio del Centro italiano di studi sull'alto medioevo* 41), 1, pp. 95-162, esp. pp. 105-106 and 154-155.
[37]   MS Bern, Burgerbibliothek, 264. On the manuscript, see: O. Homburger, *Die illustrierten Handschriften der Burgerbibliothek Bern* (Bern, 1962), pp. 136-158, and E. Beer, "Überlegungen zu Stil und Herkunft des Berner Prudentius-Codex 264", in: *Florilegium Sangallense: Festschrift für Johannes Duft zum 65. Geburtstag*, ed. O.P. Clavadetscher, H. Maurer and S. Sonderegger (St. Gallen, 1980), pp. 15-70. The three-miniature Cassian cycle is illustrated and briefly discussed in C. Hahn, "Picturing the text: Narrative in the *Life* of the saints", *Art History* 13 (1990), pp. 1-33.

tration of Prudentius's poem. There can be no question of direct influence. Rather, we are dealing with similar concerns underlying text and image. As a picture, this manuscript illustration of course does not take the same sceptical position about the visual found in Hucbald's text. Like Hucbald's version, however, the miniatures deviate from Prudentius's text to emphasize the importance of idolatry. They show that the Carolingian verbal concern about the negative power of bad images found pictorial expression as well.[38]

---

[38] Hucbald's is not the only early medieval text that retells Prudentius's story about Cassian's death. Neither the version of Gregory of Tours (*In gloria martyrum*, c. 42, ed. in: *Gregorius Turonensis Opera*, 2, *Miracula et opera minora*, ed. B. KRUSCH (Hannover, 1885: *MGH Scriptores Rerum Merovingicarum* 1.2), pp. 516-517) nor that of Flodoard of Reims (*De Christi triumphis apud Italiam*, ed. in: MIGNE, *PL* 125, col. 857) makes any mention of idols. Idols are found in the account of Cassian's martyrdom in Bede's (672/73-735) martyrology ("*qui [Cassianus] cum adorare idola noluisset ...*") and, directly following him, in a series of Carolingian martyrologies, including those of Hrabanus Maurus (780-856) (ed. J. McCULLOH (Turnhout, 1979: *CCCM* 44), pp. 80-81, whence I cite the text), Florus of Lyons († *ca.* 860), Wandalbert of Prüm (813-*ca.* 870), Notker the Stammerer (*ca.* 840-912), Ado of Vienne (*ca.* 800-875), and Usuard († *ca.* 875) (on these texts, see: BLESS-GRABHER, *Cassian*, pp. 77-82). Bede's text apparently depends on a post-Prudentian Italian passion account (*BHL* 1626; see: BLESS-GRABHER, *Cassian*, pp. 75-79). Wolfert van Egmond kindly suggested to me that such brief, formulaic mentions of idols are very characteristic of the martyrology tradition. In any event, there is no indication that Hucbald was influenced by any text other than Prudentius's in writing his account of Cassian's passion, so that his interpolation of idols into his text demands independent explanation.

Fig. 1   The martyrdom of Cassian. MS Bern, Burgerbibliothek 264, f. 61r.

Oral Tradition in Visual Art:
The Romanesque Theodoric

MICHAEL CURSCHMANN

Theodoric the Great, King of the Ostrogoths and ruler of Italy from 497 until his death in 526, stands at the centre of the most widely disseminated and most durable cycle of heroic legends known to us from the southern hemisphere of the Germanic world. There he is known as Dietrich of Bern-Verona, the city with which legend replaced his historical residence, Ravenna. At the turn of the eleventh century the influential world chronicler Fruotolf of Michelsberg paid reluctant tribute to this oral tradition by defining it as another kind of history, an indigenous way of representing the past that was at variance with that practised by learned historians, but common among "the people" even then.[1] One generation later, the anonymous vernacular *Kaiserchronik* 'solved' the resulting methodological problem through a narrative that was in effect a deliberate compromise between these two modes of historical perception, the Latinate literate and the vernacular oral.[2] In yet other

---

[1]   The best and most recent concise introduction to the matter of Theodoric/Dietrich is by J. HEINZLE, *Einführung in die mittelhochdeutsche Dietrichepik* (Berlin and New York, 1999), esp. pp. 1-28. The most recent studies on Dietrich in medieval German historiography are F. HELLGARDT, "Dietrich von Bern in der deutschen Kaiserchronik", in: *Deutsche Literatur und Sprache von 1050-1200: Festschrift für Ursula Hennig zum 65. Geburtstag*, ed. A. FIEBIG and H.-J. SCHIEWER (Berlin, 1995), pp. 83-110, and S. MÜLLER, "Helden in gelehrten Welten: Zur Konzeption und Rezeption der Heldensagenpassagen in den *Quedlinburger Annalen*", in: *Theodisca: Beiträge zur althochdeutschen und altniederdeutschen Sprache und Literatur in der Kultur des frühen Mittelalters*, ed. W. HAUBRICHS *et al.* (Berlin and New York, 2000), pp. 364-386. Cf. also V. MILLET, "Das 12. Jahrhundert und die Heldensage", *Wolfram-Studien* 16 (2000), pp. 256-281, esp. pp. 262-270.

[2]   See esp. HELLGARDT, "Dietrich von Bern".

ways this process of cultural amalgamation is reflected in the visual arts, more specifically, in Romanesque stone sculpture.

The historical Theodoric had been an Arian Christian, and the Catholic Church demonized him as a murderous heretic who, at his death, went straight to hell. At least one such narrative seems to have enjoyed popular currency as well: the earliest visual record, part of the stone frieze that frames the famous portal of San Zeno in Verona (ca. 1138), shows Dietrich/Theodoric as a hunter riding towards the gates of hell in pursuit of his quarry.[3] It holds him up as a negative example, a *"rex stultus"*, as the inscription says in part, in 'his' own city and in programmatic contrast to the Frankish warrior Roland who appears on the opposite side of the door, slaying the pagan champion Ferragut in defence of Charlemagne's Christian empire.[4] In the context of this sculpture programme, Theodoric, aligned with Old Testament scenes, represents the old order, while Roland belongs to the new.

Roland, the *miles christianus*, is the one character from early, indigenous heroic legend whom the Church could thus co-opt without qualification, and that accounts of course for the frequency with which he or events associated with him were incorporated into the architectural designs of the clergy. Theodoric, as heroic legend saw him, belongs to a different sphere of action, a world without specifically Christian connotations and populated increasingly by giants, dwarfs and dragons besides human enemies.[5] Nonetheless the grow-

---

[3]   HEINZLE, *Einführung*, fig. 1. Cf. C. VERZAR BORNSTEIN, *Portals and Politics in the Early Italian City State: The Sculpture of Nicholaus in Context* (Parma, 1988), p. 151 and fig. 228, and C.B. KENDALL, *The Allegory of the Church: Romanesque Portals and Their Verse Inscriptions* (Toronto, Buffalo and New York, 1998), pp. 294-295. Concerning Theodoric/ Dietrich in the visual arts, see: W. STAMMLER, "Theoderich der Große (Dietrich von Bern) und die Kunst", in: ID., *Wort und Bild: Studien zu den Wechselbeziehungen zwischen Schrifttum und Bildkunst im Mittelalter* (Berlin, 1962), pp. 45-70; N.H. OTT, "Epische Stoffe in mittelalterlichen Bildzeugnissen", in: *Epische Stoffe des Mittelalters*, ed. V. MERTENS and U. MÜLLER (Stuttgart, 1984), pp. 449-474, esp. pp. 464 ff. Largely without scholarly relevance are the popular publications by A. JORN, *Folkekunstens Didrek* (Koebenhavn, 1978), and A. TUULSE *et al.*, *Gotlands Didrek* (Koebenhavn, 1978), although the latter in particular contains copious pictorial material.

[4]   The standard reference work on Roland in the visual arts is R. LEJEUNE and J. STIENNON, *La légende de Roland dans l'art du moyen âge*, 2 vols. (Brussels, 1966). Cf. OTT, "Epische Stoffe", pp. 450-455. The idea that the scenes at Verona have anything to do with the fight between Hildebrand and his son Hadubrand (VERZAR BORNSTEIN, *Portals and Politics*, p. 152 and figs. 230-231) can safely be discounted.

[5]   The encounter with giants as a motif of the legend is first attested in the Old English *Waldere* fragments: *Waldere*, ed. F. NORMAN (London, 1933), ll. II, 4-10. In spite of the proliferation of ornamental dragons in historiated initials it is probably no coincidence that the twelfth-century 'portrait' initial of the *Gesta Theoderici* fragment in MS Karlsruhe, Badische

ing desire or need to engage the visual imagination of the laity through appeals to their own cultural memory brought even those traditional narrative subjects into the context of church architecture which had to be adapted in some way to become part of the evangelical message.

Five examples from the period of around 1140 to the early thirteenth century have survived that involve Dietrich, as I shall now call him, of Bern. With only one exception, they come from the heartland of the Hohenstaufen empire, the German-speaking South-West. They make up a thematic group in the sense that always the same episode from the legend was incorporated into the picture programme of local churches, in the form of sculpted stone reliefs in various architectural settings: on the margins and in prominent position, in monastic and in parish churches, but usually in broad public view. The one exception (fig. 1) is a capital in the dark recesses of the choir in the minster at Basel (ca. 1180) which nonetheless represents the basic situation very clearly: a helmeted warrior with his sword raised above his head attempts to pull another warrior from the jaws of a winged, biped dragon. The rescuer's escutcheon, a lion rampant, designates him as Dietrich of Bern, in accordance with the legend.[6] Arguably the most public representation of this heroic moment (fig. 2) occurs atop the south transept of the parish church in Rosheim, built in the second quarter of the twelfth century further down the Rhine valley, in modern Alsace. Surmounting the pillar at the west side of the facade, we see the dragon's head and (more imposing here in proportion) the two warriors. The larger of the two appears to have been swallowed, at least in part, while his rescuer, as the local guide book tells it, thrusts his sword into the dragon's mouth.[7]

Not far to the south-west of Rosheim lies the Benedictine abbey church of Andlau (fig. 3) with an extensive stone frieze on the outside, also high above the ground.[8] Created around 1140, it begins on the north wall of the nave and

Landesbibliothek, 16, f. 2v, shows a dragon above Theodoric's head. Cf. STAMMLER, "Theoderich", fig. 7. Stammler himself remained sceptical (*ibid.*, p. 57).

[6] Examples from thirteenth-century written sources in W. GRIMM, *Die deutsche Heldensage*, 4th edn. (Darmstadt, 1957), pp. 156-157. For *Thidreks saga*, see *infra*, n. 21.

[7] G. POINSOT, *Sur la route romane: L'eglise Saint-Pierre et Saint-Paul et le canton de Rosheim* (Strasbourg, 1997), p. 25. On Rosheim, see also R. WILL, *Alsace Romane*, 3rd edn. ([Paris], 1982), pp. 213-228, and figs. 62-80, and D. BRETZ-MAHLER, *Rosheim* (s.l., 1979). A detailed description of the scene can be found in E. COLSMAN, *St. Peter und Paul in Rosheim* (Köln, 1991), pp. 62-64 and 224-225. For the date see *ibid.*, pp. 231-233.

[8] There is a (composite) photograph of the whole frieze in R. FORRER, "Les frises historiées de l'église romane d'Andlau", *Cahiers d'archéologie et d'histoire d'Alsace* 1931-1932, pp. 57-67 (reproduced in TUULSE *et al.*, *Gotlands Didrek*, p. 136, and A. BRUHIN, "Die romanischen Skulpturen der Abteikirche Andlau und das geistliche Spiel", in : *Literatur und Wandmalerei* I: *Erscheinungsformen höfischer Kultur und ihre Träger im Mittelalter*, ed. E.C.

runs all the way across the west facade. We are looking at a segment from the nave where the scene is paired with the figure of another warrior on horseback, seemingly a bystander who holds the reins of a second, riderless horse. 'Our' scene looks somewhat different again. This dragon lives in a cave, his victim still holds on to his shield, and the rescuer is portrayed with two swords: one that rests in its sheath by his side, while he seems to manipulate the other precariously between the victim's chest and left arm, close to, but not into, the dragon's mouth. The gesture seems counter-intuitive and will require further comment.

At Andlau, this heroic moment is part of an extensive picture programme that still awaits consistent and convincing explication. What seems clear is that the intention was to send a strong message to the local aristocracy. This message was somehow related to the almost equally enigmatic sculpture programme of the west portal and porch below. In the two remaining cases of visual representation of Dietrich's dragon fight, the relationship to the west portal is much more direct and in that sense unequivocal.

Some 120 miles to the east of Andlau, as the crow flies, lies the village of Altenstadt in southern Swabia (fig. 4). The parish church of St. Michael was constructed in the last two decades of the twelfth century, and our scene was pictured prominently in the tympanum above the only door of the west portal, as the only figural decoration of the whole west facade.[9] And here, the artist has made this curious motif of the two swords even more explicit: While the hero wields one of these weapons above his head, as he does in Basel, another one has fallen (or is falling) to the ground.

The masons and artists who were at work in Altenstadt appear to have moved from there to Straubing, another 120 miles to the north-east, in Lower Bavaria, where they produced a very similar design for the parish church of St.

LUTZ *et al.* (Tübingen, 2002), pp. 83-113, fig. 4). Will has published good pictures of individual segments (WILL, *Alsace*, figs. 103-111). The local guidebook by E. SOMMER, *Les sculptures romanes de l'église abbatiale d'Andlau* (Andlau, 1989), has useful outline drawings. Cf. R. WILL, "Die epischen Themen der romanischen Bauplastik des Elsaß", in: *Baukunst des Mittelalters in Europa: Hans Erich Kubach zum 75. Geburtstag*, ed. F.J. MUCH (Stuttgart, 1988), pp. 323-336.

[9] Cf. M. EXNER, "Ein neu entdecktes Wandbild des Hl. Christophorus in Altenstadt bei Schongau: Anmerkungen zur frühen Christophorus-Ikonographie", in: *Monumental: Festschrift für Michael Petzet*, ed. S. BÖNING-WEIS *et al.* (München, 1998), pp. 520-529, esp. p. 521 (for the date); K. PÖRNBACHER, *Basilika St. Michael Altenstadt*, 14th edn. (München and Zürich, 1997), p. 7; H. KARLINGER, *Die romanische Steinplastik in Altbayern und Salzburg* (Augsburg, 1928), pp. 95-96 and *passim*; R. STROBEL and M. WEIS, *Romanik in Altbayern* (Würzburg, 1994), pp. 291-314.

Peter (fig. 5)[10] – with one important difference: there is no indication in Straubing of a second sword besides the one in the hand of the dragon's attacker. But the location is the same: the tympanum above the only door of the west portal where the entering congregation could not fail to see it. In this context, it should be stressed that today's modest ambiance is deceptive. As their size alone would suggest, in the twelfth and thirteenth centuries the parish churches in the villages of Rosheim and Altenstadt and in what is now an outlying quarter of the city of Straubing stood at or near the centre of substantial semi-urban settlements, serving a comparatively large and sociologically diverse citizenry.

Although nobody has yet considered these five images systematically as a group, the connection with Dietrich has been suggested repeatedly, with specific reference most often to Basel[11] and Andlau.[12] On the other hand, Wolfgang Stammler, the first scholar to explore systematically the manifold links between Theodoric the Great and the visual arts, explicitly denied this connection, exempting only the example from Andlau.[13] Following mainly Adolph Goldschmidt's classical study on the pictorial background of the Psalter of St. Albans in Romanesque symbolic sculpture,[14] Stammler preferred to see the images at Altenstadt, Basel and others mentioned along with them as anonymous, generic variations within a much older paradigm of Christian iconography, designed to symbolize man's battle against evil and echoing various passages in the psalter and elsewhere in the bible.[15] In line with that, Joachim Heinzle, the current authority on the matter of Theodoric and his afterlife in literature and the arts, concludes (somewhat more cautiously) that the identification "remains uncertain".[16] I have already stated my own conclusion that these images were indeed meant quite specifically to evoke the legend of Dietrich, but my main interest is in the argument itself. Put simply, the question is:

---

[10] KARLINGER, *Steinplastik*, pp. 96-97; STROBEL and WEIS, *Romanik*, pp. 191-198.

[11] See for example H. REINHARDT, *Das Basler Münster* (Basel, 1961), p. 25, or *Das Basler Münster*, ed. Münsterbaukommission Basel (Basel, 1982), p. 148 (D. RUDLOFF) and caption on p. 131.

[12] See for example, WILL, *Alsace*, p. 262.

[13] STAMMLER, "Theoderich", p. 61. BRUHIN, "Die romanischen Skulpturen", pp. 101 f., has recently reached the same conclusion.

[14] A. GOLDSCHMIDT, *Der Albani-Psalter in Hildesheim und seine Beziehung zur symbolischen Kirchenskulptur des XII. Jahrhunderts* (Berlin, 1895), esp. pp. 78-79 and *passim*.

[15] STAMMLER, "Theoderich", p. 61. He accepts Andlau on the basis of *Thidreks saga* (see *infra*), as does WILL, "Die epischen Themen". Rosheim has usually remained outside this discussion.

[16] HEINZLE, *Einführung*, p.142: "Doch bleibt die Deutung dieser Darstellungen auf die in Frage stehende Sage unsicher, denn das Bild-Motiv ist zunächst einmal ein Topos der christlichen Ikonographie, der seit der Spätantike breit bezeugt ist".

what constitutes visual identity in such visio-verbal contexts?[17] How do essentially unstable oral traditions[18] come to relate to an existing iconography that is itself varied and in flux, and how can we reconstruct this relationship in ways that are methodologically sound and historically plausible?

Strangely enough, what seems the most obvious argument against the identification of these images with Dietrich has never been made consistently: while the surviving verbal narratives do indeed preserve elements of the kind of adventure that appears to be depicted in these scenes, when it comes to detail, they disagree conspicuously among themselves and also with individual instances of this visual representation. The three texts in question are also much later and circulated in different parts of the Germanic world. They are: a German heroic poem titled *Virginal* in modern scholarship, one of a number of such epic accounts that sprung up around Dietrich in late medieval upper Germany;[19] a local legend from the Swiss canton of Bern, first reported in a chronicle of ca. 1420 and linked in mysterious ways to the coat of arms of the north Italian Visconti family;[20] and the Old Norse prose *Saga af Thidrek af Bern*. This saga was compiled for King Haakon of Norway around the middle of the thirteenth century, but it is based on older continental sources and contains the most detailed of these accounts. For my present purpose I shall limit comparison to this text.

Thidreks saga relates[21] that Dietrich and his companion of the moment, the giant Fasold, come across a large low-flying dragon weighed down by the body of a man whom he has "taken off his shield"[22] while he slept and swallowed up to his armpits. But the man is still alive, and, heeding his pleas for help, Dietrich and Fasold attack the dragon with their swords. It turns out, however, that the dragon's skin is too hard for these weapons and the man instructs Fasold to retrieve his own sword from the dragon's mouth.[23] This sword has magic pow

---

[17] Cf. M. CURSCHMANN, "Marcolf or Aesop? The question of identity in visio-verbal contexts", *Studies in Iconography* 21 (2000), pp. 1-45.

[18] In the form, most likely, of informal prose narrative. On this point, see: M. CURSCHMANN, "Eddic poetry and continental heroic legend: The case of the third lay of Gudrun (*Gudrunarqvida*)", in: *Germania: Comparative Studies in Old Germanic Languages and Literatures*, ed. D.G. CALDER and T.C. CHRISTY (Wolfeboro, 1988), pp. 143-160.

[19] The most commonly cited edition is that of the Heidelberg text by J. ZUPITZA, in: *Deutsches Heldenbuch*, 5 (Berlin, 1870; repr. Dublin and Zürich, 1968). See strr. 147-183.

[20] See HEINZLE, *Einführung*, pp. 141-142 and fig. 8.

[21] *Thidriks saga af Bern*, ed. H. BERTELSEN, 2 vols. (Koebenhavn, 1908-1911), 1, cc. 189-190 (pp. 196-199) and 194 (pp. 201-203), respectively. The reference to Dietrich's shield and coat of arms (*supra*, p. 3) is 1, c. 32 (p. 42).

[22] P. 197: "... *tok mic sovandi af minom scildi*".

[23] That at least is the clear implication. The text first refers to it as "a" sword (p. 198): "*Tac*

ers and Fasold and Dietrich manage to slay the beast without simultaneously wounding its victim. The man they have thus freed is called Sistram or Sintram, the three men become friends and together they soon find Sintram's shield. Eventually, Dietrich by himself also retrieves Sintram's horse and brings it back to him.

Looking again now at Andlau (fig. 3) and Altenstadt (fig. 4), we find that these visual accounts disagree in several important details with the *Thidreks saga* narrative. But there is a common core as well, a motif in which verbal and visual representation overlap. The success of the operation depends on a second sword that has to be extracted from the dragon's own jaws. The Andlau artisan offers a comparatively stylized version of this key moment. With his own sword safely back in its sheath, the attacker secures the magic weapon from Sintram's side. In other words, the second sword in the picture is Sintram's sword, and it is actually being withdrawn.[24] The Altenstadt artist chose to portray the same constellation a little more vividly and to concentrate on the next move in the epic succession. In the light of the verbal account, it seems that the sword that drops is the attacker's own sword; the sword he swings is the one he has just acquired.

The most conspicuous difference between the verbal and visual accounts of this episode is that the surviving text also features two rescuers. On the other hand that is the sort of arrangement that could easily be absorbed by the pre-existing iconographic tradition, the pictorial code into which this engagement had to be translated in order to function in this different environment. In addition, the example from Basel (fig. 1), where the rescuer bears on his shield the escutcheon that *Thidreks saga* attributes to Dietrich of Bern, makes it clear that popular consciousness did associate this adventure specifically with Dietrich. We will nevertheless have to take a closer look at both older and contemporary dragon-fight iconography to understand what exactly has happened here.

Human or superhuman figures encountering the forces of evil in the shape of dragons and other large beasts abound in Romanesque and pre-Romanesque religious art.[25] Generally speaking, there are those who are swallowed and

---

her sverd i kiefta drekanom".

[24] As noticed also by WILL, *Alsace*, p. 262.

[25] In conjunction with the dragon-fight motif in Germanic literature, a small, but useful collection of such images from the twelfth century and earlier, including our examples from Basel (fig. 12) and Andlau (fig. 13.2) as well as the Theodoric initial mentioned *supra*, n. 5 (fig. 13.1), has been assembled by M.L. RUGGIERINI, "L'eroe germanico contro avversari mostruosi: Tra testo e iconografia", in: *La funzione dell'eroe germanico: Storicità, metafora, paradigma*, ed. T. PÀROLI (Rome, 1995), pp. 201-257. An older special study that is also still useful in this context is: P. PAULSEN, *Drachenkämpfer, Löwenritter und Heinrichsage. Eine*

those who prevail. Those who are swallowed most often go headfirst,[26] a notable exception being the helmeted knight in chain-mail on a late twelfth-century tympanum that may once have been part of the entrance to the castle chapel and is now kept in the Wartburg museum (fig. 6). That the shield dangling from his neck displays the imperial eagle may be a clue to a topical context that eludes us today. Vernacular poets of the time are fond of commenting on the sometimes strange ways of the Thuringian court.[27]

Some evidently more successful combatants are related to specific textual traditions – hagiographic (and relatively late) in the case of St. George,[28] biblical in that of the archangel Michael in his battle against the dragon of the Apocalypse, as he appears, for example, in one of his two basic fighting stances on a relief of ca. 1120 in the church of St. Nicholas at Ipswich (fig. 7).[29] Many such scenes, however, are generic,[30] and in certain cases such traditions might convert into an *ad hoc* response to a particular text. The argument in favour of the generic anonymity of our composition has traditionally been made with a view particularly to a historiated initial in the Psalter of St. Albans (fig. 8).[31] Responding to the psalmist's words *"dominus, in adiutorium meum intende"* (Ps 69, 2), Christ reaches down from a cloud and rescues a human from the

---

Studie über die Kirchentür von Valthjófsstad auf Island (Köln-Graz, 1966).

[26] A splendid example is the abacus relief on the south portal of Verona cathedral from the middle of the twelfth century. See C. ENLART, *L'art Roman en Italie: L'architecture et la décoration* (Paris, 1924), Pl. 80 (2). Cf. W. ANDERSON, "Romanesque sculpture in south Sweden", *Art Studies* 6 (1928), pp. 49-70, fig. 74, where this motif is linked to Scandinavian examples. See also RUGGERINI, "L'eroe", fig. 14.1.

[27] See especially Wolfram von Eschenbach, *Parzival*, ed. K. LACHMANN (Berlin and Leipzig, 1926), ll. 297, 16-30, and Walther's poem against Gerhard Atze: *Walther von der Vogelweide, Leich, Lieder, Sangsprüche*, 14th edn. by C. CORMEAU (Berlin and New York, 1996), No. 73, III. E. NEUBAUER, *Die romanischen skulpierten Bogenfelder in Sachsen und Thüringen* (Berlin, 1972), pp. 65-67 and fig. 23, notes earlier attempts to link the scene with Dietrich or other heroic themes, but opts for "einen allgemeinen christlich-symbolischen Sinn" with secular connotations (p. 66).

[28] See for example RUGGERINI, "L'eroe", fig. 10.2, and KENDALL, *The Allegory*, fig. 19 and pp. 176-178 (tympanum in the cathedral of St. George, Ferrara; 1132-35).

[29] Apc 12, 7 ff. The example from Ipswich is also cited by RUGGERINI, "L'eroe", fig. 8.2. The dislocated stone slab that bears this relief along with an Anglo-Saxon *titulus* has been reset in the north wall of the chancel. For the date, see: K.J. GALBRAITH, "Early sculpture at St. Nicholas Church, Ipswich", *Proceedings of the Suffolk Institute of Archaeology* 31 (1967-1969), pp. 172-184, esp. p. 176. The same basic type in RUGGERINI, "L'eroe", figs. 6, 7.1 (St. Michael's in Hoveringham. A better photograph in L. MUSSET, *Angleterre romane*, II ([Paris], 1988), fig. 151) and 7.2.

[30] See for example RUGGERINI, "L'eroe", fig. 16.2, and *infra*.

[31] MS Hildesheim, Domschatz, G 1, p. 207. See *supra*, n. 14.

mouth of a winged dragon who seems submerged in water, a reminiscence perhaps of the iconography of Noah. Actually, the resemblance here is mostly thematic, not iconographic. The specific iconographic framework that was best suited to accommodate an act of armed intervention was the one associated with the archangel Michael. The relief at Ipswich (fig. 7) shows Michael attacking with a sword. More frequent, particularly on the continent, is a second basic variant where Michael thrusts a lance into the dragon's open mouth.[32] An interesting variation of this second type occurs in a prayer book written and illuminated around 1000 in north Italy (fig. 9):[33] while Michael transfixes the dragon with his lance, he simultaneously pulls a human soul from its jaws. Clearly, that is the kind of iconographic perspective from which Dietrich's legendary feat could be seen as a secular analogue with the potential for visual integration into ecclesiastical picture programmes.

There is no way of knowing whether those who recognized this possibility and effected this transformation knew the story as it surfaces in *Thidreks saga*, featuring not one, but two dragon-fighters. Narrative elaborations of the basic man-against-beast paradigm do occur in continental Romanesque stone relief sculpture, not to mention manuscript illumination,[34] and range geographically

---

[32] The earliest example of this type is a Carolingian ivory relief in A. GOLDSCHMIDT, *Die Elfenbeinskulpturen aus der Zeit der karolingischen und sächsischen Kaiser*, 2 vols. (Berlin, 1914-1918), 1, No. 11a (Pl. VI). Many more, mostly in manuscripts, have been collected by J.J.G. ALEXANDER, *Norman Illumination at Mont St. Michel 966-1100* (Oxford, 1970), pp. 88-100. A relief from the first half of the twelfth century on the south portal of the parish church of Öster Starup in Jutland, Denmark, shows this lance-bearing Michael seated (!): ANDERSON, "Romanesque sculpture", fig. 22. E. LEHMANN, *"Angelus Jenensis"*, *Zeitschrift für Kunstwissenschaft* 7 (1953), pp. 145-164, advanced the theory that the sword-wielding Michael is in fact an English 'specialty' with limited influence on the continent. While it is true that this variant is particularly frequent in England (and Scandinavia), the theory remains to be tested against a larger body of material.

[33] MS London, British Library, Egerton 3763, f. 104v. The manuscript is a psalter and prayer book supposedly made for Archbishop Arnulf II of Milan. For a description see G. WARNER, *Descriptive Catalogue of the Illuminated Manuscripts in the Library of C.W. Dyson Perrins*, 2 vols. (Oxford, 1920), 1, pp. 130-135, and 2, Pl. 51a. The most recent discussion (with bibliography) is by J. LOWDEN, "Illuminated books and the liturgy. Some observations", in *Objects, Images and the Word: Art in the Service of the Liturgy*, ed. C. HOURIHANE (Princeton, 2003), pp. 17-53, esp. pp. 33-39.

[34] Just two famous examples: The initial R at the beginning of the Dijon copy (ca. 1110-1120) of Gregory's *Moralia in Hiob*: RUGGERINI, "L'eroe", fig. 1. Colour photograph in: W. SAUERLÄNDER, *Initialen: Ein Versuch über das verwirrte Verhältnis von Schrift und Bild im Mittelalter* (Wolfenbüttel, 1994), fig. 17. The other is the even more extravagant initial A in the Canterbury copy (ca. 1130) of Flavius Josephus: SAUERLÄNDER, *Initialen*, fig. 16 (colour photograph in: *English Romanesque Art 1066-1200*, ed. G. ZARNECKI (London, 1984), p. 52). Noteworthy is Sauerländer's description of this image as "ein Buchstabenbild ..., das sozusagen

from the famous general melee that envelops the so-called *Bestiensäule* in the crypt of the cathedral in Freising to the lesser known sequence of two scenes sculpted around the bowl of a baptismal font made for the parish church of Munkbrarup, Denmark (now in north Germany):a royal personage, presumably the subsequent victim, sits on his throne in his palace. His right hand is raised and his left holds a sword. Outside, a sentinel sounds his horn. In the second scene (fig. 10), a huge lion has begun to devour a warrior who attempts to defend himself with his sword, while his companions or servants try to rescue him with lances (the second from behind).[35] Although the subject of this composition has not been identified convincingly, the general message is clear: "*Salva me ex ore leonis*".[36] Both the picture column in Freising and the font in Munkbarup date from around 1200 and offer interesting thematic and iconographic parallels to the rescue of Sintram.[37] Thus it would not have been unusual for twelfth-century sculptors to depict a two-man attack on Sintram's tormentor, had they or their instructors been motivated to do so by what they heard. But even in the unlikely event that the oral tradition current in upper Germany in the twelfth century coincided in every detail with what we read in *Thidreks saga*, in Sintram's case the transformation went in the opposite direction and, coincidentally or deliberately, focussed that particular subject in a way that allowed it to function in a variety of architectural settings. The question remains whether under those circumstances the secular subject would or could nevertheless retain its identity.

We have another, much more widespread example of this process of vernacularisation that may offer additional suggestions. In the Germanic north, another dragon slayer, Sigurd, entered church art as a highly distinctive fig-

---

zwischen dem ritterlichen Heldenepos und dem 'Libera me ex ore leonis' ... des Psalmisten oszilliert".

[35] See the fold-out diagram in K. FREYER, "Schleswigsche Taufsteine: Ein Beitrag zu den Anfängen der deutschen Plastik", *Monatshefte für Kunstwissenschaft* 12 (1919), pp. 113-124, fig. 8a. Good photographs can be found in I.-L. KOLSTRUP, "Munkbrarupfontens udsmykning", in: *1. Skandinaviske symposium om romanske stenarbeijder* (Viborg, 1989), pp. 139-154.

[36] Ps 22, 21, echoed by Paul in II Tim 4, 17: "*Et liberatus sum de ore leonis*". This has already been recognized by M. MACKEPRANG, *Danmarks middelalderlige døbefonte* (Koebenhavn, 1941), pp. 349-351. The king in question could of course be King David himself, as argued by KOLSTRUP, "Munkbrarupfontens udsmykning", but the narrative seems too elaborate and detailed for that. For bringing me up to speed on the subject of Munkbrarup I wish to thank Harriet Sonne de Torrens, Toronto.

[37] One of the scenes on the picture column in Freising, a man attacking a dragon devouring a second human, has been linked repeatedly to Dietrich. The best photographs can be found in: F. DIETHEUER, "Die 'Bestiensäule' in der Freisinger Domkrypta", *Oberbayerisches Archiv* 100 (1976), pp. 339-380.

ure.[38]From tenth-century memorial crosses on the Isle of Man to wooden church portals from the south of twelfth- and thirteenth-century Norway (fig. 11),[39] he is always seen killing 'his' dragon, Fafnir, from below and in a crouch.[40] Earlier Swedish stone carvings, especially the rune stone of Ramsund (1030) (fig. 12), show that the woodcarvers used in this instance a pre-Christian pictorial convention – pre-Christian at least in the iconographic sense. It reflects the common knowledge that Sigurd dug himself a large pit in the ground, and when the serpent-like Fafnir crawled over it, Sigurd thrust his sword into his heart.[41] That moment became the hallmark of this encounter in visual representation, so much so that it is clear whose dragon fight this is even where the motif appears entirely without context and in extreme shorthand, as it does on a Norwegian picture stone from Tanberg (ca. 1100) (fig. 13).[42] Not

---

[38] The basic modern study is E. PLOSS, *Siegfried-Sigurd, der Drachenkämpfer: Untersuchungen zur germanisch-deutschen Heldensage* (Köln and Graz, 1966), esp. pp. 79-98. S. Margeson has published more detailed comments on the Manx crosses and a critical overview in the larger context of the Volsung legend: S. MARGESON, "On the iconography of the Manx crosses", in: *The Viking Age in the Isle of Man*, ed. Ch. FELL *et al.* (London, 1983), pp. 95-106, and EAD., "The Volsung legend in medieval art", in: *Medieval Iconography and Narrative: A Symposium*, ed. F.G. ANDERSEN *et al.* (Odense, 1980), pp. 183-211. Cf. also S. MARGESON, "Saga-Geschichten auf Stabkirchenportalen", in: *Frühe Holzkirchen im nördlichen Europa*, ed. K. ALENS (Hamburg, 1981: *Veröffentlichungen des Helms-Museums* 39), pp. 459-480. K. Düwel's detailed investigation concentrates more specifically on Sigurd's dealings with Fafnir and Regin: K. DÜWEL, "Zur Ikonographie und Ikonologie der Sigurddarstellungen", in: *Zum Problem der Deutung frühmittelalterlicher Bildinhalte*, ed. H. ROTH (Sigmaringen, 1986), pp. 221-271. It includes a discussion of the various literary sources (pp. 222-229) that is lacking in the shorter English version: K. DÜWEL, "On the Sigurd representation in Great Britain and Scandinavia", in: *Languages and Cultures: Studies in Honor of Edgar C. Polomé*, ed. M.A. JAZAYERY and W. WINTER (Berlin and New York, 1988), pp. 133-156.

[39] For the Norwegian door-jambs see the new descriptions by E.B. HOHLER, *Norwegian Stave Church Sculpture*, 2 vols. (Oslo, 1999). Hylestad (I): 1, cat. No. 114 (pp. 178-180; 2, Pls. 254-256); Lardal: 1, cat. No. 123 (pp. 185-186; 2, Pl. 273); Mæl: 1, cat. No. 145 (pp. 195-196; 2, Pl. 314). Hylestad (colour photograph in MARGESON, "Saga-Geschichten", Pl. E) is generally dated before or around 1200; the others are later. The thematically related jamb planks from Austad, Uvdal and Vegusdal do not contain the killing scene.

[40] The picture type has been clearly identified and described by DÜWEL, "On the Sigurd representation", p. 134. Margeson's "diagnostic features" ("The Volsung legend", p. 184) pertain to the extended narrative context.

[41] See e.g. the prose introduction to *Fáfnismál: Edda: Die Lieder des Codex Regius nebst verwandten Denkmälern*, ed. G. NECKEL, H. KUHN, 3rd edn. (Heidelberg, 1962), p. 180. The medallion surrounding the crouching figure on the Hylestad portal is a stylistic feature and not necessarily reminiscent of Sigurd's pit, as Margeson assumes (MARGESON, "The Volsung legend", p. 196).

[42] Cf. PLOSS, *Siegfried-Sigurd*, pp. 64 and 85. In this case I side with Ploss against Margeson (stressing the fragmentary (unfinished?) character of the piece; MARGESON, "The

unlike the oral tradition that produced the image the artists who shaped and established it focussed on special, distinctive details around which narrative could cluster.

Let us now return to Dietrich. Obviously it is a similarly defining motif that imparts identity to Dietrich's dragon fight in visual representation: the need for the magic sword in the verbal account generates the duplication of weapons and the potentially ambiguous gesture we have observed in Andlau (fig. 3).[43] Other details of this negotiation between two very different, open-ended systems of signification must remain obscure. Clearly in Andlau the artist could give more narrative scope to the episode than it was accorded, for example, in Altenstadt (fig. 4). It therefore seems likely that the horseman to the right was meant to represent Dietrich as well, emerging from a subsequent episode in *Thidreks saga* in which he finds and returns Sintram's horse.[44] As for the rest – two rescuers or one? The cave behind the dragon and the shield in Sintram's hand – we simply lack the criteria to distinguish between icono-graphic convention and potential echoes of verbal storytelling.

The one significant constant linking the visual and the verbal in this in-stance is that duplication of weapons, the modus operandi that is specific to this dragon fight. It is made explicit in Andlau and Altenstadt, but it also explains,

---

Volsung Legend", p. 194) and Düwel (DÜWEL, "Zur Ikonographie", p. 247). On the other hand, what should definitely be excluded is the eleventh-century lintel at Ault Hucknall (Derbyshire), claimed for Sigurd by LEHMANN, "*Angelus Jenensis*", p. 160 (fig. 11).

[43] Although it has no bearing on the present investigation, it should be mentioned that two of the Norwegian door-jambs, from Lardal and from Mæl, show Sigurd wielding two swords. S. MARGESON, "Sigurd with two swords", *Mediaeval Scandinavia* 12 (1988), pp. 194-200, has tried to reconcile this with literary accounts. Düwel's brief comments (DÜWEL, "Zur Ikonographie", p. 245) are more nuanced. What needs further explanation is the fact that in both these cases Sigurd's crouch has been transformed into a sitting position. – A much later Swedish composition, part of a stone frieze on the west portal of the church at Dalhem (Gotland), attributed to the so-called Egypticus workshop (ca. 1330), comes very close to the continental Dietrich scenes in content and iconographic detail, including the presence of two weapons: A robed male figure sits (!) opposite a winged dragon who has begun to devour another robed male figure headfirst. The would-be rescuer keeps his left hand on the hilt of his sheathed sword, while his right arm brings down a large club on the dragon's head, an action that corresponds to the psalmist's words (Ps 73, 14), "*tu confregisti capita Leviathan*". See J. ROOSVAL, *Sveriges kyrkor: Gotland*, 4.2 (Stockholm, 1959), pp. 179-181, and figs. 200-201. Another photograph in TUULSE *et al.*, *Gotlands Didrek*, p. 62.

[44] See *supra*, p. 6, and M. CURSCHMANN, "Wort – Schrift – Bild: Zum Verhältnis von volkssprachigem Schrifttum und bildender Kunst vom 12. bis zum 16. Jahrhundert", in: *Mittelalter und frühe Neuzeit: Übergänge, Umbrüche und Neuansätze*, ed. W. HAUG (Tübingen, 1999), pp. 378-470, esp. p. 385. There is no basis in any of the surviving texts for Will's assertion that the horseman is Dietrich's mentor Hildebrand (WILL, *Alsace*, p. 262).

by implication, what we see in Rosheim (fig. 2). Adjusting in his own way to the exigencies of space this artist offers a drastically foreshortened version of the whole scene and, as a result, shows only one sword. But anyone familiar with the Dietrich story would recognize it as that second, magic one that is not thrust into, but being pulled from the dragon's mouth. Visualization of a heroic moment had introduced a significant variant into the received pictorial code, and, even in extreme shorthand, that variant signals the identity of the new subject. Similarly, its absence means loss of identity unless the artist compensated in some way. That is what the artist did in Basel, my very first example (fig. 1): taking an altogether more distant view of his subject, he identified the rescuer in chivalric fashion by 'naming' him through his coat of arms.

Special questions of identification arise as we conclude this survey with St. Peter's in Straubing (fig. 5). Although the workshop seems the same, the tympanum above the west portal there is hardly a copy of its counterpart at Altenstadt. Only the head of the victim is still visible and there is no trace of a second sword or any other visual marker to individualize the design. If one considers in addition the geographic distance from the cluster in the south-west, this may well signal a certain loss of identity. The larger context points in that direction as well. Just around the corner, in the same position above the south portal of the church, we find two large beasts, a griffin and a lion, confronting each other.[45] And only a few miles to the north-east, at the church of the Premonstratensian abbey of Windberg, stylistically close and roughly contemporaneous, a similarly conventional scene can be seen in very similar position, above the north portal (fig. 14): a single, bareheaded warrior drawing his sword to confront a lion whose head is turned outwards, towards the viewer. In other words and speaking in typological terms, while the Straubing tympanum, too, may well have been meant to evoke the memory of Dietrich's rescue of Sintram, its actual execution resorts again to the general arsenal of types of combat between human and beast where the identity of the subject is being subsumed under broader categories of visualization.[46]

---

[45] See STROBEL and WEIS, *Romanik*, fig. 49.

[46] In this sense, K.-H. Clasen has made a valid point: "Gegen eine unmittelbare Beziehung zu der deutschen Heldensage spricht wohl auch der Umstand, daß der Drache, wie in Windberg in Bayern, durch einen Löwen ersetzt werden kann" (K.-H. CLASEN, "Die Überwindung des Bösen: Ein Beitrag zur Ikonographie des frühen Mittelalters", in: *Neue Beiträge deutscher Forschung: Wilhelm Worringer zum 60. Geburtstag*, ed. E. FIDDER (Königsberg, 1943), pp. 13-36, p. 29). A comparable example from the Sigurd corpus would be the 'Spanish Sigurd', a relief at the west portal of San Guesa cathedral (eleventh/twelfth century; see PLOSS, *Siegfried-Sigurd*, fig. 24) which Margeson does not mention and Düwel excludes altogether (DÜWEL, "Zur Ikonographie", p. 248). It is true that Sigurd's posture conforms only marginally to the standard

As the Windberg analogy takes us back to the neutral zone of generic representation, it also helps explain why Dietrich's heroic feat was chosen on occasion to appear in such prominent location, as the only figural ornamentation of the main entrance into a parish church – in Altenstadt and perhaps in Straubing. What all the examples I have cited have in common is that a pre-existing formula of Christian iconography was applied and modified to remind the faithful or would-be faithful of their own, secular culture in an architectural environment devoted to visual propagation of the Christian faith. In specific instances, this adaptation of a motif from indigenous heroic legend can serve several purposes. Methodologically speaking, as long as the goal is to reconstruct their collective relationship to the verbal tradition, these images need to be considered as a group. When it comes to purpose and function, on the other hand, we need to consider them case by case, in their own programmatic context, beginning with location. But that would of course be the subject of another paper. Space allows only a few concluding remarks concerning one of these cases, Altenstadt.[47]

It will be remembered that the parish church of Altenstadt was dedicated to the archangel Michael. A parishioner who entered from the west end of the basilica (fig. 4), say, in the year 1200 and, as he did so, took with him this image of a famous act of deliverance in secular narrative will have experienced a sense of positive identification in two ways. While the secular subject engaged his sympathetic attention, the location related it to Christian teaching as an act of salvation. Here, the rescue of Sintram may signal deliverance from the forces of evil, but there is no need to think of this in allegorical or typological terms, as has been proposed for Sigurd's appearance on the portals of the Norwegian stave churches.[48] Dietrich does not become a type of Christ, for example. The relationship is both less complicated and more naturally persuasive, and in Altenstadt we can see to this day how it worked in practice. Once inside,

---

type, but the context, the smith (Regin) directly below, confirms that the Sigurd legend was indeed what the designer had in mind.

[47] It has been discussed in more detail in my paper, "Heroic legend and scriptural message: The case of St. Michael's in Altenstadt", in: *Objects, Images, and the Word*, pp. 94-104.

[48] The typology thesis has been advanced by Düwel who sees Sigurd "as an indigenous type within a semi-biblical typology, pointing at Christ as antitype". DÜWEL, "Sigurd representations", p. 147. A review of the preceding debate on these questions is provided on pp. 143-145. For J.L. Byock, on the other hand, a christianized Sigurd acts "as a symbolic protector of the church" (J.L. BYOCK, "Sigurdr Fáfnisbani: An Eddic hero carved on Norwegian stave churches", in: *Poetry in the Scandinavian Middle Ages*, ed. T. PÀROLI (Spoleto, 1990), pp. 619-628, esp. p. 628). Far more sceptical with respect to this kind of cultural appropriation are MARGESON, especially in "Saga-Geschichten", pp. 474, 478-480, and HOHLER, *Norwegian Stave Church Sculpture*, 1, pp. 22-23, and 2, pp. 57-58, 103.

the viewer would encounter the patron saint of the church in analogous action (fig. 15): one of the four reliefs that grace the lobes of the beautiful quatrefoil sandstone font shows the archangel Michael defeating the dragon of the Apocalypse, *"ille magnus serpens antiquus qui vocatur Diabolus et Satanas"* (Apc 12, 9), whose satanic soul escapes to the left, in poignant and possibly even intended visual parallel and contrast to Sintram's exodus.[49] As the imagery returns to its iconographic roots, as it were, the familiar story resonates in the not-so-familiar: a synergetic relationship has been created in which the sacred and the profane, the memory of oral culture and the precepts of scriptural culture are reconciled through visual experience.[50]

[49] Complementing this act of exorcism the three remaining main surfaces show the madonna and Christ child, Christ's baptism, and John the Baptist with the lamb of God (KARLINGER, *Steinplastik*, figs. pp. 170, 172; PÖRNBACHER, *Altenstadt*, p. 21 (colour)). The font dates from the time of construction of the building (cf. G. PUDELKO, *Romanische Taufsteine* (Berlin, 1932), pp. 112, 133, 136; the date given for both the building and the font by C S DRAKE, *The Romanesque Fonts of Northern Europe and Scandinavia* (Woodbridge, 2002), p. 97: "mid-twelfth century", is definitely wrong), as does the newly discovered and restored, gigantic Christophorus fresco on the inside of the west wall (cf. EXNER, "Ein neu entdecktes Wandbild", fig. 1). The choir fresco that shows Michael in his second major role, weighing souls on judgment day, is considerably later.

[50] The famous Arthurian frieze above the north portal of Modena cathedral has recently been shown to stand in similarly significant relationship to the legend of the patron saint of the church, St. Gemigniano, as depicted on the opposite south portal. See J. FOX-FRIEDMAN, "Messianic visions: Modena cathedral and the crusades", *Res* 25 (1994), pp. 77-95.

Fig. 1   Basel, minster, relief on a choir capital: Dietrich rescues Sintram.
Photo from *Das Basler Münster*, ed. Die Münsterbaukommission (Basel, 1982), fig. p. 131

Fig. 2   Rosheim, St. Peter and Paul's, relief atop the south transept facade: Dietrich rescues Sintram. Photo from D. BRETZ-MAHLER, *Rosheim* (s.l., 1979), fig. 23.

Fig. 3   Andlau, abbey church, segment of the outside frieze, north wall of the
nave: Dietrich rescues Sintram and returns his horse. Photo Michael
Curschmann.

Fig. 4   Altenstadt, St. Michael's, tympanum relief above the west portal: Dietrich rescues Sintram. Photo Rupert Neumayr.

Fig. 5   Straubing, St. Peter's, tympanum relief above the west portal: Dietrich
          rescues Sintram (?). Photo Michael Curschmann.

Fig. 6   Eisenach, Wartburg Museum, tympanum relief: Dragon devouring a
         knight. Photo from W. NOTH and K.G. BEYER, *Die Wartburg: Denk-
         mal und Museum* (Leipzig, 1983), fig. 94.

Fig. 7   Ipswich, St. Nicholas, relief on a dislocated slab, now in the chancel
          wall: St. Michael attacking the dragon. Photo from K.J. GALBRAITH,
          "Early sculpture at St. Nicholas Church, Ipswich", *Proceedings of the
          Suffolk Institute of Archaeology* 31 (1967-1969), p. 24.

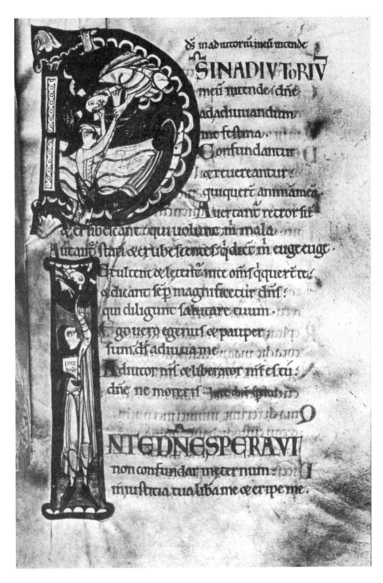

Fig. 8   MS Hildesheim, Domschatz, G 1 ('Psalter of St. Albans'), p. 207,
historiated initial at the beginning of Ps 69: Christ rescues the psalmist
from the mouth of a dragon. Photo from *The St. Albans Psalter (Albani
Psalter)*, ed. O. PÄCHT *et al.* (London, 1960), Pl. 62.

Fig. 9   MS London, British Library, Egerton 3763, f. 104v: St. Michael transfixes the dragon and rescues a soul. Photo British Library.

Fig. 10 Munkbarup (Schleswig-Holstein, north Germany), former parish
church, baptismal font: Part of a relief featuring a royal figure attacked
by a lion. Photo from K. FREYER, "Schleswegsche Taufsteine: Ein
Beitrag zu den Anfängen der deutschen Plastik", *Monatshefte für
Kunstwissenschaft* 12 (1919), pp. 113-124, fig. 8.

Fig. 11 Oslo University, Olsaksamlingen, right door-jamb from the west portal
of the (destroyed) stave church of Hylestad, detail: Sigurd killing Fafnir. Photo from D. LINDHOLM and W. ROGGENKAMP, *Stave Churches
in Norway* (London, 1969), Pl. 48.

Fig. 12 Ramsund (Södermanland, Sweden), picture stone with scenes from the legend of Sigurd. Photo from E. PLOSS, *Siegfried-Sigurd, der Drachenkämpfer* (Köln and Graz, 1966), fig. 15.

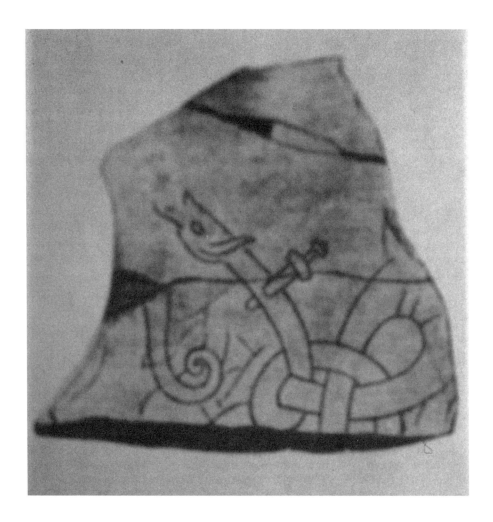

Fig. 13 Oslo University, Oldsaksamlingen, picture stone fragment from Tanberg: [Sigurd] killing Fafnir. Photo from E. PLOSS, *Siegfried-Sigurd,
der Drachenkämpfer* (Köln and Graz, 1966), fig. 7.

Fig. 14 Windberg, abbey church, tympanum relief above the north portal: A
man attacks a lion. Photo Michael Curschmann.

Fig. 15 Altenstadt, St. Michael's, baptismal font, relief scene: St. Michael
transfixes the dragon. Photo from H. KARLINGER, *Die romanische
Steinplastik in Altbayern und Salzburg* (Augsburg, 1928), p.. 171.

Perceptions of the History of the Church in the Early Middle Ages

ROSAMOND MCKITTERICK

One of the most crucial aspects of the reception and dissemination of Christian writing in the Carolingian world, that is, the area ruled by the Franks in the eighth and ninth centuries, was the perception of their original context.[1] This perception of the original impetus for, and the time and place of, the composition of Christian theology, exegesis, moral guidance and ascetic instruction was itself shaped by a small group of seminal texts concerned with the history of the Church and the Christian faith.

In a companion piece to this paper, I have focussed in detail on three of these texts in particular.[2] The most influential of them was the *Historia ecclesiastica* of Eusebius (*ca.* 260-339) in the Latin translation by Rufinus (*ca.* 345-410).[3] It is important to stress that this Latin version is essentially an interpretation and edition of Eusebius and not a literal translation,[4] quite apart from the fact that Rufinus added two new books and cut most of Eusebius's book x.[5]

---

[1] I argue the case more fully for this in my forthcoming *The Migration of Ideas in the Early Middle Ages* (Cambridge). Because this paper is part of my current research and one of a clutch of related papers, I hope I may be forgiven for citing some of the others in the course of this discussion.

[2] R. MCKITTERICK, "The Carolingian Church and the book", in: *The Church and the Book*, ed. R. SWANSON (Oxford, 2003: *Studies in Church History* 37).

[3] *Eusebius Werke*, 2: *Die Kirchengeschichte und die lateinische Übersetzung des Rufinus*, ed. E. SCHWARZ and T. MOMMSEN (Leipzig, 1903).

[4] See T. CHRISTENSEN, *Rufinus of Aquileia and the Historia ecclesiastica Lib. VIII-IX of Eusebius* (Copenhagen, 1989: *Historisk-filosofiske Meddelelser* 58).

[5] Despite F. WINKELMANN, *Untersuchungen zur Kirchengeschichte des Gelasios von Kaisareia* (Berlin, 1966: *Sitzungsberichte der deutsche Akademie der Wissenschaften zu Berlin:*

Eusebius had recounted the history of the Christian Church to the reign of Constantine († 337) and Rufinus extended it to the death of the emperor Theodosius I († 395). Secondly, Eusebius inspired and provided much of the information for Jerome (*ca.* 350-420) when the latter compiled his *De viris illustribus* ca. 392. The work, continued ca. 480 by Gennadius of Marseille, contains short accounts of a total of 234 Christian authors, in chronological order, describing where and when they lived and what they wrote.[6] Isidore of Seville (*ca.* 570-636) in the early seventh century added a further 33 authors, including some notable writers of the sixth century.[7] Lastly, there is the *Historia tripartita*, a Latin compilation and abridgement by Epiphanius for Cassiodorus (first half of the sixth century), of the ecclesiastical histories of three Greek writers, Sozomen (first half of the fifth century), Socrates (*ca.* 380-440) and Theodoret (first half of the fifth century). There is some overlap in content between this work and Rufinus's books X and XI, but the *Historia tripartita* takes the story up to the middle of the fifth century, provides complementary material for the fourth century, and a particularly dramatic presentation of the Arian conflict.[8] In the companion piece already mentioned I have suggested that these three works played a key role in creating a context for the Franks' understanding not only of the history of the Church, but also of the circumstances of the composition and dissemination of scripture and the work of the Fathers of the early Church.

Indeed, I have argued that the Church was envisaged from the fourth century onwards primarily in terms of texts and more particularly, of the writings containing the fundamental ideas of Christian faith and practice. Such a perception was a direct consequence of the distinctive presentation of the history of the Christian Church offered by Eusebius-Rufinus. Eusebius's emphasis, preserved and augmented by Rufinus, was on the writers who were the pillars of the Church, on the definition of written authority and the canon of scripture,

---

Klasse für Sprachen, Literatur und Kunst 1965 Nr. 3), who argued that Rufinus translated a now-lost Greek continuation of Eusebius' by Gelasius of Caesarea, Rufinus's authorship of books X and XI has been vindicated: see F. THELAMON, *Païens et chrétiens au IVe siècle: L'apport de l'histoire ecclésiastique de Rufin d'Aquilée* (Paris, 1981), CHRISTENSEN, *Rufinus of Aquileia*, and the useful summary of the debate in P.R. AMIDON, *The Church History of Rufinus of Aquileia, Books 10 and 11* (Oxford, 1997), pp. XIII-XVII.

    [6] Jerome-Gennadius, *Liber de viris inlustribus*, ed. E.C. RICHARDSON, *Hieronymus de viris inlustribus* (Leipzig, 1896: *Texte und Untersuchungen zur Geschichte der altchristlichen Literatur* 14, Heft 1a).

    [7] C.C. MERINO, *El "De viris illustribus" de Isidoro de Sevilla: Estudio y edicion critica* (Salamanca, 1964: *Theses et Studia philologica Salamanticensia* 12).

    [8] *Cassiodori-Epiphanii Historia ecclesiastica tripartita*, ed. W. JACOB and R. HANSLIK (Vienna, 1952: *Corpus Scriptorum Ecclesiasticorum Latinorum* 71).

and on the great doctrinal controversies and discussions by theologians of the early Church. Jerome and his continuator Gennadius consolidated this emphasis by presenting what amounts to a systematic bibliographical guide. The theme of written authority was then taken up and echoed in the *Historia tripartita* of Epiphanius-Cassiodorus. Taken together Eusebius-Rufinus, Jerome-Gennadius, and Epiphanius-Cassiodorus present a close association and essential continuation of the formation of a textual tradition within the chronological framework of the history of the Church. The development of the Church is thus also a textual history. The histories of the Church written in the fourth, fifth and sixth centuries provided both framework and context for a past and an identity built on texts.

Such a perception of the Church and its historical development accords with the clear indications that the Franks in the Carolingian period identified themselves in relation to particular texts. They recognized books as symbols of authority of the Church and of God.[9] They themselves played a fundamental role in the definition of a canon of writings. That canon was constructed with the aid also of such bibliographical guides as Jerome-Gennadius-Isidore's *De viris illustribus* and Cassiodorus' *Institutiones*[10] and rested in its turn on the ecclesiastical histories written in the fourth and fifth centuries described above.

The Franks' understanding of the significance of these histories, and the tight interweaving of texts and authors in their narratives, is amply shown by the evidence of the library catalogues and the production and dissemination of copies of Jerome-Gennadius, Eusebius-Rufinus and Epiphanius-Cassiodorus throughout the Frankish realms in the eighth and ninth centuries.[11] In consequence, it would be possible to argue that, in this fundamental conception of the history of the Church built on texts and writing, and of the Franks' place within that history, words are all. Images appear to have little place.

Similarly, in documenting responses to the various histories of the Church received and read in the Carolingian period, there is an overwhelming impression of readers of texts, and of scribes copying texts. Imaginative understanding in verbal form, however, should not be underestimated. Mental images of writers, prophets, monks, bishops, martyrs, scribes, translators and scholars emerge strongly from the *De viris illustribus*, the *Historia ecclesiastica* and the *Histo-*

---

[9]   I have discussed this at greater length in R. McKITTERICK, "Essai sur les représentations de l'écrit dans les manuscrits carolingiens", *Revue française d'histoire du livre* 86-87 (1995), pp. 37-61.

[10]   Cassiodorus, *Institutiones*, ed. R.A.B. MYNORS (Oxford, 1937); See R. McKITTERICK, *The Carolingians and the Written Word* (Cambridge, 1989), pp. 165-210.

[11]   McKITTERICK, "The Carolingian Church and the book".

ria tripartita. So does a specific spatial understanding of time and place. Naturally there is a danger of a modern reader making subjective and anachronistic assumptions about the way in which books may have been read in the past.[12] Yet the authors present the accounts of Christian writers with such consistent clarity of focus on precisely such issues as time, place and authority, that there seems little doubt about the impression an early medieval reader might gain. Because of the location of these authors in the chronological framework of the development of the Christian Church, ana also because of the geographical distribution of these various pillars of the Church, an understanding of a Christian intellectual geography was created alongside an emphasis on sacred places and on the delineation of the Holy Land.[13]

Pictorial images might reinforce these verbal pictures of authoritative writers and sacred places, but not replace them.[14] Actual images can be dissociated neither from mental images created by words nor from the texts to which the pictures are related. How text-based the Frankish understanding of the past and of historical narratives was, may be underlined by the observation of how rarely historical narratives of any kind – classical, biblical, late antique or early medieval – were illustrated in the early Middle Ages. Where illustrations are included in history books, it is in the biblical history books and more often than not as images of writers and individuals of authority in relation to scripture. A prime example is the depiction of scenes from the life of Jerome included in the Vivian Bible and the Bible of San Paolo fuori le mura, both of which were given to Charles the Bald, king of the West Franks, 840-877. Here the scenes chosen for illustration are those of the composition and dissemination of the text of Jerome's Vulgate translation of the Bible.[15] The dramatic battle scenes

---

[12] For some attempts at reconstructions of the reading process in Antiquity and the Middle Ages, see: *A History of Reading*, ed. G. CAVALLO and R. CHARTIER (Cambridge, Mass., 2000).

[13] Compare on geographical ideas N. LOZOVSKY, *"The Earth is Our Book": Geographical Knowledge in the Latin West ca. 400-1000* (Ann Arbor, 2000), A. MERRILLS, "Geography in early medieval Christian historiography", unpublished Ph.D. dissertation, University of Cambridge (2000) and P. GAUTIER DALCHÉ, *Géographie et culture: La représentation de l'espace du VIe au XIIe siècle* (Aldershot, 1997). On the Holy Land see R.L. WILKEN, *The Land Called Holy: Palestine in Christian History and Thought* (New Haven and London, 1992).

[14] I have discussed some of the issues this raises in R. MCKITTERICK, "Text and image in the Carolingian world", in: *The Uses of Literacy in Early Mediaeval Europe*, ed. R. MCKITTERICK (Cambridge, 1990), pp. 297-318. But see also the essays in *Testo e immagine nell'alto medioevo*, 2 vols. (Spoleto, 1994: *Settimane di studio del Centro italiano di studi sull'alto medioevo* 41) and, for reflections on the wider context: *Literacy, Politics and Artistic Innovation in the Early Medieval West*, ed. C. CHAZELLE (Lanham, MD, 1992).

[15] The Vivian Bible (MSParis, Bibliothèque Nationale, lat. 1), f. 3v and the Bible of San Paolo fuori le Mura, f. 3v, illustrated in H. KESSLER, *The Illustrated Bibles from Tours*

in the St. Gallen Golden Psalter and Leiden Maccabees codices, on the other hand, both produced at St. Gallen, are straightforward exceptions to this in mirroring a direct representation of what is described in the text.[16]

There are, furthermore, some striking instances from the Carolingian period of the way that the distinctive stress on texts, authors, authority and sacred places in the ecclesiastical histories, *De viris illustribus* and a number of related texts could be drawn on by readers, scribes and artists. It is on two examples of these that I wish to focus in this paper. I shall explore the way in which this written tradition of the Church appears to have shaped perceptions and attitudes, and how the particular image of the Church and the Christian faith, presented by the historical tradition I have outlined above and disseminated so zealously by the Franks, manifests itself in the Carolingian period. Let us look, therefore, at two manuscripts, MS Vercelli Biblioteca Capitolare, Cod. CLXV, a collection of canon law, and MS Munich, Bayerische Staatsbibliothek, CLM 22053, the miscellany containing the famous *Wessobrunner Gebet*.

The Vercelli canon law manuscript is a local compilation from northern Italy to be dated no later than the second quarter of the ninth century and probably to be located to the church of San Felice in Pavia.[17] The compiler drew on a library well-stocked with canon law books. He included canons from Gallo-Roman and Merovingian Church councils, papal letters, a handful of extracts from the episcopal statute of Theodulf of Orléans (750/760-821) and rare texts from Africa as well as extracts from major canon law collections from Italy and Merovingian and Carolingian Gaul, most notably in the selections from the original *Dionysiana* compiled in the first half of the sixth century by Dionysius Exiguus, the *Dionysio-Hadriana* (the eighth-century Frankish edition of the *Dionysiana*), the 'Bobbio *Dionysiana*', the so-called *Sanblasiana* collection (also from Italy), the *Breviatio canonum* compiled *ca.* 535 by Ferrandus of

---

(Princeton, 1977), Pls. 130-131.

[16] MS St. Gallen, Stiftsbibliothek 22, pp. 140-141, illustrated in: F. MÜTHERICH and J. GAEHDE, *Carolingian Painting* (London, 1976), Pls. 46-47, and MS Leiden, Universiteitsbibliotheek, Perizonius 17, ff. 9r and 46r, illustrated in: J. HUBERT, J. PORCHER and W. VOLBACH, *Carolingian Art* (London, 1970), Pls. 163-164, pp. 177-178.

[17] I have not been able so far to consult this manuscript and am reliant on the published descriptions, notably the full analysis of its contents by K. ZECHIEL-ECKES, *Die Concordia canonum des Cresconius: Studien und Edition* (Frankfurt am Main, 1992: *Freiburger Beiträge zur mittelalterlichen Geschichte* 5), pp. 172-184. This provides an essential supplement to F. MAASSEN, *Bibliotheca latina iuris canonici manuscripta* (Vienna, 1866), pp. 418-419 and IDEM, *Geschichte der Quellen des canonischen Rechts im Abendlande bis zum Ausgange des Mittelalters* 1 (Graz, 1870), pp. 799-802.

Carthage († 546/547) and the sixth-century Italian (or possibly African) compilation known as the *Concordia Canonum* of Cresconius.

The compilation is a very substantial corpus indeed. It begins with the *Canones apostolorum*, and then in sequence the canons of the councils of Nicaea, Ancyra, Neocaesarea, Gangra, Antioch, Laodicea, Constantinople, Chalcedon, Sardica and Carthage. Many of these councils of course are famous for their consideration of the Christological controversies and the efforts to define orthodoxy which racked the Church in the fourth and fifth centuries. Discussion also embraced, however, such matters as the true nature of asceticism (Gangra), discipline (Antioch), the treatment of heretics, liturgy, penance and Church order (Laodicea), and it is to these more general matters that most of the remaining texts gathered in the Vercelli collection are devoted, especially Ferrandus of Carthage's *Breviatio canonum*.

The text of the *Breviatio* in the Vercelli collection is one of three surviving manuscript copies. The second is from southern France and the third from Rhaetia; either of these two regions may have been the source of the Vercelli compiler's exemplar.[18] The *Breviatio* is a systematic arrangement of 232 extracts from the Greek and African councils of the fourth and fifth centuries organized by topic with references to the relevant conciliar canon. It thus serves as a vade-mecum to the full texts of the council records of the earlier part of the codex. Thus, there are groups of clauses on matters concerning bishops, priests, deacons and other clerics, councils, heretics, Jews and pagans, baptism, observance of Lent and behaviour in church. Number 85, for example, reads as follows:

> *Ut presbyter ante XXX annorum aetatem, quamvis sit dignus, non ordinetur. Concilio Neo Caesariensi tit.10;*

number 134:

> *Ut clerici edendi vel bibendi cause tabernas non ingrediatur, nisi peregrinationes necessitas coegerit. Concilio Laodicensi tit. 23, item 24., item 25. Concilio Carthaginensi, tit. 55;*

number 186:

> *Ut nullus a Judaeis azyma accipiat. Concilio Laodicensi tit. 36;*

---

[18] See ZECHIEL-ECKES, *Concordia canonum*, pp. 71-74.

and number 228:

> *Ut praeter scripturas canonicas nihil in ecclesia legatur. Concilio Laodicensi tit.*
> *57. Concilio Carthaginensi tit. 45.*[19]

The compiler at Pavia, therefore, drew on an extensive range of materials to provide a formidable compendium on Christian faith and practice. Zechiel-Eckes has meticulously observed how the compiler reordered into chronological sequence some of the systematic collections he used for his compilation. That is, the chronological sequence and historical development of the Church are mirrored in the ordering of his material. Not only are the conciliar canons arranged historically, but so is the decretal section from the *Concordia canonum* of Cresconius. The stress on the canonical books and orthodoxy, furthermore, is striking. The book as a whole is an eloquent exemplum of how writing and the encoding of the law of the Church contains the fundamental ideas of Christian faith and practice.

The illustrations bunched together at the beginning of the book (rather then interspersed throughout the text) are vigorous pen drawings of six scenes, namely the finding of the True Cross by Helena, the burning of the Arian books at the Council of Nicaea (325), images of Peter and Paul discussing the council of Nicaea, the burning of the books of the Macedonian heretics at the First council of Constantinople (381), the emperor Theodosius II presiding over the council of Ephesus (431), and Christ in Majesty.[20]

These pictures do not simply reflect an artist's attempt to illustrate the convening of the councils recorded in the book. They mirror the themes of the crucified and triumphant Christ, faith and devotion, the role of the emperors in supporting the Christian Church, the definition of orthodoxy, the historical place of the Church in relation to the New Testament and the apostles, and the importance of books and writing as embodiments of the faith. Thus, the pictures form a comment on the text which is itself enhanced by references to texts not in the collection at all. This is not simply a matter of the inclusion of a depiction of the discovery of the True Cross and of the Council of Ephesus which condemned Nestorius, neither of which figures in the compilation at all. The dramatic representations of the burning of the books are also not to be found in

---

[19] *Concilia Africae, a. 345-535*, ed. C. MUNIER (Turnhout, 1974: *Corpus Christianorum Series Latina* 149), pp. 287-306 at pp. 294, 298, 302, 305.

[20] Illustrated in: J. HUBERT, J. PORCHER, and W. VOLBACH, *Europe in the Dark Ages* (London, 1969), Pls. 156-161, pp. 142-147, and see also the descriptions and reproductions in C. WALTER, "Les dessins carolingiens dans un manuscrit de Verceil", *Cahiers Archéologiques* 18 (1968), pp. 99-107.

the canons of the relevant council but, at least for the Council of Nicaea, in the account of this council provided by the *Historia tripartita* of Epiphanius-Cassiodorus.

Thus, the burning of the Arian books under Constantine portrayed on f. 2v, for example, was recorded by Socrates in his ecclesiastical history and incorporated into the *Historia tripartita*.[21] The immolation of the Macedonian books, on the other hand, may be the artist's creative assumption, on analogy with the historical account of Nicaea, for neither the very full coverage of the disputes with the Macedonians (a subgroup within the Arian party) in the *Historia tripartita*,[22] nor the canons of Constantinople itself refer to the burning of the writings of these groups, only their anathematization.[23] In other words, authority was seen by this artist in terms of books, and the countering of heresy was envisaged in terms of the destruction of books. The other pictures reinforce the message of the book embodying authority. Paul displays a book in his hand, even if Peter holds the two keys. In the representation of the Council of Nicaea, Constantine is depicted with a roll in his hand and the notary writes in a codex. The illustration of the first Council of Constantinople shows Theodosius holding a book in his left hand and the notaries to his right and left inscribe what he and the assembled bishops (crowding behind the two scribes) decide in the book each of them holds. Similarly, Theodosius at Ephesus has his own codex in his hand and is flanked by two scribes, each writing in a book. These images associating the emperors with written authority and orthodoxy confirmed in codex form culminate in the representation of Christ himself, also holding a book. The link between Christ in Majesty in heaven, with an angel to his right and left, and the opening picture of this sequence, namely, the finding of the True Cross, the instrument of Christ's passion on earth, is reinforced by placing Helena and Constantine beneath Christ in attitudes of supplication. These pictures together, therefore, express the principal preoccupations of the texts in MS Vercelli CLXV in a way that reflects a wider historical knowledge and understanding of the contexts from which the conciliar canons emerged.

The detail in the scene of the discovery of the True Cross, moreover, betrays the Pavia artist's wider range of reference. He drew not only on his histor-

---

[21] *Historia ecclesiastica tripartita*, II, 15, p. 109.

[22] *Ibid.*, V, 31, 41, 42 and IX, 12-16, pp. 260-262, 285-290, 506-522.

[23] *Ecclesiae occidentalis monumenta iuris antiquissima, canonum et conciliorum graecorum interpretationes latinae*, ed. C. TURNER, 2 vols. (Oxford, 1899), 2, p. 409, and compare W. SPEYER, *Büchervernichtung und Zensur des Geistes bei Heiden, Juden und Christen* (Stuttgart, 1981: *Bibliothek des Buchwesens* 7), pp. 142-157; Speyer, p. 152, notes that a law of Theodosius II and Valentinian in 436, incorporated into the *Theodosian Code* in the aftermath of the Council of Ephesus (431) did specify the burning of the works of Nestorius.

ical understanding of the development of the Christian faith and practice as reflected in the law of the Church and at least one ecclesiastical history. Certainly the legend of the discovery of the Cross by Helena is to be found in both Rufinus, *Historia ecclesiastica* X, 7-8 and the *Historia tripartita* II, 18.[24] Rufinus recounts simply that Helena, "alerted by divine visions", journeyed to Jerusalem and there discovered the True Cross together with the crosses of the two thieves. The identity of the Cross was established by a healing miracle. Subsequently the Nails were also found, and Helena had them incorporated into a helmet for her son Constantine, and into the bridle of his warhorse. A church was then built on the site. The *Historia tripartita* adds little to this apart from reflecting on a Sibylline oracle and a prophecy of Zachariah, both of which seem to foretell the finding of the Cross and the incorporation of the Nails into war gear.

An alternative version known in the Latin West, however, was the so-called 'Cyriacus version' of the legend.[25] This introduces the character of the Jew 'Iudas' who shows Helena the spot where the Cross lay buried. Judas is subsequently converted and baptized, changes his name to Cyriacus, and becomes Bishop of Jerusalem. The earliest manuscript of the Cyriacus version is a fifth-century Syriac text, but a Latin version survives in MS Paris, Bibliothèque Nationale, lat. 2769, a sixth-century uncial manuscript probably from Italy.[26] That this version was also known in Gaul in the sixth century is clear from the reference made to it by Gregory of Tours (*ca.* 540-594) in his *Histories*.[27] Other copies of the Cyriacus legend survive in Carolingian manuscripts from St. Gallen, Paris, Langres, St. Amand and southern France. They can be divided into subgroups related only distantly and thus attest to a very wide dissemination of this version of the True Cross story during the Merovingian and early Carolingian period.[28]

In many ways the Cyriacus version complements the Rufinus version, save that the dreams at the outset are attributed to Constantine, and Judas/Cyriacus plays such a prominent practical role. That both versions of the story were

---

[24] Rufinus, pp. 967-970, and *Historia ecclesiastica tripartita*, pp. 114-115.

[25] H. and J.W. DRIJVERS, *The Finding of the True Cross: The Judas Kyriakos Legend in Syriac* (Louvain, 1997).

[26] E.A. LOWE, *Codices latini antiquiores*, 12 vols. (Oxford, 1934-1972), 5, No. 550.

[27] Gregory of Tours, *Historiarum libri decem*, I, 36, ed. B. KRUSCH, revised by R. BUCHNER, 2 vols. (Darmstadt, 1977: *Ausgewählte Quellen zur deutschen Geschichte des Mittelalters* 2-3), 1, p. 40.

[28] S. BORGHAMMER, *How the Holy Cross Was Found: From Event to Medieval Legend* (Stockholm, 1991: *Bibliotheca theologiae practicae* 47), pp. 208-228 on the manuscripts and pp. 255-71 for an edition of the Latin text.

known early on, but that some people consciously preferred one to the other, is suggested by the comment in Sozomen's *Ecclesiastical History* to the effect that there were some who said that the crosses were first discovered by a Jew who derived his information from certain documents left to him by his father. Sozomen comments, however, that divine revelation in dreams and signs is to be preferred to human information.[29] It is this preference which Epiphanius, in his abridged Latin version of Sozomen, maintains by omitting all reference to the Jew. The full version of the Cyriacus legend, however, introduces dreams and signs from God for both Constantine and Judas, quite apart from the miracle of raising the dead performed by the True Cross itself.

It is not necessary here to explore the origins or the further ramifications of these Syriac, Latin and Greek versions of the story, for they have been elucidated with great clarity by Han and Jan Willem Drijvers and by Borghammer.[30] What they do suggest, first and on a practical level, is that a version of the story probably originated in Jerusalem in the first half of the fourth century at about the time that the relics of the True Cross were discovered, no doubt while excavating for the foundations of Constantine's church of the Holy Sepulchre on Golgotha. Through Rufinus himself, who had spent many years in Jerusalem, the story reached the West but only in the form he preferred. Other variants, as recorded by others, including Sozomen, also reached the West and circulated concurrently. In the Carolingian period, a number of manuscripts containing each version were produced in widely separated centres. Secondly, the illustration in the Vercelli manuscript suggests that the legend itself was interpreted, by this artist at least, within the context of the discussions and definition of the nature and person of Christ in relation to God the Father. These discussions were precisely those given such prominence in the affairs of the early Christian Church as recounted in the ecclesiastical histories.

Other contexts for the story were provided. A small decorated initial depicting the discovery of Cross and Nails in the Sacramentary of Gellone[31] places it, as one might expect, within the liturgy of the feast for the *Inventio sanctae crucis*.[32] A further response to the Latin version of the Cyriacus legend in the

---

[29] Sozomen, *Ecclesiastical History*, II, 1, ed. R. HUSSEY, *Sozomenus Salamius Historia ecclesiastica*, 3 vols. (Oxford, 1860), 1, p. 103; English tr. C.D. HARTRANFT, in: *A Select Library of Nicene and Post-Nicene Fathers of the Christian Church*, second series, 14 vols., ed. H. WACE and P. SCHAFF, 2 (Oxford and New York, 1890), p. 258.

[30] J.W. DRIJVERS, *Helena Augusta: The Mother of Constantine the Great and the Legend of her Finding of the True Cross* (Leiden, 1992), and BORGHAMMAR, *How the Holy Cross Was Found*.

[31] MS Paris, Bibliothèque Nationale, lat. 12048, f. 76v.

[32] Illustrated in HUBERT, PORCHER and VOLBACH, *Europe in the Dark Ages*, Pl. 201,

early Carolingian period was from an artist probably based in the diocese of Augsburg. He provided the earliest-known cycle of illustrations to accompany the Latin version of the Cyriacus legend, in the famous miscellany in the *Wessobrunner Gebet*-manuscript.[33]

This codex was written in the diocese of Augsburg *ca.* 814.[34] It contains texts to do with theology, weights and measures, botany, geography, and chronology. It has been described as a "kind of scrap book or collection of fragments of useful knowledge in the liberal arts",[35] but this is to underrate the coherence of this personal and individual compilation. The first twenty-one folios contain the *Liber de Inventione S. Crucis*. There follows the famous *Wessobrunner Gebet*, which is a description of the void before God created the world, the presence of the Creator and the act of creation. The title given the poem, *De poeta* has been interpreted as 'Creator' and is thought to be a Latinization of the word used by Plato in the *Timaeus*, a text certainly available in the Carolingian period.[36] The glosses also suggest that the compiler knew Greek.

It has been suggested that the poem's composition is either the expression of conviction of a pious Christian or that it should be seen in a missionary context. Its language is predominantly Bavarian, but some have detected in certain discrepancies in the word forms either a provenance further north or else an older stratum of the language.[37] Anglo-Saxon influence has also been discerned.

---

p. 191.

[33] K. BIERBRAUER, *Die vorkarolingischen und karolingischen Handschriften der Bayerischen Staatsbibliothek*, 2 vols. (Wiesbaden, 1990: *Katalog der illuminierten Handschriften der Bayerischen Staatsbibliothek* 1.1-2), 1, No. 155, pp. 83-84 and 2, Pls. 319-336.

[34] B. BISCHOFF, *Die südostdeutschen Schreibschulen und Bibliotheken*, 3rd edn. (Wiesbaden, 1974), pp. 18-21. See also the discussion by U. SCHWAB, *Die Sternrune im Wessobrunner Gebet: Beobachtungen zur Lokalisierung des CLM 22053, zur Hs. BM Arundel 393 und zu Rune Poem V. 86-89* (Amsterdam, 1973: *Amsterdamer Publikationen zur Sprache und Literatur* 1).

[35] See J. KNIGHT BOSTOCK, *A Handbook on Old High German Literature*, 2nd edn. (Oxford, 1976), p. 128, whose discussion of the language of the *Gebet* itself and its implications I here follow.

[36] BOSTOCK, *Handbook*, p. 128. On the *Timaeus*, see: R. McKITTERICK, "Knowledge of Plato's *Timaeus* in the ninth century: The implications of Valenciennes, Bibliothèque Municipale MS 293", in: *From Athens to Chartres: Neoplatonism and Medieval Thought*, ed. H.J. WESTRA (Leiden, 1992), pp. 85-95, reprinted in R. McKITTERICK, *Books, Scribes and Learning in the Frankish Kingdoms under the Carolingians, 6th-9th Centuries* (Aldershot, 1994), chapter X, and more particularly, the important study of the manuscript tradition and its implications in A. SOMFAI, *The Transmission and Reception of Plato's Timaeus and Calcidius's Commentary during the Carolingian Renaissance*, unpublished Ph.D. dissertation, University of Cambridge (1998).

[37] See the useful summary by C. EDWARDS, "German vernacular literature: A survey", in: *Carolingian Culture: Emulation and Innovation*, ed. R. McKITTERICK (Cambridge, 1994),

Scholars have therefore looked to Fulda for links, though there are other possible centres in Franconia and there was also an Anglo-Saxon presence in Bavaria itself in the early Carolingian period. A further insular link, possibly with Fulda, however, is suggested by the manuscript tradition of the Cyriacus legend, for one of the other extant ninth-century copies is written in Anglo-Saxon and early caroline minuscule,[38] which may suggest further knowledge of the legend at a place with insular connections in the Main region in Germany. It would be tempting from this perspective as from that of the language of the *Gebet* to posit a link with Fulda itself – and thus knowledge of the historical accounts of the discovery of the Cross in both the ecclesiastical histories and the versions of the legend with the composition of Hraban Maur's extraordinary celebration of the Cross.[39] The manuscript evidence is too ambiguous for this to be stated with certainty.

At the least there is agreement that the texts of both the Cyriacus legend and the *Wessobrunner Gebet* are copied from an older exemplar, perhaps from the late eighth century. Similar to the Vercelli canon law collection, the compiler of the *Wessobrunner Gebet*-codex reveals the extent of the treasury of texts he had at his disposal for inclusion in his book. Similarly, it is the story of the True Cross which, like an invocation, starts each book, though in the case of the *Wessobrunner Gebet*-manuscript it is the whole text, amplified by the illustrations in direct response to its details, rather than simply the single but powerfully symbolic image of the very discovery of the Cross chosen by the Pavia artist.

The *Wessobrunner Gebet*-codex's pictures are simple outline pictures with a sparing use of brownish red, yellow, and blue. The pictures start with Constantine's dream. Helena is then represented in several pictures as she arrives in Jerusalem, and as she talks to soldiers and various groups of Jews. After that the pictures relate how Judas emerges from the dry well into which

---

pp. 141-170.

[38] MS Oxford, Bodleian Library, Laud misc. 129, ff. 16v-22v listed by BORGEHAMMAR, *How the Holy Cross Was Found*, p. 211. See B. BISCHOFF and J. HOFMANN, *Libri sancti Kyliani: Die Würzburger Schreibschule und die Dombibliothek im VIII. und IX. Jahrhundert* (Würzburg, 1952), p. 51. It seems clear, however, that MS Laud misc. 129 itself was not written at Fulda, nor is there any indication that it was ever there: see H. SPILLING, "Angelsächsische Schrift in Fulda", in: *Von der Klosterbibliothek zur Landesbibliothek: Beiträge zum zweihundertjährigen Bestehen der Hessischen Landesbibliothek Fulda*, ed. A. BRALL (Stuttgart, 1978), pp. 47-98, and EADEM, "Die frühe Phase karolingischer Minuskel in Fulda", in: *Kloster Fulda in der Welt der Karolinger und Ottonen*, ed. G. SCHRIMPF (Frankfurt, 1996: *Fuldaer Studien* 7), pp. 249-284, who does not include MS Laud misc. 129 in her discussions.

[39] See M. FERRARI, *Il "Liber sanctae crucis" di Rabano Mauro: Testo – immagine – contesto* (Bern, 1999).

Helena had him thrown, and excavates three crosses at Golgotha. It is then revealed, in the raising of a dead man, which cross is that of Christ. A church is built by Helena, and Judas is baptized and becomes Cyriacus. The Nails are also retrieved.

It is appropriate and a clear association of ideas that the text directly following the *Inventio sanctae crucis* in this book on ff. 22r-35v is the *De situ terrae sanctae* of Theodosius Archidiaconus concerning other sacred places in the Holy Land, written *ca.* 518-530.[40] Thus, the compiler continued to celebrate the passion of God the Son and the creation of God the Father in its many manifestations as well as the importance of knowledge of the sacred places.

These two manuscripts and their illustrations show how images were deployed to reinforce the importance of sacred place, relics, authors and books. They also serve to underline the importance of codicological context for our own understanding of any one text and its significance for its intended audience. Thereby, they incidentally add to our own knowledge of the intellectual resources of particular groups in the Carolingian world, quite apart from enlarging our understanding of the reception of late antique Christian texts in early medieval Europe. The Vercelli canon law book in particular shows how the image and understanding of the history of the Church were based not only on the compiler's readings of ecclesiastical history but also on the way a very particular perception of the history of the Church was expressed on several key issues. What seems to be reflected in both these manuscripts is a particular understanding of the Christian faith, formed by reading and expressed in written and pictorial form, certainly, but with written texts constituting its principal inspiration.

---

[40] T. TOBLER and A. MOLINIER, *Itinera Hierosolymitana* 1 (Geneva 1879-1880), pp. 353-359. MS München, Bayerische Staatsbibliothek, CLM 22053 was not used by *Itineraria et alia geographica*, ed. P. GEYER (Turnhout, 1965: *Corpus Christianorum Series Latina* 125), pp. 114-125. This version is textually related to MS Wolfenbüttel, Herzog-August Bibliothek, Weissenburg 99, ff. 144r-152v, a famous illustrated copy of the eighth-century manuscript, containing the Catholic epistles.

Saintly Images: Visions of Saints in Hagiographical Texts[1]

WOLFERT S. VAN EGMOND

In a letter to Charlemagne written at the end of the eighth century, Pope Hadrian I reported on the action taken concerning a certain monk John, who had apparently complained to Charlemagne about Hadrian. Among other things Hadrian told about two dreams recounted by John. In his first dream, John had seen the heavens open and the hand of God appear. In the second dream, a high tower and descending angels had appeared to him. Then a creature in the likeness of a man with eagle's wings had been eating a corpse. Another creature, also shaped like a man, but with wings of a dove, had declared that this dead body was the Christian faith. Pope Hadrian denied these dreams any credibility because, as attested by the Scriptures, the form of the Holy Ghost was a true dove and not some human-shaped creature with wings of a dove.[2]

---

[1]   I would like to thank Kate Dailinger and Mary Garrison for their helpful comments on earlier versions of this text.

[2]   *Codex Carolinus*, ed. W. GUNDLACH, in: *Epistolae Merowingici et Karolini Aevi* 1 (Berlin, 1892: MGH Epp 3), pp. 469-657, No. 88, at p. 625: *"Porro de revelatione eiusdem Iohannis monachi, sicut eius referebat locutio, vere fantasma esse existimatur. Dicebat enim, quia vidit primis in somnis caelos apertos et dexteram Dei; deinde vidit postmodum somnium aliud: turrem magnam et descendentes angelos; inter quibus vidit speciem hominis, alas habentes aquile, mortuumque essentem, et aliam speciem hominis, alas habentem columbe vivae et dicentem: 'Quia hic est fides christiana'. Absit enim a fidelium cordibus, ut fides christianorum mortua esse predicetur. Nos enim speciem, aquile alas habentem, sicut a sanctis suscepimus patribus, Iohannem evangelistam testamur, qui secreta caelestia hominibus predicat: 'In principio erat verbum' et cetera; in specie vero columbe spiritus sanctus visus est; nam numquam legimus speciem hominis alas columbe indutum. Quapropter nimis vestram laudantes*

Hadrian's report of John's dreams is singular because it tells about a dream which is denied credibility, whereas normally dreams in medieval texts are recounted precisely because they are considered trustworthy. Both the content of John's dreams and the pope's reaction to them raise questions about the relations between dreams (or visions) and iconography. On the one hand, it seems obvious to modern eyes that the content of John's dreams (or the account of them) was influenced by the images accessible on the walls of churches or seen in books.[3] On the other hand, the pope disqualified John's dreams because they did not fully conform to established images, that is to say: the iconography of the time. Hadrian, in other words, used iconography as a means to authenticate dreams as divine revelations. In doing this, the pope was acting on the advice given by Tertullian (ca. 150-ca. 230) always to check whether a vision's account conformed to Scripture.[4] Can such an affirmation of the legitimizing function of iconography be found also in the many visions that were given credibility by the authors of the texts in which they were reported? What reasons may there have been to use (or not to use) iconography for this purpose?

This question will be discussed here using descriptions of visions taken from early medieval hagiographical texts, written in the sixth to eleventh centuries. In contrast to the longer medieval descriptions of visions, which are mostly accounts of visits by the visionary to hell, purgatory or heaven,[5] the many short visions contained in hagiographical texts have received little attention from historians. Their function or meaning within individual texts, or within the works of one author, has been noted, but they have hardly been investigated collectively.[6] Only a few such visions can be discussed here. The sheer number

---

firmissimam atque laudabilem fidem, in hoc cognovimus, quia vos fantassma ipsas reputastis visiones".

[3] There is no way of telling how far removed this recount is from the original dream. Not only Pope Hadrian will have edited the description, while formulating his letter, but John himself will have done the same while telling his dream to Hadrian (or his representative) and even while recollecting it immediately after waking. At all these moments the description may have been changed. For an excellent consideration of these problems, see: P.E. DUTTON, *The Politics of Dreaming in the Carolingian Empire* (Lincoln, Nebraska, and London, 1994), pp. 24-25.

[4] Tertullian, *De praescriptione haereticorum*, ed. R.F. REFOULÉ (Turnhout, 1954: CCSL 1), 21, 5, pp. 186-224: "*Omnem vero doctrinam de mendacio praeiudicandam quae sapiat contra veritatem ecclesiarum et apostolorum Christi et Dei*".

[5] P. DINZELBACHER, *Vision und Visionsliteratur im Mittelalter* (Stuttgart, 1981). ID., *Revelationes* (Turnhout, 1991: *Typologie des sources du Moyen Age occidental* 57). A.A. GUREVICH, *Medieval Popular Culture: Problems of Belief and Perception* (Cambridge, 1988), pp. 104-152. C. CAROZZI, *Le voyage de l'âme dans l'au-delà d'après la littérature latine (Ve-XIIIe siècle)* (Rome, 1994: *Collection de l'École française de Rome* 189).

[6] E.g. G. DE NIE, *Views from a Many-Windowed Tower: Studies of Imagination in the*

of hagiographical texts produced in the early Middle Ages makes it a task outside the compass of the present investigation to gather a more substantial corpus, especially since accounts of dreams and visions, often rather short ones, are a very common feature in these texts. The best way to compile a comprehensive corpus of these descriptions would be to go through all 69 volumes of the *Acta sanctorum*, and to scan the texts not only for the words *visio* and *somnium*, but also for *revelatio*, *visum*, *apparuit* and the many other words used in descriptions of visionary experiences in medieval texts.[7] Soon such an undertaking may be accomplished more expeditiously, after the completion of the publication on CD-rom of the *Acta sanctorum*. All observations here will be based on a haphazardly assembled corpus.

In his ground-breaking study on medieval visions, Peter Dinzelbacher proposed a strict definition of a vision. In his view, something should only be called a vision when the visionary has the experience of being transported in a supernatural way into a different space; when he perceives this space as something which can be described; when the transportation takes place in ecstasy or sleep; and when something is revealed that until now was hidden.[8] Thus, Dinzelbacher distinguishes the vision proper from other visionary experiences such as apparitions.[9] However useful this precise definition can be for selecting and ordering the data, it carries with it the risk of distorting the evidence, since many of the visionary experiences described in medieval texts do not fully conform to this definition. In those texts there is seldom evidence whether the authors also considered phenomena different from visions to have happened. Of

---

Works of Gregory of Tours (Amsterdam, 1987), who uses visions in the works of Gregory of Tours (ca. 540-594) to reconstruct his 'outillage mental'. R. KÜNZEL, *Beelden en zelfbeelden van middeleeuwse mensen: Historisch-antropologische studies over groepsculturen in de Nederlanden, 7de-13de eeuw* (Nijmegen, 1997), pp. 225-255, who takes a vision in an exemplum by Caesarius of Heisterbach (ca.1180-1240) as the starting point for a survey into the underlying religious ideas. A notable recent study which does take in both independent accounts and visions within hagiography is: I. MOREIRA, *Dreams, Visions, and Spiritual Authority in Merovingian Gaul* (Ithaca and London, 2000). For a survey of the (Polish) literature concerning medieval visions, see: T. MICHAŁOWSKA, "Śnić w średniowiecznej pulsce", in: EADEM, *Mediaevalia i inne* (Warsaw, 1998), pp. 70-97.

[7] For the different words used to designate visions see: DINZELBACHER, *Vision und Visionsliteratur*, pp. 45-50. MOREIRA, *Dreams, Visions, and Spiritual Authority*, pp. 5-6.

[8] DINZELBACHER, *Vision und Visionsliteratur*, p. 29: *"Von einer Vision sprechen wir dann, wenn ein Mensch das Erlebnis hat, aus seiner Umwelt auf außernatürliche Weise in einen anderen Raum versetzt zu werden, er diesen Raum beziehungsweise dessen Inhalte als beschreibbares Bild schaut, diese Versetzung in Ekstase (oder im Schlaf) geschieht, und ihm dadurch bisher Verborgenes offenbar wird".*

[9] DINZELBACHER, *Vision und Visionsliteratur*, pp. 29-45.

course, authors of scientific treatises made distinctions between different sorts of experiences. Only few of such texts, however, were written in the early Middle Ages, while those from late Antiquity were seldom used.[10] As we shall see, the main concern of the authors of texts describing visions and dreams was whether these experiences had been authentic revelations of a divine origin. To them it mattered whether the things seen or heard were true, not which form they took.

There have been several appeals for a comparison between the depiction of saints seen in visions and the contemporary practices in the iconography of saints, usually accompanied by enticing suggestions about the parallels between these practices.[11] A closer look at those suggestions raises doubts about how founded these parallels are, either in the field of history or in that of art history. Part of the problem may be that most art-historical research into the early Middle Ages draws on Byzantine sources. This is quite understandable, given the relative scarcity of extant Western images, but it does make comparisons with contemporary Western texts difficult.[12] Accordingly, to avoid making weakly substantiated generalizations based on a few sources, whether pictorial or textual, this investigation will focus on a single aspect of the topic: the influence exercised by the contemporary iconography of individual saints on the depictions of saints in visions. It will become clear that, while parallels between iconography and texts can be easily found, direct influence is doubtful.

Before studying the depiction of individual saints, it is necessary to consider the representation of saints in the texts in general. Which clues are supposed to make clear that an apparition is not the figment of some overheated imagination but an actual saint? In the *Vita Radbodi*, written in the third quarter of the tenth century, two such markers can be found: an unnatural light and a sweet smell. Towards the end of the *Vita Radbodi* the story is told how one day

---

[10] MOREIRA, *Dreams, Visions, and Spiritual Authority*, pp. 7-10 and *passim*.

[11] E.g. A.J. VAN RUN, "*Imaginaria visione*: Over kunst en visioenen in de Middeleeuwen", in: *Visioenen*, ed. R.E.V. STUIP and C. VELLEKOOP (Utrecht, 1986: *Utrechtse Bijdragen tot de Mediëvistiek* 6), pp. 122-150, n. 2.

[12] E.g. H. BELTING, *Likeness and Presence: A History of the Image before the Era of Art* (Chicago, 1994) (original title: *Bild und Kult: Eine Geschichte des Bildes vor dem Zeitalter der Kunst* (München, 1990)), pp. 82-85, in a discussion of the image of saint Demetrius, made around 600 in the church dedicated to him at Thessalonika, states that the way the saint is portrayed here (life size, frontal, praying, dressed as an officer, forming the centre of the picture, timeless youth) corresponds to the way saints are portrayed in contemporary visions. This might be generally or even universally true for Byzantine texts (although I cannot judge that), but in contemporary western texts it is as easy to find examples contradicting this statement as ones confirming it.

bishop Radbod of Utrecht (900-917) fell seriously ill.[13] As he lay in bed and expected to die, he had a vision. In it, he saw the Holy Virgin accompanied by saints Agnes and Thecla enter his room. Mary told Radbod that his time had not yet come, and healed him. On Mary's arrival the room was illuminated by an unearthly light which lingered a while, accompanied by a sweet smell, after she had left. The *Vita Radbodi* claims that afterwards Radbod had described Mary's appearance, although he had to admit that he had not been able to discern her beauty completely.[14] Agnes and Thecla on the other hand he had seen quite clearly, and he had distinguished their faces as well as their clothes.[15] As usual in the texts, Radbod's description of the saints is not recounted. The light can obviously be seen as a parallel to the nimbus and aureole in the pictures of saints. A heavenly scent may be difficult to express in a picture, but the association with the incense burnt in churches springs to mind.[16] Both the light and the smell are expressions of the holy world of which the saint is part.

Early medieval pictures depicting saints and mortals at the same time, often show saints as larger than mortals. Not surprisingly, inequality between the saint and the mere mortal being is a common feature of vision texts as well. When the dreamer realizes whom he is talking to, he adopts an attitude of humility. Even more common is the presumptuous and self-assertive behaviour by the saint. The saint seems to radiate his exalted position, which entitles him to give orders to the dreamer and to expect them to be obeyed. This show of power and authority is regularly emphasized by a threat of physical violence or illness. When the dreamer has angered the saint, he is usually already suffering

---

[13] *Vita sancti Radbodi episcopi Traiectensis* (BHL 7046), c. 10, ed. O. HOLDER-EGGER in: *Suppelemnta tomorum I-II, pars III: Supplementum tomi XIII*, ed. G. WAITZ a.o., 2 vols. (Hannover, 1887-1888: *MGH SS* 15.1-2), 1, pp. 568-571[c], 571[b].

[14] *Vita Radbodi*, c. 10, p. 571[b]: *"Haec etenim cum clam suis assereret – nolens, dum viveret, palam fieri – cuius formae, cuius et habitus, cuius et ornamenti sancta virgo virginum sibi videbatur apparere, non reticuit, tamen eius pulchritudinem non posse testabatur [satis] ammirari"*.

[15] *Vita Radbodi*, c. 10, p. 571[b]: *"Sanctas vero virgines Agnem et Teclam – sic enim, ipso audiente, se fatebantur esse nuncupatas – tam vultuum qualitate quam vestium scemate posse testatus est dinoscere"*. Compare this passage with the story by Sulpicius Severus (ca. 400), who recounts how he once waited outside Martin's cell together with a monk named Gallus and heard voices within. When Martin finally came out he declared that he had been speaking to Agnes, Thecla and Mary. Martin could describe their faces as well as their clothes. Sulpicius Severus, *Dialogi*, II, c. 13, ed. C. HALM, *Sulpicii Severi libri qui supersunt* (Vienna, 1865: CSEL 1), pp. 152-216, at p. 196.

[16] However, compare for the Hebrew origins of the sweet smell associated with saints and their relics: L. ROTHKRUG, "The 'odour of sanctity' and the Hebrew origins of Christian relic veneration", *Historical reflexions - Réflexions historiques* 8 (1981), pp. 95-142.

at the time that the vision commences from the consequences of whatever his misdeed has been. A typical example of this is given by the *Passio Prisci* from the diocese of Auxerre, which must be dated to some time between the seventh and the ninth centuries. In the text's second half, the story is told how one day the nobleman Porcarius by chance entered the ruins of a church on his property and saw the beautiful tiles on the floor. He ordered his servants to collect the tiles and bring them to his house. Shortly afterwards, Porcarius fell ill. In a dream he saw the martyr Priscus, to whom the ruined church had been consecrated, and whose head was buried there. Priscus complained about Porcarius's lack of respect. Porcarius immediately expressed his regret about what had happened. He promised to restore the tiles to their original place and to rebuild the church more beautifully than it had been. Although Priscus was mollified by this promise, he left no doubt about Porcarius's fate should he fail to keep it: he would soon die a horrible death.[17]

Although the saint is always in a higher position than the mortal, the inequality between the two can vary depending on their respective status. The social status of the mortal and the rank of the saint within the heavenly hierarchy matter, as does the future rank of the dreamer in the same heavenly hierarchy. We have already seen that in Radbod's vision Mary was less visible to Radbod than Agnes and Thecla. This is undoubtedly an expression of her position as mother of Christ. A bishop and future saint such as Radbod himself is treated more or less as an equal by saints, different from a mere peasant. And a female virgin may be more polite towards mortals than a holy bishop. Such variations in the behaviour of saints towards dreamers are especially evident when the same saint visits two people of different status. When the virgin Agnes approached the peasant Amolwinus in the tenth-century *Translatio Agnetis et Benigni*, she ordered him without much ado to inform the priest Lambertus to find her relics and those of the martyr Benignus, and to ensure that they are properly venerated. Amolwinus was slow to do this, and so Agnes threatened him.[18] Later, when she visited the priest Lambertus herself, she is said to have been dressed elegantly.[19] Apparently, one should dress properly for a meeting with a priest, even if one is a saint.

---

[17] *Passio sancti Prisci et sociorum eius* (BHL 6930), c. 2, ed. in: *AASS* Maii VI, pp. 365-367.

[18] *Translatio Agnetis et Benigni Ultrajectum anno 964* (BHL 165), cc. 3-5, ed. in: *AASS* Ian. II, pp. 357-360.

[19] *Translatio Agnetis et Benigni*, c. 6, p. 358: "*Sed non longe post, finitis matutinalibus hymnis, ut bonae conversationis apud suos erat, nec vita conversationi discordabat, dum artubus strato locatis, somnus obrepsit; illi sopore leniter soporato visa est et virgo ita forma eleganti, ut nil supra esset, assistere, negligentiarum illum haud leniter redarguens; ac nisi rustici verbis assentiret, atque iussa properanter adimpleret, minitans commissi piaculum non evadere*".

The characteristics of saints appearing in visions, then, were extraordinary sensory signs such as unnatural light or scent, and the display of power and authority. The measure in which saintly authority was shown depended on the status of saint and visionary.

Let us now turn to the question of the identification of individual saints.

The idea that saints in visions could be identified with the help of existing images is not just a modern one. Pope Hadrian I, whom we have already encountered, pointed to exactly this in a discussion of the proceedings of the second council of Nicaea in 787. Calling on the authority of Ambrose's own words, Hadrian said that Saint Ambrose had recognized the apostle Paul from a picture he had seen before. According to Hadrian this was the normal way in which saints in visions were identified, and he referred to the many appearances of Mary, the apostles and other martyrs in the *Dialogi* of Gregory the Great (ca. 540-604).[20]

Another text in which pictures confirm the identity of saints appearing in a vision, is the so-called Donation of Constantine, a forgery from the middle of the eighth century which purports to have been written by emperor Constantine. In it, Constantine tells how pagan priests advised him to bathe in the blood of children to be healed from leprosy. Before Constantine could follow this advice, the apostles Peter and Paul appeared to him in a vision, instructing him to seek out the fugitive Pope Sylvester, who would heal him. Afterwards, Constantine was to build churches and convert to Christianity. Constantine found Pope Sylvester and asked him whether he had any pictures of the two apostles. Sylvester ordered such pictures to be brought, and upon seeing the images Constantine confirmed that these were the men who had appeared in his dream. He then did as they had told him. According to this text, it was not just the dream itself which prompted Constantine to convert, it was the combination of the dream and seeing the images verifying the dream.[21]

The idea that saints could be identified with the help of pictures did exist in the early Middle Ages. Indeed, in both examples pictures verify dreams, as if painted images were supposed to confirm the truth of the visions. However, in the overwhelming majority of hagiographical texts there is either no explanation of how the visionary knew the identity of the saint, or it is said that the

---

[20] *Caelo Magno et Ludowico Pio regnantibus scriptae*, ed. In: *Epistolae selectae pontificum romanorum*, ed. K. HAMPE, in: *Epistolae Karolini aevi* 3, ed. E. DÜMMLER a.o. (Berlin, 1898-1899: *MGH Epp* 5), pp. 3-84, No. 2, p. 20.

[21] Ed. in: *Das Constitutum Constantini (Konstantinische Schenkung)*, ed. H. FUHRMANN (Hannover, 1968: *MGH Iuris Germanici antiqui in usum scholarum* 10), cc. 7-8, pp. 69-74.

saint told the visionary his or her name. So far, I have come across only one hagiographical text in which a picture is explicitly adduced to identify a saint seen in a vision. This occurs in the *Gloria martyrum* written by Gregory of Tours, probably between 585 and 588.[22] Gregory tells how one day the son of a Jewish glass-worker had received the Eucharist, just as the other young boys with whom he had learned the alphabet. Upon hearing this, the boy's father was enraged and threw him into the burning oven, adding more wood to it. Christian neighbours, rushing in when they heard the boy's mother wailing, to their astonishment found him totally unhurt and reclining in the furnace as if on very soft feathers. When he was taken out, the boy declared:

> "The woman who was sitting on the throne in that church where I received the bread from the table and who was cradling a young boy in her lap covered me with her cloak, so that the fire did not devour me".[23]

"There is therefore no doubt", Gregory comments, "that the blessed Mary had appeared to him".[24] Contrary to the earlier examples, the reason for this description of Mary is not so much the need to verify the dream image – which was after all corroborated by the miracle of the boy's survival – but rather the fact that the boy was Jewish and therefore supposedly unfamiliar with the Christian faith. It is an expression of innocence rather than a verification method.[25]

Here a passage from the end of the fourth century may be noted, although a picture is not mentioned. Iconographical considerations are used to establish

---

[22] For the exact dating, see: *Gregory of Tours, Glory of the Martyrs*, tr. R. VAN DAM (Liverpool, 1988), pp. 4-5.

[23] Gregory of Tours, *Gloria martyrum*, c. 9, ed. B. KRUSCH, *Gregorii Turonensis Opera: 2. Miracula et opera minora* (Hannover, 1885: *MGH SS rer. Merov.* 1.2), pp. 34-111, at p. 44: "*Interrogantes autem infantulum christiani, quale ei inter ignes fuisset umbraculum, ait: 'Mulier, quae in basilicam illam, ubi panem de mensa accepi, in cathedra resedens, parvulum in sinu gestat infantem, haec me pallio suo, ne ignis voraret, operuit'. Unde indubitatum est, beatam ei Mariam apparuisse*". The translation is taken from Gregory of Tours, *Glory of the Martyrs*, pp. 24-32.

[24] *Ibid.*

[25] This story is one of the earliest traces of anti-jewish sentiments in the West. It was based on a similar tale in Evagrius Scholasticus (ca. 536-600), *Historia ecclesiastica*, ed.in: PG 86.2, col. 2770. MOREIRA, *Dreams, Visions, and Spiritual Authority*, pp. 101-102. Gregory's version forms the beginning of a western tradition of this story which has continued far into the modern era. Compare: E.F. WILSON, *The 'Stella Maris' of John of Garland. Edited, Together With a Study of Certain Collections of Mary Legends Made in Northern France in the Twelfth and Thirteenth Centuries* (Cambridge Mass., 1946), pp. 95-96 and pp. 157-159. M. RUBIN, *Gentile Tales: The Narrative Assault on Late Medieval Jews* (New Haven and London, 1999), pp. 2-39. With thanks to Niek Thate.

whether an apparition is what it purports to be, interestingly enough by the visionary himself. Sulpicius Severus tells us in his *Vita Martini* about an attempt by the devil to deceive saint Martin. The devil appeared in Martin's cell "preceded and even surrounded by a glittering light" and dressed in royal robes, with a serene face and a happy countenance, "so that he resembled anything but the devil".[26] Martin was dumbstruck, and the two looked at each other for some time. Then the devil declared that he was the returning Christ and had wanted to manifest himself first to Martin. As Martin kept quiet, the devil reaffirmed this claim.

> Then Martin said, understanding through a revelation by the Spirit that it was the devil, not the Lord: "The Lord Jesus has not foretold that he would return clothed in purple, nor shining with a diadem. For my part, I will not believe that Christ has returned unless in the clothes and form in which he suffered, and unless he shows the stigmata of the cross." At these words he instantly evaporated in smoke. He filled the cell with such a stench that he left indisputable evidence of having been the devil. These things as I have told them, I learned from Martin's own mouth, so that nobody may think them to be a fabrication.[27]

It is interesting to see that Martin's answer is inspired by a revelation of the Holy Spirit. One might say that this second revelation falsifies the first, diabolical one. The arguments for this falsification are of an iconographic nature. The devil poses as a triumphant Christ, dressed in what are called royal clothes, resembling fourth-century imperial vestments. According to Martin, this is not how Christ will return, and the truth of his opinion is confirmed by the devil's subsequent flight. Martin's description of the returning Christ seems familiar, as it is much like well-known depictions of this event, e.g. on Rogier van der

---

[26] Sulpicius Severus, *Vita sancti Martini*, c. 24.4, ed. J. FONTAINE, *Sulpice Sévère: Vie de saint Martin*, (Paris, 1967-1969: *Sources chrétiennes* 133-135), 1, pp. 248-344: "*Quodam enim die, praemissa prae se et circumiectus ipse luce purpurea, quo facilius claritate adsumpti fulgoris inluderet, veste etiam regia indutus, diademate ex gemmis auroque redimitus, calceis auro inlitis, sereno ore, laeta facis, ut nihil minus quam diabolus putaretur, oranti in cellula adstitit*". See Fontaine's extensive commentary on this passage in *Sulpice Sévère: Vie de saint Martin*, 3, pp. 1022-1042.

[27] Sulpicius Severus, *Vita Martini*, c. 24.7-8, ed. FONTAINE, 1, p.308: "*Tum ille, revelante sibi spiritu ut intellegeret diabolum esse, non Dominum: non se, inquit, Iesus Dominus purpuratum nec diademate renidentem venturum esse praedixit; ego Christum, nisi in eo habitu formaque qua passus est, nisi crucis stigmata praeferentem, venisse non credam. Ad hanc ille vocem statim ut fumus evanuit. Cellulam tanto foetore conplevit ut indubia indicia relinqueret diabolum se fuisse. Hoc itaque gestum, ut supra rettuli, ex ipsius Martini ore cognovi, ne quis forte existimet fabulosum*".

Weyde's (admittedly much later) polyptych for the Hôtel Dieu at Beaune. However, more than one church in Martin's own days showed an imperial Christ such as the devil was feigning to be.[28] One may wonder whether in Sulpicius's text these iconographic ideas were really intended as means of 'instant' authentication. Possibly it is rather the other way around, and the false apparition in this passage is used to advocate a specific theological and iconographic ideal, which was in line with Sulpicius's and Martin's ascetic ideals. This is certainly suggested by the marked contrast with the description of Christ's appearance in a better-known, earlier vision of Martin, in which Christ is only wearing the half mantle given by Martin to the beggar at the gates of Amiens.[29] In the story about the disguised devil, the iconographic ideas are used to falsify the apparition, but the whole story in effect validates these same iconographic ideas.

Iconography seems hardly ever to have been used explicitly to identify saints. There are, however, some traces of pictures and iconography in the descriptions of saints appearing in visions – although even those are quite rare. A text in which such traces can be found, is the ninth-century *Vita Ansgarii*, the life of Bishop Ansgar of Hamburg-Bremen (831-865) who was famous as missionary to the Danes and Swedes. The *Vita* was written by Rimbert, one of Ansgar's pupils and his successor as bishop of Hamburg-Bremen (865-888). This text is full of descriptions of dreams and visions. In one passage Christ has joined Ansgar in prayer. Christ is said to have been tall in stature, and to have had a noble face and Jewish clothes, while his divine nature shone from his eyes.[30] More interesting still is the description of the journey Ansgar made on Pentecost through a kind of purgatory and through heaven, guided by the apostle Peter and John the Baptist. This story is partly told in what, according to Rimbert, are Ansgar's own words.[31] Ansgar immediately recognized Peter and

---

[28] C. IHM, *Die Programme der christlichen Apsismalerei vom vierten Jahrhundert bis zur Mitte des achten Jahrhunderts* (Wiesbaden, 1960), pp. 11-41.

[29] Sulpicius Severus, *Vita Martini*, c. 3, pp. 256-258. For the ascetic ideals of Martin and Sulpicius, and their problematic nature for the contemporary society at large: C. STANCLIFFE, *St. Martin and his Hagiographer: History and Miracle in Sulpicius Severus* (Oxford, 1983).

[30] Rimbert, *Vita Ansgarii* (BHL 544-545), c. 4, ed. G. WAITZ, *Vita Anskarii auctore Rimberto* (Hannover, 1884: MGH SS rer. Germ. i.u.s. 55), pp. 13-79, at p. 24: *"Cumque ab oratione surrexisset, ecce vir per ostium veniebat, statura procerus, Iudaico more vestitus, vultu decorus. Ex cuius oculis splendor divinitatis velut flamma ignis radiabat. Quem intuitus, omni cunctatione postposita, Christum dominum esse credebat, atque procurrens, ad pedes eius corruit"*. Note that the *Vita Rimberti*, c. 22, edited by G. WAITZ as an appendix to *Vita Anskarii auctore Rimberto*, pp. 81-100, at pp. 97-98, ascribes visions to Rimbert as well.

[31] Rimbert, *Vita Ansgarii*, c. 3, p. 22: *"Et ut verbis ipsius utamur: Videbam, inquit, a longe diversos sanctorum ordines, ..."*.

John when they appeared. The descriptions he gives of the two roughly conform to the iconography of the age, although John is portrayed less as an ascetic than would have been possible. Peter is described as the older of the two, with "a grey head, straight and thick hair, a blooming face, a sorrowful countenance, white and coloured clothes, and a short stature". John the Baptist had "a longer stature, a prominent beard, a brown and curly head, a lean face, a charming countenance and silk clothes".[32] John's silk clothes are rather unlike the animal skins or camel hair shirts he is wearing in most pictures, but pictures did exist in which John the Baptist wore clothes made of woven fabrics. In the *Vita*, the silk clothes are probably an expression of his heavenly status. The description of his hair and beard is more in line with his ascetic image, which originated in the East and became ever more popular during the Middle Ages.[33] Most notable in the description of Peter is the absence of a tonsure and the statement that he has straight rather than curly hair, although such features can also be found in some pictures.[34]

Such precise descriptions of the outward appearances of saints are rare in hagiography. It is striking that all examples presented so far show members of the most exalted category of saints: Mary, Peter, Paul and John the Baptist. This is in line with the contemporary stage of development of the iconography of saints. Only Mary, the apostles and a few others of similarly high stature had as yet obtained characteristics and attributes. Most saints were portrayed rather impersonally. Apostles were often barefoot, martyrs could be portrayed with a palm, while bishops and abbots could be clad in their respective vestments. Apart from a few saints of high status, individual saints were either not identified at all, or identification was done with the help of written captions.[35]

---

[32] Rimbert, *Vita Ansgarii*, c. 3, p. 22: "*Quorum unus erat senior, cano capite, capillo plano et spisso, facie rubenti, vultu subtristi, veste candida et colorata, statura brevi; quem ipse sanctum Petrum esse nemine narrante statim agnovit. Alius vero iuvenis erat, statura procerior, barbam emittens, capite subfusco atque subcrispo, facie macilenta, vultu iocundo, in veste serica; quem ille sanctum Iohannem esse omnino credidit*".

[33] L. RÉAU, *Iconographie de l'art chrétien: 2. Iconographie de la bible: 1. Ancien testament* (Paris, 1956), pp. 431-463 ("Saint Jean-Baptiste"), at pp. 437-440. E. WEIS, "Johannes der Taufer (*Baptista*), der Vorläufer (*Prodromos*)", in: E. KIRSCHBAUM, *Lexikon der christlichen Ikonographie*, 8 vols. (Rome etc., 1968-1976), 7, cols. 164-190, at cols. 166-173.

[34] L. RÉAU, *Iconographie de l'art chrétien: 3. Iconographie des saints* 3 (Parijs, 1959), pp. 1076-1100 ("Pierre"), at pp. 1082-1085. E. WEIS, "Johannes der Taufer". W. BRAUNFELS, "Petrus, Apostel", in: KIRSCHBAUM, *Lexikon der christlichen Ikonographie*, 8, cols. 158-174, at cols. 161-162.

[35] L. RÉAU, *Iconographie de l'art chrétien: 1. Introduction générale* (Paris, 1955), pp. 416-420. J.J.M. TIMMERS, *Christelijke symboliek en iconografie*, second, revised edn. (Bussum, 1974), cols. 640-648.

In view of this minimal elaboration of the saints' iconography, it is hardly surprising that hagiographical texts rarely describe individual features of the saints as seen in visions. An interesting example is Saint Martin. In later images he is portrayed either as a young soldier, often in the act of dividing his mantle, or as a bishop.[36] For Gregory of Tours, writing in the second half of the sixth century, Martin was probably the greatest hero after Christ. Consequently, Martin makes an appearance in several dozens of the visions described by Gregory. Yet in all those descriptions he is only three times associated with the image of a soldier, and in one of those it is not even Martin himself who appears, but the devil in Martin's guise.[37] Martin mostly appears as a venerable old man.[38]

But what about the issue of the verification of dreams through pictures, as seems to have been the case in the *Donation of Constantine* and Pope Hadrian's letter? The question of how a dreamer or visionary knew the identity of the persons he or she saw, seems to have been of slight importance to our authors. The much more important question was, whether these persons were really what they purported to be. After all, more than once a human had been led astray by false dreams and demons disguised as saints or other heavenly creatures. Paul had already warned that Satan often disguised himself as an angel of light (II Cor. 11:14). In the sixth and seventh centuries hagiographers were in no doubt that the devil and his cronies had not forgotten such tricks. Gregory of Tours tells how the deacon Secundellus was misled by the devil, who appeared to him in a dream disguised as Christ. After that vision, Secundellus was able to perform miraculous cures. It was only after a warning by the recluse Friardus that Secundellus could expose the devil and drive him away.[39] Saints of Martin's stature could see through such disguises; lesser men could not.

Iconography would not have been of much use to hagiographers as a guarantor of authenticity. If the devil could disguise himself as Christ, he certainly

---

[36] L. Réau, *Iconographie de l'art chrétien: 3. Iconographie des saints 2* (Paris, 1958), pp. 900-917 ("Martin de Tours"), at p. 905. S. Kimpel, "Martin von Tours", in: Kirschbaum, *Lexikon der christlichen Ikonographie*, 7, cols. 572-579.

[37] Gregory of Tours, *Virtutes Martini*, 1, c. 24, ed. in: *Gregorii Turonensis Opera: 2. Miracula et opera minora*, pp. 134-211, at p. 151: Martin appears to count Alpinus of Tours attired with "his usual weapons" and heals the count's foot. *Ibid.*, 2, c. 18, p. 165: A demon appears to Landulf in the guise of a veteran and claims to be saint Martin, but Landulf sees through it. *Ibid.*, 4, c. 26, pp. 205-206: Martin appears to prisoners and liberates them. His features are not described, but he calls himself a soldier of Christ.

[38] De Nie, *Views from a Many-Windowed Tower*, pp. 213-251.

[39] Gregory of Tours, *Vitae patrum* 10, c. 2, ed. in: *Gregorii Turonensis Opera: 2. Miracula et opera minora*, pp. 211-294, at pp. 256-257. Compare: Moreira, *Dreams, Visions, and Spiritual Authority*, pp. 44-46.

could conform to iconographic conventions. In texts from the eighth century and later the devil less often seems to disguise himself as a saint. The notion of dreams being sometimes false did not, however, disappear. There is ample evidence for continuing concern about the reliability of dreams.[40] However, hagiographers usually did not take the trouble to prove that a vision was authentic. Often they recounted the visions, stating directly that they were authentic, or silently assuming that they were. This is because narrative hagiography is, up to a point, also historiography. The events it describes all took place in the past. And in the end, history is considered the best proof of the truth of matters like these. Alcuin states in the metrical part of his *Vita Willibrordi*, when he speaks about the prophecy given in a dream to Willibrord's mother before his birth:

> All things prophesied are fulfilled in the said order,
> And the outcome of events proves the dreams to be true.[41]

There is a difference between a saint having a vision and a dead saint appearing in a vision. Most hagiographers were not eager to allow for even the smallest possibility that their hero might have been in danger of deception by the devil. Instead, they used the visions their saint received as an added sign of his holiness. When the devil tries to deceive the saint through a dream, the saint immediately spots the deception. It is only when a saint appears to others after his or her death that evidence for the authenticity of the dream may be required – and given. This happens most often in texts dealing with the discovery, elevation or translation of relics. Often a dead saint gives orders to mortals concerning his or her physical remains. In such cases some strategies could be used to prove that the vision was genuine. This was yet another step towards proving that the relics were genuine, which was the first concern of the authors of these texts.[42] Iconography does not seem to have been part of such strategies. Hagio-

---

[40] Dutton, *Politics of dreaming*, pp. 40-45.

[41] Alcuin, *Vita sancti Willibrordi*, liber II, c. 34, ll. 27-28, ed. in: *Poetae Latini Aevi Carolini* 1, ed. E. DÜMMLER (Berlin, 1881: *MGH Poet. lat. medii aevi* 1), pp. 207-220, at p. 219:

> *"Omnia vatidici conplentur in ordine dicta,*
> *Et rerum eventus somnia vera probat".*

[42] A.-M. HELVÉTIUS, "Les inventions de reliques en Gaule du Nord (IXe-XIIIe siècle)", in: *Les reliques: Objets, cultes, symboles, actes du colloque international de l'Université du Littoral-Côte d'Opale (Boulogne-sur-Mer), 4-6 septembre 1997*, ed. E. BOZÓKY and A.-M. HELVÉTIUS (Turnhout, 1999: *Hagiologia* 1), pp. 293-311, at p. 296.

graphical texts had other methods to prove whether a vision was genuine or not. A very popular method of unmasking the disguised devil is the request by the dreamer to make the sign of the cross. Of course, the devil never complied and fled when the dreamer made the sign himself.

The authenticity of a vision is sometimes established by a miracle. This is the case in a late eleventh-century text on the consecration of the new abbey church of St. Denis, an event which had happened centuries earlier. This story is an embellishment of an older tale, originating with Hincmar of Reims (ca. 806-882), ascribing the consecration to an initiative by king Dagobert I (623-639).[43] According to the eleventh-century version of the story, a leper who stayed in the church saw Christ enter in the night before the planned consecration. In the company of the apostles Peter and Paul and the martyrs Dionysius, Rusticus and Eleutherius, he consecrated the church himself. Christ then ordered the leper to tell Dagobert and the congregated bishops that the consecration had already been performed. When the leper pointed out that he would probably not be believed because of his humble status, Christ healed him by pulling the affected skin from his face. This miracle convinced the king and clerics of the truth of the leper's vision. According to the text, the piece of afflicted skin was subsequently put in a reliquary and venerated as a relic.[44]

A favourite way to establish the divine origin of the vision was the triple dream. In such a scheme the saint visits the dreamer three times before the dreamer acts according to the saint's commands. This theme seems to rely on the connection with the divine Trinity, which would be too terrifying for the devil to tamper with. Its inspiration may have been the Old Testament story of the vocation of the prophet Samuel (I Sm. 3:4-10). The triple dream is already a common feature in texts from the sixth century and can be found throughout the Middle Ages.[45] However, a development can be detected in the way it is used. In the early instances, the fact that the dreamer only heeds the dream after the third occurrence is usually ascribed to the ignorance of the mortal, who at first does not realize the dream's divine origin, just as Samuel did not realize that he was called by God rather than by Heli. The third dream is a marker of its holy origin. From the tenth century onwards, one finds the variant that after the first dream the dreamer wakes up and prays for two sequels of the dream to

---

[43] G.M. SPRENGEL, *The Chronical Tradition of Saint-Denis: A Survey* (Leiden, 1978), pp. 16-20.

[44] An edition of this text can be found in: C.J. LIEBMAN, "La consécration légendaire de la basilique de Saint-Denis", *Le Moyen Age*, 3ᵉ série, 6 (1935), pp. 252-264, at pp. 259-264.

[45] E.g. Gregory of Tours, *Gloria martyrum*, cc. 22 and 86, pp. 51 and 96; ID., *Virtutes Martini*, 3, c. 42, pp. 192-193; ID., *Gloria confessorum*, c. 90, ed. in: *Gregorii Turonensis Opera: 2. Miracula et opera minora*, pp. 294-370, at pp. 355-356.

be sure of its blissful meaning.[46] Dreamers who ask for such reprises are usually clerics. The social differences between two recipients of triple dreams are clearly developed in the already mentioned *Translatio Agnetis et Benigni*. Here the peasant Amolwinus ignores the first vision of Agnes. After being threatened by her in the second vision and after having told his master about it, he is punished for sleeping during working hours. In the third vision, Agnes points out that this was only right, since he did not go to the priest Lambertus as she had told him. Shortly afterwards she visits Lambertus herself in a dream, because he had not believed the story any more than had Amolwinus's master. Lambertus's reaction upon waking is quite different from that of Amolwinus: he goes to his church and prays for two reprises of the vision. These are duly given, after which Lambertus does as he has been told.[47]

A less frequently used strategy to the same effect is a vision seen by two people, who both act as instructed in the vision. A biblical inspiration for this strategy may have been the story about the conversion of Saul (Acts 9:10-13). In it, Ananias is ordered in a vision to go to the house of Judas to heal Saul, and is told that Saul at that very moment has a vision of Ananias entering and healing him. Gregory the Great describes such a double dream in his *Dialogi*. In this case, the dreamers do not understand the importance of the fact. According to Gregory, Benedict sent some brethren to a new monastery near Tarracina. He promised to come to them on a certain day to point out where the different buildings of the monastery should be built. On the eve of that day the new abbot and prior both dreamed of Benedict telling them precisely what he had promised. Upon waking, the two told each other their dreams, but did not trust them. They waited for Benedict, who did not show up. After having travelled to him to complain, Benedict pointed out to them that he had chosen to come to them in their dream rather than physically.[48] The ignorance of the two dreamers

---

[46] *Translatio Agnetis et Benigni*, c. 6, p. 358. *Vita et translatio Ieronis*, cc. 10-11, ed. in: *Fontes Egmundenses*, ed. O. OPPERMANN (Utrecht, 1933: *Werken van het Historisch Genootschap*, 3e serie, 61), p. 51-56. In Ruopert of Mettlach, *Vita sancti Adalberti confessoris*, c. 13, ed. G.N.M. VIS in: *Egmond en Berne: Twee verhalende historische bronnen uit de middeleeuwen* (Leiden, 1987: *Nederlandse Historische Bronnen* 7), p 56, the nun Wilfsit does not ask for two reprises of the dream, but the saint sends three dreams "so that her faith shall not be offended by any doubt": "*Et ne fidem quivis forsitan ambiguitatis offendisset scrupulus, trinis feminam prefatam dignatus est certificare visionibus*". The triple dream also made its way into the vernacular literature, as, e.g. in the twelfth-century Middle-Dutch romance *Karel ende Elegast*, ed. A.M. DUINHOVEN, *Karel ende Elegast: Diplomatische uitgave van de Middelnederlandse teksten en de tekst uit de Karlmeinet-compilatie* (Zwolle, 1969), in which Charlemagne only sets out on a nightly quest after being commanded three times by an angel.

[47] *Translatio Agnetis and Benigni*, cc. 3-6, p. 358.

[48] Gregory the Great, *Dialogi*, 2, c. 22, ed. A. DE VOGÜÉ, *Gregoire le Grand, Dialogues*,

may be intended to bring out the exceptional holiness of Benedict, who is still alive when the dreams take place.

A model example of a double dream can be found in a text concerning saints Landoaldus and Landrada, written around 980 by Heriger of Lobbes (ca. 950-1007).[49] The nobleman Lantso had arranged for the bodies of saint Landoaldus and several of his companions to be elevated. About a year later, his wife Sigeburgis fell seriously ill. She had a dream in which saint Landrada complained that her body and those of two other of Landoaldus's companions had not been elevated with the others. Sigeburgis requested Lantso to have those bodies elevated as well, but he declined, saying that he had already spent so much money on the previous elevation that another one would be too expensive. Some days afterwards Sigeburgis was again visited by Landrada, who now accused her not of neglect but rather of contempt. The saint told her that, no matter how much money she would spend on doctors, she would not be healed unless all three holy bodies were elevated. Landrada also showed her where exactly their bodies could be found. Next morning, as Sigeburgis was still in doubt, one of her maidens told her that she had also been visited by Landrada and had been told the same things. This news dissolved all Sigeburgis's doubts. She immediately arranged all things necessary for the elevation.

Our conclusion has to be that the influence of iconography on the description of individual saints in early medieval hagiographical visions was small. On the one hand, the iconography was not refined enough to distinguish between most saints. On the other hand, one may wonder whether a more refined iconographic tradition would have made much difference. The need in hagiography for this kind of identification of individual saints seems to have been small, as there were other methods of authentication. This does not mean that it would be fruitless to look further into the depiction of saints in both texts and pictures: these were clearly not separate fields to the minds of our authors. This is shown quite clearly by the parallels between texts and pictures in indicating the supernatural quality of saints through heavenly light and their larger stature. Further-

---

3 vols. (Paris, 1978-1980: *Sources chrétiennes* 251, 260 and 265), 2, pp. 200-204. For a discussion of Gregory's importance for the medieval traditions concerning visions, see: MOREIRA, *Dreams, Visions, and Spiritual Authority*, pp. 34-38.

    [49] Heriger of Lobbes, *Vita sancti Landoaldi/Elevatio sanctae Landradae* (BHL 4700-4706), cc. 7-9, ed. O. HOLDER-EGGER in: *Supplementa* (MGH SS 15), pp. 604-605. For the place of these hagiographical works within the total oeuvre of Heriger, see: P. VERBIST, *Heriger van Lobbes (ca. 942–†1007): Een laat-karolinger of een vroeg-scholasticus? Een historisch onderzoek naar de religieus-culturele wereld van Luik en Lobbes in de late tiende eeuw*, licentiaatsverhandeling Leuven (1997), pp. 66-71.

more, the story of Martin seeing through the devil's disguise shows how ideas about a saint's appearance could advocate ascetic ideals. But the most important parallel between early medieval images and texts in the portrayal of individual saints is probably the lack of a strict iconography in both media.

Pictor Iconiam Litterarum:
Rituals as Visual Elements in Early Medieval Ruler Portraits in Word and Image[1]

MARIËLLE HAGEMAN

In his panegyric account of the feats of Louis the Pious from *ca.* 827, Ermoldus Nigellus, or Ermold the Black, describes the following scene: Paulinus, patriarch of Aquileia, is singing the psalms in the church at Aachen. One by one, Charlemagne's sons appear before the altar. First, Charles enters the church to pray, accompanied by a splendid retinue. With hurried steps he approaches the altar. The patriarch asks a servant who this might be. When he hears that it is the king's firstborn son, he falls silent. Charles passes before Paulinus and leaves. Then, Pippin appears, also accompanied by a following of nobles. Paulinus bows his head for the king, who hurries by, just as his brother had done. Finally, Louis approaches. He embraces the altar, throws himself down on the floor and, in tears, begs Christ for help. The patriarch, who had kept his distance in the presence of Charles and Pippin, now rises to greet the devout Louis. Louis prostrates himself at the patriarch's feet, but Paulinus raises him from the ground. Later, the patriarch tells Charlemagne what has happened, adding that it is his belief that, if God were to give the Franks a king from Charlemagne's house, Louis will be the one on the throne.[2]

---

[1] This article is based on my PhD-thesis *The Emperor's Clothes: Rituals of the Carolingian and Ottonian Rulers in Word and Image*, especially chapters 4 and 7.

[2] Ermoldus Nigellus, *In honorem Hludowici*, vv. 600-633, ed. E. FARAL, *Poème sur Louis le Pieux et épîtres au roi Pépin* (Paris, 1964: *Les classiques de l'histoire de France au Moyen Age*), pp. 48-51. This prophecy is attributed to Alcuin in the *Vita Alcuini*, c. 15, ed. W. ARNDT (Hannover, 1887: *MGH SS* 15), pp. 192-193. There, the event takes places in the year 800, when Charlemagne visits Tours accompanied by his three sons.

In this way, Ermoldus is able in his poem to outline the individuals and their mutual relations with the help of body language. He gives a characterization in which gestures play an essential part. Louis's brothers compare poorly to the future emperor because of their lack of gestures. Louis shows himself through attitude and gestures to be humble before God and the patriarch, whereas his brothers seem chiefly interested in presenting themselves with an impressive following: they hardly pay any attention to the Church or Paulinus. In response, Paulinus only bows his head for them – a gesture which was required because of their exalted position – whereas he rises out of respect for Louis. Louis's body language has told Paulinus (and Ermoldus's audience) that he will be a good ruler. He shows himself to be the ideal Cristian ruler and is recognized as such by the patriarch. Again, the patriarch makes his approval known with a gesture, by raising Louis from the ground.

Rituals and gestures could be employed to create an image of a king or emperor. The visual was the most important aspect of a ritual, as early medieval authors emphasize. It was very important that rituals were *seen*. Nithard tells us, e.g. how the Strasbourg oaths, with which the warring brothers Charles the Bald and Louis the German swore loyalty to one another in 843, were sworn before the eyes ("*in conspectu*") of the people.[3] Focusing on the prostration, this article will discuss the way in which ritual, here defined as a complex of gestures with a symbolic meaning, is presented in Carolingian texts and images;[4] how (visual) descriptions of rituals can be read; and which relations exist between rituals described in texts and those depicted in the visual arts.

Visual Elements in Panegyrics and Historiography

Throughout his poem Ermoldus, probably a cleric banned from the court of Louis's son Pippin of Aquitaine and trying to regain favour by writing a panegyric on Louis the Pious, makes use of gestures and rituals to 'paint a portrait'

---

[3] Nithard, *Historiae*, III, 5, ed. R. RAU, *Quellen zur karolingischen Reichsgeschichte* (Berlin, 1955: *Ausgewählte Quellen zur Deutschen Geschichte des Mittelalters* 5), pp. 438-443. On Nithard, see: J.L. NELSON, "Public *histories* and private history in the work of Nithard", in: EAD., *Politics and Ritual in Early Medieval Europe* (London, 1986), pp. 195-238.

[4] On Carolingian royal ritual, see, e.g. J.L. NELSON, "The Lord's anointed and the people's choice: Carolingian royal ritual", in EAD., *The Frankish World 750-900* (London and Rio Grande, 1996), pp. 99-131 and EAD., *Politics and Ritual in Early Medieval Europe*; and the work of Philippe Buc, especially his *The Dangers of Ritual: Between Early Medieval Texts and Social Scientific Theory* (Princeton, 2001).

of the ideal ruler.[5] Ermoldus was obviously interested in the visual. He valued the paintings at the aula and the chapel of the palace at Ingelheim, in which the Carolingians are placed in a context of biblical and classical rulers, and described them at length. A painting of Louis the Pious's father Charlemagne is described:

> Wise Charlemagne's frank expression is clear to see,
> His head is crowned, as his lineage and achievements demand.
> A throng of Saxons stand opposite him, waging battle,
> He subdues, vanquishes and reduces them to subjection.
> With these and other deeds that place shines brightly;
> Those who gaze on it with pleasure take strength from the sight.[6]

The painting showed Charlemagne in all his outward splendour: his facial expression, his crown. It also revealed his position of dominance over the Saxons. The visual is powerfully present in Ermoldus's poem also – and maybe even principally – in descriptions of gestures and rituals.

Ermoldus's contemporary Paschasius Radbertus explicitly compared the writing of a biography to the painting of a likeness. In the preface to his *Epitaphium Arsenii*, his cryptic account of the life of Wala, his predecessor as abbot of Corbie, he says that is has been suggested to him that

> in the manner of Zeuxis I depict as a memorial for the ages a representation of the character of our Arsenius. ... I, unworthy artist, am afraid to appear even more unworthy by giving through the medium of letters an image of a man so great, so renowned for his virtuous ornaments.[7]

---

[5] About Ermoldus, see the introduction by FARAL, pp. V-XXI; P. GODMAN, *Poets and Emperors: Frankish Politics and Carolingian Poetry* (Oxford, 1987); A. EBENBAUER, *Carmen historicum: Untersuchungen zur historischen Dichtung im karolingischen Europa* (Wien, 1978: *Philologica Germanica* 4).

[6] Ermoldus Nigellus, *In honorem Hludowici*, vv. 2160-2163, pp. 164-165. Translation in: P. GODMAN, *Poetry of the Carolingian Renaissance* (London, 1985), p. 255.

[7] Paschasius Radbertus, *Ex vita Walae abbatis corbeienses*, ed. G. PERTZ (Hannover, 1829: *MGH SS* 2), p. 533: "... *rogat Arsenii nostri morum liniamentis imaginem saeculis in memoriam more Zeuxi pingere. Nec satis igitur cogitat, quod confundor foedus pictor iconiam tanti viri, suis virtutum floribus gloriosam, litterarum in speculo posteris, ne foedior appaream, exhibere*". Elsewhere, Paschasius stresses the importance of the art of portrait painting: *Ex vita Walae*, I, 11, p. 537: "*Uti pictorum mos est, qui bene pingere norunt, qui saepe ita vultus exprimunt, ut sine litteris et voce loquantur*". Translation in: A. CABANISS, *Charlemagne's Cousins: Contemporary Lives of Adalard and Wala* (Syracuse, 1967), p. 83.

The dividing line between the literary and the visual arts seems to have been slight for these authors. Ermoldus's description of Louis the Pious could almost be called a depiction, the panegyric presenting an idealized portrait of the emperor. An important visual ingredient of the written ruler portrait was the description of gestures and rituals. The anecdote of the visual interaction between Paulinus of Aquileia and Louis the Pious is just one example chosen from many. Louis was rendered as the ideal ruler through a description of his gestures, and the poem consists of a sequence of scenes composed of descriptions of gestures and rituals. In a council scene, e.g., nobles one by one prostrate themselves before the ruler, kissing his feet.[8] When Louis is visited by pope Stephen IV at Reims, he kneels three times before the pope; this is followed by an elaborate coronation scene.[9] A battle-scene is described for its gestures.[10] In describing the reception and baptism of the Danish king at Ingelheim, Ermoldus dwells on the splendid appearance of the court. Before the white-robed clergy and the gold-clad family and retinue of Louis the Pious, the impressed Danes bow and submit to a public baptism ceremony. Complementing this display of Carolingian authority is the hunting-scene that follows, in which Louis proves himself an ideal ruler by his performance at the royal ritual event *par excellence*, the hunt.[11]

Time and again, Ermoldus's descriptions are of a visual nature: we can almost 'see the story happening before our eyes' because of his many descriptions of attitudes, gestures and rituals. The early medieval author did not simply render an account of the ruler's deeds. As Karl Morrison has discussed, medieval authors saw analogies between the writing of history – here in poetic form –, theatre and the visual arts. Writers thought they were working as dramatists did: "They were selecting, trimming, and arranging materials to portray, rather than to document, experience".[12] In panegyrical poetry especially, but in historiography as well, the ruler was characterised by his attitudes and gestures, by the rituals he performed. These also showed his relations to others - to his subjects, to other rulers, to dignitaries of the Church, and to God.

In Ermoldus's text, the influence of late antique panegyrics can be noticed. As Sabine MacCormack has shown, the role of ceremonies in panegyrical descriptions and in depictions in the visual arts increased in late Antiquity. The

---

[8] Ermoldus Nigellus, *In honorem Hludowici*, vv. 206-213, pp. 20-21.
[9] Ermoldus Nigellus, *In honorem Hludowici*, vv. 870-1100., pp. 68-87.
[10] Ermoldus Nigellus, *In honorem Hludowici*, vv. 397ff., pp. 34 ff.
[11] Ermoldus Nigellus, *In honorem Hludowici*, vv. 2252-2437, pp. 172-185.
[12] K.F. MORRISON, *History as a Visual Art* (Princeton, 1990).

emperor was praised through the representation of imperial ceremony.[13] The importance of outward appearance and rituals was 'borrowed' in Carolingian panegyric, in which, e.g. the ruler's looks and rituals are described. An illustration is provided by the famous poems by Angilbert and Theodulf in which they describe Charlemagne's court, with all the outward splendour of the palace and of the king's family and entourage.[14] The importance of outward show is especially clear in the direct forerunner of Ermoldus's poem, the so-called *Paderborn Epic*.[15] Of this poem a fragment only survives, the third book of a lost larger epic from the first decade of the ninth century. Again, the hunt and a meeting between pope and ruler – here Leo III and Charlemagne – are central scenes.[16] Charlemagne awaits the advent of the pope in a high spot, surrounded by his retinue. The pope approaches and looks at the king and his people:

He marvels at the many peoples from many lands whom he sees,
At their differences, their strange tongues, dress, and weapons.

Charlemagne embraces the pope and kisses him. When the king and the pope join hands and walk together, the entire army prostrates itself three times before the pope.[17] Just as Ermoldus, the author of the Paderborn Epic tries to conjure up a picture of the ideal king and of the ideal court, describing externals such as gestures and rituals in great detail. Modern authors cannot help describing scenes like these using 'pictorial' similes. Peter Godman, in his article on the ritual of the hunt in early medieval poetry writes about "the stylish brushstrokes of the [...] miniaturists" and their "broad canvas".[18]

Rituals play an important part as visual elements in historically oriented panegyrics, painting the portret of a ruler with words. But this is not just true for poetry, by nature a medium apt for wordpainting. Although less strikingly

[13] S.G. MACCORMACK, *Art and Ceremony in Late Antiquity* (Berkeley, 1981).

[14] Angilbert, *To Charlemagne and his entourage*, ed. and tr. GODMAN, *Poetry of the Carolingian Renaissance*, pp. 112-119; Theodulf, *On the court*, ed. and tr. *ibid.*, pp. 150-163.

[15] On the Paderborn Epic, see: D. SCHALLER, "Interpretationsprobleme im Aachener Karlsepos", in: ID., *Studien zur lateinischen Dichtung des Frühmittelalters* (Stuttgart, 1995: *Quellen und Untersuchungen zur lateinischen Philologie des Mittelalters* 11), pp. 164-183; and ID., "Das Aachener Epos für Karl den Kaiser", *ibid.*, pp. 129-163 and 419-422.

[16] P. GODMAN, "The poetic hunt: From Saint Martin to Charlemagne's heir", in: *Charlemagne's Heir: New Perspectives on the Reign of Louis the Pious (814-840)*, ed. P. GODMAN and R. COLLINS (Oxford, 1990), pp. 565-589, at p. 584.

[17] *Karolus Magnus et Leo Papa: Ein Paderborner Epos vom Jahre 799*, ed. H. BEUMANN, F. BRUNHÖLZL and W. WINKELMANN (Paderborn, 1966), vv. 487-536, pp. 94-97.

[18] GODMAN, "The poetic hunt", p. 584.

and continuously present than in panegyrics, rituals can also be found in the representation of the ruler in Carolingian historiography. An example, comparable to the anecdote from Ermoldus at the beginning of this article, can be found in Thegan's biographical work on Louis the Pious, written *ca.* 835 in defence of the emperor following his reinstatement after his public penance and imprisonment by his sons.[19] Thegan portrays Louis as a particularly pious ruler, endowed with the virtues of a monk.[20] He writes that Louis went to church every morning to pray: "genuflecting, he touched his forehead to the ground, praying humbly for a long time, sometimes with tears".[21] Here, as in Ermoldus's poem, the author uses the ritual of prostration to show his reader a humble ruler.

Proskynesis

The *proskynesis*, or prostration, was one of the most important rituals of the early Middle Ages. Subjects prostrated themselves before the ruler to show submission and reverence, or to beg pardon and favour, as Geoffrey Koziol has discussed.[22] In the examples mentioned above, however, it is the prince who prostrates himself. Just as subjects showed the exaltedness of their ruler by

[19] E. TREMP, *Die Taten Kaiser Ludwigs/Thegan, Das Leben Kaiser Ludwigs/Astronomus* (Hannover, 1995: MGH SS rer. Germ. in usum scholarum separatim editi 64), pp. 12-17; E. TREMP, "Thegan und Astronomus, die beiden Geschichtsschreiber Ludwig des Frommen", in: *Charlemagne's Heir*, pp. 691-700.
[20] T.F.X. NOBLE, "The monastic ideal as a model for empire: The case of Louis the Pious", *Revue Bénédictine* 86 (1976), pp. 235-250.

[21] Theganus, *Gesta Hludowici imperatoris*, c. 19, ed. E. TREMP, *Die Taten Kaiser Ludwigs/Thegan*, pp. 202-203: "*flexis genibus fronte tetigit pavimentum, humiliter diu orans, aliquando cum lacrimis*". Tr. in: *Carolingian Civilization : A Reader*, ed. P.E. DUTTON (Peterborough, 1993), p. 145.
[22] G. KOZIOL, *Begging Pardon and Favor: Ritual and Political Order in Early Medieval France* (Ithaca and London, 1992). About the gesture of prostration, see also: J. HORST, *Proskynein: Zur Anbetung im Urchristentum nach ihrer religionsgeschichtlichen Eigenart* (Gütersloh, 1932); A. ALFÖLDI, *Die monarchische Repräsentation im römischen Kaiserreiche* (Darmstadt, 1977); U. SCHWAB, "Proskynesis und Philoxenie in der altsächsischen Genesisdichtung", in: *Text und Bild: Aspekte des Zusammenwirkens zweier Künste in Mittelalter und früher Neuzeit*, ed. C. MEIER and U. RUBERG (Wiesbaden, 1980), pp. 209-275; G. ALTHOFF, "Das Privileg der *deditio*: Formen gütlicher Konfliktbeendigung in der mittelalterlichen Adelsgesellschaft", in: ID., *Spielregeln der Politik im Mittelalter: Kommunikation in Frieden und Fehde* (Darmstadt, 1997), pp. 99-125.

throwing themselves at his feet, just so the ruler prostrated himself before the highest king, before God. Just as other gestures, prostration was seen as an outward sign of a state of mind – of prayer and humility towards God. Einhard, another contemporary of Ermoldus, wrote in a letter to Lupus of Ferrières about the gesture of adoration. Einhard called *proskynesis* a sign of the body, a visual expression of the state of mind of veneration and humility. He writes:

> To pray, in my opinion, is to beseech in mind or voice, or at the same time in mind and voice without a gesture of the body, the unseen God; ... But to adore is to exhibit veneration to a visible thing placed before one and [actually] present either by bowing one's head or by bending or prostrating one's whole body or by extending one's arms and spreading one's hands or in any way whatsoever that constitutes a gesture of the body.[23]

Humility became an important ruler virtue.[24] Hrabanus Maurus exorted Louis the Pious in a letter to the virtues of humility and obedience. The prince's mirror Louis's son Charles the Bald received from his close adviser archbishop Hincmar of Reims included a lengthy passage on the absolute necessity of humility in rulers. The king was to show humility before other men and God. The more the king humbled himself in devotion to God, the more illustrious and exalted he became in the eyes of his subjects. Sedulius Scottus and Jonas of Orléans stressed this virtue as well. *Proskynesis* was highly appropriate to propagate the image of the ideal, humble ruler as found in Ermoldus's or Thegan's portraits of Louis the Pious. The medieval ruler found models in the biblical king David, who had humbled himself before the prophet Nathan, and in the late-antique emperor Theodosius, who had prostrated himself before St. Ambrose.[25]

In particular prostration before the cross expressed the ruler's ideal humility. In the tenth century, in Liudprand of Cremona's work, we even find an

---

[23] Einhard, *Quaestio de adoranda cruce*, ed. K. HAMPE (Hannover, 1898-1899: *MGH Epp.* 5), pp. 146-149, at p. 148: *"Orare est, ut mea fert opinio, Deum invisibilem [...] sine corporis gestu precari. Adorare vero rei visibili et coram posite ac presenti vel inclinatione capitis vel incurvatione vel prostratione totius corporis vel protensione brachiorum atque expansione manuum vel alio quolibet modo corporis tamen gestum pertinente venerationem exhibere"*.

[24] On ruler virtues, see: H.H. ANTON, *Fürstenspiegel und Herrscherethos in der Karolingerzeit* (Bonn, 1968).

[25] R. SCHIEFFER, "Von Mailand nach Canossa: Ein Beitrag zur Geschichte der christlichen Herrscherbusse von Theoderich d. Gr. bis zu Heinrich IV", *Deutsches Archiv* 28 (1972), pp. 333-370. On the David as a model, see: H. STEGER, *David Rex et Propheta: König David als vorbildliche Verkörperung des Herrschers und Dichters im Mittelalter, nach Bilddarstellungen des achten bis zwölften Jahrhundert* (Nürnberg, 1961).

example of someone who is made king because of his humble *proskynesis*. After king Hugo had been chased away by the Italians, Liudprand tells us, he sent his son Lothair to Milan and asked the people to be well disposed if not to himself, then at least to his son. Lothair prostrated himself before the cross in the cathedral of Milan. Thus, he won the sympathy of the Italians, who lifted him up and made him their king.[26]

The ideal of the virtues of the Christian ruler was influenced by monastic values. Humility was a monastic virtue, found prominently in the rule of St. Benedict. Hrabanus Maurus had himself depicted as a monk, in *proskynesis* before the cross, in his *De laudibus sanctae crucis*, a text in praise of the Holy Cross, first written in 814 and dedicated to Louis the Pious probably somewhere in the 830s (fig. 1).[27] In this treatise, text and image are combined as *carmina figurata*. On the prostrated figure of Hrabanus, the thought expressed by his attitude and gesture is put into words:

> O Christ, clement and good, I ask of you, keep me, Hrabanus, save on Judgment Day.[28]

The attitude is that of a supplicant, also expressed by the words of the prayer. Hrabanus begs Christ for protection. In the explanation of the image, Hrabanus stresses that he is a sinner in his heart, through his mouth, his hand and the attitude of his body. Through a "countergesture", the humble gesture of

---

[26] Liudprand of Cremona, *Antapodosis*, V, 28, ed. A. BAUER, R. RAU, *Quellen zur Geschichte der sächsischen Kaiserzeit* (Darmstadt, 1971: *Ausgewählte Quellen zur Deutschen Geschichte des Mittelalters* 8), pp. 476-477.

[27] Hrabanus Maurus, *In honorem sanctae crucis*, ed. M. PERRIN (Turnhout, 1997: CCCM 100/100A). About *De laudibus sanctae crucis*, see: K. BIERBRAUER, "Hrabanus Maurus, Laus sanctae crucis", in: *799: Kunst und Kultur der Karolingerzeit: Karl der Grosse und Papst Leo III. in Paderborn*, catalogue of an exhibition, ed. C. STIEGEMANN and M. WEMHOFF (Mainz, 1999), pp. 56-57; H. SPILLING, *Opus Magnentii Hrabani Mauri in honorem sanctae crucis conditum* (Frankfurt a.M., 1992: *Fuldaer Hochschulschriften* 18); *Hrabanus Maurus, Liber de laudibus sanctae crucis: Vollständige Faksimileausgabe im Originalformat des Codex Vindobonensis 652*, ed. K. HOLTER (Graz, 1972-1973: *Codices selecti* 33); H.-G. MÜLLER, *Hrabanus Maurus, De laudibus sanctae crucis: Studien zur Überlieferung und Geistesgeschichte, mit dem Faksimile-Textabdruck aus Codex Reg.Lat. 124 der Vatikanischen Bibliothek* (Ratingen, 1973: *Mittellateinisches Jahrbuch, Beihefte* 11); F. MÜTHERICH, "Die Fuldaer Buchmalerei in der Zeit des Hrabanus Maurus", in: *Hrabanus Maurus und seine Schule: Festschrift der Rabanus Maurus Schule*, ed. W. BÖHNE (Fulda, 1980), pp. 94-125; E. SEARS, "Louis the Pious as *miles Christi*: The dedicatory image in Hrabanus Maurus's *De laudibus sanctae crucis*", in: *Charlemagne's Heir*, pp. 605-628.

[28] "*Hrabanum memet clemens rogo, Christe, tuere, o pie judicio*".

proskynesis before the cross, he begs for forgiveness for his sins, as an imploring subject might beg his ruler for pardon. The miniature can be placed within a long and widespread tradition of devotional depictions. The iconography of the *proskynesis* before the cross had its origins in early Christian art. Clerics were shown before the cross in an attitude of humility.[29] But in Carolingian times, the king was depicted prostrated before the cross as well.

Ruler Humility Depicted

Proskynesis before the cross was the form in which the ideal of royal humility and veneration was expressed in ninth-century iconography.[30] Louis the Pious's son, Charles the Bald, had himself depicted in prostration before the cross. The miniature can be found in a small, but luxuriously executed prayerbook, meant for the personal use of Charles the Bald.[31] This book should probably be dated between 846 and 869, and is thus the oldest preserved royal prayerbook. The two-page miniature on ff. 38v and 39r, showing the king in *proskynesis* before Christ on the cross, is the book's most important painted decoration (fig. 2). On the left page Charles the Bald is depicted in royal attire, wearing a crown, kneeling while stretching out his hands towards the page on the right. His mantle waves behind him and one leg is placed before the other, suggesting that the king is moving towards the opposite page, where the crucified Christ is shown, being crowned by the hand of God. At the foot of the cross is a snake, a symbol of the evil that is overcome by Christ.

The miniature of Charles the Bald's *proskynesis* before the cross refers to both veneration and supplication. Both levels of meaning carry specific royal associations. The veneration of the cross was a form of devotion of an imperial nature because of its connection with Constantine the Great. The cult of the cross can be traced to the fourth century, when the cross was venerated as a

---

[29] See R. DESHMAN, "The exalted servant: The ruler theology of the prayerbook of Charles the Bald", *Viator: Medieval and Renaissance Studies* 11 (1980), pp. 385-417, pp. 386-387.

[30] For the different types of ruler depictions, see: P.E. SCHRAMM, "Das Herrscherbild in der Kunst des frühen Mittelalters", *Vorträge der Bibliothek Wartburg*, II, 1. Teil (1922), pp. 145-224.

[31] MS München, Schatzkammer der Residenz. On the manuscript: W. KOEHLER, F. MÜTHERICH, *Die karolingischen Miniaturen: V: Die Hofschule Karls des Kahlen* (Berlin, 1982), pp. 75 ff. The standard article on the miniature is DESHMAN, "Exalted servant". On the ruler ideals at the court of Charles the Bald, see: N. STAUBACH, *Rex christianus: Hofkultur und Herrschaftspropaganda im Reich Karls des Kahlen. Teil II: Die Grundlegung der 'religion royale'* (Köln etc., 1993).

symbol of victory after Constantine's vision on the *Pons Milvius*. Constantine's mother, Helena, is said to have discovered the relic of the cross in the year 320.[32] In early medieval liturgy, the cross was venerated during the festival of the Exaltation of the Cross, and also, especially, on Good Friday.[33] The miniature of Charles the Bald may allude to a Good Friday ritual, in which the king adored the cross in *proskynesis*. It marks the beginning of a series of prayers for Good Friday.[34] The portrait of the prostrated ruler is followed by a prayer in adoration of the holy cross (*Oratio ad adorandam sanctam crucem*). Charles's *proskynenis* thus expresses the adoration awarded to the cross on Good Friday. The artist probably wanted to depict the two parts of which the adoration of the cross consisted – the prostration and the kissing of the cross that followed it – by showing the figure of Charles simultaneously kneeling and moving towards the cross. Physical contact with the cross can be found often in the iconographical tradition: devotion is expressed by grasping the cross. Examples are the Byzantine depictions in which Constantine and Helena, or other members of the imperial family, hold a cross between them.[35] Charles the Bald is depicted in an attitude of veneration of the cross, and so takes his place in a tradition associated with the emperor Constantine the Great.

Charles's *proskynesis*, however, is not just an attitude of adoration of the cross. It also expresses supplication to Christ similar to the gesture of Hrabanus. The king does not kneel before an empty cross, but before a crucifixion scene. As the corpus was not depicted on the cross until about the year 1000, this probably did not correspond with liturgical practice; however, it does suit the spiritual idea expressed by Einhard, who wrote that the cross should be adored especially through prostration, while through the inner eye adoring Him who is suspended on the cross.[36] While praying, the living person was present at

---

[32] J.W. DRIJVERS, *Helena Augusta: The Mother of Constantine the Great and the Legend of Her Finding of the True Cross* (Leiden, 1992). For the iconography of the legend of the cross see: B. BAERT, *Een erfenis van heilig hout: De neerslag van het teruggevonden kruis in tekst en beeld tijdens de Middeleeuwen* (Leuven, 2001).

[33] C. CHAZELLE, *The Crucified God in the Carolingian Era: Theology and Art of Christ's Passion* (Cambridge, 2001), pp. 120-131; G. RÖMER, "Die Liturgie des Karfreitags", *Zeitschrift für katholische Theologie* 77 (1955) pp. 70 ff.

[34] DESHMAN, "Exalted servant", p. 388: *Orationes in parasceue cum crucifixo picto, et imagine uestra, et antyphonis decantandis*. The titles of the antiphones to the cross that follow the miniature are: *Ecce lignum crucis, Venite adoremus, Crucem tuam adoramus, Crux fidelis inter omnes*.

[35] DESHMAN, "Exalted servant", p. 389.

[36] Einhard, *Quaestio de adoranda cruce*, ed. K. HAMPE (Hannover, 1898-1899: MGH Epp. 5), pp. 146-149.

Christ's death, just as his death and resurrection were repeated time and again in the Eucharist following directly after the adoration of the cross in the Carolingian liturgy for Good Friday. The *titulus* that accompanies the miniature of the kneeling Charles the Bald says:

> O Christ, you who on the cross have absolved the sins of the world, absolve, I pray, all [my] wounds for me.[37]

Charles begs Christ for help in the humble attitude of a supplicant, just as his father Louis the Pious had done in Ermoldus Nigellus's description. By using the word *vulnera*, 'wounds', to suggest the ruler's sins, Charles the Bald is compared to the suffering Christ on the cross. The royal virtue of humility, expressed in prostration, is linked to the humility of Christ, who died a humiliating death on the cross. With the *proskynesis* Charles imitates Christ's humility. Amalarius of Metz points to Christ's humiliating crucifixion. Christians should imitate his death by showing humility, by prostrating before the cross "so that determined humility of mind might be shown by the deportment of the body".[38]

Already St. Paul had connected Christ's humiliation (his incarnation and crucifixion) with the *proskynesis*: Christ was exalted by God because he had shown himself to be humble, and therefore all must bend their knees for him (Phil 2, 5-11). Through a display of humility towards Christ the kneeling person is exalted in turn. The paradoxical relationship between humility and exaltation, also found in Ermoldus, is the central theme of this miniature. Christ's humiliation on the cross had led to his exaltation: his victory over evil, symbolized by the serpent at his feet, and his coronation by the hand of God. Similarly, the *proskynesis* before Christ, in voluntary imitation of Christ's humility, leads to exaltation. The Good Friday liturgy expresses the hope that human beings will share in the resurrection and the glory of Christ. The text following the miniature in the prayer book puts the adoration before Christ on the cross into words; it begs that the cross will bring deliverance from Satan. Christ's triumph over Satan through the cross was to be the means of Charles's victory over the devil and his own sins.[39] Moreover, with this moral elevation Charles shows himself to be a good ruler, by that also legitimating his worldly elevation, simi-

---

[37] *"In cruce qui mundi solvisti crimina Christe/ Orando mihimet tu vulnera cuncta resolve"*.

[38] Amalarius of Metz, *Liber officialis*, 1, 14, 4, ed. J.M. HANSSENS, *Opera liturgica omnia* (Vatican City, 1948: *Studi e testi* 139), 2, p. 100: *"Unde prosternimur ante crucem, ut fixa humilitas mentis per habitum corporis demonstretur"*. Tr. in DESHMAN, "Exalted servant", pp. 391.

[39] DESHMAN, "Exalted servant", pp. 392-393.

lar to the way Louis the Pious had legitimized his in the words of Ermoldus and Thegan.

Charles's portrait is not unique. His brother Louis the German was probably also depicted kneeling before a crucifixion (fig. 3). The so-called Psalter of Louis the German is a precious manuscript written in gold and filled with decorations, manufactured in the second quarter of the ninth century at St.-Bertin's, from where it was brought to the East-Frankish part of the realm. There, later on in the ninth century, an *oratio ante crucem dicenda* and an accompanying miniature, showing a man in *proskynesis* before the cross (f. 120r), were added to the text of the psalms.[40] Stylistic and palaeographical arguments suggest that this is king Louis the German. The ruler, dressed in a short tunic, kneels on a prie-dieu underneath the cross. He bends his upper body forward and stretches his right hand towards the cross, grasping it with his left hand. The prie-dieu and the geometrical basis on which the cross is placed refer to actual devotional practice, because just so a processional cross was placed in a standard on an altar. Although it is not certain that the kneeling figure is indeed Louis the German, the image fits well within the Carolingian tradition of royal representation. The ruler is shown as a supplicant before Christ – even more so than in Charles the Bald's miniature. The accompanying prayer is addressed to Christ on the cross; it is not an expression of adoration of the cross. In the miniature, the prostrated figure grasps the cross with his left hand, accentuating the supplicating aspect of the attitude even more.

Rituals in Word and Image

Rituals, as we have seen, have visual elements that refer to something else: an inner state of mind (such as a virtue) or the balance and legitimation of power. As such, they can be compared to images generally.

Gestures and rituals were described in texts and depicted in images, because of the ability of these forms of non-verbal communication to express thoughts, ideals and relations, and to make these clear at a glance. The visual has a large impact because of its directness and clarity. This is why rituals were employed in word and image. Through the ritual of prostration, Louis the Pious and his son Charles the Bald were characterized, in word and image respectively, as possessors of the royal virtue of humility.

---

[40] MS Berlin, Staatsbibliothek, Ms. Theol. Lat. Fol. 58. See: *Karl der Grosse. Werk und Wirkung*, catalogue of an exhibition (Aachen, 1965), Nr. 488, pp. 302-303.

Throughout the early Middle Ages, there was a continuing debate about the visual, and about images and their functioning within the Christian faith in particular. The most important Carolingian document in this discussion is the *Opus Caroli Regis*, more often called the *Libri Carolini*. This work, written between 790 and 793, is the official reaction of Charlemagne, written by Theodulf of Orléans, to the second council of Nicaea in 787. That council had reinstated the cult of images in the Byzantine empire.[41] Theodulf writes in the prologue that the Carolingians appreciate images as decocations in churches and as reminders of the deeds from the past, but they neither adore nor destroy them.[42] An image is a likeness that only brings something to mind to the extent that it resembles its subject. Images are thus necessarily confined to the material, the visible. Theodulf criticizes images, because it was impossible to represent the word of God in pictures:

> Painters ... have a certain ability to remind one of things that have happened. Such things, however, as are understood by reason are expressed not by painters, but by writers through verbal discourse.[43]

The *Opus Caroli Regis* expresses a belief in the superiority of words and written language over the visual arts as forms of communication.[44] Because no visual resemblance is necessary between a written text and its subject, the written word was thought to be more reliable that visual depictions and would, moreover, offer more possibilities: abstract matters could also be referred to. Other Carolingian authors (often writing in a reaction to bishop Claudius of Turin, who in 817 had all images removed from his churches, or in the context of the synod of Paris, where the matter of Claudius was discussed in 825) appreciated the value of images as well, and especially their function as decorations and their ability to remind one of events and persons.[45]

---

[41] T.F.X. NOBLE, "Tradition and learning in search of ideology: The *Libri Carolini*", in: *"The Gentle Voices of Teachers": Aspects of Learning in the Carolingian Age*, ed. R.E. SULLIVAN (Columbus, 1995), pp. 227-260.

[42] *Opus Caroli Regis contra synodum (Libri Carolini)*, ed. A. FREEMAN (Hannover, 1998: *MGH LL* 4, *Conc* 2, *Supplementum* I), p. 102. CHAZELLE, *The Crucified God in the Carolingian Era*, p. 42.

[43] Tr. in: DUTTON, *Carolingian Civilization*, p. 87.

[44] C. CHAZELLE, " 'Not in painting but in writing': Augustine and the supremacy of the word in the *Libri Carolini*", in: *Reading and Wisdom: The De doctrina Christiana of Augustine in the Middle Ages*, ed. E.D. ENGLISH (Notre Dame, 1995), pp. 1-22.

[45] E.g. Claudius of Turin, *Epistola* 12 (*Apologeticum atque rescriptum Claudii episcopi adversus Theutmirum abbatem*), ed. E. DÜMMLER (Berlin, 1895: *MGH Epp.* 4, *Karolini Aevi* 2),

It was probably this very ability to remind without the tedium of many words that made visual elements, such as rituals, so popular and effective. As Einhard wrote – and as we saw in Hrabanus's kneeling portrait – a gesture instantly makes clear a message that would need many words to impart. In the painting of a ruler portrait, irrespective of whether words or miniatures were used, gestures and rituals were selected because of their direct and clear way of showing ideals of rulership and relations of power.

Hans Belting has made a distinction between different types of images, between the portrait or *imago* and the narrative image or *historia*. The *imago* shows a certain presence (and therefore could be adored in the Byzantine empire), while the *historia* only shows events or things from the past. Within the history of religious images, the portrait ranked higher than the narrative picture.[46] The Carolingian and Ottonian rulers are always depicted in a portrait, never as part of a story or of history.[47] Their images are *imagines*, not *historiae*. The ruler's portrait is furnished with certain attributes and assuming a certain attitude, making certain gestures – in short, with the aid of rituals. Similarly, the ruler is presented in narrative sources in descriptions of rituals. Presenting the ruler through a ritual is like presenting an *imago* within the text.

Images played an important part within the *ars memoriae* developed in Antiquity as part of the art of rhetoric. In the Middle Ages the *ars* was adapted to remember and practice the Christian virtues. An inner, invisible, image was formed to store something in the memory and later recall it. These inner images were supplemented and prompted by visual memory aids.[48] Gregory the Great had attributed to images the task of recalling things in memory, and early medi-

---

pp. 610-613; Dungal, *Epistola* 9 (*Dungali responsa contra perversas Claudii Taurinensis episcopi sententias*, *ibid.*, pp. 583-585; Agobard of Lyon, *De picturis et imaginibus*, ed. in: *Agobradus Lugdunensis, Opera Omnia*, ed. L. VAN ACKER (Turnhout, 1981: *CCCM* 52), pp. 151-181; see CHAZELLE, *Crucified God*, pp. 120-123.

[46] H. BELTING, *Likeness and Presence: A History of the Image before the Era of Art* (Chicago and London, 1994), p. 10.

[47] See the portraits of rulers in P.E. SCHRAMM, *Die deutschen Kaiser und Könige in Bildern ihrer Zeit* (München, 1983); H. MAYR-HARTING, *Ottonian Book Illumination: An Historical Study*, 2 vols. (London, 1991); D. BULLOUGH, "*Imagines Regum* and their significance in the early medieval West", in: *Studies in Memory of David Talbot Rice*, ed. G. ROBERTSON and G. HENDERSON (Edinburgh, 1975), pp. 223-276; and H. KELLER, "Herrscherbild und Herrschaftslegitimation: Zur Deutung der ottonischen Denkmäler", *Frühmittelalterliche Studien* 19 (1985), pp. 290-311.

[48] BELTING, *Likeness and Presence*, pp. 9-10; M. CARRUTHERS, *The Craft of Thought: Meditation, Rhetoric, and the Making of Images, 400-1200* (Cambridge, 2000).

eval authors followed his example in this.[49] Rituals in early medieval ruler portraits and historiography serve as visual elements that refer to the ruler, his virtues and – through them – to the legitimation of his power. They imprint these in the audience's memory.

Gestures, then, are described and depicted because of their intended effect on the audience. The audience for the rituals that the ruler actually performed was limited. Knowledge of rituals was disseminated to a larger audience through texts and images. These media had their own conventions, knowledge of which was necessary to comprehend the represented ritual. Whom did the audience consist of, and what levels of literacy did an audience need to understand rituals expressed in words? And what levels of 'visual literacy' were needed to understand rituals through an image? In the instances of Ermoldus's poem and the miniature in Charles the Bald's prayer book, the audience must have been roughly the same: it consisted first of the king, then of his court circle. Poems and letters in verse addressed to kings were meant to be read aloud at court – first, but not exclusively so, in the monarch's hearing.[50] The prayer book was probably meant for Charles the Bald's private use. However, books did circulate at court, and the king also presented them to ecclesiastical institutions as prestigious gifts.[51]

Then as now there were of course different ways of reading poems and pictures – and I define reading here as becoming acquainted with the contents of a message; the process by which this is done and the results may differ. To give meaning to the description of a ritual, some degree of verbal literacy was required by the person doing the actual reading, even if Ermoldus's poem must have been read aloud to a larger audience. Also, one would need to comprehend the conventions of the genre of the panegyric to understand the text's author correctly. Depictions of rituals required visual literacy: the ability to recognize and identify the items depicted, to connect the images on facing pages, to understand the conventions of high and low, left and right, large and small – all things learned from seeing other, similar images. This visual literacy would operate much more instantaneously than verbal literacy, as reading words simply takes up much more time than glancing at an image. We need more time to

---

[49] L.G. DUGGAN, "Was art really the 'book of the illiterate'?", *Word and Image* 5 (1989), pp. 227-251, reprinted in this volume.

[50] P. GODMAN, *Poets and Emperors: Frankish Politics and Carolingian Poetry* (Oxford, 1987), pp. 39-40.

[51] W.J. DIEBOLD, "Verbal, visual and cultural literacy in medieval art: word and image in the Psalter of Charles the Bald", *Word and Image* 8 (1992), pp. 89-99.

read Ermoldus's description of Louis the Pious's prostration than to look at the miniature of Charles the Bald in *proskynesis*. Thus, the immediate effect of the gesture or ritual – which may be regarded as its most valuable aspect – can be more fully preserved through 'reading' pictures. But apparently the impact of the gesture was not completely lost in description. This is why a writer like Ermoldus employs gestures so often. Importantly, Ermoldus uses gestures and rituals *without* further explaining their meaning. The ability of words to explain, praised by Theodulf, is not used. The rituals are isolated images within the text; they are meant to be understood without further explanation.

This is possible because a third kind of literacy is expected from an audience 'reading' gestures in both words and images. This is what William Diebold and others have called 'cultural literacy'[52] and which in our context may be called, more specifically, 'ritual literacy'. One needed a knowledge of the meaning of rituals in general, and of the *proskynesis* and its associations in particular, to give meaning to a description or depiction of a *proskynesis*. The audience needed to know, e.g. that rituals could express royal virtues; that prosternation was an expression of humility; and that humility was a virtue that legitimated royal power, because king David and Christ possessed this virtue as well.

Because of the nature of rituals, which are meant to be apprehended directly and clearly, and because of the ritual literacy expected of the audience, there are, differences apart, striking similarities in the ways in which images and texts present gestures and rituals to their audience, and in the final effect they have on that audience. The same rituals are depicted and described. They could be called the 'standard rituals' making up the ritual side of a ruler's life, to which the *proskynesis* belonged. Also, in both images and texts, gestures are used to show the relations of the ruler with others. And to show him to be a good ruler.

This has some implications for the way we study rituals. Images and texts are usually studied separately. Either texts are employed to explain an image, or an image is used to illustrate a text. But the two forms, of course, worked together. An idea, such as the ruler's ideal of humility we have discussed here, found its outward form in a ritual. This could be – and was – represented, or employed, both in word and image. But the process did not end there. There was an interaction between descriptions and depictions of rituals, contributing to the meaning and implications of rituals, the complex of skills and under-

---

[52] DIEBOLD, "Verbal, visual and cultural literacy", pp. 95-97.

standings I would like to call 'ritual literacy'. For a clear understanding of pictures of rituals, knowledge of verbal explanations was essential to contemporaries – and therefore to scholars studying medieval ritual. On the other hand, descriptions of rituals were more effective if one knew the images. The actual ritual and its reflection in word and image together contributed to the meaning and functioning of the ritual.

What was the function of rituals? Rituals, as they have been handed down to us in word and image, tell us about the ideal ruler, exalted over his subjects because of his virtues and his power. Did the texts and images merely repeat a message that was already well known to their audience – that of a ruler elevated above and, maybe, even beyond his subjects? Possibly. But maybe descriptions and depictions of exemplary royal behaviour, expressed through gestures and rituals, also urged the ruler to act accordingly in his own life. There must have been interaction, a circle consisting of the ritual's influencing actual behaviour, its reflection in word and image, and its descriptions' and depictions' influence on actual behaviour. Through this circle of interaction, artists and writers influenced the functioning of their ruler. Rulers could be 'made' through the literary and visual processing of rituals – and sometimes they could be broken as well. This is communication at the highest level, between people who developed theories about what kingship actually implied and what royal legitimacy entailed.

This article, it may be clear, is meant as a plea against looking merely for evidence of how rituals functioned in medieval society.[53] More attention ought to be given to the fundamental role of rituals in creating the image of the persons represented – work now being done by Philippe Buc and others.[54] Texts

---

[53] As, e.g. in the work of Karl Leyser and Gerd Althoff: K. LEYSER, "Ritual, ceremony and gesture: Ottonian Germany", in: ID., *Communications and Power in Medieval Europe: The Carolingian and Ottonian Centuries*, ed. T. REUTER (London, 1994), pp.189-214; G. ALTHOFF, "Demonstration und Inszenierung: Spielregeln der Kommunikation in mittelalterlicher Öffentlichkeit", in: ID., *Spielregeln der Politik im Mittelalter*, pp. 229-257; and ID., "Ungeschriebene Gesetze: Wie funktioniert Herrschaft ohne schriftlich fixierte Normen?", *ibid.*, pp. 282-306.

[54] Cf. P. BUC, "Italian hussies and German matrons: Liutprand of Cremona on dynastic legitimacy", *Frühmittelalterliche Studien* 29 (1995), pp. 207-225; ID., "Writing Ottonian hegemony: Good rituals and bad rituals in Liutprand of Cremona", *Majestas* 4 (1996), pp. 3-38; ID., "Martyre et ritualité dans l'Antiquité Tardive: Horizons de l'écriture médiévale des rituels", *Annales ESC* 48 (1997), pp. 63-92; ID., "Ritual and interpretation: The early medieval case", *Early Medieval Europe* 9 (2000), pp. 183-210; ID., "Political ritual: Medieval and modern interpretations", in: *Die Aktualität des Mittelalters*, ed. H.-W. GOETZ (Bochum, 2000), pp. 255-272; ID., *The Dangers of Ritual*; D.A. WARNER, "Ritual and memory in the Ottonian *Reich*: The

and images worked together to propagate an *ideal* of rulership in which the visual element of the ritual was one of the main constituents.

ceremony of *adventus*", *Speculum* 76 (2001), pp. 255-283.

Fig. 1   Hrabanus Maurus, *De laudibus sanctae crucis*, 834-835. Portrait of
Louis the Pious as *Miles Christi*. MS Vatican, Reg. Lat 124, f. 4v.

Fig. 2   Charles the Bald in *proskynesis* before Christ crucified. Prayer book of
         Charles the Bald, 846-869. MS München, Schatzkammer der Residenz,
         ff. 38v-39r.

Fig. 3   Louis the German (?) in *proskynesis* before Christ crucified. Psalter of
Louis the German, MS Berlin, Staatsbibliothek, Ms. Theol. Lat. Fol. 58,
f. 120v.

Paulinus of Nola and the Image Within the Image

GISELLE DE NIE

Paulinus of Nola (*ca.* 353-431) was an immensely wealthy late fourth-century aristocrat in Aquitaine who shocked the western world by following Jesus's advice to give up secular concerns and follow Him. After giving the proceeds from the sale of most of his properties to the poor, he exiled himself to lead an ascetic life on one of his remaining estates in southern Italy.[1] In the years around 400, he built churches there around the tomb of his patron saint Felix († 260) and – signally departing from what had been the early Church's distrust of religious images as conducive to idolatry[2] – he decorated these churches with mosaics and paintings of biblical scenes and Christian symbols.[3] In his extant writings[4] he explains that his reason for doing this is to

[1] On Paulinus' life and works see now, D. TROUT, *Paulinus of Nola: Life, Letters and Poems* (Berkeley, 1999: *Transformation of the Classical Heritage* 27) and P. FABRE, *Saint Paulin de Nole et l'amitié chrétienne* (Paris, 1949). I am grateful to Professors A.P. Orbán, J.Chr. Klamt, K.F. Morrison and Dr. C. Conybeare for their suggestions concerning various earlier versions of this paper.

[2] On this, see: W. ELLIGER, *Die Stellung der alten Christen zu den Bildern in den ersten vier Jahrhunderten (nach den Angaben der zeitgenössischen kirchlichen Schriftsteller)* (Leipzig, 1930: *Studien über christliche Denkmäler*, N.F. 20)

[3] See on these: R.C. GOLDSCHMIDT, *Paulinus' Churches at Nola: Texts, Translations and Commentary* (Amsterdam, 1940).

[4] Sancti Pontii Meropii Paulini Nolani, *Carmina* (hereafter: *Carm*), ed. G. HARTEL (Prague, Vienna and Leipzig, 1894: *Corpus Scriptorum Ecclesiasticorum Latinorum* 30); translation: P.G. WALSH, *The Poems of St. Paulinus of Nola* (New York and Ramsey, N.J., 1975: *Ancient Christian Writers* 40). Sancti Pontii Meropii Paulini Nolani, *Epistolae* (hereafter: *Epp*), ed. G. HARTEL (Prague, Vienna and Leipzig, 1894: *Corpus Scriptorum Ecclesiasticorum Latinorum* 29); tr.: P.G. WALSH, *Letters of St. Paulinus of Nola* (New York and Ramsey, N.J., 1966: *Ancient Christian Writers* 35). In this paper I have adjusted the translations or made my own.

remind the illiterate peasants – via identifying verse captions which, as he explicitly states, were to be read to them – of the Christian truths and to show them examples of holy virtue to be emulated.[5]

His friend Sulpicius Severus (*fl.* ca. 400), however, was also putting pictures in the new churches on his estate in Aquitaine. When Paulinus, at Severus's request, sent him verse captions in 403 or 404 for what presumably was a portrait of St. Martin on the wall of a newly-built baptistery there, he added an intriguing comment:

> It is right that Martin should be depicted in that place of human refashioning, for he *bore the image of the heavenly man* through his perfect imitation of Christ; so that those shedding their decrepit earthly image in the baptismal basin *may encounter the to-be-imitated likeness of a heavenly soul* [italics added].

> *recte enim in loco refectionis humanae Martinus pingitur, qui caelestis hominis imaginem perfecta Christi imitatione portavit, ut deponentibus in lavacro terrenae imaginis vetustatem imitanda caelestis animae occurrat effigies.*[6]

The depicted physical appearance of St. Martin (ca. 316-397) is here conceptually distinguished from the spiritual image of his heavenly soul as a reflection of Christ, which his likeness would somehow make visible. The passage reflects the fourth-century Church's view of conversion as a return to the first man's original state of spiritual orientation as a created image of his Maker – now understood to be Christ, the consubstantial Image of the Father and his Word. Many agreed, however, that this image in man was located in the soul and as such therefore invisible.[7] As far as I could find, Paulinus is the first in the West to point to this spiritual 'image' in a *depicted* person.[8] Is this only a manner of

---

[5]   *Carm* 27. vv. 11-517, 542-567, 580-595. See on this: ELLIGER, *Stellung*, pp. 82-85.

[6]   *Epp* 32, 2. On the dating of this letter, see WALSH, *Letters*, p. 329, n. 1.

[7]   On the history of the concept of the spiritual image, see: R. JAVELET, *Image et ressemblance au douzième siècle*, 2 vols. (Paris, 1967), 1, pp. 1-63.

[8]   There is an eloquent article on the archetype in the image in Greek and later religious art: H. KESSLER, " 'Pictures fertile with truth': How Christians managed to make images of God without violating the second commandment", *The Journal of the Walters Art Gallery* 49-50 (1991-1992), pp. 53-65. Other recent articles by Kessler on the tradition of the invisible image in western Christian art, which unfortunately came to my attention too late to be used, are: H. KESSLER, "Gazing at the future: The *parousia* miniature in Vatican gr. 699", in: *Byzantine East, Latin West: Art-Historical Studies in Honor of Kurt Weitzmann*, ed. D. MOURIKI a.o. (Princeton, 1995) pp. 365-371 (reprinted in: H. KESSLER, *Spiritual Seeing: Picturing God's Invisibility in Medieval Art* (Philadelphia, 2000), pp. 88-103); IDEM, "Real absence: Early Medieval art and the metamorphosis of vision", in: *Morfologie sociali e culturali in Europa fra tarda antichità e alto medioevo*, 2 vols. (Spoleto, 1998: *Settimane di Studio del Centro Italiano di Studi sull'Alto*

speaking or does he indeed think that there is something to see? In the East, as is well known, the view arose in the following centuries that a holy portrait, through its likeness to the original, itself participated in the latter's spiritual quality and thereby made this spiritual quality present and accessible to the viewer.[9] In the sixth-century West, there are some traces of a similar view.[10] Is Paulinus pointing in this direction?

We appear to be seeing another view, however, when he speaks of the viewing of his murals of Old Testament scenes as "reading the holy stories" ("*sanctasque legentes historias*").[11] And this reminds us that, alongside his building and decorating activities, Paulinus was also among the first Latin writers to explore the 'spiritual' meanings in Scripture by discerning images of larger divine truths in its literal statements.[12] In this, he followed the tradition of the apostle Paul, who enjoined Christians to pay attention to the spirit rather than the letter of the Old Testament text. By thus recognizing what he called "shadows" ("*umbrae*"), "images" ("*imagines*") and "figures" ("*figurae*") of the living eternal Christ in its words, one would access the living reality of His

Medioevo 45) 2, pp. 1157-1211 (reprinted in: KESSLER, *Spiritual Seeing*, pp. 104-148); and IDEM, "Configuring the invisible by copying the holy face", in: *The Holy Face and the Paradox of Representation*, ed. H. KESSLER and G. WOLF (Bologna, 1998) pp. 129-151 (reprinted in: KESSLER, *Spiritual Seeing*, pp. 64-87). An older study on the concept in the medieval western material is: W. VON DEN STEINEN, *Homo caelestis: Das Wort der Kunst im Mittelalter*, 2 vols. (Bern and München, 1965). See also: M. SKEB, *Christo vivere: Studien zum literarischen Christusbild des Paulinus von Nola* (Bonn, 1997), and T. LEHMANN, "Martinus und Paulinus in Primuliacum (Gallien): Zu den frühesten nachweisbaren Mönchsbildnissen (um 400) in einem Kirchenkomplex", in: *Vom Kloster zum Klosterverband: Das Werkzeug der Schriftlichkeit*, ed. H. KELLER and F. NEISKE (München, 1997: *Münstersche Mittelalter-Schriften* 74), pp. 56-67.

[9] See on this: J. PELIKAN, *Imago Dei: The Byzantine Apologia for Icons* (New Haven and London, 1990); G.B. LADNER, "The concept of the image in the Greek Fathers and the Byzantine Iconoclastic Controversy", *Dumbarton Oaks Papers* 7 (1953), pp. 1-34; E. KITZINGER, "The cult of images in the age before iconoclasm", *Dumbarton Oaks Papers* 8 (1954), pp. 83-150; and A. CAMERON, "The language of images: The rise of icons and Christian representation", in: *The Church and the Arts*, ed. D. WOOD (Oxford, 1992: *Studies in Church History* 28), pp. 1-42. An overview of visual response in: D. FREEDBERG, *The Power of Images: Studies in the History and Theory of Response* (Chicago and London, 1989), and on the use of meditation in the high and later Middle Ages to access the invisible in depictions of the holy, pp. 161-191.

[10] See on this G. DE NIE, "The poet as visionary: Venantius Fortunatus's 'new mantle' for Saint Martin", *Cassiodorus* 3 (1997), pp. 54-59, and, more extensively, G. DE NIE, "Word, image and experience in the early medieval miracle story", in: *Language and Beyond: Actuality and Virtuality in the Relations between Word, Image and Sound*, ed. P. JORET and A. REMAEL (Amsterdam, 1998), pp. 109-116.

[11] *Carm* 27, vv. 589-590.

[12] WALSH, *Letters*, p. 20.

spirit.[13] The terms used show that such a trace or manifestation as an 'image' need not be a fully visible one but could also be understood in the sense of an outline or 'pattern'.[14] Was it perhaps this kind of consciously meditative looking through a verbal text to visualize its image-patterns as mental conduits to a greater spiritual reality, then, that was the model for Paulinus's assumption that an image of a heavenly soul – reflecting the presence of Christ in the saint – could be seen and even experienced as a living reality in a pictorial representation? To put his view in its contemporary context, it should be mentioned here that Paulinus's attitude towards pictorial representations of religious subjects contrasts sharply with that of several other Latin Christian writers. Augustine (354-430), for instance, showed a cautious reserve towards them, and the outspoken Jerome (ca. 350-420) wrote to Paulinus that the money involved in their execution was better spent on feeding the poor: for the human being, and not a building, was the real house of God.[15] As we shall see, Paulinus agreed, but – anticipating Pope Gregory the Great's view by two hundred years – hoped that his visible buildings would help especially the illiterate to build up their own invisible ones.[16]

As far as I know, Paulinus's notion of the image within the image has not yet been the focus of an investigation. In what follows, I shall attempt to discover what he may have meant with his cryptic statement by comparing the images he visualizes in St. Martin's portrait with those he sees in a symbolic representation of the Cross, in a faceless relic, and in a living person's face. That, alongside these purely mental visualizations, there may also have been a physically visible manifestation of the indwelling of Christ in a saint is shown by Paulinus's descriptions, first, of his own imagined appearance of his patron saint Felix and, second, of someone else's vision of Christ, sometimes taking on the appearance of St. Felix: they point to a perception as of radiant light. This, of course, can be suggested by certain indications in a picture. In all this, we

---

[13] Hbr 10, 1: "*Umbram enim habens lex bonorum futurorum, non ipsam imaginem rerum*"; I Cor 7, 31: "*praeterit enim figura huius mundi*". See G. BRAUMANN, "Form, substance", in: *New International Dictionary of New Testament Theology*, 3 vols. (Grand Rapids, 1975-1978), 1, pp. 703-710; and W. MUNDLE a.o., "Image, idol, imprint, example", in: *New International Dictionary of New Testament Theology*, 2, pp. 284-293.

[14] See the meanings of *imaginalis* through *imago* in: *Thesaurus Linguae Latinae*, 1- vols. (Leipzig, 1900-), 7.1, cols. 401-414.

[15] ELLIGER, *Stellung*, pp. 86-94, 80-82 respectively; Jerome, *Epistola* 58, 7, in: Jérôme, *Lettres*, ed. J. LABOURT, 8 vols. (Paris, 1949-1963), 3, p. 81. See also: H. JUNOD-AMMERBAUER, "Les constructions de Nole et l'esthétique de saint Paulin", *Revue des études augustiniennes* 24 (1978), pp. 38, 44-45.

[16] *Carm* 27, v. 647. Cf. TROUT, *Paulinus*, pp. 182-183.

shall be looking for an answer to the question: did Paulinus believe that the image of the heavenly soul could actually be seen in the picture itself or only in the beholder's mind?[17]

1. Interna Acies: *Visualizing the 'Faces' of God?*

In his description of how his craftsmen embellished the existing church for St. Felix, Paulinus makes an astonishing general statement about the religious art there. He writes: "the painter [added] divine faces borne by pictures" (*"imaginibus divina ferentibus ora"*).[18] We learn elsewhere that these representations are symbolic as well as figurative: the symbols of the Trinity (the lamb, the dove and the 'voice' – perhaps represented by the hand – of God[19]) and the deeds of biblical personages.[20] Keeping in mind that the poetic metre may influence the choice of words and case endings: does Paulinus mean here that both kinds of representation reveal the 'faces' or 'face' of God? Or does he intend the adjective 'divine' to be taken to indicate holiness, and are the faces those of the biblical figures? Since Paulinus, as we shall see, makes a habit of juxtaposing different interpretations of the same phenomenon,[21] he may mean both. But he is being cautious. For, although he gives us substantial descriptions of the Old Testament scenes depicted in Nola, he says nothing about those of the New Testament there, in which the human Christ would presumably have been depicted.[22] It has been suggested that this may have been connected with the then still ongoing controversy about the representation of the human Christ.[23] It is possible, however, that Paulinus had seen the late fourth-century depiction of

---

[17] I acknowledge my general debt to the insights in two books of Professor Karl F. Morrison: K.F. MORRISON, *'I am You': The Hermeneutics of Empathy in Western Literature, Theology and Art* (Princeton, 1988), and IDEM, *History as a Visual Art in the Twelfth-Century Renaissance* (Princeton, 1990). Conclusions similar to mine for Paulinus are reached for the sixth-century pictorial narratives in Gaul by H.L. KESSLER, "Pictorial narrative and Church mission in sixth-century Gaul", *Studies in the History of Art* 16 (1985), p. 88.

[18] *Carm* 27, v. 386.

[19] *Epp* 32, 10.

[20] *Carm* 27, vv. 511-541; *Epp* 32, 10-17.

[21] C. CONYBEARE, *Paulinus Noster: Self and Symbols in the Letters of Paulinus of Nola* (Oxford, 2000), pp. 106, 111, 117, and especially 126. I am grateful to the author for allowing me to have a pre-publication look at three chapters of this innovative and thorough study of Paulinus' imagery.

[22] Description of Old Testament scenes: *Carm* 27, vv. 517-541; mention of New Testament scenes: *Carm* 28, v. 171.

[23] JUNOD-AMMERBAUER, "L'esthétique", p. 45, with n. 66.

the human Christ in the apse of the still extant Santa Pudenziana in Rome.[24] Unfortunately, we cannot check Paulinus's words against their objects, for these no longer survive.[25] Judging from his words, he appears to have believed that his depictions – both figurative and symbolic – in one way or another made God 'visible'.[26] But not in any direct way, for he explicitly designates the painted shapes in his churches as "counterfeit pictures" (*"picturae fucatae"*).[27] He continues, nevertheless, by saying about the depictions of symbols and biblical events that

> whoever sees these, learns the truth through empty representations, and nourishes his believing mind with a by no means empty image.

> *qui videt haec vacuis agnoscens vera figuris*
> *non vacua fidam sibi pascit imagine mentem.*[28]

Whereas contemporary continuing pagan usage regarded the statue of the reigning emperor – as the early fourth-century Church Father Athanasius (295-373) had said – as making visible and thereby 'presencing' his 'idea' and 'form',[29] Paulinus appears to emphasize that the pictorial representations in his churches do not contain any reality but only point to a true image outside themselves. Also in the case of biblical events, this true image is likely to have been more than the visible appearance depicted. Since Paulinus explicitly says that he expects the beholder to be emotionally affected by the pictures, and thereby

---

[24] Depicted in R. KRAUTHEIMER, *Rome: Profile of a City, 312-1308* (Princeton, 1980), p. 41; and, in colour, in: W.F VOLBACH and M. HIRMER, *Frühchristliche Kunst: Die Kunst der Spätantike in West- und Ostrom* (München, 1958), pl. 130.

[25] The Visigoths destroyed a great deal during their Italian invasion in 410: TROUT, *Paulinus*, p. 15; JUNOD-AMMERBAUER, "L'esthétique", p. 23.

[26] Cf. TROUT, *Paulinus*, pp. 182-183. See on this in the East: KESSLER, "Pictures"; and in medieval art: C. HAHN, "Purification, sacred action, and the vision of God: Viewing medieval narratives", *Word and Image* 5 (1989), p. 75: "The frescoed narrative ... prepares the viewer to perceive the revealed scriptural narrative so that he may finally arrive at truth in a vision of God".

[27] *Carm* 27, v. 511.

[28] *Carm* 27, vv. 514-515. Cf. Virgil, *Aeneid* 1, v. 464: *"animum pictura pascit inani"* (*Virgil*, ed. and tr. H.R. FAIRCLOUGH, rev. edn., 2 vols. (Cambridge, Mass. and London, 1986: *Loeb Classical Library* 63-64), 1, p. 272). I owe this reference to Professor Karl Morrison. TROUT, *Paulinus*, pp. 182-183, stresses the vital role of the viewers' "wonderment" in the apprehension of the pictures' content.

[29] *Oratio III contra Arianos* 5, ed. in: MIGNE, *PG* 26A, col. 332 A; quoted in LADNER, "Concept", p. 8, n. 31. See on this subject also: H. BELTING, *Bild und Kult: Eine Geschichte des Bildes vor dem Zeitalter der Kunst* (München, 1990), pp. 117-122.

induced to imitate the virtue in the action shown,[30] the picture could also be understood as a true image of the invisible virtue in its sensory embodiment. This way of looking at a picture would closely resemble that of looking at a verbal communication and grasping the spiritual meaning behind the images evoked by the letter of the text. A more or less meditative looking, then, was to understand and thus 'see' the depictions – whether symbolic or historical – as images of embodied invisible divine truth: plausibly an equivalent for the more poetic phrase 'faces of God'.[31]

In Catherine Conybeare's new study of Paulinus's imagery, she argues that his concern with the pictures' captions as necessary for their understanding nevertheless shows his fundamentally "textual orientation". The text then, and not the picture, would be the starting point for an active, meditational response of the viewer-reader.[32] In his book *Picture Theory*, however, W.J.T. Mitchell has coined the term 'imagetext' to point to the experiential inseparability of image and text in visual appreciation.[33] Paulinus's writings point to the same. For, notwithstanding his own orientation towards textual images, he explicitly says that he expects the illiterate peasants to be spurred to reflection – if not also to meditation and prayer[34] – by the lifelike depictions of biblical scenes, identified by their captions. In addition, Paulinus indicates that the visible architecture and physical layout of the buildings are a sign (*"signant"*), on the one hand of theological concepts such as that of the Trinity,[35] and on the other of the "building of our hearts" (*"exstructae mentes"*).[36] The spiritual significance of all his visible representations, then, seems more important to him than their physical existence.[37] Thus he writes elsewhere: "if we build our structures, however earthly, with spiritual prayer and study, they are a blessed preparation for our heavenly dwellings" (*"beata caelestium est praeparatio mansionum"*).[38]

---

[30] *Carm* 27, vv. 582-583: *"si forte adtonitas haec per spectacula mentes / agrestum caperet fucata coloribus umbra"*; *Carm* 27, vv. 589-591: *"sanctasque legenti / historias castorum operum subrepit honestas / exempla inducta piis"*.

[31] On a similar view in Byzantine art, see KESSLER, "Pictures".

[32] CONYBEARE, *Paulinus*, pp. 95-97.

[33] W.J.T. MITCHELL, *Picture Theory: Essays on Verbal and Visual Representation* (Chicago and London, 1994), pp. 83, 197 and *passim*.

[34] As he indicates in *Carm* 27, vv. 585-586: *"dumque omnes picta vicissim / ostendunt relegunt sibi"*; ibid., vv. 596-597: *"quae facta et picta videmus, / materiam orandi pro me tibi suggero poscens"* – a long prayer, based upon the depicted scenes as archetypes for spiritual improvement, follows (vv. 607-647).

[35] *Ibid.*, vv. 455-462.

[36] *Ibid.*, v. 647.

[37] As also JUNOD-AMMERBAUER, "L'esthétique", p. 56.

[38] *Epp* 32, 18.

1.1 Prompta Fides Oculis

The deep interweave of text and image is also evident in Paulinus's explanations of the symbolic representations in his churches of the Trinity and of what must be the Last Judgment. He tells us how the objects depicted express the invisible divine qualities and actions taught by the Christian faith.[39] But it is in his elaborate description of another symbolic representation – a golden cross, significantly bearing three lamps, hanging in one of his churches – that Paulinus again explicitly speaks of an invisible image being manifested.[40] First, he tells us, the cross's intricate form as a monogram of the six letters of Christ's name points to Him through a word,[41] and perhaps also as the Word. Alongside this verbal symbolism, however, *the shapes of the letters* themselves are said to make visible the Trinity, Christ's kingship over all, and the origin and the destination of man.[42] But even now Paulinus is not finished; he continues:

> [Thus] it is wonderfully arranged to delineate the twofold likeness of the eternal Cross, so that, should it be our pleasure to gaze closely at it, *instant faith is brought forth through our eyes* ... . This representation manifests in the Cross the same shape which denotes a balance poised with equal arms, or a yoke symmetrical on its erected beam; or again, the lofty tree – with its arms extending sideways (on which the Lord hung and shed his innocent blood for sinning humankind as the

[39] *Ibid.* 32, 10 and 17.

[40] *Carm* 19, vv. 608-676. Descriptions of other representations of the Cross in Paulinus's churches are given in *Epp* 32, 10, 12 and 14. An overview of the antique representations of the Cross in: E. DINKLER and E. DINKLER-VON SCHUBERT, "Kreuz", *Lexikon der christlichen Ikonographie*, ed. E. KIRSCHBAUM, 8 vols. (Rome, Freiburg, Basel and Wien, 1968-1976), 2, cols. 562-590 (on its various forms, see col. 569; on Paulinus' luminous apsidal Cross (*Epp* 32, 10: "*crucem corona lucido cingit globo*") as a sign of the Second Coming: col. 578). A. GRABAR, *Martyrium*, 3 vols. (Paris, 1943-1946), 2, p. 287, believes that Paulinus's representations of the Cross points to a fourth-century vision of the luminous Cross: E. PAX, "Epiphanie", *Reallexikon für Antike und Christentum*, ed. T. KLAUSER, 1- (Stuttgart, 1950-), 5, cols. 885-886, lists the descriptions of its various fourth-century apparitions. M. CARRUTHERS, *The Craft of Thought: Meditation, Rhetoric, and the Making of Images, 400-1200* (Cambridge, 1998), pp. 68-70 and 151 suggests that pictures and the Cross, as well as texts, could be "meditative 'gathering' sites".

[41] *Carm* 19, vv. 628-631.

[42] *Carm* 19, vv. 632-655. CONYBEARE, *Paulinus*, p. 93, describes this as a "paradoxical multiplicitous trinitarianism". Cf. CARRUTHERS, *Craft*, pp. 165-168. J. ONIANS, "Abstraction and imagination in late Antiquity", *Art History* 3 (1980), pp. 1-23, describes a significantly increased visual response to indeterminate data in late Antiquity. Hypothetical reconstructions of this Cross's visible appearance in: G. WIMAN, "Till Paulinus Nolanus' carmina", *Eranos: Acta Philologica Suecana* 32 (1934), pp. 117-118.

world trembled) – is like the eyes bridging a face with eyebrows on the forehead.
At the very bottom of the Cross, which is formed with two bars of heavy weight, is
attached a small wreath of highly wrought metal encrusted with various jewels.
Here, too, *the Cross* of the Lord, as if wreathed with a diadem, *shines forth with its
eternal image* of the tree of life [italics added].

> *hoc opere est perfecta, modis ut consita miris*
> *aeternae crucis effigiem designet utramque,*
> *ut modo, si libeat spectari comminus ipsam,*
> *prompta fides oculis.*
>
> ...
>
> *ergo eadem species formam crucis exerit illam,*
> *quae trutinam aequato libratam stamine signat*
> *subrectoque iugum concors temone figurat,*
> *sive superciliis a fronte iugantia vultum*
> *lumina transversis imitatur cornibus arbor*
> *ardua, qua dominus mundo trepidante pependit*
> *innocuum fundens pro peccatore cruorem.*
> *huic autem, solido quam pondere regula duplex*
> *iungit, in extremea producti calce metalli*
> *parva corona subest variis circumdata gemmis.*
> *hac quoque crux domini tanquam diademate cincta*
> *emicat aeterna vitalis imagine ligni.*[43]

Both the name of Christ then, which the representation makes visible, and the
shape of the letters themselves 'delineate' the likeness of the 'eternal Cross' as
a symbol for the eternal Christ in his many aspects. The subsequent images
which Paulinus visualizes in the cross's visible contours appear to refer to the
weighing involved in the Last Judgment, to the carrying of the Cross as a way
of life, and to Christ's death on dead wood being an inversion that gives humankind access to eternal life. Again adverting to the Cross's visible shape,
Paulinus even uses its outlines to visualize a hint of what may be Christ's face.
One is reminded here, on the one hand, of Christ's face in the medallion at the
centre of the jewelled Cross in the church of Sant'Apollinare in Classe in
Ravenna,[44] and, on the other, of Augustine's references to his seeing God's face
(*facies, vultum*) in the text of Scripture.[45] Curiously, Paulinus does not exploit

---

[43] *Carm* 19, vv. 659-662; 665-676.

[44] Depicted in O. VON SIMSON, *Sacred Fortress: Byzantine Art and Statecraft in Ravenna*
(Princeton, 1987), pls. 22-23.

[45] *Confessiones* 7, 21, 27 and 9, 3, 6, ed. L. VERHEIJEN, 2nd edn. (Turnhout, 1981: *Corpus
Christianorum Series Latina* 27), pp. 110-111, 136, discussed in K.F. MORRISON, *Conversion*

the lamps hanging on the cross as, for instance, pointing to Christ as "the Light of the world" ("*lux mundi*").[46]

At the end of the passage, he returns to the tree image in the cross's shape and points to it as the cross's invisible essence as the eternal, true form of the once paradisiacal, garden-variety Tree of life. And the cross is said to "shine forth" ("*emicat*") with this invisible image. Is this an oblique reference to the jewel-encrusted wreath? For in this period, jewels (here representing flowers) were themselves thought to emit light from supernal spheres.[47] But the concept of radiance partially overlaps with the concepts of reflecting and of manifesting an image of something. This is evident, for instance, in the apostle Paul's statement about Christ who "is the radiance of the glory and the figure of[God's] nature" ("*sit splendor gloriae et figura substantiae eius*").[48] We shall return to this theme of effulgence as image below. Paulinus says something similar of the symbolic representation of the Trinity in one of his churches: "The Trinity flashes forth with all its mystery" ("*Pleno coruscat trinitas mysterio*").[49] Seeing "the image of the Tree of life shining forth" in the Cross, then, is perhaps seeing (that is: visualizing) the 'mystery' of Christ's death on the wood and subsequent resurrection as overlapping or coalescing with the dynamic archetype of accessing eternal life in the apparent death and revival of a tree every year.[50]

Paulinus's imaginative strategy invites a perception of images which are formed in the mind from the visible contours of the object – images that are visual representations of invisible extra-mental truths. His phrasing, however, also suggests a strong affective experience of the images with which the perception of the visible object is as it were overlaid. When he says that those contemplating the symbol of the Cross from close by will experience "faith brought forth through the eyes", the image seen, although in the viewer's mind only, appears to be experienced as a living manifestation of eternal life. I suggest that what he may have meant is, that an affective intimation of the tree's renewing its life every spring is directly and spontaneously experienced in the very act

---

and Text (Charlottesville and London, 1992), pp. 4-5.

[46] Io 8, 12.

[47] As in Prudentius, *Psychomachia*, vv. 851-853, ed. M.P. CUNNINGHAM (Turnhout, 1966: *Corpus Christianorum Series Latina* 126), p. 179.

[48] Hbr 1, 3. See on this R.P. MARTIN, "*Apaugasma*, radiance, effulgence, reflection", in: *New International Dictionary of New Testament Theology*, 2, pp. 289-290.

[49] *Epp* 32, 11.

[50] The conception of a visually accessible archetype in a pictorial representation was central in the later veneration of icons: KESSLER, "Pictures", p. 65. On the archetypal quality of certain religious symbols: D.L. MILLER, "Theology's ego: Religion's soul", in: *Spring* (Dallas, 1980), pp. 82-83.

itself of visualizing this image.[51] For it has been suggested that *an image is in fact a visible rendering of an affective pattern.*[52] In contemplating it, the heart spontaneously experiences its dynamic pattern – that is, the transformational leap from death to life – without the mediation of words. I would suggest that Paulinus's phrase "instant faith for the eyes" points precisely to this experience. For elsewhere, too, Paulinus shows that Christian truth can be communicated nonverbally. When words about it have not "opened one's mind (*aperit sensum*), let us then take our models (*exempla*) from the buildings", for although word and building have "different appearances (*dissimiles formae*), they concur in their similar beauty (*simili specie concurr[unt]*)".[53] Here, I think, Paulinus is pointing to an emotional rationale for his nonverbal representations of divine truths: they directly address and move the heart.

In looking at a symbolic object, then, 'God's face' could indeed become visible: not in the sensory sphere itself but in the viewer's mind, primarily through his active visualization of the biblical images associated with the visible symbol. Sometimes, these can also be precipitated by a nonverbal experience of the object's visible shapes and proportions that recall analogous ones in the biblical text. A similar strategy of visualization of the biblical text as an affective approach to invisible divine reality is found in only one other Latin writer of this period: Prudentius (348-ca. 405). And it cannot be an accident that, in contrast to Jerome and Augustine, both Paulinus and Prudentius express themselves as poets. Professor Jacques Fontaine has beautifully described their poetry as "the ultimate spiritual exercise" and "a spiritual art".[54] Augustine's view of imagination was very different. Although he recognized the mediatory role of imagination between sensation and thought, he was acutely aware of its tendency towards deception and regarded only the insight of imageless intellect as approaching infallible truth.[55]

---

[51] Cf. CARRUTHERS, *Craft*, p. 184, where she states that meditative reading tends to shade into visionary experience.

[52] As S.K. LANGER, *Feeling and Form* (New York, 1953), p. 59; and G. EPSTEIN, *Waking Dream Therapy* (New York, 1981), p. 18. On this view in the late antique period: M.R. MILES, *Image as Insight: Visual Understanding in Western Christianity and Secular Culture* (Boston, 1985), pp. 30, 44-45, 149.

[53] *Carm* 28, vv. 258-260, 265.

[54] J. FONTAINE, *La naissance de la poésie dans l'occident chrétien* (Paris, 1981), pp. 152, 143-160, respectively. CONYBEARE, *Paulinus*, pp. 124-126 similarly points to something like a poetical theology in Paulinus's writings.

[55] M.W. BUNDY, *The Theory of Imagination in Classical and Medieval Thought* (Urbana, Ill., 1928: *University of Illinois Studies in Language and Literature* 12), pp. 153-172. See also J. RIST, *Augustine* (Cambridge, 1994), p. 86.

But, like Augustine,[56] Paulinus believes that these imagistically apprehended truths are also those of one's deepest self, which is rooted in God. For
he writes:

> When you direct your mind's eye towards the heavenly sanctuary, Truth will reveal
> her face to you and disclose to you your own self, for it is through the knowing of
> divine truth that we also come to know ourselves.

> *ilico ut ad superna penetralia aciem mentis intenderis, aperiet ad te faciem suam
> veritas teque ipsum reserabit tibi. nam divinae veritatis agnitu, id quoque, ut nos-
> met ipsos noverimus, adsequimur.*[57]

Paulinus, then, appears to experience the mentally visualized images, as well as
the visible ones, as visual appearances, or 'faces', of the invisible spiritual-
affective reality of divine truth that is within and without the human self.[58] And
he believes that 'encountering' such an image can have a transformational effect.

1.2 Dum Videre Vos Cogitatis

But he can also visualize images of invisible truths when there is no pictorial take-off point. In a letter to Severus to accompany his gift to him of a relic
of the holy Cross, Paulinus gives instructions for seeing some of its invisible
dimensions:

> In this almost indivisible particle of a small sliver [of wood] take up ... the guaran-
> tee of your eternal salvation. Let not your faith be straitened because the *eyes of the
> body* behold evidence so small; let it look with *the keenness of inner vision* on the
> whole power of the Cross in this tiny segment. *While you think you are seeing* that
> wood, upon which our salvation, upon which the Lord of majesty was hanged with
> nails while the world trembled, you too must tremble and rejoice. Let us remember
> that "the rocks were rent" at the sight of this Cross, and *in emulation of the rocks,
> rend our hearts* with the fear of God [italics added].

> *in segmento pene atomo hastulae brevis sumite ... pignus aeternae salutis. non
> angustetur fides vestra carnalibus oculis parva cernentibus, sed interna acie totam*

---

[56] RIST, *Augustine*, pp. 86-90.

[57] *Epp* 16, 9.

[58] CONYBEARE, *Paulinus*, pp. 124-126, suggests that Paulinus's multivalent imagery is in
fact an ontology of an alternate, spiritual, reality.

in hoc minimo vim crucis videat. dum videre vos cogitatis lignum illud, quo salus nostra, quo dominus maiestatis adfixus tremente mundo pependerit, exultetis cum tremore. recordemur et petras fissas [Mt 27, 51] *ad huius adspectum crucis, et saltem saxorum aemulatione praecordia nostra findamus timore divino.*[59]

Here again, associative visualization is creatively invoked, this time accompanied by a purposeful affective enactment of the textual images through which past as well as eternal reality is approached. Paulinus applies the apostle Paul's statement in II Cor 3, 18 about seeing Christ in the Old Testament when he says of this relic of the Cross that "by uncovering the face of our heart (*revelata cordis facie*), we may see the mystery of the saving gifts of God (*salutarium dei munerum sacramenta videamus*)".[60] It is experienced, then, as a seeing by the heart.[61] Similarly, Paulinus elsewhere describes the meditative visualizing process that produces his poetry as "tak[ing] up the material and conceiv[ing] apprehensions of God" ("*suscipe materiam, divinos concipe sensus*").[62] But he also prays for inspiration in the metaphor of a stream of (no doubt 'living'[63]) water from the "heavenly founts" ("*superis fontibus*"),[64] and speaks of being "inflamed with the divinity of Christ God" ("*dei flammatu[s] numine Christi*") as "loosening the tongue" for poetry addressed to the Father.[65] When he counsels a friend to ascend into heaven, where "a divine light will flow through (*perfundet*) your mind, and ... you will see (*videas*) the great laws of the tremendous God ... Christ ... renewing all things",[66] we may be looking at what Fontaine calls "a quasi-mystical theory of inspiration"[67] that is reminiscent of Plato's (427-347 BC) view in his later *Dialogues* of an inspired and prophetic poetry that transcends reason.[68] According to Paulinus, then, such prayerful visualization can mentally access the living manifestation of invisible divine reality.

---

[59] *Epp* 31, 1.
[60] *Epp* 31, 1.
[61] Cf. CARRUTHERS, *Craft*, p. 50.
[62] *Carm* 22, v. 19, cited by J. FONTAINE, *Naissance de la poésie dans l'Occident chrétien* (Paris, 1981), p. 152. Similarly: *Carm* 6, vv. 25-26.
[63] As in Io 4, 10-14.
[64] *Carm* 23, vv. 20-23, 37-42.
[65] *Carm* 22, vv. 2-3, cited in FONTAINE, *Naissance*, p. 152.
[66] *Carm* 80-86.
[67] FONTAINE, *Naissance*, p. 152.
[68] BUNDY, *Imagination*, pp. 48-59.

2. Caelestis Animae Effigies: *Visible or Invisible?*

Coming now to the heavenly image in a human being: is it visible or not? Augustine said that the inner beauty of the heart transfigures a person's exterior appearance and that it therefore can be seen by the heart's eye, even in a wrinkled face and in a mutilated martyr.[69] What kind of seeing is this? In daily life, he writes, when our "mind's eye" (*"oculus mentis"*), in purity, peace and holiness, sees love in (the face of) a living person, it 'sees' God (embodied), for God is love.[70] A common late antique expression that points to an element in this hardly verbalizable experience is that the eye is "the window of the soul".[71] As we shall see, a more specific description of what is seen in eyes is that of the eyes' emission of a kind of 'light' – presumably a synonym for the experience of an invisible holy energy.

The heavenly image was regarded as a restoration of God's image in man's soul through his effort, aided by grace, to achieve similitude to Christ.[72] The phrase of "bearing the image" is, of course, that of the apostle Paul, who distinguishes between the state of the old, "earthly" man who cares about the transient things of the world, and that of the new or heavenly man, initiated through baptism, who lives in the spirit and thereby achieves eternal life.[73] Thus, he exhorts the community to "throw away the old man and his deeds, and to put on the new one which is renewed in knowing according to the image (*qui renovatur in agnitionem secundum imaginem*) of He who created him".[74] This image, as we saw, is that of Christ, who himself "is the image of the invisible God ...; in Him all things were created, in heaven and on earth, visible and invisible ...".[75] In other words, all visible phenomena would somehow manifest the image – or 'face' – of Christ.

Paulinus states that one Christ is present in all saints,[76] and that, conversely, the saints shine like glowing eyes in Christ's body.[77] When he writes to one of his correspondents that he hopes the latter's prayers will cause him to "be transformed from my earthly appearance (*a nostra terrestri specie*) into your like-

---

[69]   MILES, "Image", pp. 189-190, 236-237.

[70]   Augustine, *Epistola* 148, 18, ed. A. GOLDBACHER (Wien and Leipzig, 1904: *Corpus Scriptorum Ecclesiasticorum Latinorum* 44), p. 347.

[71]   *Thesaurus linguae latinae*, 9.2, col. 448.

[72]   LADNER, "Concept", pp. 11-12.

[73]   1 Cor 15, 45-50.

[74]   Col 3, 9-10.

[75]   Col 1, 15-16.

[76]   *Carm* 14, v. 257.

[77]   *Epp* 23, 26.

ness, so that we bear the image of the heavenly man with equal genuineness (*caelestis hominis imaginem pari veritate gestemus*)", one wonders whether he thought that this image did indeed somehow change one's visible appearance (*species*).[78] Some kind of visible distinction, too, seems implied in his statement to Sulpicius Severus, when he refuses to have his portrait painted for his friend: "Which kind of image (*qualis imago*) do you want me to send to you: that of the earthly man or that of the heavenly one?"[79] He then deplores the fact that he is "guilty of contaminating the heavenly image by earthly corruption", "by his carnal feelings and earthly acts", and asks God to "perfect his own image in me (*in nobis ... imago*), in which I would not be ashamed to be painted (*in qua nos pingi non pudet*)".[80] In conclusion, he says that he prefers the invisible image of himself in his friend's heart to any pictorial representation.[81]

2.1 Forma Nobis Conversationis et Morum

To return now to St. Martin's portrait: how does Paulinus expect the newly baptized to manage to 'see' an image of a saint's invisible heavenly soul in it? If, as he tells us elsewhere, Christ's human "life and works are the exemplar for our behaviour and manners (*forma nobis conversationis et morum*)", we should be able to see this somehow in Martin.[82] And indeed, when we look at Paulinus's inscriptions for the saint's portrait, they have specific things to say about what must constitute the heavenly image in the portrait of St. Martin. Thus they tell us that, besides being "the pattern of the perfect life" ("*perfectae ... regula vitae*") and "a model for saints" ("*exemplar sanctis*"), Martin "arms our faith with strong examples and words" ("*fidem exemplis et dictis fortibus armat*").[83] Further, the saint is designated as "the form of justice" ("*forma iustitiae*"), "the sum of virtues" ("*summa virtutum*"), and "the mirror of fortitude" ("*speculum fortitudo*").[84] Now *regula*, *exemplar*, *forma* and *speculum* are all aspects of or synonyms for the concept of pattern or 'image'. The portrait of a human figure, then, is understood to point somehow to invisible, universal qualities in their

---

[78] I Cor 15, 49; *Epp* 42, 3.

[79] *Epp* 30, 2: "*qualem cupis ut mittamus imaginem tibi: terreni hominis an caelestis?*".

[80] *Epp* 30, 5. I do not agree, therefore, with BELTING, *Bild*, p. 110, that Paulinus is saying that the heavenly image cannot be represented.

[81] *Epp* 30, 6.

[82] *Epp* 43, 7.

[83] *Epp* 32, 3.

[84] *Epp* 32, 4.

embodied form.[85] Beholding the likeness of St. Martin's physical appearance is intended to evoke all these associations – almost certainly derived from Severus's then recently completed book on St. Martin's life.[86]

Now it is not possible to visualize abstract qualities except as they are embodied in visible acts. I suggest, therefore, that the evoked memories of Martin's deeds – which presumably were not visible in the representation – were intended to be visualized in what has been called "visual hints and flashes"[87] of scenes of just, virtuous and courageous acts overlapping with congruent acts of the human Jesus. For it is difficult to imagine how else one can *see* Christ as the heavenly soul's image in Martin's justice, virtues and courage. Paulinus indeed says that "by believing, we see [Christ] with the inner eye" (or: "with our inner light") (*"credendo interno lumine conspicimus"*).[88] And when we look at Paulinus's statements about his beloved patron St. Felix, such a visualization process in fact seems to be involved. For Paulinus says that the saint is "the breath of Christ"[89] and that Christ is sweet to him through Felix's person.[90] The image (more precisely: the composite image) within the image of St. Martin, then, was one that, although triggered by the picture, was in the viewer's mind. It is highly unlikely therefore that, although Paulinus refers to Martin's portrait in Aquitaine as a "to-be-venerated image" (*"veneranda imago"*),[91] he thought that the material picture itself gave access to the spiritual quality of the depicted.

Clearly, this image was to excite admiration and emulation of the remembered deeds as a model for the new, heavenly soul of those being baptized. One background of Paulinus's thinking here may be – as it was in his thoughts about seeing salvation in the relic of the Cross – the apostle Paul's statement about the believers' recognizing of Christ's 'image' in the events and statements of the Old Testament. For in II Cor 3, 18, after having just mentioned Moses's shining face as he descended from his meeting with God on the mountain, he writes about this:

[85] Likewise for the Middle Ages: R. ASSUNTO, *Die Theorie des Schönen im Mittelalter*, tr. C. BAUMGARTH (Köln and Kleve, 1963: *DuMont Dokumente* 1.2), p. 56.
[86] Sulpicius Severus, *Vita sancti Martini*, ed. and tr. J. FONTAINE (Paris, 1967: *Sources chrétiennes* 133).
[87] R. ARNHEIM, *Visual Thinking* (Berkeley, Los Angeles and London, 1969), pp. 107-109.
[88] *Carm* 31, v. 374.
[89] *Epp* 17, 4.
[90] *Epp* 23, 1.
[91] *Epp* 32, 2.

For we all ... *beholding/reflecting* the glory of the Lord [in the text], are *being transformed into his likeness*, from brightness to brightness as though by the Spirit of the Lord.

nos vero omnes ... gloriam Domini speculantes in eandem imaginem transforma-mur, a claritate in claritatem, tamquam a Domini Spiritu.[92]

The double meaning here of *speculantes* – seeing as well as reflecting – was one and the same in late Antiquity. For its theory of vision was that a pattern through being seen impressed its likeness upon the soul, whereby the latter then reflected the pattern seen.[93] Thus, gazing admiringly at an image – even a mental one, as in meditation – would not only inspire conscious emulation of its content, but in fact *induce a spontaneous mimesis of its affective pattern in the beholder*. In other words, it would bring about the replication of the pattern of the image in the heart. The idea of becoming what one sees or contemplates was an ancient one and had also been expressed by Plato, Origen (ca. 185-254), Gregory of Nyssa (fourth century),[94] and Augustine.[95] It appears as though Paulinus and Severus hoped that something like this would happen also when the newly baptised came out of the font. Modern psychology has rediscovered this mimetic phenomenon as 'modelling' and uses it extensively in so-called guided affective imagery or waking dream therapies.[96]

2.2 Sidereum Honorem Fulgere Vultu

Nevertheless, Paulinus's image within an image in St. Martin's portrait may have had a somewhat visible aspect after all. The apostle Paul had indicated that living the likeness to Christ results in interior assimilation: it attracts or precipitates His living presence in man as a "temple".[97] And about Christ's appearance he writes: "it is the God who said 'Let light shine out of darkness' who has shone in our hearts (*inluxit in cordibus nostris*) to give the light of the knowledge of the glory of God in the face of Christ Jesus (*ad inluminationem scien-*

---

[92] II Cor 3, 18. All quotations are from the Vulgate.

[93] M. MILES, "Vision: The eye of the body and the eye of the mind in Saint Augustine's *De trinitate* and *Confessiones*", *The Journal of Religion* 63 (1983), pp. 127-128 and *passim*.

[94] JAVELET, *Image*, pp. 8, 31, 37.

[95] MORRISON, *I am You*, p. 23.

[96] See on this, for instance, EPSTEIN, *Therapy*, and R. ASSAGIOLI, *Psychosynthesis* (New York, 1962).

[97] II Cor 6, 16.

tiae claritatis Dei in facie Christi Jesu".[98] As already indicated, this radiance would itself have been regarded as the 'image' of God. Paul here assumes that, as with Moses when he descended from his meeting with God on the mountain,[99] the heavenly Christ's face reflects the dazzling light of God's glory. For during his transfiguration on Mount Tabor his human face had been seen to "shine like the sun" (*"resplenduit facies eius sicut sol"*).[100] The radiation of light, then, is understood to be a visual manifestation of the indwelling of the uncircumscribable and undepictable God.[101]

That Paulinus also regarded such radiance as a visible trace of the presence of Christ in a saint is evident when he speaks of Martin's "venerable face" (*"facies venerabilis"*) in the portrait, "through which his brightness shines with outstanding brilliance" (*"quo splendor eius ... clarius emicaret"*).[102] Perhaps this was indicated in the portrait by the then upcoming stylistic convention of a nimbus, which – in the Christian tradition – came to be associated with the uncreated light on Mount Tabor.[103] About St. Felix, Paulinus reports that the possessed cried out that Christ shone forth in the saint (*"Christum in sancto fulgere"*),[104] and elsewhere Paulinus himself says that the saint is "the glory of Christ who knows no limits" (*"immensi Felix est gloria Christi"*).[105] Elsewhere Felix is referred to as the sun and as in fact "shin[ing] ... with Christ's illumination" (*"inlustrante micat Christo"*).[106] Paulinus does not mention any portrait in his churches of his patron saint Felix; it looks therefore as though the saint's entombed body, and not a pictorial representation, mediated his 'presence'.[107] But Paulinus does visualize his long-dead hero St. Felix's appearance during life, and in these words he may actually be telling us how he 'saw' the human appearance of a heavenly soul:

> ... with his soul wholly among the stars, aware of Christ and forgetful of the world, he bore God in his heart and his bosom was filled with Christ. He was never confined to himself, and seemed [a] holy and greater [being], with his eyes and his face shining forth with a starry honour.

---

[98] Gn 1, 3; II Cor 4, 6.

[99] Ex 34, 29-30.

[100] Mt 17, 2.

[101] Cf. PELIKAN, *Imago*, pp. 78, 92-95.

[102] *Epp* 32, 2.

[103] Cf. PAX, "Epiphanie", col. 898; BELTING, *Bild*, p. 103, and PELIKAN, *Imago*, p. 100.

[104] *Carm* 14, vv. 30-31.

[105] *Carm* 14, v. 43.

[106] *Carm* 27, v. 16.

[107] As he makes clear, for instance, in *Epp* 32, 6 and *Carm* 27, vv. 440-448.

totus in astra animo, Christi memor, immemor aevi,
corde deum gestans et plenus pectora Christo.
nec iam se capit ipse, sacer maiorque videri
sidereumque oculis et honorem fulgere vultu.[108]

Here it is the radiating light that reveals the uncircumscribable and undepictable presence of divinity. It reflects what was understood to be the presence of Christ, and itself functions as his 'image', reflecting that of God. For Paulinus, then, visible reality was connected to its archetype in Christ and God through what has been called "a great chain of images".[109]

3. Videas Invisibilem: *Affective Union*

Having looked at Paulinus's strategies for discovering images of divine realities in visible objects, we now turn to his encounters with living persons. And here we find him saying that Christ can be seen in everyone! In the following passage he presents an ethical and affective way of doing this:

Raise and direct your soul to the Lord and you shall come upon Christ. *By acting according to His precepts*, you will see Him in every poor man, touch Him in every needy person, entertain Him in every guest, since He Himself bears witness that what is done to His least brethren in His name is done to Him. So now you know how you are to *see Him though He is invisible*, and to lay hold of Him though He cannot be grasped [italics added].

dirigens in dominum animam tuam, et adtinges Christum [Eph 5, 14]. *operando praeceptis ipsius videbis eum in omni paupere, tanges eum omni egeno, recipies eum in omni hospite, quoniam sibi fieri ipse testatur quae in eius nomine minimis eius fiant. ecce nosti iam contra quomodo videas invisibilem et inadprehensibilem conprehendas.*[110]

It is through love, then, that Christ may be 'seen' – Paulinus here means: sensed – embodied in every person. For although His image may be obscured by sin, He is everyone's deepest and highest self.[111] Augustine, too, says that God may be seen with an inner sight in loving one's neighbour.[112] Paulinus is speaking

---

[108] *Carm* 15, vv. 173-176.

[109] PELIKAN, *Imago*, p. 177.

[110] Cf. Mt 25, 40. *Epp* 32, 20.

[111] See on this CONYBEARE, *Paulinus*, pp. 131-160.

[112] *De trinitate* 8, 8, 12, ed. W.J. MOUNTAIN and F. GLORIE (Turnhout, 1968: *Corpus*

from experience. By extension, he tells us that he even 'sees' images in the couriers bringing his letters: "the image of the faith" (*"fidei effigies"*) of Severus and the "pattern of life" (*"formula"*) of St. Martin and Clarus. Elsewhere two hermits are said to manifest the images (*"forma"*) of John the Baptist and Christ.[113] Here again, we see that Paulinus's world cohered through images.

But his most extensive verbalization of seeing these images in living persons is that of his gazing upon the face of his visiting friend Nicetas, missionary bishop in Dalmatia.[114] He writes:

> ... when I behold the father whom I love above all others, I myself become Nicetas, bearing his heart instead of his blessed name ...

> ... *visoque parente,*
> *cuius prae cunctis amor in me regnat, et ipse*
> *Nicetes fio, benedicti nominis instar*
> *mente gerens* ... .[115]

We see here that affective union is the hinge upon which all turns. Paulinus has again 'looked through' visual appearance, this time to become one with an affective pattern he somehow senses in his friend's heart. Paulinus's instant identification with this points to one of his central assumptions: that all believers are members of the spiritual Christ and joined through their hearts in Him.[116] To give a shape and a name to his experiences, the poet Paulinus again resorts to biblical images. Here is his more elaborated description of what happens when he sees Nicetas:

> ... since my master himself sits at my side, settled close by but having come from far, and I shall *look at him* frequently *with reverent eyes*. Perhaps – as once the unproductive cattle of the shepherd Jacob – *I shall conceive* fecund thoughts in my sterile heart. For Nicetas too is like the gentle Jacob, the Lord's blessed one; like Israel, he sits as shepherd of sheep and goats before a well of living water. He, too, with a like heart collected three rods from three trees, and setting them in the water he summons his flock. When they gather, he impregnates them, and dyes the offspring with the three [variously marked] rods ... .

Christianorum Series Latina 50), pp. 286-289, cited in MILES, "Vision", p. 141.

[113] *Epp* 23, 2, 3, 4; 26, 4; 27, 3; 44, 2.

[114] *Carm* 17 is addressed to him.

[115] *Carm* 27, vv. 180-183. In *De trinitate* 8, 6, 9, quoted in MILES, "Vision", p. 139, Augustine, too, states that one cannot see spiritual qualities in others except when one recognizes them from self-knowledge.

[116] *Epp* 44, 4. See on this FABRE, *St. Paulin*, pp. 137-154.

This is how grace gives new life to sterile souls in the name of the Trinity. The Spirit as husband through coitus fills [the Church] with the Word, and the Church gives the offspring conceived for God an inner marking. So fertile in her virginal womb and the mother of salvation, with her *gaze* upon the three rods, she *drinks in the moist seed* of the Word, and her *face is signed with the eternal light* ... .
... I looked long and attentively in the face of the nourishing master, and beheld the various rods in his learned heart. *With fixed eyes, I drank in the colours I saw* [there], and his dew-laden heart sprinkled me with divine drops [italics added].

> *... quoniam lateri meus adsidet ipse magister,*
> *comminus e regione situm venerante frequenter*
> *lumine conspiciam; forsan sapientis ab ore,*
> *ut quondam effetae pecudes pastoris Iacob,*
> *concipiam sterili fecundos pectore sensus.*
> *namque et Nicetes domino benedictus ut ille*
> *mitis, ut Israel ovibus quoque pastor et haedis*
> *ante lacum viventis aquae sedet; hic etiam tres*
> *corde pari trina sibi legit ab arbore virgas,*
> *quis in aqua positis pecus advocat et coeuntes*
> *ingravidat virgisque tribus concepta colorat ... .*
> *sic animas steriles in nomine gratia trino*
> *innovat, et verbi coitu vir spiritus inplet*
> *conceptosque deo notat intus eclesia fetus*
> *virgineo fecunda utero materque salutis,*
> *dum virgis intenta tribus bibit uvida verbi*
> *semina et aeterni signatur lumine vultus ... .*
> *... adtentusque diu pascentis in ora magistri*
> *inspexi docto varias in pectore virgas*
> *conspectumque bibi per lumina fixa colorem,*
> *et me divinis sparsit mens roscida guttis.*[117]

Let me say at once that I do not think that Paulinus at that moment actually visualized the rods: the description is a literary conceit speaking of Paulinus the author. But the conceit does tell us something about Paulinus's assumptions. Nicetas's increasing his flock through his preaching with words is imaged as the impregnation and marking of Jacob's flock by letting it drink in the sight of the three variously marked rods. In the three rods, Paulinus goes on to explain, "we see the mysteries of the Kingdom [of God]" ("*inspiciamus ... mysteria regni*").[118] He explains: "the Spirit is in the plane tree, the Virgin in the storax,

---

[117] Gn 40, 37 ff. *Carm* 27, vv. 243-253; 258-263; 266-272.
[118] *Carm* 27, v. 274.

Christ in the almond" (*"spiritus in platano est, virgo in storace, in nuce Chris-tus"*),[119] and gives metaphorical motivations for this that need not concern us here. Seeing a visible representation as a symbol, then, is a "drinking" which is a being impregnated with the living truth, revealed as well as concealed by the symbol. Like a word, a visible symbol is a "seed"[120] that causes something to be generated internally. And the Church's face being "signed with eternal light" through this experience recalls the "glory" and light attending the perception of Christ in the biblical text and the resulting transformation mentioned in II Cor 3, 18. What we see in this passage, is that Paulinus uses biblical images to grasp and express his direct experience of an invisible affective pattern in a living person through looking lovingly – that is, meditatively – at his visible appearance.

4. Suo Vultu Coruscus: *Seeing the Image*

Whereas Paulinus the intellectual poet visualized and enacted biblical images of affective-spiritual truths to reach an intimation of eternal verities, it was an uneducated man who had the privilege of actually seeing Christ – in a moment of crisis and probably after intensive prayer. As Paulinus tells the story, an old sailor named Valgius was left alone, sleeping, on a storm-tossed rudderless ship. He awoke when Christ gently stroked him and tweaked his ear. Then he saw Christ, sometimes in the appearance of St. Felix, visibly guiding the ship safely to the shore. Paulinus writes that "Christ entered this ship *by means of the image* (*per imaginem*) of his confessor", apparently implying that, in this apparition at least, an image or resemblance coincided with the actual presence of the original.[121] Thus, he tells us:

> ... its rudder was the Helmsman of the universe. Yes, the Lord Himself sat at the stern, *shining* now *with his own face* and gleaming hair, as described in the Apocalypse, now with the face of His friend and confessor, my lord and our common patron, the venerable Felix ... . [italics added]

> ... *cui gubernaculum erat mundi gubernator. ipse enim dominus nunc suo vultu coruscus, ut in Apocalypsi describitur, et coma fulgidus, nunc confessoris et amici sui, domini mei, communis patroni Felicis ore venerabilis in puppi sedebat ... .*[122]

---

[119] *Carm* 277.
[120] Cf. the sower's parable in Mt 13; Lc 8, 11.
[121] *Epp* 49, 10.
[122] *Epp* 49, 3.

It is worth noting that Paulinus here does not let Valgius see the image of Christ *in* that of St. Felix: the images alternate. As an uneducated man, Valgius probably would not have been acquainted with the meditative visualizing approach of the intellectual elite – the very approach which Paulinus was introducing to the common folk through the pictures in his churches. The image of Christ informing this vision, as Paulinus reports it, is described in Apc 1, 13-16:

> ... one like a son of man, clothed with a long robe and with a golden girdle around his breast; his head and his hair were white as white wool, white as snow; his eyes were like a flame of fire, his feet were glowing like brass in an oven, ... and his face was like the sun shining in full strength.

> ... *similem Filio hominis, vestitum podere et praecinctum ad mamillas zonam auream; caput autem eius et capilli erant candidi tamquam lana, alba tamquam nix; et oculi eius velut flamma ignis, et pedes eius similes orichalco sicut in camino ardenti ... . et facies eius sicut sol lucet in virtute sua.*

Late antique literary descriptions of heavenly persons, not only of Christ, tend to point toward this image:[123] it is a visible archetype of the heavenly soul. We have already seen traces of it in Paulinus's image of St. Felix with a shining face and eyes. Here we see again that effulgence is experienced as a visible 'image' or manifestation of Christ in a person.

The old man's faith in Christ's and the saint's aid are here seen to lead to an imaginative visualization or clairvoyant vision that indeed 'sees' them as present in physical form – the former as described in Revelation, and the latter presumably as remembered from stories heard about him. In a way, this story would have been a more satisfactory one for this investigation if the old man had not been alone on the ship, and if he had seen this Christlike radiance appear on an ordinary living person's face. For that would have been an instance of seeing the spiritual image in an ordinarily visible person. What we do see in the story, however, may be one of many contemporary experiences – especially those of crisis – in which imagination shades into waking dream and/or clairvoyance: a becoming aware of intensely experienced energy patterns, in oneself or in one's surroundings, as mental images. Paulinus's story shows that for him, too, there was nothing inherently improbable about apparitions: their occurrence was accepted as a possible manifestation of the autonomous and active reality of the spiritual world.[124]

---

[123] A. Cizek, "Das Bild der idealen Schönheit in der lateinischen Dichtung des Frühmittelalters", *Mittellateinisches Jahrbuch* 26 (1992), pp. 5-35.

[124] See on this large subject Pax, "Epiphanie"; and, for instance, R.L. Fox, *Pagans and*

After a lengthy interpretation of Valgius's experience as an analogy or allegory of God's dealing with the Ark of the Church on the sea of the world, Paulinus enjoins what is probably a meditation on these images: "So let us keep before our minds and inwardly look on that most noble vision of God's work" (*"proponamus ergo nobis animo et mente cernamus pulcherrimum divini operis spectaculum"*).[125] For in these events, he writes, "mystical signs are given an embodied form" (*"mystica argumenta formantur"*).[126] Again, then, the dynamics of God's invisible works are apprehended in those of patterns or 'images' manifested in and through visible phenomena.

Characteristically, Paulinus then gives us his recipe for reliving and re-enacting Valgius's experience. Comparing the latter's body to the material places and objects in the Holy Land, he writes:

> ... if living proofs in lifeless objects demonstrate the ancient truth for today's belief, then with what reverence must this man be regarded, with whom God deigned to converse, before whom *God's face* was not concealed, to whom Christ revealed now His martyr and now His own person? Valgius is the living earth on which we see impressed the traces of the Lord's body, if *with the eye of faith and spiritual sight we scrutinize* what Christ's bosom and Christ's hands have touched in him ... [italics added]

> *si ... veterem veritatem praesenti fide conprobant in rebus exanimis viva documenta: quam religiose adspiciendus est hic, quem adloqui dei sermo dignatus est, cui se facies divina non texit, cui nunc martyrem suum, nunc semet ipsum Christus ostendit, in cuius vivente terra dominici corporis videmus inpressa vestigia, si fidelibus oculis et acie spiritali quod in eo sinus Christi, quod manus contigit perlegamus ... .*[127]

Very significantly, the recommended visualizing process is here described as "scrutiny" or a kind of (close) reading (*"perlegamus"*) – but this is a meditative 'reading' or enactment of remembered images, not words. For Paulinus, then, the *images* of Valgius's vision, *like words*, conceal as well as reveal – they are experienced and interpreted as *symbols precipitating an interior seeing of "God's face"* in that of Christ and in that of Felix.

Christians in the Mediterranean World from the Second Century AD to the Conversion of Constantine (London, 1988), pp. 102-167. Cf. P. COX MILLER, *Dreams in Late Antiquity: Studies in the Imagination of a Culture* (Princeton, 1994).

[125] *Epp* 49, 10.
[126] *Epp* 49, 11.
[127] *Epp* 49, 14.

5. Imaginibus Divina Ferentibus Ora: *The Image Within the Image*

For Paulinus, then, the portrait as well as the visible symbol, although in itself nothing more than a material configuration, is – like the word – an invitation to an inner performance and experience by the viewer. With a visible object and a pictorial representation in which an image of invisible reality is to be seen, Paulinus assumes that the imagination will construct this image or images visually from remembered models in texts or oral instruction. The imagination would then see and experience the visible object as it were overlaid with or through the shapes of these evoked images as living realities. But Paulinus's descriptions also point to the perception of a visible radiance of a saint's holy energy, which had traditionally been represented by light imagery, and which can be indicated as such in the depiction of a 'heavenly soul'.

He thus appears to have assumed that to 'see' the image of the heavenly soul in the depicted St. Martin, the viewer would not only meditatively visualize and respond affectively to the images of his remembered actions as resembling those of Christ, but also experience an indication of effulgence that was presumably visible in the picture as though it were the radiant holy energy of Christ's living presence. In the process of doing this, the beholder would enact and thereby become aware of the affective patterns which these mental images render visible as living realities. And in this way, imagination would transcend itself to become, as Paulinus intended, a seeing and experiencing of the many aspects of the invisible Christ – or 'the faces of God' – which are not in the picture, but are precipitated by the picture in the beholder's mind.

Fig. 1   Christ among the Apostles. Apsidal mosaic, Rome, Santa Pudenziana.
From W.F. VOLBACH and M. HIRMER, *Frühchristliche Kunst: Die
Kunst der Spätantike in West- und Ostrom* (München, 1958), Pl. 130.
See also Colour Plate 2.

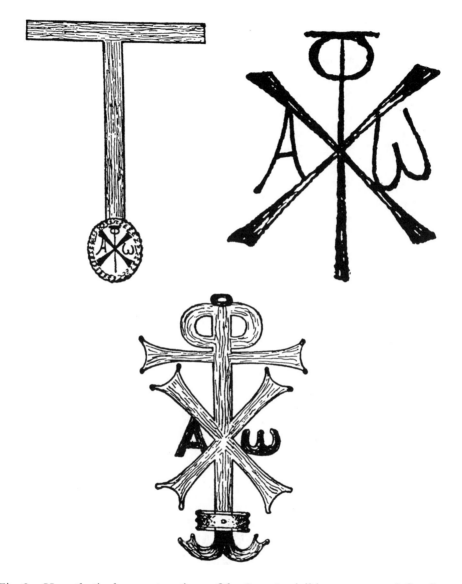

Fig. 2   Hypothetical reconstructions of the Cross's visible appearance (after G. WIMAN, "Til Paulinus Nolanus' carmina", *Eranos* 32 (1934), pp. 117-118.

Fig. 3   The apsidal mosaic of Sant'Apollinare in Classe (detail), after C.
         MARABINI, *I mosaici di Ravenna* (Novara, 1981). See also Colour Plate
         3.

Fig. 4   St. Martin (extreme left, leading the martyrs). Mosaic from Sant'Apollinare Nuovo, Ravenna, ca. 455-526, after C. MARABINI, *I mosaici di Ravenna* (Novara, 1981). See also Colour Plate 4.

Meditations on a Christmas Card:
Strategies of Empathy in a Fourteenth-Century Liturgical Illumination

KARL F. MORRISON

Last year, I found an intriguing Christmas card in a museum store. Since the manuscript leaf reproduced on the card was only a few feet away, I decided to compare the copy with the original. Naturally, there is a picture in this story. Because it is religious, I should say at the outset that I consider all art a study in anthropology. That is especially true of religious art. For, as I see it, religion in all its works and ways is something humanly made, expressing what people image and know about themselves. Surely, any religious art is anthropological, rather than theological, when, as in Christian doctrine, God is uncircumscribed, incomprehensible, and thus ineffable.

The manuscript at the heart of my story is a fragment, one page from a collection of liturgical chants (a *graduale*) now thought to have been made in Lombardy around 1400.[1] It carries portions of the opening chants (introits) for

---

[1] MS Princeton University, The Art Museum, y1929-3, now attributed to the workshop of Tomasino da Vimercate (width 0.34 m. × length 0.483 m). I am obliged to Dr. Cavin Brown, director of the Department of Prints and Drawings, and to Ms. Karen Richter for their kind assistance. For discussions of this fragment, see: A. MELOGANI, "Miniature inedite del Quattrocento lombardo nelle collezioni americane", part 2, *Storia dell'Arte* 83 (1995), p. 7, fig. 31 (attributing this fragment to the Master of the Modena Golden Book); and E.W. KIRSCH, "Milanese manuscript illumination in the Princeton Art Museum", *Record of the Art Museum, Princeton University* 53.2 (1994), pp. 23-26, figs. 1-2 (attributing it to the workshop of Tomasino da Vimercate and relating it to other manuscript fragments from the same workshop). Kirsch illustrates the fragment under review in this article and another fragment in the Princeton collection which must have followed it in the original codex, namely, the page containing the last

two consecutive masses in the Advent Season: those for *Rorate* Sunday (the fourth Sunday in Advent) and for Christmas Eve (the Vigil of Christmas). The initial letter in the Christmas Eve introit embraces an unusual picture (figs. 1 and 2). Appropriately, the illumination depicts the expectant parents counting down to the moment of birth. The Blessed Virgin sits, luxuriantly pregnant, on the ground. St. Joseph stands aside, clueless, paternally out of his element, while the ox and the ass calmly eat dinner. The Blessed Virgin's pregnancy caught my attention when I saw the Christmas card reproduction, partly because the colour of her tight frock seemed near enough a flesh-tone to be a painterly double entendre with nakedness. However, the colour on the Christmas card was slightly untrue to the original.

The results of my meditations on the Christmas card made from the manuscript fragment accent the difference between objects intended to arouse empathy. It was made for *homo mercantilis*. The manuscript from which the fragment came was made for *homo religiosus*. The card is throwaway art, not intended for meditation, and every effort has been made to desacralize it and detach it from the commercially limiting pieties of the original. The card was not made to function in a religious way; the manuscript was. The two artifacts express entirely different anthropologies.

Upon reflection, the similarities between the original and the image are only apparent. Consider the three texts of the card, visually detached by being placed on separate pages and having no relationship to one another. The section of the manuscript reproduced on the front cover has been cropped into an unsignifying decorative pattern. The pre-Nativity picture appears as a cartouche surrounded by words mutilated into unintelligibility. The second text, the single word "Rejoice", inside the card has no particular reference to anything. The third text, on the back cover, identifies the material object pictured and the collection to which it now belongs. The original and its image are dissimilar similars. Dissimilarities break through the illusion of likeness in the disparities – in the multiplicity of copies, of course, in colour, size, and texture. Even the identification on the card no longer corresponds exactly with perceived reality; for scholars have now moved the manuscript to the threshold of the fifteenth century (ca. 1400) and attributed it to a specific Milanese workshop. I am struck by how little this card, with its cropped image and atomised texts, demands of the regarding eye. By contrast, the manuscript imposes heavy demands.

words of the offertory for the Mass of Christmas Eve and the introit for the First Mass of Christmas Day (MS y1982-110). The initial (the 'D' in "*Dominus*") for the Christmas introit is also historiated with a Nativity scene.

There is good reason to think that the self-forgetting exaltation in what is called 'the aesthetic experience' depends in great part on whether viewers find something of themselves in a picture, something that snares their attention, causes them to wonder, engages their intellects and emotions, and, finally, rewards their attention, perhaps inexhaustibly.[2] At the incandescent moment of an aesthetic experience, a picture becomes a labyrinth of self-discovery. Mind and heart remain arrested, though the instant when one physically sees the picture may be brief.

Age-old tradition made hearing and seeing the two primary ways of understanding. Understanding the card requires little by way of verbal or visual recognition. The words themselves comprise three quite separate message units, and the one unit directly explaining the picture's content (on the front cover) burlesques coherence. Similarly, visual recognition of the image is not required. To be sure, those who want to know what the subject is may require recognition of visual cues, but identification of the subject itself is not required of the viewer. The interplay of verbal and visual cognition is so absent that the coloured pattern on the card's front cover might as well be art nouveau wallpaper – or any other among the countless decorative subjects in the welter of competing cards. The card, with its hodgepodge of images and texts, is little more than an indicator of one person's taste – that is, the purchaser's, coinciding perhaps with the producer's.

By contrast, the manuscript fragment, made by and for *homo religiosus*, demands much of the viewer. There is nothing personal about its objective. This fragment was an accessory of communal worship. It made sense in a collective action of cult, and at the brief moment of shared glory for which it was made. Words, image and music comprise an ensemble, each mustering distinctive skills of collective understanding. Together, the project anticipated a unified performance by a community addressing most of the five senses at one specific liturgical moment. This introit and its picture were like an enchanted, sleeping princess in some fairy tale, who had to awaken for one, incandescent moment each year if the kingdom were to live happily forever and a day.

Evidently, nothing in the manuscript – neither the words nor the picture nor the music – presupposed leisure for meditation, any more than did the Christmas card. The pace, complexity, and rhythm of liturgy, generally involving multiple participants, must be sustained. Visual contact with a picture may be fleeting, even though, after the eye moves on, the intellect and emotions may

---

[2] M. CSIKSZENTMIHALYI and R.E. ROBINSON, *The Art of Seeing: An Interpretation of the Aesthetic Encounter* (Los Angeles, 1990), esp. pp. 7-9, 113-114, 131-143, 147-158.

still be arrested, still held in a long, indeed labyrinthine, exploration opened by the picture.

This picture's cognitive demands, verbal and visual, are readily apparent if we collate the text of the introit, celebrating the sublime miracle about to happen – "Today, you shall know that the Lord will come to save us, and in the morning you shall see his glory" – with the scene of all-too-human infirmity and confusion in the picture.

In the order of time, the whole unfolding of the gospel hangs between those words in the introit, "today" and "tomorrow morning", between what you know by faith today and what you shall see tomorrow, between the self-abasement by which the Word became flesh, a child, to save his people, and his coming again, as judge of the world, in great glory. As their eyes flew across the pages, the original users of the *graduale* were themselves suspended, their minds and hearts arrested, between that "*hodie*" and that "*mane*". And yet, in the order of eternal providence, the reality known by faith today is the same as that revealed to sight tomorrow morning in glory. From beginning to end, the Incarnation of God, even the Passion, is one event, a divine comedy.

The core of that comedy appears in the picture under review; it turns precisely on the dynamic of arrest and movement. The God in whom there is no change or shadow of turning (Iac 1, 17), Jesus, "the same yesterday, today, and forever" (Hbr 13, 8) is there subject to the massive changes of gestation, birth, and the whole cycle of life.

The illuminator took advantage of the Vigil of Christmas to underscore the comedic "tomorrow morning" concealed in childbirth. It was premature to represent anything remotely glorious, the angels of the Nativity or the kings of the Epiphany. The offertory for Christmas Eve contained the words from Psalm 80, 2 referring to the Jewish people: "You who rule Israel, who lead Joseph like a sheep", and the illuminator portrayed a very different Joseph, Joseph as a very sheepish man. The parodic figure of Joseph underscores the illuminator's intent, and we find a clue to that intent in another manuscript.

There is parody, too, in the figure of the Virgin, about to give birth to the Creator of the world while she sits on a stable floor. I know one antecedent for the distinctive portrayal of the pregnant Virgin sitting upon the ground. That was an illumination for the *Meditationes Vite Christi*, also made in northern Italy in the fourteenth century, but somewhat earlier than the manuscript I am discussing (fig. 3).[3] The *Meditationes* characterize Joseph as a capable, resourceful man, an able master carpenter (*magister lignarius*).[4] There was nei-

[3] MS Paris, Bibliothèque Nationale, ital. 115.
[4] Professor Claudine A. Chavannes-Mazel kindly reminds me of a portrayal in San

ther inn nor stable in this telling of the Nativity. Finding no lodging in Bethlehem, Joseph fended for himself. One version of the *Meditationes* led him to a cave; another, to a passageway, an alley or arcade, where people took cover from the rain. In both versions, he used his skill as a carpenter to enclose a space with his own hands. The contrast between the skilful Joseph in the *Meditationes* and the parodic Joseph in the historiated initial I am discussing is stark.[5] The representation of the Virgin, pregnant and seated on the floor, is parodic in both manuscripts.

By good fortune, the page under discussion and another page bearing the introit for the next mass after Christmas Eve, the First Mass of the Nativity (figs. 4 and 5), happened to come into the same collection. The initial for that introit is historiated, appropriately enough, with a Nativity scene in which Joseph, adoring the newborn child, has been delivered from all parody.[6] The illuminator played on the fact that the word *hodie* occurred in the introit for the First Mass of Christmas and also in that for Christmas Eve. On the *hodie* (today) of Christmas Eve, we know (or believe) that the Saviour is at hand; tomorrow morning (*mane*) we shall see His glory. On the *hodie* of Christmas morning, the Lord says to me: "You are my Son. This day have I begotten you". On the *hodie* of Christmas morning, Mary and her attendant and Joseph see the glory they were promised on the 'today' of Christmas Eve. The miracle hanging in suspense between 'today' and 'tomorrow' on Christmas Eve has been realized. To choristers following the daily liturgies in sequence, the manuscript presented 'before' and 'after' pictures. (Parenthetically, I should say that these two manuscript leaves were separated by a third, which according to form should have contained the last words of the introit and the rather long gradual for Christmas Eve.)

Massimino, Ravenna, depicting the Blessed Virgin, heavily pregnant, riding on a donkey while Joseph stalwartly helps her.

[5]   I. RAGUSA and R.B. GREEN, *Meditations on the Life of Christ: An Illustrated Manuscript of the Fourteenth Century: Paris, Bibliothèque nationale MS Ital. 115* (Princeton, 1961), pp. 31-32, with illustration No. 26. John of Caulibus, *Meditaciones Vite Christi olim S. Bonauenturo attributae*, ed. M. STALLINGS-TANEY (Turnhout, 1997: *Corpus Christianorum Continuatio Medievalis* 153), pp. 30-31. Professor Pamela Sheingorn kindly referred me to the translation by Ragusa and Green. Professor Sheingorn is at work on a comprehensive study of the metamorphoses of St. Joseph in Western hagiography and iconography. She delivered an important preliminary account of her investigations in a lecture on "Tensions, ambiguities, and the pressures of history: Constructing the cultural biography of Joseph the Carpenter", on 6 May, 2000, at the Thirty-Fifth International Congress on Medieval Studies, conducted by the Medieval Institute, Western Michigan University, Kalamazoo, Michigan.

[6]   See above, n. 1.

These cross-referencing theological parodies are compounded by an artistic joke shared by both illuminations. Indeed, the painter's mimicry was part of the normal stock-in-trade of liturgical artists, used often. Looking at this manuscript, singers found that the 'O'-shapes of the initials on the pages before them mirrored the 'O'-shapes of their own mouths, and that the scenes in the pictures mimicked visually the scenes they were spelling out in words.[7] The mimicry of 'O's would have been instantly apparent to choristers who, for some weeks, had been singing the great 'O'-Antiphons of Advent, and may have known carols, some pious and others ribald, making much of the exclamation 'O', or pairing Alpha with Omega. Appropriately enough for my Christmas subjects, one of the most celebrated illustrations of singers with their mouths pursed into 'O's may be in Giotto's (1267?-1337) fresco of St. Francis instituting the crèche at Greccio – though here I admit a possible ambiguity between 'O's and 'A's (fig. 6).

There is a deep human sweetness in the transition from the Joseph of the Christmas Eve picture. There, Joseph, chewing his moustache, awkward, uneasy at the decisive moment, realized that the escape hatch of a quiet divorce was now closed. Joseph in the Nativity is at peace, led as a sheep into the network of divine parentage, spectacularly into a synonymous, though not coequal, fatherhood with God. The users of this *graduale*, too, were moving from the 'today' of faithful knowledge, with its anxieties, to the 'tomorrow' of peace, beyond the decisive moment.

The painter of the Milanese *graduale* wanted you to see that human beings are animals, of the earth, earthy, that Jesus was born in the standard way all creatures of dust, *inter urinam et faeces*. According to the *Meditationes Vite Christi*, when the time came for her to give birth, the Virgin stood leaning against a column, and the infant fell between her legs to the floor, landing safely on hay which Joseph had placed at Mary's feet.[8]

In the crack between the 'today' and the 'tomorrow morning' of the introit, the illuminator saw the whole drama of the divine comedy of redemption. But, for the moment, it was still in the liturgical moment of 'today'. Sheltered there, as was the illumination in the curved initial letter of *hodie*, the comedic sparkled with paradoxes of the sublime mystery about to happen: the Word

---

[7] I owe this observation, and suggestions for illustrations, to the generosity of Professor Michael Camille. Professor Camille provides an early fourteenth-century illumination of a choir, two of whose members' mouths are shaped into the most rotund of 'O's in M. CAMILLE, *The Luttrell Psalter and the Making of Medieval England* (London, 1998), p. 123, fig. 41. He also reminds me of the choristers carved by Donatello for the choir pulpit in Florence Cathedral (1433-1439).

[8] RAGUSA and GREEN, *Meditations on the Life of Christ*, pp. 32-33, illustration No. 27.

made flesh; the All, immensity which is everywhere, in which we live and move and have our being, confined in a womb. The paradoxes on which the illuminator focussed in the *hodie* of Christmas Eve were those of Virgin motherhood, later condensed into these lines which John Donne (1573-1631) addressed to the Virgin Mary:

> Ere by the spheres time was created, thou
> Wast in his minde, who is thy Sonne and Brother;
> Whom thou conceive'st conceived; yea, thou art now
> Thy Maker's maker, and thy Father's mother.[9]

Inevitably, comedic aspects of the illuminator's work were enriched by other paradoxes in the game of *trompe l'oeil*. Two of these paradoxes of the representational, invoked for centuries in defending the veneration of sacred images, overlapped with paradoxes of the Incarnation. Defenders of sacred images held that painted images made the invisible visible, leading viewers through matter to immaterial virtues, and that they made the absent present, as an absent emperor is present in his portrait. Similarly, theologians wrote, at the Incarnation, the invisible became visible when the Word was made flesh, and the absent became present when Christ, the mediator, bridged the gulf between divine and human, deified our flesh forever, and enabled human beings to become gods by participation.

The comedic, even carnevalesque, element in our initial invites us to recognize an anthropology largely lost, at least in European religion, since the Reformation.[10] Nietzsche's judgment that modern European culture had grown incapable of festival hangs over the change.[11] Even before Nietzsche, theology had been emptied of literalism by the application of historical criticism to the Bible, a process engendering clerical scepticism during the Enlightenment. Today, a Protestant bishop stands firmly in the Enlightenment tradition when he writes: "the virgin-birth story was never anything but the stuff of mythology".[12] Anyway, "if the Incarnation of God is no longer understood as an event that directly concerns the present lives of men, it becomes impossible, even absurd, to cele-

---

[9] John Donne, *Holy Sonnets*, 2 ("Annunciation"), ll. 9-12 (set to music by Benjamin BRITTEN, *The Holy Sonnets of John Donne: Op. 35* (London, 1946)).

[10] See a useful corrective in K.-J. KUSCHEL, *Laughter: A Theological Reflection*, tr. J. BOWDEN (New York, 1994). A recent study of the psychology of laughter is R.R. PROVINE, *Laughter: A Scientific Investigation* (New York, 2000).

[11] See J. PIEPER, *In Tune with the World: A Theory of Festivity*, tr. R. and C. WINSTON (South Bend, Ind., 1999), pp. 13-14.

[12] Bishop J. SPONG, "Face to Faith", *The Guardian: Europe*, 9 Dec., 2000, p. 10.

brate Christmas festively".[13] Since the Reformation, Christianity has become serious business, without much tolerance for laughter. An ascetic disapproval of laughter, like that in Benedict's (ca. 480-ca. 550) *Rule*, has prevailed, despite the tradition that laughter was one defining characteristic of human nature, along with reason, sensual perception and mortality, and despite the experience of laughter as an essential device of social communication, indeed of community building. The keeping of Christmas was from place to place abolished and everywhere reconstituted between the seventeenth and nineteenth centuries.

Medieval Latin Christianity was unencumbered by the particular folly of ignoring the manifest humanity of laughter and its potentials for sanctification. Reformers tried, successfully in the end, to stamp out one practice they named the *risus paschalis*.[14] The *risus* was an essential component of the Easter liturgy in which, by some device or other (including the broadest ribaldry), preachers deliberately provoked uproarious, unrestrained laughter from the faithful as their flocks expected them to do – an anticipation of the hilarity of the saints. Provocations of Easter joy had counterparts at Christmas, for example in the Boy Bishop's Feast, the Lord of Misrule's reign, and highly irreverent carols. By the seventeenth century, a different style of godly righteousness had effectively dampened the mirth of the faithful.

Michail Bachtin had a sense of this lost mirth in pre-Reformation Christian cult, though he interpreted humour as a weapon of the oppressed in their social warfare against the dominant classes.[15] Not long ago, the Dutch theologian Henri Nouwen reinvented religious humour in his book, *Clowning in Rome*.[16]

---

[13] PIEPER, *In Tune with the World*, p. 24. Pieper's fascinating, but highly condensed, argument sets forth the thesis that festival is essentially an event of worship, a religious affirmation of life. In its demand for extravagant sacrifices, festival can never justify itself on utilitarian grounds. The arts, employed in festivals, serve to adorn that affirmation, and, as stimuli of the senses, to intensify self-abandoning joy and contemplation. They were transgressive, in that they were not bound by rules of ordinary life and work. Beginning in the Reformation, and reaching a spectacular climax in the French Revolution, "rationally calculated utility" won the day in new festivals of secular religion. No longer transgressive, the arts were consciously used as vernaculars of denial, or "mendacious affirmation", or reduced to instruments of entertainment, upholding the rules of prevailing social order. Consequently, the denial of "ritual praise" in the Protestant Reformation led by stages to the "destruction of festivity" in the era of the French Revolution (PIEPER, *In Tune with the World*, pp. 3, 17, 19, 28, 30, 32, 37, 52, 54-55, 58-59, 63-72).

[14] KUSCHEL, *Laughter: A Theological Reflection*, pp. 83-87. V. WENDLAND, *Ostermärchen und Ostergelachter: Brauchtumliche Kanzelrhetorik und ihre kulturkritische Würdigung seit dem ausgehenden Mittelalter* (Frankfurt am Main, 1980), esp. pp. 59-63, 112-115.

[15] See the refutation by D.-R. MOSER, "Lachkultur des Mittelalters? Michael Bachtin und die Folgen seiner Theorie", *Euphorion* 84 (1990), pp. 89-90, 108-111.

[16] H.J.M. NOUWEN, *Clowning in Rome: Reflections on Solitude, Celibacy, Prayer, and*

He compared celibates and contemplatives, in their prayers and works of social benevolence, with circus clowns, getting into the act between the spectacular main events and evoking smiles, awakening hopes by an impractical, humanity-redeeming love.

Without recurring to Bachtin's class-bound theory of a "culture of laughter", I suggest that the empathy assumed by the illuminator and those for whom the manuscript was made required a carnevalesque sense of holiness, a *risus natalis* corresponding with the *risus paschalis*. The comedic scene in *hodie* ('today') marked a celebration of Christian joy, the hilarity of the saints, grounded in the follies of God's love.

Even so, I should repeat that the illumination under review was never intended for prolonged meditation. It did not have long to arrest singers' attentions, whether choristers or celebrants of the Eucharist. Viewing it was rather like seeing an event from a passing train, or catching a glimpse of something through a window while walking past – something sticks in the mind and will not budge. In the fleeting moment when they passed their eyes across the picture, the singers were in a mood for comedy, about to end a season of fasting and penance and cross over into the athletic rigours of the three Christmas masses. The illuminator did what he (or she) could to catch their attention on the wing, and draw it into the action depicted and the realities envisioned. Their minds and hearts could remain arrested there, after their eyes had sped along. They could stay, arrested in a labyrinth of self-discovery constructed of inexhaustible paradoxes.

Csikszentmihalyi and Robinson refer to the moment of aesthetic arrest as a "flow experience".[17] In the picture under review, we encounter another kind of flow experience, one in which there is both arrest and movement. A scene glimpsed through a window on the run, remains in the mind as the runner dashes ahead.

There are details used to snare the eye's attention such as the way the illuminator caught the light in the picture as if in a little cup, matching the contours of the painting to a dimple in the vellum, and making it sparkle by outlining the halos with raised dots, now more splendid than ever with the red underpainting accenting the flash of gold.

By contrast, the general design of the picture, and the music, were major devices for drawing the imagination into the action of the picture and their paradoxical, comedic realities and arresting it while the eye moved on.

Contemplation (New York, 2000), esp. pp. 108-109.

[17] CSIKSZENTMIHALYI and ROBINSON, *The Art of Seeing*, pp. VII, 4, and *passim*.

The picture does not cover the whole page. It is like the pupil of an eye. Someone painted a border around the picture, and wrote words around the border. The border frames the picture, a diaphragm like the iris around the pupil of an eye. The painter takes advantage of the curved 'H' in *hodie* to frame the little picture of animal indifference and confusion with three leaves of some exotic plant, bursting and unfurling with energy. One, red, the colour of love and the Holy Spirit, flares up. Another, green, the colour of life-force, drives down its roots. A third, blue, the colour of faith and truth – the pure, creative energy of what really is – charges around the picture, and whirls through the Virgin's cloak to close the focus of the diaphragm. The 'H' itself is violet, one of Advent's colours, accented with white and gold. The picture is a virtual 'eye', an *oculus*. Prevailing theories of vision endowed real, physical *oculi* with power to mingle the soul of the viewer with the object seen, to make them one, by intromission or extramission. Virtual *oculi*, like this picture, were subtypes of what St. Paul called "mirrors of enigma" through which human beings dimly saw divine truths (I Cor 13, 12). The *oculus*-construction is even more obvious in what was the next historiated initial in the manuscript: the one beginning the introit for the First Mass of Christmas. There, the almost identical encircling border, built on the frame of the letter 'D', opens to include the viewer in the circle around Jesus recumbent on the stable floor. The Virgin and an attendant kneel to the crib's right, Joseph to its left. God the Father presides above and to the rear. The viewer takes the vacant place at the front.

Liturgy is an ensemble art of visualization through opaque media, and it opens the mind's eye by several essential kinds of creative repetition. Liturgy recapitulates historically, in space and time, for it delivers all times of sacred history into the living experience of the here and now, the labyrinthine *Sitz im Leben* of participants in the liturgy.

The Milanese manuscript fragment provides a case study in how liturgy was thought to arrest and work on visual imagination. It illustrates particularly how the community that made it visualized the act of self-visualizing. The *oculus*-frame of the nativity scene is an emblem of the whole project: to draw participants in the liturgy into the composition, to enable them to see themselves, not only by looking through the dark enigma of a picture, but also by performing the mysteries of Christ repeated in the liturgy. Thus, they would reach the dynamics by which the original happiness of the human race was restored. Visualizing themselves in the mysteries of Christ, they would be transformed by being stripped of their old natures and reclothed in Christ. The external relations (for example, of time and place) which divided them were counterbalanced by internal affinities of mind and spirit.

By recapitulating, or arresting, sacred mysteries, liturgical time has the property of stripping away individual – that is, personal or local – characteristics. The mystery it arrests mitigates the uniqueness of the particular historical moment. Accordingly, the Eucharistic liturgy for which the Milanese fragment was made could have served any celebrant and congregation, since Christ was the true priest and victim. All believers were called, as the apostle Paul wrote, to put to death whatever was earthly in them and to clothe themselves with the Lord Jesus Christ (Col 3, 5; Rm 13, 14).

And still, the autonomous, historical individual was not so much suppressed in liturgical time, as it was subsumed by charisms into a communion arrested and existing beyond all times. The self-forgetting in liturgy heightened individuality by requiring introspection. It required the soul to explore deeply, earnestly, its own depths; to seek God arrested in its own inmost chamber, as the boundless Word was confined in the Virgin's womb. The apostle Paul hit upon the metaphor of the body to express how many individuals were subsumed in one communion. Believers were members of the body of Christ, he wrote, each member serving the welfare of the whole by doing the one function it was meant to do, as the hand grasps or the eye sees.

As its musical notation shows, the manuscript fragment is an artifact of a singing culture. It was made for worshippers in the act of singing. Under the aspect of harmony, the music in it suggests how to think about this manifold conversion of autonomous individuals to unity in liturgical time. The chant of a choir subsumed the voices of its individual members. And yet, like the other parts of the liturgy, chant was a religious exercise presupposing the assent of each individual will, the introspective searching by each soul of its own depths. It was unthinkable that there could be concert performances of liturgical chant, detached from the context of worship and sung by unbelievers. The movements of individual voices were subsumed in the rhythms of the whole choir, but the purpose of singing was the soul's discernment of God arrested within itself.

Thus, the chant in the Milanese fragment served the same interplay of external relationships (movement) with internal (arrest) as the words and the illumination. They comprised an art of intimacy. Occasionally, polyphony captured this complex relationship, and seldom more brilliantly than in Robert Wylkynson's (ca. 1450-ca. 1515) setting of the Creed: *Jesus autem transiens*.

This song is a study in temporal relationships – arrested, and in movement. Normally people have always said or sung the Creed one sentence after another, from beginning to end. Wylkynson thought this way of doing things missed the point. The point, he thought, was that the Creed is not a cut-and-dried set of propositions, to be ticked off one after another like items on a laundry list. He thought that all the propositions in the Creed were like windows shining with the same light, the light of Christ. The windows were blank, none of them was alive, unless Christ was both arrested and moving in every single one, and in all of them together.

That is why Wylkynson wrote his song as he did, as a series of overlays, a blending of intimacies. He set it up as a kind of drama, in which each actor had one line to say. He begins with a cantor, singing the words, "Jesus passing through the midst of them". Then, he moves through the Creed, twelve proposi-tions, each sung by a different apostle. The words "Jesus passing through the midst of them" are constantly repeated as, one by one, every sentence in the Creed sung by one apostle, joins the chorus, all singing together. They pass, Jesus arrested and moving in their midst.

To sing this song, as a choral director told me, "you have to have at least thirteen singers able to carry a part independently, and have enough sound to balance the others, and enough musicianship to sing in tune with all those parts".[18] One for all and all for one! This is strange and wonderful music, both harmony and an almost Pentecostal Babel. It climaxes, and the voices drop away, one sentence in the Creed after another, until only one voice is left, the first and the last, arrested in them all, singing "Jesus passing through the midst of them". Wylkynson treated the Creed as though it were one body made up of many members, each dependent on all the others. Each voice sings independ-ently. All voices are in balance. Each, in the spirit of the whole, has what it takes to stay in tune with all the others. Wylkynson's message is that Jesus moves simultaneously and intimately through the midst of every proposition in the Creed, through the midst of his contemporaries, the individual apostles, each of whom is given one proposition to sing, through the midst of the choris-ters he wrote for, personifying the apostles and singing then in Eton College Chapel, and arrested in every chorister who would ever sing and every hearer who would ever join with the singers in mind and heart.

At least remotely, there is a connection with vision in the idea that the apostles were eyewitnesses of Jesus's ministry, and that Scripture allowed later generations to be witnesses also, seeing through the apostles' eyes.

Time is a relationship – before, after, or simultaneous. It is a relationship of things in movement, some arrested. The eye can move on while mind and heart remain arrested by something briefly glimpsed. To give some idea of the levels of relationship encompassed by religious art, I have invited you to think about one little picture, because, playing with and against the text, it displays a luxuri-

[18] F. FOWLER SLADE, October, 1999.

ant tangle of relationships, in movement and arrested. Of course, what we see fleetingly through a window is more likely to let us discover something inside ourselves than something in what we saw.

I have contrasted this accessory of community worship with a Christmas card, an indicator of personal taste. I have underscored the difference between art that functions religiously and art that does not. Examining the dissimilar similarities between the manuscript and the Christmas card, I have suggested that this fragment cannot be understood without remembering the basic, paradoxical anthropology behind it: namely, that the human race was made for happiness, made for holy laughter, which was forfeited and restored. The whole liturgical apparatus of Christmas Vigil was designed to portray events between 'today' and 'tomorrow morning' by which happiness was restored and, indeed, to fix in the minds of members of a community, amid the flow of their experiences, that moment of arrest when, they felt to the marrow of their bones, Jesus, the same yesterday, today, and forever, came among them.

Fig. 1   Detail of fig. 2. See also Colour Plate 5.

Fig. 2   Italian (Milan), late fourteenth century, workshop of Tomasino da Vimercate, *Leaf from a Gradual, with the Virgin Mary and Saint Joseph Awaiting the Birth of Christ in Initial H.* The Art Museum, Princeton University (MS y 1929-3). See also Colour Plate 6.

Fig. 3   Italian, fourteenth century, *Virgin Mary and Saint Joseph Awaiting the Birth of Christ*. MS Paris, Bibliothèque Nationale, ital. 115, f. 18v.

Fig. 4   Detail of fig. 5. See also Colour Plate 7.

Fig. 5   Italian (Milan), late fourteenth century, workshop of Tomasino da Vimercate, *Leaf from a Gradual with Adoration of the Christ Child in Initial D*. The Art Museum, Princeton University (MS y 1982-110). See also Colour Plate 8.

Fig. 6   Giotto, *St. Francis Instituting the Crèche at Greccio* (*ca.* 1296-1303).
          Assisi, Basilica of San Francesco, upper church. See also Colour Plate
          9.

The Wall Paintings in the Campanile of the Church of S. Nicola in Lanciano (*c.* 1300-1400): Reading an Unknown Legend of the Cross in the Abruzzi

BARBARA BAERT

In 1993 frescoes were found in the bell tower of the church of S. Nicola in Lanciano, Italy, that bear great importance for our understanding of the history of the Legend of the True Cross.[1] Time has left its trace on a seem

---

[1] Restored by the *Soprintendenza dell'Aguila* (dr. Giovanna Di Matteo). Until now, the cycle has not been fully described in print. A videotape of the conference held at Lanciano on 28 June 1995 where dr. Giovanna Di Matteo spoke, is preserved by the ArcheoClub of Lanciano. Photos and identification of the cycle have appeared in R. TORLONTANO, "L'architettura in età medievale", in: *Lanciano: Città d'Arti e Mercanti*, ed. E. GIANCRISTOFORO (Lanciano, 1995), figs. 177-181. The *Cassa di Risparmio* of Teramo used several of the scenes as illustrations for its 1999 calendar (with minimal description). W. PRINZ and I. MARZIK, *Die Storia oder die Kunst des Erzählens in der italienischen Malerei und Plastik des späten Mittelalters und der Frührenaissance, 1260-1460* (Mainz, 2000), who also treat the tradition of the Legend of the Cross, have not taken note of the discovery. Without the invaluable tip from Prof.dr. Andrea de Marchi, Università di Udine, and without dr. Victor Schmidt, Rijksuniversiteit Groningen, who brought me in contact with the former, this article would not have been written. I thank them for their collegiality. I am thankful to the kind Don Leo Di Felice who offered me the opportunity on 4 August 2000 to study and photograph the wall paintings *in situ*. The Belgisch Historisch Instituut – Academia Belgica – in Rome received me in the Summer of 2000 to carry out my research. I thank Prof.dr. Valentino Pace, Università di Udine – baptized in the church of S. Nicola – for his many critical comments on the context of Lanciano. I was able to consult the licenciate thesis of Franco M. Di Paolo, under the advisement of Prof.dr. D. Benati: F.M. DI PAOLO, *Gli affreschi trecenteschi in S. Nicola di Bari a Lanciano*, Università di Udine, 1996-1997. I thank them both heartly for their cooperation. The thesis deals mainly with the style of the frescoes. My thanks also go to dr. Marco Mostert and dr. Mariëlle Hageman, Universiteit Utrecht, who gave me the opportunity to bring the wall paintings to public attention. I thank the participants of the congress for their stimulating remarks. The first results of my research were published in *Iconographia:*

ingly incoherent group of scenes which, moreover, must have been conceived in various stages throughout the fourteenth and fifteenth centuries. Nevertheless, they form an important contribution to the history of painting in the Abruzzi. In this study, attention is primarily focused on the contents of the cycle, which until this time have remained unpublished. The identification of the scenes promises to be a difficult task, for some motifs in the campanile seem foreign to any known iconographical tradition. In the context of *Reading Images and Texts*, I will discuss how the cycle illustrates the problems that arise when images seem to liberate themselves from every known literary background. Secondly, I will discuss the context of the Legend of the Cross in Lanciano. What is known about the various functions of this subject matter, which has been studied for other places in Italy and elsewhere in Europe, will then be considered in the light of the history and identity of this old commercial town on the Adriatic coast. For, however enigmatic this cycle is to the art historian today, this Legend of the Cross must have once delivered a clear message.

Word and Image: The Legend of the True Cross

The Legend of the True Cross has enjoyed a long and complex history in literature. It was formed in the period between the fourth and the twelfth centuries, and spread in countless variants and interpolations in the European vernaculars throughout the Middle Ages. This jumble of textual traditions and the impact of the written word on pictorial art attest to ways in which people were bombarded with ideas about the supposed origins of the wood of the cross of Christ. Today we group these ideas together under the epithet 'Legend of the Cross', but in reality this legend consists of three separate traditions: the Legend of the Finding of the Cross, the Legend of the Exaltation of the Cross, and the Legend of the Wood of the Cross.

The Legend of the Finding of the Cross came into existence at the end of the fourth century.[2] Initially, it could only be found in summary accounts by the

Rivista di iconografia medievale e moderna 2 (2003), pp. 108-125. I did not deal with the case study of Lanciano in my book *A Heritage of Holy Wood: The Legend of the True Cross in Text and Image* (Leiden, 2004: *Cultures, Beliefs and Traditions: Medieval and Early Modern Peoples* 22).

[2]   For what follows below, see esp. S. BORGEHAMMAR, *How the Holy Cross Was Found: From Event to Medieval Legend (with an Appendix of Texts)* (Stockholm, 1991); J.W. DRIJVERS, *Helena Augusta: The Mother of Constantine the Great and the Legend of Her Finding of the True Cross* (Leiden and Keulen, 1992).

Church Fathers. Ambrose mentions in his *De obitu Theodosii* (395) how Helena went to Jerusalem at the request of her son Constantine – a model for the late emperor Theodosius, for whom the panegyric was meant – and there, with the help of the Holy Spirit, found the cross of Christ on Golgotha. Some years before, Chrysostomos had mentioned the relic of the cross (85th *Homily on the Gospel of John*, 390), but had not yet connected the story of Helena with it. Paulinus of Nola (402) and Rufinus (403) do mention the contribution of the mother of Constantine, and respectively describe her as helped by the Jews and the local bishop Macarius. The true cross could be distinguished from the other crosses by its ability to raise the dead.

The patristic references were expanded in an anonymous variant, the Legend of Judas Cyriacus, which says that the Jewish Judas found the cross under orders from Helena. After seven days of starvation in a dry well, he had been prepared to reveal what he had heard from his ancestors: the cross of the Messiah lay buried on Golgotha. This legend, which probably had its origins in Syria, was translated into Latin, and saw an iconographical response in the Carolingian period.[3] The Sacramentary of Gellone (750-790) provides the earliest iconography of the Finding of the Cross (fig. 1).[4] Illustrating the feast of 3 May, a miniature shows Judas cutting down three crosses. The miniaturist treats the commemoration partly as an allegory. A circle refers to the holy of holies in which a red *croix pattée* with the apocalyptic letters 'alpha' and 'omega' is flanked by two green crosses.

In another Carolingian manuscript we witness the apologetic function of the tradition of the Finding of the Cross. In the *canones conciliorum* of Vercelli (ca. 800) the texts of the fourth- and fifth-century councils are introduced with drawings of the Finding of the Cross (fig. 2).[5] Both the text and the illustrations

---

[3]   A Syrian exemplar (from which subsequent texts are copied) is generally accepted on the basis of the oldest manuscript housed in the MS British Library, London, Add. 14644 from the fifth/sixth century (DRIJVERS, *Helena*, pp. 165ff). Borgehammar, on the other hand, postulates a Greek exemplar. From this, the text would be translated into Latin and Syrian. His research has shown that the Latin version must have already been known ca. 500 in Rome: BORGEHAMMAR, *How the Holy Cross Was Found*, p. 203.

[4]   Possibly made in Meaux for the abbey of Gellone; MS Paris, BN, lat. 12048, f. 76v, 259 folios, 300mm. x 180mm.; V. LEROQUAIS, *Les sacramentaires et les missels manuscrits des bibliothèques publiques de France*, 1 (Paris, 1924), p. 168; B. TEYSSÈDRE, *Le sacramentaire de Gellone et la figure humaine* (Toulouse, 1959), pp. 8ff.; *Liber sacramentorum Gellonensis. Textus*, ed. A. DUMAS and J. DESHUSSES, 2 vols. (Turnhout, 198: CCSL 159-159A), 1, p. 129, Nos. 142 and 189-190, No. 237; B. BAERT, "Le sacramentaire de Gellone (750-790): Entre le symbole et l'histoire", *Arte cristiana* 789 (1998), pp. 449-460.

[5]   MS Bibliotheca Capitolare, 165, f. 2r; 224 folios, 27cm. x 19cm.; Chr. WALTER, "Les

originated in the diocese of Milan. In the lower register, Judas reveals with an axe three parallel prone crosses, the middle one – as in the miniature of Gellone – being larger. Above, Judas hands over the true cross to Helena, who receives it with outstretched arms. The gesture illustrates the institution of a Christian state under the cloak of the emperors.

Meanwhile, in the Byzantine empire, dramatic turns of events had occurred. Around 620, the Persian king Chosroes II had stolen the relic of the cross from Jerusalem, but the Byzantine emperor Heraclius recuperated it in Ktesiphon, in present-day Iran.[6] He thereupon decapitated the Sassanidian king in his 'astrological' palace. The son of Chosroes converted to Christianity and Heraclius could return triumphant to Jerusalem. The restitution of the cross was accompanied by a miracle. An angel held the *Porta Aurea* closed for as long as the Byzantine sovereign did not, barefoot, bring the relic into the church of the Holy Sepulchre. In this version the Legend of the Exaltation of the Cross spread in the western liturgy through the work of Hrabanus Maurus (780-856).[7]

It was only in the Romanesque period that this event was given life in figural representation. In the Sacramentary of Mont St. Michel (1060), the feast of the Exaltation of the Cross is commemorated on 14 September with a miniature

dessins carolingiens dans un manuscrit de Verceil", *Cahiers archéologiques* 18 (1968), pp. 99-107, p. 99, n. 2; A. SORELLI, *Inventari dei manuscritti delle bibliotheche d'Italia*, 19-21 (Florence, 1923), p. 117, No. 165; C.M. CHAZELLE, "Archbishops Ebo and Hincmar of Reims and the Utrecht Psalter", *Speculum* 72 (1997), pp. 1055-1077, at p. 1060; f. 2r: the Finding of the Cross; f. 2v: the Council of Nicaea (*Ibidem*, fig. 4); f. 3r: Saints Peter and Paul; f. 3v and f. 4r: the first Council of Constantinople; f. 4v: the Council of Ephesus (first volume), and f. 5r: Christ in Majesty with Helena and Constantine (second volume).

    [6] A. PERNICE, *L'imperatore Eraclio: Saggio di storia bizantina* (Florence, 1905); A. FROLOW, "La vraie croix et les expéditions l'Héraclius en Perse", *Revue des études byzantines* 11 (1953), pp. 88-105; O. VOLK, "Herakleios", in: *Lexikon für Theologie und Kirche*, 5 (Freiburg, 1960), cols. 237-238; G. OSTROGORSKY, *Geschichte des byzantinischen Staates* (Munich, 1963), pp. 73-122; *The Cambridge Medieval History: 2. The Rise of the Saracens and the Foundation of the Western Empire*, ed. H.M. GUATKIN (s.l., 1964), pp. 184-302, pp. 747-758; J.J. SAUNDERS, *A History of Medieval Islam* (London, 1965); V. GRUMEL, "La reposition de la vraie croix à Jérusalem par Héraclius: Le jour et l'année", *Zeitschrift für Byzantinistik* 1 (1966), pp. 139-149; A.N. STRATOS, *Byzantium in the Seventh Century: 1. 602-634*, tr. from Greek by M. OGILVIE-GRANT (Amsterdam, 1968); W. DURANT, *Weltreiche des Glaubens* (reprint of 1935: Munich, 1981: *Kulturgeschichte der Menschheit* 5); A.H. BREDERO, *Christenheid en christendom in de Middeleeuwen: Over de verhouding godsdienst, Kerk en samenleving* (Kampen, 1986), pp. 102ff.; J. HERRIN, *The Formation of Christendom* (Princeton, 1987), pp. 183-219; M. GIL, *A History of Palestine: 643-1099*, tr. from Hebrew by E. BROIDO (Cambridge, 1992), pp. 65-74.

    [7] Hrabanus Maurus, *Homilia* LXX, ed. in: *PL* 110, cols. 131-134.

of the humbled Heraclius (fig. 3).[8] In the lower register the emperor is represented in proskynesis; the angel observes the event from the sky. This iconography became important in the time of the Crusades. People recognized in this
conflict between Christianity and Islam the earlier seventh-century struggle in
which the relic of the cross had been at stake. Although an anachronism, Chosroes served as the personification of the threatened monotheistic religion of
Islam, and Heraclius as the eample of the victor: the Saviour. For where the
precarious contact between Jerusalem, Byzantium, and Rome was at stake, that
which bound them together was also nearby: the cross, symbol and material
proof of victory.

Tangibly and sensorially spread throughout the religious community, the
relic of the cross was the antecedent for a third literary branch: the Legend of
the Wood of the Cross. For, where there was a cross, there was wood; and
where there was wood, there was a tree. And the tree of the cross could only be
the tree of all trees: the Tree of Life.

The connection between the cross and the *lignum vitae* is an early Christian
metaphor.[9] It forms the *basso continuo* of ideas which modulated on the synthesis between the cross and the Tree of Life, between Paradise and the sacrifice.
It is known that this typological exegesis received its rampant dissemination
from the twelfth century. The cross was then made part of a diachronic shadow
play between the Old and New Testaments: the cross was already there potentially in the staff of Moses, in the Tau of Aaron, etc. The idea that the material
Old Testament wood was effectively to become the bearer of the Messiah un-
folded since the twelfth century in a narrative spanning from the Book of Genesis to the Passion. The first traces of the origins of the legend are evident in the
Church histories of Petrus Comestor and Johannes Belethus.[10] Jacobus de
Voragine names them as authorities in his *Legenda Aurea* (ca. 1260). His story,

---

[8]   MS New York, Pierpont Morgan Library, 641, f. 155v; J.J.G. ALEXANDER, *Norman
Illumination at Mont St. Michel: 966-1100* (Oxford, 1970), pp. 157-159, fig. 44.

[9]   See: S.J. RENO, *The Sacred Tree as an Early Christian Literary Symbol: A Phenome-
nological Study* (Saarbrücken, 1978: *Forschungen zur Anthropologie und Religionsgeschichte*
4), *passim*.

[10]   All of the aspects of the complex literary-historical formation process of the legend are
too vast to go into here, see: W. MEYER, *Die Geschichte des Kreuzholzes vor Christus* (München, 1882: *Abhandlungen der philosophisch-philologischen Classe der königlich bayerischen
Akademie der Wissenschaften* 16.2); A.R. MILLER, *German and Dutch Versions of the Legend
of the Wood of the Cross: A Descriptive and Analytical Catalogue*, 2 vols. (Ph.D. diss., Oxford,
1992); A.M.L. PRANGSMA-HAJENIUS, *La légende du bois de la Croix dans la littérature
française médiévale* (Ph.D. diss., Assen, 1995).

for the feast of 3 May, runs as follows:[11] When Adam feels death approaching, he sends his son Seth to the earthly Paradise for solace. From the Tree of Life, Seth receives three twigs. Back home, Seth plants the twigs on the grave of his by then deceased father. The twigs grow into a wonderful tree which stands the test of time until Solomon cuts down the tree for the construction of the temple. But the wood constantly changes its dimensions, as if refusing to fit the temple. Neglected, the wood appropriately comes to lie over the river Kedron. It is here that the meeting between Solomon and the Queen of Sheba takes place. She foretells that the wood will one day support the Messiah, who shall be executed by the Jews. Full of mistrust, Solomon tosses the wood into a puddle, the *Piscina Probatica*. At the time of the Passion of Christ, however, the wood is found floating and the Jews fashion a cross from it. This is followed by the Finding of the True Cross.

With Jacobus de Voragine, the Legend of the Cross found a literary standard. The importance of the *Legenda Aurea* is clear from the fact that the text yielded more visual images than any other source. This was also the case with the Legend of the Wood of the Cross, which first manifested itself visually after 1300, when the reception of Jacobus's compendium reached its saturation point.[12] The success of the *Legenda Aurea* and the reception of the Legend of the Cross go hand in hand. As the literary counterpart of the liturgical calendar, the *Legenda Aurea* showed that the bipartite story of 3 May was actually one (i.e. the single story of the Wood of the Cross and of Helena finding it), and that the events it related had their continuation on 14 September (i.e. the story of Heraclius). With Jacobus de Voragine, the synthetic 'Legend of the Cross', that found its echo in a cyclical iconography, first took shape.

Between 1388 and 1393, the Alberti family financed a monumental cycle in the choir of the Sta. Croce in Florence. Since 1374, they had received the exclusive privilege of being buried there.[13] Agnolo Gaddi provided a cycle on

[11] *Jacobi a Voragine legenda aurea: Vulgo historia lombardica dicta*, ed. Th. GRAESSE (Osnabrück, 1969), pp. 303ff.; *Jacobus de Voragine: The Golden Legend: Reading on the Saints*, ed. and tr. W.G. RYAN, 2 vols. (New York, 1995⁵), 2, pp. 277-284.
[12] See: *Legenda Aurea: Sept siècles de diffusion, Actes du colloque international sur la Legenda Aurea: Texte latin et branches vernaculaires à l'Université du Québec à Montréal 11-12 mai 1983*, ed. B. DUNN-LARDEAU (Montreal and Paris, 1986): several case-studies.
[13] S. PFLEGER, *Eine Legende und ihre Erzählformen: Studien zur Rezeption der Kreuzlegenden in der italienischen Monumentalmalerei des Tre- und Quattrocento* (Frankfurt and Vienna, 1994: *Europäische Hochschulschriften* 18; *Kunstgeschichte* 214), pp. 53-72 on the cycle and pp. 123-129 on the patrons. A testament by Alberto di Lapo degli Alberti from 1348 (during the plague) demonstrates for certain the earliest contact between the family and the Franciscan

the right and left walls with a total of eight registers depicting the Legend of the Cross. The commission would become a key moment in the iconography of the Legend of the Cross, for never before had the legend been represented in a tripartite cyclical form. The choir shows the story of the wood of the cross, beginning with Seth and ending with Heraclius. The completeness and the compact quality of the cycle in Florence served as an exemplar or model. Emulation of Gaddi meant the spreading of the legend in nearby Volterra (Cenni di Francesco di Ser Cenni, 1410), Empoli (Masolino da Panicale, 1415)[14] and Arezzo (Piero della Francesca, before 1466). This Tuscan group is important for the iconography of the Legend of the Cross. Gaddi introduced two motifs for the first time: the task given to Seth (fig. 4) and the meeting of the Queen of Sheba and Solomon on the bridge over the Kedron (fig. 5).

Until now the exploration of the Legend of the Cross has remained within its Tuscan framework and within a Franciscan biotope, and with the *Legenda Aurea* as its literary background. However, this topographical and literary cocoon must be nuanced after the discovery of the cycle in Lanciano.

Reading Images: Tradition and Anomaly in the Frescoes at Lanciano

The frescoes in the S. Nicola church at Lanciano are found on the ground floor of the campanile – a small space of two square meters with a stone staircase. Rebuilding campaigns through the centuries have meant irrevocable damage, hindering the observer in his understanding of the direction in which the cycle is to be read, and in his identification of certain scenes. On the south side, two scenes in the upper register have to do with the construction of the temple (figs. 6-7). Below these, a duel and the worshipping of the relic of the cross are represented (figs. 8-9). On stylistic grounds the wall can be dated to 1330-1340[15]. In the corner of the entrance wall, a votive scene with St. Simon and the Sta. Croce (Helena?) has been added by a fifteenth-century hand (fig. 10). At the foot of the Sta. Croce kneels a woman with a rosary represented in minia-

---

monastery (Florence, Archivio di Stato, Diplomatico S. Croce 1348; PFLEGER, *Eine Legende*, pp. 125-126).

[14] The documents of the *Compagnia della santa Croce* in Montepulciano relate that in 1415 a journey to Florence was financed for Nanni (Giovanni) di Caccia to study Gaddi's frescoes in the Sta. Croce; A. LADIS, "Un'ordinazione per disegni dal ciclo della vera croce di Agnoli Gaddi a Firenze", *Rivista d'arte* 41 (1989), pp. 153-158.

[15] DI PAOLO, *Gli affreschi trecenteschi*, pp. 87-107.

ture (fig. 11). The remains of a horse and a dragon may also be seen, possibly depicting the story of St. George (fig. 12). Most probably the entrance wall was painted too, as the arch still shows the remnants of painted architectural decoration. On the north side, two registers with motifs from the Legend of the Finding of the Cross are represented. Here a third artist has been at work, probably around 1400 (figs. 13-14). At the lower register of the staircase one can see red colouring with a black foliage, most probably datable to the early fifteenth century.

Originally, a small S. Pellegrino chapel of *c.* 1100 stood on this site. Destroyed by fire in 1206, the chapel was rebuilt in 1242 as S. Nicola. In the same building campaign, the bell tower was rebuilt in stone. The church became a parish church in 1319. The oldest scenes on the south side may serve as the *terminus post quem* for this parish dedication. Around 1600 the present nave of the church was constructed. It is thought that the parish church of 1319 consisted only of what is now the trave bordering on the campanile. Thus, the campanile is the only remnant of the original church of S. Nicola.[16]

The oldest wall paintings were probably completed by a contemporary of the Master of Offida, who was active from 1330 onwards. He was named after his last commission in the crypt of the Sta. Maria della Rocca in Offida (1367). On his trips between the Marches (*le Marche*) and the Abruzzi, this artist blended influences from the North, i.e. Venice and Rimini, with new impulses from Tuscany.[17] As Rosanna Torlontano remarks, countless echoes of this artist's work in the area of the southern Marches (Ascoli Piceno) and the Abruzzi have until now remained without study[18] Though separated from them by barren mountain passes, the Abruzzi also border on Lazio and Umbria. Here the turn

---

[16] The campanile reveals a typical local decoration: borders with brick triangular motifs filled with polychromied ceramic (TORLONTANO, "L'architettura in età medievale", p. 106). During the restorations the remnants of the crypt of the old S. Pellegrino church were discovered. The crypt was destroyed in 1795 by the archbishop Amorosi (DI PAOLO, *Gli affreschi trecenteschi*, pp. 73-74). The vaults in the campanile refer to the gothic structures in the Sta. Maria Maggiore of Lanciano. This architecture is influenced by contemporary tendencies in Burgundy; *Ibidem*, p. 76.

[17] On painting in the Abruzzi, see: O. LEHMANN-BROCKHAUS, *Abruzzen und Molise: Kunst und Geschichte* (Munich, 1983), pp. 205-233, pp. 388-394 (with expansive thematic bibliography); V. PACE, *La pittura in Italia: Il Duecento e il Trecento*, 2 (Milan, 1986), pp. 443-450; M. ANDALORO, "Connessioni artistiche fra Umbria meredionale e Abruzzo nel Trecento", in: *Dall'Albornoz all'età dei Borgia* (Todi, 1990), pp. 305-346; *Mural Painting in Italy: The Late 13th to the Early 15th Centuries*, ed. M. GREGORI (Turin, 1995), pp. 178-179. See also, on the historical context of painting in the Abruzzi: DI PAOLO, *Gli affreschi trecenteschi*, p. 35-70.

[18] TORLONTANO, "L'architettura in età medievale", p. 178.

of the century was accompanied by influences from Romanesque painting on the one hand, as in the apse of the Benedictine church of S. Giovanni in Venere, and by the Giottesque style from Assisi on the other, as in the choir of the S. Francesco in Castelvecchio Subequo. Valentino Pace points out how this orientation towards Umbria also determined the Marian and Passion subject matter typical of the Trecento Franciscans.[19]

The 1330-1340 Master of the Construction of the Temple in the church of S. Nicola has kept the conventional facial expression and the lengthened proportions and also the noticeably elongated fingers known from the Duecento generation as seen in Atri in the Sta. Maria Assunta.[20] However, this artist also belongs to the younger Giottesque generation by virtue of the three-dimensionality of the scenes and his attempts at shading in the drapery folds. The architecture is also very sparsely decorated. The predilection for fresh and varied colours is remarkable, ranging from fluorescent green to pinkish red, from dark blue to dark green. The late fourteenth-century or 1400 Master of the Finding of the Cross brings in naturalistic facial expressions and, when allowing for the damage, has a sober palette. The generation of artists after 1400 – such as the painter of St. Simon and Sta. Croce – belong to the large movement of the International Gothic style that filtered into the Abruzzi also via Ottaviano Nelli, as shown in the Last Judgment in Sta. Maria in Piano at Loreto Aprutino.[21]

The Construction of the Temple

King Solomon sits in profile and witnesses a mysterious activity (fig. 6). A young man cuts down three boughs, the crowns of which have been freshly formed. The expression on his face betrays a melancholy appropriate for his task: the young trees have sprouted from the mouth of the deceased Adam. In the background, Solomon's men are busy modelling planks for the construction of the temple. One supervisor reports to Solomon and appears to be counting on his fingers. Perhaps he is remarking that the dimensions of the planks still are inadequate. From this the viewer infers that this living wood is awaiting its destiny as a cross later on in the story.

---

[19] PACE, *La pittura*, p. 449 and figs. on p. 447.
[20] *Ibid.*, fig. At p. 446.
[21] TORLONTANO, "L'architettura in età medievale", p. 179, fig. at p. 178.

The content of the scene is contaminated. The cutting of the tree on Adam's grave in Hebron is synchronized with the later construction of the temple in Jerusalem. Thus the artist has had to combine into one scene the living wood that has just now formed in Adam's mouth and the fashioning of the adult tree into planks. The wood which is not yet fully grown, but is already being turned into sturdy planks in the background.

Assuming that the painter consciously used a telescoping of events, the young man with the axe may be the figure of Seth. According to the legend, Seth had buried his father and, following Michael's orders, had buried the branches. Keeping in mind the logic of the story, however, the identification of the young man as Seth is not satisfactory. After all, Seth's relevance in the story of the cross is limited to the planting, not the cutting down of the tree. Seth's role is that of starting a new chapter in the history of salvation. If this is correct, it would mean that the cycle in Lanciano begins with the episode of the construction of the temple, suppressing the important initiation of the wood of the cross. However, in this damaged space, it is quite possible that a scene may be missing.[22]

Clearly the cycle in Lanciano departs from the traditions which were later to unfold in Tuscany. Whereas Agnolo Gaddi retains the role of pioneer for the Seth iconography (fig. 4),[23] the campanile reveals the earliest example of the construction of the temple. In Gaddi's cycle, this motif is omitted; after Seth, the story jumps immediately to the Queen of Sheba (fig. 5). Only later do we find the motif on Italian soil, in the Capella Farfense in Montegiorgio, in the

---

[22] The *sinopie* in the Helena chapel of the church of Santo Stefano in Empoli also begin with the construction of the temple. Elsewhere I have defended a lost Seth scene on the wall with the altar; see: B. BAERT, "Twilight between tradition and innovation: The iconography of the Cross-Legend in the sinopie of Masolino da Panicale at Empoli", *Storia dell'arte* 99 (2000), pp. 5-16. Could it be that Seth was painted at the entrance wall of the bell tower which received new masonry later on? The decorations at the arch point to a lost scene.

[23] Agnolo Gaddi shared his role of pioneer with an anonymous artist working at the same time in the modest parish church of Östofte in Denmark (Lolland). In Östofte, however, Seth functions as an interpolation in a Genesis cycle. Gn 5 is read in combination with the motif of the twig that was known since Johannes Beleth. Apart from the *Legenda Aurea*, it was spread in the translations of the Judaeo-Christian *Vita Adae et Evae*. This *vita* is a first-century apocryphal text which concentrates on the adventures of the first couple after the Expulsion. The European dissemination of the source was aided by the thirteenth-century translation of the Bohemian Lutwin. Especially in Germany and Scandinavia, this tradition had much success. See H.B. HALFORD, "The apocryphical *Vita Adae et Evae*: Some comments on the manuscript tradition", *Neuphilologische Mitteilungen* 82 (1981), pp. 417-427; B. BAERT, "The figure of Seth in the vault-paintings in the parish church of Östofte: In search for the iconographical tradition", *Konsthistorisk tidskrift* 66, 2 (1997), pp. 1-15.

southern Marches (Alberto da Ferrara (?), ca. 1425).[24] Here, too, the construction of a building under the scrutiny of Solomon is represented (fig. 15). But a dead Adam without Seth in the foreground, as found in Lanciano, is unique.

The Queen of Sheba

The following scene in the same register is partially damaged (fig. 7). On the right, a woman kneels by a tree of which she clasps the narrow trunk with one hand. On the other side of the tree stand three figures. Solomon can be recognized by the garments he also wore in the previous scene. In the corner the countenance of a black woman with a scarf around her head appears. The presence of a black companion would refer to the Queen of Sheba, who, it was believed, was from Ethiopia.[25] Her devotion to the wood is an especially important motif in the Legend of the Wood of the Cross.[26] The woman depicted in Lanciano, however, does not accord with the image of the Queen of Sheba in later Tuscan tradition. The Lanciano scene does not show a queen who meets with Solomon in royal state and reprimands him for his ignorance about the wood. Instead, it shows a simply-dressed woman with a simple headcovering who, draped in the greatest humility, pays tribute to a young (dry?) tree.

This young tree, too, is depicted in Lanciano contrary to the logic of the narrative. The wood that turned out to be useless in the construction of the temple, was sometimes described as remaining neglected in the temple (Petrus

---

[24] B. BAERT, "La cappella Farfense in Montegiorgio: Una leggenda della vera croce nelle Marche (ca. 1425)", *Arte cristiana* 804 (2001), pp. 219-233.

[25] R. KÖHLER, "Zur Legende von der Königin von Saba oder der Sibylla und dem Kreuzholze", *Kleinere Schriften* 2 (1902), pp. 87 ff.; A. CAQUOT, "La reine de Saba et le bois de la croix selon une tradition éthiopienne", *Annales d'Ethiopie* 1 (1955), pp. 137-147; A. CHASTEL, "La rencontre de Salomon et de la reine de Saba dans l'iconographie médiévale", *Fables, Formes, Figures* 1 (1978), pp. 103-122; R. BEYER, *Die Königin von Saba: Engel und Dämon: Der Mythos einer Frau* (Cologne, 1987).

[26] Because of these arguments I cannot agree with F.M. Di Paolo on a possible Seth identification for this figure (the figure is in fact rather genderless) (DI PAOLO, *Gli affreschi trecenteschi*, pp. 121-122). He refers to Seth taking a branch of the tree himself. That Seth would pluck a twig from the tree in Paradise, has no traditional support at all. I can add, however, that Gervasius of Tilbury mentions in his *Otia Imperialia* (1212) that Adam had stolen an apple from the tree of Paradise. Out of the pips the cross 'grew' (MEYER, *Die Geschichte*, p. 118). In the first-century *Apocalypse of Moses* it is also told that Adam and Eve smuggled fruit and plants from Paradise during their expulsion; A.F.J. KLIJN, *Seth in Jewish, Christian and Gnostic Literature* (Leiden, 1977), p. 19. It is a pertinent observation by P.M. Di Paolo though, that the tree seems to be dry.

Comestor, †1178).[27] Visually, the wood was usually rendered placed over the
Kedron River in Jerusalem. It is this bridge that the Queen of Sheba worships
in depictions by Agnolo Gaddi, Cenni di Francesco, Masolino da Panicale (fig.
16), and Piero della Francesca.[28] In Lanciano, however, the shoot from Adam's
mouth, cut into a useless beam, again takes root.

What does this mean? It seems as if, without any consideration for the
thread of the story, a phrase such as "and the Queen of Sheba worshipped the
wood of the Tree of Life" was rendered in visual images. Or was a now-lost
iconographical source used as a model in a corrupted way? Whatever the answer may be, if the Queen of Sheba is depicted here, the Abruzzese turned her
into a *regina della humilità*, a circumstance serving to nuance the established
iconographical traditions surrounding the queen.

[27] Petrus Comestor, *Historia scholastica*, ed. In: PL 198, cols. 1578-1579.
[28] In the cycle at Montegiorgio, the queen wades through the water on horseback. This is
only mentioned by a thirteenth-century Anglo-Norman text. It is unclear how this apparent
connection may be explained (MS Cambridge, Corpus Christi College, 66; H.H. HILTON, *Seth:
An Anglo-Norman Poem* (1941: *Studies in the Romance Languages and Literatures* 3), pp. 57,
vs. 390-404). In the northern iconography, the queen wades through the water on foot (The Book
of Hours of Catherine of Cleves, MS New York, Pierpont Morgan Library, M. 917, f. 216r; F.
GORISSEN, *Das Stundenbuch der Katharina von Kleve: Analyse und Kommentar* (Berlin, 1973),
p. 105, pp. 494-525, pp. 959-961 and pp. 999-1001; J. PLUMMER, *Die Miniaturen aus dem Stundenbuch der Katharina von Kleve* (Berlin, 1966), Nos. 79-87; and the incunable *Boec van den
Houte*, printed by Johannes Veldener, 1483, Culemborg, woodcut 25; Brussels, Koninklijke
Bibliotheek, INC A 1582; B. BAERT, *Het Boec van den Houte* (Brussels, 1995)). The motif of
wading appears in the Cologne Book of Sibyls (1321-1346). This is related to her goose foot –
a demonic remnant of which the Queen of Sheba was deeply ashamed. By immersing it in the
water of the Kedron, her foot was cured (I. NESKE, *Die Spätmittelalterliche Deutsche Sibyllen-
weissagung: Untersuchung und Edition* (Göppingen, 1985), p. 41). On the tradition of the goose
foot as an Indo-European topos for wisdom, see: B. BAERT, "*Und mal yr auch eyn gensfuss*: The
queen of Sheba's goose-foot in medieval literature and art", in: *The Authority in the Medieval
West*, ed. M. GOSMAN *et al.* (Groningen, 1999), pp. 174-192, in which I considered the figure of
David in this scene. A Cross legend in which this king figures indeed exists (for these traditions,
see the literature mentioned *supra*, n. 10). The story goes that David took the three trees from
Adam's grave back home to Jerusalem. He planted them in a well, but the following morning
they had miraculously intertwined, though still showing three crowns (an image of the Trinity).
David used to pray under the tree, and composed his psalms there. In the *Boec van den Houte* –
the only iconographical pendant of this peculiar tradition – David is kneeling under the tree
together with some servants.

The Struggle for the Cross

One register below, a battle is represented. On the left, two soldiers fight a duel (fig. 8). The man under the protection of the *manus Dei* deals a deadly blow to the other's head. In the Legend of the Cross two duels are prominent: that between Constantine and Maxentius after Constantine's vision of the cross, and that between Heraclius and the Persians.

Behind the fallen man a mysterious old man can be seen. This may be Chosroes. However, according to the *Legenda Aurea*, this Persian tyrant was had been beheaded in his palace, after which Heraclius joined battle with Chosroes's son. The battle between Constantine and Maxentius is an alternative interpretation. In both literary traditions, mention is made of a bridge over the Danube, which is absent here.

In the scene on the right, a reliquary in the form of a cross is worshipped (fig. 9). Constantine saw the cross either in a vision during battle (Eusebius) or in a dream (Lactanius) before the battle.[29] Is this the reason that one soldier points upwards, either towards the *manus Dei* or towards the relic? In twelfth-century crusader literature, the vision of the cross is a topos which is also ascribed to Heraclius. The motif is related in the *Kaiserchronik* (1146),[30] the *Eracle* of Gautier d'Arras (1175-1200),[31] and the *Eraclius* of Otte of Hessen (*c.* 1200)[32]. In the story, a messenger from God gives Heraclius the order to join battle. The worship of the recovered relic of the cross is inseparable from the figure of Heraclius. The absence of the *Porta Aurea* is also an anomaly.

Here, too, the scene from Lanciano does not conform to established prototypes, neither to those of images of Constantine, nor to those of Heraclius. Different from the Old Testament motifs, however, these two emperors knew a long visual tradition. From the twelfth century onwards, they appear frequently as *exempla* for crusaders. The intense contact with Byzantium in this

---

[29] Eusebius, *Vita Constantini*, ed. In: PG 20, cols. 909-1229, col. 943; Lactantius, *De mortibus persecutorum*, *XLIV*, ed. In: PL 7, col. 261; D. McDonald, "The vision of Constantine as a literary motif", in: *Studies in Honor of Tom B. Jones* (Neukirchen, 1979· *Alter Orient und Altes Testament* 203), pp. 289-296.

[30] E. Nellmann, *Die Reichsidee in deutschen Dichtungen der Salier- und frühen Stauferzeit: Annolied, Kaiserchronik, Rolandslied, Eraclius* (Berlin, 1963: *Philologische Studien und Quellen* 16), pp. 24-25.

[31] *Gautier d'Arras: Eracle*, ed. G. Reynaud de Lag (Paris, 1976), pp. 164-166, vs. 5323-5378.

[32] F. Maertens, *Untersuchungen zu Otte's Eraclius* (Ph.D. diss., Göttingen, 1927); D. Haacke, *Weltfeindliche Strömingen und die Heidenfrage in der Deutsche Literatur von 1170-1230* (Ph.D. diss., Berlin, 1951).

period increased influx of cross relics and also started attention for Constantine and Heraclius. On the left wing of the Triptych of the Holy Cross of Wibald (1130-1148), three enamel medallions with scenes from the life of Constantine are added: below Constantine's dream is depicted, in the centre the battle on the bridge, and above the baptism of Constantine (fig. 17).[33] On the right wing, three scenes from the Legend of the Finding of the Cross are represented. On the central panel, two Byzantine triptychs are preserved with a relic of the cross. Perhaps these were a gift Wibald received on one of his journeys to Constantinople where he was welcomed by Emperor Manuel I Comnenus? The commemoration of Constantine stimulated the dream of a single Christian empire.

Between 1240 and 1250, in the southern transept of the St. Blasius cathedral in Braunschweig, wall paintings were created for the Guelph Otto 'the Child' (1204-1252). They combine the Legend of the Finding of the Cross and that of the Exaltation of the Cross in one cycle for the first time.[34] The programme was designed by Otto's uncle, Duke Henry the Lion (1131-1195). The legend spans the plundering of the relic by Chosroes, to the duel on the bridge, the beheading in the palace, and the restitution of the relic to the church of the Holy Sepulchre (fig. 18), just as it had been told by Hrabanus Maurus and the chronicles. It is known that the Guelph court engaged in international religious politics. The *Chronica Slavorum* (after 1210) of Arnold of Lübeck († 1212) tells how Henry the Lion departed for the Holy Land on a pilgrimage in 1172.[35]

---

[33] MS New York, Pierpont Morgan Library, open: 48.4 cm. x 66 cm.; M.-M. GAUTHIER, *Emaux du moyen âge occident* (Freiburg, 1972), p. 125, Pl. 81; W. VOELKLE, *The Stavelot Triptych: Mosan Art and the Legend of the True Cross*, catalogue of an exhibition (New York, 1980); J. LAFONTAINE-DOSOGNE, "L'art byzantin en Belgique en relation avec les croisades", *Belgisch Tijdschrift voor Oudheidkunde en Kunstgeschiedenis* 56 (1987), pp. 13-47, p. 17 and fig. 2; N. STRATFORD, *Catalogue of Medieval Enamels in the British Museum: 2. Northern Romanesque Enamel* (London, 1993), Pls. 50-52; B. BAERT, "De Kruisvinding in de Maaslandse emailkunst van de 12de eeuw: Iconografie en context", *Belgisch Tijdschrift voor Oudheidkunde en Kunstgeschiedenis* 69 (2000), pp. 107-156 (with an English summary).

[34] J.-Chr. KLAMT, *Die mittelalterlichen Monumentalmalereien im Dom zu Braunschweig*, (Ph.D. diss., Berlin, 1968); S. BRENSKE, *Der Hl. Kreuz-Zyklus in der ehemaligen Braunschweiger Stiftskirche St. Blasius (Dom): Studien zu den historische Bezügen und ideologisch-politischen Zielsetzungen der mittelalterlichen Wandmalereien* (Braunschweig, 1988: *Braunschweiger Werkstücke* 25 A; *Veröffentlichungen aus dem Stadtarchiv und der Stadtbibliothek* 72); T. STANGIER, "Wand- und Gewölbemalereien in Chor, Vierung und südlichem Querarm der ehemaligen Stiftskirche St. Blasius und Johannes", in: *Heinrich der Löwe und seine Zeit: Herrschaft und Repräsentation der Welfen 1125-1235*, catalogue of an exhibition, 3 vols. (München, 1995), 1, pp. 201-202.

[35] *Ibid.*, p. 101, n. 2: *Chronica Slavorum*, I, I-XII, ed. J.M. LAPPENBERG (Hannover, 1869:

The ideal of the crusade is associated even more with Otto 'the Child' than with his uncle. In 1239 Otto, together with the Teutonic Order, undertook an expedition to Prussia to deliver the Baltic region from paganism. The success of the undertaking was a great encouragement for the restoration politics Otto wished to carry out.[36]

In a Latin *legendarium* completed between 1310 and 1320 in Palermo, the Legend of the Exaltation of the Cross is illustrated with a duel (fig. 19), the beheading, and the humble restitution. Buchtal believes this cycle to go back to a twelfth-century prototype.[37] After the coronation of Frederick II in 1296, Sicily had received virtual autonomy. The new 'national' self-confidence manifested itself artistically. In the fourteenth century, connections were sought with flourishing artistic periods of the past (the eleventh and twelfth centuries), and Byzantine and Sicilian manuscripts and mosaics from these earlier periods were used as models. The reorientation breathed new life into the Sicilian workshops and brought back older iconographies. The *legendarium* dates from approximately the same period as the wall paintings in Lanciano.

The headwear of the emperor is typical of the Palaiologan dynasty in the East. In Agnolo Gaddi's cycle, Helena wore the headdress with the protruding point in the scene of the handing over of the cross to Constantinople. In Piero della Francesca's cycle, Constantine wears the Byzantine head covering in the battle on the Danube. Johannes VIII Palaiologus wears this type of Byzantine headwear also in a Pisanello medallion datable to *c.* 1438 (fig. 20).[38] On 6 July 1439, during the ecumenical council known as that of Ferrara-Florence, Greek representatives were received. Production of the medallions has been associated with the diplomatic meetings between East and West.[39]

MGH SS 21), pp. 101 ff.

[36] BRENSKE, *Der Hl. Kreuz-Zyklus*, p. 115.

[37] MS Turin, Bibliotheca Nazionale Universitaria, I.II.17., ff. 203v-205r. H. BUCHTHAL, "Early fourteenth-century illuminations from Palermo", *Dumbarton Oaks Papers* 20 (1966), pp. 105-118; ID., "Notes on a Sicilian manuscript of the early fourteenth century", in: *Essays in the History of Art Presented to Rudolf Wittkower* (London, 1967), pp. 36 39; ID., "Early fourteenth-century illuminations from Palermo", in: *Art of the Mediterranean World: A.D. 100 to 1400* (Washington, 1983: *Art History Series* 5), pp. 105-125.

[38] London, Victoria and Albert Museum; PFLEGER, *Eine Legende*, p. 103; M. VICKERS, "Some preparatory drawings for Pisanello's medaillon of John VIII Palaeologus", *The Art Bulletin* 60 (1978), pp. 415-425, p. 418, figs. 1 and 2. The connection was first made by Aby Warburg: A. WARBURG, "Piero della Francescas Konstantinschlacht in der Aquarellkopie des Johann Anton Rambaux", in: ID., *Gesammelte Schriften*, 1 (Leipzig, 1932), pp. 251-254.

[39] PFLEGER, *Eine legende*, pp. 102-103. On two coins from the collection of the Duc de Berry (Italy, 1402), Constantine on horseback is represented on one side and on the other, the

Is it Constantine, then, who is represented in the Lanciano duel? It is an old point of contention that representations of the emperors Constantine and Heraclius are difficult to distinguish. According to Frolow, Heraclius traditionally has a more pointed beard.[40] An identification of the depicted emperor as Constantine follows the iconographical chronology, for on the opposite wall of the campanile are scenes from the Legend of the Finding of the Cross are rendered. These, however, were added some decades later by another master.

The Finding of the Cross

One scene clearly portrays the discussion between Helena and the old Judas Cyriacus on Golgotha (fig. 14). The queen, equipped with a nimbus, seems to have assumed a sitting position. She gestures in the direction of four men. These betray the man in the background, who holds his hand hesitatingly in front of his mouth. Does this refer to Judas's stubborn oath of secrecy? The Jews are not represented in a sympathetic way: they betray one another and are secretive about their topographical knowledge of the Christian Jerusalem.

The scene above this depicts a large vessel, maybe a baptismal font (fig. 13).[41] Who, then, is being baptized? Constantine's baptism was shown in the

---

head of Heraclius. Here, too, Constantine wears the Palaiologan headgear; J. VON SCHLOSSER, "Die ältesten Medaillen und die Antike", *Jahrbuch der Kunsthistorischen Sammlungen des allerhöchsten Kaiserhauses* 18 (1897), pp. 64-108, pp. 73 ff. and H.Th. COLENBRANDER, "The Limbourg brothers, the 'joyaux' of Constantine and Heraclius, the *Très Riches Heures* and the visit of the Byzantine emperor Manuel II Palaeologus to Paris in 1400-1402", in: *Flanders in a European Perspective: Manuscript Illumination around 1400 in Flanders and Abroad*, *Proceedings of the International Colloquium Leuven, 7-10 September 1993*, ed. M. SMEYERS and B. CARDON (Leuven, 1995: *Corpus of Illuminated Manuscripts* 8; *Low Countries, series* 5), pp. 171-184. See also: O. KURTZ, "An Alleged Portrait of Heraclius", *Byzantion* 16 (1942-1943), pp. 162-164; J. SEZNEC, "Youth, innocence and death: Some notes on a medaillon on the Certosa of Pavia", *The Journal of the Warburg and Courtauld Institutes* 1 (1937-1938), pp. 298-303. The medallion with Heraclius in the cart (four-in-hand) was copied in the *Belles Heures* for the Duc de Berry by the brothers Limburg (1404-1408); MS New York, The Metropolitan Museum of Art, The Cloisters, 54.1.1., f. 156r.

[40] A. FROLOW, "La déviation de la 4ième Croisade vers Constantinople: Note additionnelle: La Croisade et les guerres persanes d'Héraclius", *Revue de l'histoire des religions* 74 (1955), pp. 50-61.

[41] P.M. Di Paolo recognizes in this object the dry well of the punishment of Judas (DI PAOLO, *Gli affreschi trecenteschi*, p. 81). But why would the artist have chosen this font-like representation? One should note that Jacob of Voragine mentions the martyrdom of Judas Cyriacus: he was cooked in a barrel with boiling oil. The iconography is rare. It was represented

thirteenth-century Finding of the Cross cycle in the SS. Quattro Coronati in Rome.[42] There, the Finding of the Cross was rendered as well (fig. 21), with the crosses have taken on the exceptional form of cross-staffs. Judas Cyriacus, too, was baptized. This interpretation of the fresco, however, would not agree with the reading direction of the Lanciano frescoes, as Judas Cyriacus was converted only later, when he saw the true cross.

Although the iconographical tradition of the Finding of the Cross goes back to the Carolingian period, the first monumental cycle dates from the twelfth century. It is found in the S. Severo church in Bardolino, near Verona.[43] Besides the cycle in Braunschweig we have already had occasion to mention, drawings have been preserved from a now-lost cycle from the first quarter of the fourteenth century in the church of Sta. Eufemia in Rome, as mentioned by the sixteenth-century hand in the manuscript that copied them (fig. 22).[44] In these drawings, too, attention is paid to the interrogation by a throned queen seen in profile.

Logically, the Finding itself and the Trial are never absent in the visual tradition. One may assume, then, that these two themes in Lanciano would have been executed on the same wall, below, but have now been destroyed.

Reading in Situ

Due to the poor state of conservation, it is nearly impossible to describe or identify the cycle coherently. This is a Legend of the Cross without any pretentiousness. The motifs are not an ordered reflection of the *Legenda Aurea*. One may consider the images as rather spontaneous citations.

---

in a French *Legendarium*, ca. 1240, MS Brussels, Koninklijke Bibliotheek, 10326, f. 135v (it also contains an image of the Finding at f. 132r); cf. C. GASPAR and F. LYNA, *Les principaux manuscrits à peintures de la Bibliothèque Royale de Belgique* 1 (Brussels, 1984), pp. 131-134.

[42] A. SOHN, "Bilder als Zeichen der Herrschaft. Die Silvesterkapelle in SS. Quattro Coronati (Rom)", *Archivum Historiae Pontificae* 35 (1997), pp. 7-47.

[43] With scenes from the apocalypse as well; Y. CHRISTE, "Le cycle inédit de l'invention de la croix à S. Severo de Bardolino", in: *Académie des inscriptions et belles-lettres: Comptes rendus des séances de l'année 1978, janvier-mars* (Paris, 1978), pp. 78-109.

[44] MS Rome, Vatican, Biblioteca Apostolica, Ross. lat. 1168, ff. 7-13; H. TIETZE, *Die illuminierten Handschriften der Rossiana in Wien-Lainz* (vol. 1., 1911), pp. 163-164; PFLEGER, *Eine Legende*, pp. 93-94. C. HVELSEN, *Le chiese di Roma nel medioevo: Cataloghi ed appunti* (Rome, 2000), pp. 249-250. The early Christian church has been destroyed in 1590. The church was situated near Sta. Maria Maggiore.

Whereas the cycle at first glance offers a less structured reading, it conforms to the *Gestalt* of the space. For whoever enters the room can grasp the scenes at a glance. The paintings are synthetic and economic. The casualness of the Lanciano scenes can be likened to a narrative cycle escaping from organized norms. That cycle was grafted on oral traditions or the 'accelerated' written word, e.g. through jottings in diaries or travel literature. The resulting image-building in Lanciano is comparable to the way in which Niccolò Poggibonsi integrated the Legend of the Wood of the Cross into his report on his travels in the Holy Land (1346-1350).[45] The motif of the construction of the temple with the living wood is told when describing Adam's grave at Hebron. He briefly mentions that this was the place where the wood grew that was felled by Solomon.[46] Although the Franciscan traveller cannot have influenced the Lanciano cycle, this type of story suggests the rapid style of communication by pilgrims which may also have inspired the frescoes at Lanciano.

The motif of the dry tree with the kneeling figure – with caution identified as the Queen of Sheba – also seems to have had a particular fascination for writers of accounts of travels and pilgrimages. Odoric de Pordenone (1286-1331) mentions a "dry tree" of the cross. This tree is sometimes called the "tree of Seth". Nevertheless – as argued above – I do not read a kneeling Seth in Lanciano.[47] These motifs borrowed from the interaction between orality and literacy, surfacing as if incidentally in the memory at certain places in the

---

[45] Edition: B. BAGATTI, *Fra Niccolò da Poggibonsi: Libro d'oltramare (1346-1350)* (Jerusalem, 1945: *Pubblicazioni dello Studium Biblicum Franciscanum* 2/1), pp. 43-44.

[46] Niccolò da Poggibonsi returns to the motif during his visit to the Monastery of the Cross in Jerusalem. According to tradition, this monastery was founded by Slav monks in the seventh century. At this place, Niccolò mentions, the wood of the tree from Hebron, once planted by Seth, formed the vertical axis of the cross of Christ. The cross beam was made from a cypress planted by Lot on the site of this monastery. A third type of wood of the cross grew in the cedar woods of Lebanon; from it was made the base of the cross. A fourth type came from an olive tree – he does not mention a locale – that was used for the *titulus*. The passage about the Queen of Sheba appears in the description of the Mount of Olives near which, Niccolò mentions briefly, there was a bridge, and on the bridge the queen recognized and worshipped the wood.

[47] Marco Polo (1286-1324) says "The Province which is called Tonocail ... also contains an immense plain on which is found the *arbre Sol*, which we Christians call the *Arbre Sec*. And there, the people of the country tell you, the battle between Alexander and king Darius was fought" (H. CORDIER, *Les voyages en Asie au XIVième siècle du bienheureux frère Odoric de Pardenone* (Paris, 1891), p. 19). John Mandeville mentions a dry tree of Seth (1322) (*Mandeville's Travels*, ed. M.C. SEYMOUR (Oxford, 1967), I, 14). In the *Epistola Presbyteri Johannis* (ca 1300) of Prester John, a Christian asks what *arbor sicca* means, and the priest answers that it means the *"arbor Seth"*(E.C. QUINN, *The Quest of Seth for the Oil of Life* (Chicago and London, 1962), p. 13).

Christian world and being exchanged between travellers, may also be transformed into visual images. The resulting visuality, then, operates in a shared body of thoughts.

These reflections, inspired by the topographical experience of the cycle, now bring me to the context of the cycle.

Contextualizing Images: Lanciano and the Functions of the Legend of the Cross

Whoever thinks of the *Abruzzesi* as mere shepherds closed off from the outside world, is ignorant of an important trump card of this region: the Adriatic coast and the so-called *via degli Abruzzi*.[48] The towns on this side of Italy, such as Aquila and Sulmona, were important stopping places for merchants, crusaders and pilgrims, and thus also a dynamic meeting place between North and South, East and West.[49]

Although not situated at the *via* itself, Lanciano had its share of trade and traffic. A contract from 1153 announced the next urban phase of Lanciano: a *fiera* could be held in the city in May and September.[50] The *fiera* was a so-called 'tax-free' market, to which the town had exclusive rights. From the fourteenth century, under the crown of Anjou, Frenchmen or Italians fleeing from France because they were weary of the competition, contributed to the rise of the *fiera*. Confraternities were organized around specific products; they were associated with the patronage of their church. Thus, we know that furriers were linked to the church of S. Nicola.[51]

The wall paintings of the S. Nicola must have been embedded in the economic, social, and religious environment of Lanciano.

---

[48] P. GASPARINETTI, "La 'via degli Abruzzi' e l'attività commerciale di Aquila e Sulmona nei secoli XIII-XV", *Bullettino della Deputazione Abruzzese di Storia Patria* 54-56 (1966), pp. 5-103.

[49] See M. DE CECCO, "Brevi note sulla storia economica della città", in: *Lanciano. Città d'Arti e Mercanti*, ed. E. GIANCRISTOFORO (Lanciano, 1995), pp. 64-73.

[50] *Ibid.*; C. MARCIANI, *Scritti di Storia*, ed. R. CARABBA (Lanciano, 1974), *passim*.

[51] *Ibid.*

Liturgy and Pilgrimage

Evidently the cycle recalls the two commemorations of the cross in the medieval liturgical calendar: 3 May (Finding of the Cross) and 14 September (Exaltation of the Cross). Originally the holy feast of the Finding of the Cross in Jerusalem also celebrated the feast of the consecration of Constantine's church of the Holy Sepulchre. This is told by the pilgrim Egeria (ca. 381-384), who bears witness to an eight-day-long feast in commemoration of the consecration of the Holy Sepulchre complex in 335, which was celebrated together with the discovery of the cross of Christ (*Itinerarium Aetheriae*, 48).[52] From the seventh century onwards, this feast also celebrated the commemoration of the restitution of the relic of the cross by Heraclius.[53] In the Gelasian calendar of the Carolingians, the latter commemoration was came to be celebrated on a separate day, with Heraclius on 14 September and Helena on 3 May. This last date was taken over from an older Gallican use. Henceforth, the liturgical texts for the two feasts were transmitted under different days; they described the wood of the cross as either *lignum vitae* or, in battle, as *vexillum*. Hymns of the relic of the cross were sung as *tropaion* and as a sign of apocalyptic victory.[54]

During the various building campaigns of the church of S. Nicola, the archives were lost. Information about any special liturgical attention for 3 May and 14 September no longer exists. These were in any case stable and traditional feasts. Moreover, they were held in honour everywhere in Western Europe and therefore probably also in Lanciano.

The oldest preserved source which mentions something about religious life in Lanciano, the second chapter of *Delle feste da guardarsi* from the statutes of 1592, does not clarify things either.[55] From this document it is apparent that the

[52] *Itinerarium Egeriae*, ed. P. GEYER and O. CUNZ (Vienna, 1965: CCSL 175), pp. 1-3; *Die Pilgerreise der Aetheria*, ed. H. PETRE and K. VRETSKA (Vienna, 1958); *Itinerarium Egeriae (peregrinatio Aetheriae)*, ed. O. PRINZ (Heidelberg, 1960); J. WILKINSON, *Egeria's Travels to the Holy Land* (Jerusalem and Warminster, 1981), pp. 136-137, for the dating, see pp. 237-239; DRIJVERS, *Helena*, pp. 91-93. F. LEDEGANG, *Als een pelgrim naar het heilig land: De pelgrimage van Egeria in de vierde eeuw*, (Kampen, 1991: *Christelijke bronnen* 4), pp. 100-101.
[53] L. VAN TONGEREN, *Exaltatio Crucis: Het feest van de Kruisverheffing en de zingeving van het kruis in het Westen tijdens de vroege Middeleeuwen: Een liturgie-historische studie* (Tilburg, 1995: *Publikaties van de Theologische Faculteit Tilburg* 25), passim.
[54] J. SZÖVERFFY, "*Crux fidelis*: A prolegomena to a history of the Holy Cross hymns", *Traditio* 22 (1966), pp. 1-41; ID., "Hymns and sources of the Holy Cross", *Classical Folia* 20, 1 (1966), pp. 1-17.
[55] E. GIANCRISTOFORO, "Il folklore religioso e le tradizioni devozionali", in: *Lanciano: Città d'arti e mercanti*, ed. E. GIANCRISTOFORO (Lanciano, 1995), pp. 156-167, at p. 156.

feast of St. Nicholas was obviously important, but the same holds true, for instance, for the feast of St. Sebastian. In 1436 relics of the apostle Simon had been translated from Venice to the Sant'Agostino of Lanciano, and in 1440 the confraternity of St. Simon was founded. The fifteenth-century votive scene makes a connection between St. Nicholas, St. Simon and Sta. Croce (Helena).[56]

What sets the S. Nicola church apart is that, since its foundation in 1100, the church was an important stopping place for pilgrims on their way to Jerusalem. In the time of the Normans the S. Pellegrino was a so-called *xenodokion*, a hospital or lodgings for the travelling faithful. Precisely because of the large presence of hospitals, Lanciano was the ideal spot to rest awhile en route to other prayer sites. Furthermore, it was in the months of May and September that the *fiera* was held. Although there is no proof, it is tempting to connect both feasts of the cross with the higher concentration of pilgrims and merchants. Religion and profit are frequently partners.

According to folklore and oral tradition, pilgrims used to gather in the S. Nicola for their trip to Monte S. Gargano, a cult site for St. Michael and St. Nicholas in Bari. This was in fact the reason for the church's dedication.[57] The legend in the bell tower added a foretaste of another destination: the beloved Jerusalem. The legend also contained exemplary motifs for people far from home. Would they not have felt empathy for Helena, the archetypical pilgrim to Jerusalem? Maybe this is also why the Queen of Sheba, who travelled from the Far East to Solomon in Jerusalem, is represented in *humilitas*, as a female pilgrim who touches the tree of the cross. The touching of holy places and objects is actually an integral part of the anthropology of pilgrimage devotion.

It is not instantly clear why the cycle was conceived in the bell tower; nothing is known about the liturgical function of this space compared to the nave. We have already noted that the reconstruction of the tower had occasioned a new consecration. Authentically, the relic of the cross was connected with the consecration feast of the Holy Sepulchre in Jerusalem, and we know of other appearances of the Legend of the Cross in the context of church dedications.

The embroidery of Girona (1050), with the story of Genesis concentrically depicted around *Christus Rex*, had once been divided in two at the bottom, but five scenes are still recognizable in the context of the Finding of the Cross, and furthermore a slanted cross is held by a crowned person, whom I have identi-

---

[56] This could be a *terminus postquem* for these overpaintings, most probably ordered by the little female figure close to Helena. The devotion for the cross then became linked to the miraculous relics of the apostle (DI PAOLO, *Gli affreschi trecenteschi*, pp. 124-127).

[57] GIANCRISTOFORO, "Il folklore religioso", pp. 160-161.

fied elsewhere as Heraclius.[58] This embroidery has been replaced when the chapel of the Holy Sepulchre of the cathedral was consecrated.

In the transept of the small Romanesque church of Fraurombach (Oberhessen, ca. 1350), a Heraclius legend is preserved.[59] This foundation was the property of the abbey of the Holy Sepulchre in Fulda until 1332, after which the site was sold to the lords of Schlitz. Probably the walls were painted on the occasion of a re-dedication at this time. The contents of these paintings reminded pilgrims of the archetype of all church dedications, and of the responsibility of Europe in the East. And the Holy Sepulchre itself was even present in a copy at nearby Fulda.

Could it be that the square chapel of the bell tower of Lanciano may be seen as a reminiscence of the Sepulchre, a reminiscence reinforced by the church's role in pilgrimages towards the Holy Land? Could it be that the new dedication 'called for' a Legend of the True Cross?

The bell tower also had an important social function.[60] Bells were rung to tell the time of the church service, but they also had a more profane and even superstitious purpose. Bells brought tidings that are grafted onto the social fabric, and they were considered apotropaic: their sound chased away demons. In Lanciano the many campaniles also served to display power.[61] They embodied the pride of the city and were part of the defense structure. The S. Nicola stood at the highest point of the city, in its easternmost corner: the *porta S. Nicola*. From here, an alarm could be sounded in case of threats from the coast.[62] Moreover, not everyone went to Jerusalem with peace-loving intent: violence to Jews and Saracens was considered a legitimate goal. This social concern was also reflected in the frescoes.

---

[58] Dommuseum; B. BAERT, "New observations on the Genesis of Girona (1050-1100): The iconography of the legend of the True Cross", *Gesta: The International Center of Medieval Art* 38, 2 (1999), pp. 115-127.

[59] The cycle is related to the childhood of Heraclius, too (M. CURSCHMANN, "Constantine-Heraclius: German texts and picture cycles", in: *Piero della Francesca and His Legacy*, ed. M.A. LAVIN (Hannover and London, 1995: *Studies in the History of Art* 48), pp. 49-61).

[60] S. DE BLAUW, "*Campanae supra Urben*: Sull'uso delle campane nella Roma medievale", *Rivista di Storia della Chiesa in Italia* 47 (1993), pp. 367-414.

[61] DE CECCO, "Brevi note sulla storia economica della città", p. 90.

[62] Well into the fifteenth century, Lanciano was at war with Ortona (DE CECCO, "Brevi note sulla storia economica della città", p. 71).

The Enemy from the East

Sympathy with the crusading idea is structural in the iconography of the Legend of the Cross. The message is spread by Constantine and Heraclius, the latter being seen as a new Constantine. The scenes of the duel and the worship of the cross in Lanciano do not allow an unambiguous identification. Their meaning, however, remains the same. They concern the diplomatic contacts between Rome and Byzantium. These contacts, of changing intensity, were in large part responsible for Lanciano's strategic function.

At the end of the thirteenth century and the beginning of the fourteenth, the West was anxiously turning towards the East. In 1292, Akko had already been lost, but now the Christian enclaves in Asia Minor, conquered by the Mongols, in Russia, and in Persia came under increasing Islamic influence.[63] Nicholas IV sent bishops to the Eastern borders to promote Christian unity between the West and these Nestorian enclaves. Although the Persian religious dignitary Jabhala III was a Christian of Turkish descent, the Mongolian leader, the Ilchan Ghazan (1285-1304), converted to Islam. The Ilchan of Russia followed his example in 1313. The following decades saw an increase in diplomatic contacts and the call to arms – certainly when the Palaiologan emperor Andronikos III (1282-1328) could no longer handle the Muslims in Constantinople.[64]

The programme in the campanile of Lanciano gives expression to a shared concern for Christian cities across the Adriatic.[65] With each threat from the Muslim world, the story about the struggle for the cross was again of topical interest.[66] Trade had already been established in the early Middle Ages between

---

[63] "Mongolen", in: *Lexikon für Theologie und Kirche*, 7, cols. 549-552.

[64] A. LAIOU, "Palaiologoi", in: *Dictionary of the Middle Ages* (New York, 1987), 9, p. 33. I elaborated on this in: B. BAERT, "Das Antependium von Nedstryn (Norwegen, 1310) und die Kreuzerhöhungslegende", *Das Münster* (2001), pp. 201-209. I argued that this antependium with eight scenes of the battle between Heraclius and Chosroes II refers to the actual drama in the East.

[65] At the beginning of the fourteenth century a mural depicting the finding of the cross by Helena and Judas appears also in Romania, the Sta. Maria of Orlea. See I.C. POPA, *Christian Art in Romania: 3. The Fourteenth Century* (Boekarest, 1983), No. 50, p. 128; V. VATASIANU, *Istoria artei feudale in tarile romine: 1. Arta in perioada de dezvoltare a feudalismului* (s.l., 1959), p. 401, fig. 358; I.D. STEFANESCU, *La peinture religieuse en Valachie et en Transylvanie depuis les origines jusqu'au XIXe siècle* (Paris, 1932), pp. 223-239. See also the early fifteenth-century Legend of the Finding of the Cross in the grotto church in Andria (B. MOLAJOLI, "La crypta di S. Croce in Andria", *Atti e memoria della società Magna Grecia: Bizantina-Medievale* 1 (1934), pp. 25-35).

[66] A map of Jerusalem from 1170-1180 in a Collectar of St.-Bertin depicts the city at the time of the crusaders. Below this, George is represented as a crusading knight, stabbing the

the Muslim communities in the Balkans and far-off Persia. The townspeople of Lanciano certainly knew what it was like to live among different cultures. The relationship with the Jewish community, too, played a very relevant role in the religious and economic history of the city.

Jews and the Holy Sacrament

The Legend of the True Cross is the history of the first Christian queen and the 'first' converted Jew. It reflects the everlasting battle for the true faith. The legend was adopted in an apologetic context. I will give three examples to support this claim.

The Prayerbook of Wessobrunn (814) contains one of the oldest copies of the Legend of Judas Cyriacus in the Latin West; it is illustrated with seventeen pen and ink illustrations.[67] It is thought that this manuscript provided sermon or teaching materials for the monks. In 814, the year in which the Wessobrun Prayerbook was written, Louis the Pious commissioned the *Magister Iudaeorum*.[68] Jews could now be legalized, and in southern Germany Jewish communities flourished. The history of the Finding of the Cross of Christ by Judas Cyriacus and his baptism (fig. 23) perhaps reflected this socio-religious development.[69] The iconography of the Finding of the Cross iconography, from its conception in Carolingian times, functioned within Judaeo-Christian controversy and apology.

The Master of Tressa gives the date of November 1214 to his antependium, which was most likely intended for the choir of the cathedral of Siena (fig.

---

fleeing Muslims in the back. This saint was most probably once portrayed in Lanciano too, now partly destroyed. See MS The Hague, Koninklijke Bibliotheek, 76 F 5; 25.5cm. x 16.5cm.; S. BORRMANN, "Collectar", in: *Heinrich der Löwe und seine Zeit*, vol. 1, No. A7, p. 44, fig. 45.

[67] Pen drawings heightened in wash, unframed, MS Munich, Bayerische Staatsbibliothek, clm. 22053, ff. 1-20; drawings on ff. 2r, 3v, 6v, 7v, 9v, 10r, 10v, 12v, 13r, 14v, 15v, 16r, 16v, 17v, 18v, 19r, 20r; f. 8 is missing; unnumbered leaves between fols. 2 and 3 are also absent; ff. 4 and 5 should follow f. 7; thus, 1, 2, ?, 3, 6, 7, 4, 5, (8?), 9, etc. See *Die Handschriften des Wessobrunner Gebets*, ed. A. VON ECKARDT (facsmile) and C. VON KRAUS (introduction) (München, 1922), pp. 5-22, at p. 5; K. BIERBRAUER, *Die vorkarolingischen und karolingischen Handschriften der Bayerischen Staatsbibliothek* (Wiesbaden, 1990), pp. 83-84, cat. No. 155, figs. 219-336; M. RESTLE, "*In hoc signo vincis*: Ein Beitrag zur Illustration des Clm 22053", in: *Per assiduum studium scientiae adipisci margaritam: Festgabe für Ursula Nilgen zum 65. Geburtstag* (Santa Ottilien, 1997), pp. 27-43.

[68] R. DELORT, *Charlemagne* (Paris, 1986), p. 112.

[69] B. BLUMENKRANZ, *Le juif médiéval au miroir de l'art chrétien* (Paris, 1966), fig. 3.

24).[70] It is the oldest altarpiece surviving from medieval Italy, made during the liturgical reform of the Fourth Lateran Council, which took place in the same year. Damage to the lower part of the panel shows the physical evolution from antependium to *retabulum*. Developments within the papal curia are echoed in the subject matter of the Finding of the Cross. The central *Christus Pantocrator* is flanked on the right by three scenes, two of which are related to Helena. At the top, Helena interrogates the Jews. In the middle, the cross is found and/or tested; this part is damaged. On the left side, tableaux from the *Volto Santo* tradition are represented. This tradition told that, when a Jew had disfigured the crucifix, water and blood miraculously flowed from it, by that inciting the Jew to convert.[71]

In this altar piece, the Finding of the Cross functioned within a conversion apology concerning the Jews. In addition to the dogma of transubstantiation, this matter received much attention during the Fourth Lateran Council. The contents of the retable, dedicated to the mystery of the Passion and the Finding of the Cross, follows this dogma through the actual presence of Christ in the *Volto Santo* and through the tangibility of the cross in religious history. The Legend of the Finding of the Cross lends itself to interpretation in the light of the Jewish controversy – on the Finding of the Cross, Ambrose writes, the Jew blushes at the sight of the cross.

In this period, stories originated of Jews desecrating hosts. These legends link Christological apology with populistic mistrust. In Lanciano, too, such stories circulated from the thirteenth century onwards.[72]

Today, the tourists coming to Lanciano are Italian pilgrims who visit the local church of S. Francesco with its *santuario del Miracolo Eucaristico*. The church was built on the eighth-century church of S. Legonziano. The story goes that, when a Greek monk did not believe in the real presence of Christ, the host changed into flesh and five drops of blood appeared.[73] Since then, Lanciano has

---

[70] M. BACCI, "The Berardenga Antependium and the *Passio ymaginis* office", *Journal of the Warburg and Courtauld Institutes* 61 (1998), pp. 1-16; B. BAERT, "The retable of the Master of Tressa (Siena, 1215): Iconography and function", *Pantheon: Internationales Jahresbuch für Kunst* (München, 1999), pp. 14-21. The articles appeared independent from one another.

[71] Also related by Jacob of Voragine at the Feast of the Exaltation of the Cross on 14 September.

[72] On the Jewish legends: E. GIANCRISTOFORO, "Il folklore religioso", pp. 159-160; C. MARCIANI, "Ebrei a Lanciano dal XII al XVIII secolo", in: *Scritti di Storia* (Lanciano, 1978), pp. 266-300.

[73] The host is kept in a monstrance which in 1713 was given to the church by the wealthy merchant Domenico Coli from Norcia. See F. BATTISTELLA, "L'architettura nel XVII e XVIII secolo", in: *Lanciano: Città d'Arti e Mercanti*, pp. 126-153, p. 133.

been called the *città eucaristica*. Another eucharistic legend would soon follow. In 1273, according to this legend, on the advice of the Jew Ricciarella, the wife of a certain Jacopo Stazii stole a host for a love amulet. The women did not know any better than to bake it. To their dismay, the host turned to flesh and blood, which they hid under the floor. Seven years later, the relic was found and worshipped in the Augustinian monastery of Offida. To this day, the Lancianesi have retained the nickname *frija Criste*, those who grilled Christ.

In 1191 eighty Jewish families had been allowed to settle in Lanciano's so-called *sacca* neighbourhood.[74] Initially, the Jews were relatively well integrated into social and economic life. In 1212, Frederic II gave them the privilege to compete with Venice in the Adriatic art trade.[75] Thus, they could use the trading facilities of the *fiera*. Under the crown of Anjou, however, the balance between Christians and Jews was upset. In 1307 the Jews were obliged to wear a Jewish cap in Lanciano to distinguish them from Christians.[76] The first documentation of the expulsion of Jews dates from around 1400, the very time to which the iconography of the Finding of the Cross in the campanile can also be dated.

The Legend could be read as the story of a Judaism that, according to God's will, had to assimilate to a new covenant: their Tree of Life and their temple were transformed into the cross and the Church of the Christians. There was even the story of a Jew who was persuaded by all this and was baptized. I do not know of any documentation on forced baptisms of Jews in Lanciano, but if they ever happened, the legend would certainly have been the appropriate décor.

A hundred years later a similar situation existed up north, where we find the Legend of the Cross in the – also square – Capella Farfense of the S. Francesco in Montegiorgio (ca. 1425). Specific to this cycle is the attention given to Judas Cyriacus. Here, In contrast to other Italian cycles, the nails found by Judas are also depicted. Moreover, in contrast to the Tuscan cycles,

---

[74] L. ANTINORI, *Notizie storiche sulla città di Lanciano* (Napels, 1791), p. 13; DE CECCO, "Brevi note sulla storia economica della città", p. 95, and p. 69 for the etymology of *sacca*, perhaps *cul de sac*. In the eleventh century, the Jewish population numbered around 400 on a total population of 2000 inhabitants.

[75] D. ABULAFIA, "Il Mezzogiorno peninsulare dai bizantini all'espulsione (1541)", in: *Storia d'Italia: 11. Gli ebrei in Italia: 1. Dal'alto Medioevo all'età dei ghetti*, ed. C. VIVANTI (Turin, 1996). See also: E. DI STEFANO, "Mercanti, artigiani, ebrei: Flussi migratori e articolazione produttiva nella Camerino del primo quattrocento", in: *Atti del XX convegno di studi maceratesi (1994)* (Macerata, 1996), pp. 191-232.

[76] N. FERORELLI, *Gli ebrei nell'Italia meredionale dall'età romana al secolo XVII* (Bologna, 1915), s.p. anastatica.

Judas is portrayed as a grey old man with a long beard (fig. 25). In Tuscany, his outward appearance does not allow him to be distinguished from the other male figures depicted. The old man found in Montegiorgio, is a *topos* for the Jew. In Lanciano, too, this *topos* was expressly used.

The Franciscan church of Montegiorgio was also located near the local Jewish community, which dominated banking until the end of the fifteenth century in the *contrada* of S. Nicolò. The Franciscans organized refuges in the area – so-called *monti di pietà* – for victims of Jewish lending practices.[77] Furthermore, another influence was brought into play here. The Marches were unique in their devotion to Judas Cyriacus. Since the eleventh century, his relics were preserved in the S. Cyriaco in Ancona.[78] His role in the iconography of the Finding of the Cross led to a production of altarpieces in Sassoferrata, Matelica, and Ancona.[79] The cult of the converted Jew possibly extended to the neighbouring province of Teramo. We know that the first Franciscan Pope Nicholas IV lavishly provided the region with particles of the cross.[80] It is conceivable that the Lanciano cycle had been inspired by a very similar atmosphere.

Franciscans

The Legend of the Cross was disseminated in monumental art due to Franciscan patronage. The Franciscans used the power of the medium of the fresco to the full. The cycles in Florence, Volterra, Montegiorgio and Arezzo were all conceived within the ideology of this mendicant order.

The S. Nicola church of Lanciano was not founded by the Franciscans, but the order played a prominent role in the social and religious life of the *città eucaristica*. The Franciscan impact on the other religious foundations of the town must have been considerable. S. Nicola will have been visited by the same

---

[77] I would like to thank Prof. dr. Don Giuseppe Avarucci, Università di Macerata, who alerted me to this fact.

[78] M. POLVERARI, *Ancona e Bisanzio* (Ancona, 1993), pp. 56-57.

[79] Sassoferrato, Sta. Croce dei Conti – Giovanni Antonio Bellinzoni da Pesaro, mid-fifteenth-century, now Urbino, Pinacoteca Nazionale; Matelica, Museo Piersanti – Francesco di Gentile da Fabriano, last quarter of the fifteenth century; textile *paliotto*, Girolamo di Giovanni e Giovanni Boccati, ca. 1470, Ancona, Museo Diocesano. See L. ZANNINI, "Il paliotto di san Ciriaco di Ancona", *Studia Picena* 54/1-2 (1989), pp. 5-41.

[80] B. ORSINI, *Descrizione delle pitture sculture architetture ed altre cose rara della insigne città di Ascoli* (Perugia, 1790), p. 114.

pilgrims who wished to see the miraculous host that was guarded by the Franciscans.

Why did the Franciscans have a predilection for the subject matter of the Legend of the Cross? In the *Legenda major* (1260-1262), Bonaventure situates the stigmatization of St. Francis around the Feast of the Exaltation of the Cross.[81] In a vision, he saw the crucified Christ as a seraph. On 14 September, the Byzantine liturgy commemorates not only Heraclius but also the Discovery of the Cross by Helena. The Franciscans grouped the legends together in one cycle, reuniting the two important feasts of the cross of the East and the West. This suggests the ecumenical outlook familiar to the Franciscans,[82] but also their empathy for all aspects of the cult of the cross.

Later historical circumstances have also contributed to the 'Franciscan Legend of the Cross'. Since the beginning of the fourteenth century, the Franciscans were the 'guardians' (*Custodes*) of the holy sites in Jerusalem, i.e. of the Church of the Holy Sepulchre, the grotto of the Nativity in Bethlehem, and the tomb of Mary in the valley of Josephat.[83] Besides poverty and humility, the importance attached to missionary work is a focus of the biographies of St. Francis. This missionary aspect was felt most strongly where Saracens and Islam were concerned, but the mission was intended for all 'heretics'. This work was to be accompanied by tolerance, martyrdom, and humility,[84] qualities that could be recognized in Constantine, Helena, and Heraclius and their service to the cross. In their devotional focus on the cross and their religious engagement with other religions, the Franciscans also took an apologetic stand towards the Jews. The Franciscan presence and their recent responsibilities in Jerusalem were perhaps extra stimuli for the Legend of the Cross iconography in the S. Nicola.

---

[81] Bonaventura, *Opera omnia, o.c., Legenda major*, XIII, 3, ed. PP. COLLEGII A S. BONA-VENTURA, AD CLARAS AQUAS (Quaracchi, 1882): "*seraph unum effigies hominis crucifixi christo sub specie seraph ... circa festum exaltationis sanctae crucis*"; D.V. MONTI, "Francis of Assisi", in: *The Encyclopedia of Religion*, ed. M. ELIADE, 3 (New York and London, 1987), pp. 407-408. Also mentioned in the thirteenth-century *Fioretti* of Ugolino; *I fioretti di S. Francesco*, ed. G.D. BONINO (Turin, 1974), pp. 176, 180.

[82] L. LEHMANN, "Prinzipien Franziskanischer Mission nach den frühen Quellen", in: *Francescanesimo e profezia*, ed. E. COVI (Rome, 1985), p. 144, especially regarding the threat of Islam, but also with respect to the Byzantine orthodox Church; G. SPIERIS, "Francesco d'Assisi: Profeta dell'incontro tra Occidente e Oriente", in: *Francescanesimo e profezia*, pp. 453-489.

[83] G. ODOARDI, "La custodia di Terra Sta. nel VI. centenario della sua costituzione", *Miscellanea francescana* 43 (1943), pp. 217-256.

[84] L. LEHMANN, "Prinzipien", *passim*.

Conclusion

Until now, the discovery in the campanile of Lanciano has not received much attention. This can perhaps be attributed to the less appealing state in which the frescoes were found. Nevertheless, the contents of the cycle are not without importance. Lanciano is an asset to the iconographical map of the Legend of the Cross. Lacunae in this cycle make it difficult to follow the proper sequence of the legend. The structure of the ground floor of the bell tower has forced the artists to adjust to the available walls. 'Reading' occurs in 'snapshots' here, but the room is so small that one needs only to move one's head to take in all the tableaux.

The episode with Adam's grave and Solomon's death is the oldest known iconography that can be related to the Legend of the Wood of the Cross. Previously, it had always been assumed that Agnolo Gaddi was the first to visualize this story from the *Legenda Aurea*, in the Sta. Croce in Florence. With the discovery of the frescoes in Lanciano, the figural tradition of the Old Testament is now set at the beginning of the fourteenth century.

That in Lanciano the depiction of the construction of the temple is contaminated with the tree growing from Adam's mouth remains unique. It is an anomaly, but its synchronicity perhaps offered an elegant economic solution to the limits of space. We encounter similar 'accelerated' methods of storytelling in orality or pilgrim literature. In travel writing, a shortened version of the Legend of the Wood of the Cross was coupled with the name of the site to be visited – for example, Hebron and Jerusalem.

A solitary 'freestanding' phrase may have inspired the scene with the (supposed) Queen of Sheba. The worshipping of the tree trunk is unconnected to the previous scene. The woman's (humble) outward appearance and her action (the devotional contact with the wood) may relate to the context of pilgrimage.

The other episodes – the battle for the cross and Helena's dealings with the Jews of Jerusalem – are also oriented towards the Holy Land and the developments there. The iconography of the Finding of the Cross had enjoyed a tradition since Carolingian times; that of the Exaltation of the Cross since Romanesque times.

The context and functions of the iconography of the Legend of the Cross are known from other instances. Five prominent factors play a part in understanding the iconography: the liturgy, pilgrimage, the crusades, the apology concerning the Jews, and the support of the subject matter by the Franciscans. Obviously, the intensity of these factors fluctuated and was subject to historical developments. In Lanciano it appears that these factors may all have had their impact on the birth of the iconography in the church of S. Nicola. The S. Nicola was, moreover, the most popular gathering place for pilgrims. Could it be that some pilgrims stayed overnight in the bell tower – a safe observation post and 'foretaste' of the Sepulchre in Jerusalem?

Liturgy, pilgrimage, and crusading ideals may have burgeoned because the city was visited around the time of the *fiere* in May and September, precisely the months of the two feasts of the cross. These 'tax-free' markets brought economic impulse to the religious life of a city which largely focused on the miraculous host and which was, from the thirteenth century onwards, steeped in an anti-judaic climate. Elsewhere, the Legend of the Cross also functioned as an apology of the true faith, as e.g. in the antependium of Siena and the cycle in the Jewish area of Montegiorgio.

The Franciscans were the protectors of the host in the *città eucaristica*. At the time the frescoes in the campanile were painted, they had recently been appointed the official guardians of the Holy Sepulchre in Jerusalem. Perhaps their presence in the city gave a boost to the iconography of the Legend. That the S. Nicola not only carries the name of the most important cult in Bari, but also of the Franciscan pope who around 1300 provided the coastal area between Ascoli Picena (his birthplace) and Bari with countless relics of the cross and preached the crusade, may have been an extra stimulus for the iconographer.

Despite this reading exercise and the test of contextualization, the cycle in the campanile of S. Nicola will not divulge all its secrets. Alas, we cannot put ourselves in the shoes of the woman who is portrayed so unrecognizably small near St. Simon and Sta. Croce (fig. 11). Were some of the wall paintings perhaps painted on her commission? Which stories did she recognize in the campanile? And where did her prayers go? Did she pray that six centuries later someone would think of her?

Fig. 1   Finding of the Cross. Initial decoration *D(eus)*, atelier of Meaux, Sacramentary of Gellone, second half of the eighth century. MS Paris, Bibliothèque Nationale, lat. 12048, f. 76v.

Fig. 2   Finding of the Cross. *Canones conciliarum*, drawing without frame,
fourth quarter of the eighth century, Milan (?). MS Vercelli, Bibliotheca
Capitulare, 165, f. 2r.

Fig. 3   Heraclius restores the cross to Jerusalem. Sacramentary of Mont St.
Michel, 1060. MS New York, Pierpont Morgan Library, 641, f. 155v.

Fig. 4   Seth receives a banderole from the angel Michael and plants a twig on
          the dead body of Adam. Fresco, Agnolo Gaddi, 1388-1392. Florence,
          Sta. Croce, choir.

Fig. 5   The Queen of Sheba worships the wood on the Kedron. The wood is buried. Fresco, Agnolo Gaddi, 1388-1392. Florence, Sta. Croce, choir.

Fig. 6   Grave of Adam, and Solomon building the temple. Fresco, 1330-1340.
          Lanciano, S. Nicola.

Fig. 7   The Queen of Sheba (?) worships the living wood. Fresco, 1330-1340.
Lanciano, S. Nicola, campanile.

Fig. 8   Duel between Constantine and Maxentius or between Heraclius and
        Chosroes. Fresco, 1330-1340. Lanciano, S. Nicola, campanile.

Fig. 9   Worship of the relic of the cross by Constantine or Heraclius. Fresco,
         1330-1340. Lanciano, S. Nicola, campanile.

Fig. 10 S. Simone and Sta. Croce. Fresco, fifteenth century. Lanciano, S. Nicola, campanile.

Fig. 11 Patroness (?) in prayer. Fresco, fifteenth century. Lanciano, S. Nicola, campanile.

Fig. 12 S. Giorgio. Fresco, fifteenth century. Lanciano, S. Nicola, campanile.

Fig. 13 Baptismal font? Fresco, ca. 1400. Lanciano, S. Nicola, campanile.

Fig. 14 Helena interrogates the Jews. Fresco, ca. 1400. Lanciano, S. Nicola,
     campanile.

Fig. 15 The tree is felled and is used for the construction of the temple. Fresco, Antonio Alberti da Ferrara (?), 1425. Montegiorgio, S. Francesco, Capella Farfense.

Fig. 16 The Queen of Sheba worships the wood on the Kedron. Sinopie, Masolino da Panicale, 1424. Empoli, Sto. Stefano, Helena chapel.

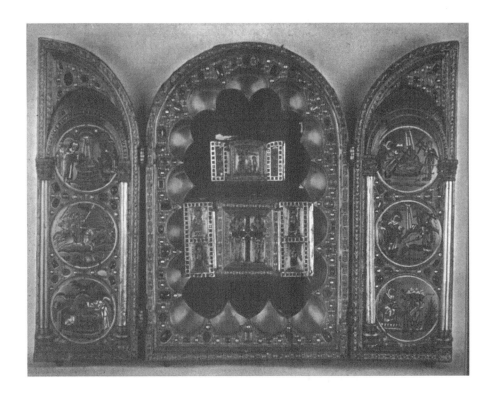

Fig. 17 Triptch of the Holy Cross for Abbot Wibald, Godfried of Huy (?), Stavelot, 1154-1158. New York, Pierpont Morgan Library.

Fig. 18 Heraclius restores the cross. Wall painting, south transept, 1240-1250.
          Braunschweig, St. Blasius.

Fig. 19 Duel between Chosroes and Heraclius. Legendarium, Palermo, 1310-1320. MS Turin, Bibliotheca Nazionale Universitaria, I.II.17., f. 203v.

Fig. 20 Johannes VIII Paleologus. Medaillon, Pisanello, 1438. London, Victoria
        and Albert Museum.

Fig. 21 Finding of the Cross. Fresco, thirteenth-century Rome, SS. Quattro Coronati.

Fig. 22 Helena interrogates the Jews. sixteenth-century drawing after a lost
        fourteenth-century cycle in the Sta. Eufemia church. MS Vatican,
        Biblioteca Apostolica, Ross. lat. 1168, f. 8r.

Fig. 23 Baptism of Judas Cyriacus. Wessobrunner Gebetbuch, pen drawing, South-German, 814. MS Munich, Bayerische Staatsbibliothek, clm. 22053, f. 16r.

Fig. 24 Antependium with Legends of the Finding of the Cross and Volto Santo. Master of Tressa, Siena, 1214. Siena, Pinacoteca.

Fig. 25 Judas Cyriacus. Fresco, Antonio Alberti da Ferrara (?), 1425. Montegiorgio, S. Francesco, Capella Farfense.

Cum ipso sunt in hac nativitate congeniti:
Dove, Throne and City in the Arch Mosaics of
Sta. Maria Maggiore in Rome (432-440)

CAECILIA DAVIS-WEYER

After nearly seventy years of modern scholarship devoted to them, the mosaics which decorate the arch of Sta. Maria Maggiore in Rome remain enigmatic. They follow neither the New Testament nor known apocryphal texts with any degree of consistency. As a result interpretations differ widely and many aspects of the mosaics' imagery have become controversial: the identity of the protagonists, whether they belong to the Old or the New Testament, the sites where events take place, whether apocryphal texts were used and if so which ones, and especially whether the mosaics should be seen as a Roman response to the Council of Ephesus.

Let me touch on the last problem first, because discussing it may help to establish a background of contemporary concerns against which the iconography of the arch needs to be seen. Theodor Klauser[1] and Richard Krautheimer[2] questioned Wilpert's thesis that Sta. Maria Maggiore and its decoration should be seen as Rome's answer to the Council of Ephesus. Ernst Kitzinger,[3] however, took a broader view and pointed out that it would be rather surprising if the mosaics of the arch, dealing with the nativity of the Saviour, and having

---

[1] Th. KLAUSER, "Rome und der Kult der Gottesmutter Maria", *Jahrbuch für Antike und Christentum* 15 (1973), pp. 120-135.

[2] R. KRAUTHEIMER, "Recent publications on Sta. Maria Maggiore", *American Journal of Archaeology* 46 (1942), pp. 373-374; and ID., *Corpus Basilicarum Christianarum Urbis Romae* III (1967), pp. 55-56.

[3] E. KITZINGER, *Byzantine Art in the Making* (Cambridge, Mass., 1977), p. 74.

been produced either at the time of the council, or shortly after that, had been created in a vacuum.

There are indeed specific indications that the iconographer of the mosaics was aware of the Christological definitions and even of some texts to come out of the Council of Ephesus. One of these was identified by Beat Brenk.[4] In its letter to pope Celestine the council offered anecdotal evidence against Nestorius. Nestorius, the Fathers wrote, had had the temerity to address a sermon to his followers in Ephesus, during which he declared, "I do not confess a two or three months' old god".[5] In the 'Adoration of the Magi' in Sta. Maria Maggiore the Christ child is not held by his mother but – contrary to fourth- and fifth-century iconographic convention – is shown seated on his own throne (fig. 6). Brenk thought that this display of the child's rank and precociousness should be seen as a rebuke to Nestorius's remark. Brenk also noted that the large number of angels surrounding the child and his mother on the arch of Sta. Maria Maggiore was likely to have been inspired by Hbr 1, 6, "And again when he brings the firstborn into the world, he says, 'let all God's angels worship him'". It is interesting that Cyril quoted this verse in his anti-Nestorian letter to the Egyptian monks,[6] and that it found its way into the patristic dossier read on 22 July 431 in Ephesus.[7]

Whatever the links between the Christological doctrines of the council and our mosaics, it might be more to the point to ask how the council and the events leading up to it were seen in Rome and the West. Writing in 1930, Erich Caspar was perplexed by the fact that Western writers, such as John Cassian and Prosper of Aquitaine – both associates of the future pope Leo, and like him already active during the two preceding papacies – held for a fact that the Nestorian heresy, the main theme of the Council of Ephesus, was closely related and more or less identical with a somewhat earlier Western heresy, Pelagianism.[8] Caspar thought that this identification of Nestorianism with Pelagianism was strange,

---

[4]   B. BRENK, Die Frühchristlichen Mosaiken in Sta. Maria Maggiore zu Rom (Wiesbaden, 1975), pp. 48-49.

[5]   Celestine, Ep. 20, 2, ed. in: PL 50, cols. 515-516 C; E. SCHWARTZ, Acta Conciliorum Oecomenicorum (Berlin, 1914 ff.), I, 3, p. 7; for an English translation see A Select Library of Nicene and Post-Nicene Fathers of the Christian Church, 2nd ser. 14 (place, year), p. 238.

[6]   Cyril, Ep. I, 28, PG 77, cols. 27-28AB; SCHWARTZ, Acta, I, 1, pp. 66-68; for an English translation see J.I. McENERNEY, in: The Fathers of the Church 76 (Washington, 1987), p. 25.

[7]   SCHWARTZ, Acta, I, 1, p.1. It was recognized as a key quote by Alcuin, who highlighted it in the Touronian MS (Paris, BN, lat. 1572) of the older Latin translation of the Ephesian acts, as he prepared himself to argue against yet another Christological heresy, Adoptionism. B. BISCHOFF, "Aus Alcuin's Erdentagen", in: B. BISCHOFF, Medieval Studies 2 (1967), pp. 12-19.

[8]   E. CASPAR, Geschichte des Papsttums (Tübingen, 1930), I, pp. 392-393.

since the two heresies were quite different and had nothing in common, except perhaps their rationalistic approach to matters of faith. Nestorius applied this approach to the Christological dilemma, while Pelagius and his monastic and aristocratic followers were interested in anthropological and ethical problems, such as free will, predestination, man's ability to justify himself, original sin or its absence, and whether the non-baptized faced certain damnation. The Pelagians, who denied the existence of original sin, did not think so and were even optimistic about the fate of children who died before being baptized.[9] Clearly Pelagianism, had it prevailed, would have brought deep changes to the whole fabric of the Church, something one can hardly say about Nestorianism. Some modern scholars, beginning with Duchesne,[10] have concluded that Nestorius was no heretic at all and that the philosophical differences between him and his orthodox enemies were small. The threat of Pelagianism frightened and energized Western churchmen – foremost among them Augustine – infinitely more than Nestorius's introduction of yet another Christological nuance. The Council of Ephesus condemned both heresies. For the West the condemnation of the Pelagian bishops who had attached themselves to Nestorius, was probably the most important outcome of the council's activities.[11]

Why and how the two heresies – Nestorianism and Pelagianism – one important to the East, the other one even more important to the West, came to be identified with each other is an intriguing question. It is quite possible that it was Nestorius himself, who by his political naivete and lack of *social skill* may have caused the entanglement which would put him into Rome's bad graces and contribute to his downfall. Of the several letters he wrote to pope Celestine to seek support against those who resisted his criticism of the term *Theotokos*, two remain.[12] Nestorius prefaced each letter with questions about what to do about a handful of Western bishops, all of them Pelagians, who had been deprived of their seats and were seeking redress in Constantinople. Caspar suggests that Nestorius did this to avoid the appearance of being a petitioner and to give the impression that he and the bishop of Rome were on equal footing when

---

[9] For a succinct overview of Pelagian positions see Marius Mercator, *Commonitorium super nomine Coelestii*, ed. in: PL 48, cols. 67-70; SCHWARTZ, *Acta*, I, 5, pp. 3-70. Not all Pelagians held such extreme views, or if they did tried to conceal them. For an analysis of the inconsistencies in Pelagius's teachings see S. THIER, *Kirche bei Pelagius* (1999: *Patristische Texte und Studien* 50).

[10] L. DUCHESNE, *Histoire ancienne de l'Église*, III (Paris, 1911). For a more recent treatment see M.V. ANASTOS, "Nestorius was orthodox", *Dumbarton Oaks Papers* 16 (1962), pp. 117-140.

[11] H. CHADWICK, **Title of article?**, *Journal of Theological Studies* NS II, 2 (1951), p. 164.

[12] *Epp.* 6 and 7, PL, 50, cols. 437-444; SCHWARTZ, *Acta*, I, 2, pp. 12-14.

exchanging information about problems of common interest.[13] In Rome Nestorius's ruse – if it was one – was seen as an attempt to question Roman jurisdic-
tion over heretical bishops in the West, and went over like a lead balloon. 'Phy-
sician, heal thyself', rather than interfere with cases which have already been
considered settled by your predecessors, was Rome's answer. From the same
letter of Celestine we also learn that the unfortunate Nestorius had not bothered
presenting his letters in a Latin translation.[14]

As a result they were sent with other Nestorian materials for an expert
opinion to John Cassian, a former member of the Church of Constantinople, a
favourite of John Chrysostomus, and now the prominent founder of two monasteries in Marseilles. The person behind this referral was the deacon Leo, who
would become pope Leo ten years therefore and to whom John Cassian refers
with expressions of affection and gratitude.[15] Cassian may have taken his lead
from Nestorius's letters, which mentioned the Pelagian bishops and Nestorius's
own problems in the same breath. Anyway he set out to prove that Nestorius
was indeed a Pelagian.

Whereas Caspar thought that this chain of events had been caused by accident, other historians[16] have wondered whether there might not have been a
more substantial link between the two heresies, since Theodore of Mopsuestia,
Nestorius's presumptive teacher, had defended Pelagius against Jerome and had
also been willing to receive the Pelagian refugees. After Theodore's death (428)
the exiles had gone to Constantinople to enlist Nestorius's help. Whatever the
details, while it was easy to imply similarities between the two heresies, it was
much harder to actually argue the point. In doing so Cassian proceeded with
extreme prejudice and without any attempt to do justice to the nuances of
Nestorius's position -- or to those of the Pelagians, or to that of a local cleric,
Leporius, who had been accused of Pelagian beliefs, and whom Cassian casts
in the role of an archetypical Pelagian.[17] According to Cassian, not only the

---

[13] CASPAR, *Kirchengeschichte*, I, pp. 392-393.
[14] Celestine, *Ep.* 13, *PL* 50, cols. 470-486, especially cols. 479-489 and 471-472;
SCHWARTZ, *Acta*, I, 2, p. 7.
[15] John Cassian, *De incarnatione domini contra Nestorium libri VII*, ed. M. PETSCHENIG
(Wien, 1888: *CSEL* 17) pp. 235-391; Praefatio pp. 235-236; ed. in: *PL* 50, cols. 10-12.
[16] O. WERMELINGER, *Rom und Pelagius* (Stuttgart, 1975: *Päpste und Papsttum* 7) pp. 244
ff.; J. SPEIGEL, "Der Pelagianismus auf dem Council von Ephesus", *Annuarium Historiae Conciliorum* 1 (1962), pp. 1-114.
[17] For Cassian's characterization of Leporius's beliefs see John Cassian, *Contra Nestorium*,
I, 2, *CSEL* 17, p. 239; ed. in: *PL* 50, col. 19A: "*solitarium quippe hominem dominum nostrum
Iesum Christum natum esse blasphemans hoc, quod ad dei postea honorum potestatemque
pervenerit, humani meriti, non divinae asseruit fuisse naturae, ac per hoc eum divinitatem ipsam*

Pelagians but also Nestorius thought that Christ was born free of sin but as a man only (*"homo solitarius"*), and that he became divine in time through personal merit.[18] Again, according to John Cassian, the Pelagians had extended this possibility to all men since they believed that each human being could justify himself through his own merit.[19] While this statement utterly misrepresents Nestorius's views, it does not paint a complete picture of the Pelagian doctrine either.[20] Historians have found the coarseness of John Cassian's judgement worrying.[21] One of them, K. H. Kuhlmann, has suggested that Cassian had been unable to find truly heterodox statements in the Nestorian material sent to him and that he had to paint Nestorius into a corner to justify attacking him.[22] It is also possible that important people in Rome had already decided to use the occasion to punish not only Nestorius but the Pelagian bishops close to him, and that John Cassian had been called upon to provide the necessary ammunition.

Cassian's identification of the Nestorian and Pelagian heresies, however wrongheaded, was accepted by Prosper of Aquitaine, an enemy of Cassian but like Cassian an associate of the future pope Leo.[23] Prosper does this explicitly

non ex proprietate unitae sibi divinitatis semper habuisse, sed postea pro praemio laboris passionisque meruisse ... blasphemaret ...".

[18] John Cassian, *Contra Nestorium*, 5, 2, CSEL, p. 303; PL 50, cols. 98-101: *"Dicis* [Cassian addresses Nestorius] *ergo Christum hominem tantummodo solitarium natum esse. Hoc utique et illa quam in primo libro evidenter ostendimus Pelagianae impietatis haeresis praedicavit, Christum hominem tantummodo solitarium natum esse. ... hoc utique etiam illa quam ante dixi haeresis asserebat, Christum non propter se colendum, videlicet quia deus esset, sed quia bonis et piis actibus deum in se habere meruisset. Ergo vides Pelagianum te virus vomere, Pelagiano te spiritu sibilare".*

[19] John Cassian, *Contra Nestorium*, 1, 3, CSEL 17, p. 239; PL 50, cols. 20-21): *"Illud sane unum praetereundum non arbitramur, quod peculiare ac proprium supra dictae illius haereseos quae ex Pelagiano errore descenderat fuit, quod dicentes quidam solitarium hominem Iesum Christum sine ulla peccati contagione vixisse eo progressi sunt, ut adsererent homines, si velint, sine peccato esse posse ...".*

[20] See above n. 9.

[21] E. AMANN, "L'affaire de Nestorius vue de Rome II", *Revue des sciences religieux* 33 (1949), pp. 226-232; and more recently K. H. KUHLMANN, *Eine dogmengeschichtliche Neubewertung von Johannes Cassianus' De incarnatione*, Diss. U. of South Africa 1983, pp. 54-55, 135-136.

[22] *Ibid.* p. 55.

[23] Prosper accused John Cassian of Pelagian leanings, because Cassian resisted extreme positions which had been developed by Augustine in the course of his crusade against the Pelagians. For a recent analysis of Prosper's outlook see P. H. WEAVER, *Divine Grace and Human Agency* (Macon, 1996: *Patristic Monograph Series* 15).

in his *Epitaph for the Nestorian and Pelagian heresies*[24] and in his *Chronicle ad a.* 431,[25] and implicitly in the entry for 428.[26] Prosper, we need to recall, was even more closely related to Leo the Great than John Cassian. He worked for years as Leo's secretary and some say as his ghost writer.[27] One might therefore assume that similar ideas might surface in the writings of Leo and in those of men who were close to him, such as Sixtus I, Leo's predecessor and the founder of Sta. Maria Maggiore. This is indeed the case.

Since the iconographer of the arch of Sta. Maria Maggiore (fig. 1) treats his material so freely, a similar freedom may be required from the modern interpreter. This approach has been tried by Nina Brodsky[28] and Suzanne Spain[29] who read the mosaics as a typological construct, playing on parallels between Isaac and Christ and Sarah and Mary. However, their interpretations have found little resonance because the iconographer of the Sta. Maria Maggiore mosaics, however unusual his approach, keeps sufficiently close to well-known events of Christ's infancy to forestall serious doubt that the events depicted are indeed the Annunciation, the Presentation in the Temple, the Adoration of the Magi, the Magi before Herod, the Massacre of the Innocents and (perhaps) the Holy Family's exile in Egypt. He does this by including key elements of existing iconography, such as the purple wool in the Annunciation scene,[30] the Persian dress of the Magi,[31] and by carefully calibrating the age of Christ in the differ-

[24] *PL* 51, cols. 153-154: "*Mecum oritur, mecum moritur, mecumque sepulchrum / intrat et inferni carceris ima subit*".

[25] *Congegrata apud Ephesum synodo ducentorum amplius sacerdotum Nestorius cum heresi nominis sui et cum multis Pelagianis qui cognatum sibi invabant dogma damnatur*, ed. Th. MOMMSEN (**place**, 1892: *MGH Auctores antiquissimi* 9), p. 473.

[26] *Ibidem*, p. 472: "*Nestorius Constantinopolitanus episcopus novum ecclesiis molitur errorem inducere, praedicans Christum ex Maria hominem tantum non etiam deum natum eique divinitatem conlatam esse pro merito ...*". The expressions "*hominem tantum*" and "*pro merito*" seem to reflect John Cassian's argument.

[27] N. W. JAMES, "Leo the Great and Prosper of Aquitaine: A pope and his advisor", *Journal of Theological Studies* N.S. 44, 2 (1993), pp. 554-584.

[28] Nina A. BRODSKY, *Iconographie oubliée de l'arc Ephésien de Sainte Marie Majeure a Rome* (Bruxelles, 1966).

[29] S. SPAIN, "'The promised blessing': The iconography of the mosaics of Sta. Maria Maggiore", *The Art Bulletin* 41 (1979), pp. 518-540.

[30] For iconographic parallels see BRENK, *Sta. Maria Maggiore*, pp. 11-13. For additional examples of Annunciation narratives which are based on pseudo-James see C. DAVIS-WEYER, J. EMERICK, "The early sixth-century frescoes at S. Martino ai Monti in Rome", *Römisches Jahrbuch für Kunstgeschichte* 21 (1964), pp. 45-48.

[31] For Magi in Persian dress on fourth-century sarcophagi see BRENK, *Sta. Maria Maggiore*, p. 27.

ent scenes: the babe in arms of the Presentation, the one or two year old of the Adoration,[32] who sits up by himself, and the seven or ten years old who walks ahead of his parents either during or after the Egyptian exile. It is only within this framework that the iconographer lets his imagination play.

Once extreme interpretations like those of Brodsky and Spain are set aside, broader areas of scholarly consensus emerge. Brenk has pointed out that the writings of Leo the Great offer an important key to the iconography of the arch.[33] Indeed, most scholars who have written about its mosaics – even those who offer contradictory readings – do quote Leo and especially his sermons, although they postdate the mosaics of the arch, in some cases by more than twenty years.[34] To do so is in a certain sense unavoidable, given Leo's large literary output and the fact that he, like Ambrose and unlike his Roman predecessors, did not hesitate to involve himself in dogmatic argument. We also know that he was already a prominent player on the Roman scene under Celestine and especially under Sixtus, the founder of Sta. Maria Maggiore. Still, the chronological problem remains troubling.

Another area of agreement has to do with A. Grabar's important proposal that the lay-out of the whole arch, its hierarchic preference for the centre and the upper registers, and also the composition of individual scenes are indebted to the iconographic conventions of late Roman public imagery (fig. 2).[35] This line of argument was successfully taken up by Beat Brenk and has never been challenged.[36] It links the mosaics of the arch to an iconographic genre which, while not entirely without textual parallels – such as panegyrics, numismatic slogans, and acclamations – is almost independent of them and was meant to be understood without recourse to a text. One might say that such an imagery, which can speak without words, represents a high point in the textualization of images. The mosaics of Sta. Maria Maggiore are far from achieving a similar level of transparency. Their opaqueness is a curious flaw, which cannot be explained away by simply pointing out that they were created before iconographic conventions had been worked out fully. One wonders whether the

---

[32] Herod ordered the killing of all male children under two years of age in Bethlehem (Mt. 2:16).

[33] BRENK, *Sta. Maria Maggiore*, pp. 44-46.

[34] See for instance J. SIEGER, "Visual metaphor as theology: Leo the Great's sermons on the Incarnation and the arch mosaics at Sta. Maria Maggiore", *Gesta* 26 (1987), pp. 83-91, who went furthest in connecting the mosaics with Leo, and S. SPAIN, "'The promised blessing'", pp. 527, 529, who argued for a very different understanding of the mosaics.

[35] A. GRABAR, *L'empereur dans l'art byzantin* (Paris, 1936), pp. 213-229.

[36] BRENK, *Sta. Maria Maggiore*, see especially pp. 24-30.

iconographer was a writer who tried to maintain the flexibility of literary expression, or whether he tried to address two different clienteles, one relatively
uninstructed and satisfied to get the broad outlines of a story, and another more
knowledgeable one, alert to novelties, hidden messages, and subtle shifts in
iconography and meaning.[37]

Apart from their reliance on the formulas of imperial and public imagery,
the mosaics may have used a body of already existing Christian iconography.
As has been pointed out by Christa Ihm,[38] the mosaics of the arch are unusual
because they combine two apparently unrelated themes: the famous nativity
cycle with its Christological overtones and a second program based on Apc. 4,
5 and 21 at the zenith and in the lowest register of the arch. This combination
is unique and its components, although doubtless related in the eyes of the
founders, need to be analyzed separately.

In dealing with the throne image above the apex of the arch Beat Brenk has
drawn detailed comparisons to other images of a similar type and especially to
mosaics in Sta. Sabina, Sta. Pudentiana and the Matrona chapel at San Prisco.[39]
None of these, however, offer quite the same combination of elements. In addition there are specific features which may have been unique to Sta. Maria Maggiore: the apocalyptic beasts, who offer crowns, the apostles Peter and Paul
standing next to the throne, the two cities in the lowest register of the arch and
the lambs waiting to enter them.

Lambs are a standard feature of early Christian iconography: they usually
proceed from two sheepfolds or from two cities towards a common goal, such
as mount Zion, the Christ Lamb, the mountain of Paradise or all three of them.
In these cases the lambs are leaving their original habitats "so there will be one
flock, one shepherd" (Io 10, 11). The cities from which the lambs depart are
usually small and plain. In Sta. Maria Maggiore, however, the cities are very
large, with splendid colonnaded interiors and golden jewel-studded walls. The
lambs are not leaving them but have assembled in front of their open gates (fig.
3). The golden jewelled walls of the two cities and their opulent interiors recall
the heavenly Jerusalem of Apc 21, 18, so do their open gates (Apc 21, 25).

---

[37] Leo acknowledges the existence of a similarly tiered audience in sermon 25, 1, *PL* 54,
col. 2).

[38] C. IHM, *Die Programme der Christlichen Apsismalerei vom vierten Jahrhundert bis zur
Mitte des achten Jahrhunderts* (Wiesbaden, 1960: *Forschungen zur Kunstgeschichte und
Christlichen Archäologie* 4).

[39] BRENK, *Sta. Maria Maggiore*, pp. 14-19.

Wilhelm Kamlah was the first to point out that the reading of Revelations underwent a massive change during the last quarter of the fourth century, when the commentary of Ticonius, or orthodox versions of it, began to replace the third-century commentary of Victorinus of Petovium.[40] As Ives Christe taught us, such a fundamental change in the interpretation of a text which provided fifth-century imagery in Rome, Ravenna and Naples with key motifs cannot be ignored by art historians.[41] Victorinus had understood the heavenly city of Apc. 21 as an eschatological and millenarian vision.[42] For him the open gates were ports through which the vanquished servants of the future saints would bring their tributes during the thousand years of Christ's rule on earth.

Victorinus's chiliastic and literal interpretation of Apc. 20 and 21 had become untenable towards the end of the fourth century. Jerome saved the Victorinus commentary from being suppressed by producing an edition which deleted the openly millenarian passages, among them Victorinus's interpretation of the golden city. Jerome replaced these passages with his own exegesis of particulars, but did not offer a coherent new interpretation of the heavenly city.[43] Although Jerome is supposed to have been already familiar with the Ticonian commentary, he avoids its identification of the heavenly Jerusalem with the Church, an identification that is typical for the commentaries of the

---

[40] W. KAMLAH, *Apocalypse und Geschichtstheologie* (Berlin, 1935).

[41] I limit myself to quoting only one of his numerous contributions: Y. CHRISTE, "Traditions littéraires et iconographiques dans l'interprétation des images apocalyptiques", in: *L'Apocalypse de Jean: Traditions exégetiques et iconographiques IIIIᵉ-XIIIᵉ siècles* (Genève, 1979), pp. 111 ff.

[42] *Victorini Episcopi Petavionensis opera*, ed. J. HAUSSLEITER (Wien, 1916: *CSEL* 49), pp. 146, 148, 150, 152, 154.

[43] *Ibid.* pp. 147, 149, 151, 153.

Ticonian tradition.[44] They also agree that the open gates of the city are a standing invitation to all, individuals and whole people, to enter the Church.[45]

This is clearly the sense of the images in Sta. Maria Maggiore, where two small flocks of lambs have assembled outside the open gates. What makes the Sta. Maria Maggiore mosaics peculiar, is the fact that there are two heavenly cities: not only "Jerusalem", the city of Christ's death and resurrection, but also "Bethlehem", the city of his birth. This doubling may refer to the twofold origin of the Church out of Jews and Gentiles, it may also be an attempt to distinguish between those who were called at the time of Christ's birth (the Magi, the Shepherds, the Innocents) and those who were called after Christ's passion and resurrection. Each group is represented by six lambs, still outside the cities but eager to enter them: All the lambs face the open gates. Some even lift their heads in a 'yearning' gesture. One might not go to far wrong in identifying them as potential Christians, desirous to become part of the Church.[46]

---

[44] The Turin fragment, the earliest and best orthodox rendering of Ticonius's commentary, lacks the text for chapters 4, 5 and 21 which are important for the Sta. Maria Maggiore mosaics. See F. LO BUE, *The Turin fragment of Tyconius' commentary on Revelation* (Cambridge, 1963: *Texts and Studies* N.S. 7). I limit myself therefore to quote from the commentaries of Caesarius of Arles (ed. in: *PL*, supplementum II, p. 392), Primasius and Bede. Caesarius, *PL* 35, cols. 2450-2451: "*Et ostendit mihi civitatem sanctam Jerusalem, descendentem de coelo a Deo'. Haec est Ecclesiae, civitas in monte constituta, sponsa Agni ...*" and "*Et suppelex muri et civitas aurum mundum, simile vitro mundo': Ecclesia enim aurea est quia fides eius velut aurum splendet, sicut septem candelabra, et ara aurea, et phialae aureae; hoc totum ecclesiam figuravit*". Primasius, *PL* 68, cols. 923A, 926C: "*'Veni ostendam tibi' novam nuptam 'uxorem Agni', id est ecclesiam ...*" and "*'Ipsa vero civitas' ex auro mundo 'similis vitro mundo'. Et licet novum non sit auro Ecclesiam figurari, quae et in candelabris aureis et phialis propter sapientiae cultum saepe concepta describitur, hoc tamen permovet quod aurum mundum vitro mundo consimilat*". Bede, *PL* 93, cols. 195CD, 197BC: "*'Veni ostendam tibi sponsam uxorem Agni', Sponsam et uxorem dicit Ecclesiam ...*" and "*'Ipsa vero civitas aurum mundum simile vitro mundo'. Ecclesia auro figuratur, quae in candelabris aureis et phialis propter sapientiae cultum saepe compta describitur*".

[45] Caesarius, *PL* 35, col. 2450: "*'Ab oriente portae tres, ab aquilone portae tres, ab austro portae tres, ab occidente portae tres': et quia civitas ista quae describitur, Ecclesia est toto orbe diffusa, ideo per quatuor partes civitatis ternae portae esse dicuntur, quia per totas quatuor partes mundi Trinitatis mysterium in Ecclesia praedicatur*". Primasius, *PL* 68, col. 923D: *Et portas duodecim et in portis angelos duodecim, et nomina scripta duodecim tribuum filiorum Israel. Scimus quidem per duodecim apostolos Dominum nostrum universis ad fidem introitum primordia aliter praebuisse*". Bede, ed. in: *PL* 93, col. 196A: "*'Habens portas duodecim'. Hae portae apostoli sunt qui suo vel scripto vel opere cunctis primordialiter gentibus Ecclesiae pandebant introitum*".

[46] Brenk suggests, that the large jewelled cities of the lost mosaic on the arch of Sta. Sabina may have served as models for the cities in Sta. Maria Maggiore. This is possible but not likely, since the message of the Sta. Sabina mosaic is less articulate. Furthermore, the date of the Sta.

This ecclesiological message is carried further by the mosaics above the apex of the arch (fig. 4). They, too, are based on Revelations and depict the throne in heaven (Apc 4, 3), the four beasts (Apc 4, 7-8), and the scroll with seven seals (Apc 5, 1). Given the Ticonian character of the golden cities in the lowest register, it is likely that the images above the arch should be seen in a similar light. However, it is somewhat more difficult to show that this is indeed the case. Victorinus had offered an extremely attractive reading of the relevant chapters. It did not contain elements which were openly chiliastic and Jerome had left it in place with only minor changes.[47] It was therefore also incorporated into commentaries which followed Ticonius in other respects. Victorinus interpreted the throne, the apocalyptic beasts, the twenty-four Elders and the book with seven seals as a coherent vision, celebrating the unity of the two testaments and the interdependence of the books of the Old and New Testaments. He also allowed that the four apocalyptic beasts might signify aspects of the person of Christ.[48]

The commentaries of the Ticonian tradition, however, even if they follow Victorinus's exegesis of chapters 4 and 5, offer an additional reading, alien to Victorinus and Jerome. It is therefore likely to be Ticonian and exhibits the ecclesiological bent which is typical for him. It interprets the elements of the vision, the throne, the twenty-four Elders and especially the four beasts as representations of the Church of the elect, Ticonius's hidden *"corpus Christi"*: the throne because it is placed in heaven,[49] the twice twelve Elders because they represent the entire Church, consisting of bishops and their flocks,[50] and the four beasts because they represent the fortitude of the Church (the Lion), her suffering (the Bull), her humility (the Man), her elevation (the Eagle).[51] Fur-

---

Sabina mosaic is by no means settled.

[47] For Jerome's version see CSEL 17, pp. 45, 47, 49, 51, 53, 55, 57, 59, 61, 63, 65, 67.

[48] *Ibid.* pp. 44, 46, 48, 50, 52, 54, 56, 58, 60, 62, 64, 66.

[49] Caesarius, PL 35, col. 2422: *"'Et ecce thronus positus erat in coelo': id est in Ecclesia. 'Et qui sedebat similis erat aspectui lapidis iaspidis vel sardii': istae comparationes in Ecclesiam conveniunt"*. Bede, PL 93, col. 113A: *"'Et ecce sedes posita erat in coelo, et supra sedem sedens'. Ecclesiam in caelesti conversatione positam Dominus inhabitat"*.

[50] Caesarius, ed. in: PL 35, col. 2422: *"Seniores totam ecclesiam dicit ... Viginti quatuor autem Seniores praepositi et populi sunt"*. Primasius, ed. in: PL 68, col. 814BC: *"Seniores totam Ecclesiam dicit ... Viginti quatuor autem praepositos complexus est simul et populos ..."*. Bede, ed. in: PL 93, col. 114D: *"'Procidebant viginti quatuor seniores' ... omnis Ecclesia, quae in praepositis constat et populis"*.

[51] Caesarius, PL 35, cols. 2422-2423: *"In animali primo simili leoni fortitudo Ecclesiae ostenditur. In vitulo, passio Christi. In tertio animali, quod est velut homo humilitas Ecclesiae significatur ... Quartum animal Ecclesiam dicit 'Similem aquilae': it est volantem et liberam*

thermore the four beasts – like the Church – praise God day and night.[52] By stressing the common meaning of throne, Elders and beasts this exegesis might have laid the ground for a corresponding combination of motifs in Sta. Maria Maggiore and especially for its unique representation of the four beasts offering crowns and assuming a role which the author of Revelations had reserved for the 24 Elders (fig. 5).

By comparing the lettering in the open book held by Peter with that in the volume of the *Ecclesia ex Circumcisione* in Sta. Sabina, Beat Brenk and others could show that the iconographer of the Sta. Maria Maggiore mosaics was interested in characterizing Peter as the apostle of the Jews and Paul – by default since we see only the binding of his book – as the apostle to the gentiles.[53] One might say that Peter and Paul have replaced the older personifications of the two Churches which appeared in Sta. Sabina, in Sta. Pudentiana, and which were also seen by Ugonio in the so-called tower of Sta. Costanza.[54] This substitution ties Ticonius's invisible Church of the Saints (his *"corpus Christi"*) tightly to the Roman see. One can only wonder what Ticonius, a brilliant but also a subversive and radical author, would have thought of this identification. To make the connection even more obvious the iconographer and his mosaicists placed portrait medallions of Peter and Paul on the small shields which decorate the front of the throne, anchoring the *corpus Christi* even more firmly in a specific geographic and historical location, Rome.

The praise of Rome and its providential role is a theme which connects the ecclesiological components of the mosaic with the childhood narrative. The portrait shields of Peter and Paul on the throne have a parallel in the image of

---

atque a terra suspensam duabus alis ... elevatam". Primasius, PL 68, col. 817B-C: *"Quocirca hinc Ecclesia regiae majestatis fortitudine fungitur et decore, quia vicit leo de tribu Juda ... Huius ecclesiae virtus in vitulo etiam, prima scilicet victima illa ratione signatur, qua adhuc quisque fidelium vincit, quando pro Christo mactatur ... 'Tertiam animal habens faciem' quasi humanum. Illam hic humilitatem Ecclesiae commendari puto ... 'Quartum animal simile aquilae volanti'. Ecclesia spiritualibus membris coelestia meditantibus volare describitur, quae nullo visu terrenae cupiditatis illecta, duorum testamentorum gubernaculis regitur sublimis provehenda"*. Bede, PL 93, col. 144 B: *"Animalia ... totam significant Ecclesiam. Cuius fortitudo in leone, victimatio in vitulo, humilitas in homine, sublimitas in aquila volante monstratur"*.

[52] Caesarius, PL 35, col. 2423: *"In animalibus ostenduntur viginti quattuor seniores 'Et requiem non habebant animalia illa': Ecclesia est quae non habet requiem, sed semper laudat Deum"*.

[53] BRENK, *Sta. Maria Maggiore*, pp. 15-16.

[54] E. MÜNTZ, "Notes sur les mosaïques chrétiennes de l'Italie", *Revue archéologique* **no?** (1878), p. 358; E. STERN, "Les mosaïques de Sainte-Constance", *Dumbarton Oaks Papers* 12 (1958), pp. 206-208.

Dea Roma, which has been smuggled into the gable of the Temple in the Presentation scene to signify the ascendency of Christian Rome over Jerusalem. Other motifs which help to connect the two branches of the program are the golden throne of the Christ child in the Adoration of the Magi, the purple clad woman in the same scene, and another highly unusual motif, the dove above Mary in the Annunciation (fig. 6). To better gauge the meaning of these elements it may be helpful to look at the iconographic background of the infancy narrative in Sta. Maria Maggiore.

A. Weis[55] was the first to notice that the infancy scenes in Sta. Maria Maggiore are related to a similar cycle on the Milan book covers, one of the few non-consular fifth-century ivories for which R. Delbrueck[56] could establish a convincing date of ca. 470-480 (figs. 7 and 8). The ivories are therefore at least 30 years younger than the mosaics of the arch. What both have in common is the use of a mix of New Testament and apocryphal stories. The Milan ivories follow the account of Pseudo-James by depicting the Annunciation in more than one episode, beginning with the scene at the well, where Mary has gone to fetch water as she prepares to spin the scarlet for the temple curtain. Our mosaics show a subsequent moment of the apocryphal account. Mary has settled down and is actually engaged in spinning the scarlet. In addition, the Milan ivories depict a third and final phase of the Annunciation with Mary and an Angel standing side by side and the Angel pointing towards a star in the sky.[57]

There are other peculiarities connecting the Sta. Maria Maggiore mosaics with the Milan ivories: the armoured Herod for instance, and Mary's festive dress, fashioned after the consular *toga picta*. In the fourth, fifth and early sixth century it was worn by women of rank (fig. 9)[58] and perhaps also by brides.[59]

---

[55] A. Weis, "Die Geburtsgeschichte Christi am Triumphbogen von Sta. Maria Maggiore", *Das Münster* 13 (1960), pp. 73 ff.

[56] R. Delbrueck, "Das fünfteilige Diptychon in Mailand", *Bonner Jahrbücher* 151 (1951), pp. 96-107; see also Davis-Weyer, Emerick, "San Martino ai Monti", p. 48.

[57] This scene includes an image of the temple with the curtain already in place, perhaps in anticipation of a subsequent scene.

[58] So for instance by Fausta on the reverse of a gold double solidus of Crispus from Trier (*Wealth of the Roman World*, ed. J.P.C. Kent, K. S. Painter, (London, 1977: *British Museum Publications*), p. 166, no. 384), by the Empress in the Cabinet des Médailles, Paris (Volbach, *Early Christian Art*, pl. 58, p. 323), and by Anicia Juliana in the dedication miniature of the Vienna Dioscurides (K. Weitzmann, *Late Antique and Early Christian Book Illumination* (New York, 1977), pl. 15).

[59] In the Old Testament mosaics in Sta. Maria Maggiore, this type of dress is given to two brides, Sephora and Rachel and to a young female attendant of Sephora (her sister?). It also appears on gold glasses which depict husband and wife, so for instance in the double portrait of

Paulinus of Nola in his poem on the marriage of Julian of Eclanum lauds the Christian simplicity of this wedding which avoids the ostentation of traditional marriage ceremonies. Within this comparison, he praises the absence of jewelled necklaces, golden dresses and fabrics interwoven with gold and purple.[60] Then there is finally the figure of Joseph. In Milan he is depicted as a carpenter who wears a *tunica exomis* and carries a large square frame-saw. In Sta. Maria Maggiore he carries a staff and wears a costume which is less class specific (fig. 6). But the sketch on the setting bed of the arch shows something quite different: a figure which holds a large square object (fig. 10). If we were in the sixth century one would think of a prophet carrying an outsized inscribed scroll in his right hand, but given the date of our mosaic and its close relationship to the Milan diptych, a frame-saw is probably the more likely reading.[61]

While the scenes of the Milan diptych follow the New Testament and the Gospel of James[62] closely, this is not true for the idiosyncratic and enigmatic Sta. Maria Maggiore mosaics. It is therefore quite unlikely that the Milan ivories depend on the Sta. Maria Maggiore mosaics. Since the date of the Milan book covers excludes a reverse relationship as well, an older model for both should be assumed. Here, the iconographer of the arch would have drawn on an existing nativity cycle combining the New Testament narrative with stories from the apocryphal Gospel of James. It already contained images of Mary in a golden *trabea* costume, the armoured Herod of the mosaics, and the carpenter Joseph of their underdrawing. In other words, two of the most discussed features of the Sta. Maria Maggiore mosaic – its use of apocryphal texts and the so-called *Maria Regina* type of the Virgin – may not have been specific choices of the mosaics' iconographer at all, but something he encountered in an older nativity cycle.

This cycle may also have provided a model for the mysterious women in purple of the Adoration scene in Sta. Maria Maggiore. In the Milan ivories,

---

Orfitus and Constantia in London (VOLBACH, *Early Christian Art*, pl. 11, p. 314). But in these cases it is impossible to know, whether the wife is depicted as a bride or whether she wears a uniform indicating her husbands rank.

[60] *Sancti Pontii Meropii Paulini Nolani carmina*, ed. W. VON HARTEL (Vienna, 1894: CSEL 30, 2), p. 239: "*Horreat inlusas auro vel murice vestes; aurea vestis huic gratia pura dei est. Respuat et variis distincta monilia gemmis, nobilis ut gemma ipsa dei*".

[61] For a discussion of this underdrawing see K. WALL, *The Iconography of the Mosaics at the Triumphal Arch of Sta. Maria Maggiore*, MA thesis, Tulane University 1983.

[62] For the Gospel of James see E. DE STRYCKER, *La forme la plus ancienne du Protoévangile de Jacques* (Bruxelles, 1961) and IDEM, "Une ancienne version latine du Protoévangile de Jacques avec des extraits de la Vulgate de Matthieu 1:2, de Luke 1:2 et 3:4", *Analecta Bollandiana* 83 (1965), pp. 365-381.

Mary's costume changes once the child is born. In the Nativity scene and in the Adoration of the Magi she wears tunic and *palla* (figs. 7 and 8) and this may also have been the case in the common model. But in Sta. Maria Maggiore Mary continues to appear in the golden *trabea* costume, perhaps in an attempt to underline her perpetual virginity.

Whatever the date and circumstances of a possible model, by the time the Sta. Maria Maggiore mosaics went up one childhood scene had a firmly established iconography: the Adoration of the Magi, which appears throughout the fourth and early fifth century on sarcophagi and in other places.[63] Always the child sits on his mother's lap. In Sta. Maria Maggiore, however, he sits by himself on a golden throne and is flanked by two women (fig. 6). The one on his right wears the golden *trabea* costume and is clearly Mary. The woman on his left wears tunic and *palla* – a type of dress, which the Milan ivory gives to the Virgin after she has become a mother. In Sta. Maria Maggiore the exalted rang of this personage is implied by the fact that she wears red shoes, a golden tunic and a purple *palla*.[64] Because she holds a scroll, Beat Brenk thought of her as the *Ecclesia ex Gentibus*. More broadly, one might think of her as Mary, "*immaculata sed nupta*",[65] personifying the Church.

An ecclesiological reading fits well with other elements of the scene, such as the presence of the Magi and the Christ child's throne, which is of the same type as the throne above the centre of the arch. Like the latter it is gilded and jewelled with a backrest and a purple cushion. It should probably be seen in the same ecclesiological and Ticonian light, as an emblem of the Church of the elect. Such a reading accords well with the presence of the Magi, who are usually understood as the first members of the *Ecclesia ex Gentibus* or of the Church as such. As the Magi bring their gifts, Christ's nascent Church – his throne – has already come into being. In other words, the iconographer of the arch connects the origin of the Church with the first appearance of Christ rather than with his death and resurrection. He may have tried to go even beyond that datum by linking the birth of the Church to the conception of Christ.

---

[63] For fourth- and fifth-century scenes of the Adoration of the Magi see VOLBACH, *Early Christian Art*, Pls. 37, 47, 103, 112, 120, 147.

[64] She is certainly not the same women as the matron in the Presentation scene, who wears neither red shoes, nor a golden dalmatic, nor a purple *palla*, but a homely mauve coloured garment.

[65] For this twofold characterization of Mary see Ambrose, *Expositio in Evangelium secundum Lucam*, II, 7, ed. C. SCHENKL (Vienna, 1897: CSEL 32, 4), p. 45; PL 15, cols. 1635D-1636A: "*Bene desponsata, sed virgo; quia est ecclesiae typus, quae est immaculata sed nupta*".

As Beat Brenk and others have pointed out, the introduction of the dove into the Annunciation scene is – as far as we know – a singular feature. It is not only without precedent, but will remain unique for several hundred years.[66] By pinpointing the moment of Mary's impregnation with a peculiar and somewhat indelicate accuracy, the presence of the dove certainly underlined Mary's role as †Mother of God' and fitted excellently into the anti-Nestorian and Christological message of the arch. It functioned just as well within the mosaics' ecclesiological programme. It may have reminded contemporary viewers of scenes of Christ's baptism, where the dove had been a fixture since pre-Constantinian times. He may also have been reminded of contemporary ecclesiological and Trinitarian images. For the likely iconographer of the arch however, somebody close to the founder, Sixtus III, or to his powerful assistant, the deacon Leo, the dove above the Mary Annunciate would have carried yet another meaning.

The *Liber pontificalis* gives a detailed but still incomplete list of foundations made by Sixtus or by third parties during his papacy. Three of them were baptisteries. In addition, Sixtus renovated a fourth, the Lateran baptistery, making it grander than it had been and adorning it with columns and a marble inscription.[67] This interest in providing multiple and occasionally luxurious settings for baptism, may have been demanded by the growth of the Christian community in Rome. It may also have been a reaction to the Pelagian challenge, since outspoken Pelagians had criticized the idea of original sin and questioned its remedy, baptism. Peter Brown[68] thought that the last lines of Sixtus's inscription at the Lateran font had an anti-Pelagian tenor. They insist on the mystical union of the baptized, and downplay the role of individual merits and demerits.[69] However, the remainder of the inscription has a strong anti-Pelagian flavour as well. It distinguishes, for instance, between personal and inherited (original) sin, and promises the sinner relief from both.[70] The first eight lines of the inscription celebrate the life-giving and regenerative power of baptism by bringing two different typologies into play. In lines 7 and 8 the

---

[66] BRENK, *Sta. Maria Maggiore*, p. 12.

[67] *Le Liber Pontificalis*, ed. L. DUCHESNE (reprint: Paris, 1955), pp. 233, 234, 235.

[68] P. BROWN, "Pelagius and his supporters", *Journal of Theological Studies* NS 19 (1996), p. 110.

[69] *Liber pontificalis*, I, p. 236: "*Nulla renascentum est distantia quos facit unum / Unus fons, unus Spiritus, una fides, / Nec numerus quemquam scelerum, nec forma suorum / Terreat Hoc natus flumine sanctus eris*".

[70] *Ibid.*: "*Insons esse volens isto mundare lavacro / Seu patrio premeris crimine seu proprio*".

baptismal water is linked to the water that flowed out of Christ's wound after his death.[71] The first four lines, however, develop a different interpretation by linking baptism not to Christ's passion, but to his conception and birth.

The *tertium comparationis* is the action of the Holy Ghost in both: the same spirit who makes the Virgin fecund also inseminates the waters of baptism. In each case a miraculous generation results: the virgin birth of Christ and the rebirth of each Christian.[72] Such metaphorical language assumes that Mary is a type of the Church. The same notion was probably suggested by the two women flanking the Christ child in the Adoration of the Magi in Sta. Maria Maggiore.

One finds very similar lines of thought in the sermons of Leo the Great. I quote from some of Leo's Christmas sermons: "As the Lord Jesus was made flesh by being born, so we are made his body by being reborn",[73] or,

> To every human being who is 'reborn' the water of Baptism is an image of the Virgin's womb – as the same Holy Spirit fills the font who also filled the Virgin, so that the mystical washing cancels in our case the sin which the holy conception lacked entirely in theirs[74]

or,

> He placed in the font of Baptism that very origin which he had assumed in the Virgin's womb. He gave to the water what he had given to his mother. For, the same "power of the most high" and "overshadowing" of the Holy Spirit that caused Mary to bear the Saviour makes the water regenerate the believer[75]

---

[71] *Ibid.*: "*Fons hic est vitae qui totum diluit orbem / Sumens de Christi vulnere principium*".

[72] *Ibid.*: "*Gens sacranda polis hic semine nascitur almo / Quam fecundatis spiritus edit aquis / Virgineo fetu genetrix ecclesia natos / Quos spirante Deo concipit amne parit*".

[73] *Sermo* 23, 5, *PL* 54, col. 203A: "*Quoniam sicut factus est Dominus Jesus caro nostra nascendo, ita nos facti sumus corpus ipsius renascendo*". English translation by J. P. FREELAND, A. J. CONWAY (Washington, 1996: *Fathers of the Church* 93), p. 99.

[74] *Sermo* 24, 3, *PL* 54, col. 206A: "*Terra enim carnis humanae, quae in primo fuerat praevaricatore maledicta, in hoc solo beatae virginis partu germen edidit benedictum, et a vitio suae stirpis alienum. Cuius spiritalem originem in regeneratione quisque consequitur; et omni homini renascenti aqua baptismatis instar est utero virginalis, eodem Spiritu sancto replente fontem, qui replevit et virginem, ut peccatum quod ibi vacuavit sacra conceptio, hic mystica tollat ablutio*". English translation by FREELAND, CONWAY, p. 95.

[75] *Sermo* 25, 5, *PL* 54, col. 211C: "*Originem quam sumpsit in utero virginis posuit in fonte baptismatis: dedit aquae quod dedit matri; virtus enim Altissimi et odumbratio Spiritus sancti, quae fecit ut Maria pareret Salvatorem, eadem facit ut regeneret unda credentem*". English translation by FREELAND, CONWAY, p. 103.

or,

> As we worship the birth of our Saviour, we find ourselves celebrating our own
> origin as well, for the Conception of Christ is the origin of the Christian people and
> the birthday of the head is the birthday of the body ... so too have we been born
> along with him in his Nativity (*cum ipso sunt in hac nativitate congeniti*).[76]

Sixtus's inscription for the Lateran Baptistery anticipated these very same ideas. Like the throne of the Christ child in the Adoration of the Magi, the dove above Mary in the Annunciation is a motif which functions not only within the Christological context of the arch but advances its ecclesiological message as well. It stresses Mary's role as Mother of God and opens the way for a baptismal interpretation of Mary's pregnancy and motherhood. In doing so it highlights the regenerative power of baptism, which had been questioned by the Pelagians. Such a reading – if correct – would link the mosaics even more firmly to Ephesus where Rome did not only add its weight to the anti-Nestorian decision but could achieve the condemnation of Pelagianism as well.

---

[76] *Sermo* 26, 2, PL 54, col. 213B: "*... et dum Salvatoris nostri adoramus ortum, invenimur nos nostrum celebrare principium. Generatio enim Christi origo est populi Christiani, et natalis capitis natalis est corporis ... Ita cum ipso sunt in hac nativitate congeniti*". English translation by FREELAND, CONWAY, p. 105. Leo revisits this complex of ideas during the Eutychian crisis. See for instance his letter to Pulcheria, 31, 3, ed. in: PL 54, col. 791A: "*De hac autem participatione mirabili sacramentum nobis regenerationis illuxit, ut per ipsum Spiritum, per quem Christus conceptus est et natus, etiam nos, qui per concupiscentiam carnis sumus geniti, spirituali rursus origine nasceremur*".

Fig. 1   Rome, Sta. Maria Maggiore. Arch.

Fig. 2   Salonica, Arch of Galerius (*c.* 297-305).

Fig. 3   Rome, Sta. Maria Maggiore, Detail of Arch. Six Lambs at the Gate of
the Heavenly Jerusalem.

Fig. 4   Rome, Sta. Maria Maggiore, Detail of Arch. Peter and Paul standing
          next to the Throne in Heaven.

Fig. 5   Rome, Sta. Maria Maggiore, Detail of Arch. The Lion offering a
         Crown.

Fig. 6   Rome, Sta. Maria Maggiore, Detail of Arch. Annunciation, Joseph and
          an Angel, Adoration of the Magi.

Fig. 7   Milan, Cathedral Treasury, Leaf of Ivory Book Cover (Rome, *c.* 470-480).

Fig. 8   Milan, Cathedral Treasury, Leaf of Ivory Book Cover (Rome, *c.* 470-480).

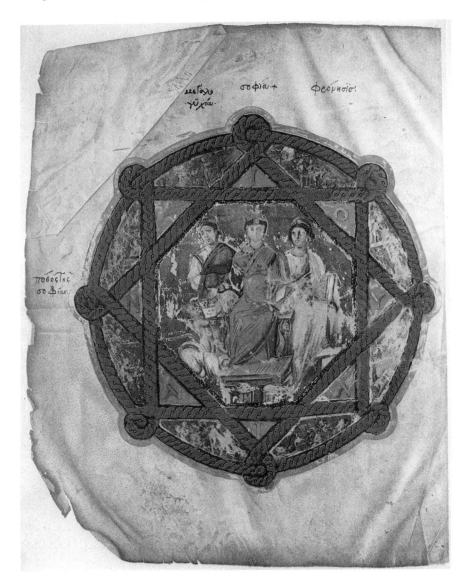

Fig. 9   MS Vienna, Österreichische Nationalbibliothek, Cod. med. grec. 1 (Vienna Dioscurides), f. 6v. Portrait of Anicia Iuliana (*c.* 520).

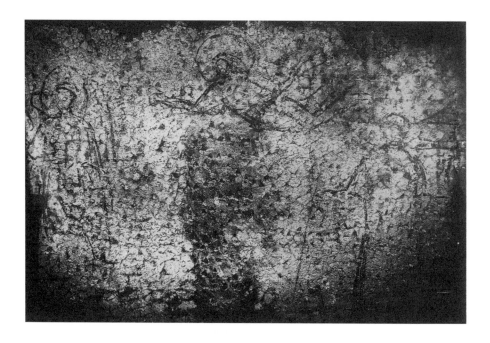

Fig. 10 Rome, Sta. Maria Maggiore. Preparatory Drawings for two Angels and
Joseph in the left upper Register of the Arch.

Les Peintures de la Crypte de Tavant:
Etat de la Question et Perspectives de Recherche

ERIC PALAZZO

A la mémoire de John Ottaway

L a réputation de l'église Saint-Nicolas de Tavant n'est plus à faire (figs. 1,
2). Tous les historiens de l'art du Moyen Age savent en effet que cette
réputation n'est pas usurpée et qu'elle s'appuie essentiellement sur le
cycle peint qui orne la crypte de l'église. De nombreux auteurs au cours du
siècle passé (le XXe!) ont à maintes reprises relevé et souligné avec force la
qualité du style de ces peintures ainsi que le grand intérêt de leur iconographie.[1]
Pour certains, le caractère exceptionnel de ce décor monumental ne peut résul-
ter que d'une 'Forgery' du XIXe siècle. C'est ce qu'a prétendu le chercheur
américain, Don Denny – spécialiste de la peinture murale médiévale –, qui voit
dans les peintures de Tavant l'oeuvre d'une main du XIXe siècle et pas
n'importe laquelle: celle de Prosper Mérimée.[2] L'un des arguments de Don
Denny pour affirmer que les peintures de la crypte de Tavant ne datent pas du
Moyen Age repose sur son incapacité à admettre que la complexité du programme iconographique résulte bel et bien d'un travail que seuls des hommes
du Moyen Age ont pu concevoir. D'autres spécialistes de l'iconographie médiévale ont rencontré, avant Don Denny, des difficultés d'interprétation face à ce

---

[1] Cet article était déjà sous presse au moment de la parution du cahier de l'Inventaire, M.
LAINÉ et C. DAVY, *Saint-Nicolas de Tavant, Indre-et-Loire* (Tours, 2002). P.-H. HENRY, *Les
fresques de Tavant: La crypte* (Paris, 1956); O. DEMUS, *La peinture murale romane* (Paris, 1970),
pp. 140-141; Dom Jean-Nesmy, "Tavant", in: *Touraine romane* (La Pierre-Qui-Vire, 1977), pp.
215-222.
[2] D. DENNY, "The Tavant crypt frescoes", *Viator* 20 (1989), pp. 327-341.

programme de Tavant, si difficile à appréhender qu'il en a découragé plus d'un.[3]

L'équipe 'Peintures murales' du Centre d'Etudes Supérieures de Civilisation Médiévale (Poitiers) a lancé en 1999 un programme de recherche interdisciplinaire autour de l'église de Tavant et de ses peintures. Faisant collaborer étroitement historiens de l'art, archéologues et historiens, ce programme propose de reconsidérer l'ensemble du dossier des peintures de Tavant. L'objectif premier consiste à étudier les peintures du triple point de vue iconographique, stylistique et technique. A côté de la recherche iconographique à proprement parler, il est indispensable de mener en parallèle une enquête stylistique – qui permettrait notamment de préciser la date des peintures – et qui sera complétée par une étude technique des peintures, ce qui n'a à ce jour jamais été réalisé. Cette étude devra essentiellement porter sur l'étude des enduits peints ainsi que sur la caractérisation des pigments. Afin de la rendre plus parlante encore, l'approche technique des peintures sera jumelée avec une étude des enduits et des mortiers de l'ensemble de l'église. Cette investigation ne pourra elle-même être menée qu'au sein d'une analyse poussée de l'architecture du monument, dossier qui reste largement à explorer. Dans ces différents cadres de recherches, il faudra encore être attentif aux apports de l'épigraphie dans la mesure où celle-ci contribue pleinement à l'approche globale d'un monument.[4] Enfin, le dossier historique du site mérite sans aucun doute d'apporter sa contribution à cette recherche interdisciplinaire. Certains chercheurs – dont Elisabeth Zadoria-Rio –[5] se sont intéressés au site de Tavant et à son histoire à cause de recherches menées sur l'abbaye de Marmoutier et ses dépendances. Malgré l'ampleur du travail déjà effectué, certains aspects de l'histoire de Tavant restent à étudier – notamment sa liturgie –, et en tout état de cause, on ne peut concevoir une étude interdisciplinaire sans une synthèse sur l'histoire du site.

---

[3]   Pour un résumé de ces questions, H. TOUBERT, "Une scène des fresques de Tavant et l'iconographie des mois", *Cahiers de Civilisation Médiévale* XVI (1973), pp. 279-286 (repris dans H. TOUBERT, *Un art dirigé, Réforme grégorienne et iconographie* (Paris, 1990), pp. 431-446.
[4]   Récemment une telle étude interdisciplinaire a été menée à Saint-Germain d'Auxerre par l'équipe dirigée par Christian Sapin, *Peindre à Auxerre au Moyen Age, IXe-XIVe siècles* (Auxerre, 1999).
[5]   E. ZADORA-RIO, "Tavant (Indre-et-Loire)", à paraître.

1. Rappels historiques et archéologiques sur le monument

Le prieuré de Tavant a été fondé en 988 par Thibault, comte de Blois qui en donna la propriété à l'abbaye de Marmoutier. L'église, qui est aujourd'hui l'église paroissiale, a été dédiée à saint Nicolas. En 1020, Burchard, seigneur de l'Ile-Bouchard, confirma la donation à l'abbaye de Marmoutier. En 1070-1071, le conflit opposant le comte de Bouchard à son oncle Geoffroy Fuel causa l'incendie de l'église, du bourg et du prieuré. En 1136, Innocent II confirma la possession de l'église Notre-Dame de Tavant et toutes ses appartenances par l'abbaye de Marmoutier. Parmi ces appartenances, il faut peut-être inclure l'église Saint-Nicolas dont on sait qu'en 1223 elle était desservie par un prêtre séculier. Dans la conclusion de cette contribution, j'évoquerai l'importance du dossier historique de Tavant pour saisir l'originalité du décor peint de la crypte et même celle des peintures ornant le choeur de l'église.

La chronologie de l'édifice est mal connue, notamment du fait de l'absence de sources textuelles. A ce jour, les spécialistes de l'architecture ont hésité entre la fin du XIe siècle, la fin du premier quart du XIIe siècle et la fin de la première moitié du XIIe siècle. Des comparaisons formelles avec certaines églises de la région et proches de Tavant sont à la base de ces propositions de datation. D'autres éléments relevant de l'étude stylistique de la sculpture de l'église de Tavant – en particulier les chapiteaux de la nef – sont venus à l'appui de l'hypothèse fréquemment admise d'une datation dans les premières décennies du XIIe siècle. A dire vrai, toutes ces hypothèses demeurent fragiles car pratiquement sans fondement autres que ceux déterminés par les historiens de l'architecture. A n'en pas douter, la reprise du dossier permettra tout d'abord la réalisation d'une véritable analyse archéologique du monument, fort complexe, et rendra plus claire la délicate question de la chronologie. L'investigation menée au sein de notre équipe sur les enduits peints et les mortiers conservés dans l'ensemble de l'édifice devrait contribuer à une lecture archéologique plus solide du monument. A l'issue d'observations faites sur place, et en particulier dans la crypte, les spécialistes de l'architecture et de l'archéologie du bâti semblent en tout cas convaincus de la relative contemporanéité de la crypte avec le choeur actuel, laissant ainsi supposer un aménagement de la crypte autour de 1120-1125 après l'achèvement de l'édifice roman et non pas comme vestiges d'un édifice antérieur (figs. 3, 4). Autrement dit, l'église primitive ne comportait vraisemblablement pas de crypte et la crypte actuelle appartient bien à la construction du XIIe siècle. On le voit, la question du rapport architectural entre la crypte et le choeur – non résolue encore aujourd'hui – est fondamentale pour la chronologie de la crypte et de ses peintures.

La datation des peintures de la crypte est un objet de controverse parfois passionnée.[6] Pour certains, oeuvres de grande innovation émergeant à partir de rien ou presque à la fin du XIe siècle, ou pour d'autres, réalisations d'un art roman 'classique' au XIIe siècle, voire de productions tardives de cet art roman (fin XIIe ou début XIIIe), les célèbres fresques de Tavant sont considérées aujourd'hui par la plupart des spécialistes comme des oeuvres de la première moitié du XIIe siècle, et même plutôt du premier quart du XIIe siècle. Le style des peintures semble les rattacher au grand courant stylistique de l'ouest de la France dans la première moitié du XIIe siècle, même si pour Don Denny ces caractères sont le fait du génial faussaire qu'aurait été Mérimée. En réalité les problèmes rencontrés par les chercheurs pour dater ces fresques touchent bien plus la question de leur lecture iconographique que de leur étude stylistique. C'est précisément ce point que je souhaite aborder succinctement ici en dressant tout d'abord l'état de la question puis en exposant les perspectives de recherches nouvelles, élaborées sur la base de réflexions méthodologiques concernant l'approche iconographique d'un programme monumental et la définition du 'lieu rituel'.

2. La lecture iconographique des peintures de Tavant: état de la question[7]

Les peintures de la crypte de Tavant rassemblent près d'une trentaine de thèmes iconographiques que l'abbé Josef Zvérina dans un article important et sur lequel je reviendrai plus loin,[8] avait classé en quatre grands groupes: le groupe biblique, comprenant notamment les représentations de David, de la Descente de Croix et de la Descente aux limbes (figs. 5, 6); le groupe hagiographique avec les représentations de saint Pierre, de saintes et peut-être de saint André (fig. 7); le groupe cosmique regroupant les atlantes et la représentation du sagittaire (fig. 8); enfin le groupe moral axé sur la représentation des vices et de la Psychomachie (fig. 9). Sans vouloir discuter la validité ou non de ces groupes, je relève simplement qu'ils laissent déjà supposer l'existence de liens iconographiques entre les sujets permettant de suggérer l'idée d'un programme iconographique global. Pour certains auteurs, tel André Grabar, la diversité

---

[6]   Voir le résumé des hypothèses par TOUBERT, "Une scène des fresques de Tavant".

[7]   Dans cet état de la question, seront seulement prises en compte les études qui ont spécialement porté sur les fresques de la crypte de Tavant.

[8]   J. ZVERINA, "Les peintures de la crypte de Tavant", *Orientalia Christiana Periodica* 13 (1947: *Mélanges G. de Jerphanion*), pp. 675-693.

iconographique du programme de Tavant ne pouvait pourtant relever que de la volonté des concepteurs de créer une sorte de florilège iconographique.[9] Pour d'autres au contraire, l'ensemble des sujets peints à Tavant tournait autour d'un thème central, la psychomachie,[10] ou bien encore, de façon plus générale, la lutte du Bien contre le Mal. Toutes ces conceptions partent de deux postulats méthodologiques qui me paraissent sans fondement réel. En premier lieu, chaque auteur à des degrés divers considère comme pratiquement établie l'identification de chacune des scènes représentées. En second lieu, tous considèrent cet ensemble peint comme un programme cohérent. Or, à mes yeux, comme déjà pour Hélène Toubert, l'existence à Tavant d'un programme iconographique cohérent n'est pas établie de façon certaine. Je reviendrai plus loin sur ce point.

Pour illustrer le premier problème, l'identification des thèmes iconographiques, je ferai à présent un bref rappel des résultats de l'article d'Hélène Toubert à propos de la représentation, insoupçonnée jusque-là, d'un couple de mois à Tavant (fig. 10).[11] A la retombée occidentale de la voûte entre la seconde et la troisième colonne à gauche de l'entrée de la crypte, les peintres ont représenté deux personnages vêtus de courtes tuniques et se dirigeant vers la droite l'un derrière l'autre. Tous deux ont en leur possession des attributs dont l'identification a été sujette à caution jusqu'à la contribution d'Hélène Toubert. Différents auteurs avant elle ont cru voir dans ces attributs des branches, des épis, des étendards et même une bourse. Le rapport entre la bourse et l'étendard a orienté certains auteurs dans la direction d'une identification iconographique liée à la Psychomachie: l'un des personnages serait l'Avarice et l'autre représenterait la *Largitas* victorieuse munie de son étendard. Soulignons que la lecture de la scène à partir de la Psychomachie s'insère idéalement dans le sens général accordé à l'ensemble du cycle de Tavant par plusieurs auteurs: la lutte du Bien contre le Mal. Evitant le piège d'une identification iconographique déterminée à l'avance par le prétendu sens global du programme peint de la crypte, Hélène Toubert s'est livrée à une enquête iconographique serrée de cette scène. Passant notamment en revue la tradition iconographique des mois de l'année durant l'Antiquité et le haut Moyen Age, l'auteur propose d'identifier le premier personnage avec le mois d'avril ou de mai, ou bien encore avec la saison du printemps tenant dans sa main une gerbe composée de trois éléments (feuilles, branches, fleurs). Le second personnage quant à lui est identifié comme la personnification du mois d'octobre ou de février, notamment à cause

---

[9]   A. GRABAR, *La peinture romane* (Paris, 1958), p. 102.
[10] M. WEBBER, "The Frescoes of Tavant", *Art Studies* III (1925), pp. 83-92.
[11] TOUBERT, "Une scène des fresques de Tavant".

de son attribut: une perche sur laquelle des canards sont suspendus. En conclusion, la scène de Tavant figurerait un couple de bon et de mauvais mois ou de bonne et de mauvaise saisons. L'évocation du cycle des saisons à Tavant trouverait sa justification dans la volonté d'inscrire le programme iconographique, axé sur le rapport entre le Bien et le Mal, dans le temps des hommes comme dans le temps cosmique, signalé à Tavant par la représentation du sagittaire.

Peu de temps après la parution de l'article d'Hélène Toubert, un musicologue de renom, Jacques Chailley, publiait un article où il proposait une nouvelle interprétation de la scène de David jouant de la harpe (fig. 11).[12] Comme le précédent auteur, Jacques Chailley poursuivait un double objectif: proposer une lecture inédite d'une scène de ce programme pour le moins complexe et tenter de comprendre cette scène à partir de la signification globale du cycle peint de la crypte. A l'instar des autres auteurs, Jacques Chailley comprend le programme de Tavant à partir d'une répartition des thèmes dans les catégories du Bien ou du Mal. A propos de l'ensemble des thèmes représentés, l'auteur relève des couples de scènes dont certaines entrent dans la catégorie du Mal et d'autres dans celle du Bien. A côté de cela, Chailley introduit une idée nouvelle, relativement peu présente dans la littérature sur Tavant avant lui et sur laquelle je reviendrai dans la dernière partie de cette contribution. Selon Chailley, la clé de lecture du programme de la crypte de Tavant est l'image du pèlerin représenté en tenue de voyage près de la porte d'entrée (fig. 12). Cette image constituerait une sorte d'image générique du pèlerin arrivant à Saint-Nicolas de Tavant et effectuant dans la crypte de l'église un parcours guidé par la succession des images, à forte connotation moralisatrice et le menant vers la Rédemption, symbolisée par le thème du Christ en gloire. L'essentiel du propos de Chailley repose cependant sur la lecture de l'image de David musicien, représenté ici selon une tradition iconographique déjà ancienne à l'époque, couplée avec celle qui lui fait face: la représentation d'un danseur. Pour Chailley, David symboliserait ici la musique bienfaisante dédiée à la louange divine, opposée à son antithèse, la musique malfaisante représentée par le danseur ou jongleur. La démonstration de Chailley semble convaincante et l'on peut ainsi se rallier à cette identification nouvelle de David opposé à la Musique pernicieuse. Pour Chailley enfin, le symbole du Bien et du Mal s'opposant dans l'ensemble du programme de Tavant, l'affrontement de la bonne et de la mauvaise Musiques trouve ici normalement sa place.

---

[12] J. CHAILLEY, "Le David de Tavant et l'*utriusque Musica*", *Bulletin de la Société Archéologique de Touraine* 39 (1981), pp. 761-779.

Dans son livre sur l'iconographie de la psychomachie dans l'art médiéval, Joanne Norman a insisté à son tour sur le rôle central de David dans la signification globale du programme de la crypte.[13] Pour cet auteur, les thèmes développés à Tavant démontre l'étendue des possibilités de l'iconographie de la psychomachie au Moyen Age. Pour elle, l'ensemble des scènes sont à lire à partir de leur connotation bonne ou mauvaise et en rapport direct avec la psychomachie. Dans cet ensemble, la figure de David est en quelque sorte le noyau, le pivot du programme iconographique. A l'appui de sa démonstration, Norman cite des textes d'auteurs médiévaux notamment, dont Hugues de Saint-Victor, où David est présenté comme la préfiguration du Christ, considéré comme le vainqueur de la mort et du mal. Sans m'étendre ici sur les hypothèses de Norman, je souligne simplement son désir de faire de David la figure de référence du programme de la crypte.

En 1947, un savant tchèque, Josef Zverina, a publié un article sur les peintures de Tavant qui me paraît sans doute comme l'un des plus importants publiés à ce jour sur ces fresques.[14] Comme tous les auteurs ou presque, Zverina commence par rappeler les trois enjeux majeurs de l'étude des peintures de Tavant: l'identification iconographique des sujets, l'idée directrice du programme et la date. Je n'entrerai pas ici dans le détail de l'article de Zverina du point de vue de son apport à la compréhension de l'iconographie des scènes, d'autant plus que l'apport essentiel de l'auteur me paraît résider dans la double interprétation liturgique et historique qu'il propose. Pour Zverina, il n'existe pas à proprement parler dans la crypte de Tavant d'idée directrice du programme iconographique, je cite:

> Nous avons à Tavant un inventaire de pensée universaliste romane, des échantillons iconographiques tirés du domaine biblique, moral, hagiographique et cosmologique qui constituent la conception du monde de l'époque. En ce cas, il n'existe pas un thème unique, précis, complet, reliant les sujets entre eux.[15]

Selon Zverina, la liturgie du lieu – une crypte – explique pour une large part le programme peint. Dans ce cadre, Zverina tente en premier lieu un rapprochement fort lointain entre les sujets des peintures et le rituel de la dédicace dont certains aspects théologiques – mais certainement pas les plus importants – tournent autour de la lutte des fidèles, constituant l'Eglise au sens ecclésiolo-

---

[13] J. NORMAN, *Metamorphoses of an Allegory: The Iconography of the Psychomachia in Medieval Art* (New York, Berne, Frankfurt and Paris, 1988), pp. 59-63 et 164-169.

[14] ZVERINA, "Les peintures de la crypte de Tavant".

[15] ZVERINA, "Les peintures de la crypte de Tavant", p. 693.

gique du terme en même temps que le bâtiment, contre le démon. En second lieu, Zverina croit détecter dans les thèmes de Tavant des liens, là encore plus ou moins clairs, avec les textes de la liturgie funéraire. Il en conclut que cette crypte avait peut-être une fonction funéraire et que la liturgie commémorative devait constituer le liant entre les différents sujets des peintures: l'Homme pécheur face à la mort.

Je terminerai ce rapide panorama sur l'historiographie des recherches sur l'iconographie des fresques de Tavant en faisant la critique de l'article de Don Denny que j'ai déjà mentionné au début de cette contribution.[16] D'emblée, je rappelle que pour l'auteur les peintures de la crypte de Tavant sont des faux certainement réalisés par Prosper Mérimée autour de 1845 alors qu'il avait en charge, en tant qu'Inspecteur général des Monuments Historiques, la restauration de monuments prestigieux du Moyen Age. A la base de l'hypothèse pour le moins surprenante mais non dénuée d'intérêt du savant américain, on rencontre l'idée qu'un tel programme, aussi complexe et difficile à cerner dans sa globalité, ne peut expliquer ses incohérences qu'en considérant qu'il a été réalisé à une autre époque que le Moyen Age. En conséquence, Don Denny suggère d'une part que les concepteurs de programmes peints du Moyen Age ne pouvaient penser de manière complexe l'iconographie et que, d'autre part, ils étaient déjà emprisonnés dans des systèmes de lectures iconographiques que des historiens de l'art plusieurs siècles après eux allaient construire. En disant simplement cela, on mesure la difficulté réelle qui oblige, pour ma part en tout cas, à ne pas suivre Don Denny dans sa démarche et son hypothèse. La seconde partie de l'article représente selon moi une géniale intuition, une belle construction intellectuelle, mais malheureusement pour l'auteur, celle-ci est rendue fragile par la critique formulée précédemment. Denny est manifestement fasciné par Mérimée qui aurait reproduit à Tavant des motifs connus de lui à cause de sa fréquentation des peintures de Saint-Savin et des sculptures de Vézelay. Malheureusement pour Denny, les motifs stylistiques ou iconographiques de Saint-Savin et de Vézelay qu'il croit repérer à Tavant sont tellement généraux et répandus dans l'ensemble de l'art roman qu'on ne peut que rejeter cette interprétation. Enfin, pour Don Denny, Mérimée appartenait à cette catégorie des grands faussaires érudits de la seconde moitié du XIXe siècle qui s'étaient alors surtout illustrés dans le domaine de la littérature. Je ne peux en dire plus à ce propos, mais Marco Mostert a relevé que Mérimée avait vigoureusement défendu Guglielmo Libri – il fut même emprisonné pour cela – soutenant l'innocence de son ami, pourtant grand voleur de manuscrits.[17]

[16] D. DENNY, "The Tavant crypt frescoes".
[17] P. A. MACCIONI RUJU, M. MOSTERT, *The Life and Time of Guglielmo Libri (1802-1869)*

3. Pour une nouvelle lecture de l'iconographie des fresques de Tavant: réflexion méthodologique et perspectives de recherche

Dans une église médiévale, le décor monumental contribue largement à la création d'un espace liturgique spécifique que l'on peut appeler le 'lieu rituel'.[18] La définition du lieu rituel tient tout d'abord à la valeur structurante de l'image. Un cycle de fresques ou un programme sculpté rythment chacun à leur manière l'espace intérieur et extérieur de l'église. Le décor monumental détermine des zones particulières dans le lieu rituel par excellence qu'est l'église, participant ainsi à la création de lieux rituels particuliers à l'intérieur du lieu rituel pris dans sa globalité. Dans l'abside par exemple, on rencontre majoritairement des thèmes iconographiques relatifs à la célébration de l'eucharistie.[19] Par exemple, de nombreuses voûtes ou clefs de voûtes d'églises gothiques comprennent une représentation de l'Agneau, symbole par excellence du sacrifice offert au cours de la messe.[20] Le décor des voûtes ou des chapiteaux de la nef obéit généralement à une iconographie différente de celle observée dans l'abside. Dans cette zone de l'église en effet, ce sont principalement les thèmes de l'Ancien et du Nouveau Testaments qui occupent l'espace rituel, offrant ainsi une narration synthétique de l'Histoire du Salut. Ce parcours visuel de l'histoire biblique n'exclut cependant pas la possibilité d'insérer ponctuellement à l'intérieur des cycles peints ou sculptés des images de nature théologique. A la jonction entre le choeur et la nef, l'espace du transept est parfois décoré de peintures présentant aussi des liens avec la liturgie, comme c'est le cas par exemple avec les fresques du XIIᵉ siècle placées sur le mur extérieur de l'une des baies du transept nord de Saint-Sernin de Toulouse et dont l'iconographie présentent des liens étroits avec la liturgie pascale.[21] Les

(Hilversum, 1995), pp. 274-279.

[18] Sur la notion de 'lieu rituel', cf. J. BASCHET, *Lieu sacré, lieu d'images: Les fresques de Bominaco (Abruzzes, 1263): Thèmes, parcours, fonctions* (Paris and Rome, 1991); E. PALAZZO, *Liturgie et société au Moyen Age* (Paris, 2000), pp. 144-147, 156-159; voir aussi J.-M. SPIESER, "Liturgie et programmes iconographiques", *Travaux et Mémoires* 11 (1991), pp. 575-590.

[19] U. NILGEN, "Texte et image dans les absides des XIᵉ-XIIᵉ siècles en Italie", *Epigraphie et iconographie*, Actes du colloque de Poitiers (1995) (Poitiers, 1996: *Civilisation Médiévale* II), pp. 153-165.

[20] P. SKUBISZEWSKI, "Le thème de la parousie sur les voûtes de l'architecture 'Plantagenêt', *De l'art comme mystagogie: Iconographie du Jugement dernier et des fins dernières à l'époque gothique*, Actes du colloque de Genève (1994) (Poitiers, 1996: *Civilisation Médiévale* III), pp. 106-153.

[21] T. LYMAN, "Theophanic iconography and the Easter liturgy: The Romanesque painted program at Saint-Sernin in Toulouse", in: *Festschrift für Otto von Simson* (Berlin, 1977), pp. 72-93.

revers de façades étaient généralement consacrés à la représentation du Jugement dernier et de l'Enfer.[22] La thématique eschatologique propre à ce 'lieu
rituel' spécifique se justifie par la fonction de façade, fortement connotée
comme 'lieu de passage', à cause de la présence des portes.[23] Ainsi, à l'intérieur
comme à l'extérieur, le mur de façade a reçu des programmes où domine la
thématique eschatologique ou, plus largement, celle des fins dernières.[24] Dans
certains cas, ces programmes sont également marqués par la théologie de la
liturgie. Par exemple, aux façades de grandes cathédrales gothiques, la succession des personnages en pied des sacrificateurs de l'Ancien Testament amène
à considérer le programme iconographique en rapport avec la liturgie
eucharistique, rappel des sacrifices offerts par les figures vétéro-testamentaires
du prêtre: Abraham, Moïse, Aaron.[25] Restons à l'intérieur de l'église pour
constater l'existence d'une zone pénitentielle déterminée au sein de la topographie liturgique de l'édifice cultuel. La localisation au portail nord des églises
de la liturgie pénitentielle n'est plus à démontrer. Plusieurs programmes sculptés sur ces portails attestent les liens étroits entre iconographie et liturgie.[26]
L'analyse minutieuse de certains éléments du mobilier liturgique ou bien d'éléments appartenant au décor monumental temporaire, telles que les tapisseries,
précisent encore notre vue de l'organisation spatiale de l'église médiévale en
fonction de la liturgie et de la notion de 'lieu rituel'. Par ces différents exemples, on voit clairement le rôle central tenu par le décor monumental dans la
définition d'espaces liturgiques particuliers appartenant tous à un seul et même
'lieu rituel', l'église.

A partir du cadre théorique que je viens rapidement d'évoquer, de quelle
manière doit-on interpréter les fresques de Tavant? A quel 'lieu rituel' global
appartiennent-elles? Participent-elles à la définition d'une zone liturgique particulière réservée à la pratique d'un rituel propre? Loin de pouvoir ici donner des
réponses satisfaisantes à toutes ces questions, on peut cependant envisager une

---

[22] P.K. KLEIN, "L'emplacement du Jugement dernier et de la seconde parousie dans l'art
monumental du haut Moyen Age", in: *L'emplacement et la fonction des images dans la peinture
murale du Moyen Age*, Actes du 5° séminaire international d'art mural, Saint-Savin 1992 (Saint-
Savin, 1993), pp. 89-101.
[23] J.-M. SPIESER, "Portes, limites et organisation de l'espace dans les églises
paléochrétiennes", *Klio* 77 (1995), pp. 433-445.
[24] P.K. KLEIN, "Programmes eschatologiques, fonction et réception historiques des portails
du XIIᵉ siècle: Moissac, Beaulieu, Saint-Denis", *Cahiers de Civilisation Médiévale* 33 (1990), pp.
317-349.
[25] L. PRESSOUYRE, "La *Mactatio Agni* aux portails des cathédrales gothiques et l'exégèse
contemporaine", *Bulletin Monumental* 132 (1974), pp. 49-65.
[26] O.-K. WERCKMEISTER, "The lintel fragment representing Eve from Saint-Lazare, Autun",
The Journal of the Warburg and Courtauld Institutes 35 (1972), pp. 1-30.

lecture nouvelle de l'iconographie du programme de Tavant à partir de ce cadre théorique au centre duquel se trouve la notion de 'lieu rituel'.

Les fresques qui nous occupent sont peintes dans un espace particulier de l'édifice, la crypte. Comme je l'ai dit plus haut, les rapports architecturaux entre cette crypte et le choeur surélevé de l'église restent à éclaircir. Mais ce *locus proprius* de l'église Saint-Nicolas de Tavant est-il véritablement assimilable à une crypte? La définition de ce lieu de l'église médiévale est certes fluctuante étant donné la grande variété de sa typologie architecturale. La 'crypte' de Tavant est bien un espace voûté à demi-enterré mais que savons-nous au juste de l'affectation rituelle de ce lieu? L'évocation par Josef Zvérina d'une crypte à vocation funéraire reste à prouver et les arguments liturgiques généraux qu'il avait en son temps invoqués ne suffisent pas pour emporter l'adhésion. A vrai dire, on ne sait si cet espace de l'église a abrité des reliques, ce qui pourrait justifier qu'on la classe parmi les cryptes étant donné leur vocation première: servir d'écrins à des reliques, permettant ainsi le développement d'un culte avec son corollaire rituel habituel, les processions. Sur ce point, l'hypothèse formulée par Jacques Chailley d'un programme peint destiné à guider visuellement le cheminement de pèlerins repentant et en voie de rédemption n'est attestée par aucune source ni par aucun élément archéologiquement observable sur place. Il est pour le moins remarquable de constater, dans l'état actuel de la 'crypte', l'absence de toutes traces d'autel. A la vue de ce qui précède, on est légitimement en droit de s'interroger sur la fonction rituelle précise de cet espace dont l'usage liturgique pour la vénération de reliques, pour la commémoration des défunts ou pour des processions de pèlerins ne semble pas attesté.

Pour sortir de cette impasse je crois nécessaire en premier lieu de procéder à de nouvelles enquêtes sur les sources archéologiques et historiques du lieu. Pour ce qui concerne l'enquête archéologique, j'ai déjà dit l'importance de la question du rapport entre le choeur liturgique et sa 'crypte'. Le dossier historique de l'église Saint-Nicolas de Tavant est quant à lui pratiquement à reprendre. En effet, aucun auteur ou presque ne s'est à ce jour interrogé sur la fonction paroissiale de l'édifice ni sur ses rapports avec le prieuré voisin qui dépendait de Marmoutier. Le vocable de saint Nicolas demeure inexpliqué. Que sait-on en effet du culte de saint Nicolas dans la région et à Tavant en particulier? Quels sont les rapports éventuels entre ce culte et l'histoire de Marmoutier qui a pendant longtemps eu la main-mise sur Tavant? Autant de questions qu'il est urgent de se poser afin de proposer des éléments d'interprétation historique du monument et de son décor.

Enfin, pour ce qui concerne l'iconographie des fresques de la crypte, je préconise une méthode consistant à réétudier chaque scène indépendamment des autres afin de cerner au mieux l'identification. Je suis pour ma part convaincu que pour un grand nombre de ces scènes la méthode donnera des résultats concluants, d'autant plus que le relevé archéologique des peintures devrait fournir des indices supplémentaires pour cette nouvelle lecture iconographique. Traiter individuellement chaque thème me paraît encore donner la meilleure garantie pour ne pas forcer l'interprétation dans un sens ou dans l'autre, en fonction d'une idée directrice du programme peint. A ce propos, l'existence d'un programme cohérent dans la crypte de Tavant reste à démontrer car tous les auteurs, Hélène Toubert exceptée, ont jusqu'à présent considéré comme acquise l'identification de la plupart des scènes et en même temps l'existence d'un programme axé autour de la lutte du Bien contre le Mal. Dans ce cadre précis, peut-être arriverons-nous à en savoir plus sur l'étrange chapiteau sculpté surmontant la colonne de droite de la première travée. L'iconographie de ce chapiteau demeure énigmatique: on y voit un homme chevauchant un animal et fouettant une femme à demie-agenouillée devant lui (fig. 13). S'agit-il là d'un thème 'marginal' à l'ensemble du programme, à l'instar des nombreuses scènes peintes dans les marges des manuscrits médiévaux,[27] ou bien s'agit-il d'une scène faisant partie intégrante du programme peint? A côté de l'identification précise de chaque thème, on peut également penser de manière nouvelle la signification de scènes dont l'identification ne fait pas problème. Tel est le cas de l'image de David dont on a vu précédemment qu'il était interprété par certains auteurs comme une préfiguration du Christ, devenant ainsi le noyau du programme peint organisé autour de la lutte du Bien contre le Mal. Pourtant, au Moyen Age, David est par excellence une figure polysémique, certes préfiguration du Christ, mais pas seulement. Par exemple, l'*Apologia David* d'Ambroise de Milan (IVe siècle) développe le thème du souverain pénitent, nouveau David.[28] Ce texte a été bien diffusé au Moyen Age, ce dès l'époque carolingienne. J'ignore s'il était connu dans la région de Tavant au XIIe siècle – ou peut-être à Tours, grand centre théologique –, mais le David de Tavant ne serait-il pas aussi la figure du souverain pénitent? Si tel était le cas, alors la fonction liturgique de la crypte aurait à voir avec la liturgie pénitentielle.[29] Une fois l'investigation iconographique nouvelle effec-

---

[27] M. CAMILLE, *Images dans les marges: Aux limites de l'art médiéval* (tr. fr., Paris, 1997).

[28] H. YAGELLO, "Histoire, exégèse et politique, l'Apologie de David d'Ambroise de Milan et les carolingiens", *Sources et Travaux historiques* 49/50 (1999), pp. 103-122.

[29] La position de la figure féminine n'est pas sans rappeler la position d'Eve sur le linteau d'Autun dont WERCKMEISTER, "The lintel fragment" a montré la signification pénitentielle.

tuée, il sera nécessaire de repenser les liens existants ou pas entre chaque thème. Là encore, les auteurs ont relevé à de multiples reprises des couples de thèmes, généralement des scènes proches sur l'espace de la voûte. Je ne suis pour ma part pas convaincu du bien-fondé de cet unique système de lecture, procédant par binomes iconographiques, et je ne serais pas surpris qu'apparaissent des connexions entre des thèmes éloignés sur la 'géographie' de la voûte. Au total, c'est une nouvelle façon de lire les fresques de Tavant qui devrait apparaître, laissant peut-être entrevoir d'autres manières de penser le ou les modes de fonctionnement de l'image, du parcours visuel proposé à l'intérieur de cet espace.

A partir de là, il faudra repenser entièrement la fonction de ce 'lieu rituel' et la façon dont son décor participe à sa définition. Pour cela, seule une comparaison avec d'autres lieux du même genre et pour lequel nous avons une meilleure documentation liturgique qu'à Tavant permettra de proposer des hypothèses sur la place et le rôle de cet espace particulier dans la topographie liturgique de l'église de Tavant.[30] Pour terminer, j'ajouterai que la lecture iconographique et l'interprétation rituelle de la 'crypte' de Tavant ne peut faire l'économie d'une investigation approfondie des rapports qu'entretient cet espace avec le choeur situé juste au-dessus (figs. 14, 15). D'autant plus que cet autre 'lieu rituel' est lui aussi marqué du sceau des images. Leur iconographie devra dans ce cadre faire l'objet d'une recherche précise. Au premier regard, le thème central des images du choeur semble être celui de l'eucharistie. En soi, cela n'est pas une originalité. En revanche les modalités iconographiques développées le sont peut-être: tels, par exemple, ces anges qui portent eux-mêmes les hosties et les patènes (fig. 16). Or depuis l'époque carolingienne, la région tourangelle a été l'un des foyers théologique de réflexion autour de la présence réelle du Christ dans l'hostie. Au IXe et au XIe siècles, diverses formules iconographiques locales attestent le rôle joué par les images au sein de ces débats.[31] Les peintures du choeur de Saint-Nicolas de Tavant ne reflètent-elles pas une fois de plus les tensions causées par ce débat propre à la théologie de l'eucharistie? Quelle que soit la réponse apportée à cette question, on ne peut exclure que les images d'un 'lieu rituel' particulier – celui de la 'crypte' – aient entretenus des rapports étroits avec celles localisées dans la zone litur-

---

[30] Voir par exemple le programme peint de la crypte de l'église paroissiale de Saint-Aignan-sur-Cher, autour de 1200, cf. M. KUPFER, "Symbolic cartography in a medieval parish: From spatialized body to painted church at Saint-Aignan-sur-Cher", *Speculum* 75 (2000), pp. 615-667.

[31] H. TOUBERT, "Dogme et pouvoir dans l'iconographie grégorienne: Les peintures de la Trinité de Vendôme", *Cahiers de Civilisation Médiévale* 26 (1983), pp. 297-326 (repris dans TOUBERT, *Un art dirigé*, pp. 365-402, 381-386).

gique du choeur et qu'à un certain moment la dynamique visuelle de l'espace de l'église ait pu les faire entrer dans un rapport dialectique et avec elles, les deux 'lieux rituels' particuliers: la crypte et le choeur.

On le voit, beaucoup de travail reste à accomplir pour tenter d'élucider cette énigme de l'art médiéval que représente le programme peint de la crypte de Tavant dont on peut légitimement penser qu'il appartient bien à la complexité de la pensée médiévale et non pas à l'esprit nostalgique du Moyen Age qui a caractérisé une partie du XIXe siècle.

Fig. 1   L'église Saint-Nicolas de Tavant. Cliché J.-P. Brouard, CESCM -
Poitiers.

Fig. 2   L'église Saint-Nicolas de Tavant Cliché J.-P. Brouard, CESCM - Poitiers.

Fig. 3   L'église Saint-Nicolas de Tavant, Intérieur. Cliché J.-P. Brouard, CESCM - Poitiers.

Fig. 4   L'église Saint-Nicolas de Tavant, Crypte. Cliché J.-P. Brouard, CESCM
- Poitiers.

Fig. 5   L'église Saint-Nicolas de Tavant. Représentation de David. Cliché J.-
         P. Brouard, CESCM - Poitiers.

Fig. 6   L'église Saint-Nicolas de Tavant, La Descente de croix. Cliché J.-P.
Brouard, CESCM - Poitiers.

Fig. 7 L'église Saint-Nicolas de Tavant. Le groupe hagiographique avec les
représentations de saint Pierre, de saintes et peut-être saint André. Cliché J.-P. Brouard, CESCM - Poitiers.

Fig. 8   L'église Saint-Nicolas de Tavant. Représentation du sagittaire. Cliché
         J.-P. Brouard, CESCM - Poitiers.

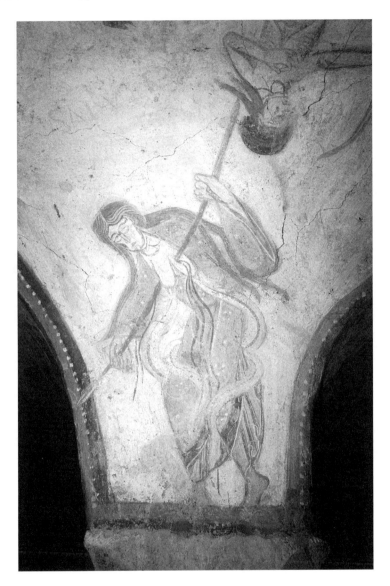

Fig. 9 L'église Saint-Nicolas de Tavant. Groupe moral (détail). Cliché J.-P. Brouard, CESCM - Poitiers.

Fig. 10 L'église Saint-Nicolas de Tavant. Représentation d'un couple de mois.
Cliché J.-P. Brouard, CESCM - Poitiers.

Fig. 11 L'église Saint-Nicolas de Tavant. David jouant de la harpe. Cliché J.-P. Brouard, CESCM - Poitiers.

Fig. 12 L'église Saint-Nicolas de Tavant. Image du pèlerin. Cliché J.-P. Brouard, CESCM - Poitiers.

Fig. 13 L'église Saint-Nicolas de Tavant. Iconographie énigmatique du chapiteau sculpté surmontant la colonne de droite de la première travée.
Cliché J.-P. Brouard, CESCM - Poitiers.

Fig. 14 L'église Saint-Nicolas de Tavant. Le choeur et le 'crypte'. Cliché J.-P.
Brouard, CESCM - Poitiers.

Fig. 15 L'église Saint-Nicolas de Tavant. Choeur. Cliché J.-P. Brouard, CESCM - Poitiers.

Fig. 16 L'église Saint-Nicolas de Tavant. Choeur (détail). Cliché J.-P. Brouard,
CESCM - Poitiers.

La Piété Princière dans l'Image et dans la Parole: Le Pavement Orné de Wiślica (Petite Pologne) de la Deuxième Moitié du XIIᵉ Siècle

ANNA ADAMSKA

E
n Pologne profonde, à environ 60 km au nord-est de Cracovie, au bord de la rivière Nida, se trouve le petit village de Wiślica. Lors des fouilles archéologiques menées dans les années 1959-1960, effectuées dans le sous-sol de l'église collégiale actuelle, on a découvert un monument extraordinaire de l'art roman. C'est un pavement orné en plâtre,[1] composé de dessins et d'une inscription (fig. 1).

Sans doute, l'analyse de ce monument (nommé couramment la 'plaque' de Wiślica) peut nourrir la réflexion à propos des manières de 'lire' une image médiévale et le texte qui l'accompagne. La lecture n'en est pas facile à cause de difficultés méthodologiques. Les instruments de recherche, élaborés par les historiens de l'art d'une part, et par les spécialistes de la littérature de l'autre,

---

[1] Pour des descriptions accessibles au lecteur occidental, voir: H. KIER, *Der Mittelalterliche Schmuckfussboden* (Düsseldorf, 1970), pp. 50-51, 64-65, 75, 138-139 et pl. 149. J.I. DONIEC, "The 20th century discovery of a 12th century Romanesque work of art at Wiślica in Poland", *The Polish Review* 1-2 (1976), pp. 113-127. A. TOMASZEWSKI, "Fouilles de Wiślica", *Cahiers de Civilisation Médiévale* 5 (1962), p. 71. Les études de base en polonais sont: *Odkrycia w Wiślicy: Rozprawy Zespołu Badań nad Polskim Średniowieczem Uniwersytetu Warszawskiego i Politechniki Warszawskiej*, 1 (Warszawa, 1963). L. KALINOWSKI, "Romańska posadzka z rytami figuralnymi w krypcie kolegiaty wiślickiej", dans: ID., *Speculum artis: Treści dzieła sztuki średniowiecza i renesansu* (Warszawa, 1989), pp. 175-214. W. ZALEWSKI et M. STEC, *Rytowana romańska posadzka w kolegiacie wiślickiej* (Kraków, 1994: *Studia i Materiały Wydziału Konserwacji i Restauracji Dzieł Sztuki ASP w Krakowie*), *passim*. Z. ŚWIECHOWSKI, *Architektura romańska w Polsce* (Warszawa, 2000), pp. 282-285.

sont très utiles pour l'historien de la communication, mais pas suffisants. Pour ce dernier, 'lire' l'image et le texte ne veut pas dire seulement 'décoder' la grammaire interne de l'image et donner l'exégèse du texte, mais aussi examiner la relation entre les deux. En ce qui regarde cette relation, l'historien de communication pose des questions concernant la cohérence d'un message, qui est porté par l'image et l'écrit en même temps, ainsi que sur l'accessibilité de ce message au public et sur les circonstances de sa réception.[2]

1. Description de l'Objet

Le pavement orné en question fut découvert dans le bourg de Wiślica, qui pendant le haut Moyen Âge polonais était un des sièges principaux du système administratif de la monarchie.[3] Probablement dans les années 50 du XIIe siècle, le prince Henri de la dynastie de Piasts (env. 1130-1165) a bâti à Wiślica une petite église romane composée d'une nef dédiée à Notre Dame. A la fin des années 60, son successeur Kazimir le Juste (1138-1194)[4] a ajouté une crypte sous le presbytère qui était soutenue par quatre colonnes. Sur le sol de cette crypte fut trouvé l'image qui nous intéresse, située au pied de l'autel, dont les restes sont encore reconnaissables (fig. 2). L'usage de la crypte dura environ 70 ans. Dans les années 30 du XIIIe siècle on a embrassé la première église dans un nouveau bâtiment, une deuxième église romane beaucoup plus grande, et on a détruit une partie de la crypte existante jusque là. Un siècle plus tard fut construite une troisième église, cette fois une grande église gothique, qui existe toujours de nos jours.

---

[2] A côté de l'épanouissement des études comparatives sur l'image et le texte, les médiévistes et les historiens de l'art qui s'occupent de l'histoire sociale des images sont conscients de l'existence de ces problèmes méthodologiques. Voir p. ex.: J.-Cl. SCHMITT, "Rituels de l'image et récits de vision", dans: *Testo e Imagine nell'Alto Medioevo*, 2 vols. (Spoleto, 1994), 1, p. 419. E. PALAZZO, "Tituli et enluminures dans le haut Moyen Age (IXe-XIe siècles): Fonctions liturgiques et spirituelles", dans: *Epigraphie et iconographie: Actes du colloque tenu à Poitiers les 5-8 octobre 1995*, éd. R. FAVREAU (Poitiers, 1996), pp. 168-170. En Pologne, l'étude comparative du sujet reste toujours mal devéloppée. Cf. B. HOJDIS, *O współistnieniu słów i obrazów w kulturze polskiego średniowiecza* (Gniezno, 2000).

[3] A. WĘDZKI, "Wiślica", dans: *Lexikon des Mittelalters*, 8.2 (München, 1998), col. 257-258. J. LEŚNY, "Wiślica", dans: *Słownik Starożytności Słowiańskich*, 6, éd. G. LABUDA et Z. STIEBER (Wrocław, Warszawa et Kraków, 1977), pp. 491-499.

[4] A propos des fondations de Kazimir le Juste et de son rôle de mécène, voir J. DOBOSZ, *Działalność fundacyjna Kazimierza Sprawiedliwego* (Poznań, 1995).

Le pavement orné de Wiślica, appartenant à la période de 'maturité' de l'art roman en Pologne,[5] est très proche du groupe de sols ornés qui sont connus en France et dans la région rhénane.[6] Très probablement, il ne fut pas le seul monument de ce type en Pologne médiévale.[7] Le pavement, de 412 cm sur 244 cm, est composé de trois éléments, dont chacun demande une description à part. Ce sont: l'image centrale de six personnes en deux 'champs', la bordure (avec une décoration florale et des représentations zoomorphiques) et l'inscription, dont on ne garde aujourd'hui qu'une partie.

Dans la partie supérieure de l'image on voit un adolescent, un ecclésiastique et un vieillard, tandis que dans la partie basse un artiste inconnu a 'dessiné' un garçon, un homme et une femme, qui tous regardent en haut, et qui tiennent leurs mains en geste de prière. Quant à la bordure, dans sa partie gauche nous pouvons voir les images symétriques de quelques animaux: un griffon en vis-à-vis d'un animal inconnu, puis une femme-centaure vis-à-vis d'un lion,[8] accompagnés par des branches et des feuilles. La bordure supérieure représente deux lions auprès d'un arbre qui est d'habitude interprété comme l'Arbre de Vie. A gauche, vers le nord, dans la bordure et le dessin des personnages, il y a une inscription en hexamètres qui est pratiquement invisible sur les photos puisqu'elle n'a pas été imprégnée de couleur noire comme le sont les dessins.

2. Problèmes de Genèse Artistique

La découverte du pavement de Wiślica a ouvert un débat entre des représentants de différentes disciplines, qui dure jusqu'à nos jours. On peut dire qu'à part l'admiration universelle pour les qualités artistiques de l'image, tout est objet de controverse: la datation précise, les artistes qui ont exécuté l'ouvrage, la technique de travail, la genèse iconographique, l'identification des personnes représentées. Après 40 ans de recherche intensive entreprise par des archéologues, des historiens de l'art, des historiens médiévistes et des philologues,[9] nous regardons cette image toujours avec la même sensation de d'impuissance vis-à-vis de l'inconnu.

---

[5] L. KALINOWSKI, "Treści ideowe sztuki przedromańskiej i romańskiej w Polsce", *Studia Źródłoznawcze* 10 (1965), p. 4.

[6] KIER, *Der Mittelalterliche Schmuckfussboden*, p. 51.

[7] Des traces de pavements ornés du XIᵉ et XIIᵉ siècle, ont été retrouvées dans la cathédrale de Gniezno et dans l'église abbatiale de Tyniec. Pour une description, voir: KIER, *Der Mittelalterliche Schmuckfussboden*, pp. 95-96.

[8] Si ce n'est pas un sphinx.

[9] Voir *supra*, n. 1.

Dans l'état actuel de la recherche, le pavement de Wiślica est considéré comme ayant été fait entre 1178-1182.[10] La technique utilisée pour le dessin n'est pas tout à fait manifeste. D'une part on parle d'une technique du dessin du contour, comparable à la technique des enluminures dans les manuscrits.[11] D'autre part, les historiens de l'art évoquent une technique de *niellage*, c'est-à-dire le mélange du borax, du cuivre, du plomb et du soufre dont l'usage est bien attesté pour l'orfèvrerie médiévale. Avec ce mélange on comblait souvent les gravures.[12] La possibilité de l'usage d'une telle technique est très importante pour la tentative d'identifier les auteurs potentiels de l'image.

Le problème des auteurs est leur anonymat. Dans les premières années après la découverte du pavement, l'attention des spécialistes qui tentaient de les identifier, fut surtout dirigée vers l'étranger, à la recherche en Occident,[13] notamment en Allemagne et Bohême[14] (mais aussi à Byzance[15]) d'analogies et de ressemblances de style qui permettraient d'identifier les artistes. Ainsi a été établie une liste de pavements ornés, fabriqués surtout en Allemagne, qui auraient pu servir de modèle pour celui de Wiślica. Cette direction des recherches semblait justifiée, puisque l'architecture de l'église de Wiślica a été inspirée de celle des églises de la région rhénane.[16] Parmi les sols ornés de cette région il y a les objets célèbres comme ceux d'Ilsenburg, de Hildesheim et de Helmstedt.[17] Dans

---

[10] Pour une analyse des différentes possibilités de datation, voir: J. DOBOSZ, *Działalność fundacyjna*, pp. 56 et 218. Dans la publication la plus récente on donne "1175-1177" (ŚWIECHOWSKI, *Architektura romańska*, p. 283).

[11] KALINOWSKI, "Romańska posadzka", p. 177.

[12] KIER, *Der Mittelalterliche Schmuckfussboden*, p. 50. L. KALINOWSKI, " 'Hi conculcari querunt', czyli kto pragnie być deptany na posadzce wiślickiej", dans: ID., *Speculum artis*, p. 218.

[13] KALINOWSKI, "Romańska posadzka", pp. 176 et suiv.

[14] Hélène, la femme de Kazimir le Juste, le fondateur présupposé du pavement de Wiślica, était probablement d'origine bohémienne. De la chapelle de Znojmo, siège de la famille d'Hélène, provient un cycle de fresques faites après 1130, illustrant l'histoire de la dynastie des Přemyslides. Ce cycle montre des analogies fortes avec l'image de Wiślica (voir B. KRZEMIEŃSKA, A. MERHAUTOVÁ et D. TŘESTIK, *Moravstí Přemyslovci ve Znojemske Rotundě* (Praha, 2000). Pourtant il n'y a pas d'arguments assez forts pour prouver que l'inspiration venait de la Bohême. Voir T. WASILEWSKI, "Helena księżniczka znojemska, żona Kazimierza II Sprawiedliwego", *Przegląd Historyczny* 69 (1978), p. 120.

[15] T. MROCZKO, *Polska sztuka przedromańska i romańska* (Warszawa, 1978), pp. 135-142, et planches 149, 158.

[16] La genèse architectonique de l'église de Wiślica fut analysée par A. TOMASZEWSKI, *Romańskie kościoły z emporami zachodnimi na obszarze Polski, Czech i Węgier* (Wrocław, Warszawa et Kraków, 1974), pp. 87 et suiv.

[17] Pour la description et une documentation photographique de ces objets, voir KIER, *Der Mittelalterliche Schmuckfussboden*, pp. 98-105.

tous ces cas la technique du travail est la même,[18] mais dans le cas polonais le programme iconographique est différent.

Dans une autre perspective de recherche on a tenté de trouver des artistes d'origine locale. Cette orientation devint de plus en plus populaire dans les deux dernières décennies, au fur et à mesure que les médiévistes polonais se montrèrent de plus en plus capables de reconstruire et apprécier les acquis de la culture des XIe et XIIe siècles en Pologne.[19] Dans la seconde moitié du XIIe siècle, les princes et les grands seigneurs fondèrent de nombreux monastères et églises et firent réaliser des objets liturgiques. Ces fondations et donations furent fréquemment mémorisées par des images de dédicace et des inscriptions.[20] On connaît des cas où le même atelier d'artistes (ou artisans), travaillait pour le même fondateur deux ou trois fois.[21] Il est donc possible que le pavement de Wiślica, lui aussi, soit l'ouvrage d'un groupe d'artistes qui travaillait pour les élites laïques et ecclésiastiques dans plusieurs régions de la Pologne. En plus, le même prince Henri qui avait bâti la première église romane à Wiślica, a implanté en 1166 à Zagość (environ 10 km à l'est) l'hôpital des frères de Saint-Jean de Jérusalem, la première maison des johannites en Pologne. Parmi les nombreux servants 'étatiques' qu'il a légués au service de l'hôpital dans l'acte de fondation, il y avait "*quatuor aurifices*", quatre orfèvres qui jusqu'ici travaillaient pour la cour princière.[22] Puisque la technique utilisée pour la réalisation du pavement de Wiś-

---

[18] G. BINDING et U. KIER, "Fussboden", dans: *Lexikon des Mittelalters* 4.5 (Zürich et München, 1988), col. 1062: il s'agit de "verschieden gefärbte Gipsmasse in einen Gipsestrich".

[19] *Kultura Polski średniowiecznej X-XIII wiek*, éd. J. DOWIAT (Warszawa, 1985), *passim*. A. ADAMSKA, " 'From memory to written record' in the periphery of medieval Latinitas: The case of Poland in the eleventh and twelfth centuries", dans: *Charters and the Use of the Written Word in Medieval Society*, éd. K. HEIDECKER (Turnhout, 2000: *Utrecht Studies in Medieval Literacy* 5), pp. 83-100.

[20] Une partie considérable de cette vague de fondations provient de la Silésie, surtout de Wrocław. Voir H. MANIKOWSKA, "*Princeps fundator* w przedlokacyjnym Wrocławiu: Od Piotra Włostowica do Henryka Brodatego", dans: *Fundacje i fundatorzy w średniowieczu i epoce nowożytnej*, éd. E. OPALIŃSKI et T. WIŚLICZ (Warszawa, 2000), pp. 11-36; T. PŁÓCIENNIK, "Les inscriptions des tympans polonais relatives aux fondations d'églises", dans: *Epigraphie et iconographie*, pp. 201-210.

[21] P. ex. l'inscription votive sur le tympan de l'église de Saint-Anne à Strzelno, qui fut fondée par Piotr Wszeborowic (1151-1175). Du point de vue de la technique épigraphique, l'inscription est identique avec l'inscription de la colonne en pierre sur la route entre Kruszwica et Kalisz, fondée par le même grand seigneur (1151). Voir B. KÜRBIS, "Inskrypcje", dans: *Słownik Starożytności Słowiańskich*, 2, éd. G. LABUDA, W. KOWALENKO et T. LEHR-SPŁAWIŃSKI (Wrocław et Warszawa, 1964), pp. 272-275.

[22] Z. KOZŁOWSKA-BUDKOWA, *Repertorium polskich dokumentów doby piastowskiej*, 1 (Kraków, 1937), n° 62.

lica semble typique pour l'orfèvrerie, on a souvent vu ces quatre artisans de Zagość comme ses auteurs.[23]

Il existe aussi plusieurs hypothèses concernant l'identité des personnes visibles dans le dessin de Wiślica. Les opinions diffèrent, pour commencer, sur la question: Est-ce qu'on a affaire à l'image de personnes vivantes ou bien mortes? Probablement nous voyons des vivants dans le carré du bas, et des morts dans le carré du haut. D'après les identifications les plus convaincantes,[24] un homme d'âge moyen, au centre de l'espace du bas, est probablement Kazimir le Juste, alors prince de Wiślica (qui depuis 1177 régnait aussi à Cracovie) et commanditaire du pavement. La dame à droite serait sa femme Hélène († env. 1206),[25] tandis que le garçon à gauche serait leur fils Boleslas, tragiquement disparu en 1182.[26]

La place centrale dans le carré du haut fut donnée à l'ecclésiastique. Le plus souvent on l'identifie à Gedko, évêque de Cracovie (mort en 1186), qui était le plus important conseiller politique de Kazimir le Juste.[27] Le vieillard à droite est probablement le prince Henri de Sandomierz († 1165), le fondateur de l'église de Wiślica et, comme un vrai *miles christianus*, présent en Terre Sainte en 1154.[28] Enfin, l'adolescent à gauche serait le fils aîné de Kazimir le Juste, lui aussi dénommé Kazimir († 1168).[29]

3. Le Message Porté par le Pavement Orné de Wiślica

L'Image

Au premier coup d'oeil l'interprétation du monument de Wiślica ne pose pas de grandes difficultés. Son programme iconographique est très simple comparé

---

[23] Voir DOBOSZ, *Działalność fundacyjna*, p. 56, n. 133.

[24] *Ibid.*, p. 56.

[25] WASILEWSKI, "Helena", pp. 115 et suiv. Z. BUDKOWA et Z. PERZANOWSKI, "Helena", dans: *Polski Słownik Biograficzny*, 1- (Kraków, 1935-) [désormais *PSB*], 9 (1960-1961), pp. 358-359.

[26] A. MARZEC, "Bolesław", dans: *Piastowie: Leksykon biograficzny*, éd. S. SZCZUR et K. OŻÓG (Kraków, 1999), p. 180. Pour d'autres propositions d'identification, voir DOBOSZ, *Działalność fundacyjna*, p. 56.

[27] Voir R. GRODECKI, "Gedko", dans: *PSB* 7 (1948-1958), pp. 367-370. Une autre hypothèse veut que l'ecclésiastique soit le prévôt anonyme du chapitre collégial de Wiślica (voir KALINOWSKI, "Hi conculcari", p. 194).

[28] J. MITKOWSKI, "Henryk Sandomierski", dans: *PSB* 9, pp. 408-409.

[29] A. MARZEC, "Kazimierz", dans: *Piastowie*, p. 180.

à ceux des sols ornés de la région rhénane.[30] La scène visible ici est une image de dévotion, représentant la prière collective, facilement reconnaissable par la position des corps et, surtout, par les gestes des mains. Les personnes représentées sur le pavement restent debout, les bras levés dans la position de l'orant. Grâce aux études de F. Garnier et J.-Cl. Schmitt (pour ne mentionner que ces deux noms) nous savons que cette attitude corporelle exprimait la disposition d'écouter la parole du Dieu.[31] Liée à la résurrection du Sauveur, elle devait exprimer aussi l'espoir de la résurrection de tous les croyants.

Le message symbolique de la bordure échappe aux interprétations faciles et peut-être à cause de cela on a développé l'opinion que sa fonction fut avant tout esthétique, comme une sorte d'encadrement de l'image principale.[32] Les animaux réels et fantastiques représentés, tels que lions et griffons, apparaissent souvent dans l'art polonais de l'époque.[33] A Wiślica, les animaux dans la partie gauche en bas, sont juxtaposés symétriquement, d'une façon que l'on rencontre relativement souvent dans l'art de l'époque. Le griffon, la femme-centaure et le lion sont bien connus des bestiaires médiévaux. Les deux premières bêtes appartenaient à un groupe plus large d'animaux fantastiques et de monstres, qui stimulait l'imaginaire de l'époque. Comme les sirènes, le Scylla, le triton et les Gorgones, le griffon, lui aussi, et surtout le centaure proviennent indirectement de la civilisation classique. Pourtant dans l'iconographie médiévale ils transmettent des associations négatives, symbolisant la folie et la duplicité.[34] La symbolique du lion est plus ambivalente.[35] Son emplacement parmi les bêtes fantastiques, en juxtaposition à la femme-centaure, suggère dans ce cas des liens avec les forces du mal. Tous les animaux représentés dans cette partie de la bordure ont la langue tirée, ce qui fait penser à l'eau comme *fons et origo rerum*, comme source de vie.[36] La bordure dans la partie droite en haut a été détruite. Ce qu'on

---

[30] Voir la typologie des programmes iconographiques établie par Kier, *Der Mittelalterliche Schmuckfussboden*, pp. 56 et suiv.

[31] F. GARNIER, *Le langage de l'image au moyen âge*, 1 (Paris, 1982), p. 223; J.-Cl. SCHMITT, *La raison des gestes dans l'Occident médiéval* (Paris, 1990), p. 290.

[32] KALINOWSKI, "Romańska posadzka", p. 185.

[33] ŚWIECHOWSKI, *Architektura romańsku*, pp. 50, 130, 132, 231, 236, 264, 269, 308, 312.

[34] Voir D. HASSING, *Medieval Bestiaries: Text, Image, Ideology* (Cambridge, 1995), p. 113.

[35] Voir U. LIEBL, "Löwe", dans: *Lexikon des Mittelalters*, 5.10 (München, 1991), col. 2141-2142; P. REUTENSWÄRD, "The lion, the lily and the Tree of Life", *Konsthistorisk tidskrift* 54 (1985), pp. 147-151.

[36] Il faut souligner que la bordure en question n'était pas la seule représentation graphique de monstres d'origine antique en Pologne. L'ornement sculpté de l'église des johannites à Zagość représente la sirène et le triton, de la même manière que les animaux à Wiślica. En plus, on trouve l'image de la sirène sur la monnaie de Kazimir le Juste, datée environ 1177-1194. Voir P. STRÓŻYK, "O fryzie z joannickiego kościoła w Zagości, monetach Kazimierza Sprawiedli-

peut voir à droite en bas est une sorte de décoration florale, sortant du corps d'un dragon, un autre animal inspirant des associations négatives.

Pourtant, pour des raisons simples de perception, notre attention est attirée surtout vers l'image de la bordure en haut, représentant deux lions auprès de l'Arbre de Vie (fig. 3). Cette partie du pavement orné de Wiślica semble différente du reste. Le dessin est moins subtil, presque brutal, peut-être effectué par une autre main.[37] L'image des lions peut être interprétée ici comme une image apotropaïque, puisque d'après l'interprétation la plus répandue le lion, roi de tous les animaux, inspire respect et repousse les démons. Pour cette raison on le voit dans la sculpture romane toujours debout, avec ses yeux ouverts. Les yeux des lions wisliciens semblent être fermés, ou bien aveugles, mais leur fonction de gardiens de l'Arbre de Vie est évidente.

Les profondeurs de la symbolique de l'Arbre de Vie, envisagées très schématiquement dans le dessin, sont bien connues.[38] Il suffit ici de dire que toute cette représentation de l'Arbre et de lions qui l'entourent, renforce la symbolique de la Résurrection et de la vie éternelle.[39]

Si l'identification des personnages est correcte, presque toutes les personnes représentées furent des membres très proches de la famille du prince-commanditaire (sa femme, ses deux fils, son frère – et lui-même). Si les choses se présentent ainsi, et si l'ecclésiastique fut imaginé sans vêtements liturgiques, on peut lire cette scène comme un acte de la dévotion privée,[40] exprimant les sentiments religieux de la famille du fondateur, sans souligner qu'il s'agit de la famille princière. Sans doute peut on approfondir cette interprétation. La composition générale, à trois niveaux verticaux, transmet un message par beaucoup plus complexe. L'ensemble des vivants au niveau le plus bas ainsi que l'ensemble des morts (au deuxième niveau) est en train d'adorer l'Arbre de Vie et, indirectement, Dieu, présent sur l'autel dans son Corps et son Sang pendant l'eucharistie. On serait enclin à penser qu'on ne regarde pas seulement le portrait collectif[41] de

---

wego i bordiurze posadzki z kościoła w Wiślicy", dans: *Flora i fauna w kulturze Średniowiecza od XII do XV wieku*, éd. A. KARŁOWSKA-KAMZOWA (Poznań, 1997), pp. 107-111.

[37] Il semble tout à fait possible que cette bordure ait été faite plus tôt, pour une autre oeuvre d'art; voir ŚWIECHOWSKI, *Architektura romańska*, p. 283.

[38] Voir R. BAUERREISS, *Arbor Vitae: Der "Lebensbaum" und seine Verwendung in Liturgie, Kunst und Brauchtum des Abendlandes* (München, 1938). Voir aussi B. BAERT, "The wall paintings in the campanile of the church of S. Nicola in Lanciano (ca. 1330-1400): Reading an unknown legend of the Cross in the Abruzzi" (dans ce volume).

[39] A propos de la connotation du lion avec la Résurrection du Christ, voir HASSING, *Medieval Bestiaries*, p. 135.

[40] KALINOWSKI, "Romańska posadzka", p. 191.

[41] Voir P. MROZOWSKI, "Przesłanie symboliczne portretu w kulturze Polski średniowiecznej", dans: *Człowiek w społeczeństwie średniowiecznym*, éd. R. MICHAŁOWSKI *et*

la famille en prière, mais aussi la communauté des vivants et des morts, qui fut présentée de manière hiérarchique sur une échelle d'êtres terrestres et célestes, circonstances qui dépassent les limites de la dévotion privée. La placement, dans la bordure, d'animaux fantastiques qui furent *grosso modo* liés à la symbolique du mal, renforce la présupposition que, peut-être, on voit ici l'image symbolique de l'église des élus, entourée par les forces du mal.

L'Inscription

Bien sûr, la lecture du sol orné de Wiślica ne peut pas se limiter seulement à l'image. On doit analyser le message de l'inscription pour juger à quel type "d'interaction entre l'image et le texte écrit" – en citant l'expression de Leslie Brubaker[42] – on a affaire ici.

L'inscription accompagnant l'image sur le pavement fut placée entre le dessin de l'Arbre de Vie et le niveau le plus haut de l'image propre, en continuant le long du bord droit qui, malheureusement, a subi une destruction (voir fig. 2). Elle a été gravée en capitales romanes. Seulement pour deux lettres, notamment pour le *E* et le *H*, on a choisi l'onciale.[43] Le texte, reconstruit par Brygida Kürbis,[44] se présente comme suit:

HI CONCVLCARI QUERVNT VT IN ASTRA LEVARI POSSINT
ET PARITER VE[RSVS CELVM CAPESCERE ITER]

Nous trouvons donc des vers en hexamètres léonins, un mètre qui fut présent très souvent dans les inscriptions latines de l'Europe Occidentale depuis le XIe siècle.[45] On rencontre des inscriptions composées de cette manière relativement souvent en Pologne au XIIe siècle,[46] mais pour celle-ci on n'a trouvé aucune analogie, ni de style, ni du lexique employé.

---

al. (Warszawa, 1997), p. 204.

[42] L. BRUBAKER, "Conclusion: Image, audience and place: Interaction and reproduction", dans: *The Sacred Image, East and West*, éd. R. OUSTERHOUT et L. BRUBAKER (Chicago, 1995), p. 206.

[43] U. ZGORZELSKA, "Wiślica", dans: *Corpus Inscriptionum Poloniae*, 1, pars 3 (Kielce, 1980), n° 198.

[44] KÜRBIS, "Inskrypcje", p. 273.

[45] R. FAVREAU, *Epigraphie médiévale* (Turnhout, 1997: *L'atelier du médiéviste* 5), pp. 100 et suiv.

[46] Cf. KÜRBIS, "Inskrypcje", pp. 272-273. Voir aussi *supra*, n. 19.

Il n'y a pas de doute qu'un tel texte, accompagnant une image de prière, possède un caractère fortement informatif. Très frappant est le contenu de ce message écrit. L'inscription ne nous informe ni sur l'identité des personnes représentées, ni sur la scène. Elle nous transmet quelque chose de plus important: les intentions et les désirs les plus profonds du commanditaire.

La construction du texte s'appuie sur deux termes juxtaposés, c'est-à-dire "*conculcari*" et "*in astra levari*", des termes qui appartiennent à des traditions mentales différentes. *Conculcari* nous renvoie à la tradition judéo-chrétienne. Dans la Bible, la forme active et passive du verbe, "*conculcare*", *conculcari*", apparaissent dans deux contextes principaux. Le premier est le contexte négatif: c'est le serviteur de Dieu, ou bien Dieu même qui est foulé, déshonoré, humilié, par les forces du mal.[47] Dans un autre contexte, c'est justement le Dieu, ou bien un homme 'juste' qui peut fouler le mal, comme on peut lire au Psaume 80:

> *Super aspidem et basiliscum ambulabis*
> *conculcabis leonem et draconem*[48]

et dans les plusieurs commentaires patristiques sur ce verset.

"*In astra*" semble appartenir plutôt à l'héritage de l'antiquité classique païenne, faisant penser au proverbe célèbre "*per aspera ad astra*" et aux spéculations philosophiques de la Grèce antique. On peut y retrouver l'idée de la transformation des âmes en étoiles qui fut développée par le néo-platonisme gréco-romain, et qui fut aussi connue de la tradition chrétienne (par exemple de Grégoire le Grand).[49] La conjonction dans l'inscription de deux traditions mentales, dont le néo-platonisme, laisse présupposer que l'érudition de l'auteur, dont l'identité reste inconnue, pouvait profiter du mouvement intellectuel qu'on nomme d'habitude 'la Renaissance du XIIe siècle'.

3. Le Caractère du Message

En résumant les observations précédentes, on pourrait dire que dans le cas étudié il existe une cohérence profonde entre le message de l'image et celui du texte, et aussi, entre ces deux messages et les moyens d'expression artistique qu'on a choisis.

---

[47] Voir p. ex. Ps 7, 6; Ps 55, 2-3; Is 63, 18; Jr 12, 10; Dn 7, 23; I Mcc 3, 51; Mt 7, 6; He 10, 29.

[48] Ps 90, 13. Voir aussi Is 28, 3; Is 63, 3.

[49] KALINOWSKI, "Treści ideowe", p. 18.

Sans aucun doute, l'inscription est extrêmement importante dans le processus de 'lecture' du message du pavement de Wiślica. C'est l'inscription qui change une image relativement simple dans une scène dramatique de *descensus* et *ascensus* des âmes au ciel. Et c'est l'inscription qui rend compréhensible l'usage économique des moyens artistiques dans cette image, privée des détails considérés superflus, comme par exemple un arrière-plan ou bien des signes de position sociale. Grâce à la technique du dessin *dal sotto al su*, les silhouettes des orants semblent libérées de leur poids, et nous témoignent leur *transitus* vers le royaume céleste. Ainsi prit forme la fonction principale de l'image comme telle, c'est-à-dire le passage vers des réalités invisibles à travers des choses visibles.[50] L'écrit, de sa part, approfondit le message du programme iconographique en confirmant les associations avec la vie éternelle, portées, entre autres, par les symboles de l'Arbre de Vie et des lions.[51]

Dans le cas étudié, les deux instruments de communication, l'image et l'écrit, tentent d'exprimer la même chose: le désir de la vie éternelle qu'on peut gagner seulement par l'humilité. Et le désir et l'humilité sont si profonds que les personnes représentées le pavement n'hésitent pas à être foulées aux pieds, puisque d'après le principe du *pars pro toto*, si leur effigie était foulée, elles étaient humiliées, elles aussi.

Ce message, transmis de façon comparable en Occident,[52] semble conforme à l'emplacement du pavement, précisément dans la crypte et devant l'autel. La présence des cryptes dans les églises polonaises du XIe et XIIe siècles est bien confirmée, mais leurs fonctions ne sont pas manifestes. Probablement, comme dans les églises occidentales, on y déposait des reliques, ainsi que dans l'autel.[53] Malheureusement, il n'existe pas de sources confirmant la présence des reliques

---

[50] J. BASCHET, "Introduction: L'image-objet", dans: *L'image: Fonctions et usages des images dans l'Occident médiéval*, éd. J. BASCHET et J.-Cl. SCHMITT (Paris, 1996), p. 8.

[51] La composition strictement verticale de toute l'image, basée sur la répétition des éléments verticaux des silhouettes, inspire l'association avec la symbolique et la valorisation du 'haut' et du 'bas' au Moyen Age. Voir A. GOUREVITCH, *Les catégories de la culture médiévale* (Paris, 1983), pp. 77 et suiv.

[52] Cf. X. BARRAL I ALTET, "Marcher sur l'image du Pape au XIIe siècle", dans: *Les images dans les sociétés médiévales: Pour une histoire comparée*, éd. J.-M. SANSTERRE et J.-Cl. SCHMITT (Bruxelles et Rome, 1999: *Bulletin van het Belgisch Historisch Instituut te Rome 69*), pp. 203-214.

[53] *Sztuka przedromańska i romańska w Polsce*, éd. M. WALICKI (Warszawa, 1971), p. 143. Voir aussi J. MICHAUD, "Culte des reliques et épigraphie: L'exemple des dédicaces et des consécrations d'autels", dans: *Les reliques: Objets, cultes, symboles: Actes du colloque international de L'Université du Littoral-Côte d'Opale (Boulogne-sur-Mer) 4-6 septembre 1997*, éd. E. BOZÓKY et A.-M. HELVÉTIUS (Turnhout, 1999: *HAGIOLOGIA: Études sur la Sainteté en Occident – Studies on Western Sainthood* 1), p. 208.

dans la crypte de l'église wiślicienne au XIIe siècle.[54] Nous ne savons rien, non plus, sur la façon de célébrer la liturgie dans la crypte, à part le fait que, probablement, elle fut célébrée par les chanoines du chapitre collégial.

Pour élaborer l'interprétation du message comme une manifestation de l'humilité chrétienne, nous devons retourner aux personnes qui désiraient être représentées sur le pavement, et surtout au prince Kazimir le Juste. Il n'est pas tout à fait clair de quelle manière il a été "le maître de l'image" (l'expression est de J.-Cl. Schmitt).[55] Pourtant des indices suggèrent que le programme iconographique et textuel du pavement est le témoignage fidèle de la spiritualité de sa cour princière.

On peut reconstruire le caractère de cette spiritualité grâce à plusieurs sources textuelles, dont la plus éminente reste la chronique érudite du maître Vincent dit Kadłubek, écrite probablement après 1190.[56] Cet ouvrage ne contient cependant aucune liste des fondations pieuses de Kazimir le Juste. Grâce à d'autres sources[57] nous savons par contre qu'il était fondateur ou bien co-fondateur de huit monastères, protecteur de la réforme de la *vita canonica*, et promoteur de la translation des reliques de Saint Florien à Cracovie, et tout ça, en dépit du fait qu'il vivait à une époque caractérisée par l'instabilité politique profonde, liée aux débuts du démembrement féodal de la Pologne. Ce qui est bien manifeste dans la chronique de maître Vincent elle-même, c'est le portrait psychologique du prince, d'ailleurs établi sous l'influence très forte des *specula principum* du XIIe siècle.[58] Le chroniqueur a ressemblé plusieurs anecdotes pour convaincre le lecteur que la formation spirituelle de Kazimir avait été plus riche que la

---

[54] A cause de l'absence des sources, il faut juger comme spéculation la proposition de l'historien d'art polonais L. Kalinowski. D'après lui, l'objet de culte dans la crypte de Wiślica aurait pu être une statue de la Vierge Marie, détruite et 'remplacée' par la statue 'miraculeuse' de la fin du XIIIe siècle qui existe aujourd'hui. Une autre spéculation est sa thèse que l'autel dans la crypte contenait des reliques apportées de la croisade par le prince Henri. Voir KALINOWSKI, "Romańska posadzka", pp. 193 et suiv.

[55] J.-Cl. SCHMITT, "Introduction", dans: *Les images dans les sociétés médiévales*, p. 19.

[56] L'édition la plus récente est: *Magistri Vincenti dicti Kadłubek, Cronica Polonorum*, éd. M. PLEZIA (Cracoviae, 1994: *Monumenta Poloniae Historica, series nova 9*). La littérature, très riche, est résumée dans l'introduction à la traduction polonaise de la chronique: voir B. KÜRBIS, "Wstęp", dans: *Mistrz Wincenty (tzw. Kadłubek), Kronika polska*, éd. et trad. B. KÜRBIS (Wrocław, Warszawa et Kraków, 1992), pp. III-CXXXI. On discute toujours la question du genre littéraire du texte: "... bien que, conservant l'ordre chronologique, c'est plutôt un traité, une moralité, un discours raisonné, que ce que nous avons l'habitude d'attendre des chroniqueurs" (B. KÜRBIS, "Maître Vincent dit Kadłubek, disciple des humanistes français du XIIe siècle", dans: *Gli Umanesimi Medievali: Atti del II Congresso dell'Internationales Mittellateinerkomitee, Firenze, 11-15 settembre 1993*, éd. C. LEONARDI (Firenze, 1997), p. 316).

[57] Pour une analyse détaillée, voir DOBOSZ, *Działalność fundacyjna*, pp. 19-63.

[58] Voir KÜRBIS, "Maître Vincent", *passim*.

moyenne de l'époque. Par exemple, il aurait aimé discuter avec les évêques les secrets de la foi et il serait décédé inopinément pendant le banquet, étant justement en train de poser une question à propos de l'immortalité des âmes.[59] Parmi les vertus monarchiques incarnées en Kazimir, ce sont la magnanimité et l'humilité qui prennent la première place.[60] Il semble qu'on peut comprendre cette vertu de manière double. D'une part l'humilité fut, chez Vincent, une vertu strictement politique, ayant la fonction dans le 'miroir du prince' qu'il voulait lui donner dans son ouvrage. Dans une telle perspective, la manifestation de l'humilité sur le pavement de Wiślica fut pour Kazimir un moyen d'expression du pouvoir politique.[61] D'autre part, on peut retrouver les traces d'un autre contexte, dépassant les limites de la 'religion politique'. Il s'agit notamment du rôle appréciable joué par la culture monastique dans la formation spirituelle du milieu princier, en premier lieu par la dévotion cistercienne.

C'est précisément lorsque Kazimir le Juste était enfant (les années 50 du XIIe siècle), que les cisterciens formèrent leurs premières communautés en Pologne. Dès le début ils ne reçurent pas seulement de riches donations des princes et des grands seigneurs, mais ceux-ci leur témoignèrent aussi un respect profond, et ils furent traités comme une élite spirituelle de la société chrétienne.[62] On connaît bien les contacts entre le milieu ecclésiastique cracovien et Saint Bernard,[63] même si on ne peut pas prouver directement que ses textes furent lus à Cracovie. Quant à Kazimir, il a fondé le grand monastère cistercien de Sulejów. Il entrete-

---

[59] Magistri Vincentii, *Chronica Polonorum*, IV, 19 (éd. M. PLEZIA, dans: *Monumenta Poloniae Historica, nova series* 11 (Kraków, 1994), p. 169).

[60] *"regem plus humilitate decorum, quam purpura conspicuum; immo nec hominem censeri, nedum principem, quem ab aliis non secernit humilitas"* (Magistri Vincentii, *Cronica Polonorum*, IV, 9 (éd. PLEZIA, p. 144). Voir J.B. KOROLEC, "Ideał władcy w 'Kronice' Mistrza Wincentego: Rola cnót moralnych w legitymizacji władzy", dans: *Pogranicza i konteksty w literaturze polskiego średniowiecza*, éd. T. MICHAŁOWSKA (Wrocław, Warszawa et Kraków, 1989), pp. 71-87.

[61] A propos du rôle des images dans l'expression du pouvoir politique, voir entre autres J.-Cl. SCHMITT, "Translation d'image et transfert du pouvoir: Le crucifix de Waltham (Angleterre, XIe-XIIIe siècle)", dans: *Les images dans les sociétés médiévales*, p. 245. Sur les fonctions politiques et idéologiques des fondations monarchiques en Pologne pendant le haut Moyen Age, voir R. MICHAŁOWSKI, *Princeps fundator: Studium z dziejów kultury politycznej w Polsce X-XIII wieku* (Warszawa, 1993), et *supra*, n. 20.

[62] Cf. B. KÜRBIS, "Cystersi w kulturze polskiego średniowiecza: Trzy świadectwa z XII wieku", dans: *Historia i kultura cystersów w dawnej Polsce i ich europejskie związki*, éd. J. STRZELCZYK (Poznań, 1987), pp. 321-342. Pour l'histoire des monastères cisterciens en Pologne, voir: *Monasticon Cisterciense Poloniae*, 2 vols., éd. A.M. WYRWA, J. STRZELCZYK et K. KACZMAREK (Poznań, 1999).

[63] Voir ADAMSKA, "From Memory", p. 94.

nait aussi des liens très forts avec les autres communautés cisterciennes dans sa principauté.[64]

En considérant toutes ces données, on peut se demander si la manifestation de l'humilité sur le pavement de Wiślica ne fut pas influencée par l'enseignement de Saint Bernard de Clairvaux.[65] Et si pour Saint Bernard l'humilité fut la voie de la contemplation,[66] peut-on interpréter l'image du pavement comme une illustration de l'expérience mystique?

Même si cette interprétation ne reste qu'une hypothèse, la connaissance des activités de prince Kazimir comme bienfaiteur de l'Église et mécène permet de conclure que le sol orné de la crypte à Wiślica s'inscrit très bien dans l'atmosphère de sa cour, où l'on savait exprimer la piété profonde par des oeuvres de haute qualité artistique.

4. Incohérences du Message et Problèmes de sa Transmission

On aimerait bien pouvoir terminer avec la conclusion optimiste et simple que l'image et l'écrit furent deux moyens choisis consciemment pour exprimer la piété princière. Pourtant, il nous faut retourner au problème général des relations entre l'image et le texte qui dans le cas étudié sont plus compliquées qu'on n'aurait pu penser.

L'analyse épigraphique nous force à prendre au sérieux la possibilité que l'inscription, ayant tellement d'importance pour l'approfondissement du message, n'a pas été réalisée en même temps que le dessin. Il semble possible qu'elle ait été ajoutée plus tard, peut-être avec un délai de dix ou vingt ans.[67] En plus, son emplacement, ainsi que la dimension modeste des lettres (3,5 cm), suggèrent que dans le plan de l'ornement l'inscription n'ait pas été prévue du tout. Si le texte a été ajouté plus tard, la question se pose immédiatement: pourquoi? Est-ce-que l'image seule n'était pas suffisamment compréhensible? Est-ce que, dans le milieu du commanditaire, soit apparu tout d'un coup un littéraire doué, et que l'on a décidé de profiter de sa présence?

[64] Pour les détails, voir DOBOSZ, *Działalność fundacyjna*, pp. 63-80. De même maître Vincent, un proche du prince, avait des liens très forts avec les cisterciens (voir KÜRBIS, "Wstęp", p. CVIII).

[65] A propos des inspirations théologiques de l'art cistercien, voir P. REUTERSWÄRD, "The forgotten symbols of God (III)", *Konsthistorisk tidskrift* 54 (1985), pp. 99-121.

[66] Voir P. ADNÈS, "Humilité: Le Moyen Age", dans: *Dictionnaire de spiritualité, ascétique et mystique, doctrine et histoire* 7 (Paris, 1969), col. 1165.

[67] LEŚNY, "Wiślica", p. 497.

L'historien pose encore une autre question: comment percevait-on un message aussi profond et aussi pieux que celui porté par l'image et le texte de l'objet? Autrement dit, comment l'a-t-on 'lu' à l'époque? Pour répondre à cette question, il serait utile d'introduire la distinction entre la lecture intentionnelle (désirée par le commanditaire) et la lecture réelle par le public, qui avait à franchir plusieurs obstacles pour recevoir le message. Le commanditaire présupposé du pavement wislicien, le prince Kazimir le Juste, était désireux de perpétuer sa mémoire et celle de sa famille sur le chemin menant au ciel.

Le public avait une tâche double: reconnaître la scène, ainsi qu'identifier les personnes représentées. Même si l'image était relativement simple et accessible, pour sa réception correcte était nécessaire une certaine capacité de comprendre et interpréter les images, et surtout le langage des gestes.[68] Quant à la capacité d'identifier les personnes du dessin après une ou deux générations, nous pouvons être relativement optimistes, sachant que la mémoire collective en Pologne médiévale pouvait embrasser une période d'environ 150 ans.[69]

Par contre, on peut sérieusement douter de l'accessibilité de l'inscription. Dans les dernières décennies du XIIᵉ siècle, à Wiślica, en raison de la présence de la cour princière et du chapitre collégial, le milieu des *litterati* en possession d'un certain niveau de *textual literacy*[70] aurait pu être relativement large. Pourtant, la mise en oeuvre de l'inscription rend sa lisibilité extrêmement difficile. Le texte, gravé mais pas imprégné de couleur contraste par rapport au fond, était visible et lisible uniquement pour quelqu'un qui se penchait directement sur lui.[71] Quand on se demande comment l'unité des images et des textes médiévaux était 'lue' et ressentie par les contemporains, dans ce cas précis il faut dire que, probablement, le texte, si important pour la pleine réception du message, n'était

---

[68] Dans ce cas le terme anglais *visual literacy* est très utile. Voir W.J. DIEBOLD, "Verbal, visual and cultural literacy in medieval art: Word and image in the Psalter of Charles the Bald", *Word and Image* 8 (1992), p. 89. Voir aussi les remarques de M. HAGEMAN, "Rituals as visual elements in early medieval texts" (dans ce volume) à propos de *ritual literacy*, ainsi que EAD., *De kleren van de keizer: Rituelen van de Karolingische en Ottoonse vorsten in woord en beeld* (diss. Utrecht, 2001), pp. 398-400 (une traduction anglaise de cette thèse est en préparation pour *Utrecht Studies in Medieval Literacy*).

[69] Cette capacité est attestée par les dépositions des témoins pendant le procès de Varsovie de 1339, du Roi de Pologne contre l'Ordre des Chevaliers Teutoniques. Voir A. ADAMSKA, "The Kingdom of Poland versus the Teutonic Knights: Oral tradition and literate behaviour in the later Middle Ages", dans: *Oral History of the Middle Ages: The Spoken Word in Context*, ed. G. JARITZ and M. RICHTER (Krems et Budapest), pp. 67-78.

[70] Toujours d'après la terminologie de W.J. DIEBOLD, "Verbal, visual and cultural literacy in medieval art".

[71] Cette difficulté est comparable à l'accessibilité discutable du plafond peint à l'église de Saint-Martin à Zillis, en Suisse.

pas du tout présent dans la conscience du public. La raison en est des plus simples: l'inscription sur le pavement de Wiślica était très mal visible.

Sans approfondir le problème de savoir qui, à vrai dire, était ce public,[72] on peut supposer que pour les gens qui venaient à la crypte pour les célébrations liturgiques, c'était l'image qui comptait. L'image belle, ascétique, qui inspirait la dévotion et la concentration. Si les yeux du spectateur suivaient la direction des regards des personnes représentées, le regard partait de l'image de l'Arbre de Vie au pied de l'autel, pour arriver à l'autel même, où se produisait le Mystère des Mystères, où Dieu même était présent dans son Corps et son Sang. La fonction essentielle de l'image, notamment celle d'émouvoir les esprits, était accomplie. Dans une telle perspective le rôle de l'inscription était tout à fait secondaire.

Conclusion

Sans doute, de chaque interprétation du pavement orné de Wiślica surgissent plutôt des questions nouvelles que des réponses définitives. Notre analyse avait pour but de démontrer les relations compliquées entre l'image et le texte qui l'accompagne. Ce qui est le plus frappant, c'est la disproportion pour le public entre l'accessibilité de l'inscription et celle de l'image. Peut-être a-t-on affaire ici à un de ces cas confirmant la règle que, de même que toutes les images médiévales n'ont pas été nécessairement faites pour être vues, tous les textes qui les accompagnent n'ont pas été nécessairement écrits pour être lues par tout un chacun. Est-il possible que le pavement orné de Wiślica confirme l'idée que les textes sont destinés aux élites et les images aux illettrés?[73]

Quand on se demande comment les contemporains lisaient cette unité de l'image et de l'écrit, on est confronté à un autre mystère encore. Comment est-il possible qu'un objet aussi extraordinaire que notre pavement soit tombé dans l'oubli total? Comme nous l'avons signalé, la démolition partielle de la crypte eut lieu dans les années 30 du XIIIe siècle. Le chroniqueur Jan Długosz, connaisseur excellent de l'histoire locale, qui écrivait dans les années 70 du XVe siècle,

[72] La question de savoir si l'accès à la crypte était réservé uniquement pour les chanoines de la communauté et pour la famille princière, ou bien pour toute la population du bourg, reste ouverte.
[73] Voir L. DUGGAN, "Was art really the 'Book of the Illiterate'?" (dans ce volume) et ID., "Reflections on 'Was art really the "Book of the illiterate"?' (également dans ce volume), ainsi que M. CAMILLE, "The Gregorian definition revisited: Writing and the medieval image", dans: L'image: Fonctions et usages, pp. 89-107.

connaissait encore l'existence de la crypte – mais seulement de la crypte.[74] Dans une absence totale d'informations le concernant, la découverte du pavement en 1959 fut une véritable surprise pour les historiens. Et, en dehors de toute hypothèse, cette unité de l'image et du texte reste un témoignage impressionnant du désir de Dieu – et de l'amour de l'art.[75]

---

[74] "*Fabricata autem erat praefata Visliciensis ecclesia a primaeva sui fundatione quadro lapide, anguste tamen et obscure, cum cripta subterranea in priscorum et praesertim Graecorum more*" (Jan Długosz, *Liber Beneficiorum Dioecesis Cracoviensis*, éd. dans: ID., *Opera omnia*, 7, éd. A. PRZEŹDZIECKI (Cracoviae, 1863), pp. 403-404.

[75] J'aimerais exprimer ma reconnaissance à M. Mieczysław STEC de l'Académie des beaux-arts de Cracovie pour les photos du pavement de Wiślica.

Fig. 1   Le pavement orné de Wiślica

Fig. 2   Le pavement orné de Wiślica (détail). Cliché M. Stec (Cracovie)

Fig. 3   Le pavement orné de Wiślica (détail). Cliché M. Stec (Cracovie)

The Ambiguity of Eros:
An Image of the Antique God of Love
in a Christian Encyclopaedia

ESTHER MULDERS

E ros, the ever-famous god of love, is probably the most ambiguous deity in the pagan Pantheon. First, there are as many aspects to his person as there are to love. Secondly, he is both the cause and the personification of the idea of love. This idol of many faces found his way into a Christian encyclopaedia (fig. 1). Apparently, the ancient god could also function adequately in a medieval Christian context.

In the image, Eros is depicted between the goddess Venus and the god Pan. The illustration is taken from an eleventh-century copy after Hrabanus Maurus's Carolingian encyclopaedia *De universo*, also known as *De rerum naturis*.[1] The Carolingian original has been lost; this copy, now kept in the monastery of Montecassino, is the oldest specimen of only three illustrated copies still extant.[2] The three gods look rather stiff and motionless. They are lining up orderly in frontal positions, while showing their attributes to the observer. They show roughly the same hairstyles, and their gowns are draped in simple folds. The accompanying text, much like the image itself, draws a very plain, descriptive picture of the god of love.

[1] Hrabanus Maurus, *De universo*, ed. in: PL 111.
[2] The Montecassino manuscript (MS Montecassino, Biblioteca dell'Abbazia, cod. 132) was, in its turn, copied in the fifteenth century. This copy is kept in the Vatican (MS Vatican, Pal.lat. 291). Another image of the god of love that was copied after the Montecassino manuscript, survives in a fragment made in Catalonia at the end of the fourteenth century and is now kept in Berlin (MS Staatsbibliothek Preussischer Kulturbesitz, lat. fol. 930).

The significance of this static image has to be understood against the background of the changing interpretation of Eros in the earlier Middle Ages. His presence in a Christian encyclopaedia is compatible with medieval tradition. Image and the text contain a similar message: the image seems a visual translation of the text. I will concentrate on the relations between the image and the text and consider the question whether this 'literal' visual image might also have been understood by itself, without the accompanying text.

Introducing the Pagan God of Love to the Christian Mind

Already at the beginning of his career, the god of love was a great expert. Hesiod (ca. 700 BC) was the first to describe Eros as a person. This Greek author regarded him as the basic impulse that caused the union between Chaos and Gaia; he saw him as the deep and creative love behind the genesis of life.[3] According to Plato, the idea of Eros was that of the regulating and uplifting principle at the basis of all good.[4] However, in later mythology a more earthly view of the deity came into being. Eros gradually turned into a troublesome child, held responsible for many cases of unhappy infatuation. The Roman poets, who were to become an important source for mythological information in the Middle Ages, gave the god a moral significance. Propertius (ca. 50-15 BC), e.g. added an allegorical explanation to his description of Eros's features.[5]

The Church Fathers transformed the Platonic idea of love into a theory of divine love that they named *agape* or *caritas*. This *caritas* became the counterpart of the various forms of earthly love they called *cupiditas*.[6] In medieval moralizing texts, such as, e.g. encyclopaedias, the god Eros personified the inferior aspect of love. As early as the fourth century, in Prudentius's very influential *Psychomachia*, Eros was the personification of the comparatively powerless *cupiditas*.

---

[3]   Hesiod, *Theogonia*, 120-123, tr. S. LOMBARDO (Cambridge, 1993), p. 64.
[4]   See, e.g. Plato, *Symposium* 178 B, 199 C-212 C, tr. T. GRIFFITH (New York, 2000), p. 15.
[5]   Cf. E. PANOFSKY, *Studies in Iconology: Humanistic Themes in the Art of the Renaissance* (New York, 1962), pp. 104-105.
[6]   PANOFSKY, *Studies in Iconology*, pp. 99-100; R. BERLINER, "God is love", *Gazette des Beaux Arts* 56 (1953), pp. 9-26; J.C.M. VAN WINDEN, *Wat heet liefde? Over eros en agape in het vroeg-christelijke denken* (Amsterdam, 1993: *Mededelingen van de afdeling Letterkunde/Koninklijke Nederlandse Academie van Wetenschappen* nieuwe reeks 56.3), pp. 5-27; A. NYGREN, *Eros and Agape* (London, 1953), pp. 41-48.

The interpretation of Eros as the weak and inferior vice of earthly love must have been what Hrabanus Maurus (780-856) had in mind when he introduced the god into his *De universo*. Hrabanus, abbot of Fulda and later archbishop of Mainz, was a most important ninth-century theological and educational author. Under his direction the monastic school of Fulda developed into a leading centre of learning. Hrabanus considered the arts and sciences important means to convey the message of Christianity.[7] *De universo* is his most comprehensive didactic work, meant for students in the monastic school who were to teach the laity after finishing their studies. *De universo* is an encyclopaedia consisting of twenty-two books, synthesizing and christianizing the entire body of knowledge inherited from Latin Antiquity.

The text accompanying the image of the god of love harks back to the beginning of the great medieval encyclopaedic tradition. Hrabanus based his encyclopaedia – including his description of the god Eros – largely on the *Etymologiae* written by Isidore of Sevilla, the first of the medieval encyclopaedists, not long before his death in 636.[8] Isidore gathered and systematized all knowledge available ito him, hoping to educate the newly converted Visigoths. In doing so, for the sake of preservation and completeness, he 'reconciled' paganism with Christianity. Of his *Etymologiae*, however, no illustrated copies survive.[9]

Image and Text

The eighth book of Isidore's *Etymologiae* is devoted to the Church. In it, Isidore lists many pagan gods. He describes of the appearance of most of them, with a short account of their significance. Hrabanus, in the fifteenth book of *De universo*, faithfully copied his predecessor.

---

[7] F. SAXL, *Lectures* (London, 1957), I, pp. 233-234.

[8] M. REUTER, *Text und Bild im Codex 132 der Bibliothek von Montecassino "Liber Rabani de originibus rerum"* (München, 1984), pp. 175-176.

[9] It has been argued that a large number of the images of *De universo*, including the image of Eros, were based on a now lost illustrated specimen of the *Etymologiae*. Be this as it may, it is generally accepted that the miniatures in the Montecassino manuscript were copied after an illustrated Carolingian specimen which in its turn reached back to a model (or models) conceived in the Mediterranean area. Cf., e.g. F. SAXL, *Lectures* (London, 1957), I, pp. 228-241; N. HIMMELMANN, *Antike Götter im Mittelalter* (Mainz, 1986), pp. 8-11; REUTER, *Text und Bild*, pp. 22-32.

Both authors mention Aphrodite and Pan with Eros. From Antiquity onwards, Eros had usually been associated with Aphrodite.[10] The appearance of
the goddess, however, is not described in either of the two medieval
encyclopaedias. Pan, the amorous pastoral god, is depicted – as he is also described – with goat's feet and pan pipes. The beams of the sun and the moon
shine from his temples. The staff in his left hand, possibly a shepherd's crook,
is not mentioned in the texts.[11] In both encyclopaedias, the god Eros is described as a lascivious demon. He is winged, because he is a flighty and whim-
sical demon. He is depicted as a child, because he is unwise and irrational. He
is shown carrying an arrow and a torch. With his arrow he stabs the heart. With
his torch he sets the heart on fire:

> *Cupidinem vocatum ferunt propter amorem. Est enim daemon fornicationis. Qui*
> *ideo alatus pingitur, quia nihil amantibus levius, nihil mutabilius invenitur. Puer*
> *pingitur, quia stultus est et irrationabilis amor. Sagittam et facem tenere fingitur.*
> *Sagittam, quia amor cor vulnerat; facem, quia inflammat.*[12]

In writing about the god of love, Isidore was inspired by the Roman poet
Propertius.[13] In the second book of his *Elegies*, in which Propertius mainly
sings of his beloved Cynthia (also known as Hostia), he gives a description of
a painting of Eros. He also furnishes the appearance and the attributes of the
deity with a meaning:

> *Quicumque ille fuit, puerum qui pinxit Amorem,*
> *nonne putas miras hunc habuisse manus?*
> *is primum vidit sine sensu vivere amantis,*
> *et levibus curis magna perire bona.*
> *idem non frustra ventosas addidit alas,*
> *fecit et humano corde volare deum:*
> *scilicet alterna quoniam iactamur in unda,*
> *nostraque non ullis permanet aura locis.*
> *et merito hamatis manus et armata sagittis,*
> *et pharetra ex umero Cnosia utroque iacet:*
> *ante ferit quoniam tuti quam cernimus hostem,*

---

[10] In Hesiod, *Theogonia*, 201, Eros was a witness to her birth and became her companion.
Later mythological traditions describe Eros as her son.
[11] Cf. REUTER, *Text und Bild*, pp. 175-176.
[12] Isidori Hispalensis Episcopi, *Etymologiarum Sive Originum, libri XX*, ed. W.M. LINDSAY,
2 vols. (Oxford, 1911), 1, VIII, 80, and Hrabanus Maurus, *De Universo*, XV, 6, *PL* 3, col. 432.
[13] Cf. PANOFSKY, *Studies in Iconology*, pp. 104-105.

nec quisquam ex illo vulnere sanis abit.

Whoever he was who painted Love as a boy, think you not that he had won-
drous skills? He was the first to see that lovers behave childishly and that great
blessings are lost through their petty passions. He also added fluttering wings,
and made the god to fly in the human heart, since in truth we are tossed by the
waves this way and that, and with us the wind never sits in the same quarter.
And justly his hand is armed with barbed arrows, and a Cretan quiver is suspended from his shoulders, since he strikes while we feel save and do not see
the enemy, and from that wound no one departs unscathed.[14]

Propertius compares the childlike nature of the god to the thoughtlessness of
lovers. His wings, flying in the wind, show how fancifully the god flits about
in the heart; and lovers, too, lack all direction. His arrows suggest the pain the
god inflicts on the heart.

Indirectly, therefore, the text about the god of love in Hrabanus's
encyclopaedia, copied from Isidore, goes back to a tangible painting of the god.
Such paintings were probably meant to illustrate, or to call to mind, a myth
about Eros. Propertius, trying to reveal his own feelings, gave a moral meaning
to the outward appearances of the god in the visual image. In doing so, he un-
wittingly made his work into a fascinating source of information for writers
such as Isidore, whose self-appointed task it was to adjust ancient learning to
the Christian mind by explaining its underlying moral meaning. Propertius does
not mention the torch depicted in the Montecassino image; it was, however, one
of Eros's usual attributes in Antiquity.[15] Apparently Isidore, with his exceptional knowledge of the Greek and Latin writings (in the *Etymologiae* he cited
as many as 154 ancient authors), must have come across the torch in the work
of another author. He explains the torch in a familiar moralizing fashion: it is
used by Eros to set the heart on fire.[16]

Clearly the text accompanying the image of Eros in the Montecassino
manuscript reaches back to an antique personification of love as an annoying
toddler who attacks people at random, hurting them with his arrows, and man-
aging to transmit his infantility to his victims, in whose hearts he will flit

---

[14] Propertius, *Elegiae*, II, 12. Translation adapted from Propertius, *Elegies*, ed. and transl.
G.P. GOULD (Cambridge, 1990).

[15] The torch can be found, e.g. in Ovid, *Metamorphoses* I, 461 ff. or in the *Ars Amatoria*,
I, 22, of the same author.

[16] PANOFSKY, *Studies in Iconology*, pp. 104-105.

around capriciously. Seen in this way the god of love is the cause and personification of infatuation.

The Eros figure in the Montecassino image, then, is a personification. He is a supernatural, winged person. He carries attributes that must have hidden meanings. This Eros is showing his weapons to the observer, while looking straight at him. The god of love himself seems to suggest that a deeper meaning should be read into his appearance. What this meaning might be is explained in the accompanying text.

When one looks at the image, not much is left of the foolish amorousness the god had personified in Propertius's text – the ultimate source of Hrabanus's text as copied in the Montecassino manuscript. This Eros is hardly about to shoot one of his arrows, nor can we imagine him flying about lightheartedly. In the Montecassino image, Eros is hardly a reckless toddler. He is a static entity, an icon of his own self.

The Defeated Eros

Eros's symbolic meaning as expressed by Propertius must have appealed to medieval authors. Hesiod had described the love represented by Eros as life, and as present before time and space; the Eros of Plato was the ordering principle at the basis of all good. Both of these interpretations are reminiscent of the creative love of the Christian God. This connection between divine creative love and earthly reproductive love was neglected by medieval scholars. The Church Fathers seized on the duality of love, emphasizing the existence of a divine love and an earthly love. Eros was dissociated from divine love and turned into a symbol of earthly love.[17] In Christian medieval thinking he did not enjoy a very high reputation.

Both Propertius and Isidore and his follower Hrabanus refer to Eros's earthly aspect in their descriptions of the god of love. The deity changed position as time went on. The static Eros in the Montecassino manuscript has become a symbol of the medieval vice of earthly love, no longer connected to either the active deity known from early classical mythology or the personification of Propertius's fanciful emotions.

Prudentius's *Psychomachia* showed the god for the first time as the personification of the vice of *cupiditas*, and, for the last time in centuries, showed him

---

[17] PANOFSKY, *Studies in Iconology*, pp. 99-100; BERLINER, "God is love"; VAN WINDEN, *Wat heet liefde?*, pp. 5-27; NYGREN, *Eros and Agape*, pp. 41-48.

in action.[18] Prudentius reworked the antique notion of the perpetual mental battle between good and evil into a Christian setting. In his *Psychomachia*, female personifications of the virtues and vices are staged as warriors in an arena, fighting a bloody battle. Eros appears on the scene as a follower of the vice of Luxuria (Voluptuousness), which has taken the form of the goddess Venus. The other vices are shooting arrows, but Luxuria strews rose petals and violets. These unexpected tactics confuse the virtues. They are about to surrender to Luxuria when, just in time, the virtue of Sobrietas (Modesty) leaps in front of Luxuria's chariot, carrying a cross in her hand. The horses are frightened and jump; the chariot topples over and Sobrietas kills Luxuria with one blow of a stone. Luxuria's flock is terrified and is forced to flee. Eros, pale with fear, throws off his bow and arrows. At the end of the battle the virtues are triumphant.[19]

The defeat of the vices in the *Psychomachia* marks an important shift in the interpretation of Eros. The motionless Eros of the Montecassino image is the personification of the vice of earthly love, beaten by Christianity and imprisoned inside the system of a Christian encyclopaedia. Eros, whom not even the Olympic gods could resist, could not lord it over medieval Christianity. The perpetual battle in the mind seemed to have come to its conclusion. The high-handedness with which the ancient god used to shoot his arrows seems finished. And had the god still succeeded in penetrating the heart, he would no longer have found any room there to flit about as whimsically as he used to. Both love and lover had been encapsulated into a new moral system, the framework of Christianity, one of the symbols of which was the Christian encyclopaedia.

Eros as a Medieval Symbol

The medieval predicament of earthly Eros differed from the Roman one. It must be noted that the interest taken by Propertius, Isidore and Hrabanus in the deity, stemmed from different motives. To Propertius, the god of love had been

---

[18] The interpretation of Eros as a passive and impotent vice did not change until the thirteenth century. Then, within the context of courtly love, a new synthesis was found between the earthly and the divine aspects of love. At the same time, the old antithesis persisted. The new reconciliation between the two extremes within the concept of courtly love was by no means a rebirth of the ancient glory of Eros, but a medieval, 'encyclopedic' construct meant to harmonize the worldly with the religious. See PANOFSKY, *Studies in Iconology*, p. 100; J. HUIZINGA, *Herfsttij der Middeleeuwen* (repr. Groningen, 1984), pp. 103-116.

[19] Prudentius, *Psychomachia*, 310-438, ed. M. LAVARENNE (Paris, 1933), pp. 158-168.

a suitable personification of his own emotions. An image of the god inspired the poet to a very personal statement. To Isidore and Hrabanus, Eros was a common reality. The ancient god of love was part of the pre-Christian inheritance that was to be preserved – and to be pressed into Christian morality's service. Similarly, both image and text in the Montecassino manuscript conjure up Eros as a figure from the classical past whose presence was meant to remind the audience of his prevailing Christian significance. This early medieval attitude towards antique learning marks the beginning of the mythological exegetic tradition that was to grow to enormous proportions in the twelfth century.

Propertius and Isidore were free to choose or to create any interpretation of Eros to answer their needs. As we have seen, the idea of the god of love had a most malliable content. The image of the deity, on the other hand, is very constant. Eros is consistently depicted as winged, carrying his bow and arrows and possibly his torch. His apparent meaning as the cause of love is equally unchanging. The kind of love he causes and personifies, however, is subject to change to such a degree that one might even say that the personification – the 'image' of love – is more real than the realities referred to. Eros can be seen as a natural phenomenon that could be furnished with variable symbolic meanings. This manoeuvres the god in a special position. In Antiquity he could be regarded as a visible reality. Propertius saw a painting of Eros which most likely referred to a myth, but the poet considered the painting a suitable means to impart real feelings to his readers. Propertius did not create a personification but found an existing figure, whose content could be modified to such an extent that it could be used as a symbol of his own emotions. In doing so, he imbued an existing figure with renewed meaning.

The inactive Eros in the Montecassino manuscript hardly reminds one of either a myth or a human emotion. The accompanying text is a bare catalogue of Eros's distinguishing marks, supplied with an unadorned explanation of their meaning. This image shows an Eros consisting of the sum of the traits of his character as represented in his outward features. He is placed between other motionless pagan gods, who also show their personal appearance to the viewer with the purpose of calling to mind their moral meaning.

Different from Propertius, Isidore had not been seeking to personify an abstract idea – quite the contrary. Isidore had been confronted with a fairly real Eros, a part of existence he was expected to interpret in an appropriate way, and to fit it into the system of Christian thought. Although both authors provided the 'image' of a pre-existing Eros with symbolic significance, Isidore looked at the ancient god from a totally different perspective. Thus, he turned the god into a 'medieval' symbol, admitting him into the first veritable Christian encyclopaedia. Eros existed in the reality God had created, a reality imbued with meaning; Eros was therefore allowed its role in the encyclopaedia, a symbol of God's creation.[20]

Conclusion

The static Eros in the Montecassino image forms part of an encyclopaedia. It should be understood as a reality furnished with Christian meaning. The image cannot be seen as an illustration of the accompanying text – which was influenced by a passage in the work of Propertius, which in turn was inspired by a painting of Eros. Nor can it be said that the Montecasino image inspired the accompanying text. Indeed, the image hardly adds anything to the understanding of the text. Yet the image was not meant to be understood in isolation from the text: its sole audience was that of the literate monks studying in the monastic school.

Text and the image in the Montecassino manuscript have a similar meaning. Both 'describe' Eros. In addition, the text provides an explanation of the symbolic content of Eros's outward features, and by that explains the image. Here, we may touch on the question why books meant for literates should be illustrated at all? Considering the medieval perception of creation as a visible image of a deeper cause needing explation, e.g. in encyclopaedias, images seem fundamental to the medieval literate mind. Although an image of Eros such as the one in the Montecassino encyclopaedia was probably not the inspiration for the accompanying text, the passage *does* explain the 'image' of Eros as a real, existing figure, part of the visible world. From this point of view his depiction in the encyclopaedia – as the depiction of any other aspect of the physical world – seems very appropriate to medieval thought.

Eros's features in the Montecassino image may be read as if they were words, and yet their significance cannot be understood as a matter of course. The 'reader' of this image needs to know the content of the added text, and through the words of the text the prevailing symbolic readings of the image's 'words'. But the symbolic readings cannot be isolated from their context. Clearly the text may help: after all, the encyclopaedia was an educational device

---

[20] E. MÂLE, *L'Art religieux du XIIIᵉ siècle en France* (Paris, 1913). Although this book focusses on the art of the thirteenth century, Mâle nonetheless drew a very beautiful and comprehensive general picture of this well-nigh universal attitude in medieval thinking.

meant to familiarize believers with the Christian world picture. More important still, the encyclopaedia is itself symbolic of the image of the world it provides. The writers of medieval encyclopaedias aimed to unveil the harmony of God's creation, and by that to reconcile present, past and future. From this perspective a pagan god such as Eros was as alive as he had ever been. Reading about the god may have given some clues as to the kind of love he was meant to personify, but this cannot of itself give insight into the living harmony Eros had to be fitted into. The encyclopaedia was designed to be studied as a whole. Only thus its content could gradually become acceptable knowledge.

Fig. 1   Hrabanus Maurus, *De rerum naturis*, XV, 6, *"de diis gentium"*, illustration showing Venus, Cupid (Eros) and Pan, MS Montecassino, Biblioteca dell'Abbazia, cod. 132, f. 398r.

Ottonian *Tituli* in Liturgical Books

HENRY MAYR-HARTING

The *tituli*, that is the legends or inscriptions, accompanying images in Ottonian liturgical books, are not an entirely neglected subject. Eric Palazzo, for instance, in an important paper, has made a survey of the various functions of these *tituli*, such as explanation of novel iconography, memorials of the dead, and aids to prayer including aids to prayer for the celebrant during mass.[1] It is with the last of these that I am at present concerned, in order to try to advance the description of this phenomenon in Ottonian religious culture. A very large proportion of the finest surviving illustrated Ottonian books are liturgical, and *tituli* were amongst other things an attempt to focus the mind of the celebrant and help him to meditate.[2] They imply that in the Ottonian period we can easily exaggerate the distinction between liturgical and private prayer, between external and interior religion. Ottonian society and culture, as Karl Leyser has shown, was highly ritualistic, with enormous importance attached, in all spheres of life and art, to the external gesture.[3] Not for nothing did

---

[1]   E. PALAZZO, "Tituli et enluminures dans le Haut Moyen Âge (IXᵉ-XIᵉ siècles): Fonctions liturgiques et spirituelles", in: *Epigraphie et iconographie: Actes du Colloque International de Poitiers, 5-8 Octobre 1995, Civilisation Medievale II* (Poitiers, 1996), pp. 167-190. I have written about the *tituli* of the Hitda Codex as aids to prayer and meditation, albeit not in the context of the public liturgy, in H. MAYR-HARTING, *Ottonian Book Illumination: An Historical Study* 2 vols. (London, 1991), 2, pp. 101-117. I am grateful to Eric Palazzo for drawing my attention to, and giving me a copy of his paper, during the colloquium in Utrecht in December 2000.

[2]   PALAZZO, "Tituli", p. 186, n. 110, has very relevantly drawn attention to the analogy between the *tituli* of liturgical books (and frescoes) and the *tituli psalmorum* as aids to meditation.

[3]   K. LEYSER, "Ritual, ceremony and gesture: Ottonian Germany", in: IDEM, *Communications and Power in Medieval Europe: The Carolingian and Ottonian Centuries*, ed. T. REUTER (London, 1994), pp. 189-213.

Hans Jantzen see as characteristic of Ottonian figural art what he called the *Gebärdefigur*, the figure whose point was in its gesture.[4] But we must not be swept off our feet so much by Ottonian ritualism, that we overlook the strong element of interiority in its religious culture, and suppose that this element was a development only of the Twelfth-Century Renaissance.

As so often with Ottonian matters, the roots of the problem lie in the Carolingian period. In the Drogo Sacramentary of ca. 845 or 850, for instance, the initial "O" for the collect of Palm Sunday has an image of the Crucifixion and the blood flowing from Christ's side being collected into a chalice by a personification of *Ecclesia* (fig. 1).[5] This is only the second known time that that scene occurs in Christian art, the first being in the Utrecht Psalter.[6] In the ordinary way this might be considered dangerously iconodulistic, particularly as the Byzantine iconoclasts of 754, whose arguments were of course known in the West, had regarded the presence of Christ in the Eucharist as his only valid representation.[7] However, nobody but an educated priest or bishop celebrating the mass could have seen this initial. It was not something to which those prone to idolatrous superstition would be exposed. It was made not long after the so-called Eucharistic Controversy of Paschasius Radbertus (ca. 790-ca. 860) and Ratramnus († after 868), both of Corbie, and at first sight it might seem, in its corporeality, to support the position of Paschasius. In reality, however, its rationale as an illustration fits much better to Ratramnus's memorialist view, that the bread and wine are a figure or memorial of the Lord's death, so that what was done in the past may be recalled to the memory in the present. When we have arrived at the point of seeing Christ face to face, then we shall have no need of aids by which we are reminded of his measureless love, and shall not be moved by any outward remembrances of things temporal, seeing the truth itself through contemplation.[8] So this initial letter was an aide-memoire of the Passion, in line with the teaching about legitimate illustration in the *Libri Carolini*, something on which the priest or bishop could meditate, perhaps while the

---

[4] H. JANTZEN, *Ottonische Kunst* (München, 1947; paperback edn. Hamburg, 1959), pp. 73-75.

[5] MS Paris, Bibliothèque Nationale, lat. 9428, f. 43v; and Cf. F. UNTERKIRCHER, *Zur Ikonographie und Liturgie des Drogo-Sakramentars* (Graz, 1977), pp. 17-19.

[6] Utrecht Psalter (ca. 830): MS Utrecht, Universiteitsbibliotheek 32, f. 67r, before Psalm 115.

[7] C. MANGO, *The Art of the Byzantine Empire 312-1453* (Englewood Cliffs, NJ, 1972), p. 166.

[8] Ratramnus, *De Corpore et Sanguine Domini*, c. 100, ed. in: MIGNE, *PL* 121, col. 170C.

Kyrie was sung and he waited to recite the collect from the book. For the collect was apparently said in that period at the altar.[9]

One could give other examples of the insinuation of private prayer into public worship under the Carolingians, but I prefer to turn to the Ottonian period: in Ivrea there is an (I think) little known prayer book of Bishop Warmund of Ivrea, a close supporter of Otto III, dating from ca. 1000. It is a book of prayers to be said by the bishop privately before and during the celebration of mass. There is a prayer for when he approaches the altar (fig. 2). The parchment is here water-damaged, but the purport of the prayer is clear: "O God who makes of the unworthy the worthy, of sinners the repentant, of the unclean the clean, make me a worthy minister at your altar" etc. When the *Gloria in Excelsis* is intoned, there is a prayer that the celebrant's sins may be forgiven. When he puts incense into the thurible before the Gospel, he says, "may God kindle in us the odour of celestial inspiration, and fill our hearts" etc.. And later on in the mass there are prayers for his household, the sick etc., reminding one of Hrabanus Maurus's (780-856) observations that when the priest stands at the altar he must remember that he is there as a mediator between man and God. There are many other similar prayers besides.[10] This is so far as I know a unique survivor of its kind, but I am sure that the idea which it reflects was far from unique in its age. One has only to think of how Thietmar of Merseburg (975-1018) loved to retail stories of the recollection with which bishops and abbots celebrated mass;[11] or how interested Hrabanus Maurus was, in his widely known and used *De institutione clericorum*, in what ought to be going on in a priest's mind during his celebration of mass.[12] Above all the evidence of liturgical manuscripts, their illustrations and *tituli*, strongly suggest that its approach was not unique.

The Ottonians did not scatter *tituli* around like confetti without purpose. Sometimes the art itself was so expressive that they were not needed, and the

[9]   At least he stood at the altar during the Kyrie (and Gloria, though this obviously not on Palm Sunday): Ordo X (prob. Mainz, ninth/tenth century), edited in: M. ANDRIEU, *Les Ordines Romani du Haut Moyen-Age*, 5 vols. (Louvain, 1931-1961: *Spicilegium Sacrum Lovanense* 11, 23-24, 28-29), 2, p. 355.

[10]   MS Ivrea, Biblioteca Capitolare, Cod. IV see See MAYR-HARTING, *Ottonian Book Illumination*, 2, 89-90. a) f. 6r: "*Deus qui de indignis dignos facis, de peccatoribus ... , de inmundis ... , fac me dignum sanctis altaribus tuis mynistrum etc*". b) ff. 11v-12v. c) f. 19v: "*Odore celestis inspirationis sue accendat dominus et impleat corda nostra etc*". d) ff. 28r-28v.

[11]   *Thietmari Merseburgensis Episcopi Chronicon*, ed. R. HOLTZMANN (Berlin, 1955), e.g., III, 9, p. 108 (Liudolf abbot of Corvey); IV, 28, p. 165 (Adalbert of Prague's dream of himself celebrating mass before his martyrdom); VI, 65, p. 354 (Tagino of Magdeburg).

[12]   Hrabanus Maurus, *De Clericorum Institutione* I, c. 32, ed. in: MIGNE, *PL* 107, cols. 321-322.

artists knew it. In the illustration of the heavenly and earthly Church which the celebrant could look at while he waited to recite the collect of the patronal feast of All Saints in the Fulda Sacramentary now at Udine (fig. 3), the marvellous contrast of greens, and the arresting figure of the earthly Church standing like the conductor of a great double choir, would speak for themselves. Also, however, any celebrant would be expected to know of Bede's allegorical commentary on the Temple, treating of the duality of the Church on earth and the Church of the Resurrection, swathes of which the Fuldan Hrabanus Maurus had lifted without acknowledgment for his own commentary on the Books of Chronicles.[13]

Contrast this with the frontispiece of a Fulda pericopes book now at Aschaffenburg (ca. 970). It is an illustration of the Apocalypse, chapter five. There is the Lamb who was slain, worthy to open the book of seven seals; the angels who proclaim his worthiness; the four living creatures, and – not the Twenty-four Elders who fell on their faces in adoration, but *Ecclesia* whom they typify. The titulus above the Lamb ("the Lamb that was slain is worthy to take the book and break its seven seals") would be particularly applicable to the meditation of a deacon, who opened the book to read the Gospel and who thus in a sense stood in place of the Lamb. *Ecclesia* collecting the blood in her chalice would be more relevant to the *priest*'s action later in the ceremony, and one must remember that the celebrant kissed the Gospel Book when he first approached the altar and again after the gospel reading.

The Aschaffenburg manuscript has only ten folios of which this page is a singleton, although certainly belonging to it. It contains eighteen gospel readings for major feasts throughout the year, written in the finest Fulda calligraphy.[14] There is no evidence that it ever had an early permanent binding. If this booklet were on a stand on the altar, unbound, our page would have a considerable impact at many metres – I have tested it at Aschaffenburg – with its deep purple ground, and the gold shimmering behind the rose-tinted Lamb in its roundel.

The *titulus* below the Lamb is of some interest too. The problem here is that the artist, not in every respect a genius, has tried to combine two motifs for *Ecclesia*, her bowing down in worship of the Lamb, and her holding up a chal-

---

[13] MS Udine, Archivio Capitolare, MS. 1, f. 66v. See MAYR-HARTING, *Ottonian Book Illumination*, 2, pp. 151-152 and Colour Plate XV.

[14] H. HOFFMANN, *Buchkunst und Königtum im ottonischen und frühsalischen Reich* (Stuttgart, 1986), p. 138. Also MAYR-HARTING, *Ottonian Book Illumination*, 2, pp. 148-150 (but I advance, I hope, on that discussion here) and Colour Plate IX, where the *tituli* or legends are entirely legible.

ice to collect the blood. It is not at all easy to do both things at once, and the Church is not falling on its face but falling over backwards. Here if anywhere a *titulus* was needed for her support! The *titulus*, written in golden letters around the figure of *Ecclesia*, reads: "Behold the bowing Church (*ecclesia cernua*) worthily receives the blood of the Lamb". The adjective, *cernuus*, was a surprisingly rare one, never otherwise used for bending backwards, but only, when used at all, for bowing forwards. It is used by Thomas Aquinas (1224/5-1274) in that sense in the *Tantum ergo* – "*veneremur cernui*".[15] The use of the word here obviously seeks to convey the bowing down at the same time as the blood is collected in the chalice (fig. 4 and Colour Plate 10).

In sacramentaries, the "T" at the beginning of the Canon of the Mass lent itself to representations of the Crucifixion. Immediately before the Canon, during the singing of the *Sanctus*, the celebrant stood at the altar with practically nothing else to look at but the sacramentary.[16] Sometimes the Crucifixion was so powerful that any *titulus* would be superfluous, and the artist knew it. This Corvey crucifixion, albeit an intelligently designed page, is not quite in that league. The hand of God represents the presence of the Father, and the *titulus* on either side of this hand gives the celebrant one of the last sayings of Jesus on the Cross for his reflection: "Father, into thy hands I commend my spirit". In the bottom roundel is the celebrant himself, clad in liturgical dress, a maniple over his left hand to indicate his priesthood, looking up and contemplating the scene, as though the celebrant would look through the eyes of this depicted priest at the Crucifixion (fig. 5).[17]

The Sacramentary of Bishop Sigebert of Minden (1022-1036) has a Crucifixion before the Canon, and then very unusually, two full-page miniatures at the end of the canon, one of the Lamb of God with blood flowing from his side, and after it this remarkable image of Sigebert standing at the altar of his cathedral on which lies the communion bread, taking the chalice with the blood of the Lamb from a very *kämpferisch*-looking *Ecclesia* (fig. 6).[18] The legend in the margins reads:

---

[15] Patrick Wormald reminded me of this.

[16] Ordo X, edited in: ANDRIEU, *Les Ordines Romani*, 2, No. 49, p. 360.

[17] MS München, Bayerische Staatsbibliothek, Clm 10077, f. 12r, in colour in MAYR-HARTING, *Ottonian Book Illumination*, 1, Plate XIII.

[18] MS Berlin, Deutsche Staatsbibliothek, theol. lat. fol. 2, ff. 8v and 9r, i.e. on facing pages. R. MEYER, "Die Miniaturen im Sakramentar des Bischofs Sigebert von Minden", in: *Studien zur Buchmalerei und Goldschmiedekunst des Mittelalters: Festschrift für Karl Hermann Usener*, ed. F. DETTWEILER, H. KÖLLNER and P.A. RIEDL (Marburg, 1967), esp. pp. 186-88; and HOFFMANN, *Buchkunst und Königtum*, p. 374.

Receive, Sigebert, the gifts of eternal life, through which the mother of graces
gently refreshes you.

Sigebert could contemplate all this during the singing of the Agnus Dei. And
then what would be almost the next words he would recite in the public liturgy
as he took the chalice? "*Quid retribuam domino*": "What return shall I make to
the Lord for all he has given me. I shall take *the chalice of salvation* and call
upon the name of the Lord" (Ps. 116).[19]

What I have been describing is not a universal but a characteristic feature
of Ottonian liturgical books. But one more example I must give, because it lets
the cat out of the bag about the function of sacramentary illustrations. Before
the magnificent pages which bear the Easter prayers in the St. Gereon
Sacramentary, made at Cologne in the last years of the tenth century, is a series
of three pictures: the Crucifixion, Pilate's ordering a guard on Christ's tomb (a
rare one), and the two women at the tomb. This last contains the *titulus*: "*Hic
erit contemplandum*": "Here it is to be contemplated how the heavenly angel
testified that Christ had risen from the dead" (fig. 7).[20] I do not say that such
pictures were a source of meditation only during mass, as distinct from, say, in
the sacristy beforehand, or at some quite other time of private prayer. I would
argue that the pictures of that greatest of all Cologne works, the Hitda Codex,
could only have been used for meditation, and that only outside any liturgical
celebrations, because of how they are placed in the book. What I do say is that
there was some kind of continuum between meditation outside and meditation
within the performance of the liturgy.

It is not clear that a Book of Epistles was ever given the same prominence
as the Gospel Book during the solemnities of a pontifical mass. No *ordo*, for
instance, states that this should be proffered to the bishop after the reading as
the gospel book was. But there was no reason why it should not be so, and it is
possibly implied by the frontispiece of the epistolary which archbishop Everger
of Cologne gave to his cathedral. This represents the archbishop, dressed in
mass vestments, in full prostration before the saints Peter and Paul, who sit like
two disputing scholars of Antiquity. The *tituli* read, "Dear father (i.e. Peter),
absolve me from the nexus of my sins; Paul, elect of God, you also absolve me

---

[19] J.A. JUNGMANN, *Missarum Sollemnia*, 2 vols., 2nd edn. (Vienna, 1949), 2, p. 429, says
that this prayer was widespread in this place at mass from the beginning of the eleventh century.
One could make a case, indeed, for its going back to the ninth century. That the celebrant would
still be standing at the altar during the *Agnus Dei* is clear from Ordo X (ed. ANDRIEU, *Les
Ordines Romani*, 2, p. 362), for only after communion does it say that, "the bishop sitting down",
his hands are washed.

[20] MS Paris Bibliothèque Nationale, lat. 817, f. 60r.

from my guilt that I may obtain heavenly pardon by the gift of Christ"; and "Bishop Everger, in whose name I am written, calls these, with devout mind, his patrons" (fig. 8).[21] At the very least we have to say that Everger wanted to enfold these very personal pleas for forgiveness within his performance of the liturgy. The splendid 1998 catalogue of Cologne manuscripts tells us that what this is all about is *"noch unerforscht"* (still unresearched).[22] But one can make a shrewd guess, without much *Forschung!* Thietmar of Merseburg tells us that when Everger was cathedral provost at Cologne, archbishop Gero became ill and committed himself to be looked after by Everger, who, finally thinking him dead, ordered him to be washed, laid in a coffin, and carried to the church to be buried on a subsequent day. In the night, "as people say", Gero, as if waking from a deep sleep on hearing the sound of a bell, shouted that they should let him out quickly. The man who heard it was astonished and rushed to Everger. But Everger asserted that it was a pack of lies and struck the man with a large staff. And so Gero died, on 29 June 976, actually the feast of saints Peter and Paul, none other than the saints whom in his Book of Epistles Everger calls his patrons.[23]

I end with the Regensburg Uta Codex of ca. 1020. The pictures in several of the greatest Ottonian Gospel Books, or pericopes books, were clearly not made directly for the embellishment of the liturgy, but for private meditation outside the context of the liturgy. And it is obviously significant that two of these were made for abbesses who could never have been celebrants, Hitda of Meschede and Uta of the Niedermünster in Regensburg. The brilliant article of Bernhard Bischoff on St. Emmeram of Regensburg in this period, where he proved that the *schemata* of illustrations and the accompanying texts in the four great pages of the Uta Codex were the work of a Regensburg monk, Hartwic, pupil of the great liberal arts expert Fulbert of Chartres,[24] has led to a certain amount of learned overkill in their interpretation.

They have sometimes come to seem more like an intellectual exercise in the liberal arts than what they surely are, spiritual meditations for someone who could use her own knowledge of the liberal arts for the enlargement of her reflections. It is true that the pages other than the crucifixion page do show a

---

[21] MS Köln, Dombibliothek, Cod. 143, ff. 3v and 4r.

[22] *Glaube und Wissen im Mittelalter: Die Kölner Dombibliothek*, ed. J.M. PLOTZEK und U. SURMANN (München, 1998), p. 385.

[23] Thietmar of Merseburg, III, 4, ed. HOLTZMANN, p. 100. Evidently the funeral itself was postponed until after the feast.

[24] B. BISCHOFF, "Literarisches und künstlerisches Leben in St. Emmeram (Regensburg) während des frühen und hohen Mittelalters", in: IDEM, *Mittelalterliche Studien* 2 (Stuttgart, 1967), pp. 77-115.

considerable knowledge of the works of John Scotus Eriugena (ca. 810-ca. 877). Regensburg was one of the great centres of study of these works in the early eleventh century.[25] But this page is like a great meditation on the Crucifixion in which, as in the Resurrection, every cosmic opposite or discord – sun and moon, grace and law, life and death, church and temple – is resolved (fig. 9).[26] Most of the *tituli* refer to the Bible,[27] but one, that accompanying the representations of life and death, has two direct references to the Roman/Gregorian collect of Easter Sunday:

Titulus: Mors devicta *peris quia Christum vincere gestis;* spirat *post dominum sanctorum vita per aevum.*

(Death you are conquered and perish because you sought to conquer Christ; after the Lord the life of the saints breathes for ever).

Easter Collect: *Deus qui hodierna die per unigenitum tuum aeternitatis nobis aditum* devicta morte *reserasti; vota nostra, quae praeveniendo* aspiras, *etiam adjuuando prosequere.*

(O God who this day through Thine only-begotten Son conquered death and opened for us the way to eternity, help us to continue in those desires which Thou hast in the first place breathed into us).

Hence we are not far removed from the liturgy in the Crucifixion page of the Uta Codex. Indeed, the book is a liturgical book, both in having a *capitulare*, and in the texts of each gospel being divided up into pericopes for gospel readings. It is as if the onlooker were being given food for meditation which would presumably carry over from private prayer into her thoughts during the liturgy of Good Friday and Easter Sunday and vice versa.

It was an inspiration amidst all this to represent, in diagrammatic form on either side of the cross, the perfect harmonies of music. Again, there has been a temptation here to treat this diagram more as a learned exercise and less as a meditation on creation and salvation than it deserves. Ulrich Kuder, for instance, thinks it likely that the source of the diagram was Boethius's *De Musica*,[28] a difficult liberal arts text to master. But in Boethius's *De Musica* (II, 27)

---

[25] MAYR-HARTING, *Ottonian Book Illumination*, 1, pp. 126-128.

[26] MS München, Bayerische Staatsbibliothek, Clm. 13601, f. 3v.

[27] A.S. COHEN, *The Uta Codex: Art, Philosophy and Reform in Eleventh-Century Germany* (University Park, PA, 2000), esp. pp. 60-67.

[28] U. KUDER, "Der spekulative Gehalt der vier ersten Bildseiten des Utacodex", in: *St. Emmeram in Regensburg: Geschichte, Kunst, Denkmalpflege* (Kallmünz, 1992), pp. 163-178.

the succession of numbers given as representing the perfect intervals is 3, 6, 8, 9; whereas in our diagram it is 4, 6, 8, 12. More reasonably, Adam Cohen cites the *Musica Enchiriadis*, a basic music theory text found in three eleventh-century manuscripts at St. Emmeram, as a probable source.[29] As a general proposition I accept this, but his citation of it is not in itself quite adequate to cover our diagram. The text which does cover the case precisely is Boethius's *De Arithmetica*, widely known and much studied.[30] It should not be overlooked that in the early Middle Ages the ordinary run of educated people were much more likely to have acquired an elementary knowledge of musical theory from this relatively easy work, which was to some extent an introduction to the whole quadrivium, than from the *De Musica*. And here (*De Arithmetica*, II, 49, 3), in one short paragraph the whole explanation of the series 4, 6, 8, 12 is laid out with complete clarity. I give it in Michael Masi's translation:

> We will find all the musical symphonies (i.e. harmonies) in this disposition (i.e. 6, 8, 12). A diatesseron is 8 to 6, since this is a sesquitertian proportion (i.e. 1-1 1/3); the diapente is 12 to 8, which is called a sesquialter comparison, and such a comparison contains a diapente. A diapason is born from a duplex produced from the placing together of 12 and 6. The diapason and the diapente, which maintain the ratio of a triple, come from the difference of the extremities compared to the smaller difference. The difference between 12 and 6 is 6, and the smaller difference between 8 and 6 is 2. Six to two is a triple, and the diapason with the diapente sound a consonant. The major consonance, that is a double diapason, comes from a quadruple (i.e. 4), and is seen in a compari middle term, that is 8, and the difference which is found between 8 and 6.[31]

How many of those who ever studied the Crucifixion page would have had the patience to follow even this short and easy explanation of its diagram of musical harmonies we cannot know. But all could be assured that there existed an explanation, ready to hand in Boethius's deeply Platonist work, of those consonances of the universe which were re-established in the triumphant death of the Crucifixion.

Only the Holy Spirit knows how powerful Ottonian celebrants of the public liturgy actually were. But what we can see from the liturgical books is that

---

[29] COHEN, *The Uta Codex*, p. 69, and p. 220, n. 71.

[30] This will be discussed in detail in my *Ottonian Church and Cosmos: The View from Cologne* (forthcoming, 2003).

[31] Ed. J.-Y. GUILLAUMIN, *Boèce, Institution Arithmétique* (Paris, 1995), p. 164; M. MASI, *Boethian Number Theory: A Translation of the De Institutione Arithmetica* (Amsterdam, 1983), pp. 179-180.

there was a whole world of private prayer which was *supposed* to impinge on public celebration. At many points they are only intelligible if we understand them in this light.

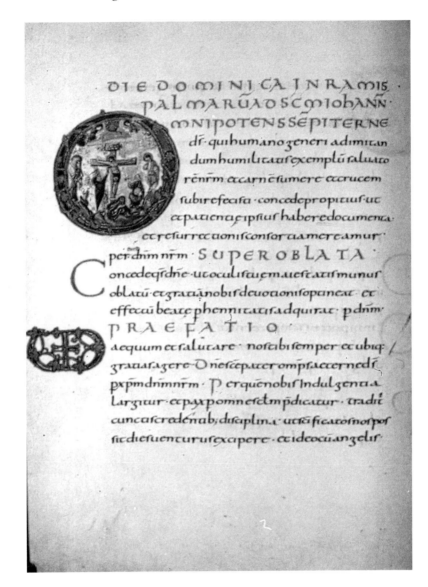

Fig. 1   Crucifixion in letter "O", Drogo Sacramentary, MS Paris, Bibliothèque
Nationale, lat. 9428, f. 43v. Metz, *c.* 845-850.

Fig. 2   The bishop approaches the altar. Prayer Book of Bishop Warmund of
          Ivrea, MS Ivrea, Biblioteca Capitolare, Cod. iv f. 4v. Ivrea, *c.* 1000.

Fig. 3   Illustration for All Saints, Sacramentary, MS Udine, Archivio Capitolare, MS. 1, f. 66v. Fulda, late tenth century.

Fig. 4   Frontispiece, *Ecclesia* holding a chalice to receive the blood of the
Lamb, Pericopes Book, MS Aschaffenburg, Hofbibliothek MS. 2, f. 1v.
Fulda, *c.* 970. See also Colour Plate 10.

Fig. 5 Crucifixion for the *Te Igitur*, Corvey Sacramentary, MS München, Bayerische Staatsbibliothek, Clm 10077, f. 12r. Corvey, late tenth century.

Fig. 6   Bishop Sigebert of Minden offers the chalice to *Ecclesia* at Mass,
Sacramentary of Sigebert, MS Berlin, Deutsche Staatsbibliothek, theol.
lat. fol. 2, ff. 8v and 9r. Minden/St Gall, 1022-1036.

Fig. 7 The two women at the Tomb, St Gereon Sacramentary, MS Paris
Bibliothèque Nationale, lat. 817, f. 60r. Cologne, shortly before 1000.

Fig. 8   Archbishop Everger of Cologne prostrates himself in penitence before
          Saints Peter and Paul, Everger's Epistolary, MS Köln, Dombibliothek,
          Cod. 143, ff. 3v and 4r. Cologne, 985-999. See also Colour Plate 11.

Fig. 9   Crucifixion page, Uta Codex, MS München, Bayerische Staatsbibliothek, Clm. 13601, f. 3v. Regensburg, prob. *c.* 1020.

Texte et Image dans le Manuscrit de Madrid de la *Chronique* de Skylitzès

MICHEL KAPLAN

L e manuscrit qui est au centre de notre propos est sans doute le plus célèbre manuscrit enluminé de la codicologie byzantine,[1] le plus souvent
utilisé dans l'illustration des ouvrages d'histoire byzantine sinon le plus
souvent étudié par les savants.

Outre la richesse de l'illustration sur laquelle nous reviendrons et qui suffit
à justifier sa célébrité, ce manuscrit contient l'ouvrage de l'un des chroniqueurs
byzantins les plus notables.[2] Jean Skylitzès était un haut fonctionnaire de
l'administration byzantine: drongaire de la veille, donc chef de la garde, il reçut
la haute dignité de curopalate. Il vécut pour l'essentiel durant la seconde moitié
du XIe siècle et il a produit dans les années 1070 une chronique présentée par
règne d'empereur, qui va de 811 (avènement de Michel Ier) à 1057 (chute de
Michel VI qui marque la fin de la dynastie macédonienne). Pour la période qui

---

[1] L'illustration du manuscrit de Madrid a été intégralement publiée par S. CIRAC
ESTOPAÑAN, *Skylitzes Matritensis*, t. 1, *Reproducciones y miniaturas* (Barcelone-Madrid, 1965).
L'étude de référence pour les miniatures est celle de A. GRABAR, M. MANOUSSACAS, *L'illustration du manuscrit de Skylitzès de la Bibliothèque Nationale de Madrid* (Venise, 1979: *Bibliothèque de l'Institut Hellénique d'études byzantines et post-byzantines de Venise* 10). Un fac
simile complet du manuscrit a été récemment publié par A. TSÉLIKAS (Athènes, 2000) aux
éditions Milètos. Voir aussi V. TSAMAKDA, *The Illustrated Chronicle of Ioannes Skylitzes in
Madrid* (Leiden, 2002). Je n'ai pu avoir accès à la dernière étude parue: E.N. BOECK, *The Art of
Being Byzantine: History, Structure and Visual Narrative in the Madrid Skylitzes Manuscript*
(diss. Yale University, 2003).

[2] Cf. avant tout l'introduction à l'édition de I. THURN, *Ioannis Scylitzae Synopsis historiarum* (Berlin and New York, 1973: *Corpus Fontium Historiæ Byzantinæ* 5, *Series Berolinensis*),
pp. IX-XI et désormais l'introduction à *Jean Skylitzès, Empereurs de Constantinople*, texte traduit
par B. FLUSIN et annoté par J.-C. CHEYNET (Paris, 2003: *Réalités byzantines* 8).

commence en 813 et jusqu'au milieu du Xe siècle, où nous prendrons l'essentiel de nos exemples secondaires, il utilise comme source principale la Continuation de Théophane. En revanche, pour le règne de Michel Ier (811-813), que couvre la chronique de Théophane proprement dite et où nous prendrons le sujet principal de notre discussion, la source n'est pas clairement déterminée. Même si l'auteur s'écarte assez peu de ses sources, il rédige en général avec un grand souci d'exactitude.

La datation du manuscrit est assez discutée.[3] Avant d'aboutir en Espagne au XVIIe siècle, il a certainement été en possession du monastère du Sauveur de Messine au XVe siècle où il est peut-être arrivé peu de temps après sa confection. En tout état de cause, le manuscrit a été l'objet d'une restauration, qui a permis de changer les quaternions 12 et 25; pour ceux-ci, la main semble d'Italie du Sud, sûrement postérieure au milieu du XIIe siècle, et les cartons laissés en blanc pour l'illustration lors de la réfection n'ont finalement pas été remplis. Cela ne prouve évidemment pas que le reste, écrit par un autre scribe et intégralement enluminé, ait été confectionné en Italie méridionale. En tout, le manuscrit compte 574 miniatures. Le travail originel a été divisé en deux entre la copie, effectuée en laissant vides les cartons pour l'illustration, et qui est à l'origine d'une seule main, et l'illustration, réalisée après coup, qui est au contraire due à deux artistes différents. Les inscriptions qui commentent les illustrations ont été écrites par le scribe principal; comme nous le verrons, elles comportent parfois des termes qui ne sont pas dans le manuscrit de Madrid, mais dans d'autres manuscrits connus de la chronique. Il paraît donc vraisemblable que les artisans qui ont confectionné le manuscrit de Madrid avaient au moins deux modèles, en gros l'un pour le texte et l'autre pour l'illustration. En tout état de cause, ce dernier ne nous est pas parvenu. Cette présence simultanée de deux manuscrits dans le *scriptorium* où s'effectuent copie et enluminure renforce l'hypothèse selon laquelle le manuscrit a été confectionné à Constantinople.[4]

---

[3] Pour ce qui suit, je me réfère à l'article de N. OIKONOMIDÈS, "Ἡ στολή του ἐπάρχου καὶ ο Σκυλίτζης της Μαδρίτης", dans: *Εὐφρόσυνον. Ἀφιέρωμα στὸν Μανόλη Χατζηδάκη* (Athènes, 1992: *Δημοσιεύματα τοῦ Ἀρχαιολογικοῦ Δελτίου* 46) t. 2, pp. 422-434 (avec résumé en Anglais).

[4] I. ŠEVČENKO, "The Madrid manuscript of the Chronicle of Skylitzes in the light of its new dating", dans: *Byzanz und der Westen: Studien zur Kunst des Europäischen Mittelalters*, éd. I. HUTTER (Vienne, 1984: *Österreichische Akademie der Wissenchaften, Philosophisch-Historische Klasse Situngsberichte* 432), pp. 117-130 le fait confectionner vers 1150 dans la Palerme normande. Même si l'argumentation d'Oikonomidès (cf. note précédente) semble la plus convaincante, signalons toutefois qu'un autre manuscrit de Skylitzès est conservé à Naples, ce qui renforcerait l'intérêt de l'Italie normande pour Skylitzès. GRABAR, MANOUSSACAS, *L'illustration*, p. 9, démontrent, à partir d'une différence entre le texte de la chronique et la

Dans une large mesure, Skylitzès était un écrivain officiel, qui a dédié son *Histoire* aux empereurs. Il n'est donc pas étonnant que l'on confectionne un manuscrit aussi luxueux, vraisemblablement dans l'entourage immédiat de l'Empereur, voire pour le souverain lui-même. L'influence occidentale sur l'iconographie, qui a été souvent utilisée pour faire du Skylitzès de Madrid un manuscrit originaire d'Italie normande, n'est pas surprenante: dès l'époque de Manuel Comnène (1143-1180), qui est la plus haute que l'on puisse attribuer à ce manuscrit,[5] les Latins sont nombreux à Constantinople, y compris dans la plus haute aristocratie et jusque dans l'entourage impérial. Quant au passage au monastère du Sauveur de Messine, qui compte dans ses archives au moins cinq manuscrits venus d'Orient, elle s'explique soit directement par l'effort des moines bénédictins, soit indirectement par les nombreux cadeaux faits à la cour normande. De toute façon les erreurs ou insuffisances dans les légendes apportées à l'illustration ne peuvent être attribuées à la maladresse ou au manque de compétence d'un copiste qui ne serait pas byzantin et, partant, peu au fait d'une histoire. Au reste, les byzantins eux-mêmes n'ont pas forcément une connaissance approfondie et détaillée d'événements vieux de presque quatre siècles en dehors des manuscrits qu'ils ont sous les yeux.

Pour l'essentiel, les enluminures du Skylitzès de Madrid collent parfaitement au texte.[6] Nous en prendrons l'un des cas les plus célèbres, celui des cartons qui illustrent l'épisode de la riche péloponnésienne communément appelée Danilis (fig. 1 et Planche 12). Pour expliquer les origines de la fortune accumulée par Basile Ier[7] avant son accession au trône, dans le cours du chapitre consacré au fondateur de la dynastie macédonienne, Skylitzès, suivant fidèlement Constantin Porphyrogénète, rédacteur de la vie de son grand père dans la Continuation de Théophane, raconte les relations entre l'épouse d'un aristocrate de la région de Patras, nommé Daniel,[8] et Basile. Ce dernier, alors modeste

légende de l'illustration au folio 232 v, carton b, que l'illustrateur a sous les yeux un autre manuscrit que celui de Naples.

[5] Grabar et Manoussacas adoptent la datation généralement admise au moment où ils écrivent, le XIIIe siècle.

[6] Les deux auteurs cités à la note précédente établissent à partir des 517 miniatures comportant une légende (sur 574) les statistiques suivantes: dans 250 cas, l'illustration compte deux légendes; dans 120, une seule plus ou moins développée; dans 111, trois légendes, dans 25, 4 légendes; dans 6 cas, 5 légendes; dans 4 cas, 6 légendes; enfin, dans un cas, 7 légendes.

[7] Sur les débuts de la dynastie macédonienne, notamment l'avènement de Basile Ier, cf. en dernier lieu S. TOUGHER, *The Reign of Leo VI (886-912): Politics and People* (Leiden, New York and Cologne, 1997: *The Medieval Mediterranean* 15), pp. 23-41, où l'on trouvera la bibliographie la plus récente.

[8] La femme n'est jamais appelée que par le nom de son mari au génitif: madame "de

fonctionnaire du fisc, fait l'objet, dans l'église Saint-André de Patras, d'une prédiction de la part d'un moine qui promet un destin impérial Danilis, informée de ce somptueux avenir, adopte spirituellement Basile, qui devient ainsi le frère spirituel de Jean, son fils, et fait cadeau à Basile de biens meubles et d'esclaves domestiques.[9] Lorsque, conformément à la prédiction, Basile est devenu empereur, s'insère le récit ici illustré:

> Le fils de Danilis, à qui l'unissait le lien de fraternité spirituelle, [Basile Ier] l'honora de la dignité de protospathaire et lui accorda une grande facilité d'accès auprès de lui. Il fit venir à lui la vieille Danilis. Celle-ci n'était pas capable de monter à cheval. Elle se coucha sur une litière, choisit trois de ses esclaves jeunes et vigoureux pour la porter et se mit en route. Ils se relayaient pour porter la litière. Arrivée à la ville impériale, reçue, selon l'habitude, à la Magnaure, elle fut introduite avec les honneurs auprès de l'Empereur, apportant des cadeaux de toute sorte; raconter chacun produirait un récit de mauvais goût. Elle était accueillie selon son désir. Elle circula dans la ville impériale autant que ce fut à son goût puis retourna dans sa propre région. Il lui arriva de revenir dans la ville impériale. L'Empereur était mort et son fils Léon avait hérité du pouvoir. La vieille femme revint avec de semblables cadeaux. Elle le salua et l'inscrivit comme héritier de sa fortune, puis elle rentra chez elle et, peu de temps après, elle mourut. Mais c'est plus tard.[10]

Nous sommes au folio 102 du manuscrit. Le carton du haut nous montre Danilis, durant son trajet, portée sur une litière par huit serviteurs (et non trois comme dit le texte); l'inscription porte seulement "ἡ Δανιλίς". Le carton du milieu représente l'entrevue avec Basile où se fait l'offrande des cadeaux. À gauche: "ἃ ἤνεγκε τῷ βασιλεῖ δῶρα ἡ Δανιλίς" ("les cadeaux qu'apporta Danilis à l'empereur") et "ἡ Δανιλίς"; à droite: "Βασίλειος ὁ βασιλεύς" ("Basile l'Empereur"). Le troisième carton nous montre le second voyage de Danilis pour rencontrer Léon VI, où seul le dessin du palais est un peu différent. À gauche: "ἃ ἔφερε δῶρα ἡ Δανιλίς Λέοντι βασιλεῖ" ("les cadeaux

---

Daniel". Nous avons étudié longuement ce dossier du point de vue de la fortune de cette femme, que, à dessein, nous n'appelons pas "veuve" comme l'essentiel de la bibliographie disponible, car rien ne dit qu'elle l'est, dans M. KAPLAN, "L'aristocrate byzantine et sa fortune", dans: *Femmes et pouvoirs des femmes à Byzance et en Occident (VIe-XIe siècle)*, éd. S. LEBECQ, A. DIERKENS, R. LE JAN, J.-M. SANSTERRE (Lille, 1999), pp. 205-226. Voir en dernier lieu: B. KOUTAVA-DÉLIVORIA, "Qui était Daniélis?", *Byzantion* 71 (2001), pp. 98-109. Cet article s'applique avec bonheur à réfuter l'hypothèse d'une femme à la tête d'une principauté slave.

[9] Skylitzès, Basile Ier, c. 6, p. 122.

[10] *Ibid.*, c. 41, pp. 161-162. Nous adoptons pour l'essentiel la traduction de B. Flusin citée *supra*, n. 2. Pour ne pas surcharger notre propos, nous nous abstenons ici de commenter le cérémonial.

qu'apporta Danilis à l'empereur Léon"); à droite: "Λέων ὁ υἱὸς Βασίλειου ὁ βασιλεύς" ("Léon, fils de Basile, l'Empereur"). La correspondance entre le texte et son illustration est donc parfaite.

Il arrive que les légendes soient fautives, en tout cas sensiblement différentes du texte et de l'illustration, qui, elle est conforme au texte. Skylitzès raconte le baptême de Boris, tsar des Bulgares, en 864 (fig. 2 et Planche 13). Le chroniqueur ne parle que d'un évêque qui a catéchisé Boris et l'a ensuite baptisé.[11] L'enluminure du folio 68v est conforme au texte: un personnage, revêtu de l'habit épiscopal, baptise Boris dans une cuve baptismale. Le tsar est représenté enfant alors qu'il a tout de l'adulte en âge de combattre et de vendre sa conversion au plus offrant, Rome ou Constantinople. Mais la légende porte "ὁ μοναχὸς Μεθόδιος βαπτίζων τὸν ἄρχων τῶν Βουλγάρων" ("le moine Méthode baptise le chef des Bulgares"). L'erreur peut venir du texte de Skylitzès: quelques lignes plus haut, le chroniqueur parle du moine Méthode, un Romain, à qui le tsar avait donné l'ordre de décorer les murs d'un nouveau pavillon de chasse et qui peint le jugement dernier. Selon le chroniqueur, c'est cette comparaison entre l'enfer et le paradis qui conduit Boris à recevoir de l'évêque catéchèse puis conversion. L'enluminure figure à la fin de cet épisode. On peut émettre une autre hypothèse. Trois siècles au moins se sont écoulés entre les événements et l'enluminure. Les événements sont devenus quasi légendaires pour les Byzantins. Il s'agit du type de récit que n'importe quel enlumineur connaît. Certes, ce n'est pas Méthode, l'aîné des 'frères moraves', qui a baptisé Boris, car Méthode était alors en Moravie, deux cents kilomètres au nord, mais Méthode a bien été consacré évêque par le pape Nicolas Ier et passe, dans l'inconscient collectif des Byzantins, avec son frère Constantin-Cyrille, pour l'apôtre des slaves. Ce sont les disciples de Méthode, ultérieurement chassés de la Moravie voisine, qui ont accompli le gros de la christianisation en profondeur des populations bulgares. L'erreur du scribe qui écrit la légende et qui est pourtant celui qui a copié le texte, mais qui revient légender l'enluminure longtemps après, une fois le travail du peintre accompli, est sans doute inconsciente. C'est d'ailleurs moins une erreur du scribe qui écrit la légende qu'une interprétation. Il convient de ne pas la surinterpréter à son tour. On pourrait faire la même remarque pour la quasi totalité des quatorze cartons pour lesquels Grabar

---

[11] *Ibid.*, Michel III, c. 7, p. 91. Le texte est ici mal composé. Le chroniqueur évoque une première fois le baptême de Boris, suite à la famine qui ravage son peuple, par un évêque qui lui a été envoyé par les Byzantins. Trouvant la cause trop profane, Skylitzès, comme son modèle, rajoute l'épisode du moine Méthode.

et Manoussacas ont relevé une divergence entre l'enluminure et le texte:[12] il s'agit non d'une erreur du dessinateur mais d'une inexactitude de la légende.

Une vraie difficulté surgit néanmoins pour une enluminure qui est la première du manuscrit (fol. 10 v) et qui illustre le couronnement d'un co-empereur[13] durant le règne de Michel Ier Rhangabè (fig. 3 et Planche 14). La scène est d'une grande simplicité: six personnages élèvent sur le pavois un empereur qui couronne un autre personnage légèrement plus petit. L'officiant porte la chlamyde tandis que le bénéficiaire ne porte que le *lôros*, mais il s'agit bien dans les deux cas d'un habit strictement impérial; l'un et l'autre tiennent un *velum* et ont leur tête nimbée. Cette élévation sur le pavois[14] s'accompagne de l'acclamation par des dignitaires dont deux portent la coiffe caractéristique des officiers impériaux. Rangés derrière ceux-ci, des personnages accompagnent cette acclamation au son des trompettes. L'enluminure ne comporte pas de légende, mais elle suit immédiatement le titre du paragraphe suivant du chapitre que Skylitzès consacre à Michel Rhangabè: "Πόλεμος 'Ρωμαίων καὶ Βουλγάρων καὶ ἀποστασία Λεόντου τοῦ 'Αρμενίου" ("guerre des Romains et des Bulgares et trahison de Léon l'Arménien").

Avant de débattre de la principale difficulté, celle qui vient de l'invention pure et simple par rapport au texte, intéressons-nous à la cérémonie telle qu'elle est représentée et que l'on peut utilement comparer aux autres enluminures du même manuscrit illustrant une scène analogue, aux traités byzantins sur les cérémonies auliques et au récit des chroniqueurs. Nous avons deux récits de la façon dont Michel III fait de Basile le Macédonien, qu'il vient d'adopter, son co-empereur. Dans le récit relatif au règne de Michel III, on lit: "en effet, Michel, auquel la nature refusait une descendance et qui était incapable de conduire les affaires, fit de lui son fils adoptif après lui avoir conféré la dignité de *magistros*, puis, peu après, il le ceignit du diadème à la Grande Église".[15] Cette scène donne matière à enluminure (fol. 80 r, carton b, fig. 4 et Planche 15). Michel trône au centre, accompagné d'un porte enseigne; à sa droite, Basile arrive à la tête de ses guerriers, en position de triomphe; à gauche, le patriarche

---

[12] GRABAR, MANOUSSACAS, *L'illustration*, pp. 19-21.

[13] C. WALTER, "The coronation of a co-emperor in the Skylitzes Matritensis", dans: *Actes du XIVe congrès international des Études byzantines*, Bucarest, 6-12 septembre 1971, éd. M. BERZA, E. STĂNESCU, vol. II (Bucarest, 1975), pp. 453-458, repris dans C. WALTER, *Studies in Byzantine Iconography* (Londres, 1977) XI.

[14] Sur l'élévation sur le pavois, cf. C. WALTER, "Raising on a shield in Byzantine iconography", *Revue des Études Byzantines* 33 (1975), pp. 133-175, repris *Studies in Byzantine Iconography*, XII.

[15] Skylitzès, Michel III, c. 23, p. 113.

bénit et couronne Basile, devant Sainte-Sophie, car il eût été difficile de représenter la cérémonie à l'intérieur de la cathédrale. La légende se limite aux noms des deux protagonistes. L'événement est raconté une seconde fois dans le livre relatif à Basile Iᵉʳ:

> L'empereur [Michel III] ... se rendant compte qu'il était incapable de s'occuper des affaires du monde et craignant aussi une révolte, décida d'associer quelqu'un à son gouvernement et à son règne. Et comme il venait d'adopter Basile ainsi que je l'ai dit plus haut et qu'il savait que son courage et son intelligence hors du commun le rendaient capable de compenser sa propre insuffisance à gouverner le navire du monde, comme, surtout, la puissance suprême de Dieu le poussait à cela, voici qu'il distingue ce Basile du glorieux honneur de l'onction impériale: au jour de la Pentecôte, il se rendit en cortège public dans l'illustre église de la Sagesse de Dieu où il le ceignit de la couronne des empereurs.[16]

Mais il s'agit de l'un des cahiers où les cartons n'ont pas été remplis (fol. 88 à 95). Dans la suite du récit relatif à Michel III, le chroniqueur nous raconte que l'empereur se méfie:

> il se mit en tête de se débarrasser de Basile, qui l'empêchait de faire ses volontés. Il amena en public un certain Basilikinos, rameur sur la galère impériale, qu'il revêtit de la pourpre et ceignit du diadème, puis qu'il conduisit au Sénat en le tenant par la main.

C'est cette dernière scène qui est illustrée dans le carton du bas: au centre, le rameur assis sur un trône, revêtu du *lôros* et couronné; à sa gauche, Michel III suivi de sénateurs; à sa droite, le patriarche fait un geste de bénédiction. La légende est sans équivoque: au dessus de Basilikinos, "Βασιλικῖνος στέφεται" ("Basilikinos couronné"); au dessus de Michel, "Μιχαὴλ βασιλεύς ὁ υἱὸς Θεοφίλου" ("Michel, empereur, le fils de Théophile").

Cette scène ressemble à la deuxième représentation de l'avènement de Léon V, toujours dans le même chapitre du livre consacré à Michel Iᵉʳ. Ce dernier a subi une grave défaite face aux Bulgares, que Skylitzès attribue à la trahison de Léon. Léon suborne les soldats et déclenche la révolte. Les soldats conspuent Michel et acclament Léon empereur. Celui-ci semble hésiter à s'emparer définitivement du trône, mais Michel le Bègue, commandant de l'un des corps d'armée et futur assassin de Léon en 820, le menace de l'épée et le force à monter sur le trône. "Et c'est ainsi que Léon ceignit le diadème et qu'il fut

---

[16] Skylitzès, Basile Iᵉʳ, c. 13, p. 129.

proclamé empereur des Romains".[17] Cette scène donne matière à un carton, où Léon V est représenté sur le trône, au milieu de la scène, entouré de personnages habillés comme des fonctionnaires, l'un portant la coiffe, qui l'acclament (fol. 12v, fig. 5 et Planche 16). La légende est la suivante: "Léon est proclamé empereur par le peuple". Elle est semblable pour le texte comme pour l'enluminure à la proclamation de Théophile en 829 ou à celle de Basilikinos.

Pour en revenir au lien entre le texte et l'image, il est clair que, dans les deux cartons proches situés à la fin du règne de Michel III, il y a une différence entre le texte et l'image. Dans le cas de Basile, le texte évoque seulement le couronnement par Michel III tandis que l'image montre le patriarche accomplissant cet acte. Dans le cas de Basilikinos, où le couronnement n'est pas représenté, mais seulement la proclamation, l'enlumineur fait intervenir le patriarche, qui n'est pas non plus mentionné dans le texte. L'artiste se différencie donc nettement du texte. Reste à savoir ce qu'il a en tête. Non point l'état du cérémonial à l'époque de Basile Ier, que nous relate de *De Cerimoniis* de Constantin Porphyrogénète: certes, le patriarche bénit la chlamyde et la couronne, mais c'est l'empereur principal qui revêt son co-empereur de la chlamyde et le ceint de la couronne, le tout à Sainte-Sophie.[18] Plus proche de l'époque de l'illustrateur, puisque datant de XIVe siècle, mais recueillant des traditions antérieures, le Pseudo Kodinos montre l'empereur régnant et le patriarche plaçant le *stemma* sur la tête du nouvel empereur.[19] Bref, l'illustrateur est avant tout tributaire d'une tradition plus proche de son époque que des événements illustrés. Toutefois, le texte, même quelque peu trahi, fournit encore le support de l'image.

---

[17] Skylitzès, Michel Ier, c. 2, p. 7. Michel le Bègue deviendra l'empereur Michel II (820-829), fondant la dynastie d'Amorion dont Michel III sera le dernier représentant.

[18] Constantin Porphyrogénète, *De Cerimoniis* I, 38, éd. et trad. A. VOGT, *Constantin Porphyrogénète: Le Livre des Cérémonies* (Paris, 1939), t. II, p. 3. Voir le commentaire de G. DAGRON, *Empereur et prêtre: Étude sur le 'césaropapisme' byzantin* (Paris, 1996: *Bibliothèque des Histoires*), pp. 74-79. Notons toutefois que, précisément, pour Théophylacte, fils de Michel Ier, c'est le patriarche Nicéphore qui le couronne; cf. *infra*, n. 21.

[19] Pseudo Kodinos, éd. et trad. J. VERPEAUX, *Pseudo Kodinos: Traité des Offices* (Paris, 1976: *Le monde byzantin* 1), c. VII, p. 259. À cette époque, résultat de l'influence latine, le couronnement est précédé par le sacre sous la forme d'onction au saint chrême par le patriarche. Notons que le Pseudo Kodinos prévoit l'élévation sur le pavois, mais du seul co-empereur, le bouclier étant alors tenu par l'empereur principal et le patriarche. Le principe dynastique est alors suffisamment évident pour que le couronnement soit de façon prioritaire celui d'un co-empereur, fils de l'empereur régnant; c'est au contraire l'absence d'empereur de la génération précédente qui paraît l'exception.

Il en va autrement dans l'illustration du folio 10.[20] Le titre qui la surmonte est en parfaite contradiction avec l'enluminure, puisqu'il annonce non pas le couronnement de Léon V par Michel Ier, qui suppose une entente minimale, mais l'*apostasia*, donc la trahison, de Léon. L'enluminure ne peut pas plus illustrer le paragraphe précédent, qui raconte le choix par le peuple et le Sénat de Michel, gendre de Nicéphore Ier, mais seulement une fois mort Staurakios, fils de l'empereur tué face aux Bulgares le 26 juillet 811 et alors grièvement blessé. Certes, dès ce moment, Michel voulait céder la place à Léon, stratège des Anatoliques, mais celui-ci a refusé. D'autre part, Michel Ier fit couronner trois mois plus tard son fils Théophylacte, mais le texte de Skylitzès ne mentionne aucun des enfants à cet endroit et donc pas cette association au trône.[21] L'événement eut lieu à la Noël 811. Le couronnement fut pratiqué par le patriarche Nicéphore à Sainte-Sophie.[22] Le paragraphe qu'ouvre l'enluminure raconte la défaite de Michel face aux Bulgares à Versénikeia le 22 juin 813 en attribuant le retournement d'une bataille apparemment gagnée à la trahison de Léon l'Arménien, suivie de l'usurpation déjà racontée.[23] Le décalage demeure complet entre le texte et l'image.

L'enlumineur illustre-t-il la suite du récit? Au paragraphe 3, Michel rentre à Constantinople après sa défaite. Il annonce avoir laissé l'armée à son fidèle Léon l'Arménien. On lui rapporte alors l'usurpation et, malgré les objurgations de sa femme Prokopia qui retrouve les accents de Théodora face à la sédition Nika de 532,[24] il décide de ne pas résister: "il envoya l'un des proches les plus intimes porter à Léon les insignes de la dignité impériale, le diadème, la robe de pourpre et les brodequins rouges".[25] Tandis que Léon entre dans Constantinople en triomphateur par la Porte d'Or, acclamé par l'armée, le peuple et le Sénat, et gagne le Palais, Michel se réfugie à l'église de la Théotokos du Pharos[26] d'où

---

[20] On ne peut évidemment reprendre ici l'hypothèse d'ailleurs peu soutenable de Walter selon qui l'illustrateur a sous les yeux un manuscrit enluminé non de Skylitzès mais de la continuation de Théophane; en effet, celle-ci ne traite pas de Michel Rhangabè.

[21] Cela n'empêche nullement W. TREADGOLD, *A History of the Byzantine State and Society* (Stanford, 1997), p. 430, qui illustre son propos de cette miniature, de mettre en légende: "proclamation de Michel Ier Rhangabè et de son fils Théophylacte".

[22] Théophane, *Chronographie*, éd. C. DE BOOR (Leipzig, 1883), p. 494.

[23] Tardif, le récit de Skylitzès n'est évidemment pas le meilleur. On trouvera une analyse détaillée des sources relatives à l'avènement de Léon V dans D. TURNER, "The origins and accession of Leo V (813-820)", *Jahrbuch der Österreichischen Byzantinistik* 40 (1990), pp.171-203. Voir aussi W. TREADGOLD, *The Byzantine Revival, 780-842* (Stanford, 1988), pp. 177-189.

[24] "L'Empire est un beau linceul", citation exacte des paroles prêtées à Théodora.

[25] Skylitzès, Michel Ier, c. 3, p. 8.

[26] Sur l'église de la Vierge du Pharos, cf. R. JANIN, *La géographie ecclésiastique de*

il sera exilé au monastère de l'île de Prôtè, l'une des îles des Princes,[27] et ses fils sont castrés, notamment le futur patriarche Ignace. Il n'y a pas de place pour la cérémonie décrite par l'enluminure.

Les autres sources disponibles n'offrent pas plus matière à une telle enluminure.[28] Théophane présente la particularité d'être un strict contemporain des événements. Il écrit à une époque où, ne sachant pas que Léon V sera iconoclaste, il se révèle un chaud partisan de ce général visiblement apte à combattre le danger bulgare. Il en fait non pas un traître, mais le sauveur que viennent implorer les officiers que Michel a abandonnés. Léon résiste quelque temps, mais, voyant les Bulgares s'avancer vers Constantinople, il demande la bénédiction du patriarche Nicéphore. Proclamé empereur à l'Hebdomon par l'armée,[29] il entre à Constantinople par la porte d'Andrinople[30] et arrive au palais, tandis que Michel se fait tonsurer à la Théotokos du Pharos le 11 juillet 813. Le 12 juillet, le patriarche Nicéphore couronne Léon à Sainte-Sophie comme le voulait la tradition. Le nouvel empereur et le patriarche mettent la capitale en défense contre les Bulgares.[31]

La version du *Scriptor Incertus de Leone Armenio*, iconodoule militant et, lui, averti de l'iconoclasme de son client, offre une version un peu différente.

---

l'Empire byzantin. Première partie: le siège de Constantinople et le patriarcat œcuménique, t. 3: les églises et les monastères, 2ème éd. (Paris, 1969), pp. 232-236.

[27] Sur Prôtè, cf. R. JANIN, *Les églises et les monastères des grands centres byzantins (Bithynie, Hellespont, Latros, Galèsios, Trébizonde, Athènes, Thessalonique)* (Paris, 1975), pp. 70-72.

[28] Nous laisserons de côté les sources romaines, analysées avec bonheur par J.-M. SANSTERRE, "Les informations parvenues en Occident sur l'avènement de l'empereur Léon V et le siège de Constantinople par les Bulgares en 813", *Byzantion* 66 (1996), pp. 373-380: l'auteur conclut en effet qu'il ne faut "pas se faire une trop haute idée de la qualité de l'information – particulièrement celle de caractère profane – en provenance du monde byzantin" et que reflètent les Lettres du pape Léon III et les *Annales Regni Francorum*.

[29] Sur le *Tribounalion*, le champ de parade militaire proche du monastère et du palais de l'Hebdomon, cf. R. DEMANGEL, "Au Tribunal de l'Hebdomon", *Bulletin de Correspondance Hellénique* 63 (1939), pp. 275-284. Sur l'Hebdomon en général, cf. R. JANIN, *Constantinople byzantine, développement urbain et répertoire topographique*[2] (Paris, 1964: *Archives de l'Orient Chrétien* 4A), pp. 446-449.

[30] Léon V évite d'entrer par la Porte Dorée, celle des empereurs triomphants, pourtant celle qui est la plus proche de l'Hebdomon, pour ne pas créer la confusion. Les sources ultérieures, qui vont le charger, le feront passer par la Porte Dorée pour bien marquer son mépris d'usurpateur pour les bons usages. La porte d'Andrinople offre l'avantage d'ouvrir sur la branche nord de la Mésè, la grande artère triomphale qui conduit au choix au Palais, à l'Hippodrome ou à Sainte-Sophie après avoir rejoint la branche sud, que l'on emprunte en venant de la Porte Dorée, au Philadélphion.

[31] Théophane, *Chronographie*, pp. 501-503.

Comme Skylitzès, il attribue la défaite de Versénikeia à la défection de Léon, mais de façon plus discrète, car les soldats du thème des Anatoliques ne furent pas les premiers à prendre la fuite. De plus, ce sont les soldats, non leur chef, qui sont accusés de défection. Il confirme que, rentré à Constantinople, Michel ne pense qu'à abdiquer. Le thème des Anatoliques se révolte, proclame son stratège empereur, ouvre les portes de la ville. La foule acclame Léon, tandis que Michel fuit et se fait tonsurer. Léon entre dans la ville, reçoit les insignes impériaux, mais pas de Michel, qui a fui, puis se fait couronner par le patriarche.[32] Cette version, elle aussi proche des événements, confirme le récit de Théophane et ne laisse pas de place pour notre enluminure.

Avec la Vie du patriarche Nicéphore,[33] que Léon V forcera à démissionner en 815 lors du rétablissement de l'iconoclasme, écrite par Ignace le Diacre peu après la restauration des images en 843, on passe à la version qui fait de Léon un véritable traître sur le champ de bataille. Par la suite, le stratège des Anatoliques adresse des discours à ses soldats pour les soulever tandis que l'empereur est rentré à Constantinople. Cette Vie ne décrit évidemment aucun contact entre l'usurpateur et sa victime.

Les événements de 813 apparaissent dans les deux versions de la Vie de Iôannikios, dernier tenant affiché, quoique discret, de l'iconodoulie au moment

[32] *Scriptor Incertus de Leone Armenio*, éd. I. BEKKER (Bonn, 1842), pp. 336-341. L'oeuvre est difficile à dater, mais a pu être écrit pour l'essentiel sous Michel II par Serge le Confesseur, père du futur patriarche Phôtios. À la lumière de ce passage, il nous semble antérieur aux sources hagiographiques que nous mentionnons par la suite. Mais ce problème mériterait d'être repris. Pour cette datation, cf. A. MARKOPOULOS, Ἡ χρονογραφία τοῦ Ψευδοσυμεών καὶ οἱ πηγές της (Ioannina, 1978), pp. 155-157 et, en dernier lieu, A. MARKOPOULOS, "La chronique de l'an 811 et le *Scriptor Incertus de Leone Armenio*: Problèmes des relations entre l'hagiographie et l'histoire", *Revue des Études Byzantines* 57 (1999), pp. 255-262, notamment p. 259, n. 25 et p. 261-262 avec une note additionnelle.
[33] Vie du patriarche Nicéphore (*BHG* 1335), éd. C. DE BOOR, *Nicephori archiepiscopi Constantinopolitani opuscula historica* (Leipzig, 1880), pp. 139-217. Sur l'oeuvre abondante d'Ignace le Diacre, qui fit plusieurs aller et retours entre iconoclasme (de qui lui valut la métropole de Nicée) et iconodoulie, cf. en dernier lieu l'introduction de C. MANGO, S. EFTHYMIADIS, *The Correspondence of Ignatios the Deacon: Text, Translation and Commentary* (Washington, 1997: *Corpus Fontium Historiæ Byzantinæ* 39, *Dumbarton Oaks Texts* 11) et l'introduction à l'édition d'une autre oeuvre d'Ignace, la Vie de Taraise (*BHG* 1698) par S. EFTHYMIADIS, *The Life of Patriarch Tarasios by Ignatios the Deacon: Introduction, Text, Translation and Commentary* (Aldershot, 1998: *Birmingham Byzantine and Ottoman Monographs* 4). Voir en dernier lieu M. KAPLAN, "Quelques remarques sur la vie rurale à Byzance au XIe siècle d'après la correspondance d'Ignace le Diacre", dans *The Dark Centuries of Byzantium (7th-9th c.)*, éd. É. KOUNTOURA-GALAKÈ (Athènes, 2001: *National Hellenic Research Foundation, Institute for Byzantine Research, International Symposium* 9), pp. 365-376.

du rétablissement des Images en 843. La première version, écrite entre 843 et 847 par un iconodoule modéré et proche du patriarche Méthode, Pierre, mentionne les événements brièvement en deux endroits proches. D'abord pour dire qu'après le très court règne de Staurakios, fils de Nicéphore Ier, Michel Ier lui succéda, puis devint moine après s'être fait voler son empire par le sauvage Léon (jeu du mot sur le prénom de celui qui est présenté peu ou prou comme un usurpateur). Au paragraphe suivant, Pierre précise que Michel et Léon, commandant du thème des Anatoliques, partent combattre les Bulgares. Il ne mentionne pas la défaite, mais, que "par la suite, avec la permission de Dieu, Léon chassa Michel, un homme ami du Christ, du pouvoir impérial; il s'empara de façon tyrannique de la couronne impériale".[34] Malgré le ton modéré d'un auteur qui voit ici la volonté de Dieu, il n'y a pas de place pour le couronnement de Léon par Michel.

Dans la Vie de Iôannikios par Sabas, écrite après 847, l'hagiographe suit une tradition proche de celle d'Ignace le Diacre, celle de la trahison:

> Aussitôt après l'engagement des hostilités, il [Léon V] fournit sciemment aux ennemis la force et, aux Romains, il apporta la défaite, et pour lui même tissa le vêtement précieux de la tyrannie qui est imprégnée du sang des chrétiens.[35]

Là encore, Léon V usurpe le trône sans plus qu'il soit question de Michel Ier.

La Vie d'Ignace[36] par Nicétas David le Paphlagonien,[37] écrite au début du Xe siècle, souligne que Michel a nommé Léon stratège des Anatoliques, que

---

[34] Vie de Iôannikios par Pierre (*BHG* 936), éd. J. VAN DEN GHEYN, *AASS Novembris* 2,1 (Bruxelles, 1984), c. 15 et 16, p. 392.

[35] Vie de Iôannikios par Sabas (*BHG* 935), *ibid.*, p. 347. La bibliographie sur Iôannikios est abondante (cf. *Byzantine Defenders of Images: Eight Saints' Lives in English Translation*, éd. A.M. TALBOT (Washington, 1998: *Byzantine Saints' Lives in Translation* II), pp. 253-254), mais les questions des rapports entre les deux Vies, de leurs sources et de la date de rédaction de la Vie par Sabas méritent encore d'être reprises. Cf. C. MANGO, "The two lives of St. Ioannikios and the Bulgarians", *Harvard Ukrainian Studies* 7 (1983), pp. 393-404 et M. KAPLAN, "Les saints en pèlerinage à l'époque mésobyzantine (VIIe-XIIe siècles), *Dumbarton Oaks Papers* 56 (2002), pp. 109-128.

[36] Ignace est le troisième fils de Michel Ier; contrairement à Théophylacte, il n'a pas été couronné empereur du vivant de son père, selon la Vie; en 813, il est castré comme son frère (l'aîné, Staurakios, était mort avant l'avènement de son père), et entre au monastère sous le nom d'Ignace. Il devient patriarche à la mort de Méthode en 847. Forcé de démissionner en faveur de Phôtios en 858, il redevient patriarche lorsque Basile Ier renvoie Phôtios en 867 et le reste jusqu'à sa mort en 877.

[37] Vie d'Ignace (*BHG* 817), *PG* 105, cols. 488-573. Nicétas David est l'un des prédicateurs les plus réputés de son époque.

celui-ci a voulu le renverser et que Michel lui a laissé volontiers le pouvoir.[38] La Vie ne fait que résumer, sans détails, la version du *Scriptor Incertus*. Quant à la continuation de Théophane[39] et à son parallèle de la même époque ou légèrement antérieur, Génésios,[40] elle est la source qu'utilise Skylitzès, de préférence à Théophane, pour décrire le règne de Michel Ier. Elle ne contient donc pas davantage de scène de rencontre entre Michel et Léon pour transmission du pouvoir qui corresponde à notre enluminure.

Celle-ci reste donc un complet mystère. Elle n'a aucun rapport ni avec le texte qu'elle illustre, ni avec le reste du texte, ni avec aucune tradition concernant l'avènement de Léon V, ni même avec aucun cérémonial connu de proclamation d'un co-empereur. Car si c'est bien l'empereur régnant qui couronne le co-empereur, c'est lors d'une cérémonie religieuse, en général à Sainte-Sophie, éventuellement à l'Hippodrome,[41] bien distincte de l'élévation sur le pavois, rite de proclamation par l'armée qui précède le couronnement. Le télescopage de trois notions sur cette enluminure reste encore aujourd'hui inexpliqué.

---

[38] Vie d'Ignace, cols. 489C-492A.

[39] Théophane Continué, éd. I. BEKKER (Bonn, 1838), pp. 11-21.

[40] Génésios, *Histoire impériale*, éd. A. LESMÜLLER-WERNER, A. THURN, *Iosephi Genesii Regum Libri Quattuor* (Berlin, 1978: *Corpus Fontium Historiæ Byzantinæ, series Berolinensis* XIV). Sur les relations entre les deux auteurs, cf. F. BARISIĆ, "Les sources de Génésios et du Continuateur de Théophane pour l'histoire du règne de Michel II (820-829)", *Byzantion* 31 (1961), pp. 93-106 et "Génésios et le Continuateur de Théophane", *Byzantion* 27 (1958), pp. 119-133.

[41] Cédant à l'amicale pression de ses partisans, Léon IV finit par couronner son fils Constantin VI, âgé de 6 ans, en 776, pour faire pièce aux prétentions de ses propres frères. Le dimanche de Pâques, 24 avril, l'empereur se rend avec le patriarche à l'Hippodrome; le prélat dresse un autel portatif, prononce sur les attributs impériaux les bénédictions usuelles; puis Léon IV couronne son fils. Théophane, *Chronographie*, pp. 449-450; cf. G. DAGRON, *Empereur et prêtre*, n. 17, pp. 97-99. Nous avons vu toutefois ci-dessus que, dans le cas du fils de Michel Rhangabè, c'est le patriarche qui procède au couronnement.

Fig. 1   MS Madrid, Biblioteca Nacional, Codex Matritensis Vitr. 26-2, f. 10 v.
         Voir aussi Pl. 12.

Fig. 2   MS Madrid, Biblioteca Nacional, Codex Matritensis Vitr. 26-2, f. 12 v.
          Voir aussi Pl. 13.

Fig. 3   MS Madrid, Biblioteca Nacional, Codex Matritensis Vitr. 26-2, f. 68 v.
         Voir aussi Pl. 14.

Fig. 4   MS Madrid, Biblioteca Nacional, Codex Matritensis Vitr. 26-2, f. 80 r.
Voir aussi Pl. 15.

Fig. 5   MS Madrid, Biblioteca Nacional, Codex Matritensis Vitr. 26-2, f. 102 r.
          Voir aussi Pl. 16.

'Reading' Images and Texts in the *Bibles moralisées*: Images as Exegesis and the Exegesis of Images

JOHN LOWDEN

Introduction

To consider complex illuminated manuscripts such as the *Bibles moralisées* under the heading of 'communication' is to raise in some form virtually every question that could be put to the material.[1] Some of these questions are of a genus both specific and familiar, applicable in different ways to all illuminated books. Who was doing the communicating (in the *Bibles moralisées*), and to whom? What was being communicated, and how? Why was it being communicated, where, and when?[2] All these questions draw atten-

---

[1] I am most grateful to Marco Mostert and the other members of the Pionier Project Verschriftelijking for the invitation, at the suggestion of Michael Clanchy, to speak at the very stimulating symposium whose proceedings are published here. Its organisation allowed for exceptionally constructive debate. The paper as published is slightly fuller than was possible in the time available, and includes ideas discussed at the 89th College Art Association meeting in Chicago, the 36th International Congress of Medieval Studies at Kalamazoo, and in a Work-in-Progress Seminar at the Courtauld Institute, London. The resources of the Warburg Institute and the Palaeography Room of the University of London Library were of particular help in the preparation of both the lecture and subsequent publication. The annotation is as supplied on submission of the text in September 2001. The paper is dedicated to the memory of Michael Camille, who enlivened the conference as he did every subject he considered in a life of wonderful productivity, cruelly cut short. [For reference to important publications since 2001 see 'Bibles Moralisées: Electronic Bibliography' at http://www.courtauld.ac.uk/people/lowden_john/bibliography.html]

[2] Compare the list of questions in the introductory essay by M. MOSTERT, "New

tion to important and worthwhile topics which invite exploration. There are also other broader questions that are raised, which go beyond the history of any single book to embrace patterns of medieval production and consumption. Why was there a desire for this type of book under those circumstances? How were such manuscripts related by those who commissioned and used them to other books that they might have possessed, or seen, or made? Were illuminated manuscripts such as the *Bibles moralisées* normative in terms of medieval communication, or exceptional? Potentially, our field of enquiry is in fact so vast as to be almost unlimited, because illuminated manuscripts are unquestionably forms of communication not merely in terms of their initial production and first destination (the usual foci of enquiry), but also because they continue to communicate under all the contingencies and circumstances that surround them right up to the present day. In order not to be completely overwhelmed by the topic, therefore, I am going to approach it initially from an oblique angle. To begin with I will take up the term 'form' from the general title of the proceedings, and ask what was special about the *form* of the *Bibles moralisées* as witnesses to the communication of medieval images and texts. I will then look in detail at a few images in one *Bible moralisée* in order to explore specific issues of communication. The first case to be investigated will be image-and-text, the second purely image, and in both some basic exegetical techniques will be applied at a range of levels. Finally I shall turn to a more general consideration of the viewer as exegete and offer some proposals that will stand in place of a conclusion.

The Form of the Bibles Moralisées: A Framework for Ideas

At the outset it can be stated categorically that no illuminated manuscripts communicate in quite the same way as the *Bibles moralisées*.[3] The significance

---

approaches to medieval communication?", in: *New Approaches to Medieval Communication*, ed. M. MOSTERT (Turnhout, 1999: *Utrecht Studies in Medieval Literacy* 1), pp. 15-37, esp. pp. 20-21. See also M. MOSTERT, "A bibliography of works on medieval communication", in: *New Approaches*, pp. 193-318, esp. Nos. 417-37, to which many further studies could be added.

[3]   In general see J. LOWDEN, *The Making of the Bibles Moralisées*, 2 vols. (University Park, 2000), with further bibliography in vol. 1, pp. XVI, 333-51. This study provides the essential foundations upon which the present essay is based. To the works cited in the above study should be added the recent publications of Y. CHRISTE, "L'Héxaméron dans les Bibles moralisées de la première moitié du XIIIᵉ siècle", *Cahiers archéologiques* 47 (1999), pp. 177-198; Y. CHRISTE, "Les Bibles moralisées et les vitraux de la Sainte-Chapelle: Le vitrail de l'Exode", *Bulletin monumental* 157 (1999), pp. 329-346; Y. CHRISTE, "Le portail Saint-Étienne à la cathédrale de

of this point can hardly be overemphasized. Far from being normative, the *Bibles moralisées* are utterly exceptional. It does not follow, however, at least in my opinion, that we should therefore dismiss their evidence as erratic. Precisely because the *Bibles moralisées* are so unusual they bring other illuminated books into sharper relief. And in addition they enable us to see medieval producers and consumers at work on a scheme of unmatched ambition and complexity.

The defining features of the form of a *Bible moralisée* are as follows (figs. 1, 8).[4] Each large page has eight quite small images of identical size and shape, and each image is flanked by a relatively short text. There is an absolutely regular alternation on every page between a biblical image, and its accompanying biblical text, and a moralizing interpretation of that image and text in the form of another image and accompanying text. There are seven manuscripts of this type surviving (some now divided between different libraries). In order of relative chronology they are:

Vienna, Österreichische Nationalbibliothek (ÖNB) cod. 2554;[5]
ÖNB cod. 1179;[6]
Toledo, Tesoro del Catedral (*Biblia de San Luis*) + New York, Pierpont Morgan
Library MS M. 240;[7]

Chartres au regard des Bibles moralisées", in: *Arte d'Occidente: Temi e metodi: Studi in onore di Angiola Maria Romanini* (Rome, 1999), pp. 847-856; Y. CHRISTE and L. BRUGGER, "Quelques images de la Genèse, de l'Exode et du Lévitique dans la Bible moralisée napolitaine de Paris et les Bibles moralisées du début du XIIIe siècle", in: *Iconographica: Mélanges offerts à Piotr Skubiszewski*, ed. R. FAVREAU and M.-H. DEBIÈS (Poitiers, 1999), pp. 49-61; S. LIPTON, *Images of Intolerance: The Representation of Jews and Judaism in the Bible moralisée* (Berkeley and Los Angeles, 1999); Y. ZALUSKA, "Le Psautier Manchester, John Rylands University Library, ms. lat. 22 et les Évangiles dans la Bible moralisée", in: *Iconographica*, pp. 231-250.

 [4] LOWDEN, *Making of the Bibles moralisées*, 1, pp. 22-30, 65-70; see also Index, s.v. BIBLES MORALISÉES, critical approaches to, text/picture block.

 [5] For reproductions see R. HAUSSHERR, *Bible moralisée: Faksimile-Ausgabe im Originalformat des Codex Vindobonensis 2554 der Österreichischen Nationalbibliothek* (Graz, 1973: *Codices selecti* XL-XL*), R. HAUSSHERR, *Bible moralisée: Codex Vindobonensis 2554 der Österreichischen Nationalbibliothek*, commentary by R. HAUSSHERR, trans. of the French text by H.-W. STORK (Graz, 1992: *Glanzlichter der Buchkunst* 2); G.B. GUEST, *Bible Moralisée: Codex Vindobonensis 2554, Vienna, Österreichische Nationalbibliothek*, Commentary and tr. by G.B. GUEST (London, 1995). See also LOWDEN, *Making of the Bibles moralisées*, 1, pp. 11-54.

 [6] Relatively few of the pages of this manuscript have been reproduced; in general see the studies by LIPTON, *Images of Intolerance*; and LOWDEN, *Making of the Bibles moralisées*, 1, pp. 55-94.

 [7] A complete facsimile of the Toledo manuscript, *La Biblia de San Luis*, is in preparation by M. Moleiro (Barcelona), with a multi-authored commentary edited by R. Gonzálvez. A complete facsimile of the Morgan fragment already exists: H.-W. STORK, *Die Bibel Ludwigs des*

Oxford, Bodleian Library MS Bodley 270b + Paris, Bibliothèque nationale de
France (BnF) MS lat. 11560 + London, British Library (BL) MSS Harley
1126-1127 ('Oxford-Paris-London' or 'OPL');[8]
BL MS Add. 18719;[9]
BnF MS fr. 167 ('Bible of Jean le Bon');[10]
BnF MS fr. 166.[11]

Of the seven *Bibles moralisées* only one of them, the Bible of Jean le Bon, is
still complete.[12] It contains 5112 images on 642 pages, and because all its texts
are in both Latin and French, it has 10224 texts. The *Bibles moralisées* are by
far the most ambitious attempt to accompany the biblical text with images and
commentary and that commentary with images ever to be brought to fruition.
It should be noted that there are other types of book considered under the heading *'Bible moralisée'* by R. Haussherr and others, but they differ in fundamen-

*Heiligen: Vollständige Faksimile-Ausgabe im Originalformat von MS M. 240 der Pierpont
Morgan Library, New York* (Graz, 1995: *Codices selecti* CII-CII*). See also LOWDEN, *Making of
the Bibles moralisées*, 1, pp. 95-137. A short but helpful discussion, clarifying the manuscript's
appearance in the various Toledo inventories, has now been provided by R. GONZÁLVEZ RUIZ,
Hombres y Libros de Toledo (1086-1300) (Madrid, 1997: *Monumenta Ecclesiae Toletanae
Historica* ser. 5, studia 1), pp. 561-571.
    [8]   The manuscript was reproduced in its entirety in black and white by A. DE LABORDE, *La
Bible moralisée illustrée conservée à Oxford, Paris et Londres: Reproduction intégrale du
manuscrit du XIIIe siècle accompagnée de planches tirées de Bibles similaires et d'une notice*, 5
vols. (Paris, 1911-27: *Société française de reproductions de manuscrits à peintures*), Pls. 1-624;
vol. 5 is entitled *Étude sur la Bible moralisée illustrée*. See more recently LOWDEN, *Making of
the Bibles moralisées*, pp. 139-87.
    [9]   The manuscript is little known. See recently LOWDEN, *Making of the Bibles moralisées*,
1, pp. 189-219; p. STIRNEMANN, "Note sur la Bible moralisée en trois volumes conservée à
Oxford, Paris et Londres, et sur ses copies", Scriptorium 53 (1999), pp. 120-124; C.F. WAUGH,
*Style-Consciousness in Fourteenth-Century Society and Visual Communication in the Moralized
Bible of John the Good*, PhD thesis, University of Michigan (2001).
    [10]   Still mostly unreproduced; see LOWDEN, *Making of the Bibles moralisées, 1, pp. 221-250*;
WAUGH, Style-Consciousness. Still fundamental is the article by F. AVRIL, "Un chef-d'oeuvre de
l'enluminure sous le règne de Jean le Bon: La Bible Moralisée manuscrit français 167 de la
Bibliothèque Nationale", *Monuments et Mémoires* 58 (1972), pp. 91-125.
    [11]   Still little reproduced apart from the opening folios painted by the Limbourg brothers:
e.g., M. MEISS, *French Painting in the Time of Jean de Berry: 3. The Limbourgs and Their
Contemporaries* (London, 1974), pls. 278-325. Recently see LOWDEN, *Making of the Bibles
moralisées*, 1, pp. 251-284. Some further discussion in J. LOWDEN, "Beauty or Truth? Making
a *Bible moralisée* in Paris around 1400", in: *Patrons, Authors and Workshops: Books and Book
Production in Paris circa 1400*, ed. G. CROENEN (forthcoming).
    [12]   Quire diagrams in LOWDEN, *Making of the Bibles moralisées*, 1, pp. 298-302.

tal ways from the core group, and from one another, and are, in my view, best considered apart.[13]

The seven surviving *Bibles moralisées* were made in Paris for the kings and queens of France and their closest relatives between the early 1220s and the end of the fifteenth century generally by teams of craftsmen. No expense was spared to make them monuments of unforgettable splendour. The vast scale of the demands they made on their manufacturers at times suggested various unusual procedures to bring them to completion, which I will not go into here.[14] It is striking (in contrast to many other ambitious programmes of illumination) that only one of the *Bibles moralisées*, the last, BnF fr. 166, was left unfinished, and I think this is noteworthy. Fundamental to our understanding of the entire group of manuscripts, I believe, is an argument, advanced elsewhere,[15] that although often closely related textually and/or visually the *Bibles moralisées* do not descend from a lost perfect archetype nor bear witness to a gradual impoverishment in 'accuracy' according to the classic *stemma codicum*, but rather they represent the reverse process, by which an initial idea, exemplified in the oldest surviving *Bible moralisée*, was successively and systematically revised, refined, improved, corrected, elaborated upon, and generally made more splendid in each successive exemplar (obviously this has profound implications for how we study these books). The motivation for making a new *Bible moralisée* was not, for example, the desire to reach a larger audience (these books were never intended for a wide public), but rather to surpass the precedents commissioned by royal forebears. There is a distant parallel, perhaps, in the contemporary building boom in the great churches of North-East France in which the ever taller vaults of one building stood, metaphorically speaking, on the shoulders of its predecessors, rather than 'descending' from some lost perfect prototypical cathedral.

---

[13] R. Haussherr published and argued for his list of Bibles moralisées in numerous places, e.g. R. HAUSSHERR, "Drei Texthandschriften der Bible Moralisée", in: *Festschrift für Eduard Trier zum 60. Geburtstag* (Berlin, 1981), pp. 35-65. His *stemma codicum* was widely disseminated through the commentary to the facsimile *Bible Moralisée: Codex Vindobonensis 2554*, where it is reproduced on pp. 28 and 31. For the dominance of this construct see, e.g. H.-W. STORK, *Die Wiener französische Bible moralisée Codex 2554 der Österreichischen Nationalbibliothek* (St. Ingbert, 1992: *Saarbrücker Hochschulschriften* 18), pp. 61-64. For a critical discussion of Haussherr's stemma see LOWDEN, *Making of the Bibles moralisées*, 2, pp. 204-206.

[14] On matters of production see LOWDEN, *Making of the Bibles moralisées*, 1, *passim*; for the remarkable use of pressure tracing in the Toledo and Oxford-Paris-London manuscripts see 1, pp. 119-121, 167-180, colour plates XI-XX, figs. 70-83.

[15] LOWDEN, *Making of the Bibles moralisées*, 2, *passim*.

The physical form or *mise en page* of a *Bible moralisée* with its eight images and accompanying texts is its defining feature, but the problems of interpretation that it raises for us, because it is unique, are considerable. Medieval
viewers of illuminated manuscripts, like us, had certain expectations of the role
of images in books: as frontispieces, for example, or to mark textual divisions,
in historiated initials, or in marginal or *bas-de-page* areas, and so forth.[16]
Whereas different viewers undoubtedly looked at different books in different
ways over the centuries, nonetheless the limitless supply of surviving material
at our disposal and decades of study have provided us with various paradigms
about how images and texts communicated in these very varied circumstances.
For the *Bibles moralisées*, however, we have to ask how and why the special
form (the characteristic *mise en page*) was developed before we even ask the
usual questions about what it was communicating, how, to whom, and so forth.
I say we need to do this *before*, because the *mise en page* had been carefully
measured and drawn on the parchment before any image or text was supplied.
It was the conceptual foundation for everything we see.

We have a range of precedents for aspects of the *mise en page* of the *Bibles
moralisées*. Probably everybody who has looked at a thirteenth-century *Bible
moralisée* with its images in medallions has been forcibly struck by a visual
parallel with the ambitious glazing programmes of the period.[17] Yet there is not
a single window with paired medallions that combine biblical and moralizing
images in a comparable manner. The window analogy, striking as it is, thus
operates at only a generic level in terms of communication. Medallions as a
formula for organising images were used quite widely, notably in metalwork
and manuscript illumination, to pair up, or otherwise to organise images, and
sometimes to make broadly typological parallels.[18] But any parallel with the

---

[16] Useful starting points are H. TOUBERT, "Illustration et mise en page", in: *Mise en page
et mise en texte du livre manuscrit*, ed. H.-J. MARTIN, J. VEZIN (Paris, 1990), pp. 335-420; J.J.G.
ALEXANDER, *Medieval Illuminators and Their Methods of Work* (New Haven and London, 1992).

[17] LOWDEN, *Making of the Bibles moralisées*, 2, p. 207 and notes; on the question of
possible specific iconographic (rather than conceptual) parallels, see further the recent (and
forthcoming) work by Y. Christe on the possible links between the *Bibles moralisées* and the
Sainte-Chapelle, cited above, n.3. More generally, A. JORDAN, "Material girls: Judith, Esther,
narrative modes and models of queenship in the windows of the Ste-Chapelle in Paris", *Word &
Image* 15 (1999), pp. 337-50; this is one of a number of studies deriving from her PhD thesis: A.
JORDAN, *Narrative Design in the Stained Glass Windows of the Ste-Chapelle in Paris*, Bryn
Mawr College (1994).

[18] LOWDEN, *Making of the Bibles moralisées*, 2, pp. 206-207, 268 n. 21; recently see
ZAŁUSKA, "Le Psautier Manchester"; also an article in press for the Mélanges Kalinowski: F.
BOESPFLUG, Y. ZAŁUSKA, "Les Évangiles dans la Bible moralisée et le Diatessaron latin" (I am
grateful to the authors for a typescript of this text).

Bibles moralisées is again a generic, not a specific one: medallions were not used in other contexts to contain moralisations, nor were they organized in the characteristic pattern of eight with every biblical and moralization image accompanied by a biblical and moralization text. It follows, therefore, that the invention of the distinctive form of the *mise en page* of the *Bible moralisée*, and the book's distinctive purpose – to moralize the Bible visually and textually for a thirteenth-century viewer – are inextricably entwined. We have a perfect link in terms of communication between design and function/purpose.

Moralizing the Bible, so crucial to the concept of the *Bible moralisée* (the title is not original, if undoubtedly appropriate)[19] is characteristic of that tendency in Parisian biblical study of the decades around 1200 sometimes loosely termed the 'biblical-moral school'.[20] This is one of the factors that has led to the conclusion, mistaken in my view, that the *Bibles moralisées* are themselves the product of university-trained biblical scholars, and represent a fairly high level of biblical exegesis.[21] In truth, most of the textual exegesis represented in the moralisations is banal and repetitive. Nonetheless, when we come to 'read' the images and texts it will be convenient to use some basic thirteenth-century exegetical approaches.[22]

Since we are dealing in the *Bibles moralisées* with a thirteenth-century invention, it is important to try to establish as clearly as possible the circumstances that brought that invention about. Here the extraordinary nature of the *Bibles moralisées* is of help. The surviving books are related to one another in a complex but analytically definable manner which leaves little doubt that the well-known Vienna ÖNB 2554 (conveniently available in various facsimile publications) is the earliest surviving such book.[23] Furthermore, it appears that

---

[19] For discussion of the title see LOWDEN, *Making of the Bibles moralisées*, 1, pp. 2-3 and notes on p. 305; HAUSSHERR, "Drei Texthandschriften", pp. 56-58.

[20] The term comes from M. GRABMANN, *Die Geschichte der scholastischen Methode* (Freiburg, 1909), 2, pp. 476-501, chapter title: "Die von Petrus Cantor ausgehende biblisch-moralische Richtung der Theologie". The problems of the term were highlighted by B. SMALLEY, *The Study of the Bible in the Middle Ages* (Oxford, 1952, 1983³), pp. 196-263, esp. p. 197. See also J.W. BALDWIN, *Masters, Princes and Merchants: The Social Views of Peter the Chanter and his Circle*, 2 vols. (Princeton, 1970).

[21] General observations in LOWDEN, *Making of the Bibles moralisées*, 2, pp. 8-9, 207-208, with references to earlier discussion. The most carefully argued presentation of the possible role of university-trained theologians is by R. HAUSSHERR, "Petrus Cantor, Stephan Langton, Hugo von St. Cher und der Isaias-Prolog der Bible moralisée", in: *Verbum et Signum*, ed. H. FROMM, W. HARMS, U. RUBERG (Munich, 1975), 2, pp. 347-364. See also STORK, *Die Bibel Ludwigs des Heiligen*, pp. 20-21 (on Guillaume d'Auvergne).

[22] See first G. DAHAN, *L'exégèse chrétienne de la Bible en Occident médiéval* (Paris, 1999).

[23] See above n. 5. For the arguments see LOWDEN, *Making of the Bibles moralisées*, 1, pp. 8-

Vienna 2554 was itself quite probably the first *Bible moralisée* to be made. Certainly there is no evidence that is more easily explained by the hypothesis that Vienna 2554 could be a copy of some lost archetypal *Bible moralisée*.

Accepting for the sake of discussion that Vienna 2554 is the original *Bible moralisée* it might seem obvious to ignore the six other examples of the genre, on the assumption that they are in various ways derivative descendants, and hence less interesting or important, and to put to Vienna 2554 alone the various questions of communication with which we started (the How? Why? What? Where? When? By whom? For whom? etc. questions). But I do not want to attempt that here, in part because of general methodological reasons.[24] Vienna 2554, as it happens, is less ready to yield up answers to such questions than are some of its later relatives, in part because of its fragmentary condition, and in part because of its obscure later history. Let us instead take the *Bible moralisée* in Toledo as our focus.

An Exegetical Approach to Aspects of Communication in a Pair of Texts and Images in the Toledo Bible Moralisée

On the last page of the Apocalypse in the three-volume Toledo *Bible moralisée* (fig. 2 and Colour Plate 18), a book seemingly made at the command of the queen of France, Blanche of Castille, for her son king Louis IX, and possibly completed in 1234, there are four biblical excerpts from Apc. 22, starting at the top left with verses 10-11. (All of this final quire of the Toledo manuscript is now in New York, and forms MS Morgan M. 240.) Neither text nor image can communicate without our active participation – this is crucial – so at this point we must turn our attention closely to the page in question.[25] The first text reads (fig. 1):

> *Et dixit m(ih)i, Ne signaueris u(er)ba p(ro)phetie huius, temp(us) eni(m) p(ro)pe est. Qui nocet noceat adhuc, et q(u)i in sordibus est sordescat adhuc, et iustus i(us)tificetur adhuc.*

9, 50-52, and passim in vols. 1 and 2.

[24] The point is exemplified at length in the comparative discussion of the manuscripts in volume 2 of LOWDEN, *Making of the Bibles moralisées*.

[25] See also discussion in STORK, *Die Bibel Ludwigs des Heiligen*, pp. 71-72.

(And he said to me Do not seal the words of this prophecy, for the time is near. He who does evil, let him do evil still, and he who is sordid let him be sordid still, and the righteous let him be righteous still.)

The adjacent image (here we must verbalize what we see) shows St. John seated at the left, addressed by an angel who points up to heaven and holds a bundle of unexplained objects in his left hand. In the centre a couple embraces. At the right a Dominican friar holds a book and preaches to an unseen audience. Above, Christ, attended by an angel, blesses a bishop, attended by two tonsured figures.

Below we read the moralisation:

Hoc q(uod) dicit ne signaueris libru(m), sig(nifica)t q(uod) p(re)dicatores n(on) debe(n)t dimitt(er)e ueritatem p(re)dicare p(ro)pt(er) scel(us) malorum.

(That it [or he] says "Do not seal the book" signifies that preachers ought not to abandon preaching the truth because of the wickedness of evil doers).

In the image, at the left, within a stylized church a Franciscan preaches from an open book. He appears to be in dispute with a sword-bearing layman. At the right a kneeling saint is martyred by a coiffed and belted swordsman. Above are four naked souls in heaven.

Traditionally, at this point an art historical analysis would bring to bear a number of visual and textual comparanda, notably (for the page in question) two other *Bibles moralisées*, the twin of the Toledo manuscript, Oxford-Paris-London, and the Latin manuscript Vienna ÖNB 1179, the earliest *Bible moralisée* to contain the Apocalypse (fig. 8 and Colour Plate 17);[26] and an illustrated English Apocalypse manuscript, Paris BnF fr. 403, because the moralization texts are excerpted from a commentary found in an Old French version in this Apocalypse and its relatives.[27] For other pages of the *Bibles moralisées* we

[26] See above, notes 6 and 8. For a recent example of the comparative approach in the Apocalypse see Y. CHRISTE, "L'Apocalypse dans les Bibles moralisées de la première moitié du XIIIe siècle", *Bulletin archéologique du comité des travaux historiques et scientifiques*, NS, 25 (1997), pp. 7-46.

[27] Still fundamental is the study by G. BREDER, *Die lateinische Vorlage des altfranzösischen Apokalypsenkommentars des 13. Jahrhunderts (Paris B.N. Ms fr. 403)* (Münster, 1960: *Forschungen zur romanischen Philologie* 9). For a facsimile reproduction of the manuscript see Y. OTAKA and H. FUKUI, *Apocalypse (Bibliothèque nationale, fonds français 403* (Osaka, 1981). See also L. DELISLE and P. MEYER, *L'Apocalypse en français au XIIIᵉ siècle (Bibl. Nat. fr. 403)* (Paris, 1900-1901). Further bibliography in N.J. MORGAN, *Early Gothic Manuscripts: 2. 1250-1285* (London, 1988: *Survey of Manuscripts Illuminated in the British Isles* 4.2), pp. 63-66, cat.

would have to consider other textual comparanda, such as the *Glossa Ordinaria*, and quite possibly other works by, for example, Peter Lombard, perhaps Hugh of St. Cher, and so forth.[28] But in terms of communication this comparative approach would be tangential. The consumers of the Toledo *Bible moralisée* would, like us, have been looking at this page – or rather opening (figs. 1-2) – without collating it with other manuscripts. It will be instructive, therefore, to continue with a highly focussed viewing and reading. As it happens, a comparative approach to the texts and images would produce a very different sort of discussion, one which can, perhaps, be reserved for some other occasion.

First we can observe that the biblical image is not merely a literal or historical accompaniment to the biblical text. For example, there is no mention in the biblical text of Christ blessing the bishop and religious in Heaven, nor, of course, is the presence of the preaching Dominican cited. Conversely, the angel's explicit instruction in the text that St. John not seal up his prophecy is not represented. The couple embracing in the centre surely represents literally the sordid and/or evildoers. But the artist has clothed them, like the Dominican and the bishop above, in recognizable thirteenth-century dress. Clearly, therefore, this image is not primarily literal or historical (in exegetical terms) but tropological, in that it seeks to interpret the biblical text in a contemporary Christian moralizing mode, most explicitly by identifying the righteous man of the text as a preaching Dominican. The image is also clearly anagogical and eschatological, in that it implies that the actions of those who, like the Dominican, persevere in righteousness, will receive divine blessing in heaven, and there may also be a spiritual and allegorical element in the representation here of Christ. The biblical image, therefore, is a quite sophisticated piece of exegesis.

Turning to the moralization text and image we find that the text is relatively simple. We note, however, that the *verba prophetie* of the biblical text, the words of the prophecy that St. John is not to seal, have become *librum* (the book), that is to say the specific object in which, to a thirteenth-century reader, the prophecy was (or would have been) written. This might be the result of a thought process based on literal exegesis: *verba prophetie id est librum*. The signification that the text then goes on to offer, however, is a tropological or moral one: it concerns preachers and preaching. Here the text seems to be drawing on the previous image, taking up the visual suggestion (not explicit in the Bible of course) that *iusti significant predicatores* (my wording, not that of

---

No. 103. See also J. LOWDEN, "The Apocalypse in the early-thirteenth-century *Bibles moralisées*: A re-assessment", in: *The Millennium, Social Disorder and the Day of Doom*, ed. N. MORGAN (*Harlaxton Medieval Studies*), forthcoming.

[28] LOWDEN, *Making of the Bibles moralisées*, 2, pp. 8-9, 207-208, with further references.

the manuscript). Since in the biblical text the *iusti* are told to persevere in just-ness, it is appropriate that in the moralization the preachers should persevere in preaching, but, oddly, the text then offers a reason for this: they are under threat from evildoers. This is not at all what the biblical text implies, where the evil-doers and the just are treated quite separately. But it *is* what the adjacent image represents. The wording could even be considered a quite apt description of what the image shows.

Initially the image appears to relate to the text quite literally: the Franciscan preaches despite the threatening presence of a man with a sword. But at the right a figure dressed as a biblical saint is martyred. What is the relationship of the martyrdom to the preaching? Is the Franciscan preaching about a saint's life and martyrdom? Or is the threatened Franciscan about to suffer a martyr's fate? If that is the case why is the figure at the right not dressed as a friar? Above are souls in heaven. Doubtless these are saints and martyrs. But are they also the subject of the Franciscan's preaching? Or, looking at the gestures, is this an anagogical parallel to the role of the Franciscan and his congregation (the sword-bearer excluded) below?

Our exploration needs to operate at a further level too, because in a *Bible moralisée*, just as the moralization text takes up and interprets the wording of the biblical text (by the procedure of routinely repeating certain words and phrases – in this case "Do not seal the book" – followed by formulae such as 'this signifies that'), so, as a general principle, does the moralization image in some sense take up and interpret visually the biblical image. In the present instance the position is complex. Starting at the right side, we can see that the preaching Dominican with his head in profile is a striking visual parallel to the kneeling martyr. This makes sense in interpretative terms too, for it suggests that the Dominican is saintly in his preaching. As he has a halo, he might even be intended for a specific Dominican saint; unfortunately Peter of Verona (who would be appropriate to this image) is out of the question since the page was certainly made some twenty years before his martyrdom, but Dominic himself, who died in 1221 and was canonized in 1234 might be represented here – al-though I have to say I think the image is more likely to be generic than specific. Even this preacher/martyr link is problematic, however, since it appears to reverse the analogy we would expect to find between biblical and moralization images: to explain, the martyr in the moralization image (in his biblical dress) has to be seen as somehow moralizing the preacher in the biblical image, al-though the preacher, as we have seen, is already a moralizing interpretation of the biblical text.

A similar problem besets our analysis of the relationship between the embracing evildoers in the biblical image and the executioner in the moralizing image. What the images should, I guess, suggest is that to martyr a saint is to make yourself like the evildoers described by the angel to St. John. But because the evildoers have already been moralised as an embracing couple the argument works additionally in the opposite direction: it suggests that to give yourself over to bodily lust (like these contemporaries of yours) is to make yourself not just one of the evildoers mentioned in the Apocalypse, but like those who martyred the saints of old.

Moving to the left part of the image the preaching Franciscan is clearly intended to be like and to moralize St. John, for just as St. John did not seal up his prophecy, so the Franciscan does not close up his book, but continues to preach. The man who threatens him is surely an evildoer, to be related perhaps to the lecherous man above, but the presence of the instructing angel finds no close visual parallel in the moralization image. Perhaps the church that frames and holds the preacher and his congregation is like the wing of the angel that extends somewhat protectively over St. John. As for the souls in heaven, they are reminiscent of the heavenly group seen above, but quite how this is to be understood I am not sure.

The discussion has selectively used terms of biblical exegesis that would doubtless have been familiar to some of those responsible for the making of the *Bibles moralisées*. But in applying them to the visual material there is an element of playfulness. Initially they seemed to work quite well – we found literal, anagogical, and tropological elements – but then the position became increasingly uncertain. The more we look at these images, I think, the more complex and ill-defined the 'reading' becomes. This, of course, is the difference between the verbal and the visual. The words of the texts are there, and the rules of grammar and syntax limit the ways we can read them. Of course we allow that they can mean different things to different people, or even to the same people, at different times. But what these particular texts can never say is, for example, 'lasciviousness is sordid'. When we turn to the images, however, we face the opposite problem: we can never be clear what it is they say, because in a real sense they *say* nothing at all. It is we who do the saying.

An Exegetical Approach to the Visual Colophon of the Toledo Bible Moralisée

At this point I want to move to a consideration of the facing page in the Toledo manuscript, an often mentioned and frequently reproduced image (fig. 3 and Colour Plate 19).[29] My particular concern is to consider how this page might communicate within the special context of this *Bible moralisée*. The image shows a king and queen, Louis IX and most probably his mother Blanche of Castille, above a religious who is instructing a layman in the production of a book, clearly identifiable by its unique layout as a *Bible moralisée*, i.e. this book.[30] The page faces the end of the Apocalypse. The only text on the page is that partially legible on the book on the lectern of the religious, which I have suggested can be reconstructed to read: "*Laist ci a foi teindre*", "Let it be left here to faith to paint", implying verbally what the image communicates unambiguously: that the book was produced under religious supervision.[31]

Once again, we can attempt to 'read' the image using some of the approaches of thirteenth-century biblical exegesis. Starting at a literal or historical level, the two figures above seem to be Blanche of Castile (whom I believe ordered the book to be made (fig. 4)) and her son Louis IX (whom I believe to have been the book's intended recipient (fig. 5)). They are crowned and enthroned. He holds the sceptre and a small gold disk, and appears relatively youthful.[32] Blanche communicates with him by gestures seemingly evocative, but also imprecise.[33] At a moral or tropological level, however, the couple represent generically the king and queen of France, their power and their splendour, and what we might call the 'close working relationship' between them. Furthermore, at an anagogical level the relationship between this king and this queen (his mother), resembles that between Christ and *his* mother, the Queen of

---

[29] See first STORK, *Die Bibel Ludwigs des Heiligen*, pp. 75-79; LOWDEN, *Making of the Bibles moralisées*, 1, pp. 127-132; *In August Company: The Collections of the Pierpont Morgan Library* (New York, 1993), pp. 88-90.

[30] At the symposium William Voelkle asked why the layout of the page (fig. 7) appears to be upside down; I think this is the result of a simplification meant to make the medallions (the defining feature, here about 3 mm. in diameter) as visible as possible.

[31] The basis of the reconstruction of the text is explained in LOWDEN, *Making of the Bibles moralisées*, 1, p. 129.

[32] For a possible interpretation of the gold disk see LOWDEN, *Making of the Bibles moralisées*, 1, p. 128.

[33] G. WOLF, *Salus Populi Romani: Die Geschichte römischer Kultbilder im Mittelalter* (Weinheim, 1990), p. 190, interpreted (improbably in my view) the queen's gesture as one of intercession or advocacy on behalf of her people.

Heaven. This last is a point that could hardly be made so explicitly in a text, but which in iconographic terms is unavoidable: the parallels between this image of Louis and Blanche and numerous contemporary images of Christ's Coronation of the Virgin, or the Virgin as Queen of Heaven, are extraordinarily vivid and specific.[34] Neither the makers nor the viewers of the image could have failed to notice the similarity.[35]

There is a further level too, for the standard image of Christ enthroned in Heaven with his mother shares (indeed exploits) many visual and semantic parallels with that of Christ enthroned in heaven with his bride, *Ecclesia*, the Church, the couple seen typologically as *Sponsus* and *Sponsa*, the bride and groom of the Song of Songs.[36] In our image, therefore, the queen is both the mother of the king and also his wife. And at a spiritual or mystical level the relationship between the king and queen of France is seen to be likened to that between Christ and *Ecclesia*.

Below, in the same miniature, starting our reading again at the literal/historical level, we see a religious (fig. 6) and a lay craftsman (fig. 7). Given that this particular image was actually made by such a craftsman, a degree of self-referentiality in what is depicted is certain: one of the people involved in making the book represented himself, or at least a figure like himself, in the act of making the book. The image could be said to be 'auto-historical'. The image can also be seen to be self-referential at the literal/historical level in terms of the religious: the artist was presumably instructed by a religious such as we see to make the image of the religious giving instruction. At a moral or tropological level what the image shows is the relationship in thirteenth-century Paris between religious knowledge (on the left) and art made in the service of religion (on the right). The moral level in this case remains close to a certain literal/historical truth, closer indeed than the literal level itself, because many craftsmen collaborated on the making of the book, not just one, and quite likely several religious had control over its content, rather than one.[37] According to

---

[34] In general see P. VERDIER, *La couronnement de la Vierge: Les origines et les développements d'une thème iconographique* (Paris and Montreal, 1980); M.-L. THÉREL, *Le triomphe de la Vierge-Église: Sources historiques, littéraires et iconographiques* (Paris, 1984).

[35] They needed to look no further than the tympanum of the north portal of the west front of Notre Dame at Paris: reproduced in W. SAUERLÄNDER, *Gothic Sculpture in France, 1140-1270* (London, 1972), figs. 152-153.

[36] See first D. GERMANIER, "L'*Ecclesia* comme *Sponsa Christi* dans les Bibles moralisées de la première moitié du XIIIe siècle", *Arte Cristiana* 84 (1996), pp. 243-252, although this particular image is not discussed.

[37] The idea of a 'team' of compilers goes back to R. HAUSSHERR, "Sensus Litteralis und sensus spiritualis in der Bible moralisée", *Frühmittelalterliche Studien* 6 (1972), pp. 356-380, at

Hans-Walter Stork the religious encapsulates the 'authorial' role (or the 'team leadership') of the theologian Guillaume d'Auvergne, Bishop of Paris (1228-1249), but I have proposed that this identification is not cogent on textual or chronological grounds.[38] At a more general spiritual level we see how a symbiosis of religious learning (represented in the clothing and book), and vernacular communication (symbolized by the French text on the book) is required to bring the laity to serve the Church. Word (the book held by the religious) and image (the sheet on which the craftsman works) are represented separately, but they operate in harmony.

At this point we can begin to consider further levels of exegesis, specific to this image's position in a *Bible moralisée*, by applying the four-way pattern that elsewhere links biblical and moralization texts and images. That this is a legitimate procedure is suggested not merely by the weight of evidence of the hundreds of preceding pages, but by a specific *Bible moralisée* precedent, the end of the Apocalypse in Vienna 1179, a book made some ten years before for Louis IX's father, King Louis VIII, in which the final pair of medallions were given over to an image of the king (figs. 8-9), holding the completed *Bible moralisée*, with below him the craftsman engaged in its manufacture.[39] Applying the four-way pattern to the full-page image we see that the religious (with his text) is to the craftsman (making the image) as elsewhere in the book every text (at the left) is to its image (to its right). That is to say, in theory at least, we read and scan from left to right, and we treat the image as in some ways subsidiary to the text. By implication, and I do not think we can avoid this reading, so also is the king of France somehow under the control of the woman to the left, his mother. She does not hold a text, but she does gesture actively. His legitimacy as king comes from her, he is in some sense her image.

Because we are in a *Bible moralisée*, we also need to scan up and down as well as side to side. This scanning suggests that it is the relationship between the queen and king that has given rise to that between the religious and the craftsman. As the Bible is to its thirteenth-century moralizing (i.e. the indispensable cause and justification), so are the queen and king of France to the making of this *Bible moralisée*. The religious and the craftsmen are communicating in contemporary terms of the mid 1230s what these and other Christian

pp. 371-372.
    [38] STORK, *Die Bibel Ludwigs des Heiligen*, pp. 20-21; LOWDEN, *Making of the Bibles moralisées*, 1, p. 318, n. 60; 2, p. 9.
    [39] LIPTON, *Images of Intolerance*, pp. 7-8; LOWDEN, *Making of the Bibles moralisées*, 1, pp. 88-90.

monarchs have established over time (for this is but one of a series of such *Bibles moralisées* going back at least to ca. 1220).

There is also a deeper but still recoverable level of exegetical reading. I have said that images are in some sense subsidiary to texts in these books, because the eye scans from left to right, and indeed this is true, but only up to a point. The situation in the *Bibles moralisées* is extremely unusual. In practice, even if not in theory, the texts are in fact subsidiary to the images in all the early *Bibles moralisées*.[40] The texts were only written in by the scribes, a little like captions, after the images had been completed. In part as a result there are all kinds of strange anomalies.[41] Sometimes a 'biblical' text is not excerpted from the Bible at all, but is merely descriptive of the adjacent image. Sometimes it is absurdly inaccurate. There are entire pages on which all the texts were carefully erased and rewritten.[42] All this would have been well known to the craftsmen involved, and symbolically represented on the full-page image. Faith was supposed to be directing the painting, but in practice there were all kinds of problems. The image may have been intended to be subservient to the word, but that was not what happened. In terms of its consumers the book may have worked, so to speak from left to right, but for its producers it was the other way round. The artist, in placing himself in the position of the image, at the right, is in the position of greater power, even, given that it is a picture book, of greater prestige. So, by implication, is the king above. He may have been the son, ruling under his mother's guidance, but he was king: when she acted she acted in his name, not vice versa.

I think there is yet a further level of exegetical reading to explore. Gathered together on this superbly executed page are four figures: a queen and a king, a religious and a craftsman. The page is divided precisely into quarters, in each of which sits a figure on a gold ground within the same architectural fantasy. The religious and the craftsman are, it is true, a little smaller than the royal couple, but only a little. At a literal/historical level the implication of the image is that the book was made in the royal palace on the Île de la Cité in Paris (not an impossible scenario, I think). At a moral level it is implied that to be involved in the making of such a book is to bring yourself into the orbit of royalty. At an anagogical and eschatological level, especially because of the image's place at the end of the Apocalypse, the implication is that the palace we see is in Heaven, Paris is the heavenly Jerusalem, and that the making of such

---

[40] LOWDEN, *Making of the Bibles moralisées*, 1, pp. 30, 33, 42, 77, 163, 165.

[41] Detailed in LOWDEN, *Making of the Bibles moralisées*, 2, *passim*.

[42] E.g., LOWDEN, *Making of the Bibles moralisées*, 1, p. 123 (in volume III of the Toledo manuscript).

a book is an exercise that carries one from the temporal and mundane to the eternal and divine.

The Viewer as Exegete

Starting from the assumption that Louis IX was the intended recipient of the Toledo *Bible moralisée*, it would be possible, if very time-consuming, to consider every image and text in the book in terms of reading and communication by/with Louis. Bulk apart, there is, however, a major drawback to such an undertaking, which only becomes apparent if we consider both the later history of the book (and ask to whom it was communicating?) and its current condition. The Toledo *Bible moralisée* is (it is generally agreed) mentioned in the 1284 will of Alfonso X, king of Castille and León, who refers to it as the "illustrated Bible in three volumes which the King of France (Louis IX) gave to us" (*"la otra [Biblia] en tres libros estoriada que nos dio el rey Luis de Francia"*).[43] It is cited along with the crowns and other noble things that pertain to the king. It seems likely, even if undocumented, that the book was given in connection with one of the two marriages arranged after Blanche of Castille's death between the children of Louis and Alfonso. The first involved the betrothal of Louis, eldest son and heir of Louis IX, to Berenguela, eldest child and heir of Alfonso X, and the marriage was to join the kingdoms of France and Castille (but the young Louis died before it could be celebrated). The second, arranged in 1266 took place in 1269, and joined Blanche, daughter of Louis IX, with Fernando, son and heir (supplanting Berenguela) of Alfonso X, but he died before his father, and Blanche never became queen of Castille.

When Louis IX gave this book to Alfonso X its final image (along with all its other pages) gained an audience that its makers could not have envisaged. In such circumstances it might seem that the generic or – one could say – moral and anagogical qualities of the image would have become more important than any specific or literal/historical interpretation. But the true situation was probably more complex. I suggest that by originating from Louis IX the book and its colophon image would have gained, rather than losing, communicative power. When the book was finished, perhaps in 1234, Louis was a young man still

---

[43] LOWDEN, *Making of the Bibles moralisées*, 1, pp. 132-133 and p. 319 nn. 77-78. GONZÁLVEZ RUIZ, *Hombres y Libros de Toledo*, pp. 567-569. See also the lengthy discussion in P. BÜTTNER, *Bilder zum Betreten der Zeit: Bible Moralisée und kapetingisches Königtum*, Ph.D. thesis, Basel University (1996), pp. 45-50, 54. I am grateful to the author for sending me a copy of parts of his thesis.

ruling, in effect, through his mother. By the time the book was given to Alfonso X, Louis was Europe's leading ruler. Alfonso would have recognized in the tailpiece, therefore, images of his distinguished relatives in a book intimately linked to both of them: Blanche, his great-aunt, and her son the saintly Louis, his brother-in-law. By this date the Toledo manuscript had probably begun to acquire a relic-like status to add to its dynastic symbolism.

Alfonso seems to have deposited the *Bible moralisée* at Toledo, where it has remained. There is no evidence in the writings associated with him (for example the *General Estoria*)[44] of knowledge of the *Bible moralisée*, but this is not in itself evidence that he did not study the book. As it is now on display, it is difficult to gain permission to consult the *Bible moralisée*, but this does not always seem to have been the case. Around 1400 its entire Latin text was transcribed in a (royal?) book that still survives in Madrid (Biblioteca Nacional MS 10242), accompanied by a translation of all the moralisations (but not the biblical passages) into Castilian.[45] All the images, however, were ignored. Madrid BN 10232 is thus communicating something very different from its *Bible moralisée* model. In 1422-1433 a different type of illustrated Bible with text and gloss in Castilian was made in Toledo for Don Luis de Guzmán. This was a full Bible of familiar type, not a collection of short biblical excerpts like a *Bible moralisée*.[46] The translation, as we know from a long preface, was the work of a learned rabbi, Moses Arragel, while the provision of images was organized by a Franciscan of the Toledo house, Fra Arias de Enzinas.[47] Rabbi Moses was to leave spaces in the book for images, and Fra Arias was to instruct the artists. "I will show them" he said "the Bible of the *sagrario* of the great church [i.e. the Toledo *Bible moralisée*], which is very well illustrated (*muy bien ystoriada*), and it and my written instruction (*escriptura*) will inform them in what they have to paint and illustrate".[48] As it happens, since the resulting book, the Bible of the Duke of Alba, survives, we can be sure that this was *not*

---

[44] LOWDEN, *Making of the Bibles moralisées*, 1, p. 134.

[45] LOWDEN, *Making of the Bibles moralisées*, 1, pp. 3, 105, 135-136 with further references. P. MIGUEL VIVANCOS is preparing a complete transcription of the Castilian texts for the commentary volume of the facsimile Biblia de San Luis (see above n. 7).

[46] LOWDEN, *Making of the Bibles moralisées*, 1, pp. 134-135.

[47] A. PAZ Y MELIA, *Bible of the House of Alba*, 2 vols., Roxburghe Club (Madrid, 1918), 1, pp. XIII-XXVII.

[48] PAZ Y MELIA, *Bible of the House of Alba*, 1, p. XVII (see also p. 15). To the study of this manuscript by C.-O. NORDSTRÖM, *The Duke of Alba's Castilian Bible* (Uppsala, 1967), should be added two important critical reviews: by J. GUTMANN in *Art Bulletin* 51 (1969), pp. 91-96; and by T. METZGER, "The 'Alba Bible' of Rabbi Moses Arragel", *Bulletin of the Institute of Jewish Studies* 3 (1975), pp. 131-155.

what happened, because its images bear no relation to those in the Toledo *Bible moralisée*, but clearly that book was in some sense accessible to Fra Arias, and he intended to make it communicate directly with others (i.e. artists) and indirectly, via the copying of its images, to Luis de Guzmán.

The Toledo *Bible moralisée* was also accessible to lay visitors to Toledo, as we know from accounts of travellers from the second half of the fifteenth and early sixteenth century.[49] Information about the book seems to have been presented to such people in a standardized form (a little like a modern press release), to judge from parallels between the otherwise completely unrelated accounts. The book they saw was "the most precious Bible in all Christendom".[50] Its artist was "the most famous the world had ever seen".[51] It was in three volumes.[52] It had a costly silk and jewel-encrusted binding.[53]

Putting these disparate sources together we would seem to have good evidence for the continuing visibility and potential communicative power of the Toledo *Bible moralisée* over the three centuries or so after its manufacture. To be sure, it was visible to very different types of people, who had very different motives for their viewing. And yet the manuscript itself belies some aspects at least of this extensive 'history of communication'. On examination the book's condition is found to be very inconsistent and very remarkable. Volume I has lost 33 of what were originally 224 leaves, about 15% of its content.[54] These losses are from different quires in different parts of the book, and some of the pages seem to have been removed roughly. One surviving folio is even torn in half horizontally. Most, but not all, of the missing leaves had already been removed by the time the text was translated into Castilian, around 1400, in

---

[49] LOWDEN, *Making of the Bibles moralisées*, 1, p. 136. Note the earliest Toledan inventory entry on the Bible (there called the Briuia Rica) is that of 1504: GONZÁLVEZ RUIZ, *Hombres y Libros de Toledo*, p. 570. The "Bible moralisée" was specifically cited as in the *sagrario* of the cathedral in the description by Blas Ortiz of 1549: R. GONZÁLVEZ and F. PEREDA, *La Catedral de Toledo 1549 según el Dr Blas Ortiz "Descripcion Graphica y Elegantissima de la S. Iglesia de Toledo"* (Toledo, 1999), pp. 202-203.

[50] *The Travels of Leo of Rozmital*, trans. and ed. M. LETTS (Cambridge, 1957: Hakluyt Society, 2nd. ser. 108), p. 126; compare the remark of Hieronymus Müntzer (Monetarius) in J. GARCÍA MERCADEL, *Viajes de Extranjeros por España y Portugal*, 3 vols. (Madrid, 1952), 1, pp. 399-400 and n. 1.

[51] *Travels of Leo of Rozmital*, p. 126.

[52] A key element in all the descriptions.

[53] GARCÍA MERCADEL, *Viajes de Extranjeros*, 1, pp. 399-400, n. 1; 462-463. In a similar way, later inventories simply repeated the wording of the description in the inventory of 1504: GONZÁLVEZ RUIZ, *Hombres y Libros de Toledo*, p. 570.

[54] LOWDEN, *Making of the Bibles moralisées*, 1, p. 103, and diagrams on pp. 288-291.

Madrid BN 10232.[55] These losses, I think, represent piecemeal removals: pages
that could be purchased (or perhaps stolen) as religious memoria. The condition
of volumes II and III of the Toledo *Bible moralisée*, however, is totally different
from that of volume I. By around 1400, as shown again by the Castilian translation, volume III, it is true, had already lost its final quire, that part now in New
York including the colophon image. It has even been suggested that this was
done before the book was sent to Alfonso,[56] but this seems improbable since it
would have disguised the specific personal and historical qualities that made
the book so valuable to him, and which he explicitly recorded in his will. Volume II is complete and is today extraordinarily well preserved, the margins of
its leaves completely unmarked by the traces of sebum or dirt we might expect
to have been left by the fingers of readers. Now it is true that a worn or damaged manuscript, like Volume I of Toledo, may have received very different
degrees of wear at different times, and it is unusual and helpful to have in this
case the evidence of the Castilian translation to act as a control and dating terminus for the losses. But a manuscript that *appears* virtually unused, especially
if there is no reason to believe that it has been cleaned, must I think *be* virtually
unused. Here the student of illuminated manuscripts is at a real advantage:
whereas evidence of wear and tear on a panel painting or a piece of metalwork
may indicate extensive use, it does not follow that good condition indicates that
the object has been little seen, or that its power to communicate with viewers
has been in some way limited. Gazing at a panel painting does not leave traces
of wear. But an unused book, made evident by unturned pages, means its words
and images have gone unseen: it has been incommunicado. Such a book has
probably communicated largely through aspects of its external appearance (its
size, its cover, together perhaps with a single opening chosen for display).
Quite probably, therefore, all those thousands of images and texts in the Toledo
Bible moralisée went largely (or in the case of Volume II completely) unstud-
ied. Page after page their surfaces worked to create an immediate and overwhelming impression to even the most cursory viewer: all that gold, all that
blue, all that learning. But the users, from Louis IX onwards, may never have
been systematic. Probably the full-page tailpiece was looked at in the Middle

---

[55] That the losses had not *all* occurred by ca. 1400 is important: contrast the remarks of
HAUSSHERR, "Drei Handschriften", p. 38. LOWDEN, *Making of the Bibles moralisées*, 1, pp. 135
and 320-321, nn. 100-101.

[56] HAUSSHERR, "*Sensus Litteralis*", p. 365. See also the recent work of GONZÁLVEZ RUIZ,
Hombres y Libros de Toledo, pp. 569-570, who considers the note at the end of Volume III of the
Toledo manuscript, referring to the missing Apocalypse leaves, to be of the late thirteenth
century. Were the note indeed datable ca. 1300 this would be important evidence; LOWDEN,
Making of the Bibles moralisées, 1, pp. 109, 112.

Ages (as today) with more attention, in part because it made fewer demands than the rest of the book. By extension, the facing final page of the Apocalypse (partially considered above) may well have benefited from some scrutiny as well. In sum, however, the demands made on the viewer by the thousands of images and texts were just too great.

One of the most striking aspects of the power of the *Bibles moralisées* to communicate is that the only manuscripts, illuminated or not, that appear to show a knowledge of them are the few that are derived from them directly.[57] As a result, by far the richest source of evidence as to how the images and texts in these books communicated comes not from analysing them in terms of their intended royal recipients, but from considering how they were made, and how they were then used by those who made subsequent *Bibles moralisées*, taking one or other of the surviving manuscripts as a model. It was the books' makers, rather than their users, whom we can be certain looked at every image and text with interest and attention.

How then was the characteristic eight-to-a-page schema of images and texts of a *Bible moralisée* expected by its makers to communicate at a more than superficial level (for we can hardly suppose that they intended such costly and complex books to remain largely unused)? What I think we have in these picture books is not merely images as accompaniments to and exegesis of scripture, for that would be true for many illuminated books, but a schema that presents text and image as material for discussion. By 'discussion' I mean not the familiar tripartite treatment of the Bible in and around the university of Paris in the thirteenth century, which took the form of *lectio, disputatio, predicatio*, with the emphasis very much on public activity.[58] Instead I have in mind something formal but not formalized: the sensitive and private discussion before the open codex between a king or queen and his or her favourite chaplain or confessor, who stood ready to turn the book's pages, and looked with the royal viewer sometimes carefully, sometimes not, and intervened with appropriate words as he or she sought for explanations: "What does it say here? What does that mean? Tell me about this". Speaking sometimes briefly, sometimes at length, as the occasion made appropriate, the religious would expound the page from his biblical and exegetical knowledge, always sympathetic to the specific

---

[57] LOWDEN, *Making of the Bibles moralisées*, 1, p. 9.

[58] SMALLEY, *Study of the Bible*, pp. 196-213; BALDWIN, *Masters, Princes and Merchants*, 1, pp. 88-116; see more recently L.-J. BATAILLON, "Early scholastic and mendicant preaching as exegesis of Scripture", in: *Ad Litteram: Authoritative Texts and their Medieval Readers*, ed. M.D. JORDAN and K. EMERY Jr. (Notre Dame, 1992), pp. 165-198; L. SMITH, "The use of Scripture in teaching at the medieval university", in: *Learning Institutionalized: Teaching in the Medieval University*, ed. J. VAN ENGEN (Notre Dame, 2000), pp. 229-243.

requirements of his royal audience. I am not sure that we have a term for this kind of use of a book. It is not merely pedagogical, it is not merely devotional, it is not simply instructional, it is not entirely private, but it is certainly not public. It is all these things and more, a mode of use appropriate to the opportunities presented and the rewards offered by these extraordinary picture books.

It takes a few moments to read a *Bible moralisée* text, but once that text is embedded in its gold and blue and red surroundings its potential is transformed. It is now no longer merely text as definition or text as information; alongside its image it becomes text as caption, as label, as *aide-mémoire*, and especially as starting point for discussion. In the *Bibles moralisées* art is unquestionably a form of communication, but to make that art communicate we, like the people for whom such books were made, must be its exegetes.

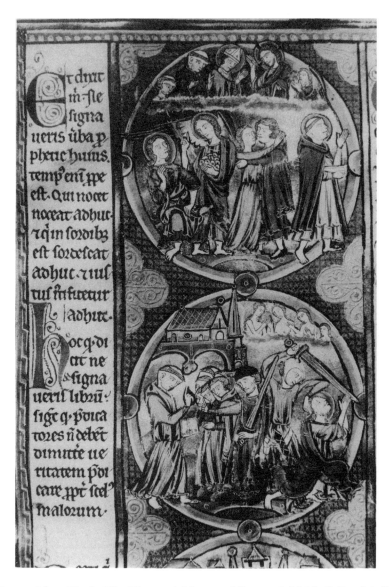

Fig. 1   MS New York, The Pierpont Morgan Library, M 240, f. 7v, detail.

Fig. 2   MS New York, The Pierpont Morgan Library, M 240, f. 7v. See also
Colour Plate 18.

Fig. 3   MS New York, The Pierpont Morgan Library, M 240, f. 8r. See also
Colour Plate 19.

Fig. 4   MS New York, The Pierpont Morgan Library, M 240, f. 8r (detail).

Fig. 5   MS New York, The Pierpont Morgan Library, M 240, f. 8r (detail).

Fig. 6   MS New York, The Pierpont Morgan Library, M 240, f. 8r (detail).

Fig. 7   MS New York, The Pierpont Morgan Library, M 240, f. 8r (detail).

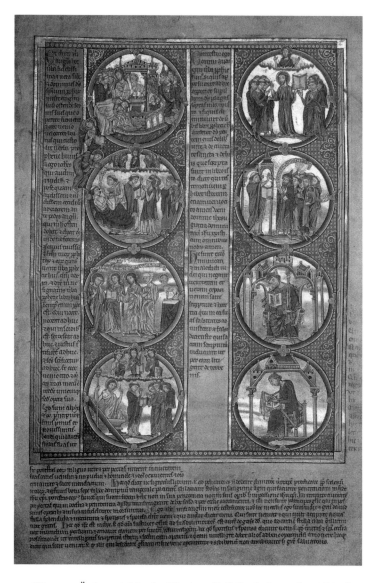

Fig. 8   MS Vienna, Österreichische Nationalbibliothek, cod. 1179, f. 246r. See
          also Colour Plate 17.

Fig. 9   MS Vienna, Österreichische Nationalbibliothek, cod. 1179, f. 246r, detail.

Les Images de la Porte Romane comme un Livre Ouvert à l'Entrée de l'Église

XAVIER BARRAL I ALTET

Des oppositions typologiques entre l'Ancien et le Nouveau Testament, des cycles complémentaires de la doctrine chrétienne, comme ceux de l'Enfance et de la Passion du Christ font l'objet d'un déploiement à l'entrée de l'église romane, sous le tympan à l'iconographie synthétique et visionnaire et la façade avec sa multitude d'images destinées à être admirées et découvertes dans la distance, à servir de cadre monumental pour la prédication et de référence quotidienne générale sur le message de l'Église. Les portes, en revanche, affichent les détails de la doctrine; elles sont destinées, par leur composition comme une bande dessinée, à être lues par le fidèle grâce aux images et aux inscriptions.

Les portes à deux vantaux sont particulièrement indiquées pour accueillir, donc, les diverses correspondances iconographiques qui constituent le noyau principal de l'iconographie romane. La présentation des deux vantaux d'une porte reproduit en grand format, d'une part, les deux plats d'ivoire utilisés comme reliure d'un livre et, d'autre part, la double page ouverte d'une bible illustrée romane. Le livre ouvert ou fermé joue le même rôle iconographique que la porte monumentale. La porte par rapport à l'église est en quelque sorte le frontispice du manuscrit qui accompagne le fidèle en entrant puis, comme un livre ouvert, la porte instruit le fidèle quand elle est fermée. Ouvertes, les deux portes servent de cadre monumental à celui qui pénètre dans l'édifice, comme les deux faces latérales d'un arc de triomphe. Lorsque les portes sont fermées, elles deviennent comme une grande affiche, comme un livre ouvert agrandi à l'entrée de l'église. Le tympan à l'iconographie synthétique couronne les portes qui sont le support de la narration. La correspondance entre le tympan et les

portes est la même que celle qui existe entre la calotte absidiale et les murs de
la nef pour les thèmes iconographiques présentés dans l'église (l'iconograhie
synthétique couronnant la narration), ou entre le niveau supérieur d'un arc de
triomphe et ses jambages inférieurs (pour l'utilisation idéologique qui est faite
de la composition). Au sein du vaste univers de l'iconographie romane, la porte
est l'un des endroits où le texte et l'image sont à la fois le plus étroitement
imbriqués et le mieux mis à la portée de tous. C'est le lieu où le programme
doit être le plus populaire; le livre monumental dans lequel l'image et le texte
sont vraiment conçus pour être regardés de près.

Les portes des églises, en bois ou en bronze, font partie intégrante de
l'iconographie de toute la façade et leur étude permet une meilleure compréhension globale du programme iconographique d'ensemble. L'ornementation de la
façade est la grande conquête iconographique de l'époque romane. Tel un écran
qui s'étend à l'extérieur de l'édifice, elle est décorée d'une iconographie
propre, d'un véritable programme théologique qui sépare l'intérieur de l'église
du monde extérieur. La façade se prête admirablement au déploiement d'un
décor sculpté ou peint et les pouvoirs ecclésiastiques et civils s'en servent au
Moyen Age avec dextérité pour leur propagande politico-religieuse. Les portails, les tympans, les archivoltes, les chapiteaux sculptés, les portes figurées,
sont le support de l'organisation d'un message destiné à transmettre la doctrine
chrétienne, à marquer le seuil de la demeure de Dieu. Les portes sont les gar-
diennes de l'entrée de l'église. Qu'elles soient en bronze ou en bois, elles se
présentent comme la double page d'un manuscrit ouvert devant lequel le fidèle
est invité à prier avant d'entrer dans l'édifice. De plus, étant l'un des derniers
éléments à être mis en place dans l'église lors de sa construction, les portes sont
souvent porteuses des signatures de l'artiste roman et du commanditaire, dans
un esprit de fierté, d'ostentation et de recherche de reconnaissance.

Les portes de l'église de Saint-Michel de Hildesheim, coulées en bronze,
résument à elles seules l'importance accordée aux portes dans l'édifice médiéval. Ce type de porte se rencontre souvent en Italie: portes de bronze des cathédrales de Pise et de Monreale (1186), exécutées par Bonanus, celles de la cathédrale de Ravello et de la cathédrale de Trani par Barisanus, de la basilique de
Saint-Marc à Venise ou de Saint-Zénon à Vérone.

Les portes en bronze de la cathédrale de Gniezno, en Pologne (fig. 5), exécutées vers 1175, montrent, par le relief plat et la distribution des images, que
le traitement iconographique des portes en bronze conservées est souvent tout
à fait similaire à celui des portes en bois. Celles-ci, en revanche, ont parfois
cherché à imiter la richesse des portes de bronze par la polychromie, comme à

la cathédrale de Gurck (Carinthie) vers 1220. Les portes de la cathédrale du Puy-en-Velay (fig. 3-4) offrent des registres plus cycliques (comme à Gniezno) dans la mesure où ils sont disposés d'après le découpage qui est donné par les panneaux de bois. Les scènes sont quand même disposées sur des grands registres horizontaux comme dans les illustrations des manuscrits des bibles romanes. Dans certains cas, comme à Blesle, dans la même région, la couleur semble imiter les portes en bronze. La polychromie des portes s'accorde avec celle de la façade et d'une manière très vaste avec celle de l'édifice auquel s'intègre cette structure de type narratif.

Une autre manière de concevoir la relation du décor de la porte avec le public, par l'agressivité du relief très puissant, se manifeste de manière précoce dans une oeuvre célèbre, déjà évoquée, les portes en bronze de Saint-Michel de Hildesheim en Basse-Saxe. Au XIe siècle, la nef principale de l'église fut modifiée et, entre 1022 et 1054, on dota l'édifice d'un massif occidental modifié au XIIe siècle. Les célèbres portes en bronze que conserve cet édifice sont des ouvrages qui furent commandés pour l'église abbatiale Saint-Michel par Bernward (933-1022). Exécutées en 1015, chaque battant (4,72 m × 1,15 m) fut fondu d'une seule pièce. Leur iconographie illustre l'histoire du péché originel mise en opposition avec celle de la Rédemption (vie du Christ). Le style est fortement expressif, proprement ottonien, et s'inspire probablement de manuscrits carolingiens. Les divers panneaux historiés ressemblent à des miniatures fondues dans le métal, faisant état d'une façon de transposer des scènes d'une technique dans une autre qui produit des formes tranchées et tendues, annonciatrices d'une nouvelle esthétique clairement romane par la naïveté des attitudes et la vivacité des gestes, rythmées par la composition, qui unissent déjà avec bonheur abstraction et réalité.

Parmi les portes romanes figurées, les plus luxueuses, on l'a vu, étaient en bronze, soit incisées et incrustées, en Italie notamment, au Mont Cassin et à Venise par exemple, soit moulées avec des reliefs forts, saillants, comme à Hildesheim, ou faibles, comme à Gniezno. Cette production était très coûteuse et nous ne savons pas si celle des portes en bois l'était beaucoup moins. Celles-ci étaient très fréquentes à l'époque romane, sous la forme parfois de simples vantaux en bois ornés de ferronneries ou, d'autres fois, sous celle de séries complètes de scènes à l'iconographie très riche. Peu d'exemplaires en bois d'époque romane ont survécu dans la mesure où le bois situé à l'extérieur des édifices a beaucoup souffert au cours des siècles. Le bronze des portes a également disparu en grande quantité, fondu et transformé à des moments de nécessité.

L'exemple le plus ancien parmi ceux qui sont à l'origine de l'iconographie médiévale appartient à l'Antiquité tardive, et présente déjà tous les éléments de l'iconographie médiévale des portes; il s'agit de l'exemplaire conservé à l'entrée de l'église Sainte-Sabine à Rome (fig. 1). Il appartient à la seconde moitié du Vᵉ siècle, et est un des rares vestiges conservés des hautes époques; on doit mentionner également les trois panneaux en provenance de l'église des Saints-Gervais-et-Protais de Milan conservés à Saint-Ambroise. Hors d'Europe, on peut se référer aux portes de Sainte-Barbara du Vieux Caire ou encore à celles du monastère de Sainte-Catherine du Sinaï.

L'entrée de la basilique paléochrétienne de Sainte-Sabine à Rome se faisait sous le portique qui semble protéger symboliquement les monumentales portes en bois. Dans un encadrement de marbre d'époque sévèrienne orné de délicats motifs végétaux, la porte offre sans doute au fidèle une imitation de modèles antiques, un exemple aujourd'hui exceptionnel parce que seul conservé de son époque en Italie; les comparaisons les plus proches à prendre en considération étant d'un tout autre format: les ivoires des Vᵉ et VIᵉ siècles. La porte de Sainte-Sabine est composée de quatre vantaux alternant verticalement à l'origine quatre panneaux petits et trois plus grands sur chaque volet. Sur le modèle de l'encadrement d'ensemble de la porte, les panneaux sont placés dans des cadres plus petits de bois sculpté de motifs végétaux représentant des feuillages dans l'entourage des petits panneaux, et des ornements floraux autour des plus grands. Comme c'est souvent le cas pour les portes en bois, les parties basses ont disparu au contact du sol et de l'eau. À Sainte-Sabine, seuls dix-huit panneaux ont été conservés, les dix manquants sont ceux des parties inférieures de la porte. Le matériau est un bois dur, sans doute du cèdre ou du cyprès.

La thématique générale des scènes met en relation l'Ancien et le Nouveau testament, avec des épisodes centrés principalement sur les histoires d'Elie, de Moïse, et du Christ, soit, la relation de la Loi des prophètes avec l'Evangile et une présentation qui oppose les deux Testaments. Les vantaux racontent ainsi principalement des épisodes de l'exode (Moïse sur le mont Horeb, la traversée du désert et l'exode d'Egypte), de la Passion (le Christ en Croix, le jugement de Pilate, l'annonce du reniement de Pierre, le Christ devant Calife) et de la résur-rection (l'incrédulité de Thomas, l'ange et les femmes au sépulcre, le Christ ressuscité et les deux Marie, le retour de Pierre du tombeau (?), l'ascension, les pèlerins d'Emmaüs). Sur le dernier panneau se trouve la représentation de l'Ascension d'Elie et du vol d'Habacuc. On conserve également deux panneaux de la vie du Christ, le premier représentant trois miracles (Cana, la multiplication des pains et la guérison de l'aveugle), l'autre, l'Epiphanie. Caractéristique du Vᵉ siècle, le relief de ces figures est plat et le trait est incisé et griffé.

La mise en place générale, la disposition et le contenu iconographique des portes de l'église Sainte-Sabine, restaurées en 1836 mais non modifiées si l'on en croit le dessin publié par le père Tommaso Mamachi en 1799, sera repris, avec les variantes de style ou de qualité correspondantes tout au long du Moyen Age. L'opposition Ancien-Nouveau Testament, mise déjà en place à Sainte Sabine, sera toujours le noyau essentiel de l'iconographie des portes romanes avec, comme à Sainte-Sabine, une insistance particulière sur le second, autour de la vie du Christ, au détriment du premier.

Au cours des XIᵉ et XIIᵉ siècles, les portes des églises ornées, en bronze ou en bois, sont des témoins majeurs de l'art roman occidental, mais aussi de ses contacts avec le monde byzantin, et prouvent l'importance qui était accordée par les commanditaires ecclésiastiques à la porte de l'église et à son décor. Symbole des portes du Paradis, en les poussant, le fidèle entrait dans la nouvelle Jérusalem, matérialisée par l'architecture de l'église. Parmi les exemples majeurs en bois, les portes de l'église de Sainte-Marie-au-Capitole de Cologne (fig. 2), datées peu avant 1065, sont aujourd'hui déposées à l'intérieur de l'église. Dans un tout autre contexte culturel, des portes mudéjares en bois ont été conservées dans la Péninsule Ibérique. Pour l'Italie, Emile Bertaux avait déjà signalé les portes également en bois de Santa Maria in Cellis, actuellement conservées au Musée National d'Abruzzo à l'Aquila, après avoir été mises en dépôt entre 1910 et 1948 au Palazzo comunale de Carsoli, et celles de San Pietro à Alba Fucense. Les portes de Santa Maria in Cellis, non loin de Carsoli, datées précisément de 1132, ont été remontées, et les anciennes planches ont été replacées dans de nouveaux vantaux. De largeur inégale, chaque panneau de bois présente cinq épisodes à l'iconographie christique. Suivant un sens de lecture de gauche à droite, les bas-reliefs représentent l'Annonciation, la Visitation, la Nativité, l'Annonciation aux bergers, l'Adoration des Mages, le massacre des Innocents et le baptême du Christ. La dernière scène offre cinq personnages debout qui ont été habituellement interprétés comme la présentation au Temple, mais il s'agirait plutôt peut-être de la dispute des docteurs. Comme partout ailleurs, les panneaux situés dans la zone inférieure sont désormais fort abîmés; on peut juste distinguer sur le panneau de droite trois figures sous des arcatures. Les scènes sont accompagnées d'inscriptions dont certaines sont des imitations ornementales de l'écriture coufique; un choix esthétique que l'on retrouvera utilisé comme décor et ornement évocateur, loin de là, à Notre-Dame du Puy.

Toujours dans les Abruzzes, la porte de l'église de San Pietro d'Alba, conservée au Musée de l'Aquila, daterait également de la première moitié du XIIᵉ siècle. L'iconographie n'a rien d'exceptionnel dans son ensemble compte tenu du type d'images préférées pour les portes des églises à l'époque romane. Ici, chacun des deux vantaux est divisé en quatorze panneaux plus ou moins carrés ornés de figures isolées, qui se répondent généralement deux à deux. Les panneaux sont encadrés de palmettes sur le battant de gauche, et de rinceaux sur celui de droite. L'iconographie des scènes présente un ensemble de représentations dominées par la référence aux évangiles. On y trouve également un répertoire fantastique (centaures), animalier et des cavaliers jouxtant une représentation de saint Benoît – l'église est une possession bénédictine – le tout surmonté des quatre symboles des évangélistes. Souvent, comme ici, la porte est aussi un lieu pour l'affirmation de l'histoire locale et du prestige de la communauté religieuse concernée.

La cathédrale du Puy, dans le Velay, au sud de l'Auvergne, conserve deux portes en bois chacune à deux vantaux à l'intérieur du grand porche, à l'entrée des deux chapelles latérales qui se situent de part et d'autre de l'entrée principale, et qui offrent une sorte de double diptyque monumental sous le porche, sous la grande façade, avant d'entrer dans la basilique.

Chaque porte se compose de deux vantaux à deux battants avec une large bordure et huit panneaux historiés. La porte de la chapelle Saint-Gilles, à gauche de l'entrée à l'église, est dédiée à l'enfance du Christ (Annonce aux bergers, Adoration des Rois mages, Hérode, Massacre des Innocents, Présentation au Temple) tandis que celle de la chapelle Saint-Martin, à droite, offre des épisodes de la Passion. Dans ce deuxième ensemble, on découvre la Résurrection de Lazare, l'Entrée à Jérusalem, la Cène, l'Arrestation de Jésus, le Christ devant Pilate, le Portement de Croix, la Crucifixion, la Résurrection, l'Ascension et la Pentecôte.

On a déjà vu que l'idée d'opposer le cycle de l'Enfance du Christ à celui de la Passion en utilisant les possibilités de représentation qu'offrent les portes est fréquemment utilisé à l'époque romane (portes de Sainte-Marie au Capitole à Cologne et diverses portes italiennes). Au Puy, chaque cycle occupe toute une porte au lieu de se cantonner à un seul des deux vantaux comme c'est parfois le cas ailleurs. On y trouve la volonté d'exprimer la totalité du programme chrétien de l'oeuvre de Salut du Christ sur terre qui au Puy a été mise en avant à l'entrée de l'église, dans une disposition inspirée probablement de l'illustration d'une bible romane de grand format. La technique employée se rapproche de celle du champlevé ou technique du méplat; il en résulte des représentations

très plates qui ressortent sur un fond creusé. A l'origine, les décors et les mode-
lés étaient soulignés par une riche polychromie. Sa perte explique le manque de
nuances dans la taille du bois. On conserve cependant quelques vestiges de
couleur. Ce qui peut être saisi du style des vantaux du Puy s'accorde aussi avec
une date dans le troisième quart du XIIᵉ siècle vers laquelle convergent plusieurs
indices stylistiques, archéologiques et historiques.

Les portes du Puy et celles de Sainte-Marie-au-Capitole de Cologne, possèdent un programme iconographique identique, mais elles diffèrent sur le plan
de l'ordonnance et du style. A Cologne, les deux portes en bois sont sculptées
de vingt-six panneaux qui conservent peu de polychromie et qui représentent
des scènes de la vie du Christ. Les panneaux en bois possèdent un relief très
saillant et alternent les images d'une manière propre ce qui produit un effet très
différent de celui des portes du Puy. À Cologne le relief est très fort, dans
l'héritage de la tradition ottonienne, issue de l'Antiquité tardive et qui se situe
dans un contexte très bien représenté par les portes de bronze de Hildesheim,
par exemple. Au Puy, en revanche, le relief est nettement moins marqué, le
méplat domine, rapprochant la technique de celle des portes d'Italie précédemment citées. A la différence de l'ensemble de Sainte-Marie-au-Capitole de
Cologne, au Puy chaque cycle occupe une porte toute entière et se déploie sur
les deux vantaux faisant de la porte fermée une véritable double page de manuscrit enluminé; à Cologne, chaque cycle se cantonne sur un seul des deux
vantaux de la même porte, d'où une lecture différente par rapport aux portes du
Puy. La porte de Cologne et celles du Puy, un siècle plus tard, sont les deux
exemples majeurs conservés d'une technique de décor des portes romanes en
bois, qui devait être assez fréquente dans les grands édifices religieux du
Moyen Age comme le prouvent d'autres vestiges (par exemple, ceux vers 1220
de la cathédrale de Gurk en Carinthie).

Walter Cahn avait étudié d'autres portes romanes conservées dans la région, en Haute-Loire et en Auvergne méridionale, à Lavoûte-Chilhac, à Blesle
et à Chamalières-sur-Loire, par exemple. D'autres églises au delà de la cathédrale du Puy conservent des vantaux en bois sculptés de motifs ou de scènes
bibliques polychromes, à l'iconographie plus ou moins proche de celle de la
cathédrale ponote. Ces images faisaient partie aussi, ici également dans le cas
d'édifices moins notables, du programme iconographique général de l'ensemble de l'édifice religieux et tout particulièrement de la façade dans l'esprit
d'une tradition de la symbolique des portes du royaume de Dieu qui trouve son
origine dès l'Antiquité tardive.

On trouve parfois sur ce type de portes apparemment moins narratives une iconographie plus proche de celle des façades proprement dites, des pavements ou des plafonds des églises avec des animaux ou des cavaliers affrontés et souvent une croix qui domine la scène. Ces croix que nous trouvons parfois au sommet des façades sculptées de l'époque romane imitent sur les portes bien souvent les grandes croix d'orfèvrerie du Moyen Age. Elles se réfèrent ici au répertoire de la sculpture monumentale et se rapprochent des grands décors que l'on trouve sur les façades mêmes.

La porte de Lavoûte-Chilhac est un autre grand vestige du décor que j'évoque dans cette communication; elle est conservée dans la sacristie de l'ancien monastère. Le noyau original de l'oeuvre est formé de la croix grecque, aux bras s'élargissant, et des quatre éléments qui l'entourent dans le haut du panneau. La croix est décorée de quatre ornements géométriques en entrelacs sur chaque bras, incrustés entre les cinq lobes et situés respectivement sur chacun des bras de la croix et en son centre. On possède à nouveau ici un témoignage de cette volonté d'imiter les décors prestigieux en orfèvrerie. Les quatre panneaux autour sont ornés d'un jeu de clous qui traversent chaque décor dans ses diagonales. L'inscription visible sur l'ensemble de la porte commémore la fondation du monastère par Odilon de Cluny au XIe siècle. Le motif de croix décorées de lobes en relief se retrouve sur les portes de Chamalières-sur-Loire, où chacun des deux vantaux est orné en son sommet d'une croix grecque aux bras rectilignes sur lesquels on retrouve les lobes, moins aplatis qu'à Lavoûte-Chilhac.

Les portes en bois de Saint-Pierre de Blesle, toujours de la même région du Centre de la France, sont encore un exemple de ce type d'ornementation. Les quatre panneaux autour des croix des deux battants de la porte figurent, en bas relief, des motifs géométriques, mais aussi le signe du capricorne et celui du sagittaire aux extrémités de la porte, comme une évocation de l'ensemble du zodiaque. Les dates de ces monuments sont très proches de celles des portes de la cathédrale du Puy et la technique également.

Le rapport entre le travail du bois et celui d'autres matériaux est au centre de notre réflexion concernant l'iconographie des portes et l'utilisation qui est faite des images représentées, car plusieurs matériaux différents sont utilisés pour la réalisation des portes ce qui implique un choix stricte dans la manière de planifier le décor et sa réalisation. Il n'est pas envisageable en effet que les mêmes ateliers aient travaillé les portes en bois et les portes en bronze, par exemple, car à l'époque romane les ateliers spécialisés dans le travail du bois semblent déjà séparés, à en croire le traité de Théophile, de ceux qui travaillent d'autres matériaux. *Le livre des métiers* d'Étienne Boileau témoigne de la spé-cialisation de plus en plus grande qu'atteignent les artisans du bois au-delà des XIIᵉ et XIIIᵉ siècles lorsque la menuiserie et la charpenterie n'avaient plus rien en commun depuis un certain temps déjà.

Plus encore que le bronze, le bois est en général, au-delà des portes, d'une grande importance au Moyen Age pour la construction et le décor des édifices religieux. Toujours utilisé sous forme de planches et de troncs d'arbres comme éléments de charpentes et de toitures, le bois intervient même parfois dans la construction – en Norvège par exemple – de toute l'église. Des quantités im-menses de bois étaient utilisées sur les chantiers du Moyen Age ce qui imposait parfois le choix de lieux situés à proximité des forêts pour la construction.

Nous ne savons pas si les artisans qui travaillent les portes en bois corres-pondent au nom de *carpentarius*, terme utilisé souvent dans les sources pour désigner les artisans du bois, et nous ne savons pas non plus si dans ces ateliers spécialisés était produit également le décor architectural et le mobilier qui cons-tituaient, avant le XIIIᵉ siècle, avec la statuaire, les principales occupations des artisans du travail du bois taillé.

En ce qui concerne les portes en bois, mais aussi également celles en bronze, il y a un aspect essentiel dans la mise en place de l'ouvrage après la planification de son iconographie qui est celui de l'assemblage des panneaux après la taille pour le bois, ou la fonte, pour le bronze. Sauf cas exceptionnel, les portes en bois sont exécutées dans des ateliers régionaux avec du bois local, tandis que celles en bronze, notamment italiennes, ont dans certains cas fait l'objet d'une exportation de panneaux prêts à être montés à partir d'ateliers ayant acquis une réputation suffisante.

Pour que la porte, surtout lorsqu'elle est en bois, puisse assurer pleinement son rôle de livre-ouvert à l'entrée de l'église, une attention extrême devait être accordée à la polychromie car la couleur, comme sur l'ensemble de la façade en pierre, était probablement l'élément principal qui aidait à la compréhension des images. Parfois même, la couleur apportait des compléments indispensables au travail du sculpteur du bois, par l'ajout d'éléments décoratifs, et surtout d'inscriptions qui donnaient la touche finale sur place à l'ouvrage non fini en atelier. En effet, le bois n'est pratiquement jamais destiné à être montré nu une fois taillé. Il était toujours pensé, conçu, pour recevoir un habillage peint, stu-qué, en métal ou parfois même en tissu. Assemblage des panneaux et poly-chromie sont également étroitement associés car la couleur cachait les irrégula-rités dans la planification des différents éléments. Cette planification est essen-tielle dans le cas des portes romanes car ici, comme pour le travail de l'ivoire, le matériau, le tronc d'arbre dans ce cas, détermine le format maximal de chaque panneau. C'est la même planification qui permet de destiner la partie la plus large du tronc aux panneaux narratifs et les formats plus étroits aux bordures et assemblages.

De nombreuses pièces détachées, jusqu'au morceau le plus petit de bois, étaient assemblées pour constituer les portes. Dans le cas des Christs en Croix, par exemple, on utilisait, comme on le voit sur les statues et comme le dit *Le Livre des métiers*, une pièce pour le corps et deux autres pour les bras du Christ, au-delà de l'assemblage de deux troncs pour former la croix. Bien que *Le Livre des métiers* se réfère sur ce point à la statuaire, nous devons retenir qu'il insiste sur le fait que l'assemblage est la qualité principale du métier; le mauvais assemblage désignant d'après cette source, le mauvais ouvrier. Dans le cas des portes, la qualité de l'assemblage devait être également l'une des exigences principales du commanditaire dans le but de donner l'impression qu'une iconographie organisée par petits panneaux devenait en réalité une grande image unique pour chacune des portes, pour chaque volet du livre monumental qui accueille le visiteur à l'entrée de l'église.

Les portes en bois décorées du Velay sont taillées dans une technique proche du champlevé dans laquelle les représentations se détachent sans relief sur le fond creusé. Celles de Sainte-Marie-au-Capitole de Cologne, ou de Santa Maria in Cellis a Carsoli en Italie utilisent le décor en relief. Dans les deux cas l'assemblage est un élément très important au même titre que celui de certains plafonds en bois. Mais l'oeuvre en bois une fois taillée et assemblée n'était pas finie avant d'accueillir la polychromie qui complétait et élargissait l'iconographie ou même parfois, dans le cas des portes sculptées, de recevoir des éléments de ferronnerie qui l'enrichissaient davantage sur le plan décoratif tout en lui donnant solidité sur le plan technique. Le titre LXII du *Livre des métiers*, est consacré plus particulièrement aux peintres de sculptures sur bois en montrant bien les liens qu'il y a entre imagiers et peintres, bien qu'ils appartiennent à deux branches différentes. Même si cette donnée concerne une période bien plus tardive que celle que nous étudions ici et que l'accent y est mis sur la relation entre imagier et peintre de statuaire, nous pouvons nous en servir pour évoquer certains aspects de l'organisation du travail des ateliers spécialisés dans l'exécution de portes monumentales d'église, assez immobiles au cours des différentes périodes du Moyen Age.

Retenons donc que la mise en place de portes monumentales, souvent de très grand format, à l'entrée des églises, était, à l'époque romane, une étape essentielle du programme iconographique global du monument car c'est là que l'Eglise affichait son livre ouvert le plus lisible et pédagogique. Mais la réalisation de ces ouvrages était une tâche spécialisée et complexe dont le résultat devait être à la hauteur de l'enjeu. Le passage du format du livre illustré ouvert à celui des grandes dimensions d'une porte à deux vantaux permettait d'afficher beaucoup plus de scènes que celles qui pouvaient être offertes à la contemplation des fidèles lorsque le prêtre montrait entre ses mains ou à l'aide d'un lutrin la double page d'un livre, d'une Bible, pour servir à la méditation de tous ceux qui, surtout en période d'oralité dominante, avaient besoin des images représentées pour comprendre l'histoire du Salut chrétien.

Éléments de bibliographie sur les questions traitées dans cette communication

Deux colloques ont fait le point sur les questions relatives aux portes et aux façades romanes: *La façade romane: Actes du colloque international de Poitiers = Cahiers de Civilisation médiévale* 34 (1991) et *Le porte di bronzo dell' Antichità al secolo XIII*, ed. S. SALOMI, 2 vols. (Roma, 1990), actes du colloque, *Trieste, porta latina sui mondi slavo e germanico: le porte di bronzo dall'antichità al secolo XIII*, Trieste, 13-18 aprile 1987, et les remarques d'A. IACOBINI dans *Arte medievale* 2.2 (1988), pp. 273-286. Trois articles de *l'Enciclopedia dell'Arte Medievale*, 9 (Roma, 1998), apportent la bibliographie essentielle et une mise au point scientifique: A. IACOBBINI, "Porta", pp. 655-672, M. BERNARDINI, "Islam (porta)", pp. 672-675 et Y. CHRISTE, "Portale istoriato", pp. 675-695. Moi-même, j'ai consacré précédemment deux études à la question: *La cathédrale du Puy-en-Velay*, ed. X. BARRAL I ALTET, (Paris, 2000), pp. 255-262, 305-310; ID., "La porte-récit en bois dans la façade romane", dans *Medioevo: Immagine e racconto (I convegni di Parma 3, 2000)*, ed. A.C. QUINTAVALLE (Parme, 2003), pp. 278-286.

Parmi l'abondante bibliographie je voudrais citer: X. BARRAL I ALTET, "Remarques sur le travail du bois à l'époque romane", dans *Artistes, artisans et production artistique au Moyen Age: colloque international [du] Centre National de la Recherche Scientifique, Université de Rennes II-Haute-Bretagne, 2-6 mai 1983*, ed. X. BARRAL I ALTET, 3 vols. (Paris, 1986-1990), 2, *Rapports préliminaires du colloque, Rennes, 1983*, pp. 1359-1374. ID., "Le bois: De l'artisanat au chef-d'oeuvre", dans F. AVRIL, X. BARRAL I ALTET et D. GABORIT-CHOPIN, *Le monde roman 1060-1220: Les Royaumes d'Occident* (Paris, 1983: *L'univers des formes*), pp. 343-358. C. BELLANCA, *La basilica di Santa Sabina e gli interventi di Antonio Muñoz* (Rome, 1999). V. PACE, dans E. BERTAUX, *L'art dans l'Italie méridionale: Aggiornamento dell'opera di Émile Bertaux*, ed. A. PRANDI, 3 vols. (Rome, 1978) et *Indici* (Rome, s.d.), 2, livre IV, chap. III. J.J. BERTHIER, *L'église de Sainte-Sabine à Rome* (Rome, 1910). *Blesle, visite dans son passé*, édité par Les amis du vieux Blesle (Blesle, s.d.). W. CAHN, *The Romanesque Wooden Doors of Auvergne* (New York, 1974: *Monographs on Archeology and Fine Arts* 30). ID., "Les portes en bois", dans *La cathédrale du Puy-en-Velay*, pp. 260-262. C. CAZORLA, "Puertas mudéjades con inscripción eucarística", *Archivo español de arte y arqueología* 3 (1927), pp. 197-220. F. DARSY, *Sainte-Sabine* (Rome, 1961). A. ESCU-DERO, "Portes mudèjares de l'Annunciata", dans *Thesaurus: L'Art als Bisbats de Catalunya 1000-1800*, catalogue d'exposition, *Estudis* (Barcelone, 1986), p. 118. M. FRA-ZER, "Church doors and the Gates of Paradise: Byzantine bronze doors in Italy", *Dumbarton Oaks Papers* 27 (1973), pp. 154 et suiv. J. GARDNER, " 'Magister Bertucius Aurifex' et les portes en bronze de Saint-Marc, un programme pour l'année jubilaire", *Revue de l'art* 134.4 (2001), pp. 9-26. U. GÖTZ, *Die Bildprogramme der Kirchentüren des 11. und 12. Jahrhunderts* (diss. Tübingen, 1971). G. JEREMIAS, *Die Holztür der Basilica S. Sabine in Rom* (Tübingen, 1980). J.P. LECLERCQ, J.F. LUNEAU et B. YTHIER, *Canton de Blesle Haute-Loire, Inventaire général des monuments et des richesses artistiques de la France* (Paris et Clermont-Ferrand, 1994: *Images du Patrimoine*). A.S. LABUDA et A. BUJAK, *Porta regia: Die Bronzetür zu Gnesen* (Gniezno, [1997]). G. MATTHIAE, *Le porte bronzee bizantine in Italia* (Rome, 1971). U. MENDE, *Die Bronzetüren des Mittelalters 800-1200*, 2ᵉ éd. (Munich, 1994; 1ᵉ éd. Munich, 1983). B. DE MONTESQUIOU-FEZENSAC, "Les portes de bronze de Saint-Denis", *Bulletin de la Société nationale des antiquaires de France* (1945-1947), pp. 128-137. J. VILLARD, *Chamalières-sur-Loire* (Chamalières, 1988).

Fig. 1   Portes en bois de l'église Sainte-Sabine à Rome (Vᵉ siècle)

Fig. 2   Portes en bois de l'église Sainte-Marie-au-Capitole de Cologne (XIᵉ
siècle)

Fig. 3   Portes en bois de la Cathédrale du Puy. Cycle de l'Enfance du Christ (XIIe siècle). Document graphique

Fig. 4   Portes en bois de la Cathédrale du Puy. Cycle de la Passion du Christ (XIIᵉ siècle). Document graphique

Fig. 5   Portes en bronze de la cathédrale de Gniezno (Pologne), vers 1175

Plates

Pl. 1   Russian icon, seventeenth century, present whereabouts unknown.

Pl. 2   Christ among the Apostles. Apsidal mosaic, Rome, Santa Pudenziana.
From W.F. VOLBACH and M. HIRMER, *Frühchristliche Kunst: Die
Kunst der Spätantike in West- und Ostrom* (München, 1958), Pl. 130.

Pl. 3   The apsidal mosaic of Sant'Apollinare in Classe (detail), after C. MARABINI, *I mosaici di Ravenna* (Novara, 1981).

Pl. 4   St. Martin (extreme left, leading the martyrs). Mosaic from
         Sant'Apollinare Nuovo, Ravenna, ca. 455-526, after C. MARABINI, *I
         mosaici di Ravenna* (Novara, 1981)

Pl. 5   Detail of Pl. 6.

Pl. 6 Italian (Milan), late fourteenth century, workshop of Tomasino da Vimercate, *Leaf from a Gradual, with the Virgin Mary and Saint Joseph Awaiting the Birth of Christ in Initial H.* The Art Museum, Princeton University (MS y 1929-3).

Pl. 7   Detail of pl. 8.

Pl. 8   Italian (Milan), late fourteenth century, workshop of Tomasino da
        Vimercate, *Leaf from a Gradual with Adoration of the Christ Child in
        Initial D*. The Art Museum, Princeton University (MS y 1982-110)

Pl. 9   Giotto, *St. Francis Instituting the Crèche at Greccio* (*ca.* 1296-1303).
Assisi, Basilica of San Francesco, upper church.

Pl. 10   Frontispiece, *Ecclesia* holding a chalice to receive the blood of the Lamb, Pericopes Book, MS Aschaffenburg, Hofbibliothek MS. 2, f. 1v. Fulda, *c.* 970.

Pl. 11   Archbishop Everger of Cologne prostrates himself in penitence before
Saints Peter and Paul, Everger's Epistolary, MS Köln, Dombibliothek,
Cod. 143, ff. 3v and 4r. Cologne, 985-999.

Pl. 12   MS Madrid, Biblioteca Nacional, Codex Matritensis Vitr. 26-2, f. 10 v.

Pl. 13   MS Madrid, Biblioteca Nacional, Codex Matritensis Vitr. 26-2, f. 12 v.

Pl. 14   MS Madrid, Biblioteca Nacional, Codex Matritensis Vitr. 26-2, f. 68 v.

Pl. 15   MS Madrid, Biblioteca Nacional, Codex Matritensis Vitr. 26-2, f. 80 r.

Pl. 16   MS Madrid, Biblioteca Nacional, Codex Matritensis Vitr. 26-2, f. 102 r.

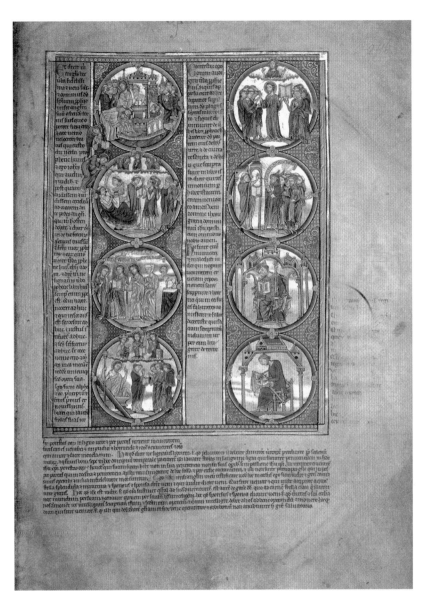

Pl. 17   MS Vienna, Österreichische Nationalbibliothek, cod. 1179, f. 246r.

Pl. 18   MS New York, The Pierpont Morgan Library, M 240, f. 7v.

Pl. 19   MS New York, The Pierpont Morgan Library, M 240, f. 8r.